ORGANIZED CRIME

Nelson-Hall Series in Law, Crime, and Justice

Consulting Editor: Howard Abadinsky
Saint Xavier University, Chicago

ORGANIZED CRIME

Fourth Edition

Howard Abadinsky

Nelson-Hall Publishers ■ Chicago

Project Editor: Rachel Schick
Production/Design Manager: Tamra Campbell-Phelps
Photo Research: Nicholas Communications
Illustrations: Bill Nelson
Composition: E.T. Lowe
Manufacturer: The Maple Press
Cover Painting: *Two Men Talking* by Kim Pruitt

Library of Congress Cataloging-in-Publication Data

Abadinsky, Howard, 1941–
    Organized crime / Howard Abadinsky. — 4th ed.
      p. cm.
    Includes bibliographical references and index.
    ISBN 0-8304-1385-5
    1. Organized crime—United States—History. I. Title.
HV6446.A224 1994
364.1'06'0973—dc20   93-35757
                                                        CIP

Copyright © 1994 by Nelson-Hall Inc.
Reprinted 1996

Manufactured in the United States of America

10 9 8 7 6 5 4 3

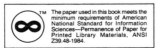

To Donna, Alisa, and Sandi

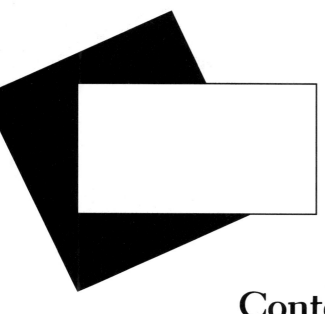

Contents

CONTENTS

Chapter 6 · The Business of Organized Crime: Gambling, Loansharking, Theft, and Sex 293

Chapter 7 · The Business of Organized Crime: Drugs 325

Chapter 8 · Organized Crime in Labor and Business 389

CONTENTS

Chapter 9 · Responding to Organized Crime: Laws and Law Enforcement   433

Chapter 10 · Organized Crime: Committees, Commissions, and Policy Issues   493

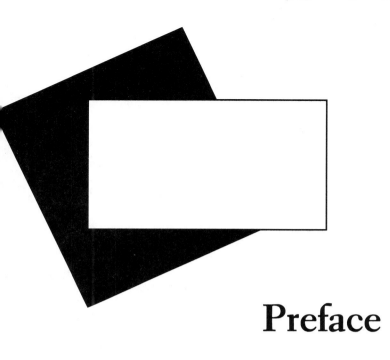

Preface

In 1964, fresh out of college, I was sworn in as a New York State parole officer. Soon afterward, equipped with a badge and a .38, I was assigned to the waterfront section of South Brooklyn known as Redhook. As I struggled to become familiar with the neighborhood, I noticed that my presence on certain streets seemed to generate a great deal of curiosity (I am six feet one inch tall, and in those days weighed an athletic 200 pounds) and, at times, activity—windows opening and closing, people on the streets suddenly melting into doorways or shops. I discussed Redhook with my more experienced colleagues and some of the naivete faded.

Redhook was dominated by a faction of one of New York City's five organized crime "Families." Prior to my arrival, this faction had been involved in a conflict with the rest of the Family, and Redhook had been the scene of a great deal of violence. A tentative truce was in effect when I appeared on the scene. I became familiar with such terms as "wise-guy" and "made-guy," *capo* and *con-sigliere*, and names like "Crazy Joey," "Blast," "The Snake," "Punchy," and "Apples."

After fourteen years as a parole officer and supervisor, I left New York for Western Carolina University and an academic career. My interest in organized crime continued, and I began to teach a course on the subject. However, a single text, one that was both comprehensive and accurate, was unavailable. Like so many others presenting courses on organized crime, I had students purchase the classics by Francis Ianni (1972), Donald Cressey (1972), Joseph Albini (1971), and Humbert Nelli (1976). Nevertheless, there were still gaps, particularly with respect to emerging organized crime and the statutes and techniques used in organized crime law enforcement.

The first edition of this book (1981) was the result of a need for a basic text that covered all of the important dimensions of organized crime and its control. But organized crime changed; hence a second edition was published in 1985, when I was teaching at Saint Xavier University and becoming familiar with organized crime through contacts developed as a (part-time) Cook County deputy sheriff/inspector.

Ever dynamic, organized crime continued to change, with efforts to combat one aspect of the phenomenon, traditional organized crime, reaching new levels of prosecutorial success. Public officials and media presentations began to talk of the demise of traditional organized crime, while emerging criminal groups were becoming an even more serious threat.

A third edition of this book was published in 1991, a time when traditional organized crime was being battered by federal law enforcement using the RICO statute. Since that time, the ranks of some organized crime units have been decimated; for all practical purposes a few have ceased to function. According to some observers, the end is in sight—but is it? A number of crime "Families" have succeeded in recruiting new members and continue to be viable—and dangerous—entities. Meanwhile, emerging groups of criminals have become more sophisticated and more threatening, and additional crime groups have been added to the pantheon we refer to as organized crime.

This new edition reflects changes that have occurred and updates information and analyses of organized crime. For ease of classroom presentation, the ten chapter curriculum format has been retained, although several chapters have been reorganized. An Instructor's Resource Manual with a test bank is available. I would like to thank Nelson-Hall President Steve Ferrara for his continued confidence in the author, and a most proficient editor, Rachel Schick.

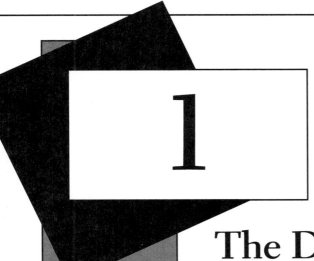

1

The Definition and Structure of Organized Crime

The walls were clear, there were no systems or dogs. We moved into the compound and checked each window of the house. Only servants were home. I entered from the balcony, the French doors were open, locked the hall door, and found nothing in the dressing room. I entered the master bedroom and saw this big elegant piece of furniture. . . . I began taking out the velvet cases and placing the jewelry in a pillowcase. I dropped the pillowcase off the balcony to Don, unlocked the hall door after sliding the back of the dresser under the bed. Everything was left real neat and we made our way back to the boat for the return trip to Connecticut with about $200,000 in jewels. (Abadinsky 1983: 44)

I gave Harry one end of the rope, and I hold the other end. Puggy is kicking and fighting. He is forcing his head down, so we can't get the rope under his throat. Bugsy holds his head up, so we can put the rope under. Then me and Harry exchange the ends, cross them, so we made a knot, a twist. Then we cross them once more. Then we rope around his throat again, to make two loops.

Bugsy gets Puggy by the feet and me and Harry get him by the head. We put him down on the floor. He is kicking. Harry starts finishing tying him up. I am turning him like, and Harry gets his feet tied up with the back of his neck. He tied him up like a little ball. His head is down on his chest. His knees are folded against his chest. His hands are in between. The rope is around his neck and under his feet. If he moves the rope will **tighten up around his throat more.** (Turkus and Feder 1951: 308–309)

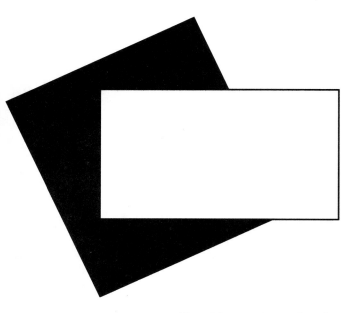

Two felony crimes—burglary and murder—but the motives are as different as the perpetrators. In the first example, Pete and Don are professional jewel thieves. Their goal is simple and direct: to secure their victim's jewelry and sell it to a fence. Along with their getaway driver, they were dubbed (by the newspapers) the "Dinner Set Bandits." In the second example, Abraham ("Kid Twist") Reles is describing how he, Harry ("Pittsburgh Phil") Strauss, and Martin ("Bugsy") Goldstein murdered "Puggy," an ex-fighter and small-time gambler, at the behest of syndicate boss Albert Anastasia. They were part of a murder unit dubbed "Murder, Inc." The Dinner Set Bandits ended with the incarceration of its leader, Pete Salerno. The syndicate, organized crime, continues—the death or incarceration of Abe Reles or Albert Anastasia does not end its operations. This is one of the distinguishing characteristics that makes organized crime a distinct form of criminality.

The criminality of persons in organized crime differs from that committed by conventional criminals "because their organization allows them to commit crimes of a different variety [labor racketeering, for example] and on a larger scale than their less organized colleagues" (M. Moore 1987: 51). In this chapter we will explore the elements that enter into defining organized crime. We will review the origins of American organized crime groups with the greatest longevity by examining the criminal organizations of southern Italy: Mafia, Camorra, and 'Ndrangheta. We will then consider two contrasting organizational models—bureaucratic and patron-client networks—in order to better understand the structure of contemporary organized crime in the United States.

DEFINING ORGANIZED CRIME

Whether researching or investigating organized crime, one is faced with the problem of defining the phenomenon. Oddly enough, a great many works on organized crime (OC) avoid this problem, as if the obvious need not be

ORGANIZED CRIME: FBI DEFINITION

Any group having some manner of formalized structure and whose primary objective is to obtain money through illegal activities. Such groups maintain their position through the use of violence or threats of violence, corrupt public officials, graft, or extortion, and generally have a significant impact on the people in their locales or region of the country.

defined. The federal Organized Crime Control Act of 1970 (discussed in chapter 9), for example, fails to define organized crime. "The problem in defining organized crime," states the President's Commission on Organized Crime (hereafter PCOC), "stems not from the word 'crime,' but from the word 'organized.' While society generally recognizes and accepts certain behavior and actions as criminal, there is no standard acceptance as to when a criminal group is organized. The fact that organized criminal activity is not necessarily organized crime complicates that definition process" (PCOC 1986a: 25).

The lack of an adequate definition is highlighted by the Task Force on Organized Crime (1976), which noted the inadequacies of state efforts at defining OC. These range from the simple definition of the state of Mississippi—"Two or more persons conspiring together to commit crimes for profit on a continuing basis"—to the more elaborate definition offered by the state of California, which stresses the types of activities that fall under the term "organized crime":

> Organized crime consists of two or more persons who with continuity of purpose, engage in one or more of the following activities: (1) The supplying of illegal goods and services, i.e., vice, loansharking, etc.; (2) Predatory crime, i.e., theft, assault, etc. Several distinct types of criminal activity fall within this definition of organized crime. The types may be grouped into five general categories:
>
> 1. *Racketeering*. Groups of individuals which organize more than one of the following types of criminal activities for their combined profit.
> 2. *Vice-Operations*. Individuals operating a continuing business of providing illegal goods or services such as narcotics, prostitution, loansharking, and gambling.
> 3. *Theft/Fence Rings*. Groups of individuals who engage in a particular kind of theft on a continuing basis, such as fraud and bunco schemes, fraudulent documents, burglary, car theft, and truck hijackings, and

3

associated individuals engaged in the business of purchasing stolen merchandise for resale and profit.

4. *Gangs*. Groups of individuals with common interests or backgrounds who band together and collectively engage in unlawful activity to enhance their group identity and influence, such as youth gangs, outlaw motorcycle clubs, and prison gangs.

5. *Terrorists*. Groups of individuals who combine to commit spectacular criminal acts, such as assassination and kidnapping of public figures, to undermine public confidence in established government for political reasons or to avenge some grievance.

Criminologists, too, have their definitions. Donald R. Cressey (1969: 319) is concerned less with the criminal activities than with their perpetrators and the relationships among them:

> An organized crime is any crime committed by a person occupying, in an established division of labor, a position designed for the commission of crime providing that such division of labor also includes at least one position for a corrupter, one position for a corruptee, and one position for an enforcer.

Michael Maltz (1976) is also concerned more with organization than the actual criminal behavior. He points out a problem of semantics: we call a specific behavior or act organized crime, but when we refer to organized crime in the generic sense, we usually mean an entity, a group of people. In his "tentative" definition of organized crime (1976: 76), Maltz is especially concerned with the dynamics of such groups—their means and ends:

> A crime consists of a transaction proscribed by criminal law between offender(s) and victim(s). It is not necessary for the victim to be a complainant or to consider himself victimized for a crime to be committed. An organized crime is a crime in which there is more than one offender, and the offenders are and intend to remain associated with one another for the purpose of committing crimes. The *means* of executing the crime include violence, theft, corruption, economic power, deception, and victim participation. These are not mutually exclusive categories; any organized crime may employ a number of these means.
>
> The objective of most organized crimes is power, either political or economic. These two types of objectives, too, are not mutually exclusive and may coexist in any organized crime.
>
> There are a number of *manifestations* that objectives may take. When the objective is political power it may be of two types: overthrow of the existing order, or illegal use of the criminal process. When the objective is economic power, it may manifest itself in three different ways: through common crime (*mala en se*), through illegal business (*mala prohibita* or vices), or through legitimate business (white collar crime).

This definition is quite broad—it fails to provide a basis for distinguishing between the James Gang (of "Wild West" fame) and the Capone organization

A depiction of the death of Jesse James as his brother Charles looks on. When Jesse was killed by Robert Ford, the James gang died as well. Crime organizations tend to continue after the death or imprisonment of their founders.

(of Prohibition fame). While our predilections permit us to accept Al Capone as an "organized crime figure," Jesse James does not seem to fit the conventional model. Indeed, when Jesse was killed in 1882 in St. Joseph, Missouri, by Robert Ford (a member of the gang and "the dirty little coward who shot Mr. Howard," Jesse's alias), that ended the "James Gang." When Al Capone was imprisoned fifty years later, the "Capone Organization" continued, and in its more modern form (the "Outfit") it continues to operate in Chicago. Perhaps, then, what is needed is a definition that includes Al Capone while excluding Jesse James. Such a definition will be presented with eight attributes, and in this book organized crime will refer to groups of criminals having all or most of these eight particular attributes.

ATTRIBUTES OF ORGANIZED CRIME

While there is no generally accepted definition of organized crime, there have been a number of attributes identified by law enforcement agencies and researchers as indicative of the phenomenon. There is a practical dimension to offering these attributes: they provide a basis for determining if a particular group of criminals engages in organized crime and, therefore, needs to be approached in a way different from the way one would approach other groups of criminals. Organized crime

1. is nonideological
2. is hierarchical
3. has a limited or exclusive membership
4. perpetuates itself
5. exhibits a willingness to use illegal violence and bribery
6. demonstrates specialization/division of labor
7. is monopolistic
8. is governed by explicit rules and regulations

Let us examine each of these attributes.

Nonideological. An organized crime group does not have political goals nor is it motivated by ideological concerns; its goals are money and power. While political involvement may be part of the group's activities, the purpose is to gain protection or immunity for its illegal activities. This distinguishes groups of persons who may be organized and are violating the law to further their political agenda—for example, the Ku Klux Klan or terrorist groups (contrary to the California definition)—from organized crime.

Hierarchical. An organized crime group has a vertical power structure with three or more permanent ranks, each with authority over the level beneath. The authority is inherent in the position and does not depend on who happens to be occupying it at any given time.

Limited or exclusive membership. An organized crime group has significant limitations on who is qualified to become a member. These may be based on ethnic background, kinship, race, criminal record, or similar considerations. Those who meet the basic qualification(s) for membership usually require a sponsor, typically a ranking member, and must also prove qualified for membership by their behavior—for example, willingness to commit criminal acts, obey rules, follow orders, and maintain secrets. There is a period of apprenticeship that may range from several months to several years. If the OC group is to remain viable, there must be more persons who desire membership than the OC group is willing to initiate.

Perpetuates itself. An organized crime group constitutes an ongoing criminal conspiracy designed to persist through time; that is, beyond the life of the current membership. Permanence is assumed by the members, and this provides an important basis for interesting qualified persons in becoming members, thus perpetuating the group's continued existence.

Willingness to use illegal violence and bribery. In an organized crime group, violence is a readily available and accepted resource. Access to private violence is an important dimension that allows the group to actively pursue its goals. When necessary, the OC group will resort to bribery in order to protect its operations or members. The use of violence or bribery is not restricted by ethical considerations, but is controlled only by practical limitations.

Specialization/division of labor. An organized crime group will have certain functional positions filled by qualified members. Given the nature of an OC group, the position of *enforcer* is often crucial. This person carries out difficult assignments involving the use of violence, including murder, in a rational

A concrete-filled barrel containing the remains of car-thief Joseph Scorney is hoisted to a Staten Island dock in the early 1980s. Scorney's murder was one of an estimated two hundred "jobs" of private violence performed by the Roy DeMeo crew of the Gambino Family.

manner. The enforcer may use members or nonmembers to accomplish the assignment. He may turn over assignments for murder to specialists, persons holding the position of *executioner* (for example, Murder, Inc.). Less difficult assignments involving violence can be carried out by any member. The enforcer does not act independently but receives assignments, directly or indirectly, from the head of the OC group.

If the group is sophisticated enough, it may also have positions for *fixer* and *money mover*. The fixer excels in developing contacts with criminal justice and/or political officials and, when appropriate, arranges for corruption. The money mover is an expert at "laundering" illicitly obtained money, disguising its origin through a string of transactions and investing it in legitimate enterprises (discussed in chapter 8). Certain OC groups, for example, outlaw motorcycle clubs (discussed in chapter 5) also have a position equivalent to *intelligence analyst*.

Monopolistic. An organized crime group eschews competition. It strives for hegemony over a particular geographic area (a metropolitan area or section of a city) or over a particular "industry," legitimate or illegitimate (for example, gambling, trucking, loansharking), or over a combination of both (for example, loansharking in a particular area). A monopoly, of course, restrains "free trade" and increases profits. An OC monopoly is maintained by violence or the threat of violence or by corrupt relationships with law enforcement officials. A combination of both methods may be employed. Although an OC group may

DEFINITION OF ORGANIZED CRIME

Organized crime is a nonideological enterprise involving a number of persons in close social interaction, organized on a hierarchical basis with at least three levels/ranks, for the purpose of securing profit and power by engaging in illegal and legal activities. Positions in the hierarchy and positions involving functional specialization may be assigned on the basis of kinship or friendship, or rationally assigned according to skill. The positions are not dependent on the individuals occupying them at any particular time. Permanency is assumed by the members who strive to keep the enterprise integral and active in pursuit of its goals. It eschews competition and strives for monopoly on an industry or territorial basis. There is a willingness to use violence and/or bribery to achieve ends or to maintain discipline. Membership is restricted, although nonmembers may be involved on a contingency basis. There are explicit rules, oral or written, which are enforced by sanctions that include murder.

strive for a monopoly, this may not be possible given the nature of competing groups or the type of industry, for example, drugs (discussed in chapter 7).

Governed by rules and regulations. An organized crime group, like legitimate organizations, has a set of rules and regulations that members are expected to follow. In an OC crime group, however, a rule-violating member is not fired but, more likely, fired upon.

These attributes are arrayed in a structure that enables the organized crime group to achieve its goals—money and power. There are a number of criminal organizations that have many, if not all, of the attributes that have been discussed. Examples include Mexican and Colombian crime Families, outlaw motorcycle clubs, and Asian crime groups. They will be examined in chapter 5; in this chapter we will look at the structure of the longest continuously existing OC group, Italian-American crime units/Families.

THE STRUCTURE OF ORGANIZED CRIME

The attributes of organized crime that we have examined can fit two contrasting organizational models: the *bureaucratic/corporate* and the *patrimonial/patron-client network*. There is some dispute over the model that best fits the oldest continuing criminal syndicate, Italian-American organized crime (sometimes referred to as "traditional organized crime"). But before we can discuss this issue, it is necessary to examine the etiology of traditional organized crime. This requires that we travel to the area south of Rome known as the

Mezzogiorno—in particular, Sicily, the city of Naples and its surrounding Campania area, and the province of Calabria. More than 80 percent of the Italians who came to the United States were from the south of Rome, and every important Italian-American OC figure had cultural roots in the *Mezzogiorno*.

The Mezzogiorno

The history of southern Italy is one of political, social, and economic repression and exploitation—a succession of foreign rulers culminating in a revolution in 1860 against (Spanish) Bourbon rule that eventually united Italy. For the people of the *Mezzogiorno*, however, little changed. Instead of foreign repression, the *contadini* (peasants) were repressed by other Italians: "The political foundation of the new Italian state," notes Judith Chubb (1982: 16), "was an alliance between the northern industrial bourgeoisie and the southern landed aristocracy." The south "was brought into the Italian nation dragging its feet as the new government issued edict after edict that affected the southerners adversely" (Mangione and Morreale 1992: xv). Thus, the north imposed upon the island of Sicily a tax policy that had the "overall effect of taking money out of Sicilian agriculture for investment in the north" (Finley, Smith, and Duggan 1987: 186). Landowners escaped heavy taxation, which fell disproportionately on the peasants (Catanzaro 1992). Meanwhile, the landed aristocracy, actually absentee landlords who preferred to reside in the urban areas of Palermo, Naples, or even northern Italy, employed what later became known as the *Mafia* to protect their estates and their political interests.

The southern Italian experience dates back more than a thousand years, and it led to the development of a culture that stressed variables necessary for survival in a hostile environment. Neither government nor church was to be trusted. The only basis of loyalty was the family (*famiglia*)—"blood of my blood" (*sangu de me sangu*). Richard Gambino (1974: 3) describes the family of southern Italy:

> The *famiglia* was composed of all of one's blood relatives, including those relatives Americans would consider very distant cousins, aunts, and uncles, an extended clan whose genealogy was traced through paternity. The clan was supplemented through an important custom known as *comparatico* or *comparaggio* (godparenthood), through which carefully selected outsiders became, to an important (but incomplete) extent, members of the family.

The family patriarch, notes Gambino (1974: 4), the *capo di famiglia*, arbitrated all ambiguous situations, and the family was organized hierarchically: "One had absolute responsibilities to family superiors and absolute rights to be demanded from subordinates in the hierarchy." Luigi Barzini (1977: 36) describes the dynamic qualities of the southern Italian family:

> The family, first source of power, had to be made prosperous, respected, and feared with antlike tenacity; it was enlarged (like dynasties of old) by suitable

marriages, strengthened by alliances with families of equal status, by negotiated submission to more powerful ones, or by establishing domination over weaker ones.

In the *famiglia*, physical aggression was rewarded and the strongest member of the domestic group assumed the dominant status.

The southern Italian developed an ideal of manliness, *omertà*, which included noncooperation with authorities, self-control in the face of adversity, and the *vendetta*—any offense or slight to *famiglia* had to be avenged, no matter what the consequences or how long it took. Out of this history and culture developed the famous "secret societies" of southern Italy.

Mafia

The word *Mafia*, states Norman Lewis (1964: 25),

> probably derives from the identical word in Arabic and means "place of refuge." As such, it no doubt recalls the predicament of the relatively civilized Saracens after the conquest of Sicily by the Normans in the eleventh century. The Arabs had introduced small holdings and scientific irrigation. Their rule by comparison with anything the island had known before (or has known since) was mild and beneficent. Had they remained, there is no reason why the property and civilization of Sicily should not have equaled that of Spain, but the Normans dislodged them and plunged the country back into the polar night of feudalism. Most of the Arab small holders became serfs on the reconstituted estates. Some escaped to "the Mafia."

According to James Inciardi (1975: 112–13), "explanations of *Mafia* come from Sicilian historical and literary works that link its root and meaning to elements prevailing within Sicilian culture." The word *Mafia* is apparently Sicilian-Arabic derived from terms meaning to protect and to act as guardian; a friend or companion; to defend; and preservation, power, integrity, strength, and a condition that designates the remedy for damage and ill. As a dialect term in pre-1860 Palermo, *mafia* "expressed 'beauty and excellence,' united with notions of 'superiority' and 'bravery'; in reference to a man it also meant: 'the consciousness of being a man,' 'assurance of the mind,' 'boldness' but never 'defiance,' and 'arrogance' but never 'haughtiness.'" In sum, Inciardi notes, *mafia* means "protection against the arrogance of the powerful, remedy to any damage, sturdiness of body, strength and serenity of spirit, and the best and most exquisite part of life."

Thus, *mafia* is a state of mind, a way of life—not a secret criminal organization. A play in 1863 describing prison life in Palermo, *I Mafiusi della Vicaria*, "gave national currency to a local dialect word that until then had lacked criminal overtones" (Finley, Smith, and Duggan 1987: 182). While a criminal organization known as the "Mafia" did not exist, there were most certainly *mafiosi* who exploited the gap left by an ineffective state, and whose main function was to impose some form of rudimentary order on the anarchy of Sicilian life.

Barzini (1965: 253) separates *mafia* as a state of mind from Mafia as an illegal secret organization. The former (*mafia*) is shared by all Sicilians, the honest and the criminal: "they must aid each other, side with their friends, and fight the common enemies even when the friends are wrong and the enemies are right; each must defend his dignity at all costs and never allow the smallest slight to go unavenged; they must keep secrets and beware of official authorities and laws." In Mafia areas, notes Pino Arlacchi (1986: 13), the issue is never who is "right" and who is "wrong." Instead, "preference tended to be given to whichever party proved victorious in the end, irrespective of the original conflict." Thus, in Mafia areas, at bottom nothing could really be unjust, and honor "was connected less with justice than with domination and physical strength": a Hobbesian world ruled by the credo "might is right."

Barzini points out that the two (Mafia and *mafia*) are closely related, that Mafia could not flourish without *mafia*. Eric Hobsbawm (1976: 92) notes that *mafia* represents a general attitude toward the state:

> A *mafioso* did not invoke State or law in his private quarrels, but made himself respected and safe by winning a reputation for toughness and courage, and settled his differences by fighting. He recognized no obligation except those of the code of honor or *omertà* (manliness), whose chief article forbade giving information to the public authorities.

The absentee landlord who was unwilling to manage his land—many never even visited their fiefs—or unable to do so because of Mafia intimidation, either hired or rented his estate to a *gabelloto*, a manager who had already gained the reputation of *uomo inteso*—"a strong man." The *gabelloto* ruled over the estate with brute force, protecting it from bandits, peasant organizations, unions, and other *mafiosi*. He was assisted by *famiglia*, *amici* (friends), and *campieri* (lawfully armed mounted guards). The *campieri* were hired because they were *uomini di rispettu*, "men of respect," meaning they were quick to use violence and people feared them. An important—that is, widely feared—*campiere* could become a *gabelloto*, a manager. The *gabelloto* did not perform his overseer's functions in person—often he did not even show up on the estate that had been entrusted to his custody; "he simply allowed his name to be mentioned, with the declaration that the estate was under his protection" (Catanzaro 1992: 28). The *gabelloto* was a patron to his peasants, controlling access to scarce resources, in particular farming land, and he acted as a mediator between official power and government and the peasantry, a position he maintained by the exercise of force. In league with the landlords, he fought land reform, labor unions, and revolution (Servadio 1976). The *gabelloto* is a *capomafioso*, and the network of relationships surrounding him, *campieri*, *famiglia*, and *amici*, became known as the Mafia.

While its roots are clearly discernible during the colonial period, the Mafia is the result of unification and democracy (Hobsbawm 1976: 92): "In lawless communities power is rarely scattered among an anarchy of competing units, but clusters round strong points. Its typical form is patronage, its typical holder the private magnate or boss with his body of retainers and dependents and the network of 'influence' which surrounds him and causes men to put themselves under his protection."

The *mafioso* brought order, albeit in a conservative if not reactionary form, and dispensed primitive justice in a lawless society. "The question of lawlessness in Sicily was complicated by the fact that this was a society in which honour, power and mistrust sometimes played a greater role in crime than the mere pursuit of gain" (Finley, Smith, Duggan 1987: 157). *Mafiosi* were frequently not only tolerated by their communities, but "respected to the point where they could parade as standard bearers of a more equitable system of justice than that provided by the state." Outsiders were baffled and governments frustrated by this phenomenon, leading to the development of a myth: that of a widespread secret criminal association (1987: 157) which they called "The Mafia." In terms of structure, however, the Mafia is not a formal organization but rather a collection of groups, or *coche*, plural of *cosca* (Catanzaro 1992).

The Cosca

At the center of the Mafia is the *padrino* or *capomafioso*, around whom other *mafiosi* gather, thereby forming a *cosca*. The word *cosca* alludes to the leaves of an artichoke, the *capomafioso* being the plant's heart. The structure consists of a network of two-man—that is patron-client—relationships based on kinship, patronage, and friendship (Catanzaro 1992). Henner Hess (1973) notes that Mafia is neither an organization nor a secret society—it is a *method*. *Mafiosi* come together in some type of instinctive solidarity to form a *cosca*, a small, cliquelike association to support one another in the pursuit of their aims. The typical *cosca*, notes Arlacchi (1986), rarely has more than fifteen or twenty members, at the center of which are four or five blood relatives. Anton Blok (1974) states that one becomes a member of a *cosca* gradually and not through any type of formal initiation. The *cosca* is devoid of any rigid organization: it is simply *gli amici degli amici*—"friends of friends." The "members" are *gli uomini qualificati* ("qualified men"). Flexibility prevents the *cosca* from becoming bureaucratic: "the need continually to broaden the scope of the networks of social relationships reinforced the impossibility of creating stable organizational structures" (Catanzaro 1992: 40). The *mafioso* succeeds because he commands a *partito*, a network of relationships whereby he is able to act as an intermediary—a broker—providing services, which include votes and violence for the holders of institutionalized power. All he requests in return is immunity to carry out his activities (Hess 1973).

According to Hobsbawm (1976), standardized rituals developed in the 1870s. Once initiated into the *cosca*, the *mafioso* became a *compadre*; this practice is based on the custom of *comparatico* (fictional kinship or godparenthood).

Capomafioso Tommaso Buscetta, born in 1928, describes the ceremony. The initiate is brought to a secluded spot.

> Then a finger is pricked on one of the hands of the person being sworn and the blood is made to fall on a sacred image. Then the image is placed in his hand and is burned. At this time the neophyte must endure the fire, passing the sacred image quickly from one hand to the other until it goes out, and he swears to remain faithful to the principle of the Cosa Nostra, stating solemnly, "May my flesh burn like this holy picture if I am unfaithful to this oath." (Shawcross and Young 1987: 34–35)

The remnants of pre-unification power in western Sicily—*gabelloti, campieri,* and in some instances clergymen, form the *cosche.* Each village has its own *cosca,* larger ones have two, and collectively they are the Mafia.

Barzini (1965) delineates four levels of organization that constitute the Mafia. The first, the family, constitutes the nucleus. Some families, he notes, have belonged to the *società degli amici* for generations, each *padrino* bequeathing the family to his eldest son. The second level consists of a group of several families who come together to form a *cosca;* one family and its *padrino* is recognized as supreme. The *cosca* establishes working relationships with other *cosche,* respecting territories and boundaries. The third level is achieved when *cosche* join in an alliance called *consorteria,* in which one *cosca* is recognized as supreme and its leader is the leader of the *consorteria—capo di tutti capi,* the boss of bosses. "This happens spontaneously... when the *cosche* realize that one of them is more powerful, has more men, more friends, more money, more high-ranking protectors.... All the *consorterie* in Sicily... form the *onerata società.*" A sense of solidarity unites all *mafiosi:* "they know they owe all possible support to any *amico degli amici* who needs it... even if they have never heard of him, provided he is introduced by a mutual *amico*" (Barzini 1965: 272).

Every *mafioso* demands *rispetto,* indeed, is referred to as a *uomo di rispetto*—a man worthy of respect. Cesare Mori (1933: 69) noted that *rispetto* requires "a concrete recognition of the prerogative of immunity belonging to the *mafioso,* not only in his person, but also everything that he had to do with or that he was pleased to take under his protection. In fine, evildoers had to leave the *mafioso* severely alone, and all the persons or things to which, explicitly or implicitly, he had given a guarantee of security." As a man of respect, Mori states, "the *mafioso* is in a position to provide protection where the state is unwilling or unable; to provide arbitration services superior to those available from local judges, especially to the poor person who cannot afford a lawyer, or for those whose justice is of a social, not a legal, nature—the pregnant daughter whose seducer refuses to marry. The *mafioso,* and in particular the *capomafioso,* can put it all right, and his services are speedy and final." The legendary *capomafioso* Calogero ("Don Calo") Vizzini (1877–1954) explained his role as a broker: "In every society there must exist a category of

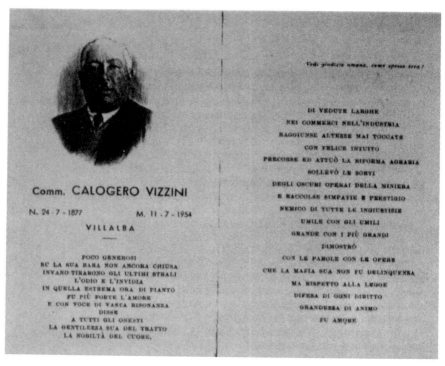

A card commemorating Sicilian *capomafioso* Calogero Vizzini was distributed among friends and relatives in America after his death in 1954. The last part of the eulogy on the right reads: "He was humble with the humble, mighty with the mightiest, and showed with his words and deeds that his mafia was not delinquency but respect for the law, defence of every right, nobleness of spirit, love."

persons who smooth out situations when they become complicated" (Catanzaro 1992: 31).

The constitutional state and elected parliament that accompanied Sicily's union with Italy, notes Gaia Servadio (1976: 17), provided a crucial step in the rise to power of the Mafia—Sicily's special kind of middle class. "With an electorate of little more than 1 percent, the landlords and their friends and employees [*mafiosi*] were often the only voters. If there were any doubt about the result of an election, intimidation was usually effective. As early as January 1861, when the very first parliamentary elections were held, the whole paraphernalia of mafia influence was employed" (Finley, Smith, and Duggan 1987: 183). Because of its ability to control elections, the Mafia was courted by political powers in Rome. Lewis (1964: 41) reports that "the Mafia became the only electoral force that counted in Sicily and the government was realistic in acceptance of the fact." The situation remained unchanged until the rise of Benito Mussolini and the Fascist state.

Mussolini and the Mafia

The rise to power of Mussolini in the 1920s had important implications for the Mafia and Italian-American organized crime. While the south was resistant to Fascism, "Once it became clear that the Fascists would obtain a major share in national power, the entire south became Fascist almost overnight" (Chubb 1982: 25). Jack Reece notes that "during the years immediately after 1922, the Mafia supported Fascism more or less freely. When they were not encumbered with too notorious a prison record or sunk in absolute illiteracy, individual *mafiosi* openly joined the local party organization and at times attained leading positions in it." Reece points out that "alliance with Fascism appeared not only to be the best guarantee of preserving their property, advantages, and prestige, but it also provided a timely opportunity for the acquisition of social and political respectability" (1973: 266). The impact of the Mafia can be seen by comparing the elections of 1922, when no Fascist was elected to Parliament from Sicily, to the elections of 1924, when thirty-eight Fascists were elected out of fifty-seven from Sicily (Servadio 1976).

Mussolini visited Sicily in 1924 and was introduced to Ciccio Cuccia, a *capomafioso* who was also a local mayor. Don[1] Ciccio accompanied *Il Duce* on a tour and, after seeing the large number of police officers guarding him, is reputed to have said: "You're with me, so there's nothing to worry about" (Lewis 1964). To Don Ciccio, the large police escort indicated a lack of *rispetto*. When Mussolini declined to discharge the police contingent, the *capomafioso* arranged for the town piazza to be empty when *Il Duce* made his speech: "When Mussolini began his harangue he found himself addressing a group of about twenty village idiots, one-legged beggars, bootblacks, and lottery-ticket sellers specially picked by Don Ciccio to form an audience" (1964: 72).

A totalitarian regime does not tolerate pockets of authority that are not under its control, and Mussolini quickly moved to destroy the Mafia. Elections were abolished in 1925, depriving the Mafia of its major instrument of alliance with government and an important basis for its immunity from criminal justice. The other important basis was intimidation: "Fascist courts trying criminal cases in which members of the Mafia were implicated found it just as impossible to obtain convictions as it had been for the democratic courts of old" (Lewis 1964: 68). Mussolini responded by investing Prefect Cesare Mori of Lombardy, a career police officer, with emergency police powers and sending him after the Mafia. Christopher Duggan (1989) stresses general lawlessness in western Sicily and a request by a delegation of war veterans as the bases for Mussolini's intervention.

Mori assembled a small army of agents and set about the task of purging the island of *mafiosi*. "Under the jurisdiction of Prefect Mori, repression

---

1. The appellation *Don* is an honorific title used in Sicily to refer to clergymen, government officials, and important *mafiosi*. It derives from the Latin *dominus*, "lord," and is used with the person's first given name.

became savage. Many mafiosi were sent to prison, killed or tortured, but also many left-wingers were called 'mafiosi' for the occasion, and were disposed of. . . . In many cases the landowners provided Mori with information against the mafiosi they had so far employed, who had been their means to safeguard their interests against the peasantry. This was logical because they saw that the regime would provide a better and cheaper substitute" (Servadio 1976: 74). Thus, the Fascists replaced the Mafia as intermediaries and maintainers of Sicilian law and order.

Mori swooped down on villages and with the free application of torture reminiscent of the Inquisition was able to arrest hundreds of *mafiosi*. He arrested Don Ciccio and other important *capomafiosi*. The *gabelloti* were required to be free of any police record, and in 1928 Mori declared that the Mafia had been destroyed. However, the reality was otherwise, and the Mafia began to reassert itself by 1941. When questioned by Allied officials at the end of World War II, Mori stated: "I drove the mafia underground all right. I had unlimited police powers and a couple of battalions of Blackshirts. But how can you stamp out what is in people's blood?" (Sciascia 1963: 6).

The campaign against the Mafia did succeed in driving out of Sicily some important *mafiosi*. They travelled to the United States at an opportune time, during the Prohibition era. (The impact of these men on organized crime in America will be discussed in chapter 3.) Judith Chubb (1982: 27) notes, however, that many Mafia bosses assumed important positions within the regime, and the Fascists failed to significantly transform social and economic conditions upon which the Mafia depended: "It was no surprise that the mafia rapidly reemerged as soon as Fascism fell." Many *mafiosi* awaited "liberation," which came in the form of the Allied landing in 1943. (The post-World War II Mafia will be discussed in chapter 5.)

Camorra

While the Mafia began as more of an idea than an organization, and while it evolved along cultural lines in western Sicily, the Camorra was a deliberately structured criminal society. The term *camorra* is believed to have derived from the Castillian *kamora*, meaning "contestation," and was imported into Naples during the years of Spanish domination (Serao 1911a). Ernest Serao reports that the forbears of the Neapolitan Camorra were the Spanish brigands of the Sierras known as the *gamuri* (1911a: 723): "Not a passer-by nor a vehicle escaped their watchful eye and their fierce claws, so that traveling or going from one place to another on business was impossible for anyone without sharing with the ferocious watchers of the Sierras either the money he had with him or the profits of the business that had taken him on his journey."

While there are several versions of how the term *camorra* came into being (Walston 1986), it seems clear that the Camorra developed in the Spanish prisons during Bourbon rule of the Two Sicilies (the *Mezzogiorno*), early in the nineteenth century. The members of this criminal society eventually moved their control of the prisons into Naples proper (a phenomenon that has its parallel with prison gangs in the United States, discussed in chapter 5). Eric Hobsbawm notes that they were "rather tightly, centrally, and hierarchically organized" (1959: 55). John McConaughy reports (1931: 244):

> The Camorra of Naples was organized as openly and carefully as a public school system, or an efficient political machine in one of our own cities. Naples was divided into twelve districts, and each of these into a number of sub-districts. Although burglary and other remunerative felonies were not neglected, extortion was the principal industry; and the assassination of an inconvenient person could be purchased by anyone with the price. In the case of a friend in need, a murder could be arranged without any charge—a simple gesture of affection.

One English diplomat in Naples (quoted in Hibbert 1966: 181–82) during the 1860s observed:

> There was no class, high or low, that did not have its representatives among the members of the Society which was a vast organized association for the extortion of blackmail in every conceivable shape and form. Officials, officers of the King's Household, the police and others were affiliated with the most desperate of the criminal classes in carrying out the depredations, and none was too high or too low to escape them. If a petition was to be presented to the Sovereign or to a Minister, it had to be paid for; at every gate of the town *Camorristi* were stationed to exact a toll on each cart or donkey load brought to market by the peasants; and on going into a hackney *carrosel* in the street, I have seen one of the band run up and get his fee from the driver. No one thought of refusing to pay, for the consequences of a refusal were too well known, anyone rash enough to demur being apt to be found soon after mysteriously stabbed by some unknown individual, whom the police were careful never to discover.

The Camorra was "more efficiently organized than the police," notes Francis Ianni (1972: 22), "and set up a parallel system of law in the typical southern Italian style." When Giuseppe Garibaldi (1807–82) became active in the Two Sicilies, in Naples the Bourbon king actually turned police powers over to the Camorra, and those members in jail were set free. The Camorra constituted not only the *de facto* but also the legally constituted police power in Naples (McConaughy 1931). James Walston (1986) states that the *camorristi* had been freed upon the proclamation of the constitution in 1860, and it was the new prefect who used the Camorra to maintain order. The Camorra welcomed Garibaldi and his "Red Shirts" in 1860, and after his success their power increased. Gambino (1974) states that the Camorra was at its peak of power from 1880 until 1900. "If they so decided, there would not be, in some regions, a single vote cast for a candidate for the Chamber of Deputies who was opposed to their man" (Ianni 1974: 246). Walston (1986) reports that the Camorra is still very much involved in politics, but does not exert the same level of influence as the Mafia does in western Sicily or the 'Ndrangheta in southern Calabria.

According to Serao, in contrast with the Mafia, the Camorra was highly organized and disciplined (1911a: 724): "There is a *capo'ntrine*—a sectional head—and a *capo in testa*, or local head-in-chief of the Camorra, a kind of president of the confederation of all the twelve sections into which Naples is divided and which are presided over by the *capi'ntrini*." The lowest or entry level of the Camorra is the *picciuotto*, which requires an act of daring—often simply a bloody deed, including "very dreadful crimes committed against very peaceful and quiet people" (1911b: 781). The *picciuotto*

> has no share in the social dividend. If he wishes to live on other people's money, he must do the best he can by stealing, cheating, or swindling whom he can, giving, however, to his superiors of the Camorra proper *shruffo* or proportionate percentage.
>
> Only the regular Camorrist participates in the social dividends. In the prisons, when there are *picciuotti* and Camorrists, the former must make the beds and wait upon the latter, collect the dues from the non-associates and give them to the *cuntaiuola*, treasurer, who will pass the amount to his superiors. The *cuntaiuola* must produce every Saturday a balance-sheet giving an account of all the dues collected during the week. . . . Thus, the imprisoned Camorrists often send out to their families handsome sums of money. These families enjoy just the same the "right of Camorra" (*shruffo*), and the wives and children of the Camorrist receive every week from the *cuntaiuola* of the gang to which he belonged the sum of money which would have been due to him had he been at liberty. (1911b: 781)

Below the *picciuotti* are specialized associates of the Camorra such as the *batista*—a person who can plan burglaries because of his access to the homes of wealthy persons. The Camorra has its own authorized fences, usually dealers in second-hand goods, who arrange for the auction of stolen articles.

The Camorra also differed from the Mafia in the style of dress and comportment of its members. While even a *capomafioso* exuded an air of modesty in both dress and manner of speaking, the camorrista was a flamboyant actor whose manner of walking and style of dress clearly marked him as a member of the *società*. In the United States, the public profile of important Italian-American organized figures with a Neapolitan heritage have tended toward Camorra, while their Sicilian counterparts have usually been more subdued. Al Capone, for example, and, in more recent years, John Gotti, boss of the Gambino crime Family, are both of Neapolitan heritage.

In 1912, in the "Cuocolo Case," a key witness allowed the *carabinieri* (federal police) to prosecute the entire Camorra hierarchy (Walston 1986). Given its highly formal structure, this was devastating to continuity. Ianni (1972) states that the Camorra did not survive Mussolini, since, like the Mafia, it required weak government control. McConaughy (1931: 248) writes that the Camorra welcomed the Fascists as they had Garibaldi; after that there was not a

Camorra: "They are all Fascists, and everything they do is legal." While there are still criminals operating in Naples identified as being part of the Camorra, Ianni (1972) states that they have no direct links to the criminal society of the past.

Vincenzo Ruggiero (1993: 143) states that the last boss of the traditional Camorra died of natural causes in 1989 "after having acted for years as an informal 'justice of the peace' in one of the most crowded areas of the city. He settled disputes and, it is said, helped the poor." In an interview shortly before his death, "he mourned an end of an era—that of the men of honour who succored the people—and condemned the present, dominated by cruel, greedy and unscrupulous individuals."

Postwar Naples has been plagued with violence attributed to a "New Camorra," *Nuova Camorra Organizzata*. The leader of one of the important Camorra groups, Don Raffaele Cutola (born in 1941), reportedly has been running his Family while serving a twenty-four-year sentence for murder and extortion. His expansionist activities brought him into conflict with other New Camorra groups—in 1980 and 1981 there were 380 murders attributed to the "Camorra War." Consistent with its historical origins, Cutola's group, which numbers about two thousand (Walston 1986), does most of its recruiting in jails. Naples has always had a reputation as a major center for smuggling, and the New Camorra is involved in the smuggling of narcotics (in cooperation with the Mafia), cigarettes, and other consumer goods; gambling; and especially extortion from illegitimate and legitimate enterprises (Schmetzer 1982; Kamm 1982c; Walston 1986).

'Ndrangheta

A third part of the *Mezzogiorno*, Calabria, is the home of the *Onerate Società* ("Honored Society") or *'Ndrangheta* ("Brotherhood"), another "cousin" of the Mafia. In Calabria the term *'ndrangheta* is used to indicate a high degree of heroism and virtue as embodied in the *'ndranghetisti* who are ruled by *omertà* (Arlacchi 1986).

Actually several bands that grew out of government repression, the *'Ndrangheta* gained popular support because of its political stance against the central government. Gambino states (1974: 289):

> In 1861 the new Italian government sent troops to police Calabria. The old economic order had collapsed under the strains of national unification, and the number of gangs had increased. Because of the government's deliberate policy of favoring the North over the South of Italy in its programs of economic development, and because of its ignorant and arrogant insensitivity to the customs of the South, the Calabrians soon grew to hate the new government in the North. They naturally turned to the gangs.

These gangs mixed political insurrection with banditry and were supported and romanticized by the repressed peasantry. Hobsbawm notes (1969: 56), however, that the *'Ndrangheta* had no positive program; its sense of social justice was basically destructive: "In such circumstances to assert power, any power, is itself a triumph. Killing and torture is the most primitive and personal assertion of ultimate power, and the weaker the rebel feels himself to be at bottom, the greater we may suppose, the temptation to assert it." The present day 'Ndrangheta differs little, if at all, from the "New Mafia" discussed in chapter 5 (see Arlacchi 1986), and is often referred to as the "Calabrian Mafia."

With the lessons of southern Italy serving as important background, let us return to our discussion of the structure of traditional organized crime and two contrasting organizational models: the *bureaucratic/corporate* and the *patrimonial/ patron-client network*.

Bureaucratic/Corporate Model

The corporation, the police, and the military are examples of bureaucracies, that mode of organization essential for efficiently carrying out large-scale tasks. All bureaucracies share a number of attributes; they are rationally organized with:

- a complicated hierarchy
- an extensive division of labor
- positions assigned on the basis of skill
- responsibilities carried out in an impersonal manner
- extensive rules and regulations
- communication from the top of the hierarchy to persons on the bottom, usually in written (memo) form

While traditional organized crime "is not merely the Sicilian Mafia transplanted," Donald Cressey (1969: 8) states, "the similarities between the two organizations are direct and too great to be ignored." According to Cressey (1967a: 7–8) traditional organized crime groups are bureaucratic, the basic unit being a monopolistic corporation called the *Family*, consisting of men of Italian heritage (figure 1.1):

Each family is headed by one man, the "boss," whose primary functions are maintaining order and maximizing profits. Subject only to the possibility of being overruled by the national advisory group, which will be discussed below, his authority in all matters relating to his family is absolute.

Beneath each boss is an "underboss," the vice-president or deputy director of the family. He collects information for the boss; he relays messages to him; and passes his instructions down to his own underlings. In the absence of the boss, the underboss acts for him.

On the same level as the underboss, but operating in a staff capacity, is the *consigliere*, who is a counselor or adviser. Often an elder member of the family who has partially retired from a career in crime, he gives advice to family members, including the boss and underboss, and thereby enjoys considerable influence and power.

Below the level of the underboss are the *caporegime*[2], some of whom serve as buffers between the top members of the family and the lower-echelon personnel. To maintain their insulation from the police, the leaders of the hierarchy (particularly the boss) avoid direct communication with the workers. All commands, information, complaints, and money flow back and forth through a trusted go-between. A *caporegime* fulfilling this buffer capacity, however, unlike the underboss, does not make decisions or assume any authority of his boss.

Other *caporegime* serve as chiefs of operating units. The number of men supervised in each unit varies with the size and activities of particular families. Often the *caporegime* has one or two associates who work closely with him, carrying orders, information, and money to the men who belong to his unit. From a business standpoint, the *caporegime* is analogous to plant supervisor or sales manager.

The lowest level "members" of a family are the *soldati*, the soldiers or "button" men who report to the *caporegime*. A soldier may operate a particular illicit enterprise—e.g., a loan-sharking operation, a dice game, a lottery, a bookmaking operation, a smuggling operation—on a commission basis, or he may "own" the enterprise and pay a portion of its profit to the organization, in return for the right to operate. Partnerships are common between two or more soldiers and between soldiers and men higher up in the hierarchy. Some soldiers and most upper-echelon family members have interests in more than one business.

Beneath the soldiers in the hierarchy are large numbers of employees and commission agents who are not members of the family and are not necessarily of Italian descent. These are the people who do most of the actual work in the various enterprises. They have no buffers or other insulation from law enforcement. . . .

The highest ruling body of the twenty-four families is the "commission." This body serves as a combination legislature, supreme court, board of directors, and arbitration board; its principal functions are judicial. Family members look to the commission as the ultimate authority on organizational and jurisdictional disputes. It is composed of the Nation's most powerful bosses, but has authority over all twenty-four.

Ralph Salerno, a former police officer with the New York City Police Department's Central Intelligence Bureau and, like Cressey, a consultant to the Task Force on Organized Crime, also emphasizes the corporate analogy (Salerno and Tompkins 1969: 84–85):

The major difference between the diagram of an organized crime family and the chart of a major corporation is that the head of the enterprise—the Boss—does not have a box over him labeled "stockholder." Many of the other boxes are paralleled in the underworld. The Underboss serves a function similar to that of executive vice-president. The Counselor off to one side is much like a

---

2. The plural of *caporegime* is *capiregime*, although it is often Anglicized as caporegimes. It is often used interchangeably with *capodecina* or "chief of ten."

THE LAWYER AS *CONSIGLIERE*

In the *Godfather* saga, the Irish attorney Tom Hagen served as a *consigliere* for the Corleone Family. In real life, the PCOC (1985b: 3–4) points to attorneys who appear to have played a similar role. According to the President's Commission there are

a small group of attorneys who have become integral parts of criminal conspiracies, using their status as sworn officers of the court to advance the criminal purposes of these criminal organizations. It is clear that traditional organized crime and narcotics traffickers depend upon, and could not effectively operate without, these attorneys. [They] also have a network of tested auxiliaries to draw upon, including former police officers and investigators. These private investigators use their contracts within the investigative agencies to gather information to which they are not legally entitled.

vice-chairman of the board or a special assistant. He is an advisor but has no command authority. . . .

The lieutenants or captains farther below are equivalent of divisional vice-presidents or general managers. There are different staff jobs corresponding to personnel director, public relations manager, general counsel, security officer, and the like, but they are not assigned permanently to any one man. . . .

Cressey notes that "not everyone who wants to participate in the business conducted by crime syndicates can do so. One cannot 'just decide' to become a member of Cosa Nostra[3] . . . any more than he can 'just decide' to become a professional baseball player. . . . His desires must be matched by his competence, and by the desires of those who control membership" (1969: 242). Cressey points out that the incarceration or death of a member of any crime Family does little to affect the Family's activities, because for each membership position there are at least a hundred applicants.

Every bureaucratic organization has an elaborate set of rules and regulations that govern the behavior of its members. Cressey (1967a: 40) admits, however, that "we have been unable to locate even a summary of the code of conduct which is used in governing the lives of American crime families." This

---

3. Cosa Nostra, literally "Our Thing," or La Cosa Nostra (LCN), which is grammatically incorrect, is how Cressey and the Federal Bureau of Investigation refer to Italian-American crime units/Families.

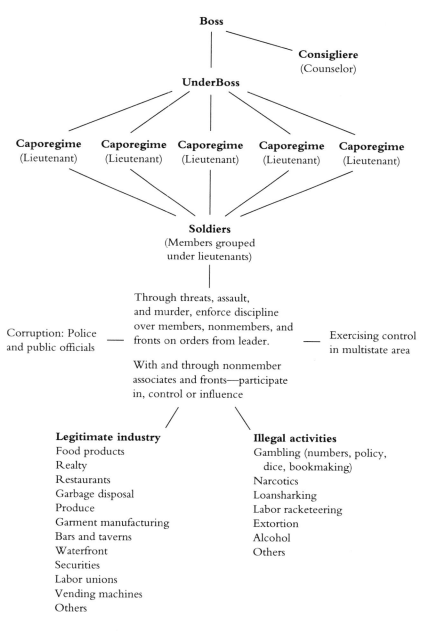

Figure 1.1. An Organized Crime Family

Boss

Consigliere
(Counselor)

UnderBoss

Caporegime
(Lieutenant)

Caporegime
(Lieutenant)

Caporegime
(Lieutenant)

Caporegime
(Lieutenant)

Caporegime
(Lieutenant)

Soldiers
(Members grouped
under lieutenants)

Corruption: Police
and public officials —

Through threats, assault,
and murder, enforce discipline
over members, nonmembers, and
fronts on orders from leader.

— Exercising control
in multistate area

With and through nonmember
associates and fronts—participate
in, control or influence

Legitimate industry
Food products
Realty
Restaurants
Garbage disposal
Produce
Garment manufacturing
Bars and taverns
Waterfront
Securities
Labor unions
Vending machines
Others

Illegal activities
Gambling (numbers, policy,
  dice, bookmaking)
Narcotics
Loansharking
Labor racketeering
Extortion
Alcohol
Others

Source: Task Force on Organized Crime, 1967, 9.

deficiency is corrected by assuming commonality between the code of prison inmates and that of organized crime (1967a: 41):

> The snippets of information we have been able to obtain have convinced us that there is a striking similarity between the code of conduct and the enforcement machinery used in the confederation of organized crime and the code of conduct and enforcement machinery which governs the behavior of prisoners. This is no coincidence for . . . both the prisoner and the confederation governments are responses to strong official governments which are limited in their means for achieving their control objectives. In order to maintain their status as governors of illegal organizations, the leaders of the two types of organization must promulgate and enforce similar behavior codes.

Based on this analogy, Cressey suggests five rules of conduct (1969: 175–76; italics deleted):

1. Be loyal to members of the organization. Do not interfere with each other's interests. Do not be an informer. . . .
2. Be rational. Be a member of the team. Do not engage in battle if you cannot win. . . .
3. Be a man of honor. Always do right. Respect womanhood and your elders. Do not rock the boat. . . .
4. Be a stand-up guy. Keep your eyes and ears open and your mouth shut. Do not sell out. . . .
5. Have class. Be independent. Know your way around the world. . . .

Assuming the analogy to be correct, these rules appear to be more of a value system than a formally organized set of operating instructions for guiding a bureaucratic organization.

Before turning to the second model of organized crime, we should note some important ramifications of describing Italian-American OC as bureaucratic/corporate. Ianni (1972: 110) states that the bureaucratic analogy "may arise from honest attempts to explain syndicate organization in terms that are familiar to the public." But Ianni is suspicious: a widespread belief in the existence of an evil corporation with a set of goals aimed at corrupting and subverting the American way of life can enhance the efforts of law enforcement agencies to increase their budgetary allocations. And Dwight Smith (1975: 88) argues that "proving" the existence of such an organization can justify the use of certain law enforcement techniques that otherwise might be severely limited if not curtailed; for example, electronic eavesdropping. Richard Quinney (1974: 104), writing from a conflict perspective, argues that the "war" against organized crime "further extends the power of the government over the lives of citizens, overturning even constitutional protections."

Patrimonial/Patron-Client Networks

Francis Ianni (1972) argues that the Italian-American version of organized crime is a traditional social system organized by action and by cultural values that have nothing to do with modern bureaucratic or corporate principles. He maintains that Italian-American crime syndicates are better explained through an examination of kinship networks: the subtitle of Ianni's (1972) book is *Kinship and Social Control in Organized Crime*. In other words, the structure of traditional organized crime is based on the traditions and experiences of southern Italy.

Instead of bureaucratic, Italian-American OC can be seen as *patrimonial* (Collins 1975: 65n):

> Patrimonial organization, most characteristic of traditional societies, centers around families, patrons and their clients, and other personalistic networks. The emphasis is on traditional rituals that demonstrate the emotional bonds among men; the world is divided into those whom one can trust because of strongly legitimated personal connections, and the rest of the world from whom nothing is to be expected that cannot be exacted by cold-blooded bargaining or force. In modern bureaucratic organization, by contrast, personal ties are weaker, less ritualized and emotionally demonstrative; in their place is the allegiance to a set of abstract rules and positions. The different class cultures in patrimonial and bureaucratic organizations are accordingly affected. Patrimonial elites are more ceremonious and personalistic. Bureaucratic elites emphasize a colder set of ideals.

Many aspects of a bureaucracy are impractical for organized crime, in which there must be constant concern with the very real possibility that communications are being monitored. The use of the telephone must be limited (often used only to arrange for in-person meetings). Written communication is avoided. Information, orders, money, and other goods are transmitted on an intimate, face-to-face basis. Lengthy chains of command, characteristic of modern bureaucracy, are impractical for organized crime, and this limits the span of control. Randall Collins (1975: 293) points out that control is a special problem for patrimonial organizations. Bureaucracies develop, he argues, to overcome such problems: "Patrimonial organizations cannot be very well controlled much beyond the sight of the master." He notes that when the geographic range becomes too great, the organization collapses into feudalism. In organized crime this can have deadly consequences: When Lucchese crime boss Vittorio ("Little Vic") Amuso lost control of the New Jersey faction of his Family, he declared them outlaws and ordered the entire crew headed by *caporegime* Anthony Accetturo executed.

In fact, says Mark Moore (1987: 53), a highly centralized organization "tends to make the enterprise too dependent on the knowledge and judgment of the top management, and wastes the knowledge and initiative of subordinate managers who know more about their own capabilities and how they fit into a local environment of risks and opportunities." But the very informality of organized crime brings with it other dangers. In 1977, for example, Ruby Stein, a major loanshark for the Gambino crime Family, was murdered by the Westies, a group of Irish-American criminals from New York's West Side—the Westies owed Stein a considerable amount of money. The murderers dismembered their victim and stole his "black book" containing records of Stein's loans. As a result, the Gambino Family was unable to claim millions of dollars in outstanding loans—there were no duplicate or backup records (English 1990).

Decentralization in a criminal organization can be advantageous for both business and security reasons, notes Joseph Albini (1971: 285). He points out that the bureaucratic model would be a relatively easy target to move against: "All that would be necessary to destroy it would be to remove its top echelon." Instead, Albini argues, the syndicate's real power lies in its amorphous quality: "If a powerful syndicate figure is incarcerated, all that has really been severed is his position as a patron to his clients." If it so happens that another individual is in a position to assume this role, the clients may continue in the enterprise. The alternative is to find a new patron-boss or *caporegime*—or to develop their own enterprises.

Every person is embedded in a social network, notes Jeremy Boissevain (1974: 24): "the chains of persons with whom a given person is in contact." Since contact can be through a chain of persons, an individual can send "messages" to far more people than he or she actually knows on a direct basis. These are the "friends of friends," a phrase that refers to *mafiosi* in Sicily. Boissevain (1974: 147) writes: "Every individual provides a point at which networks interact. But not everyone displays the same interest in and talent for cultivating relationships with strategic persons for profit." To be successful, each member of organized crime from the boss down to a soldier—just like Sicilian *mafiosi*—must display such interest and talent. This is done by acting as a patron. When the social exchange relationship (see Homans 1961; Blau 1964) becomes unbalanced, we have a patron-client relationship. The patron "provides economic aid and protection against both the legal and illegal exaction of authority. The client, in turn, pays back in more intangible assets," for example, esteem and loyalty. He may also offer political or other important support, thus making the relationship reciprocal (Wolf 1966: 16–17). The patron—whether a *mafioso* in Sicily or his American equivalent—acts as a power broker between the client and the wider society, both legitimate and illegitimate.

The member of an Italian-American OC unit, acting as a patron—like the Sicilian *mafioso*—controls certain resources as well as strategic contacts with people who control other resources directly or who have access to such persons. The member-as-patron can put a client "in touch with the right people." He can bridge communication gaps between the police and criminals, between businessmen and syndicate-connected union leaders; he can transcend the world of business and the world of the illegitimate entrepreneur. He is able to perform important favors and be rewarded in return with money or power.

Boissevain (1974) and Hess (1973) refer to this network surrounding patrons as *partito*: a circle of dyadic relationships orbiting the OC member in which most clients have no relations with each other except through the patron.

The patron needs a great deal of time to manage such a network adequately, notes Boissevain (1974), to develop and maintain contacts, provide services and enhance power and income, and to keep well informed. Since OC members do not usually have to maintain conventional schedules, they are free to "hang around," to pick up and disseminate important information. An OC patron may dominate a particular geographic area or industry. He will have available a network of informants and connections, for example, with the police and other officials, as well as specialized criminal operatives such as *papermen* (persons who convert stolen "paper," for example, stocks, bonds, checks, into cash), *torches* (professional arsonists), *muscle-men* or *legbreakers*, and *enforcers*. He is in a position to fence large amounts of stolen goods or to lend out various amounts of money at usurious interest—loansharking. He will act as a center for information (providing targets for professional burglars, for example), "license" criminal activities (for example, allow a high-stakes dice game to operate), and use his position to assist criminals in linking up for specialized operations (for example, finding a driver for a robbery or hijack team). He can provide stolen firearms and cars and other items necessary for conventional criminal activity. A single member of OC can be the center of, and act as a catalyst for, a large amount of criminal activity.

Criminal activities in *his* territory not under his patronage are "outlaw" operations whose participants act without his grace. If they are arrested he will not intervene; if their activities conflict with those under his patronage, police raids or violence will result. When Joe Aiello of the Genovese Family decided to deal with an independent bookmaker not under his patronage, he called upon New York City Police Department (NYPD) detective John Manca (with Cosgrove 1991: 129):

> Later that day I drove down to Union Square. The bookie was so independent and small-time that he was running his own slips. I followed him into an apartment house, stuck a gun in his back, and forced him down to the basement. His knees were practically knocking. I grabbed this big manila envelope he was carrying, then handcuffed him to the boiler. He was begging me not to kill him. I emptied the envelope—money and slips fell out. There was about twelve hundred dollars. I scooped the money up, put it in my pocket. Then I picked up the betting slips and threw them in the boiler. The guy started to cry. I left him there, cuffed to the boiler.

Independent criminal operatives may be forced to pay tribute for "protection" —protection from violence that the OC member can inflict or cause to be inflicted. Professional criminals who are not necessarily part of organized crime will often pay financial tribute to an OC patron, indicating *rispetto*. This show of *rispetto* enables criminals to secure vital information and other assistance and ensures that other criminals will not jeopardize their operations.

27

Vincent Siciliano (1970: 55) provides an example. He and his gang held up a card game that was under the patronage of the Genovese crime Family in New York—a "connected" game. And he was summoned:

> When we got to the cafe and those big shots started laying down the law and telling us we knocked over one of their games, butter wouldn't melt in my mouth. I told them I was careful to ask if the game has any connections, and the other guys agreed that nobody had any idea in the whole world that the game had any connections.
>
> The way we always put it (the way you still put it) is that we didn't know they were "good people," which is like saying the guy is an American or an official something. Part of some organization. Not an outlaw.
>
> First they made us give back the money.

In sum, at the center of the patrimonial/patron-client network model of organized crime is the boss—the *pater familias*—who may be assisted by an underboss (*sottocapo*) and counselor (*consigliere*). The boss is the "patron's patron." In a structure that resembles a model of the universe, the boss is surrounded by clients; for example, captains (*capiregime*) to whom he acts as a patron. The captains are surrounded by members or soldiers (*soldati*), to whom they act as patrons. This crime unit is tied together in a network that includes nonmember associates who are clients of each of the members, including the boss and captains. In the Italian-American version of OC, each of the bosses is connected (by kinship, friendship, mutual respect) to every other boss. This structure represents what W. Richard Scott (1981) refers to as a *natural system*: members are not necessarily guided by their organization's goals, but they share a common interest in the survival of the system and engage in collective activities informally structured to secure this end. In organized crime as a natural system, the OC unit is more than an instrument for attaining defined goals; it is fundamentally a social group attempting to adapt and survive in a dangerous environment.

Italian-American Crime Groups/Families

The basic unit within Italian-American crime is the "Family" or *borgata*. The actual name by which a group is known, however, may vary. In New England, for example, it is the "Office"; in Chicago, it is the "Outfit." Groups in the New York metropolitan area are known as "Families." While any number of members may be related, the term Family does not imply kinship by blood or marriage (which is why we distinguish the term by using upper case "F"). According to the President's Commission there are twenty-four of these groups—"LCN Families"—with a total membership of about 1,700; about one-half of the strength is in the five New York Families (PCOC 1986a).

The reference to twenty-four separate "LCN" groups is troubling; it is a number that has been used for decades despite obvious changes that have occurred in traditional OC. In a number of cities that have historically had

Figure 1.2. Patron-Client Network of Italian-American Organized Crime

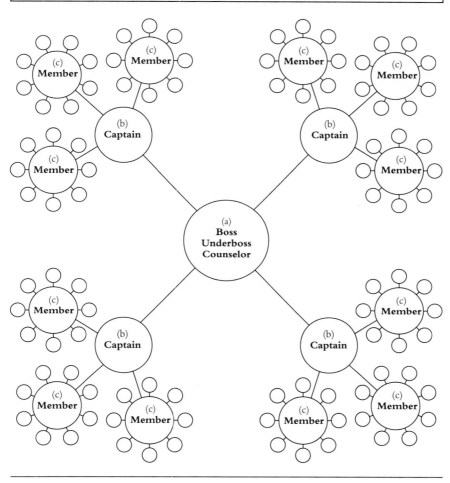

(a) At the center of each organized crime unit (*famiglia:* Family) is the boss (*capo*).
   He is assisted by an underboss (*sottocapo*) and a counselor (*consigliere*).
(b) Surrounding the boss are his clients, the captains (*capiregime*).
(c) Orbiting around each captain are his clients, the lowest-ranking members who
   have been formally initiated into the Family (*soldati:* "made-guys").
(d) The members act as patrons to nonmember clients.
(e) Each unit is tied to other Families throughout the country by the *capo*, whose
   sovereignty is recognized by the other bosses.

traditional OC units, these are either no longer viable, for example, Denver,
Cleveland; or totally absent, for example, Madison, Wisconsin; Springfield,
Illinois; Dallas. And although the government has identified a traditional crime
group in New Orleans, the amorphous structure characteristic of the Carlos

Marcello[4] Family has defied efforts to describe it or assess its strength (Ridenhour 1992). Jay Albanese (1989) elaborates on the contradictions that exist as to the number of "LCN families" operating in the United States. Each crime unit is composed of members and associates.

Membership

The concept of "membership" may provide an important key to understanding traditional organized crime and its peculiar ability to survive as a dominant force for more than six decades. In crime circles the importance of membership is revealed by the numerous terms and phrases to indicate membership status: "made-guy," "wise-guy," "button" or "receiving his button," "being straightened out," "goodfella," "*amico*," and "friend of ours." And there is also a ceremony, described by Joseph Valachi, who was initiated by Joseph Maranzano (discussed in chapter 3) into what became the Genovese Family. It is strikingly similar to that described above by *capomafioso* Tommaso Buscetta:

> "Which finger do you shoot with?"
> I said, "This one," and I hold up my right forefinger. I was still wondering what he meant by this when he told me to make a cup out of my hands. Then he put a piece of paper in them and lit it with a match and told me to say after him, as I was moving the paper back and forth, "This is the way I will burn if I betray the secret of this Cosa Nostra." (Maas 1968: 95–95)

At a 1991 trial, Philip Leonetti, a member of the Philadelphia crime Family of Nicky Scarfo, described his initiation at the home of a Family captain in South Philadelphia:

> Entering a room of family members, he was shown a gun and a knife, and he swore to use them to help his friends. As part of the ceremony, he was supposed to hold the picture of a saint in his hands while the picture was burned, symbolizing what would happen "if I betray my friends." But they did not have a saint's picture, so they just burned a tissue paper in his hands and told him to "make believe the tissue paper is the picture of a saint." (Lubasch 1991a: 16)

At the 1992 trial of John Gotti, Salvatore Gravano recalled being made a member of the Gambino Family:

> He [boss Paul Castellano] asked me if I liked everybody there. I told him yes. He asked me a few questions. One of the last questions he asked me was would I kill if he asked me to. I told him yes.
> He told me what [sic] was my trigger finger. I pointed to my trigger finger. He pinched it [with a needle], blood came out. He put it on the saint, and started to burn the saint in my hand. He said, honor the oath. He said to me,

---

4. Eighty-three-year-old Carlos Marcello died of natural causes on March 2, 1993. Many popular sources linked the New Orleans crime boss to the assassination of President John F. Kennedy, a link that has never been proven.

BEING "MADE" IN NEW ENGLAND

On October 29, 1989, two electronic eavesdropping devices were placed in the basement ceiling of a house in Medford, Massachusetts, a Boston suburb. The bugs recorded the initiation of four men into the crime Family then headed by Raymond Patriarca, Jr., who presided at the ceremony. Apparently, the induction was an effort to bring peace to the Family, which had been racked by internal divisions since the death of long-time boss Raymond Patriarca, Sr.

> [Patriarca] We're all here to bring in some new members into our Family and more than that, to start maybe a new beginning. Put all that's got started behind us. 'Cause they come into our Family to start a new thing with us. . . .

The prospects were introduced to the gathered Family members and *consigliere* Joe Russo asked each to individually take an oath in Italian/Sicilian (translated):

> I want to enter into this organization to protect my family and to protect all of my friends. I swear not to divulge this secret and to obey with love and *omertà*.

He was then assigned to a *caporegime*.

Each candidate was then asked which finger he shoots with, and that finger was pricked to draw blood. A holy card with the image of the Patriarca family saint was burned. The prospect was told that he was required to keep secrets and could only leave the Family dead. Some details of mob protocol and rules were explained: introduce other members as "a friend of ours" and associates as "a friend of mine"; kill anyone who betrays the Family, even if he is your brother, if ordered; respect the female relatives of other members—under penalty of death; memorize the chain of command; keep your *caporegime* informed of your whereabouts; all crime Families in America are related; avoid kissing other members in public—too conspicuous.

On December 3, 1991, Patriarca pleaded guilty to racketeering charges related to this ceremony.

> that if I divulge any of the secrets of this organization that my soul should burn like the saint.
>
> I kissed him on both cheeks. I kissed everybody. I went around the table and kissed everybody. I sat down. They got up. They locked hands. They unlocked hands. They made me get in the middle of it.
>
> They locked hands again and told me, at that point, I was part of the brotherhood. I was a made member and I belonged.

Michael Franzese of the Colombo Family reports a two-stage process. First, he was formally proposed: taken by an old-time member to meet the Family boss who explained the rules. "After the meeting, my name, along with those of the other potential inductees, was circulated around the other five families" (1992: 124). Franzese was then assigned to a *caporegime* for a probationary period of nearly a year. In 1975, he was formerly inducted in a ceremony similar to those already described.

According to Ianni (1974), childhood gangs in the ghetto are sources of OC membership. Salvatore Giangana, more widely known as Sam ("Momo") Giancana[5], Chicago OC boss, began his career in the "42 Gang" in the Irish neighborhood known as "The Patch"—which was gradually adding more and more Italian families. Salerno (1969) reports that recruitment into OC involves the careful study of neighborhood youngsters by those who control membership. A potential recruit must exhibit a recognition of the authority of the organization and a willingness to perform various criminal and noncriminal functions (usually minor at first) with skill and daring and without asking questions. Robert Woetzel (1963: 3) points out that "the standards of the teenage gang from which the potential criminals come are the same as those of an adult conspiracy": a code of loyalty and exclusive "turf" (territory). The gang boy may also have a criminal record and antisocial attitude, which indicate that he is a "stand-up" kid, the proper credentials for a career in organized crime.

Raymond Martin, a former ranking officer with the NYPD, describes why recruitment is made easy in certain Italian neighborhoods in Brooklyn (1963: 61):

> On so many street corners in Bath Beach, in so many luncheonettes and candy stores in Bensonhurst, boys see the mob-affiliated bookies operate. They meet the young toughs, the mob enforcers. They hear the tales of glory recounted—who robbed what, who worked over whom, which showgirl shared which gangster's bed, who got hit by whom, the techniques of the rackets and how easy it all is, how the money rolls in. What wonder is it that some boys look forward to being initiated into these practices with the eagerness of a college freshman hoping to be pledged by the smoothest fraternity on campus. With a little luck and guts, they feel, even they may someday belong to that splendid, high-living band, the mob.

One recruit, raised in the OC neighborhood of Brooklyn's East New York-Brownsville section, recounts (Pileggi 1985: 13):

> At the age of twelve my ambition was to be a gangster. To be a wiseguy. To me being a wiseguy was better than being president of the United States. It meant power among people who had no power. It meant perks in a working-class neighborhood that had no privileges. To be a wiseguy was to own the world. I dreamed of being a wiseguy the way other kids dreamed about being doctors or movie stars or firemen or ball players.

---

5. Whenever appropriate, I will make note of nicknames, since they are important in organized crime, and often the only way to properly identify OC figures with any accuracy.

An undercover FBI agent describes the day Jilly Greca was "made" —became a member of the Colombo crime Family (Pistone 1987: 64): "When he came back, he was ecstatic, as proud as a peacock. 'Getting made is the greatest thing that could ever happen to me,' he said. 'I've been looking forward to this day ever since I was a kid.' . . . That night we partied together for his celebration. But now everybody treated him with more respect. He was a made guy now." After completion of his initiation, Jimmy ("The Weasel") Fratianno "was so excited that he could feel his legs tremble." Becoming a member of the Los Angeles crime Family of Jack Dragna "made him a special person, an inheritor of enormous power. It was something he had wanted for as long as he could remember" (Demaris 1981: 3).

To be eligible for membership, a young man (there are no female members) must be of Italian descent (although it is not certain how many of one's grandparents must be of Italian blood to qualify). He needs a sponsor and must have a long history of successful criminal activity or possess certain skills required by the group. Jimmy Fratianno, for example, possessed an important "skill": the ability to execute persons in an efficient, impersonal, and dispassionate manner (Demaris 1981). Every potential member, however, is expected to participate in a murder—although not necessarily as the actual executioner. Such participation serves to more closely bind the person to the ongoing conspiracy that is organized crime, and it precludes government agents from becoming members. (There are indications that certain members may have avoided this requirement.) An OC group is also interested in criminals who have proven to be money-makers, "earners" who can increase the group's income.

In New York's five crime Families and perhaps in other traditional crime groups, each member is an independent operator, not an employee—he receives no salary from the group. Instead, the made-guy or wise-guy has a form of "franchise": he is authorized by the group to make money by using the Family connections that come with membership, bolstered by the status (that is, fear) that membership generates. While part of a particular crew (discussed shortly), he is an independent entrepreneur, violent and aggressive, who is constantly on the prowl for opportunities for making money. In a typical pattern, a made-guy, a franchised member, will attract nonmembers who are eager to associate with him, to become "connected," since an associate enjoys some of the status and connections that the crime Family enjoys. In a discussion with an associate of the Gambino Family, Dominick ("Little Dom") Cataldo of the Colombo Family reported on his recent change in status: "Since I got made I got a million fuckin' worshippers hanging around" (Iannuzzi 1993: 172). The member-as-patron thus sits at the center of a network of nonmember clients that constitutes an action-based unit for coordinated criminal activities. If the member is able to generate considerable income, he gains greater status in the Family and can become a candidate for advancement to *caporegime*. If successful associates are Italian, they become candidates for membership.

Because of their acquisitive and violent nature, members of organized crime can easily come into conflict with members in the same or another OC unit. The more members a group has, the greater the likelihood of conflict—too many made-guys in search of too few money-making opportunities. Under such circumstances, members are more likely to become involved in high-risk ventures that can be a threat to the safety of the group. This dynamic serves to place natural limitations on membership. Furthermore, each new member is a potential threat to the security of the group—a potential informant—so new members are selected with caution and great care. A prospective member may have to serve the group for many years before achieving membership status.

According to FBI recordings released at the 1992 trial of John Gotti, the "making" of prospective members requires passing the list around to other Families. But this is complicated by the very informality that characterizes OC—men are typically known only by their nicknames, which may not be precise enough to identify a particular person for such an important function as determining fitness for membership. In fact, just before a ceremony for the making of new members, Gambino Family underboss Sam Gravano reported to *consigliere* Frank Locascio: "I don't have it right, Frank. I don't have their last names. I don't have the proper spellings. I ain't got the, the guys all down." (recorded January 4, 1990).

According to Cressey (1969), the "membership books" were closed in 1931 and since then new members have been initiated on a very limited basis and with the approval of the commission. Cressey states that this was an effort by the most powerful bosses, heads of the largest groups, to maintain the status quo. Michael Franzese, who became a *caporegime* in the Colombo Family, states that "from 1955 to 1972, the Mob was a closed shop; virtually no one was inducted during that quarter century. . . By 1972, with the ranks thinning by death, age, and imprisonment, the doors were opened" (Franzese and Matera 1992: 122–236). Membership, as opposed to some type of associate status, provides the rewards associated with being an "insider." As one member told this writer, "a made-guy is considered more honorable," meaning there is a greater level of trust—and *rispetto*. Only members are allowed to attend certain important meetings and be privy to important conversations and information, and information is an important basis of power. The basic mechanism for resolving disputes is arbitration—a *sitdown* or *table*—and a nonmember needs a member to represent him. A nonmember associate in dispute with a made-guy is at a distinct disadvantage—a disadvantage that can be life threatening. This can become balanced if the associate is an "earner"—a source of substantial funds.

Considerable "psychic gain" is associated with being a member. Within criminal and certain legitimate circles, being "made" conveys a great deal of prestige, if not fear. The President's Commission notes that although a soldier is the lowest-ranking member of the organization, "he is a considerable figure on the street, a man who commands respect and fear" (PCOC 1986a: 44). In testimony before the commission, a witness elaborated:

GOODFELLAS

Clearly the most realistic portrayal of organized crime to date, this motion picture actually centered on the activities of men who were not even made members of—in this case—the Lucchese Family. Only "Paulie" (in real life Paul Vario, a Lucchese *caporegime*), played by Paul Sorvino, was a made-guy.

[Q:] How did you come to know that Greg Scarpa [soldier in the Colombo crime Family] is a "made" individual while someone in his crew is not "made"?

[A:] Conversation—you could just see the way that everybody answers to him; I mean, he has a club on 13th Avenue [in Brooklyn] and everyone comes up to him, and no one—they don't double park their car without getting his permission, so to say. In other words, no one does anything without getting his permission. So you could just see the respect he gets.

There are a number of otherwise legitimate persons who are attracted by the mystique that surrounds organized crime. Popular sources report that many young women are attracted to OC figures and to the bars and nightclubs that are owned or frequented by them. For similar reasons young men may aspire to membership in OC—reasons that go beyond economic advantages—out of a desire to be part of the mystique reinforced by media representations such as *The Godfather* and *Goodfellas*.

There are also important disadvantages associated with membership. Law-enforcement agencies take great interest in a criminal if they discover he is a made-guy. Any insult or assault on a member requires that he kill the offender. He is also required to obey the orders of his boss, even if this requires participation in the murder of a complete stranger or perhaps a close friend or relative. But, of course, the member is protected by the boss, who will respond to any attack on one of his soldiers as a personal affront, a fundamental lack of *rispetto*, requiring mobilization of the group's resources for violence. It is the ready availability of private violence that makes the OC group a viable entity.

The continuation of traditional organized crime in the United States is dependent upon the ability of crime units to recruit new members which, in turn, is dependent upon the availability of a pool of qualified applicants. For at least some Italian-American crime groups, this is becoming more difficult. On January 4, 1990, John Gotti, boss of the Gambino Family, was recorded decrying the paucity of qualified candidates for membership to *consigliere* Frank Locascio:

35

ORGANIZED CRIME AND GRATUITOUS VIOLENCE

"But you know Paul, I think some guys just take so much pleasure from breaking heads that they'd almost rather not get paid."—*Caporegime* Joe ["Piney"] Armone to Gambino Family boss Paul Castellano.

Source: Joseph F. O'Brien and Andris Kurins, *Boss of Bosses: The FBI and Paul Castellano*. New York: Dell, 1991.

And where we gonna find them, these kinda guys? Frank, I'm not being a pessimist. It's gettin' tougher, not easier. We got everything that's any good. Look around, ask your son someday, forget who you are, what you are. Talk to your son like his age. Put yourself in his age bracket, and let him tell you what good kids in the neighborhood other than the kids that are with you. Or good kids in the neighborhood other than with him. You know what I'm trying to say? I told you a couple of weeks ago, we got the only few pockets of good kids left.

This issue will be examined in chapter 4 in a discussion of "ethnic succession" in organized crime.

Crews

Members and associates are organized into crews, semi-independent units, nominally headed by a *caporegime*, *capodecina*, street boss, or even a soldier. Crews generate finances, which they share with their crew chief who shares it with the *caporegime* or with the boss. These crews have been described in a number of popular books on OC. FBI agent Joseph Pistone (1987: 51–52), who used the name "Donnie Brasco" in his undercover role, describes the crew of soldier Jilly Greca of the Colombo Family, whose "headquarters" was the back room of a store stocked with expensive clothing—stolen merchandise: "Although these were lower-echelon guys in the mob, they always had something going. They always had money. They were always turning things over. They always had swag around. . . . You name it, they stole it. Jilly's crew would hit warehouses, docks, trucks, houses. . . . There wasn't one hour of one day that went by when they weren't thinking and talking about what they were going to steal, who or what or where they were going to rob. . . . The mob was their job."

The crew headed by Paul Vario, a *caporegime* in the Lucchese crime Family, used a drab, paint-flecked storefront cabstand and dispatch office in Brooklyn as its headquarters. Nicholas Pileggi (1985) notes that the Vario crew did most of the strong-arm work for the Lucchese Family. At the cabstand there were always young tough guys ready to go out and break a few heads whenever Paul gave the order and killers who were happy to take on the most violent of assignments. The persons in Vario's crew "had always been outlaws. They were the kids from the neighborhood who were always in trouble. As youngsters they were the ones invariably identified as toughs by the police and brought into the precinct for routine beatings, whenever some neighborhood store burglary or assault moved the station house cops into action" (1985: 35).

The crew headed by John Gotti, a *caporegime* and later boss of the Gambino Family, was headquartered at the Bergin Hunt and Fish Club, a (very) private storefront in the Ozone Park section of the New York City borough of Queens: "The Bergin men were good customers in the small cafes and stores operating on slim margins. Around his neighbors, Gotti acted like a gentleman; around him they acted as though he were a successful salesman. He began saluting the community with Fourth of July fireworks displays and barbecues; some residents began saluting him by alerting the club when men resembling undercover detectives were around" (Mustain and Capeci 1988: 112).

The Boss

At the center of the universe of an Italian-American crime group is the boss. In the past, the boss has usually been a senior citizen—he needs many years to

MEMBERSHIP AND OC IN CLEVELAND

In Cleveland, while there may have been eligible candidates, the crime Family headed by John Scalish failed to induct new members for almost two decades, which made his group vulnerable to a challenge by other criminals. Scalish died of natural causes in 1976, and his replacement as boss, James T. Licavoli ("Jack White"), was challenged by the sixty-one-year-old secretary of a Teamster Union local, John Nardi. Nardi was angry because, despite his qualifications, he had not been inducted into the Cleveland crime Family. He was aided by ("Irish") Danny Green (b. 1929), an ex-Marine marksman and Teamster's Union official who had his own gang of racketeers.

Jimmy ("The Weasel") Fratianno came in from the West Coast to aid Licavoli in quickly inducting new members for the ensuing struggle with the Nardi-Green forces. In 1977, Nardi was the victim of a bomb triggered by remote control; Green met the same fate later in the year. The murders of Nardi and Green, and other victims of the feud, resulted in a massive investigation and convictions against Licavoli, his underboss Angelo Lonardo, and Fratianno—the latter two subsequently became federal witnesses, their testimony leading to further convictions and an end to the Cleveland crime Family.

gain the respect of members and the knowledge and connections needed by the group. It is a sign of weakness that many of the current heads of important Italian-American crime groups are relatively young, as well as volatile and violent. Typically, the boss operates out of a fixed location: a restaurant, a private club, or his own business office. Raymond Patriarca, the New England crime boss who died of natural causes in 1984 at age seventy-six, operated out of his vending-machine business, the National Cigarette Service, in the "Little Italy" of Providence, Rhode Island. Vincent Teresa (1973: 95) states that the entire area around Patriarca's headquarters was an armed camp: "It was impossible to move through the area without being spotted and reported." Throughout the day he received visitors, sometimes legitimate persons asking for a favor, usually to resolve a dispute, but more frequently "a parade of the faithful bearing tithes: cold cash for the middle drawer in the dirty back room of a cigarette vending-machine business in a run-down section of Providence. It could be the receipts from a wholly owned subsidiary or rent from a franchise.

Joe N. Gallo, New York City *consigliere* for the Gambino family, at work in his Astoria, Queens, neighborhood. He is standing in front of Sperazza's Luncheonette.

In a complex maze of interests, he completely controlled some markets, especially those involving gambling, loansharking, and pornography, and dabbled in others such as truck hijacking and drug trafficking in which free-lancers negotiated fees to do business." (O'Neill and Lehr 1989: 43).

The head of the Genovese Family in New York operated out of an Italian restaurant in lower Manhattan. The boss was driven every day from his home in Long Island by a chauffeur-bodyguard. In the back of the restaurant was a table reserved for him. Persons having business with the boss would come in all day long and sit at the table for varying periods of time. Strangers were not welcome in the restaurant, which was located in the heart of an Italian neighborhood dominated by the Genovese crime group. There was no place to park; all parking spaces were taken by members of the Family or their associates. Anyone walking in the area who was not recognized would be reported to the Family members at the restaurant. If a stranger entered the restaurant, he or she was told that a reservation was needed—but the restaurant did not take reservations (Abadinsky 1983). Joseph Colombo, whose crime Family bears his name, operated out of a neighborhood real estate firm, Cantalup Realty Co., in the Bensonhurst section of Brooklyn. He was on the books as a licensed real estate salesman—the licensing test was fixed (Cantalup and Renner 1990). Gambino Family boss John Gotti operated out of the Ravenite Social Club on Mulberry Street in Manhattan's Little Italy; every Wednesday, Gotti would hold court at a gathering of Family captains. To avoid being electronically surveilled, Gotti would discuss business on the street or in an apartment upstairs from the club; however, the apartment was bugged by the FBI (Coffey and Schmetterer 1991).

A boss has a number of men who report directly to him. They carry messages and perform assignments as necessary; they also serve to physically protect the boss. In many crime groups, particularly those in New York where five Families operate, most of the activities of Family members are not under the direct or indirect supervision of the boss. He often finds out about many of the activities of members only as the result of periodic briefings by the *capiregime*.

Joseph Bonanno (1983: 157) describes how he operated as a boss ("Father") of his Family:

> Internal disagreements between Family members were solved at the grass-roots level by group leaders or by the *consigliere*. A Family member's personal or business problems were usually handled in this manner, and the problem rarely had to be brought to my attention.
>
> On the other hand, if a Family member wanted to go into business with a member of another Family, such an association would need the approval of the Fathers of the respective Families. A Family member's relations with non-Family members was his own affair.
>
> Other than meeting with other Fathers and meeting with group leaders within my Family on an ad hoc basis, being a Father took up relatively little of

> my time. Family matters were largely handled by the group leaders under me. Indeed, there were many Family members I never met.
>
> If I convened a Family meeting, I met only with the group leaders, who in turn passed the information to the people in their groups.

Peace-keeping, notes Bonanno, was his main responsibility as head of the Family. According to the PCOC (1985b), the family boss is also responsible for making all important decisions on trial strategy when a Family member is the defendant. This responsibility is for the purpose of protecting Family interests during the trial.

Crime boss Carlo Gambino would often conduct briefings in a moving car to reduce the possibility of surveillance. Very important or sensitive operations, for example, those that could result in conflict with other crime Families or attract undue law enforcement attention, are cleared with the boss in advance. And as noted above, in all but the smallest units, the boss will be assisted by an underboss (*sottocapo*) and a counselor (*consigliere*).

The boss, like many other members of a crime Family, has investments in illegitimate and legitimate enterprises, often in partnership with other members from his own or other crime groups, or with nonmember associates. He receives a portion of the illegal earnings of all the members of his group, roughly between 10 and 15 percent if he has no stake in the activities. With activities that he directs personally, the share will be considerably higher. Soldiers will share their earnings with their *capiregime*, who will pass on a portion to the boss. Sitting in the back of his restaurant headquarters, the head of the Genovese Family would receive visitors who passed sealed envelopes filled with money to his bodyguard—their show of *rispetto* (Abadinsky 1983). As opposed to bureaucratic organizations, the money goes only in one direction—upward. When the boss gives someone money, it is for investment purposes on which a substantial return is expected—or violence is guaranteed.

The boss demands absolute respect and total obedience. His working day is spent in exchanges with numerous persons. With a word or two, a sentence, a shake of the head, a smile, or a gesture, he can set in motion a host of activities and operations involving dozens, if not hundreds, of persons. The boss is treated with a great deal of deference. People rise when he enters the room and they never interrupt when he is speaking. If they are close, a kiss on the boss's cheek is considered an appropriate gesture of respect. If the boss rises, all rise. If the boss rises and embraces an individual, this is considered a great honor, often reserved only for other bosses.

The Commission

All crime bosses are linked in a rather informal arrangement known as the "commission," but only the bosses of the most powerful groups—particularly those in New York, Chicago, Buffalo, and Philadelphia—are considered actual commission "members." "The national commission regulates joint ventures between families, intervenes in family disputes, approves the initiation of new

COMMISSION CASE

On January 13, 1987, Anthony ("Fat Tony") Salerno, at age 75 boss of the Genovese Family, was sentenced to 100 years (he died in 1992); Anthony ("Tony Ducks") Corallo, at age 73, boss of the Lucchese Family, 100 years; Carmine ("Junior" or "The Snake") Persico, at age 53, boss of the Colombo Family, 100 years (he was already serving a 39-year sentence); Gennaro ("Gerry Lang") Langella, at age 48, underboss and acting boss of the Colombo Family, 100 years (he was serving a 65-year sentence); Anthony ("Bruno") Indelicato, at age 38, *caporegime* in the Bonanno Family, 40 years; Ralph Scopo, at age 58, member of the Colombo Family and president of a Cement Workers Union local, 100 years; Salvatore ("Tom Mix") Santoro, at age 72, underboss of the Lucchese Family, 100 years; Christopher ("Christie Tick") Funari, at age 62, *consigliere* of the Lucchese Family, 100 years. Paul Castellano, boss of the Gambino Family, was indicted in the commission case, but was murdered before he could stand trial. Because of ill health, the case of Philip Rastelli, at age 69, boss of the Bonanno Family, was separated; he was sentenced to 12 years for labor racketeering in a different case. Joseph Bonanno, the former boss of the crime Family that bears his name, refused to honor a subpoena to testify about the commission during the trial and was jailed for contempt of court. The prosecutor, Rudolph Giuliani, sought to question Bonanno with respect to information contained in the crime boss's 1983 autobiography, A *Man of Honor.*

members, and controls relations between the U.S. and Sicilian branches of *La Cosa Nostra* (PCOC 1986a: 37)." The commission, reports Bonanno (1983: 159), can arbitrate disputes. Having no direct executive power, however, it has to depend on influence: "It had respect only insofar as its individual members had respect. More than anything else, the Commission was a forum."

In addition to the "national commission," which is a body that rarely, if ever, meets as a group, the bosses of the New York Families also constitute a commission that serves to arbitrate disputes and deal with joint ventures between their Families. On November 19, 1986, in what became known as the "Commission Case" (*United States v. Salerno*, 85 CR 139, S.D.N.Y. 1985), a number of New York bosses were convicted of conducting the affairs of "the commission of La Cosa Nostra" in a pattern of racketeering that violated the RICO statutes (discussed in chapter 9).

The case revealed the role of the commission in New York:

1. Regulate and facilitate relationships between the five Families;
2. Promote and facilitate joint ventures between Families;
3. Resolve actual and potential disputes among Families;

4. Regulate the criminal activities of the Families;
5. Extend formal recognition to newly chosen Family bosses and resolve leadership disputes within Families;
6. Authorize the execution of Family members; and
7. Approve of the initiation of new members into the Families.

The Chicago Outfit

In Chicago, and perhaps elsewhere, traditional organized crime is less ritualized, tending toward the bureaucratic—Camorra rather than Mafia. Under the control of a boss and his "board of directors," Chicagoland (Cook County, surrounding "collar counties," and parts of Indiana and Wisconsin) is divided into spheres of interest or territories. Ranking members are assigned to oversee specific activities, usually gambling, loansharking, and, in some areas, extortion from entertainment spots featuring sexual activities. Members and associates are organized into five crews, each under direct control of an Outfit street boss: Twenty-sixth Street, Taylor Street/Elmwood Park, Chicago Heights, North Side, and Grand Avenue. Each street boss is aided by his top assistant or underboss. While everyone in the Outfit is associated with a particular crew, the concept of "territory" has become fluid and members may move from one crew to another.

Each street boss may also be directly involved in other activities, such as labor racketeering, on an "industry" as opposed to a territorial basis. For example, Vincent Solano was boss of the North Side (a territory which extends into the northern suburbs and Wisconsin) as well as president of Local 1 of the Laborer's Union. In his syndicate position he received tribute from pornography and related businesses through Michael Glitta, who was in charge of such operations for Solano. (Glitta died of natural causes in 1988 at age sixty-eight; Solano in 1992 at age seventy-two.) Members of the crew may be on "salary," receiving a portion of the income generated by the activities of the street boss. They may derive other income from additional activities that are permitted by their street boss, although direct involvement in drug trafficking has generally been considered off limits. (This appears to have changed during the three-year reign of Outfit boss Joseph ["Joe Negal"] Ferriola, 1986–89.) Some crews have developed specialties which, in the past, included cartage theft, particularly from railroads that crisscross the Chicagoland area. In more recent years, juke boxes, amusement machines, and, particularly, electronic poker games have proven important Outfit money-makers.

The terms *caporegime, consigliere,* and underboss are not typically used in Chicago, certainly not by criminals or local enforcement officials. The Chicago Crime Commission points out: "The Chicago Outfit does not call itself La Cosa Nostra. It is not exclusively Italian. It is not governed by familial relationships. Initiates are not assigned to 'godfathers.' They do not take ritual oaths" (1990: 3). While membership has been associated with a formal initiation ceremony, as described above, there is no evidence of such ceremo-

TAYLOR STREET CREW OF ROCKY INFELICE

Until his death in 1989, Joseph Ferriola of Cicero, Illinois, was boss of the Taylor Street crew of about twenty persons and head of the Outfit. He was replaced by his top assistant, Rocco Ernest Infelice (b. 1922), a former paratroop combat veteran with a $250,000 home in suburban River Forest and a vacation home in Fort Lauderdale, Florida. Information from Infelice's trial indicated the extent of his profits: $570,000 from bookmaking alone in 1983 and 1984. He paid $1,000 a month to the police chief of Forest Park to allow high stakes dice games in the Chicago suburb. A major bookmaker for his crew, the Republican Party boss and town assessor of Cicero (a Chicago suburb with a long history of OC influence) acted as a fixer and provided warnings of police raids. In 1993, a year after Frank Maltese pleaded guilty to gambling-conspiracy charges, his wife was elected Cicero town president. Before he could begin serving a nine-month prison sentence, the ailing Maltese died of cancer.

Infelice lieutenant for Lake County, Illinois, Salvatore DeLaurentis (b. 1938) of suburban Inverness, demanded $6,000 a month in "street taxes" from a wealthy bookmaker, Hal Smith (age forty-eight): "Or you're 'trunk music!'"—alluding to the sound of flesh decomposing in the trunk of a car. Smith made a counteroffer, $3,500; the offer was rejected—Smith was found stuffed into a car trunk, stabbed, beaten, and strangled. When the crew expanded into Lake County, they encountered two gamblers already operating in this suburban county—the body of one was later found in the trunk of a car. Gamblers were typically given a choice: pay the street taxes, split the gambling business fifty-fifty, turn it all over to the Outfit—or die. In Lake County similar overtures were also made to the proprietors of houses of prostitution and marginal businesses, such as bars with sex shows or adult book stores. The crew included feared enforcers such as Gerald Scarpelli and Harry Aleman, who were experts at intimidation.

Scarpelli, an enforcer and collector for the Infelice crew, was born in New York in 1938 and raised on Chicago's West Side. Arrested seventeen times since 1960, Scarpelli served prison sentences for armed robbery and counterfeiting. His responsibilities for Infelice included fifteen individual accounts, most of whom were bookmakers. (Because of law enforcement activity, the Infelice crew had backed away from loansharking.) The actual payments were collected by two other enforcers/collectors who turned the money over to Scarpelli. He also collected payments directly from the operator of several houses of prostitution. The total sum collected varied from $20,000 to $60,000 per month. The two collectors each received $1,200 per month and Scarpelli received $2,000. The remainder of the money was turned over in person to Infelice around the first of each month. As part of his obligation to the Outfit, Scarpelli performed a variety of violent activities—murders, beatings, destruction of property. His income was supplemented by armed robbery, burglary, and some legitimate business activities. In 1989, while in federal custody, and after providing information to the FBI, Scarpelli committed suicide.

Harry Aleman (b. 1939), nephew of the late Outfit boss Joseph Ferriola, is believed responsible for at least fifteen homicides. His looks belie a fearsome reputation, and the mob hitman fancies himself an artist whose canvases usually depict outdoor scenes; after high school, Aleman attended art school in Chicago. This did not prevent him from being sentenced to a twelve-year term in 1992 after pleading guilty to RICO violations.

(continued on next page)

43

TAYLOR STREET CREW OF ROCKY INFELICE *(Continued)*

The fringes of the Infelice crew included men such as Ronald DeRosa (b. 1943), who in 1992 pleaded guilty to federal gambling and tax fraud charges and was placed on probation. A former truck dispatcher in Cicero, DeRosa accepted bets and handled money for the crew. Another member, Paul Spano (b. 1931), used his Cicero trucking company as a front for a sports betting operation; the firm's safe was used to store profits from gambling and loansharking. In 1993, Spano was sentenced to seven months imprisonment followed by five months of home confinement. Other members of the crew ran gambling operations, including card and dice games in various locations, and they were involved in loansharking, usually related to a gambling debt, making loan rates as high as 5 percent a week. They made the mistake of lending $50,000 to an undercover IRS agent. Robert Salerno collected debts and street taxes for Infelice; his son Alex, an attorney, assisted in Salerno's legal defense.

In 1992, Infelice and several members of his crew were found guilty of racketeering and murder conspiracy—they had killed numerous gamblers. The conviction was largely the result of the testimony of William ("B.J.") Jahoda, a member of the crew who became an informant. Among other charges, Jahoda admitted to falsely filing an income-tax statement that reported a gambling income of $126,000, when the actual amount was substantially higher. Infelice was sentenced to sixty-three years; Robert Bellavia, age fifty-three, to thirty years; and Louis Marino, age sixty-one, received twenty-eight years. At his sentencing hearing, Infelice castigated the judge and made a veiled threat against Jahoda, who is in the witness protection program. Salvatore DeLaurentis was sentenced to eighteen years and six months.

---

nies being used in Chicago. Chuck Giancana, younger brother of Chicago crime boss Sam Giancana, reports:

> [B]ecause Chicago didn't have a formal "initiation" and "secret society" like New York, or adhere to some hocus-pocus Old Country rules for being "made," it was hard to tell who was a member of the Outfit and who wasn't. You just knew. You knew how high up the ladder a guy was by the men he hung around with, by how many soldiers he required to conduct business, or by the job he had. . . . Chicago's Outfit was a fluid, ever-changing animal with no spoken rules and no formalities. There were no conferences as there were in the movies. It was a look, a walk, the cut of a guy's clothes; whom he had dinner with and whom he didn't. (1992: 254, 243)

In Chicago, a made-guy is feted at a luncheon or dinner by ranking members in recognition of his new status, and being "made" is equivalent to being a supervisor or what elsewhere would be a *caporegime*, a management position.

Rules

An elaborate system of written rules and regulations is one of the important characteristics of a bureaucracy. While traditional organized crime does not have written rules, it has an elaborate set of norms that govern behavior. Ianni (1972) argues that the rules of OC are actually standards of conduct based on the traditions of southern Italy, particularly the concept of family loyalty. However, my research (Abadinsky 1981a, 1983) indicates that the rules are not

RULES OF TRADITIONAL ORGANIZED CRIME

1. Always show *rispetto* to those who can command it.
2. Report any failure to show *rispetto* to one's patron immediately.
3. Violence must be used, even if only of a limited type, to ensure *rispetto*.
4. Never ask for surnames. Underboss Sam Gravano testified that there were many people in his crime Family whose last names he did not know.
5. Never resort to violence in a dispute with a member or associate of another Family.
6. Never resort to, or even threaten, violence in a dispute with a member of your Family.
7. Do not use the telephone except to arrange for a meeting place, preferably in code, from which you will then travel to a safe place to discuss business.
8. Avoid mentioning specifics when discussing business—for example, names, dates, and places—beyond those absolutely necessary for understanding.
9. Keep your mouth shut—anything you hear, anything you see, stays with you, in your head; do not talk about it.
10. Do not ask unnecessary questions; the amount of information given to you is all you need to carry out your instructions.
11. If your patron arranges for two parties to work together, he assumes responsibility for arbitrating any disputes between the parties.
12. The boss can unilaterally direct violence, including murder, against any member of his Family, except that he cannot engage in murder-for-hire; that is, make a profit from murder. And the murder need not be related to business: Paul Castellano ordered his son-in-law murdered, believing Frankie Amato's philandering to be responsible for his daughter's miscarriage.
13. The boss cannot use violence against a member or close associate of another Family without prior consultation with that Family's boss.

Sources: Howard Abadinsky, *The Mafia in America: An Oral History.* New York: Praeger, 1981; Howard Abadinsky, *The Criminal Elite: Professional and Organized Crime.* Westport, CT: Greenwood, 1983; Joseph Coffey and Jerry Schmetterer, *The Coffey Files: One Cop's War Against the Mob.* New York: St. Martin's, 1991; transcripts from the 1992 trial of John Gotti.

traditional but quite rational and sometimes run counter to southern Italian tradition. For example, loyalty to the crime Family supersedes loyalty to one's own blood family. According to the rules, if required by the boss, a member *must* participate in the murder of a relative (usually by helping to "set him up"). When Vincent Siciliano (1970: 74) discovered who had killed his father, he swore vengeance, but later found out that the hit had been "authorized," the killers carrying out Family orders. Finding one of them at a restaurant, Siciliano told him: "Look, I came here to talk to you. I want to apologize about the noise I was making." His father's murderer responded: "Hey, don't worry about it. I know how you felt about your father. I understand. There are no hard feelings, Vinnie." In Philadelphia, Frank ("Chickie") Narducci was killed on orders of Family boss Nicky Scarfo; yet his sons, Philip and Frank, Jr., continued to work as enforcers for Scarfo (Anastasia 1991). After John Gotti had *caporegime* Thomas Gambino's uncle, Paul Castellano, murdered, Gambino continued to report and show deference to Gotti, who subsequently became boss of the Gambino Family.

This is all contrary to the southern Italian credo *sangu du me sangu* ("blood of my blood"), which actually means *famiglia* (family) above all: *o tortu o gridu difenni i to* ("right or wrong, defend your own" kin). In fact, the rules of traditional organized crime have succeeded in preventing the emergence of a violent southern Italian tradition: *vendetta*, the irrational blood feud that is "bad for business." Since the 1930s there have been no "wars" between traditional OC groups, although there has been a great deal of intragroup violence such as the "Gallo-Profaci war" and the "Banana war" (to be discussed in chapter 3).

ANALYSIS OF THE STRUCTURE

In this chapter, the type of structure that has been outlined for traditional organized crime is rather fluid, similar to that of the real estate development business. "A great deal of illegal activity within the illegal industries is not routine production and distribution carried on under the auspices of a specific firm, but instead the result of many ad hoc deals and projects" (Moore 1987: 54). The firms (crews) are not consistently in one business, but intermittently in several. They are not organized as a "production line," but as a "job shop." Annelise Anderson (1979) found that the formal organizational structure of the Philadelphia crime Family was not the same as its economic structure. There was a relatively clear hierarchy within the Family, but its income-generating activities involved several smaller, operationally independent crews involved in gambling and loansharking. Ronald Goldstock (Stone 1992: 29), Director of the New York Organized Crime Task Force, says that OC is less like a corporation and more like a government: "In a corporation, people at the bottom carry out the policies and perform tasks assigned to them by the executives at the top. In the Mob, the people at the bottom are the entrepreneurs. They pass a percentage of their income upward as taxes in return for government-type

---

Figure 1.3. The Structure of Organized Crime

patron-client/ --bureaucratic/
   networks   corporate

---

services: resolution of disputes, allocation of territories, enforcement and corruption services." Anderson (1979: 46) argues that the most threatening aspect of this type of organized crime is the "group or organization's capacity for forming a quasi-government," giving it a competitive advantage that may explain the success of Italian-American crime groups.

In sum, traditional organized crime, and the criminal groups to be discussed in chapter 5, can range from the patrimonial/patron client structure of New York's crime Families to the more bureaucratic (but far from corporate) organization of the Chicago Outfit.

Now that we have examined the definition and structure of organized crime, in the next chapter we will discuss explanations for its existence.

REVIEW QUESTIONS

1. What characteristics make organized crime a distinct type of criminality?
2. Why is it difficult to define "organized crime"?
3. What is the important difference between the gang headed by Jesse James and the organization headed by Al Capone?
4. What are the practical advantages of examining a criminal group with respect to the eight attributes of organized crime?
5. What are the eight attributes of an organized crime group?
6. What are the responsibilities of an *enforcer*, a *fixer*, and a *moneymover*?
7. What is meant by the *Mezzogiorno*?
8. How does the history of Sicily help explain the phenomenon known as *mafia*?
9. What is the difference between the term *mafia* and an organization referred to as the "Mafia"?
10. How does the concept of *partito* explain the power of a *mafioso*?
11. What is the concept of *rispetto* and why is it important to a *mafioso*?
12. What was the impact of Mussolini on the Mafia?
13. How did the Camorra differ from the Mafia?
14. What are the attributes of a bureaucracy?
15. What are the aspects of traditional organized crime that are "bureaucratic"?
16. According to Donald Cressey, how is an organized crime Family structured?
17. What are the important ramifications of describing the structure of organized crime as "bureaucratic"?
18. What are the characteristics of a patrimonial organization?
19. In what ways can organized crime be considered a government?

20. What is the role of a patron in organized crime?
21. How can a member of organized crime act as a catalyst for a great deal of conventional criminal activity?
22. What is the primary role of a boss in an Italian-American (traditional) crime Family?
23. What is the function of the "commission" in traditional organized crime?
24. Why is the concept of "membership" important in traditional organized crime?
25. What are the advantages and disadvantages of membership in traditional organized crime?
26. What are the basic qualifications for membership in traditional organized crime?
27. What is a "crew" in traditional organized crime?
28. How does organized crime in Chicago differ from that in New York?

2

Organized Crime:
Theories and
Antecedents

In this chapter we will examine some explanations for the continued existence of organized crime in the United States. Then we will explore three overlapping slices of American history—the robber barons, urban machine politics, and Prohibition—that provided the fertile soil necessary for the growth of organized crime.

THEORIZING AND ORGANIZED CRIME

Organized crime, as we have discussed the phenomenon in chapter 1, has been subjected to only limited attempts at explanation. While sociologists have offered a number of theories to explain crime and criminal behavior, rarely were they directed specifically at *organized* crime. Nevertheless, some theories of crime and deviance provide insight into the existence of organized crime, and they will be examined in this chapter.

Anomie

Building on a concept originated by the French sociologist Émile Durkheim (1951) back in the nineteenth century, in 1938 Robert K. Merton set forth a social and cultural explanation for deviant behavior in the United States. He conceived of organized crime as a *normal* response to pressures exerted on certain persons by the social structure. Merton points to an American preoccupation with economic success—*pathological materialism*. It is the goal that is emphasized, not the means, which are at best only a secondary consideration. "There may develop a disproportionate, at times a virtually exclusive, stress upon the value of specific goals, involving relatively slight concern with the institutionally appropriate modes of attaining these goals" (1938: 673).

This being the case, the only factors limiting goal achievement are technical, not moral or legal. According to Merton, "emphasis on the goals of monetary success and material property leads to dominant concern with technological and social instruments designed to produce the desired result, inasmuch as institutional controls become of secondary importance. In such a situation, innovation flourishes as the *range of means* employed is broadened" (1938: 673).

Thus, in American society, "the pressure of prestige-bearing success tends to eliminate the effective social constraint over means employed to this end. 'The-ends-justifies-the-means' doctrine becomes a guiding tenet for action when the cultural structure unduly exalts the end and the social organization unduly limits possible recourse to approved means" (1938: 681). Later in this chapter we will review the activities of earlier "godfathers," the "robber barons" who exemplified the spirit that Merton refers to as *innovation*. Taking advantage of every (legitimate and illegitimate) opportunity, these men became the embodiment of the great American success story. However, the opportunity for economic success is not equally distributed, and the immigrants who followed these men to America found many avenues from "rags to riches" significantly limited if not already closed. Some immigrants recognized that the cards were stacked against them and as a result, organized crime flourished (Taylor, Walton, and Young 1973).

Writing several years before Merton, Louis Robinson (1933: 16) spoke of an American credo according to which "We dare not or at least will not condemn the criminal's goal, because it is also our goal. We want to keep the goal ourselves and damn the criminal for pursuing it in the only way he knows how."

> The methods which criminals use in attaining our common goal of wealth may, of course, differ from those which the non-criminal classes use. But this is to be expected. They are probably not in a position to employ our methods. We can think of a variety of reasons why a man without capital or without education or without industrial skill or without this or that advantage or handicapped by any one of several factors which anyone could easily name would be forced to seek the common goal by means differing from those employed by another man better situated or endowed. In other words, he would *play the game differently*. (1933: 15–16; emphasis added)

Anomie results when numbers of people are confronted by the contradiction between goals and means and "become estranged from a society that promises them in principle what they are deprived in reality" (Merton 1964: 218). Despite numerous success stories, "we know in this same society that proclaims the right, and even the duty, of lofty aspirations for all, men do not have equal access to the opportunity structure" (1964: 218). Yet, those with ready access to success ("born with a silver spoon") *and* those who are at a distinct disadvantage are constantly exposed to the rewards of "fame and fortune" by the mass media. For some, particularly the disadvantaged, anomie is the result. Merton states there are five modes of individual adaptation to this phenomenon: conformity, ritualism, rebellion, retreatism, and innovation. We are concerned only with the last adaptation, since it includes organized criminal activity for those who would *play the game differently.*

Ian Taylor and his colleagues, British sociologists, summarize the anomic condition in the United States (1973: 97): "The 'American Dream' urges all citizens to succeed whilst distributing the opportunity to succeed unequally: the result of this social and moral climate, inevitably, is innovation by the citizenry—the adoption of illegitimate means to pursue and obtain success." However, "routine" pedestrian criminal acts do not lead to any significant level of economic success. Innovation, then, is the adoption of *sophisticated,* well-planned, skilled, organized criminality. A question remains: Why do some persons suffering from anomie turn to criminal innovation, while others do not? Edwin Sutherland, the "father" of American criminology, provides an answer: *differential association.*

Differential Association

According to Sutherland (1973), the principal part of learning criminal behavior occurs within intimate personal groups. What is learned depends on the intensity, frequency, and duration of the association. The actor learns the techniques of committing crime and the drives, attitudes, and rationalizations that add up to a favorable precondition to criminal behavior. Thus, the balance between noncriminal and criminal behaviors is tipped in favor of the latter.

Sutherland presents the nine basics of differential association:

1. Criminal behavior is learned.
2. Criminal behavior is learned in interaction with other persons in a process of communication.
3. The principal part of the learning of criminal behavior occurs within intimate groups (for example, family and gangs).
4. When criminal behavior is learned, the learning includes (a) the techniques of committing crime, which are sometimes very complicated, and (b) the specific direction of motives, drives, rationalizations, and attitudes.
5. The specific direction of motives and drives is learned from definitions of legal codes as favorable and unfavorable. Sutherland notes that in America, attitudes toward rules are usually mixed, and this results in culture conflict with respect to legal codes.
6. A person becomes delinquent/criminal because of an excess of definitions favorable to violation of law over definitions unfavorable to violation of law.
7. Differential association may vary in frequency, duration, priority, and intensity.
8. The process of learning criminal behavior by association with criminal patterns involves all the mechanisms that are involved in any other learning.
9. Though criminal behavior is an expression of general needs and values, it is not explained by those general needs and values, since noncriminal behavior is an expression of the same needs and values.

In a capitalistic society, socioeconomic differentials relegate persons to an environment wherein they experience a *sense of strain*—anomie—as well as differential association. In the environment that has traditionally spawned organized crime, this "strain" is intense. Conditions of severe deprivation are coupled with readily available success models that are innovative; for example, racketeers and drug dealers. However, learning the techniques of sophisticated criminality also requires the proper environment—ecological niches where delinquent/criminal subcultures flourish and this education is available.

Subcultures and Social Disorganization

Culture refers to a source of patterning in human conduct. It is the sum of patterns of social relationships and shared meanings by which people give order, expression, and value to common experiences. The strength of a culture is determined by the degree of commitment of its members: culture is a valued heritage. Culture involves beliefs and moral values as opposed to the social structure, which includes roles, class, political and economic arrangements. "A subculture implies that there are value judgments or a social value system which is apart from a larger or central value system. From the viewpoint of this larger dominant culture, the values of the subculture set the latter apart and

Members of a Latino gang in South Los Angeles demonstrate hand signals used for identification—part of the tradition of their subculture. Like traditional organized crime groups, adolescent street gangs' attitudes and behaviors are culturally transmitted.

prevent total integration, occasionally causing open or covert conflicts" (Wolfgang and Ferracuti 1967: 99). James Short (1968: 11) explains that "subcultures are patterns of values, norms, and behavior which have become traditional among certain groups. These groups may be of many types, including occupational and ethnic groups, social classes, occupants of 'closed institutions' [for example, prisons, mental hospitals] and various age grades." They are "important frames of reference through which individuals and groups see the world and interpret it."

Central to the issue of culture versus subculture are *norms*, "group-held prescriptions for or prohibitions against certain conduct" (Wolfgang and Ferracuti 1967: 113). Norms are general rules about how to behave and expectations that are predictive of behavior. These rules and expectations are approved by the vast majority of a society, which provides rewards or punishments for conformity or violation. "The 'delinquent subculture' is characterized principally by conduct that reflects values antithetical to the surrounding culture" (Wolfgang and Ferracuti 1967: 110). Subcultural theory explains criminal behavior as learned—the subcultural delinquent has learned values that are deviant. Ideas about society lead to criminal behavior. A number of studies indicate that delinquent youths hold values that differ markedly from nondelinquents. Indeed, they may view their criminal behavior as morally wrong, but this is not the controlling attitude. Being right or wrong in terms of the wider society is simply not a guidepost for behavior. Nonconventional behavior is admired—the ability to fight, to win at gambling (Elliott, Huizinga, and Ageton 1985).

Clifford R. Shaw and Henry D. McKay, sociologists at the University of Chicago, used that city as a "laboratory" for their study of patterns of criminality during the 1920s and 1930s. They found that certain clearly identifiable neighborhoods maintained a high level of criminality over many decades despite changes in ethnic composition. Thus, although one ethnic group replaced another, the rate of criminality remained constant. What was it about the environment of these neighborhoods that made them criminogenic?

According to Shaw and McKay (1972: 72), such neighborhoods are characterized by attitudes and values that are conducive to delinquency and crime, particularly organized crime:

> [T]he presence of a large number of adult criminals in certain areas means that children there are in contact with crime as a career and with the criminal way of life, symbolized by organized crime. In this type of organization can be seen the delegation of authority, the division of labor, the specialization of function, and all the other characteristics common to well-organized business institutions wherever found. . . .
>
> The heavy concentration of delinquency in certain areas means that boys living in these areas are in contact not only with individuals who engage in proscribed activity but also with groups which sanction such behavior and exert pressure upon their members to conform to group standards. (1972: 174).

A disruption of the social order is associated with high rates of delinquency in a community, the result of a breakdown in mechanisms of social control. In many U.S. cities around the turn of the century, the social order was disrupted by the combined interactive effects of industrialization, immigration, and urbanization. Deviant traditions developed and competed with conventional norms; in some communities, deviant norms won out. Once established, these norms took root in areas which, according to Shaw and McKay, are characterized by attitudes and values that are conducive to delinquency and crime—a subculture of crime. The attitudes and values, as well as the techniques of organized criminality, are transmitted culturally: "[D]elinquent boys in these areas have contact not only with other delinquents who are their contemporaries but also with older offenders, who in turn had contact with delinquents preceding them, and so on back to the earliest history of the neighborhood. This contact means that the traditions of delinquency can be and are transmitted down through successive generations of boys, in much the same way that language and other social forms are transmitted" (1972: 174).

Back in the 1920s, John Landesco (1968) found that organized crime in Chicago could be explained by the prevalence of social disorganization in the wider society (during the period of Prohibition), and the distinct social organization of urban slums from which members of OC emerge. "Once a set of cultural values is created and established—either because of economic factors or intellectual or moral transformations—they tend to become autonomous in their impact. From that point on, they can influence human relations independently of their original sources. And since they are, as a rule, accepted uncritically and through the most inadvertent process of socialization, they are regarded as normal and inevitable within each cultural system" (Saney 1986: 35). In other words, the roots and culture of particular neighborhoods explain why gangsters come from clearly delineated areas "where the gang tradition is old" (Landesco 1968: 207), and where adolescents, through differential association, can absorb the attitudes and skills necessary to enter the world of adult organized crime.

Inadequate familial socialization prevents some persons from conforming to the conventional norms of the wider society. Through differential association, some of these persons organize their behavior according to the norms of a delinquent or criminal subculture with which they identify or to which they belong. This is most likely to occur in environments characterized by relative social disorganization, where familial and communal controls are ineffective in exerting a conforming influence. In his classic study of Chicago street gangs originally published in 1927, Frederic Thrasher (1968: 270) notes: "Experience in a gang of the predatory type usually develops in the boy an attitude of indifference to law and order—one of the basic traits of the finished gangster." Thrasher (1968: 273) points out: "If the younger undirected gangs and clubs of the gang type, which serve as training schools for delinquency, do not succeed in turning out the finished criminal, they often develop a type of personality which may well foreshadow the gangster and the gunman." In the Chicago of the Prohibition era there was no hard-and-fast dividing line between gangs of boys, youths, and adult criminal organizations (1968: 281): "They merge into each other by imperceptible gradations."

In order for an organized crime group to survive, it must have "an institutionalized process for inducting new members and inculcating them with the values and ways of behaving of the social system" (Cressey, 1969: 263). Donald Cressey notes (1969: 236) that "in some neighborhoods all three of the essential ingredients of an effective recruiting process are in operation: inspiring aspiration for membership, training for membership and selection for membership." In his research, Gerald Suttles (1968) refers to areas from which members of organized crime have typically emerged as *defended neighborhoods*: recognized ecological niches whose inhabitants form cohesive groupings and seal themselves off through the efforts of delinquent gangs, restrictive covenants, and a forbidding reputation. Such neighborhoods have traditionally provided the recruiting grounds that ensure the continuity of traditional OC. In such communities, notes Solomon Kobrin (1966: 156), the conventional and criminal value systems are highly integrated. Leaders of organized criminal enterprises "frequently maintain membership in such conventional institutions of their local communities as churches, fraternal and mutual benefit societies, and political parties." Formal and informal political, economic, and religious ties provide both illegitimate and legitimate opportunities. These leaders are able to control violent and delinquent behavior in their domain. "Everyone," particularly would-be miscreants, "knows" not to "mess around" in certain neighborhoods. And those who do not "know" have suffered serious consequences—selling drugs in one Chicago suburb, for example, resulted in mutilated corpses.

Nicholas Pileggi (1985: 37–38) describes a defended neighborhood in Brooklyn:

> In Brownsville-East New York wiseguys were more than accepted—they were protected. Even the legitimate members of the community—the merchants, teachers, phone repairmen, garbage collectors, bus depot dispatchers, housewives, and old-timers sunning themselves along the Conduit Drive—all seemed to keep an eye out to protect their local hoods. The majority of the residents, even those not directly related by birth or marriage to wiseguys, had certainly known the local rogues most of their lives. There was the nodding familiarity of neighborhood. In the area it was impossible to betray old friends, even those old friends who had grown up to be racketeers.

The extraordinary insularity of these old-world mob-controlled sections, whether Brownsville-East New York, the South Side of Chicago, or Federal Hill in Providence, Rhode Island, unquestionably helped to nurture the mob.

Recruitment into OC is made viable because "in the type of community under discussion, boys may more or less realistically recognize the potentialities for personal progress in the local society through success in delinquency. In a general way, therefore, delinquent activity in these areas constitutes a training ground for the acquisition of skill in the use of violence, concealment of offense, evasion of detection and arrest, and the purchase of immunity from punishment" (Kobrin 1966: 156).

Robert Lombardo, an expert on organized crime for the Chicago Police Department, points out that prospective members of OC "typically come from communities which share collective representations and moral sentiments which allow them to recognize the pursuit of a career in the underworld as a legitimate way of life" (1979: 18). According to Irving Spergel (1964), in such communities life in OC is considered acceptable and therefore a legitimate avenue of aspiration for young persons. While these communities provide an appropriate learning environment for the acquisition of values and skills associated with the performance of criminal roles, integration into OC requires selection and tutelage in the process of acquiring recognition—and only a select few are given recognition by those who control admission. Entry into organized crime is characterized by *differential opportunity*.

Differential Opportunity

In agreement with Merton, Richard Cloward and Lloyd Ohlin (1960: 107) note that American preoccupation with economic success, coupled with socioeconomic stratification, relegates many persons to an environment wherein they experience strain: "Many lower-class male adolescents experience extreme deprivation born of the certainty that their position in the economic structure is relatively fixed and immutable—a desperation made all the more poignant by their exposure to a cultural ideology in which failure to orient oneself upward is regarded as a moral defect and failure to become mobile as proof of it."

Conditions of severe deprivation with extremely limited access to ladders of legitimate success result in collective adaptations in the form of delinquent subcultures. Cloward and Ohlin distinguish three types:

1. *Retreatist subculture*: Activities in which drug usage is the primary focus; the anomic condition leads the sufferer to reject the goal of economic success in favor of a more easily obtainable one—the "high."
2. *Conflict subculture*: Gang activities devoted to violence and destructive acting out as a way of gaining status; as with retreatism, the anomic condition leads to a rejection of economic success in favor of a more easily obtainable goal.
3. *Criminal/rackets subculture*: Gang activity devoted to utilitarian criminal pursuits; an adaptation that begins to approximate organized crime.

Anomie alone, note Cloward and Ohlin, is not sufficient to explain participation in organized crime. What is necessary is *cultural transmission* (Shaw and McKay) through *differential association* (Sutherland). However, Cloward and Ohlin point out that illegitimate opportunity for success, like legitimate opportunity, is not equally distributed throughout society (1960: 145): "Having decided that he 'can't make it legitimately,' he cannot simply choose from an array of illegitimate means, all equally available to him." In other words, access to criminal ladders of success is no more freely available than access to noncriminal alternatives:

> Only those neighborhoods in which crime flourishes as a stable, indigenous institution are fertile learning environments for the young. Because these environments afford integration of different age-levels of offender, selected young people are exposed to "differential association" through which tutelage is provided and criminal values and skills are acquired. To be prepared for the role may not, however, ensure that the individual will ever discharge it. One important limitation is that more youngsters are recruited into these patterns of differential association than the adult criminal structure can possibly absorb. Since there is a surplus of contenders for these elite positions, criteria and mechanisms of selection must be evolved. Hence a certain proportion of those who aspire may not be permitted to engage in the behavior for which they have prepared themselves. (Cloward and Ohlin 1960: 148)

Why do young men who have the opportunity not become contenders for positions in organized crime? *Social control theory* offers an explanation.

Social Control Theory

Perhaps, as social control theorists argue, the relevant question is not why persons become involved in crime, organized or otherwise, but rather, why do most persons conform to societal norms? If, as control theorists generally assume, most persons are sufficiently motivated by the potential rewards to commit criminal acts, why do only a few make crime a career? According to control theorists, "delinquent acts result when an individual's bond to society is weak or broken" (Hirschi 1969: 16). The strength of this bond is determined by internal and external restraints. In other words, internal and external restraints determine if we move in the direction of crime or law-abiding behavior.

Internal restraints include what psychoanalytic theory refers to as the *superego* (Freud 1933): an unconscious, yet powerful, conscience-like mechanism that provides a sense of *guilt*. According to Sigmund Freud, conscience is not something that is a part of us from the very beginning of our lives. It is a controlling mechanism that develops out of the relationship with, and influence of, our parents. In the adult who experienced "healthy" parental relationships as a child, the superego takes the place of the controlling parental function. Dysfunction during early stages of childhood development, or parental influences that are not normative, result in an adult who is devoid of prosocial internal constraints; some refer to this as psycho- or sociopathology. (There is also evidence tying psychopathology to a brain defect.) The murderous behavior, devoid of remorse, engaged in by persons in organized crime can be explained according to this dimension. Whether they are conceived of in terms of psychology or sociology, internal constraints are linked to the influence of the family (see, for example, Hirschi 1969), an influence that can be supported or weakened by the presence or absence of significant external restraints.

External restraints include social disapproval linked to public shame and/or social ostracism and fear of punishment. In other words, people are typically deterred from criminal behavior by the possibility of being caught and the punishment that can result, ranging from public shame to imprisonment (and in extreme cases, capital punishment). In neighborhoods or among subcultural groups with moral sentiments favorable to organized crime, such public shame/social ostracism is ineffective.

The strength of official deterrence—force of law—is measured according to two dimensions: risk versus reward. Risk involves the ability of the criminal justice system to detect, apprehend, and convict the offender. The amount of risk is weighed against the potential rewards. Both risk and reward, however, are relative to one's socioeconomic situation. In other words, the less one has to lose, the greater is the willingness to engage in risk. And the greater the reward, the greater is the willingness to engage in risk. This theory explains why persons in deprived economic circumstances would be more willing to engage in criminal behavior. However, the potential rewards and a perception of relatively low risk can also explain why persons in more advantaged economic circumstances would engage in remunerative criminal behavior such as corporate or organized crime.

Instead of conforming to conventional norms, some persons organize their behavior according to the norms of a delinquent or criminal group to which they belong or with which they identify. This is most likely to occur in environments characterized by relative social disorganization, where familial and communal controls are ineffective in exerting a conforming influence. In certain areas—ecological niches with strong traditions of OC—young persons stand a greater chance of being exposed to criminal norms. In these areas, Kobrin (1966) points out, persons exhibiting criminal norms are often well-integrated into the community, and such areas are the breeding ground for entrants into organized crime.

HISTORICAL ANTECEDENTS OF ORGANIZED CRIME: THE ROBBER BARONS

"Al Capone," notes Michael Woodiwiss (1978: 8), "was not the first ruthless entrepreneur to combine with thugs, gunmen and government officials and carve out an illegal fortune. But the expression—'organised crime'—was not commonly used until the 1920s and the Prohibition era when academics and newspaper editors found it to be a convenient new label for an old phenomenon." While contemporary organized crime has its roots in Prohibition (1920–33), unscrupulous American business entrepreneurs provided role models and created a climate conducive to the growth of the phenomenon. Earlier generations of predatory Americans with English, Scottish, Scandinavian, or German ancestry paved the way for later generations of Irish, Jewish, or Italian criminals who, in turn, are being emulated by criminals of African, Hispanic, or Asian ancestry. An examination of these antecedents is necessary if we are to place contemporary organized crime and the ethnic and racial groups who drive it in the proper historical perspective. While no assertion is made for a direct link from "Carnegie to Capone," balance requires an examination of the former before we presume to judge the latter.

John Jacob Astor

John Jacob Astor (1763–1848) arrived from Germany penniless and died the richest man in America: "The first great self-made millionaire whose career whetted the ambitions of a host of young Americans" (Rugoff 1989: 40). The Astor fortune was based on alcohol and fraud: drunken Native Americans were systematically cheated by agents of Astor's American Fur Company. When the Native Americans complained to the government, Astor's agents resorted to violence. When the Native Americans retaliated, troops were sent to quell the "Indian disorder." In addition to exploiting Native Americans, Astor succeeded in forcing his employees in the western wilderness to buy from company-owned stores at exorbitant prices. By the time they returned east, most employees were actually in debt to Astor (Myers 1936; Rugoff 1989).

Astor was able to monopolize the fur trade and "was never prosecuted for the numerous violations of both penal and civil law invariably committed by his direction and for his benefit. With the millions that rolled in, he was able not only to command the services of the foremost lawyers in warding off penalties of law, but also to have as his paid retainers some of the most noted and powerful politicians of the day" (Myers 1936: 103). For example, he paid Lewis Cass, then governor of the territory of Michigan, $35,000 for unexplained services. David Loth (1938: 104) notes that the money was well-invested. Later, as Secretary of War, "Cass was to hear, and dismiss, many charges of corruption, extortion, trespass and violence against the [American Fur] company and its representatives." The money gained through lawlessness and violence against Native Americans in the western fur trade was used for real estate speculation in New York, where easily corrupted officials helped Astor become America's greatest "slumlord," extracting money from poor immigrants for the privilege of living in the vilest of tenement housing. The Astor-inspired slums became a spawning ground for organized crime.

Cornelius Vanderbilt

Cornelius Vanderbilt (1794–1877) came from a small farming family on Staten Island (now part of New York City). He parlayed profits from a ferryboat venture into shipping and shipbuilding, and at age forty-seven, the "Commodore" was a rich man. The government of Nicaragua had given his Accessory Transit Company a monopoly over transportation across the isthmus connecting the two great oceans. In 1853, while Vanderbilt was on a European vacation, two members of his board of directors, in accord with business practices of the day, usurped control of Accessory Transit. Vanderbilt retaliated by setting up a competing line, and by cutting prices forced the two directors, C.K. Garrison and Charles Morgan, to withdraw. They retaliated by financing an insurrection in Nicaragua where Accessory Transit was chartered. The revolutionary forces, led by an American adventurer, William Walker, achieved a great victory. Early in 1856, the Vanderbilt charter was cancelled and his property confiscated. Vanderbilt responded that summer by persuading the governments of Honduras, San Salvador, and Costa Rica to form an alliance against Nicaragua. Then, on Vanderbilt's orders, two American mercenaries led an invasion of Nicaragua. By the end of the first year the invasion force was progressing quite well; then the Nicaraguans counterattacked. Vanderbilt thwarted the offensive by persuading the State Department to send in the U.S. Marines, who succeeded in deposing the revolutionary government. Vanderbilt's charter was restored (Andrews 1941). Even Mario Puzo's godfather of fiction did not use "muscle" on this scale.

Like many other successful businessmen of the era, Vanderbilt was a "war profiteer." During the Civil War he acted as an agent for the Union Army, securing unfit and rotting vessels for the transportation of federal troops at exorbitant prices. However, his primary interest was civilian transportation, and Vanderbilt moved from shipping to railroads. Striving for monopoly, he gained control of the Hudson River and Harlem lines and forced the competing New York Central to sell out. In 1866 he sought to complete his transportation stranglehold by taking over the Erie Railroad line, which was a direct competitor. Vanderbilt, however, was ambushed by the Erie Ring, comprised of three of America's greatest pirate capitalists: Daniel Drew, James Fisk, and Jay Gould.

The Erie Ring

As part of a scheme to fleece Vanderbilt, the Erie Ring secretly authorized the issuance of ten million new shares of Erie stock while Vanderbilt was busy buying up shares to gain control of the Erie Railroad. The more stock he purchased, the more stock was issued by the ring, which declared their actions in accord with the First Amendment—"freedom of the press." In 1868, Vanderbilt realized he had bought more Erie stock than was known to exist and still did not control the line. An obliging New York Supreme Court judge, part of the "Tweed Ring," issued an injunction against further issue of Erie stock. The judge also ordered the ring to return to the treasury one-fourth of what they had already issued. "When Vanderbilt needed a court order in a hurry or a special bill or a joker in a franchise, he could rely on the 'Boss' to have it in stock" (Loth 1938: 196). ("Boss" William M. Tweed was the head of Tammany Hall, an organization that dominated New York City politics and government for more than one hundred years; it is discussed in chapter 3.)

The injunction, however, simply drove up the price of Erie stock, but it did not stop the ring. They had "their judge" issue a counterinjunction, and chaos swept Wall Street. Trading in Erie stock was suspended by the stock exchange, but not before Vanderbilt had lost between $5 and $7 million (that was a significant sum in those days). He responded by having "his judge" issue contempt-of-court arrest warrants for the members of the ring.

The Erie Ring withdrew all of its combined funds from New York banks, took all its securities and documents from safes, and crossed the Hudson to Jersey City with its printing press—out of range of the Tweed Ring. Arriving just ahead of pursuing sheriff's deputies, Gould, Drew, and Fisk set up headquarters in Taylor's Castle Hotel, dubbed "Fort Taylor." In Jersey City they were guarded by railroad police and cooperative city police officers. Cannons were mounted on piers to thwart any landings from New York, and the ring counterattacked. They reduced fares to Buffalo, undercutting the hard-pressed Vanderbilt line. Vanderbilt retaliated by ordering a band of thugs into New Jersey, and the members of the Erie Ring fled to New York, where the field of battle shifted to the state capital, Albany.

In Albany the ring spread $1 million worth of "good will" in an effort to legalize their theft of the Erie from Vanderbilt. Jay Gould "drew the 'Boss' [Tweed] away from the Commodore's New York Central by the present of a block of Erie stock, a directorship and a retainer of many thousands as counsel" (Loth 1938: 197). Vanderbilt joined the fray, but soon grew tired of trying to satisfy the seemingly insatiable appetites of state legislators for bribe money. The ring achieved a "legislative victory," and Vanderbilt sued for peace. In return for $4.5 million, he relinquished his interest in the Erie and the arrest warrants were quashed (Josephson 1962; Rugoff 1989).

Daniel Drew

The oldest member of the Erie Ring, Daniel Drew, was born in Carmel, New York, in 1797. An illiterate raised in poverty, Drew began his business career as a cattle drover, buying cattle on credit from New York farmers and driving them to market for sale. He often failed to pay his debts and was forced to move operations to Ohio where he perfected the technique that resulted in the term *watered stock*. His cattle were kept thirsty by a liberal diet of salt and very little water. Before arrival at the drover's market, the cattle were allowed to quench their thirst and increase their poundage accordingly. With money thus earned, Drew purchased a tavern and also became a moneylender, a steamship owner, and a stockbroker. He gained notoriety by his comments on the advent of the Civil War: "Along with ordinary happenings, we fellows on Wall Street now have in addition the fortunes of war to speculate about, and that always makes great doings on the stock exchange. It's good fishing in troubled waters" (O'Connor 1962: 51).

Drew became treasurer and, according to W.A. Swanberg (1959: 24), virtual "dictator" of the Erie Railroad. He would issue stock for new steel rails and other vital equipment and divert the money for his own speculative investments. As a result, the Erie's "schedules were fictional, its rolling stock ruinous, and its rails so weak and chipped as to invite derailment." For his own enrichment, Drew ran what had been considered a technological marvel, the Erie Railroad, into the ground (Ackerman 1988). The Erie ran from Jersey City to Lake Erie. In 1866, the line was in financial trouble and borrowed $3.5 million from Drew. As collateral, he received 28,000 shares of unissued stock and $3 million in convertible bonds. The securities had been entrusted to him only as collateral; they were not to be sold. Drew converted the bonds into 30,000 more shares of stock and, with Jim Fisk as his broker, began selling short—speculating that the price of the stock would go down. To ensure that this would happen, Drew dumped all 58,000 shares on the market and realized a profit of almost $3 million (at a time when most workingmen earned less than $25 a week and New York State legislators were paid $300 a year).

Drew was an ardent Methodist churchgoer and was responsible for the founding of the Drew Theological Seminary in New Jersey, now part of Drew University. As a pious fraud, notes Milton Rugoff (1989), Drew offered to endow the seminary with $250,000, but wound up giving the institution only the 7 percent interest on this amount. He founded a brokerage firm, but the panic of 1873 wiped out his fortune. While Cornelius Vanderbilt died leaving an estate valued at $90 million and a university named in his honor, Drew was a pauper when he died in 1879 (Swanberg 1959).

James Fisk

James Fisk, Jr., was born in Vermont in 1834 to a family of English ancestry. He left home at age fifteen to join the circus, returning a few years later to join his father as an itinerant peddler. His success at this trade led to a job as a salesman for Jordan Marsh & Company of Boston. During the Civil War he acted as an agent for Marsh to the Union Army, lobbying congressmen and generals with lavish entertainment and liberal spending. This led to lucrative contracts for Marsh and advancement for the young Fisk. While other young men were dying by the thousands defending the Union, Fisk was operating an enormous smuggling operation moving southern cotton to the northern mills of Jordan Marsh, and a fortune was made. At the end of the war, a grateful Marsh presented Fisk with a bonus of $65,000.

Fisk took his Civil War profits and used them to swindle buyers of Confederate bonds in Europe. After the fall of Richmond, he sold short to Englishmen who did not know that the Confederacy had collapsed. Although he had successfully avoided military service during the Civil War—when a man could get killed—in peacetime he and his fortune assumed command of a national guard militia unit. "The Ninth New York," notes Richard O'Connor (1962: 116), "was up for sale; without transfusions of men and money it would have to be disbanded." The newly elected Colonel Fisk, in uniform and astride his horse, was at the head of his militiamen during the Orangemen parade of 1871. When the English loyalists were attacked by Irish Catholics, Fisk reacted by throwing away his sword and fleeing. Three of his militiamen died in the fighting, and the colonel prudently absented himself from their funeral.

Known as a *bon vivant*, Fisk was murdered in 1872 by the paramour of his favorite mistress, the actress Josie Mansfield. He left an estate valued at $1 million. Although his wife was reputed to be worth $2 million, she died in 1912, a poor woman living on an income of $50 a month from some rental property (Swanberg 1959).

Jay Gould

The third member of the Erie Ring, Jay Gould, was born in Roxbury, New York, in 1836, the son of a poor farmer. The Golds (the original family name) had roots in America dating back to 1674 when the family first settled in Connecticut (Klein 1986). At age sixteen, with a neat hand and a good head for figures, the future member of the Erie Ring was working as a clerk for a village storekeeper. Gould discovered that his employer had negotiated to buy a piece of property for $2,000. Gould secured a loan from his father, purchased the land for $2,500, and sold it to his employer for $4,000. Taking advantage of positions of trust was to become the basis for Gould's early financial success. At age twenty he took $5,000 he had accumulated and entered the leather market in New York.

Gould was befriended by a wealthy businessman who, impressed with the young man's ability, provided him with $120,000 to establish a large tannery in Pennsylvania. "Early in life," writes Maury Klein (1986: 43), "he revealed a talent for charming people." According to Matthew Josephson (1962), the company did well, but no profits were received by the owner in New York—Gould was systematically diverting the funds for his own speculative investments. (Klein states, however, that there is no evidence to support this conclusion.) When he traveled to Pennsylvania, the investor found the books in disarray. Fearing for his investment, he offered to sell the company to Gould for only $60,000—money that Gould didn't have. Gould found other backers, paid off the original owner, and continued to divert funds for his own use, until the new owner attempted to physically take back his property. Using hired thugs and idle workers, Gould resisted the effort until officers of the law finally ousted him (Josephson 1962). Klein states that Gould was blameless, and that it was his financial backer who used hired thugs, Gould relying on the tannery's workers. However, notes Klein, "Jay came out of the episode in better financial shape than when he began it. The tannery may have lost money, but Jay did not" (1986: 60). In fact, Gould was soon able to enter a new partnership worth about $80,000—a considerable sum of money in those days.

Gould entered the railroad business, first buying mortgage bonds of the Rutland and Washington Railroad. For ten cents on the dollar Gould was able to gain controlling interest of this small, bankrupt line. He then hired men with managerial ability, improved the railroad's rolling stock, and consolidated it with other small lines whose stock he had also purchased. By complex stock manipulations, Gould was able to drive up the price of his holdings. He then purchased a controlling interest in the Cleveland and Pittsburgh Railroad, using profits from bond speculation, and manipulated the line's stock to an all-time high. Gould then sold it to the Pennsylvania Railroad Company (Myers 1936). His next great enterprise involved him as part of the Erie Ring in its battle with Cornelius Vanderbilt.

In 1869, the United States had an unfavorable balance of trade—a problem that has again gained widespread attention. In order to trade successfully, American importers had to make payments to European exporters in gold. Gould discovered that there was only about $15 million in gold in the New York market, and he plotted to corner that market. Gould already owned $7 million worth of gold, and using the Erie's resources and that of his backers, he could easily absorb the outstanding $15 million and drive the price of gold sky high. Only one ingredient remained to be dealt with—President Ulysses S. Grant. The president had the power to release some of the $100 million in gold reserves, which the federal government did periodically in the interest of fostering trade and commerce. Gould attempted to influence the president through a financial relationship with Grant's brother-in-law. He also had stories placed in newspapers that the government was going to refrain from releasing any gold reserves. These activities, in addition to his own feverish buying and that of Jim Fisk, caused a "bull market," and the price of gold skyrocketed (Loth 1938).

Gould discovered, however, that Grant had not been influenced—the president would not permit the price of gold to rise freely. He began to sell off his gold and, suddenly, on September 24—known as "Black Friday"—the bottom fell out and the price of gold plummeted. Enraged mobs of investors sought to lynch Gould and Fisk, who were protected by their paid thugs from the Erie line. Gould, of course, made a handsome profit—$1 million—from the entire venture (Swanberg 1959; Rugoff 1989). In 1886, the Knights of Labor demanded a minimum wage of nine dollars a week. Gould responded with wholesale firings at one of his holdings and the union called a strike. Violence broke out, and with the help of private detectives and strikebreakers, Gould broke the strike and the union (Rugoff 1989).

When Gould died in 1892 he left an estate valued at $70 million (Josephson 1962). His progeny, however, fought costly legal battles over the estate, and frequently mismanaged what they inherited. Nevertheless, the last surviving son, Howard, who died in 1959, left an estate of more than $62 million to twenty-eight relatives (O'Connor 1962). On January 3, 1984, the *New York Times* reported that the jewelry collection of the late daughter-in-law of "railroad magnate Jay Gould" would be auctioned at Christie's on April 11. The widow of the youngest son of Jay Gould had a jewelry collection insured for more than $100 million, in addition to an art collection of one hundred twenty works by van Gogh, Renoir, Manet, Degas, Goya, and others of like quality. The bulk of the estate went to the Gould Foundation to promote Franco-American friendship (Reif 1984). The Gould family also provided generous endowments to New York University from which Frank, Jay's youngest son, was graduated in 1899. Several of the school's buildings bear the Gould name.

Russell Sage

Russell Sage was born in 1816 in Oneida County, New York. He worked in his brother's grocery store as a clerk, and in 1839 became a partner in a wholesale grocery business. In 1851 he engaged in the first of his major swindles, and the resulting legal action reached the United States Supreme Court. For seven years Sage held the office of alderman in the city of Troy and was treasurer of Renesselaer County in New York. Using his public positions and chicanery, he succeeded in getting the city of Troy to sell its Troy and Schenectady Railroad, which had been constructed at great public expense. Through intermediaries, Sage bought the line for a mere $200,000—$50,000 down and fourteen years to pay. He then arranged for sale of the line to the New York Central Railroad for $1 million.

In 1853 Sage was elected to Congress, and during his stay enormous grants of land and financial subsidies were given to railroad corporations. When he left Congress after serving two terms, Sage was a major stockholder of the La Crosse and Milwaukee Railroad, which had received land grants from the state of Wisconsin worth more than $17 million—which cost about $1 million in bribes. Sage eventually gained control of the line and swindled stockholders and creditors. The line was driven into bankruptcy and turned over to the major bondholders, who were Sage front men. The line was then renamed and (on paper) reorganized, and the whole scam was repeated. Although the overplundered line was unsafe and inefficient, its owner became a multimillionaire. He was also involved in a number of stock and railroad schemes with Jay Gould.

Using his accumulated railroad wealth, Sage became one of America's greatest usurers, charging as much as 2 percent per day to hard-pressed businessmen. Upon his death in 1906, $50 million in personal property was inherited by his widow and second wife, Margaret. She devoted much of her husband's wealth to philanthropy, particularly Russell Sage College and the Russell Sage Foundation "for the improvement of social and living conditions in the United States." Through the efforts of the foundation, small-loan acts were passed to protect workers from the usurious practice known as "salary lending."

Leland Stanford

The railroading tradition of Vanderbilt, Drew, Fisk, Gould, and Sage was not reserved for the eastern portion of the United States. But in the West there was none of the cutthroat competition that pervaded the East. Leland Stanford was born in Watervliet, New York, in 1824. He practiced law in Wisconsin for a time, and finally moved to California where he became involved in Republican politics and was elected governor in 1861. According to Myers (1936: 250), Stanford was "one of the arch-bribers and thieves of the time." His major coup, accomplished while he was governor, involved the Central Pacific Railroad. He formed the Pacific Association with three colleagues who, like himself, were devoid of any railroading background or significant financial assets. What assets they did have, $200,000, were used prudently—but not to build a railroad. The money was "laid out in bribes to Congressmen or others with influence" in the nation's capitol. David Loth (1938: 159) states: "The Central Pacific had thrown its $200,000 upon Congressional waters and lo! it had returned in the form of a land grant for 9,000,000 acres and a loan of Federal bonds for $24,000,000."

The Central Pacific would run from the ocean to as far as it could reach in a race east, with the Union Pacific racing west. The lines linked up in 1869. For every mile of track, the lines received a subsidy from the government. This did not satisfy Stanford and his associates. They intimidated local governments into providing millions of dollars by threatening to have the line bypass their communities. San Francisco, for example, provided $550,000 (Myers 1936; Josephson 1962). Nevertheless, in 1885 Stanford was elected to the U.S. Senate by the legislature and reelected in 1890. In 1885, he established Leland Stanford, Jr. University—now known as Stanford University—in memory of his son, who had died in 1884 at age fifteen. Stanford died in 1893.

John D. Rockefeller

John D. Rockefeller was born in Richford, New York, in 1839, the son of a vendor of patent medicines. A studious, hardworking youngster, at age sixteen he secured a job as a bookkeeper for a produce merchant. He saved meager earnings and became a successful commodities broker, buying and selling grain and produce. During the Civil War, Rockefeller made a fortune selling grain to the military while avoiding conscription. In 1862, he invested in a technique to extract kerosene from crude oil and in 1865 sold his share in the produce business to devote all his time and money to oil. His remarkable success in the oil business was aided by the Vanderbilt-owned railroad, which shipped the Rockefeller oil at a discount. A portion of the shipping costs were rebated—"kickbacks"—allowing Rockefeller to undercut his competitors.

In 1870, Rockefeller and Henry Flagler incorporated the Standard Oil Company, and during the following year they conspired to control the entire oil industry in the United States. First, they obtained the Pennsylvania charter of a defunct corporation that had been authorized to engage in a plethora of business activities—the South Improvement Company (SIC). Then, in collusion with railroad officials, they doubled shipping rates for competing oil companies, but the increase for the SIC was rebated. By 1872, Rockefeller was intimidating rival oil companies into selling out to SIC. An "oil war" resulted, as independent oil dealers fought the SIC by refusing to sell their oil to the

Rockefeller-controlled refineries. The oil boycott hurt the railroads, which rebelled against Rockefeller. The Pennsylvania legislature finally revoked the SIC charter (Lloyd 1963).

The great monopolist struck again, this time conspiring with refinery owners to gain control over the setting of railroad oil shipping rates. The owners of the fifteen strongest oil firms in the United States swore an oath of secrecy and became part of what became known as the Standard Oil conspiracy. In league with the railroads, they controlled the delivery of oil, forcing competitors to sell out to Standard or pay exorbitant shipping costs that would render them noncompetitive. Those who were stubborn enough to resist were harassed with price wars and, if that didn't work, dynamite. The Rockefeller trust—Standard Oil—extended its vertical control of the oil industry to include

These late nineteenth-century cartoons reflect popular attitudes toward two of the most powerful and ruthless robber barons of the day. Railroad magnate Cornelius Vanderbilt (left) tightens his stranglehold on the American public, while oil monopolist John D. Rockefeller (right) balances the world in the palm of his hand.

pipelines, oil terminals, and direct marketing. By 1876 Standard Oil controlled 80 percent of the oil production in the United States, and by 1878 Rockefeller dominated the entire industry.

In 1877, a great oil boom threatened to break the Standard Oil monopoly. Rockefeller fought the new independents by refusing them use of railroads, pipelines, and storage facilities. The independents organized and fought back, financing the construction of the Tidewater Pipe Line to break Rockefeller control over railroad rates. They attacked Standard Oil in the courts, and Flagler and Rockefeller were indicted in Pennsylvania for conspiracy in restraint of trade.

Undaunted, Rockefeller built a rival pipeline, slashed prices, attacked Tidewater credit in the money market, and "his" judges enjoined the issuance of Tidewater bonds. In the finest tradition of direct action, Standard Oil operatives plugged up Tidewater pipelines. Under siege, Tidewater finally capitulated and was bought out by the National Transit Company, which was owned by Standard Oil (Lloyd 1963). By 1890 the Rockefeller trust controlled about 90 percent of the petroleum production in the United States, a situation that led to the passage of the Sherman Anti-Trust Act that same year.

John D. Rockefeller died in 1937, and his legacy lives on in the form of the University of Chicago, Rockefeller University, and the Rockefeller Foundation. His progeny have served as governors of New York, Arkansas, and West Virginia, as U.S. senator from West Virginia, and as vice president of the United States.

J. Pierpont Morgan

J. Pierpont Morgan (1837–1913) was born in Connecticut and educated in Germany. His father was a wealthy banker, and by virtue of the family fortune Morgan was able to escape conscription during the Civil War —"he saw the Civil War as an occasion for profit, not service" (Chernow 1990: 22). Morgan became a war profiteer, financing the sale of defective carbines to the Union Army (Loth 1938). In 1869 he engaged Gould and Fisk in a battle over a railroad line that had been constructed with public funds. The contest over the Albany and Susquehanna's stock moved into the courts as each side accused the other of fraud. The ensuing battle threw the railroad into chaos, and it had to be shut down. Unfortunately for Gould and Fisk, the court fight took place upstate, not in the Tammany courts of New York City. As a result, the Morgan-influenced judges handed him control of the line. Morgan continued to feed at the public trough, and his banking firm (Drexel, Morgan & Co.) earned $5 million for acting as brokers in the sale of government bonds that Myers (1936: 560) argues the government "could have disposed of . . . without intermediaries."

In 1889, Morgan convened a secret meeting of the major banking houses in order to form a cartel—a monopoly designed to corner federal gold reserves. The cartel began buying up government gold reserves by redeeming bonds for gold coin. By 1895, they had $120 million in gold hoarded away in bank vaults. Morgan, through an emissary, offered to release the gold in negotiations with President Grover Cleveland. The only thing he wanted in return was exclusive rights to a government bond issue of over $62 million. Cleveland agreed, and the cartel sold the bonds for a net profit of $18 million—money that would have otherwise gone to the government.

By his control over banking and, thus, sources of credit, Morgan wielded more power than Andrew Carnegie or John D. Rockefeller. By merely threatening to withhold credit, he could destroy companies or coerce them into submission. As a result, Morgan was able to control railroads and steel production: about half the nation's railroad mileage and, as a result of his great "Steel Trust" (United States Steel), 75 to 100 percent of the market for finished steel. His enormous wealth permitted Morgan to collect great works of art and a considerable number of mistresses. He generously endowed Manhattan General Hospital "so that any little mistakes could be looked after" (Sinclair 1989: 90). When Morgan died while vacationing in Rome in 1913, he left an estate valued in excess of $131 million, while his son Pierpont, Jr., inherited an empire worth about $2.5 billion (Myers 1936; Josephson 1962).

Kindred Spirits

This sampling of earlier "godfathers" and some of their activities is far from complete. For example, we could have included the Du Ponts, who made vast fortunes during the War of 1812 and the Civil War, and who arranged for the formation of a cartel of gunpowder manufacturers, the "Powder Trust." After the Civil War, the cartel drove competition out of business by cutthroat pricing, bribery, and sabotage—competing companies disappeared in mysterious explosions (Zilg 1974). We could have given "dishonorable mention" to Scottish-born Andrew Carnegie (1835–1919), who gained control over a more efficient steel competitor by sending to railroads throughout the country a libelous circular warning that his competitor's product was unsafe. This lie enabled Carnegie to buy out his rival at bargain prices. Carnegie steelworkers put in twelve-hour days, seven days a week, "and Carnegie went on giving to libraries and wondering why so few adults made use of his magnificent gifts" (Wall 1970: 579).

We could have provided details about James Jerome Hill (1838–1916) of the Great Northern Railroad and Edward H. Harriman (1848–1909) of the Union Pacific and their battle to monopolize the rails, a battle that began in the stock exchange, moved to the courts, and finally was fought through melees and killings by thugs from both sides (Holbrook 1953). Harriman later joined with Hill and J. Pierpont Morgan to form a combine (Northern Securities Company) to monopolize railroads, but the trust was ordered dissolved by the U.S. Supreme Court in 1904. Edward's son, Averell Harriman, was elected governor of New York in 1954. He was defeated in a reelection bid by Nelson Rockefeller, grandson of John D.

We could have mentioned Henry Ford (1863–1947), icon of the American capitalist spirit, as well as a notorious anti-Semite, whose credo was: "There is something sacred about big business. Anything which is economically right is morally right" (Sinclair 1962: 369). In that spirit Ford hired Harry Bennett, known for his street-fighting abilities, who employed a small army of gangsters to beat and terrorize Ford workers and union organizers. (For Bennett's version of Ford, see Bennett 1951.) We could have discussed publishing magnate William Randolph Hearst (1863–1951), who employed Max and later brother Moses ("Moe") Annenberg to handle circulation for his *Chicago American*: "To persuade news dealers to find room for the *American* on their stands he recruited prizefighters, bouncers, muggers, and other street athletes, armed them with blackjacks, brass knuckles, and handguns, and sent them out in the *American* circulation wagons with instructions to give each news dealer a fair choice—he could either sell the bundle of newspapers tossed to him or he could eat them" (Gies 1979: 35). The Annenberg brothers were subsequently hired away from Hearst by the legendary publisher of the *Chicago Tribune*, Colonel Robert McCormick (1880–1955), who used their skills to engage in his own "circulation war" with Hearst. In the ensuing battle, "dozens of thugs, news dealers, and passing citizens got hit and an indeterminate number killed" (1979: 36). The Annenbergs' success in business included a number of racing sheets and a wire service indispensable for bookmaking. When Moe died in 1942, his son Walter inherited the empire, adding *TV Guide* and other popular publications. A philanthropist who gave millions to charity, Walter Annenberg was appointed ambassador to Great Britain in 1969 by President Nixon (Fox 1989). The Annenberg School of Communications at the University of Pennsylvania is part of his legacy.

We could have moved our historical review to the West, where cattle barons and land grabbers were not above using any means at their disposal to achieve their ends, as evidenced by the sensational escapades of the "Lincoln County War" (1876–78) in New Mexico, and the "Johnson County War" (1891–92) in Wyoming. William H. Bonney (1859–81), born Henry McCarty, but better known as "Billy the Kid," began his murderous career in the Lincoln County War (see Nolan 1992 for the fascinating history of this Wild West epic).

And if we wanted to update our review, we could have included more recent *corporate crime*—"crime in the suites," organized, "white collar" crime. We will examine business racketeering in chapter 8.

Conclusion

What does all this add up to—what are we to conclude? First, we must understand that the United States, as the Eisenhower Commission[1] pointed out, is quite a violent country (see also, Hofstadter and Wallace 1971). Im-

---

1. National Advisory Commission on the Causes and Prevention of Violence (1969). See also Graham and Gurr (1969).

FAMILY LEGACY

In the first edition of this book (1981b: 29), after noting the important foundations and universities named after the men we have just discussed, I theorized that "we may yet experience the Meyer Lansky Foundation and Carlo Gambino University."

In 1991, Thomas Gambino, then age sixty-two, a graduate of Manhattan College and president of the Gambino Medical and Science Foundation, donated $2 million to Long Island Jewish–Hillside Medical Center and thousands more to Mount Sinai Medical Center in Manhattan. Thomas Gambino is reputed to be a captain in the crime Family that bears his father's name. In 1992, he and his brother Joseph, then fifty-five, agreed to quit New York City's garment center and pay a fine of $12 million in exchange for not being imprisoned. The brothers had been accused of restraint-of-trade violations.

Source: Ralph Blumenthal, "When the Mob Delivered the Goods." *New York Times Magazine,* July 26, 1992: 22–23, 31–34; Howard Abadinsky, *Organized Crime.* Boston: Allyn and Bacon, 1981.

portant features of the development of America have hinged on violence, both figurative (for example, "financial piracy"), and literal (for example, the use of gunmen, thugs, private police, law-enforcement agents, the National Guard, and the military) to further *private* ends.

Lincoln Steffens, writing in 1902, noted that the "spirit of graft and of lawlessness is the American spirit" (1957: 8). With the western frontier closed, with the wealth of the "robber barons" now institutionalized and their progeny firmly in control of the economy, there has been only modest opportunity for the poor but ambitious adventurers of our urban frontiers. Among these later immigrants—Irish, Jewish, Italian—some have sought to innovate, not on the grand scale of the Vanderbilts, the Goulds, and the Rockefellers, but in a manner more consistent with available opportunity. Many found this opportunity in the politics and vice of urban America beginning in the latter half of the nineteenth century.

HISTORICAL ANTECEDENTS OF ORGANIZED CRIME: URBAN MACHINE POLITICS

Organized crime in America, notes Gus Tyler (1962: 89), "is the product of an evolutionary process extending more than a century." The roots of organized crime can be found in the politics of urban America prior to Prohibition, in the exemplary patron-client network known as the political machine. The underpinnings of this phenomenon are found in immigrant America and the role of the Irish.

Immigration

Immigration into the United States, except for brief depressions, grew dramatically in the years from 1820 to 1850, particularly in urban areas. During those three decades, the population of cities in the East and West quadrupled—New York's population rose to half a million (Bennett 1988). Immigrants and their offspring comprised more than two-thirds of the population of the largest cities in the northeast and more than three-quarters of the population of New York, Boston, and Chicago (Buenker 1973).

These urban immigrants found employment in the most dangerous, monotonous, and poorly paid industries; women and children often labored as well. John Buenker (1973: 3) points out that the new immigrants were forced into slum housing reserved for their own ethnic group. Their culture, customs, and religious beliefs and practices were subjected to virulent attack by Americans of older stock. "Beset by hostility and discrimination on virtually all sides, the immigrant gradually found that he possessed at least one commodity that some native Americans coveted: his vote." A new breed of broker—the political boss—emerged to channel these votes into a powerful entity known as the "machine," and this boss was not necessarily of immigrant stock. In New York, for example, William Magear ("Marcy") Tweed, the quintessential machine politician, was the scion of an American-born Scottish Episcopalian father and a mother whose maiden name was Eliza Magear (Hershkowitz 1978).

The necessities of urban America, notes Richard Hofstadter (1956), the need for construction workers, street cleaners, police and firemen, and service workers of all kinds, provided the immigrant with his livelihood and the political boss with patronage. During the 1880s, for example, New York's Tammany Hall had more than 40,000 municipal jobs at its disposal (Erie 1988). "The immigrant, in short, looked to politics not for the realization of high principles but for concrete and personal gains, and he sought these gains through personal relationships. And the boss, particularly the Irish boss, who could see things from the immigrant's angle but could also manipulate the American environment, became a specialist in personal relations and personal loyalties" (Hofstadter 1956: 182).

The Irish

There are strong historical parallels between the repression suffered by Sicilian peasants and that endured by their Irish counterparts. In both cases, this helped to shape their culture. Ireland fell under foreign domination in the twelfth century, although it was not until the latter half of the sixteenth century and the reign of Elizabeth I (1533–1603) that England tried to impose Protestantism on the largely Catholic Irish. England used the religious dispute to seize large tracts of the most fertile land in Ireland. Thousands of Protestant Lowland Scots (and to a lesser extent, English) were encouraged to settle in northern Ireland, and they soon owned most of the land. In the South, Oliver Cromwell crushed an Irish rebellion and parceled out two-thirds of the land to his soldiers and followers (Shannon 1989). Ireland was reduced to "a country of peasants who were constantly oppressed by excessive rents, taxes, and tithes, and for whom poverty was a general condition" (Levine 1966: 5). Prior to Queen Elizabeth's rule, the people of the island identified themselves as followers of a particular local chieftain; afterward, they became *Irish*.

Paradoxically, this environment of misery gave rise to a culture of hospitality and openhandedness. The Irish looked forward to opportunities for social gatherings; events as sad as death meant gathering for an "Irish wake." As in the *Mezzogiorno* of Italy, a certain attitude developed: let outsiders, the government, and the world be damned (Shannon 1989). Finding no justice in the formal system of government imposed by the British, the Irish turned to informal mechanisms, bargaining and negotiating, for favorable outcomes. The Irish resorted to secret and open organizations on a local and national level as part of their continuous efforts to deal with British oppression. When the franchise was extended to Ireland, the Irish were caught up in the corrupt politics fostered by the British, and they became a thoroughly politicized people (Levine 1966). Two centuries of close personal experience with Anglo-Saxon Protestant government led to a disdain for law and provided the knowledge necessary for an important role in the rough-and-tumble politics of America's urban areas. "The Irish political personality," notes Lawrence McCaffrey (1976: 8), "was shaped by confrontation with British imperialism and colonialism . . . In their efforts to free themselves from anti-Catholic Penal Laws and to achieve national independence, the Irish learned to compete within the context of the Anglo-Saxon political system. They became particularly adroit in the techniques of mass agitation, political organization, confrontation, and liberal, democratic politics."

When the Irish potato crop failed, 1845–47, there was widespread famine. The workhouses, supported by taxes on landowners, were overflowing. The landlords encouraged and sponsored Irish immigration to the United States as a way of easing their tax burden (Wyman 1984). Once in the United States the Irish tended to settle in urban areas. Uneducated and often illiterate—the British had denied them educational opportunity—the Irish immigrants secured employment as unskilled labor (McCaffrey 1976). But, William Shannon points out, "Irish immigrants came to America with a live political tradition" (1989: 15). They "were the world's greatest experts in the art of warfare without confrontation. They could make alliances without formal conferences, agreements, or treaties that would leave a record. They could act in concert without giving commands but with a clear understanding of who was in charge. These were the lessons they had learned while living under repression. It did not take very long to learn how to apply their underground tactics to a democracy" (Reedy 1991: 22).

Between 1840 and 1844 about a quarter of a million persons from mostly Catholic districts in Ireland entered the United States (Bennett 1988). In a single decade, 1845–54, almost 1.5 million Irish immigrants entered the United States, and from 1855 until the turn of the century more than 3 million more arrived. They constituted the first large-scale immigration of non-Anglo-Saxon Protestants to arrive in the United States. And "although generally peasants in their homeland," notes Buenker (1973: 2), "most of the new arrivals lacked either the resources or the desire to resume agrarian life. Arriving at a time when available land was scarce and agriculture mechanized, most sought work as unskilled laborers in the burgeoning industrial metropolises"; only 6 percent would become farmers (Erie 1988). "By 1870, while only about 10 percent of the country's 29 million native-born whites lived in the big cities, 42 percent of the nation's 1.8 million Irish-born lived in the twenty-five cities with populations greater than 50,000" (Erie 1988: 25). By 1850, more than one-third of New York City's population was Irish (Shannon 1989).

In the United States the Irish found themselves restricted from upward mobility, which was reserved for middle-class Protestants. In response, Irish immigrants remained in close-knit neighborhoods, where they joined the Democratic Party as an outlet for social and economic advancement. However, instead of using politics as an avenue to integration into the middle class, politics enveloped the Irish, and the Irish social structure became an integral part of the process of recruiting other Irishmen into both the party and government. As the Irish swarmed into city politics, political office was recognized as *the* career among them, and politics became the secular extension of their essentially religious identity" (Levine 1966: 5).

Like southern Italians, Irish Catholic immigrants distrusted the public education system, which was dominated by Protestants: "most Irish took a dim view of the usefulness of education and left its destiny in the hands of the clergy" (Levine 1966: 87). While Catholic parochial education promoted Irish solidarity, it did not encourage secular intellectual pursuits and higher education. "Before World War I," notes McCaffrey (1976: 82), "few Irish boys and girls went on to secondary schools and before World War II few of them enrolled in college." Politics and government employment provided the most readily available road to social mobility. Irish success in politics coincided with a decrease in the substantial crime rate among Irish immigrants; that is, until Prohibition in 1920 suddenly offered a new fast track to economic—albeit crime-based—success. "The Irish, the most numerous and advanced section of the immigrant community, took over the political party (usually the Democratic Party) at the local level and converted it into virtually a parallel system of government" (Shannon 1989: 62). The clan system welded the Irish into a community capable of acting in concert while disregarding the formal governmental and legal structure (Reedy 1991).

Irish success in politics was also advanced by an ability to speak English, knowledge of Anglo-Saxon government, and the timing of their arrival in the United States. They were also "community-minded, gregarious by nature, fond of visiting and talking" (McCaffrey 1976: 65). The Irish were "neutral outsiders in the traditional ethnic antipathies and hostilities which the Central and East European ethnic groups brought to America from their homelands. 'A Lithuanian won't vote for a Pole, and a Pole won't vote for a Lithuanian,' according to a Chicago politician. 'A German won't vote for either of them—but all three will vote for a 'Turkey,' an Irishman'" (Rakove, 1975: 33). And then there was the Irish connection to the saloon: "For many years the saloon was as important a link in the communications process of the Irish social structure as was the parish church" (Levine 1966: 119). "Irish politicians used Catholic solidarity as a voting base, saloons as political clubs." (McCaffrey 1976: 140).

The Saloon and the Machine

Throughout much of urban America a similar pattern developed. The saloon-keeper, gambling-house operator, and politician were often the same person. The saloon was a center of neighborhood activity, an important social base for political activity. Saloon-keepers became political powers in many cities. Larry Englemann (1979: 4) points out:

In turn-of-the-century New York and Chicago, saloons were a center of neighborhood activity and an integral cog in the urban political machine. Saloon-keepers and politicians were often the same people.

Part of the appeal of the saloon was due to the social services it provided. In saloons files of newspapers in several languages were available along with cigars, mail boxes for regular patrons, free pencils, paper, and mail services to those wishing to send letters, and information on employment. Saloons provided a warm fire in the winter, public toilets, bowling alleys, billiard tables, music, singing, dancing, constant conversation, charity and charge accounts, quiet corners for students, and special rooms for weddings, union meetings, or celebrations. No other institution provided such a variety of necessary services to the public.

City government was fragmented, and power dispersed. The city was divided into wards or districts, which were both electoral and administrative units containing relatively small numbers of people. The police and police (lower) courts operated on the ward/district level (Haller 1990a). These wards/districts were divided into electoral precincts. In this environment saloon-keepers were in a position to influence their customers and their votes—they could deliver their precincts and, thus, control the wards or districts. It was only a slight exaggeration to jest that in New York the easiest way to break up a meeting of Tammany Hall leaders was to open the door and shout: "Your saloon's on fire."

The Constitution does not provide for or even make mention of political parties. Indeed, the Founding Fathers perceived the political party as an unnecessary, if not divisive, element in the democratic process. As a result of this constitutional omission, political parties enjoyed the same degree of autonomy as that of any other voluntary association, despite the reality that a political party often determined the outcome of an election. The procedures used to nominate candidates favored those who controlled the party apparatus. Until the late 1880s, a political party was a private association, and as such determined the method for nominating candidates. The methods used lacked state control; they were informal and often effectively disenfranchised the electorate.

Throughout most of the nineteenth century, each political party provided its own ballots and ballot boxes at the general election. Prior to ballots, there was voice voting in which a voter stated his preference. Parties printed their own ballots, called "tickets," in different colors. Voters chose one and placed it in the ballot box under the careful eye of party workers. This system virtually precluded split party voting and facilitated the buying of votes since party workers could readily see which ballot a voter chose to cast.[2] This system

2. From 1888 to 1890, states began providing the ballots for general elections, placing party labels on these ballots. This made the ballot secret and gave formal recognition to political parties, but only the major political parties. Laws were enacted to restrict third-party access to the new ballot. The treatment of political parties as public entities provided legal justification for government control of the primary elections that followed: "By 1896 all states but one had statutory regulations for nominating candidates for elective office" (Epstein 1986: 166).

enabled ward politicians, often with the help of street corner boys and gangs that proliferated in urban ghettos, to deliver lopsided votes that helped the machine to dominate the city. Politicians frequently employed the gangs for such legitimate purposes as distributing campaign literature, hanging posters, and canvassing for votes. They were also used as "repeaters" who voted early and often and as sluggers who attacked rival campaign workers and intimidated voters. "Elections," notes Michael Johnston (1982: 46), "were held at odd hours in odd places, including bars and brothels. Voters seldom were informed of their franchise, and there was frequent intimidation of voters whose loyalties were suspect." With a small following and a willingness to engage in "political hardball," he argues, machine politicians could easily win power. "Powerful ward chieftains," notes Steven Erie (1988: 26), "were often rewarded with a share of the patronage commensurate with their district's share of the total party vote."

The machine politician was usually a popular figure who, in the days before social welfare programs, provided important services to loyal constituents—jobs, food, and assistance with public agencies, including the police and the courts. All that he asked for in return were votes and a free hand to become wealthy in politics. To the impoverished and powerless ghetto dweller, this was a small price to pay for services that would otherwise not be available. And even when they became available through government agencies during the Great Depression, the loss of self-respect that this entailed was often too high a price for assistance. On the other hand, the precinct captain "asks no questions, exacts no compliance with legal rules of eligibility and does not 'snoop' into private affairs" (Merton 1967: 128). Robert Merton (1967: 128) points out:

> The political machine does not regard the electorate as an amorphous, undifferentiated mass of voters. With keen sociological intuition, the machine recognizes that the voter is a person living in a specific neighborhood, with specific personal problems and personal wants. Public issues are abstract and remote; private problems are extremely concrete and immediate. It is not through the generalized appeal to large public concerns that the machine operates, but through the direct quasi-feudal relationships between local representatives of the machine and voters in their neighborhood.

"There is nothing satanic about the Chicago machine," notes newsman Len O'Connor (1984: 114):

> The basis of its success has always been the machine's dedication to a policy of doing little favors for the people. If a humble householder is getting the runaround from City Hall when he complains about a crew from the Department of Streets and Sanitation smashing up his curbing, a ward committeeman who learns of this will instantly raise hell with "somebody downtown" and get the curb fixed. The widow who is struggling to make ends meet will get a food basket delivered from the ward office.

The very personal nature of the machine is highlighted by one day in the life of George Washington Plunkitt, a Tammany district leader at the turn of the century who died a wealthy man in 1924 at the age of eighty-two (Riordon 1963: 93):

2:00 A.M. Aroused from sleep by ringing on his doorbell; went to the door and found a bartender, who asked him to go to the police station and bail out a saloon keeper who had been arrested for violating the excise law. Furnished bail and returned to bed at three o'clock.

6:00 A.M. Awakened by fire engines passing his house. Hastened to the scene of the fire, according to the custom of the Tammany district leaders, to give assistance to the fire sufferers, if needed. Met several of his election district captains who are always under orders to look out for fires, which are considered great vote-getters. Found several tenants who had been burned out, took them to a hotel, supplied them with clothes, fed them, and arranged temporary quarters for them until they could rent and furnish new quarters.

8:30 A.M. Went to the police court to look after constituents. Found six "drunks." Secured the discharge of four by a timely word with the judge, and paid the fine of two.

9:00 A.M. Appeared in the Municipal Court. Directed one of his district captains to act as counsel for a widow against whom dispossess proceedings had been initiated and obtained an extension of time. Paid the rent of a poor family about to be dispossessed and gave them a dollar for food.

11:00 A.M. At home again. Found four men waiting for him. One had been discharged by the _____ for neglect of duty, and wanted the district leader to fix things. Another wanted a job . . . The third sought a place on the Subway and the fourth . . . was looking for work. The district leader spent nearly three hours fixing things for the four men, and succeeded in each case.

3:00 P.M. Attended the funeral of an Italian. . . . Hurried back to make his appearance at the funeral of a Hebrew constituent . . . and later attended the Hebrew confirmation ceremonies in the synagogue.

7:00 P.M. Went to the district headquarters and presided over a meeting of election district captains. . . .

8:00 P.M. Went to a church fair. . . .

9:00 P.M. At the clubhouse again. . . . Listened to the complaints of a dozen pushcart peddlers who said they were persecuted by the police and assured them he would go to Police Headquarters. . . .

10:30 P.M. Attended a Hebrew wedding. . . . Had previously sent a handsome wedding present to the bride.

12:00 P.M. In bed.

The very personal nature of the machine is also noted by John McConaughy (1931): "In the midst of the current depression, an Irish alderman named

Moriarity distributed unleavened bread [matzah] to hundreds of Jewish families in his district, so that they might keep the feast of Passover. This will not cost him any votes" (1931: 312). Tom Foley was a Tammany district leader in Manhattan at the turn of the century and, note Norman Hapgood and Henry Moskowitz (1927: 41), he understood the business of being a political leader: "His job was to see that politics in his district were run efficiently for the purpose for which primarily politics existed. That purpose was to look after the welfare of individuals who resided in the district":

> Almost any family was likely to want something. Perhaps the father had died and there was not money enough for the funeral. Perhaps one of the boys had been arrested, justly or unjustly. Perhaps a man who had a job on the police force had been dropped or moved to an undesirable location. Perhaps laborers had to be placed in the street cleaning department, or a transfer effected for one of his constituents from one department to another, or an increase in salary negotiated.

And no job was too unpleasant or demanding for machine Alderman Charley Weber of Chicago, as newsman Len O'Connor (1984: 117) reports:

> When he hung up the phone, Charley looked at me with sadness and said, "That woman's lived in the ward for more than twenty years and she's Republican. . . . Now she's got a dead rat in the alley behind her house—and she don't call no Republican to come over and take care of her dead rat; she calls the alderman.
> "So what are you going to do, Charley?"
> "What can I do?" he replied. "I got to go over there, like I said, and pick up her rat and find a good garbage can with a top on it and, well take care of it."
> "With one phone call," I said, "you could get somebody to do this."
> . . . "You crazy?" he said. "It's a good chance, dealin' with the rat. This woman'll be peekin' out the kitchen window and see the alderman drive up in his Cadillac and get out and pick up her dead rat and drive away with it. She'll tell everybody."

And when challenged, the machine could fight back with "hard ball" tenacity:

> Besides voter fraud, emerging machines used repression to weaken their opponents. Irish party bosses were famous for the ingenuity with which they systematically weakened labor and socialist parties. Machine-controlled bureaucrats and judges denied parade and meeting permits. The party's plug-uglies armed with brass knuckles waded into peaceful assemblies. Opposition leaders were frequently arrested on trumped-up charges. For insurgent Jews and Italians, the Irish machines specialized in rigorous enforcement of Sunday closing laws and in punitive denial of business permits. (Erie 1988: 11)

By 1890 most big-city Democratic machines were controlled by Irish bosses.

Underworld and Upperworld

The machine leader was a master at keeping his ward/district organized, a broker par excellence who was in a key position to perform services for both the captains of industry and the captains of vice. The machine leader mediated between unorganized urban masses, underworld, and upperworld. Earlier in this chapter we saw the vital services performed by Boss Tweed for Cornelius Vanderbilt and Jay Gould. Lincoln Steffens (1931) described the interrelationship between big business and the machine that could deliver franchises, access to underdeveloped land sites, government contracts, tax abatements, and other special considerations. In Chicago this was exemplified by the relationship between Samuel Insull (1859–1938), the president of Commonwealth Edison, and both Democratic and Republican political machines: "Both had accepted huge campaign-fund contributions from the utility magnate, in return for which they left him relatively unmolested to pursue his economic ends" (Gosnell 1977: 5). Once entrenched, the Irish machine bosses quickly built alliances with older-stock business interests (Erie 1988).

In fact, notes Harold Gosnell, dishonest, corrupt, and inefficient government in Chicago was actually promoted by business interests: "All factions, Republican and Democratic, were the handmaidens of the business interests" (1977: 8). And Fletcher Dobyns (1932: 8) states: "Populous and efficient as the underworld is, it could not wield the influence it does if it were not for its financial and political alliance with the inhabitants of Chicago's upper world. . . . The deal is that the underworld shall have a 'liberal government' and a 'wide open town' and its upper world allies shall be permitted to plunder the public treasury and appropriate wealth belonging to the people." In most cities, particularly New York, Philadelphia, St. Louis, and Pittsburgh, "the rough and tumble ward and city bosses allowed the private utilities and favor-seeking men of wealth as well as the purveyors of vice to exploit the great mass of citizens" (Douglas 1974: ix; also Steffens 1957). Merton (1967: 135) notes the irony: "[T]he supporters of the political machine include both the 'respectable' business class elements who are, of course, opposed to the criminal or racketeer and the distinctly 'unrespectable' elements of the underworld."

"Just as the political machine performs services for 'legitimate' business," notes Merton, "so it operates to perform not dissimilar services for 'illegitimate' business: vice, crime and rackets" (1967: 132). In fact, the relationship between the racketeer and the machine was symbiotic. Gosnell states that "not only are the contributions from the underworld interests an important item in the campaign funds of the dominant party, but the services of the underworld personnel are also significant. When word is passed down from the gangster chiefs, all proprietors of gambling houses and speak-easies, all burglars, pick-pockets, pimps, fences, and their like, are whipped into line. In themselves they constitute a large block of votes, and they frequently augment their value to the machine by corrupt election practices" (1977: 42).

In Kansas City, John Audett, a professional criminal, received his orders

James Pendergast testifies before the Kefauver Crime Investigating Committee in Kansas City, Missouri, 1950. He was asked, among other things, what his Democratic organization had done to solve vote frauds twelve years after the outrage of the 1934 election.

from gangster chief John Lazia, who was an important part of the Pendergast machine. Audett looked up vacant lots (1954: 120): "I looked them up, precinct by precinct, and turned them lists in to Mr. Pendergast—that's Tom Pendergast, the man who used to run Kansas city back in them days. When we got a precinct all surveyed out, we would give addresses to them vacant lots. Then we would take the addresses and assign them to people we could depend on—prostitutes, thieves, floaters, anybody we could get on the voting registration books. On election days we just hauled these people to the right places and they went in and voted—in the right places." In return for "delivering the vote," the ward boss was rewarded with patronage and recognized as lord of his area in a system that resembled feudalism. He appointed, directly or indirectly, police officials in his area, so he was in a position to protect vice activity (gambling, prostitution, liquor-law violations), which he "licensed."

In Kansas City, James Pendergast began his political career as a saloon-keeper. He became a dominant power in the First Ward, and his ability to deliver the vote enabled him to provide police protection for organized gambling. The police acted on his behalf, forcing independent operators to join the gambling combine or get out of business. Between 1900 and 1902, Pendergast named 123 of the 173 policemen on the Kansas City force. The Pendergast machine, under brother Tom, received support of the gang bosses, and they in return secured police protection (Dorsett 1968). This led to the election day outrage of 1934. Despite an estimated 50,000 to 100,000 fake registrations, the machine was taking no chances (Steinberg 1972: 307):

> In the streets that morning, long black limousines cruised slowly past voters on their ways to the polls and created an atmosphere of fright, for none of the cars had license plates and their passengers looked like gangsters. One of the cars did more than cruise. When it rolled past the opposition's headquarters in downtown Kansas City, seven shots were fired through the big window, though miraculously no one inside the crowded office was hit by a bullet. Another car pulled up at the ninth ward center of the opposition, and its passengers rushed inside to beat several persons with blackjacks.

With repeat voters, the beating of opposition voters, guns and baseball bats at polling places, the Pendergast machine won an overwhelming victory; four persons were killed and dozens beaten.

In Chicago:

> The police department generally, and the [thirty-eight] district stations in particular, were parts of the Democratic political machine. The department was a source of patronage jobs, while alderman and ward committeemen controlled law enforcement in their districts. In effect, each alderman functioned as the mayor of a community, with the district captain acting as his chief of police. Alderman would choose their own captains and controlled promotions, assignments, and transfers of personnel. (Bopp 1977: 91)

In New York:

> In each district of the city, saloon keepers, owners of houses of prostitution, grocers who wanted to obstruct sidewalks, builders who wanted to violate the building regulations of the City, paid tribute at election time to the district leaders, who turned the money over to the general campaign fund of Tammany Hall. The organization collected not only from those who wished to violate the laws, but also from those who wished to live peacefully without having the windows of their shops smashed by the district leader's gang, or without being unnecessarily molested by the police. (Werner 1928: 293–94)

In Chicago, New York, and elsewhere, gambling operators paid heavily for protection with the understanding that an occasional police raid would have to be staged "for appearances." The raiding squads were careful not to damage furniture or equipment, and policemen obligingly guarded the resort while the gambling operators and their customers made a brief perfunctory appearance before a friendly magistrate before returning to the gaming house to resume play (Commission on the Review of the National Policy Toward Gambling

1976). An extraordinary Kings County (Brooklyn) Grand Jury, which sat for four years (1938–42) investigating police corruption in that borough, found bookmaking and policy operations flourishing. Furthermore, the police had "a tendency to make unfounded arrests in order to create a record of apparent efficient law enforcement," and they had a "practice of presenting the evidence in such a manner that a conviction cannot possibly result." An "examination of the plainclothes policemen who were assigned to gambling cases in Kings County during the period covered by this investigation revealed that in all except a few cases the assignment to plainclothes work on gambling violations was accompanied by a distinct change in financial status" (Supreme Court of the State of New York 1942: 5–6). A special grand jury in Philadelphia in 1928 found that certain members of that city's police department received a total of $2 million in bribes annually (Haller 1985b).

The National Commission on Law Observance and Enforcement concluded (1931: 45):

> Nearly all of the large cities suffer from an alliance between politicians and criminals. For example, Los Angeles was controlled by a few gamblers for a number of years. San Francisco suffered similarly some years ago and at one period in its history was so completely dominated by gamblers that three prominent gamblers who were in control of the politics of the city and who quarrelled about the appointment of the police settled their quarrel by shaking dice to determine who would name the chief for the first two years, who for the second two years, and who for the third.

The alliance between business interests and the machine during the latter part of the nineteenth century caused the political bosses to move in the direction of fiscal conservatism, which in turn reduced city revenues and their ability to dispense patronage. Faced with the need to provide important services to maintain constituent loyalty, but constrained by fiscal conservatism, the machine turned to the vice entrepreneurs to help keep the wheels of the machine well-oiled. During the first decades of the twentieth century, new political machines emerged, and they abandoned the fiscal constraints under which their immediate predecessors had operated. Greatly expanded city budgets bloated with borrowed funds provided the machine with an enormous payroll army (Erie 1988), but the relationship with underworld interests continued.

Reform

In cities dominated by machine politics, the same ones that would spawn organized crime, there was a pattern of corruption-reform-corruption-reform, often interspersed with investigations and widely-publicized hearings. It is important to recognize the political motivation, and the not insignificant degree of hypocrisy, behind many of these exposés and reform efforts. In New York, investigations were often initiated by upstate, rural, Protestant Republican interests against downstate (New York City) urban, Catholic and Jewish Democrats.

For example, in 1894 the New York State Senate appointed a special committee, five Republicans and two Democrats, headed by Senator Clarence Lexow of (heavily Republican) Rockland County, to investigate charges of vice and corruption leveled by the Reverend Charles H. Parkhurst. The hearings revealed a sordid tale of corruption. A report released in January of 1895 stated (Fogelson 1977):

1. Instead of maintaining the peace at polling places, the police acted as agents of Tammany seeking to influence elections.
2. Instead of suppressing gambling and prostitution, the police systematically licensed the activities in return for a share of the proceeds.
3. Detectives would seek out stolen property only when the owner offered a reward and agreed to repay the pawnbroker.
4. Police frequently intimidated, harassed, and otherwise oppressed defenseless and law-abiding citizens.

However, the recommendations of the committee, given its findings, were actually quite modest, since they were designed not to correct the problem but to enable Republicans to share in the rich patronage created by the Democratic machine (Fogelson 1977).

The Republicans were able to dominate the state legislature in New York and many other northern states by gerrymandering[3] districts in a most outrageous manner, a practice eventually declared unconstitutional by the U.S. Supreme Court in the landmark "one-man-one-vote" decision (*Baker v. Carr* 369 U.S. 186, 1962). In New York, for example, one voter in rural Putnam County had as much representation as seven in some districts of New York City (Cashman 1981). The threat of investigation and public disclosure was often used to secure the support of city politicians for legislation favored by rural or big business interests. Corruption was real and often rampant, but many of the efforts purporting to deal with it were just as corrupt morally, if not legally.

This is exemplified by legislation, passed as a result of the efforts of New York Governor Charles Evans Hughes, which banned betting on horses and bookmaking. In 1909, the law was vigorously enforced during the metropolitan racing season; that is, when horses ran in the New York City area. In Saratoga, a Republican stronghold just north of Albany, gambling continued unabated; the racetrack was big business and an important tourist attraction (Katcher 1959). In fact, gambling continued to be an important business in Saratoga

---

3. During the second term of Governor Elbridge Gerry of Massachusetts (1744–1814), the Democratic-Republicans created senatorial districts that greatly disadvantaged the Federalists. One district in northeast Massachusetts had the appearance of a salamander (an amphibious lizard), hence the origins of the term "gerrymandering." Gerry, a signer of the Declaration of Independence, went on to serve as vice president under James Madison.

where Arnold Rothstein, Meyer Lansky, and Lucky Luciano had an interest in gambling casinos that were protected by the Republican machine (Lacey 1991). Historically, in industrial states of the North, the urban masses had to place their bets illegally with a bookmaker, while their more affluent brethren enjoyed the "sport of kings" in the sunshine of the great outdoors at the racetrack, where they could bet legally. Illegal casino gambling continued unabated in Saratoga even while the racket-busting Republican Thomas E. Dewey (1902–1971) was governor. The state police found six casinos operating in 1947 but would not intercede without a special order from the governor, an order that was never issued (Kefauver 1951).

Even so-called political reformers sometimes showed a considerable amount of hypocrisy. New York's reform mayor Fiorello H. La Guardia (1882–1947) moved against gangster Frank Costello, a Democratic stalwart, but did not bother racketeers in East Harlem where his Republican protégé, Congressman Vito Marcantonio, held sway. In Brooklyn Joe Adonis (born Giuseppe Doto), a *caporegime* in the Luciano Family, was equally untouchable until 1937, when he switched his support to La Guardia's opponent. The "Little Flower" had the police drive him out of New York, and Adonis stayed in New Jersey until 1945, the year La Guardia's term ended (Repetto 1978). Enoch J. ("Knucky") Johnson, the racketeer overlord who "owned Atlantic County and Atlantic City, [New Jersey] lock stock, and barrel" (Irey 1948: 245), was a Republican stalwart. As such, he avoided prosecution until Democrat Franklin D. Roosevelt became president, at which time Johnson was convicted and imprisoned for income tax evasion. Treasury agents counted the number of towels sent to the laundry from local brothels. They were thus able to determine the number of customers and hence Johnson's estimated income (Irey 1948). The tax weapon was used freely against Roosevelt's political enemies, such as Tom Pendergast of Kansas City, James Mitchell Curley of Boston, and Huey Long of Louisiana. Friendlier politicians of the same stripe, such as Frank Hague of Jersey City, Ed Crump of Memphis, and Edward J. Kelly of Chicago, escaped criminal sanctions.

Reform was typically fostered by business leaders for their own ends. The machine leaders, notes Loth (1938: 280), had to be paid to defeat legislation opposed by business interests: "municipal ownership, labor legislation, adequate health regulations, better schools, new parks, decent housing, aid to the needy. . . . Business men in politics were eager without bribes to oppose anything that raised taxes or threatened private enterprise. They wanted to stop paying graft, but keep all the favors graft bought. They demonstrated that the perennial demand for business methods in government was as logical as a cry that penitentiaries ought to be run by criminals." In Chicago, notes Gosnell (1977: 8), dishonest, corrupt, and inefficient government was actually promoted by business interests: "All factions, Republican and Democratic, were the handmaidens of the business interests."

"Reform" was frequently a favorable label applied by the newspapers to the efforts of two, sometimes overlapping, interest groups: businessmen and white,

Anglo-Saxon, Protestants whose voting strength was in rural America. "Most immigrant voters," notes Buenker (1973: 26), realized instinctively that honesty, efficiency, and economy in government would do nothing to alleviate their condition and could severely cripple the system's ability to dispense favors."

Nativism

"Reformers" were often part of the rampant nativism that at times intertwined with Social Darwinism, a dogma that stressed "survival of the fittest" and, thereby, justified not assisting persons of "inferior stock," in this case recent immigrants. Nativism helped tie urban dwellers—immigrants in general, Catholics (and often Jews) in particular—to the political machine. Attitudes of extreme religious prejudice have a long history in our country, dating back to the first colonists. While settlers came to the New World in search of religious freedom, they sought only *their* religious freedom. In the seventeenth century, mass could not be publicly celebrated anywhere in Colonial America except in Pennsylvania. Virulent anti-Catholicism was an important part of colonial America. Certain Protestant school primers vilified Roman Catholicism, and many Roman Catholic children were encouraged to dislike Protestants. It was only the Revolutionary War and the rebel colonists' alliance with Catholic France that generated a new attitude of Roman Catholic–Protestant tolerance. But anti-Catholicism reappeared, and in 1834 a mob of Protestant workmen in Charlestown, Massachusetts, ransacked and burned a convent, the first fruit of Catholic educational enterprise in New England (Bennett 1988).

Samuel Morse (1791–1872), distinguished painter, inventor of the telegraph, and son of a prominent minister, wrote that "we are the dupes of our hospitality. The evil of immigration brings to these shores illiterate Roman Catholics, the tools of reckless and unprincipled politicians, the obedient instruments of their more knowing priestly leaders" (quoted in Bennett 1988: 40). Francis Walker (1840–97), a prominent economist, statistician, and president of the Massachusetts Institute of Technology, referred to the American immigration and naturalization process as "the survival of the unfit" (McCaffrey 1976: 104–105). In 1886, the Reverend Josiah Strong quoted Herbert Spencer, a British philosopher and Social Darwinist, decrying the increasing immigration that "not only furnishes the great portion of our criminals," but permits domination of our cities by the Catholic church. "The Roman Catholic vote," the reverend stated, "is more or less perfectly controlled by the priests" (McCaffrey 1976: 14).

Early in this century, the president of the National Association of Manufacturers referred to "an unrestricted invasion of our national household by foreign hordes, many of whom have brought and kept inferior moral and political conceptions, ideals, and habits" (Grant and Davison 1930: 5). From the Carnegie Institution came a condemnation of the American policy of admitting "cheaper" stocks: "We must expect the ever-broadening appreciation of the value of hereditary quality to support henceforth the policy of limited and selected immigration" (1930: 53). The president of the American Museum of Natural History, Henry Fairfield Osborn, warned "native" Americans "of the threat to American institutions by the influx of alien elements of population with alien ideas and ideals in the principles of self-government" (1930: 204). These sentiments aided in passing the 1920 Immigration Act designed to halt the influx from Southern and Eastern Europe in general, and Jews and Italians in particular.

In an attack on machine politics, Osborn pointed to "what is going on in our large cities in which the original American element has entirely lost control and the alien or foreign-born element is in absolute power" (Grant and Davidson 1930: 208). In 1928, Bishop James A. Cannon of the Methodist Episcopal church verbally attacked Governor Alfred A. Smith, a product of Tammany Hall and the Democratic candidate for president. Bishop Cannon told his audience: "Governor Smith wants the Italians, the Sicilians, the Poles and the Russian Jews. That kind has given us a stomach ache. We have been unable to assimilate such people in our national life, so we shut the door to them. But Smith [an Irish Catholic] says, 'give me that kind of people.' He wants the kind of dirty people that you find today on the sidewalks of New York" (Cashman 1981: 197). In contrast, the machine politician "cultivated the immigrant's ethnic pride by defending him against nativist attack, observing his customs, and concerning himself with conditions in the homeland" (Buenker 1973: 5). The most successful campaign waged by nativist interests involved prohibiting the beverages most favored by immigrants—whiskey, wine, and beer.

HISTORICAL ANTECEDENTS OF ORGANIZED CRIME: PROHIBITION

The acrimony between rural and urban America, between Protestants and Catholics, between Republicans and (non-Southern) Democrats, between "native" Americans and more recent immigrants, and between business and labor, reached a pinnacle with the ratification of the Eighteenth Amendment in 1919. Efforts at limiting or prohibiting alcohol consumption, however, date back to the earliest days of our Republic. Residents of the United States have traditionally consumed large quantities of such beverages. In 1810, for example, the per capita intake was almost five gallons (Asbury 1950). In 1785, Dr. Benjamin Rush, surgeon general of the Continental Army and signer of the Declaration of Independence, wrote a pamphlet decrying the use of alcohol. The pamphlet helped to fuel the move toward prohibition and inspired the establishment of the first temperance society in 1808, the Union Temperance Society. The Society was superseded by the American Temperance Union in 1836, and the work of the Union was supported by Protestant churches throughout the country.

The temperance movement made great progress everywhere in the country, often accompanying the nativist sentiments that swept over the United States during the late 1840s and early 1850s. In 1843, nativist feelings led to the formation of the American Republican Party in New York, which spread nationally as the Native American Party. By 1850, the party was known as the Order of the Star Spangled Banner, and also the "Know-Nothings." (Many clubs were secret, and popular belief was that when outsiders inquired about the group, they were met with the response: "I know nothing.") Allied with a faction of the Whig Party, the Know-Nothings almost captured New York in 1854, and succeeded in Delaware and Massachusetts. They also won important victories in Pennsylvania, Rhode Island, New Hampshire, Connecticut, Maryland, Kentucky, and California. In 1855, the city of Chicago elected a Know-Nothing mayor—Dr. Levi D. Boone, grandnephew of the frontiersman Daniel Boone. In addition, prohibition legislation was enacted in the Illinois legislature but was defeated in a public referendum that same year (Asbury 1942; Lindberg 1991; Anbinder 1992). Temperance and nativism arose again strongly during the 1880s and led to the formation of the American Protective Association, a rural-based organization that was strongly anti-Catholic and anti-Semitic. (For an excellent history of nativism in the United States, see Bennett 1988.)

In 1869, the Prohibition Party attempted, with only limited success, to make alcohol a national issue. In 1874 the Women's Christian Temperance Union was established, and in 1893 the Anti-Saloon League was organized. Around the turn of the century, both of these groups moved from efforts to change individual behavior to a campaign for national prohibition. After a period of dormancy, the prohibition movement was revived in the years 1907–1919 (Humphries and Greenberg 1981). By 1910, the Anti-Saloon League had become one of the most effective political action groups in American history. It had mobilized America's Protestant churches behind a single purpose: the enactment of national prohibition (Tindall 1988). In 1915 nativism and prohibitionism fueled the rebirth of the Ku Klux Klan, which spread into northern states and exerted a great deal of political influence, including control of state politics in Indiana (see Tucker 1991). During the First World War, anti-German feelings were strong, and made more intense because brewing and distilling were associated with German immigrants (Cashman 1981).

According to William Chambliss (1973: 10), Prohibition was accomplished by the political efforts of an economically declining segment of the American middle class: "By effort and some good luck this class was able to impose its will on the majority of the population through rather dramatic changes in the law." Andrew Sinclair (1962: 163) points out that "in fact, national prohibition was a measure passed by village America against urban America." Prohibition also resulted from the struggle of Protestant America against Catholic (and, to a lesser extent, Jewish) America: "Thousands of Protestant churches held thanksgiving prayer meetings. To many of the people who attended, prohibition represented the triumph of America's towns and rural districts over the sinful cities" (Coffey 1975: 7; Gusfield 1963). "Prohibition not only reflected revulsion at drunkenness and contempt for the drinking immigrant masses, not only the power of the Women's Christian Temperance Union and its role in the emerging women's movement, but also an assault on the pleasures and amenities of city life" (Bennett 1988: 204).

Big business was also interested in Prohibition; alcohol contributed to industrial inefficiency, labor strife, and the saloon that served the interests of machine politics:

> Around 1908, just as the Anti-Saloon League was preparing for a broad state-by-state drive toward national prohibition, a number of businessmen contributed the funds essential for an effective campaign. The series of quick successes that followed coincided with an equally impressive number of wealthy converts, so that as the movement entered its final stage after 1913, it employed not only ample financing but a sudden urban respectability as well. Substantial citizens now spoke about a new discipline with the disappearance of the saloon and the rampaging drunk. Significantly, prominent Southerners with one eye to the Negro and another to the poorer whites were using exactly the same arguments. (Wiebe 1967: 290–91)

Workmen's compensation laws also helped to stimulate business support for temperance. Between 1911 and 1920, forty-one states had enacted workmen's compensation laws. Sean Cashman (1981: 6) points out: "By making employers compensate workers for industrial accidents the law obligated them to campaign for safety through sobriety. In 1914 the National Safety Council adopted a resolution condemning alcohol as a cause of industrial accidents."

The Eighteenth Amendment to the Constitution was ratified by the thirty-sixth state, Nebraska, on January 16, 1919. Subsequently it was ratified by an additional ten states. According to its own terms, the amendment became effective on January 16, 1920:

> *Section 1.* After one year from the ratification of this article the manufacture, sale, or transportation of intoxicating liquors within, the importation thereof into, or the exportation thereof from the United States and all territory subject to the jurisdiction thereof for beverage purposes is hereby prohibited.

> *Section 2.* The Congress and the several States shall have concurrent power to enforce this article by appropriate legislation.

Ten months after ratification, over a veto by President Woodrow Wilson, Congress passed the National Prohibition Act, usually referred to as the Volstead Act after its sponsor, Congressman Andrew Volstead of Minnesota. The Volstead Act strengthened the language of the amendment and defined as intoxicating all beverages containing more than 0.5 percent alcohol. It also provided for federal enforcement: the Prohibition Bureau, an arm of the Treasury Department, was created. The bureau soon became notorious for employing agents on the basis of political patronage. According to Loth (1938:

346), this patronage provision helped to pass the act, and almost 18,000 federal jobs were exempted from civil service restrictions: "The clause had been passed by dry votes in Congress. The lobbyists who cracked the whip over the legislators later explained that Congress had insisted upon the exemption in return for passage of the Volstead Act." The treasury agent who brought down Al Capone commented that the "most extraordinary collection of political hacks, hangers-on, and passing highwaymen got appointed as prohibition agents" (Irey with Slocum 1948: 5).

In addition to being inept and corrupt, Prohibition Bureau agents were a public menace: they ran up a record of being killed (by 1923 thirty had been murdered) and for killing hundreds of civilians, often innocent women and children. By 1930, the figure rose to eighty-six federal agents and two hundred civilians killed. Prohibition agents set up illegal roadblocks and searched cars; drivers who protested were in danger of being shot. Agents who killed innocent civilians were rarely brought to justice—when they were indicted by local grand juries, the cases were simply transferred and the agents escaped punishment (Woodiwiss 1988).

The bureau was viewed as a training school for bootleggers because agents frequently left the service to join their wealthy adversaries. The Treasury

In general, law enforcement during Prohibition was a haphazard affair; few speakeasies met fates like this one. "The Great Experiment" sparked more sophisticated and violent forms of organized crime.

Department was headed by the banking magnate Andrew Mellon (1855–1937), a man who had millions invested in the liquor trade before Prohibition and was not interested in enforcing the new law (Sinclair 1962). Neither were most local police agencies, and very little money was allocated to enforce the most sweeping criminal law ever enacted in the United States (Asbury 1950). Ten days after the Eighteenth Amendment went into effect, three Prohibition agents were indicted in Chicago for bribery and selling seized liquor to bootleggers. And it got worse. Prohibition agents escorted liquor trucks and helped smugglers to unload cargoes: "On salaries averaging less than three thousand dollars a year, prohibition agents bought country homes, town houses, city and suburban real estate, speedboats, expensive automobiles, furs, and jewelry for their women, and fine horses; many reported to work in chauffer-driven cars" (Asbury 1950: 176). According to Elmer Irey, one agent had been a worker on a garbage truck before being appointed: "he worked three months as an agent and then took a six-month leave so that he and his wife could tour Europe" (Irey with Slocum 1948: 6).

Herbert Packer (1968: 263) reminds us that people do not necessarily respond to new criminal prohibitions by acquiescence. He points out that resistance can be fatal to the new norm, and moreover, when this happens "the effect is not confined to the immediate proscription but makes itself felt in the attitude that people take toward legal prescriptions in general." Thus, primary resistance or opposition to a new law such as Prohibition can result, secondarily, in disregard for laws in general: *negative contagion*. During Prohibition, notes Sinclair (1962: 292), a "general tolerance of the bootlegger and a disrespect for federal law were translated into a widespread contempt for the process and duties of democracy." This was exemplified by the general lawlessness that reigned in Chicago:

> Banks all over Chicago were robbed in broad daylight by bandits who scorned to wear masks. Desk sergeants at police stations grew weary of recording holdups—from one hundred to two hundred were reported every night. Burglars marked out sections of the city as their own and embarked upon a course of systematic plundering, going from house to house night after night without hindrance. . . . Payroll robberies were a weekly occurrence and necessitated the introduction of armored cars and armed guards for the delivery of money from banks to business houses. Automobiles were stolen by the thousands. Motorists were forced to the curbs on busy streets and boldly robbed. Women who displayed jewelry in night clubs or at the theater were followed and held up. Wealthy women seldom left their homes unless accompanied by armed escorts. (Asbury 1942: 339).

The murder rate rose every year until Prohibition was repealed, going from 6.8 per 100,000 persons in 1920 to 9.7 in 1933 (Chapman 1991).

In the ninety days preceding the date when the Eighteenth Amendment became effective, $500,000 of bonded whiskey was stolen from government warehouses; afterward it continued to disappear (Sinclair 1962). Thomas Coffey

(1975) reports that less than one hour after Prohibition went into effect, six armed men robbed $100,000-worth of whiskey from two Chicago boxcars. He notes that in February of 1920, a case of whiskey purchased in Montreal for ten dollars could easily be sold in New York for eighty dollars. In fact, Canadians began making so much money from American Prohibition that provinces with similar laws soon repealed them (Sinclair 1962). Almost immediately, notes Herbert Asbury (1950), stores sprang up selling hops, yeast, malt, corn meal, grains, copper tubing, crocks, kettles, jugs, bottle tops, and other equipment for home distilling and brewing. Within one week of the onset of Prohibition, portable stills were on sale throughout the country.

Organized Crime

While America had organized crime before Prohibition, it "was intimately associated with shabby local politics and corrupt police forces"; there was not organized-crime activity "in the syndicate style" (King 1969: 23). The "Great Experiment" provided a catalyst of opportunity that caused organized crime, especially violent forms, to blossom into an important force in American society. Prohibition acted as a catalyst for the mobilization of criminal elements in an unprecedented manner. Pre-Prohibition crime, insofar as it was organized, centered around corrupt political machines, vice entrepreneurs, and, at the bottom, gangs. Prohibition unleashed an unparalleled level of competitive violence and served to reverse the power order between the criminal gangs and the politicians. It also led to an unparalleled level of organization.

The liquor business, licit or illicit, demands large-scale organization. Raw material must be purchased and shipped to manufacturing sites. This requires trucks, drivers, mechanics, warehouses, and laborers. Manufacturing efficiency and profit are maximized by economies of scale. This requires large environments where the whiskey, beer, or wine can be manufactured, bottled, and placed in cartons for storage and distribution to wholesale outlets or saloons/speakeasies. If the substances are to be smuggled, ships, boats, and their crews are required, as well as trucks, drivers, mechanics, warehouses, and laborers. And there is the obvious need to physically protect shipments through the employment of armed guards. "As illegal entrepreneurs," notes Mark Haller (1985a: 142), bootleggers "also had to learn to use legal institutions to service their illegal enterprises": "they had to learn banking to handle their money, insurance to protect their ships, and the methods of incorporation to gain control of chemical and cosmetics companies from which they diverted industrial alcohol. They also dealt with varied legitimate companies to purchase trucks, boats, copper tubing, corn sugar, bottles, and labels." Haller (1974) found that businessmen who had previously been involved in the legal liquor industry did not remain in business during Prohibition; this left the field open to opportunistic amateurs, often violent young men who had heretofore been left behind in the race for economic success. Bootlegging, notes Haller, "was a relatively open field of endeavor and allowed ambitious young Italians

CHANGES IN THE SOCIAL ORDER

Pre-Prohibition
Machine Politicians
Vice Entrepreneurs
Gangs

Prohibition
Gangs
Machine Politicians
Vice Entrepreneurs

Note: There was often no explicit delineation between politicians and vice entrepreneurs. In Chicago, for example, Billy Skidmore was a saloon-keeper/gambler and Democratic leader of the Thirteenth Ward. Until his

1939 conviction for income tax evasion, Skidmore remained one of the city's most important gambling operators as well as a major political power.

Sources: John Landesco, *Organized Crime in Chicago.* Chicago: University of Chicago Press [originally published in 1929]; Mark H. Haller, "Illegal Enterprise: A Theoretical and Historical Interpretation." *Criminology*, vol. 28, May 1990: 207–35.

and Jews (as well as some Poles and Irishmen) to catapult to quick success" (1974: 5).

Furthermore, Prohibition encouraged cooperation between gang leaders from various regions—syndication. Legal or illegal, the liquor business was international in scope. Smuggled rum and whiskey from Canada, the Caribbean, or Europe had to be moved across the Great Lakes or from the Atlantic onto beaches along the East Coast. Shipments then had to be trucked intra- and interstate to warehouses at distribution points. At each juncture the shipment required political and physical protection. Only the criminal organization dominant in the local area could provide such protection. Syndication arose out of these needs, and a number of meetings between important organized figures have been documented (Nelli 1976: 212): "Meetings were held for a number of reasons—to settle disputes, choose successors for slain or deposed leaders, divide local or regional markets, or discuss production, supply, and distribution problems. Some gatherings consisted of Italian criminals and limited their discussions to problems of interest to them. Others involved only Jews or Irish or some other ethnic group; still others were formed of members of a variety [of] ethnic syndicates."

With the onset of the Great Depression (1929) and the subsequent repeal of Prohibition (1933), the financial base of organized crime narrowed considerably. Many "players" dropped out. Some went into legitimate enterprises or employment; others drifted into conventional criminality. Bootlegging, as noted above, required trucks, drivers, mechanics, garages, warehouses, bookkeepers, and lawyers—skills and assets that could be converted to noncriminal endeavors. For those who remained in the "business," reorganization was necessary. Haller points out (1974: 5–6):

When Prohibition ended in 1933, bootleggers were still young men—generally in their thirties—yet with wealth and nationwide contacts that had grown out of their bootlegging enterprises. In addition to their liquor interests, they already had substantial investments in restaurants, night clubs, gambling, and other profitable businesses. In the 1930s and 1940s, then, they used their national contacts, diverse interests, and available capital to cooperate in a variety of entrepreneurial activities, legal and illegal.

Some entrepreneurial bootleggers simply continued in the newly legitimate liquor trade. Sam Bronfman moved the Seagrams main office from Canada to New York and paid $1.5 million in taxes that the United States said he owed on Prohibition-era shipments. His bootlegging confederate, Lewis Rosenstiel, continued to operate Schenley Distillers Company. The Reinfeld syndicate—Joe Reinfeld and Longie Zwillman—became Renfield Importers, Ltd. Joseph P. Kennedy, father of a future president, moved from bootlegging to head Somerset Importers (Fox 1989).

Just prior to the end of Prohibition, gang leaders began meeting throughout the United States in anticipation of the new era. On April 19, 1932, the Chicago Police Department detained a number of gangsters, including Paul Ricca of the Capone syndicate, Lucky Luciano, and Meyer Lansky, for questioning. In 1934, reports Burton Turkus (Turkus and Feder 1951: 99), the major leaders of OC in the East gathered at a New York hotel with Johnny Torrio presiding, and they came to an understanding:

> Each boss remained czar in his own territory, his rackets unmolested, his local authority uncontested. In murder, no one—local or imported—could be killed in his territory without his approval. He would have the right to do the job himself or permit an outsider to come in—but only at his invitation. In fact, no lawlessness on an organized scale could take place in his domain without his sanction and entire consent, unless he was overruled by the board of governors. . . .
>
> Each mob leader now had behind him not just his own hoods, but a powerful amalgamation of all hoods. Every gang chieftain was guaranteed against being interfered with in his own area—and against being killed by a rival mobster.

Furthermore, Turkus states (1951: 99):

> The Brooklyn stoolpigeons told us a second meeting was called in Kansas City to hear from the Western executives. The Capone crowd from Chicago and the Kansas City mob liked the idea. Reports came from Cleveland and Detroit that the Mayfield Gang and the Purple Mob wanted in. Boston and Miami, New Orleans and Baltimore, St. Paul and St. Louis—all flocked to the confederacy of crime, until it was nationwide.

Hank Messick (1967: 32) adds that "the country was divided into territories. Wars ended between regional groups, between religious groups, between national groups." There are several significant indications of this cooperation: the founding of modern Las Vegas (discussed in chapter 6); labor racketeering on a national level (discussed in chapter 8); establishment and joint ownership of illegal casinos such as the Colonial Inn in Hallendale, Florida, by Irish, Jewish, and Italian criminals from New York, Detroit, and Chicago (Haller 1990a); and a group of Jewish and Italian criminals known as *Murder, Inc.*

The Pinnacle of Organizing Crime: Murder, Inc.

The setting is the East New York–Brownsville section of Brooklyn, a Jewish ghetto, and the adjoining neighborhood of Ocean Hill, an Italian ghetto. The story begins in the spring of 1930, when Abe ("Kid Twist") Reles, Martin ("Buggy") Goldstein, and Philip ("Pittsburgh Phil") Strauss decided to make some "easy" money by going into the pinball-machine business—renting the machines to candy stores and poolrooms. It was a good idea, but hardly original. In fact, the pinball business and organized criminal activities in that part of Brooklyn were controlled by the notorious Shapiro brothers, Irving, Meyer, and Willie. To deal with the anticipated problem, the boys from East New York–Brownsville teamed up with a crew of Italian criminals from the Ocean Hill section of the borough led by the Maione brothers, Harry ("Happy") and "Duke," and Frank ("The Dasher") Abbandando. Together they began to make inroads into the business controlled by the Shapiros, and with profits from the pinball machines they entered the loansharking business. The Shapiro brothers responded.

On June 11, 1930, a member of the Reles group was killed, and Reles and Goldstein were wounded. Meyer Shapiro then abducted Reles' girlfriend, whom he beat and raped. The Reles group struck back—during 1930 and 1931 eighteen attempts were made on the life of Meyer Shapiro; the nineteenth was successful. Brother Irving's demise followed, and Willie was abducted, severely beaten, and buried alive. The Reles group took over gambling, loansharking, and prostitution in the East New York–Brownsville section, and they soon became involved in labor racketeering; their specialty, however, became murder.

The "Boys from Brooklyn" were used as staff killers by the newly formed confederation of organized crime leaders that emerged in New York and went nationwide. In addition to their various criminal enterprises, the "Boys" received a retainer to be "on call" whenever the occasion arose—and it arose often. In a ten-year period they murdered more than eighty persons in Brooklyn alone. They were so efficient that gang leaders from across the country made use of their services.

There were full-dress rehearsals; getaway routes were carefully checked. A "crash car" followed the stolen vehicle containing the actual killers in the event of a police pursuit. Guns were rendered untraceable, although ropes and ice-picks were often the preferred weapons. One of the group's members describes the "contract system" (Berger 1940: 5): The killer ("trooper") is directed to take a plane, car, or train to a certain place to meet "a man." The man points out ("fingers") the victim for the trooper, who kills him when it is convenient. He then leaves town immediately, and when local hoodlums are questioned, their alibis are perfect. For the "Boys from Brooklyn," murder was an art form. Pittsburgh Phil, for example, delighted in roping a victim like a little ball so that any movement pulled the line tighter and he eventually strangled himself (Turkus and Feder 1951).

Jenna Joselit (1983: 153) stresses the level of intergroup cooperation, noting that the Jewish and Italian members of the group "worked side by side on a daily basis, physically molesting tardy borrowers and stubborn union leaders." Moreover, the gang took its orders from Albert Anastasia, even though Reles was considered the leader of the "Boys from Brooklyn." Louis Capone was Anastasia's personal representative and served as a buffer between the Reles and Maione parts of Murder, Inc.

In 1940 several of the "Boys from Brooklyn" were indicted for the 1933 murder of Alec ("Red") Alpert. The nineteen-year-old had been "convicted" of talking to the authorities. Quite to the surprise of Burton Turkus, chief of the Homicide Bureau of the Brooklyn District Attorney's Office, one of the group's members agreed to become a government witness; he was reputedly the toughest of the "Boys." Abe Reles, upon being granted immunity from prosecution, began to disclose the sensational details of Murder, Inc. His information and subsequent testimony led to the conviction and electrocution of seven men, including Louis Capone. Before any case could be made against Albert Anastasia (discussed in chapter 3), Reles had an accident. On November 12, 1941, while under constant police guard, he fell out of the sixth floor window of a Coney Island hotel. His death remains officially unexplained.

In the next two chapters we will examine the details of the history of organized crime in New York, Chicago, and Philadelphia.

REVIEW QUESTIONS

1. How does Robert Merton's theory of anomie explain organized crime?
2. How is differential association (Edwin Sutherland) relevant to explaining entry into organized crime?
3. How does cultural transmission (Shaw and McKay) explain the continuity of organized crime in certain neighborhoods?
4. What are the qualities of the delinquent subculture that correlate well with the prerequisites of organized crime?
5. What is meant by the "defended neighborhood"?
6. In what ways are the Irish similar to southern Italians?
7. What explains the success of the Irish in American machine politics?
8. What was the relationship between the political machine and organized crime?
9. What was the relationship between the saloon and machine politics?
10. What was the relationship between the political machine and big business?
11. Why did business interests often support reform politics?

12. How did nativist sentiments influence immigrant support for the political machine?
13. What were the conflicts between urban and rural America that helped to fuel the prohibition movement?
14. What was the relationship between Prohibition and the development of organized crime?
15. How did Prohibition change the relationship between politicians and gang leaders?
16. How did Prohibition lead to criminal syndication?
17. How did the onset of the Great Depression affect organized crime?
18. How does Murder, Inc., provide an example of intergroup cooperation in organized crime?

3

The History of Organized Crime: Part One

The task of presenting an accurate history of organized crime in the United States is insurmountable. This is not for lack of material, which is abundant. But quantity cannot replace quality, and the latter is the problem. Alan Block (1978) notes that when it comes to organized crime, there is a reliance on unsubstantiated accounts of informers or the ideological preconceptions of law enforcement agencies. John Galliher and James Cain (1974: 69) point out the lack of scholarly material relating to organized crime, noting that the dominant literature is either journalistic, tending toward sensationalism, or else consists of government documents. "There are two troublesome aspects to this reliance on such sources, one empirical, the other political. In arriving at conclusions and statements of fact, the journalist or political investigator is not bound by the canons of scientific investigation as is the social scientist." They note the journalist's need to quickly produce exciting copy even at the expense of "careful accumulation and sifting of information characteristic of scientific investigation."[1]

The executive editor of the *New York Times*, Max Frankel, is troubled by information from law enforcement sources who request anonymity. He says, "[we are] getting stuff out of law enforcement agencies who are letting that information out for reasons of their own or because of carelessness but are not prepared to take responsibility for it" (Rosenthal 1988: 9). Even the President's Commission on Organized Crime, at a briefing for reporters, insisted that information be attributed to an unnamed official ("Washington Talk" 1986).

---

1. This is highlighted by two reports in the *Chicago Tribune*. The first, on November 3, 1948, declared Thomas E. Dewey the victor over Harry S. Truman; the second, on April 23, 1989, declared that Vito Marzullo, a former Chicago alderman and a legend of Chicago's political machine, had died. The ninety-one-year old Vito read the report and was only slightly amused.

MEDIA GONE AWRY

According to eastern newspapers during the 1870s, Palisades, Nevada, was the toughest town west of Chicago. Passengers travelling west on the Central Pacific Railroad, upon alighting in Palisades, found street brawls, gunfights, bank robberies, and shootouts between Native Americans and soldiers. The press demanded that something be done. However, Palisades never even elected a sheriff—it didn't need one. The brawls, robberies, and shootouts were staged: local Indians and army troops were in on the joke—the eastern press was not (Wallace and Wallechinsky 1983). In 1990 newspapers and television stations in New York reported on a $35 million lottery winner without confirming the information. It was a hoax deliberately engineered by a man who had done it before (Jones 1990).

Christopher Byron (1992a, 1992b) reported how the media—*Time*, ABC, NBC—carried stories on alleged U.S. government complicity in the bombing of Pan Am Flight 103 over Lockerbie, Scotland in 1988, an incident that claimed the lives of 259 passengers. According to the story, which made the cover page of *Time*, U.S. intelligence agents helped smuggle the bomb aboard. In fact, reports Byron, the story was bogus, promoted by lawyers for Pan Am and the airline's insurance company.

In 1981 it was revealed that a reporter for the *Washington Post* had fabricated a story about an eight-year-old heroin addict she called "Jimmy." The story won the reporter a Pulitzer Prize (which was revoked after the fabrication was disclosed). In 1968 newspaper headlines reported that a strike on Chicago's Belt Line Railroad had resulted in 10,000 employees being laid off at the 324 industrial plants served by the line. The information, which

ECOLOGICALLY CORRECT FRAUD

"The earth is our mother," said the television narrator, quoting an 1854 speech by Chief Seattle, after whom the state of Washington named its largest city. "I have seen a thousand rotting buffalos on the prairie, left by the white men who shot them from a passing train." These and other ecological homilies of Chief Seattle have been widely quoted and appear in a best-selling children's book, *Brother Eagle, Sister Sky: A Message From Chief Seattle*.

While they may be ecologically correct, they were not spoken by Chief Seattle, who lived in the Pacific Northwest and never saw a buffalo. The quotes, in fact, were written by a screenwriter.

Source: Malcolm Jones and Ray Sawhill, "Just Too Good to be True." *Newsweek*, May 4, 1992: 68.

came from the Chicago Association of Commerce, was a lie. A simple telephone check by the *Wall Street Journal* revealed that fewer than one hundred employees had been laid off as a result of the strike (Rottenberg 1983). In 1991, it was revealed that *The Education of Little Tree*, a best-selling book—No. 1 on the *New York Times* paperback nonfiction list—purporting to be based on the childhood of a Native American raised in the Tennessee mountains, was a fraud, actually written by an ex-Ku Klux Klan member (Lee 1991).

THE MEDIA AND ORGANIZED CRIME

In one week in 1977, major news stories appeared in the *New York Times* (Franks 1977) and *New York* (Meskil 1977) revealing that Carmine ("Lilo") Galente, who they reported headed the Bonanno Family, and who was born in New York in 1910, was emerging as the new *capo di tutti capi*, "boss of bosses." In 1962, Galente, then Bonanno Family underboss, was imprisoned in a drug case that also netted Vito Genovese. Galente had been out of prison only a few months. Paul Meskil, an investigative reporter, stated that law-enforcement officials thought Galente's immediate goal was to bring all five New York crime Families under his direct control. According to these officials, he would succeed: "Soon, federal agents predict, Carmine Galente's peers on the Mafia Commission will elect him boss of all bosses" (1977: 28). Lucinda Franks, a reporter for the *New York Times*, stated: "Officials say that Mr. Galente is moving to merge the five New York crime families under his own leadership and aims to become a national chieftain who would try to restore the Mafia to a position of power it has not held in at least 20 years" (1977: 34).

Writing in 1991, Joseph Coffey and Jerry Schmetterer report that Galente was not the boss of the Bonanno Family—instead, they maintain, the imprisoned Phil Rastelli was the boss. Galente was resented by other Family bosses for his extensive drug trafficking enterprises. Instead of distancing himself from the trade, Galente directed his men to expand drug operations.

Jerry Capeci (1978: 28), writing in *New York*, reported the *real* "godfather" to be Frank ("Funzi") Tieri, a seventy-four-year-old Brooklyn mob leader. He stated that Carmine Galente was being proclaimed boss of all bosses as "the result of a well-planned 'leak' by the Drug Enforcement Administration of a 'confidential' report by its Unified Intelligence Division." Capeci added: "It now turns out that the report was based on quite old information and was leaked in self-interest by the drug agency." On July 12, 1979, Galente was dining in the backyard of Joe and Mary's Restaurant in the Bushwick section of Brooklyn, a Bonanno Family stronghold. As he pushed away his empty plate and placed a cigar in his mouth, "four Bonanno button men, including the father-and-son hit team of 'Sonny Red' and Bruno Indelicato, swung open the small wooden door leading from the restaurant and entered the backyard. Without warning they opened fire with shotguns and automatic pistols" (Coffey

ORGANIZED CRIME 101

Federal prosecutors hoped that the former Colombo associate would prove to be a credible witness in a racketeering case. But the imprisoned would-be informant needed information—*about the inner workings of organized crime.* He asked a fellow prisoner, an OC informant, for help. In response, that inmate wrote a six-page manual describing crime Family structure, operational strategies, mediation of disputes, etc. The document was full of such phrases as "hierarchy form of government," and "inborn Machiavellian guilefulness."

Source: New York *Daily News* editorial, January 18, 1993: 24

and Schmetterer 1991: 32). The would-be *capo di tutti capi* was dead. Joe and Mary's Restaurant has closed as the once Italian and German neighborhood has changed. While the neighborhood continues to be a stronghold for criminal organizations, they are primarily Puerto Rican and Dominican drug trafficking groups.

Anthony Villano (1978), an FBI agent for twenty years who specialized in organized crime, states that the bureau regularly leaked false reports to the press in order to stir up dissension among organized crime figures. This subterfuge was made possible by the use of the journalistic convention known as "sources." Sources, under the protective cloak of anonymity, notes David Shaw (1984: 57), "are permitted to use the press for personal and political purposes—to grind axes, advance ambitions, attack rivals and mislead the public." In 1988 it was revealed that the DEA had arranged for staged seizures to generate false news reports and, thus, protect the identity of undercover operatives. "The undercover operatives sometimes pose as middlemen and ship loads of narcotics into the United States for major South American traffickers. The agency on occasion then arranges for the local law-enforcement authorities to seize the incoming drug shipments in an attempt to insulate the operatives from disclosure" ("U.S. Looking Into Undercover Drug Manipulation" 1988: 9).

Jonathan Rubinstein and Peter Reuter (1978a: 57) state that "the difficulty the government had in obtaining accurate information on the reserves of energy-producing companies in the wake of the 1973 oil boycott should serve as a sober reminder of how difficult it is to collect accurate information even from legitimate organizations operating in a highly regulated environment. The challenges are immeasurably greater in collecting information about people who are consciously involved in illegal activities."

103

Rubinstein and Reuter report on a United States Department of Justice effort to determine the amount of illegal gambling revenues. In the past, the Justice Department frequently asserted that organized crime derives its major income from gambling. After noting the totally unscientific basis for the estimate, the authors conclude that (1978a: 62): "In truth, we suspect that the real failing of the estimate was that no one really cared precisely how it was developed, but only that it produce a large number. The assumption that the details of the calculation would not be subjected to any scrutiny led to a cavalier use of the available data. Also, the estimate had no possible consequences; it was produced for rhetorical purposes and has served these purposes well."

In 1974, a book by Martin Gosch and Richard Hammer purported to be *The Last Testament of Lucky Luciano* dictated by Luciano himself during the final months of his life. The book's introduction explains that in 1961 Luciano made a decision to provide the details of his life as a crime boss to Martin Gosch. According to the introduction, the syndicate, acting on orders from Meyer Lansky, vetoed a movie that Gosch was producing titled *The Lucky Luciano Story*. Luciano, who was living in exile in Italy at the time, was to be technical advisor, and now he was angry. However, according to Gosch, who died of a heart attack before publication, Luciano extracted a promise that his autobiography not be published earlier than ten years after his death; he died in 1962. The book earned more than $1 million before it was even published, and paperback rights were auctioned for an additional $800,000 (Gage 1974).

On December 17, 1974, in a front-page article, Nicholas Gage of the *New York Times* questioned the authenticity of the book by pointing to numerous errors of fact: "It is widely known that Mr. Gosch met on a number of occasions with Mr. Luciano on the aborted film project, and presumably the gangster recounted some of his experiences during these meetings. But contradictions and inaccuracies in the book raise questions to the claim that Mr. Luciano told his whole life to Mr. Gosch and that everything in the book attributed to Mr. Luciano actually came from him." For example, the book was incorrect on how and when Luciano gained the nickname "Lucky," and contained an alleged firsthand account about one event that actually occurred two years after Luciano died.

In 1981, Grossett and Dunlop published *Mafia Kingpin*, the autobiography of Sonny Gibson. Sonny claimed to have been an enforcer for the Chicago Outfit, but this was the least of his claims: he was sent to Sicily to be trained by the Mafia; executed twenty-four persons; ran 150 different corporations; threw nine prison guards over the wall. He appeared on national television, the *Today* and *Tomorrow* shows, where he was taken seriously. Perhaps his interviewers were hoping for a private discussion of his wildest claim: sex with 10,000 different women.

In 1986, a book by James Mills claimed to present the entirely factual story of *The Underground Empire: Where Crime and Governments Meet,* an expose of global drug trafficking networks. In almost twelve-hundred pages (paperback edition), the reader is treated to the fascinating details of the operations of CENTAC, the Drug Enforcement Administration's Central Tactical Units. Its director reveals: "We write an operational plan, select our staff, marshal our forces, and attack. From that moment on, the target is doomed" (1986: 15). In fact, of the three cases tracked in the book, only one, a marijuana ring headed by Donald Steinberg, resulted in U.S. convictions, although the Mexican government managed to convict the second major trafficker, Alberto Sicilia-Falcon. A great deal of the book is devoted to the activities of Michael Decker, a self-described former U.S. Navy (SEAL) commando with extensive combat experience in Vietnam, and an assassin for Sicilia-Falcon. However, an investigation by the *Los Angeles Times* (Johnston 1986) revealed that Decker never served with the SEALS, and many of his other statements were found to be pure fantasy—that he was an assassin; participated in a shootout in Mexico that left twenty-one persons, some of them law enforcement officers, dead; that he drove a car equipped with fully automatic shotguns concealed beneath the headlights that could fire 140 rounds in forty seconds.

The situation has been further complicated by the rash of "true crime" portrayals and the publicity-seeking activities of those peddling their stories: "The thirst for reality-based entertainment has created an entertainment-based reality—book and movie projects about celebrated cases now become issues in those cases, as defense lawyers point to Hollywood money as a motive for cops to twist investigations or for witnesses to lie on the stand." Eric Pooley (1992: 45) points out, "just about every wiseguy entering the federal witness-protection program thinks about selling his memoirs."

The problem inherent in presenting an accurate history of organized crime is highlighted by a 1931 incident. On September 10, 1931, Salvatore Maranzano, the self-appointed American Mafia boss of bosses, was killed by gunmen dispatched by Meyer Lansky and Bugsy Siegel at the request of Lucky Luciano—a historic event in interethnic criminal cooperation. Donald Cressey (1969: 44) reports: "On that day and the two days immediately following, some forty Italian-Sicilian gang leaders across the country lost their lives in battle." Fred Cook (1972: 107–108) refers to this episode as the "Purge of the Greasers" and states: "Within a few short hours, the old-time crime bosses who had been born and reared in Sicily and were mostly illiterate—the 'Mustache Petes' or 'the greasers,' as they were sometimes called—were liquidated by the new breed of Americanized, business-oriented gangsters of the Luciano-Costello-Adonis school." Cook adds: "Beginning on September 11th and lasting through the next day, some thirty to forty executions were performed across the nation." A special publication of *New York* (Plate 1972) adds to the story: "During the bloodbath nearly 40 of the Old Guard were executed in various *ingenious ways*" (emphasis added). In 1978 this episode was reported as *historical fact*—"The 'Night of the Sicilian Vespers,' so named because Luciano had not only engineered the slaughter of Salvatore Maranzano for the night of September 10, 1931, but had gone ahead and wiped out 40 of the 'Mustache Petes' across the country." This last quote is from Jerry Capeci (1978: 26), the journalist for *New York* who could not be "duped" by the Drug Enforcement Administration in the Galente incident discussed earlier.

In fact there was no nationwide purge of "Mustache Petes"; only three murders, all occurring in New York and reported by that city's newspapers, could be traced to the Maranzano execution. "A careful examination of newspapers issued during September, October, and November of 1931 in twelve large cities... turned up evidence of only one killing that occurred at about the time Maranzano died and might have been [but apparently wasn't] linked to the death of the 'Boss of Bosses'" (Nelli 1976: 183). Thus, concludes Humbert Nelli, the "purge" applied only to New York and the message was clear: "any oldtimers still permitted to live had better accept and adjust to the new order" (1976: 182). Nevertheless, the story continues to be presented in popular books on organized crime. In *Mafia Dynasty*, John Davis (1993: 42) tells us of the Luciano-ordered purge: "By the time it was over, sixty [sic] Maranzano loyalists had been killed." (Davis is also confused about the source of Luciano's nickname and other details.)

The remainder of this chapter and chapter 4 contain a history of organized crime in New York, Chicago, and Philadelphia, cities where the most extensive information is available. What is presented represents the best available literature on the topic. When the literature conflicts, the divergence of opinion will be noted. Otherwise, the material will be presented as "history," although we have already seen the weakness inherent in much that passes for the history of organized crime. *Caveat emptor.*

In order to understand the development of organized crime in New York, we need to examine a most unique political organization—the Society of Saint Tammany, usually referred to as Tammany Hall.

TAMMANY HALL

In 1790, a group of white men decked out in feathers and bucks' tails sat cross-legged in wigwams pitched along the Hudson River. They were there at the request of President George Washington "to smoke the peace pipe" with a delegation of Creek Indians. The Creeks had been harassing American settlements in Georgia and Florida, and the "white Indians" were members of the Society of Saint Tammany, named for a legendary Delaware Indian chief. For several days the Creek delegation was treated to banquets, concerts, theater, and the wonders of Tammany's New York. The result was a peace treaty transmitted to President Washington. Tammany, which began as a fraternal and patriotic society in 1789, with chapters in a number of states, quickly emerged as a full-fledged political organization in New York. The guiding genius behind the scene in Tammany's rise to power was Aaron Burr (Peterson 1983a), who in 1800 became vice-president of the United States. In 1836, Tammany leader Martin Van Buren was elected the eighth president of the United States (Connable and Silberfarb 1967). Tammany eventually became synonymous with the Democratic Party of New York City.

In post-Revolutionary War New York, only landowners could vote, an obvious handicap to an organization striving for broad-based support. Tammany responded with "collective property"—the title to a house might list the names of a number of persons and they became enfranchised as freeholders. Tammany established a system of district leaders and precinct captains in each assembly district, and by 1838 had a reputation for dispensing favors and social services from funds extorted from vice entrepreneurs and a 6 percent kickback from all city employees. The tie-in between criminals and politicians was now firmly established.

During the latter half of the 1840s and early 1850s, large numbers of immigrants fled famine and British repression in Ireland for New York. Despite nativist and anti-Catholic sentiment in the Tammany society, the Irish quickly rose to leadership positions, and by the turn of the century clearly dominated "The Hall." The Irish immigrant spoke English and was quite at home in a saloon; his willingness to engage in fisticuffs made him a "natural" for the rough-and-tumble politics of that period. And there was also an Irish genius for politics. "It is in close, warm, personal contact with local life that the Irish had excelled. That the Irish in New York have been almost altogether Democrats has been one element in making the character of the Democratic party in that city" (Hapgood and Moskowitz 1927: 43). The Irishman, because of his stature and ability to speak English, also dominated the city's police force, which was in effect an adjunct of Tammany Hall.

The Tammany Police

In 1844, the New York State legislature authorized the creation of a police force for New York City patterned after the London Metropolitan Police of Sir Robert Peel (from which they get the nickname "Bobbies"). Whereas the London model centralized the police command, in New York the police in each of the city's wards were under the domination of the alderman, who could hire and fire police officers. "Even after aldermanic appointment was formally discontinued, local politicians continued to exercise de facto control" (Repetto 1978: 41). Positions on the police force were sought after. The salary, compared to that of skilled laborers, was good, qualifications were almost nonexistent, discipline was lax, and opportunities for graft extensive (however, hours tended to be long: nine hours on patrol and seven hours on reserve).

Antagonism between the Irish Catholics and Germans of New York City, who dominated Tammany Hall, and the rural-oriented, Protestant-controlled legislature led to an 1857 statute creating a metropolitan police department encompassing Manhattan, Brooklyn, Staten Island, and Westchester County, under a board of commissioners appointed by the governor. The Tammany mayor, Fernando Wood, resisted, threatening to fire any fireman or police officer who accepted state jurisdiction—only 300 of 1,100 did. In June of 1857, a city official secured a warrant for Mayor Wood for obstructing the appointment of a street commissioner, and a former city police captain working for the

107

metropolitan police attempted to enforce the warrant. The mayor refused to submit to arrest and the captain was ejected from city hall.

With the aid of fifty "metros," the captain attempted to gain entry to city hall, but they were met by more than one hundred city policemen who drove them out. A National Guard unit participating in a nearby parade was enlisted in the struggle and the mayor finally submitted to arrest. For several weeks afterward, however, both police departments patrolled the streets of New York. The metros soon ran into conflict with the street gangs who were typically aligned with Tammany. In response, the metros selected six powerful officers, placed them in plain clothes, and authorized them to "slug on sight" every gang member they encountered (Repetto 1978).

In July 1863, the Irish population of New York rioted in protest against a draft law that permitted those with the necessary funds to buy their way out of military service. Burning, looting, and lynching of blacks ensued. The half-Irish metro police force, which numbered 2,400 members, mostly strong supporters of the Union cause, was a special target of the rioters. The police, however, with some help from the military, maintained control of the city with a loss of three officers. In 1870, the now Democrat-controlled legislature returned control over policing to the city and the metropolitan district was dissolved. While the new police board was in theory bipartisan, the two Republican commissioners, like their Democratic counterparts, were usually responsive to Tammany ward leaders (Repetto 1978).

The police not only tended to be corrupt, but also were brutal toward the poor and the helpless, as the story of Alexander ("Clubber") Williams high-lights. This vicious and corrupt officer, who rose to the high rank of inspector, told his recruits: "Boys, there's more justice in the end of this nightstick than there is in all of the courts of the land" (Logan 1970: 106). The police received very little public support and were often subjected to abuse by Tammany-linked street gangs. An arrest frequently required the officer to physically subdue the suspect: "A tradition of police brutality developed out of this disrespect. Officers sought to gain with their billy clubs the deference to their authority that was not freely given" (Walker 1980: 63). The police manhandled and brutalized prostitutes, miscreants, and members of the underclass in general. In return, they were abused by the Tammany politicians. Police brutality, notes Samuel Walker, was a "delegated form of vigilantism" tolerated by the "respectable" middle-class citizenry who perceived a need to control the "dangerous classes." "Many a morning," noted reporter Lincoln Steffens at the turn of the century (1957: 207), "when I had nothing else to do, I stood and saw the police bring in and kick out their bandaged, bloody prisoners, not only strikers and foreigners, but thieves too, and others of the miserable, friendless, troublesome poor."

Tammany Hall protected the wealthy of uptown from the radical elements of downtown. In 1872 the Tammany police proved reliable in putting down a strike of some 70,000 workers (out of a city population of 1 million) who were demanding that employers comply with an 1870 state law requiring an eight-hour day. Police officers worked overtime without extra compensation to suppress the strikers. In 1874 club-swinging police officers broke up a peaceful demonstration called by organized labor in Tompkins Square. Steven Erie (1988) notes that organized labor posed a threat not only to industrialists, but also to the machine.

"Cops who chose not to take graft," notes Thomas Repetto (1978: 75), "had to immerse themselves in areas of policing where they did not need to deal with vice—quiet precincts or special units such as the homicide squad— and to ignore any corruption they saw. To be a squealer in a predominantly Irish police force was a fate worse than death." Andy Logan (1970) points out that during the years prior to the First World War, the New York City Police Department was more or less a branch of Tammany; indeed, to secure a job as a policeman a fee of $250 to Tammany was required, and promotions were handled in a similar manner. For $15,000, "Clubber" Williams effected a transfer to the midtown Manhattan area where lucrative graft was available from gambling establishments and brothels. Williams informed an inquiring newspaper reporter: "I've had nothin' but chuck steak for a long time, and now I'm going to get a little bit of the Tenderloin" (Connable and Silberfarb 1967: 215), as this section of Manhattan was known. When he was called to testify before a legislative committee investigating corruption in New York City (Lexow Committee), Williams acknowledged that he had more money and property than could have been accounted for by his salary. And how did he manage this? Land speculation, he responded, *in Japan* (Steffens 1957). Williams was eventually dismissed from the force by New York City Police Commissioner Theodore Roosevelt, a Republican appointed during a reform administration.

The Tammany Gangs

From the mid-1800s until the First World War, old-style gangs were an important feature of the Tammany-criminal tie-in. By the 1920s, when they were disappearing, the *New York Times* could wax nostalgic about the "old breed" of gang with its twisted sense of valor, as compared to the current (1923) variety that operated with "the calculation and efficiency of an industrial tool for breaking strikes or wrecking factories" ("New Gang Methods Replace Those of Eastman's Days" 1923: 3). The *Times* article referred to the demise of the Shirt Tails, Dead Rabbits, Plug Uglies, Bowery Boys, Hudson Dusters, Cherry Hill Gang, Gophers, Five Points, and Whyos. The last gang used printed price lists for mayhem commissions; for example, punching, $2; leg or arm broken, $19; murder, $100 and up (Asbury 1928).

On election days, Tammany used these gangs as "repeaters" and "sluggers," a situation that led the notorious, apelike Lower East Side gang leader Monk Eastman (born Edward Osterman in 1873) to utter: "Say, I cut some ice in this town. Why, I make half the big politicians" ("New Gang Methods Replace Those of Eastman's Days" 1923). Logan notes that gangs such as the Whyos were so useful on election day that the politicians made natural alliances with them (1970: 56): "To keep gang members in funds between elections, the politicians found jobs for them in the off-season months." They worked as lookouts, steerers, and bouncers—resident thugs for the gambling houses and brothels under the patronage of Tammany.

One of the more infamous of the Tammany gangs was the Five Points, with an estimated 1,200 members, led by Paul Kelly, an ex-pugilist born Paolo Vaccarelli. It was not unusual for prize fighters or criminals to assume Irish names. Before he left for Chicago, Al Capone was a member of the Five Points gang (Kobler 1971), as was Lucky Luciano. The Five Points refers to a neighborhood on the city's Lower East Side, in what today is Chinatown. Kelly eventually left the mayhem of lower Manhattan for Harlem, where he founded the Harlem Branch of the Paul Kelly Association. He became a labor organizer and, with the help of some of his Five Pointers, a vice president of the International Longshoremen's Association (a union discussed in chapter 8). One of the highlights of New York gang history is the feud between Kelly and his Italian Five Points gang and the Jewish gang led by Monk Eastman over a small piece of Lower Manhattan real estate that each claimed as its "turf." When their political patrons insisted that they cease the bloodshed, Kelly and Eastman fought it out in a fracas that lasted two hours and ended in a draw when both combatants collapsed from exhaustion.

Eastman fell into disfavor with his Tammany patrons and was imprisoned for a 1904 robbery attempt. After his release in 1909, he was unable to reestablish himself as a gang leader. Enlisting under an alias, Eastman served with distinction in the First World War, during which his gang faded. Eastman received a full pardon from Tammany Governor Alfred E. Smith for his outstanding military service. He was shot to death by an old crony after a petty quarrel that followed a Christmas Eve drinking bout. The friend, a federal Prohibition agent, escaped with a three- to ten-year sentence by claiming self-defense—he thought the unarmed Monk was reaching for a gun (Lee 1963). Peterson (1983a) states that Monk was killed for encroaching on the territory of a bootlegger.

Gambling and house prostitution in Manhattan was "licensed" by Tammany state senator Timothy Sullivan with the support of Police Chief William Devery. When Devery's post was abolished by the state legislature, Sullivan notified city Democratic leader "Boss" Richard Croker of Tammany Hall that unless Devery was reappointed to head the police, "ten thousand gamblers in the Sullivan-Devery syndicate would make no further campaign contributions to Tammany" (Connable and Silberfarb 1967: 224). Devery was reappointed to head the police department. When a Tammany alderman, Paddy Divver, opposed brothels in his heavily Irish district, Sullivan organized a primary election fight against him. With Tom Foley as his candidate, Sullivan sent in the Kelly and Eastman gangs to beat and intimidate Divver supporters while the Tammany police remained passive. Foley won by a margin of three-to-one (Connable and Silberfarb 1967).

In addition to Eastman and Kelly, Sullivan used Charles Becker, a New York City police lieutenant in charge of Special (vice) Squad No. 1, to "muscle" uncooperative gamblers. Sullivan eventually became insane, was committed, escaped, and died on some railroad tracks in Westchester County, New York, in 1912.[2] In 1911, while Sullivan was ill, Lieutenant Becker moved to take over his operations. This move was thwarted on July 5, 1912, the day Herman ("Beansy") Rosenthal was murdered. Rosenthal, a well-known gambler, was an associate of Sullivan. When his gambling establishment was raided by the ambitious Becker, Rosenthal went to the newspapers and implicated Becker as his gambling partner; he claimed the raid was a double-cross. This brazen violation of the "code of silence" resulted in the inevitable—Rosenthal's murder. The four gunmen, Harry ("Gyp the Blood") Horowitz, Louis ("Lefty Louie") Rosenberg, Jacob ("Whitey Lewis") Seidenshner, and Frank ("Dago Frank") Cirofici, represented the ethnic makeup of New York's underworld. The four were convicted and electrocuted. Becker was convicted of ordering the murder—although Logan (1970) argues that he was framed—and became the only American policeman ever put to death by the state.

Charles Murphy, a former saloon-keeper, became Tammany boss in 1902, replacing Richard Croker. He remained in that position until his death twenty-two years later, amassing a personal fortune of $2 million (Van Devander 1944). Murphy changed Tammany operations: open gambling and prostitution were ended and total immunity for gangsters was withdrawn. He also moved to cut down the power of the police who, like Charles Becker, had occasionally challenged Tammany (Katcher 1959). Murphy "concluded that the use of the police as major graft collectors was an antiquated concept" (Logan 1970: 340). Modern organization was needed—a conduit between the politicians and the gamblers, who would be organized into a dues-paying trade association as were the brothel owners. That conduit was Arnold Rothstein—organized crime was beginning to evolve.

From the mid-nineteenth century through World War I, gang activity and political activity were well coordinated. In Manhattan, organized criminal activities were presided over by a three-man board: a representative of Tammany, a police member, and Frank Farrell, the bookmaking czar who represented gambling interests (Logan 1970). Leo Katcher (1959) points out that at this time gangsters were merely errand boys for the politicians and the gamblers; they were at the bottom of a highly stratified social milieu. The gamblers were under the politicians, who were "kings." This would all change with the onset of Prohibition.

Prohibition changed the relationship among the politicians, vice entrepreneurs, and gang leaders. Before 1920 the Tammany ward boss acted as a patron for the vice entrepreneurs and gangs. He protected them from law enforcement, and they assisted him with financial and electoral support. The Irish ward boss was at the top of an unofficial structure that included Jewish and

---

2. Sullivan is best remembered in New York as the author of a state ("Sullivan") law prohibiting the carrying of concealed firearms without a permit. This law was enacted to enable Tammany to better control the behavior of its street-gang allies.

Italian vice operators and gang leaders. The onset of Prohibition, however, unleashed an unsurpassed level of criminal violence, and violence is the specialty of the gangs. Physical protection from rival organizations and armed robbers was suddenly more important than protection from law enforcement. Logan (1970) notes that Prohibition turned gangs into empires. The *New York Times* ("Schultz Product of Dry Era" 1933: 23) noted the transition made by Arthur Flegenheimer, better known as "Dutch Schultz." In 1919 he was a street thug sentenced to imprisonment for unlawful entry; by 1923 he was "a wealthy man with widespread interests." Schultz had become the "beer baron" of the Bronx, owner of speakeasies, a bail-bond business, and an architectural firm.

JEWISH ORGANIZED CRIME IN NEW YORK

At the turn of the century, the Irish still comprised the dominant force in the dominant political organization, Tammany Hall. But in organizing gamblers and brothels, Jews began to gain a niche. They not only helped rationalize illicit activities but provided a conduit between local crime personnel and Tammany. Among Jewish organized criminal operatives, Arnold Rothstein was the most important organizer and innovator.

Arnold Rothstein

The specter of Arnold Rothstein looms so large over organized crime in New York that it would not be much of an exaggeration to call him its "Godfather." Jenna Joselit (1983: 143–44) states:

> Rothstein transformed criminal activity from a haphazard, often spontaneous endeavor into one whose hallmarks—specialized expertise, administrative hierarchy, and organizational procedure—correspond to the classic sociological model of a bureaucracy. Thus, Rothstein's illegal business had a definite administrative structure based on specific skills; competence and not ethnic pedigree determined one's rank and, of course, one's position in his outfit.
>
> Rothstein's office . . . in the middle of the midtown business district, employed a staff comparable to that of any large (and legitimate) commercial firm, replete with secretaries, bookkeepers, and legal counsel. . . . A decision to enter some new illegal venture tended to be based not on personal motives of revenge or power but on strictly commercial considerations: the amount of profit to be made and the length of time it would take to make it. Finally, by investing the money he earned through illegal channels into legal enterprises such as real estate and the theater, Rothstein made it difficult to ascertain where the illegal enterprise left off and the legitimate ones began.

When this writer was researching Rothstein in the *New York Times*, his name was usually found in the business and sports sections of that newspaper.

Arnold Rothstein, shortly before his death in 1928. His specter looms so large over the New York OC scene that it would not be much of an exaggeration to call him its "Godfather."

"A.R.," or "The Brain," as Damon Runyon called him, was born in New York in 1882 and served as the inspiration for Meyer Wolfsheim in F. Scott Fitzgerald's *The Great Gatsby* and for Sky Masterson in *Guys and Dolls*. His father, an Orthodox Jew born of immigrant parents, was a respected and successful businessman. Arnold was also respected and quite successful, but his business was comprised of gambling, bootlegging, drug smuggling, and labor racketeering (Katcher 1959).

As a young man, Rothstein worked in poolrooms and became a "shark," an expert billiard player. Poolrooms were places where lottery or "pool" tickets were sold. The drawings were held in the evenings, and the owners installed billiard tables to help customers pass the time while waiting for lottery results (Katcher 1959). The money he earned was used to finance usurious loans, and Monk Eastman was employed as a collector. Rothstein would later employ Waxey Gordon (born Irving Wexler), the Diamond (Nolan) brothers, "Legs" and Eddie, and other important criminals of the day. Rothstein began running dice games and became a bookmaker and the owner of a gambling house. He was associated with Tim Sullivan, which afforded him political-police protection. He later became a "bookmaker's bookmaker," handling "layoff" bets from other bookmakers. Rothstein contracted a crew of thugs for unions, using a gang led by Jacob ("Little Augie") Orgen, who employed, among other prominent hoodlums, Louis ("Lepke") Buchalter and Jacob ("Gurrah") Shapiro. Eventually, Rothstein went into the bail-bond business, insurance, and real estate (Katcher 1959).

Rothstein's power was enormous. In 1919, he was overseeing one of his floating dice games when a police raid was announced. Incredulous that the police would raid one of *his* games, and fearing a ruse by robbers, Rothstein opened fire, wounding several policemen. The actual evidence against Rothstein was not very strong, but the case was pursued by Inspector Dominick Henry, an honest police officer working for anti-Tammany Mayor John F. Hylan. The grand jury reviewed the evidence and handed down an indictment—of Inspector Henry for perjury. Needless to say, (even honest) policemen became rather reluctant to tangle with "A.R." (Katcher 1959), and he was never convicted of a crime. He is probably best remembered for his alleged involvement in the "Black Sox Scandal," the fixing of the 1919 World Series.

Rothstein also fenced stolen bonds and securities, and when Prohibition arrived he organized the importation of liquor from England and Canada. At the same time, diamonds and drugs, which took up very little space, were smuggled in on his whiskey ships, and he established an international drug-smuggling network. His buyers overseas shipped the drugs into the United States, where they were distributed to criminal organizations in several states: to Johnny Torrio and Al Capone in Chicago; Harry Stromberg ("Nig Rosen") in Philadelphia; Charles ("King") Solomon in Boston; and Lucky Luciano in New York. "This was not the integrated empire of a czar or a J. P. Morgan. . . . Rothstein put Meyer Lansky in one doorway, Charlie Luciano in another. . . . Each of Rothstein's deals was separate, flexible, and detached. His protégés and partners might operate individually or together. It was a question of what worked. Fueled by the riches of Prohibition in the 1920s, Arnold Rothstein set new and historic standards in the development of organized crime in America" (Lacey 1991: 50).

Rothstein played the role of broker, not only between Tammany and the gamblers, but between two of New York's political-crime factions. One faction was headed by James J. Hines,[3] a Tammany renegade with ties to Owney ("Killer") Madden, his partner Bill Dwyer, Dutch Schultz, Vannie Higgens, and Larry Fay—important non-Italian gangsters. The other faction was headed by Tammany stalwart Albert C. Marinelli, a port warden, district leader, and (later) county clerk, with ties to mainly Italian gangsters: Joe ("The Boss") Masseria, Lucky Luciano, Frankie Yale, Frank Costello, and Albert Anastasia (Katcher 1959). Alfred Connable and Edward Silberfarb (1967) report that

---

3. On February 25, 1939, James J. Hines was convicted for his activities on behalf of the Dutch Schultz organization. He was paroled from Sing Sing Prison in 1944 and died in 1957 at the age of eighty (Peterson 1983a).

MAGISTRATE VITALE OF TAMMANY HALL

In 1929 Bronx magistrate Albert H. Vitale was sitting down to a political dinner in his honor at a Democratic clubhouse when masked gunmen burst into the room and staged a holdup. Among the notables seated at the festive board were half a dozen or so hoodlums, the most notorious of them being Ciro Terranova, who was known by the engaging sobriquet, King of the Artichoke Racket.

Why the holdup took place still remains a mystery, but a few hours later Vitale arranged to have the stolen items returned, including the service revolver of a detective who had been one of the diners!

Source: Arthur Mann, *La Guardia Comes to Power: 1933*. Philadelphia: Lippincott, 1965: 45.

---

during Prohibition, nearly half of the Tammany clubs were controlled by gangsters. Rothstein was tied to both factions and did favors for both—pistol permits, bail bonds, fencing stolen merchandise, and financing illegal operations. In 1929 it was publicly revealed that Rothstein had loaned nearly $20,000 to a Bronx magistrate, Albert H. Vitale, who had helped Tammany get out the Italian vote (Mann 1965).

On Sunday night, November 4, 1928, Arnold Rothstein was found staggering in the service entrance of the Park Central Hotel, where he resided. He had been shot once in the abdomen with a small-caliber gun. At age forty-six, Rothstein died after refusing to name the person who shot him, and the murder was never solved. It has been attributed to Rothstein's refusal to pay a gambling debt in excess of $300,000—he maintained that the card game was rigged ("Gamblers Hunted in Rothstein Attack" 1928). After his death, federal officials opened many of his safes and files. Papers found in his apartment linked Rothstein to what United States Attorney Charles H. Tuttle called "the largest drug ring in the United States" ("Unger Indicted in Drug Conspiracy" 1928: 1; see also "$4,000,000 in Narcotics Seized Here, Traced to Rothstein Ring" 1928). Tuttle, in 1930, became the Republican candidate for governor of New York. He lost to Franklin Delano Roosevelt primarily over the issue of Prohibition (Sinclair 1962). Rothstein left a public estate appraised at $1,757,572; his hidden assets, of course, are not known (S. Smith 1963).

Dutch Schultz

At the beginning of Prohibition, Schultz worked for Otto Gass, who moved from trucking into the beer business in response to the new opportunities. In

1928 Schultz went into partnership with Joe Noe, and they became owners of a Bronx speakeasy. The partners soon bought trucks and garages and became major beer distributors, aided by a vicious crew of gunmen including Legs Diamond, the Weinberg brothers—Bo and George—and the Irish-born Coll brothers—Vincent ("Mad Dog") and Peter. Next they began to expand into the territory of rival beer businesses. Joe Rock was one unfortunate rival. The Schultz gang kidnapped him, beat him severely, hung him by his thumbs, and eventually blinded him—a message that was not lost on other recalcitrant beer distributors.

While Prohibition was in full swing, important gangsters did not pay attention to the numbers (illegal lottery), often referring to it as "nigger pool" since many of its followers were black and Hispanic. With Prohibition on the way out, however, Schultz began searching for new areas of profit. His attorney, Dixie Davis, also represented some numbers operators, and engineered Schultz's takeover of the business in Harlem from independent black, Hispanic, and some white numbers bankers. Schultz was able to offer political and physical protection as well as financing—several operators had had a run of costly bad luck. Eventually, the operators were reduced to being employees of the Schultz organization (Sann 1971). By 1932, political protection and fire-power enabled Schultz to centralize policy operations in Harlem (Schatzberg 1993). Schultz also moved into labor racketeering, and on January 31, 1934, the *New York Times* reported on an alliance between officials of the restaurant workers union and the Schultz organization ("Gang Linked to Union Charged at Trial" 1934).

In 1931, the Coll brothers rebelled against Schultz and began killing off the Dutchman's drivers and payoff men: the "band of killers would wake the Schultz employees in their homes at the dead of night and kill them in their own bedrooms" (Berger 1935: 17). In a five-month period in 1931, seven Schultz men were murdered ("Schultz Aide Slain; 7th in Five Months" 1931). Schultz responded by placing a $50,000 contract on Coll and began to return the gunplay ("Woman, 2 Men, Slain as Gang Raids Home in Coll Feud" 1932). It was during this feud that Vincent Coll received his nickname, "Mad Dog." Coll's men opened fire at a leader of the Schultz organization, Joe Rao, who was standing in the street near a group of playing children. Rao escaped injury, but a five-year-old child was killed and four other children were wounded. Coll was arrested as one of the shooters, but his attorney, Samuel J. Leibowitz, who later became a judge noted for his "toughness" on criminals, disclosed that the witness to the shooting had a criminal record and a history of providing false testimony. Coll went free (O'Connor 1958).

Owney Madden

Another important Prohibition figure would soon play a role in the Schultz-Coll War. Owney Madden, born in England of Irish parents in 1892, began his career in crime as head of the Gophers, a notorious and widely feared gang that controlled an area of Manhattan's West Side appropriately called "Hell's

Kitchen." The neighborhood stretched roughly from Twenty-third to Fifty-ninth Street, west of Eighth Avenue. Their name was derived from the habit of holing up in basements and cellars (Sante 1991). In 1915, Madden was sentenced to Sing Sing Prison for ordering the murder of one of his rivals. In 1923 he was paroled and began to hijack liquor trucks, including those of Vincent ("Bill") Dwyer, a major bootlegger. Instead of a violent response, Dwyer, ever the rational businessman, chose to make Madden part of his organization (Peterson 1983a). Madden also became a partner of George Jean ("Big Frenchy") de Mange, a bootlegger and speakeasy owner who saw the need for the services that Madden and his Hell's Kitchen stalwarts could provide (O'Connor 1958).

As a result of his partnership with Bill Dwyer, Madden became a millionaire during Prohibition, and he continued his operations until 1932, when he was arrested for parole violation and returned to prison. A year later he was paroled again and retired to Hot Springs, Arkansas, a town known for corrupt machine politics and illegal gambling. There, according to Stephen Fox (1989), he controlled the rackets, married, and lived out his days in comfort. In 1935, Lucky Luciano found temporary refuge from a New York indictment by hiding out in Hot Springs. On April 24, 1965, the front page of the *New York Times* reported that Madden, an "ex-gangster" who had given big contributions to charity, had died of emphysema.

In need of money to help finance his campaign against Schultz, Coll kidnapped de Mange and demanded ransom from Madden, who turned over $35,000 for "Big Frenchy's" return. Coll then tried to extort money from Madden by threatening to kidnap him. The outraged Madden joined forces with Schultz in an all-out war against Coll. They divided the city into zones and dispatched their gunmen to find the "Mad Dog." In the interim, Madden fled to Florida, while Schultz barricaded himself in a bordello surrounded by bodyguards. In the end, Coll's bodyguards "fingered" him for Schultz. On February 9, 1932, Coll stepped into a drugstore phone booth and made a call. As he was busy on the telephone, his bodyguard discreetly left, and two men entered. One carried a Thompson submachine gun. They ordered the customers to remain calm, and several bursts of machine-gun fire entered the phone booth. Coll was almost cut in half by the barrage (O'Connor 1958).

Waxey Gordon

With Coll out of the way, Schultz began to expand into midtown Manhattan until he ran into the area controlled by Irving Wexler, better known as Waxey Gordon. In 1933, warfare finally broke out as Schultz gunmen made an unsuccessful attempt on Gordon's life ("2 Women Wounded as Gang Opens Fire in Upper Broadway" 1933).

Gordon was another Prohibition success story. In 1933, the *New York Times* cited him as an outstanding example of "what golden opportunities of the prohibition era could do for a man without scruples and anxious to get ahead" ("Gordon Made by Dry Era" 1933: 6). Born in 1889 in New York's teeming Lower East Side, the son of poor tenement dwellers, Gordon took to the streets. On October 5, 1905, he was arrested for practicing his trade, picking pockets, and sent to the Elmira Reformatory. As an adult he was sent to Sing Sing Prison for robbery and released in 1916 ("Gordon Says He Got Up to $300 a week" 1933). Gordon married the daughter of a rabbi, but his future looked bleak—then came Prohibition.

Gordon teamed with Max Greenberg, a hijacker and member of the notorious St. Louis gang known as "Eagan's Rats." The two were financed by Arnold Rothstein and soon had a fleet of rum ships riding the seas and making them rich. Gordon controlled the beer business in New Jersey (with the help of New Jersey racketeer Abner "Longie" Zwillman) and much of New York City. To avoid legal problems, Gordon ceased importing liquor from abroad and began to invest in breweries, producing legal "near beer" (0.05 percent alcohol and therefore legal). However, brewing near beer requires manufacturing the real thing and then removing its alcoholic content. The potential for illegal profit is obvious, and Gordon produced thousands of gallons of beer each year (Joselit 1983).

As befitting a multimillionaire, Gordon lived in a castle, complete with a moat, in southern New Jersey. He owned extensive property in New Jersey and Philadelphia, as well as nightclubs and gambling casinos. However, he paid an average of only $33 a year in income taxes from 1928 to 1930 (Schnepper 1978). A second mistake was his feud with Meyer Lansky, who reputedly fed information to the Internal Revenue Service about the source of Gordon's enormous income (Hammer 1975). In 1931, apparently worried about federal efforts to prosecute gangsters for tax violations, Gordon paid $35,000 in federal taxes. But it was too little, too late. Elmer Irey, head of the Treasury Department's Special Intelligence Unit, and the man who "got" Capone, began to work on Gordon. Thomas E. Dewey, a Columbia Law School graduate and Wall Street lawyer, was appointed chief assistant in the United States Attorney's Office for the Southern District of New York. Based on Irey's investigation, on November 20, 1933, Gordon was brought to trial; Dewey personally prosecuted the case. That same year, in a feud with Dutch Schultz, Greenberg was killed in an ambush that Gordon escaped (Irey 1948; Fox 1989).

Among other charges that Dewey was able to prove was that Gordon had spent $36,000 to install a bar in his $6,000 a year apartment; this was during the Depression (Schnepper 1978). It took the jury only fifty-one minutes to find Gordon guilty, and on December 1, 1933, he was sentenced to ten years' imprisonment ("Waxey Gordon Guilty; Gets 10 Years. Is Fined $80,000 for Tax Evasion" 1933). By the time Gordon was released from federal custody, Prohibition was over, and he looked for other areas of profit. During World War II he was convicted for black-market operations (Hammer 1975), and following the war he was active in heroin trafficking. In 1952, Gordon was one of twenty-three persons indicted in a nationwide drug trafficking case. On December 13, 1951, he was sentenced in a New York State court for narcotics violations. Under New York's "Baume's Law," as a fourth-felony offender, Gordon was sentenced to a term of twenty-five years to life. On April 10, 1952, a federal detainer brought him to Alcatraz to await trial on the federal drug charges. On June 24, 1952, Gordon became ill and died in the prison hospital ("Waxey Gordon Dies in Alcatraz at 63" 1952).

With Coll and Gordon out of the way, Schultz began to experience a new problem—the Internal Revenue Service. He went into "hiding"—at least law enforcement officers were unable to find him. Paul Sann (1971) reports that for eighteen months the Dutchman was actually in Harlem watching over his business interests. On November 29, 1934, the front page of the *New York Times* reported "Dutch Schultz Surrenders." He subsequently succeeded in obtaining a change of venue based on his notoriety in New York City. The case was moved to Syracuse, New York, where a mistrial (hung jury) resulted. The retrial was moved to the small upstate community of Malone, New York. Schultz travelled to Malone in advance of his trial, bought candy and flowers for the children he visited in the hospital, held a grand ball to which he invited the entire town, and generally endeared himself to the good people of Malone. Schultz was acquitted, a verdict that led Frederick Bryant, the presiding judge, to admonish: "Your verdict is one that shakes the confidence of law-abiding people. You will go home with the satisfaction—if it is a satisfaction—that you have rendered a blow against law enforcement and given aid and encouragement to the people who flout the law. In all probability, they will commend you. I cannot" (R.N. Smith 1982: 166).

Schultz could not safely return to New York; the federal government had several counts of the original indictment held in abeyance and, to avoid possible double-jeopardy problems, indicted Schultz for a series of misdemeanors. In addition, New York State had a warrant outstanding for income-tax evasion; Schultz owed the state $36,937 in back taxes. It was understood that if Schultz could be arrested in New York City, the authorities would be able to institute a prohibitive bail and thus keep him in custody. Schultz travelled to New Jersey and surrendered to the federal charges; bail was set at an amount that enabled him to remain at liberty (Sann 1971). The *New York Times* reported that Schultz could not return to New York City because of Mayor La Guardia's threat to have him arrested if he showed up ("Schultz Succumbs to Bullet Wounds Without Naming Slayers" 1935). La Guardia often made outrageous public pronouncements—poor civil liberties, great politics. The Dutchman set up headquarters in a Newark tavern, but faced threats from two sources: Thomas E. Dewey and Lucky Luciano.

In 1935, Dewey, a Republican, was appointed special prosecutor by Governor Herbert Lehman, an anti-Tammany Democrat. The man who prosecuted Waxey Gordon was now after Schultz. Dewey threatened to convene a special grand jury to investigate the Dutchman's activities. Luciano and his colleagues expected Schultz to be convicted and imprisoned as a result of his trials in Syracuse and Malone. They were planning to move in on his numbers and restaurant rackets, and his acquittal presented them with a serious

LA GUARDIA

In a well-publicized crime "clean-up" campaign, New York City Mayor Fiorello La Guardia dumped five thousand firearms taken from criminals, along with hundreds of slot machines and other gambling devices, into Long Island Sound in 1934.

Fiorello La Guardia was born in New York City in 1882. He attended high school in Arizona and worked for a while as a reporter in St. Louis. Endowed with language skills, he worked for the U.S. consulates in Budapest, Trieste, and Fiume (Rijeka), and then as an interpreter at New York's Ellis Island. In 1910 La Guardia graduated from New York University Law School and began aiding immigrants with legal problems. In 1916 La Guardia was elected to the House of Representatives as a progressive Republican. In the House he fought for child labor laws, women's suffrage, and the protection of labor unions.

In 1929, La Guardia ran for mayor as a reformer against Tammany Mayor Jimmy Walker, whose administration was racked with scandal. Although La Guardia lost the election to Walker, the rising tide of scandal forced Democratic Governor Franklin Roosevelt to call for investigations. From 1930 to 1932, the Seabury investigations uncovered rampant municipal corruption intertwined with organized crime, and Mayor Walker was forced to resign.

For the 1933 election, Samuel Seabury, the crusading investigator and scion of a prominent New York family, helped put together a formidable reform slate under the Fusion Party label, which swept into office. A colorful campaigner who used his language skills to appeal to a variety of ethnic groups, La Guardia was reelected twice, serving as mayor for twelve years. A cornerstone of his administration was highly publicized efforts against organized crime.

setback. The independent and violent Schultz, for his part, became even more unpredictable, personally murdering one of his men, Jules Martin, in a dispute over money, and his top aide, Bo Weinberg, whom he (correctly) suspected of dealing with Luciano. The Dutchman was also threatening to kill Dewey, an idea that had been rejected by the other leading gangsters in New York sitting as a commission; they were fearful of the "heat" that would result (R.N. Smith 1982).

On the evening of October 25, 1935, Dutch Schultz entered the Palace Chop House and Tavern in Newark, where he had established his headquarters "in exile." With him were his bodyguards Bernard ("Lulu") Rosenkrantz and Abe Landau, as well as the financial wizard of the Schultz organization, Otto ("Abbadabba") Berman. As Schultz left the group and entered the men's room, two men suddenly entered the tavern—Charles ("Charlie the Bug") Workman, a top professional killer, and (it is believed) Emanual ("Mendy") Weiss, who worked for Lepke Buchalter. The pair opened fire with handguns and a shotgun, and the Schultz men were mortally wounded. Workman entered the men's room and shot the Dutchman, who died about twenty hours later. Less than two hours after the Newark attack, a top Schultz aide, Martin Krompier, was shot and seriously wounded in a Manhattan barber shop. The *New York Times* reported that Krompier's shooting was connected to the takeover of loansharking operations in Schultz's territory by Luciano and Buchalter ("Usury Racket Stirred Gang War" 1935).

Workman was tried for the Schultz murder six years later, and during his trial suddenly entered a plea of guilty. The thirty-four-year-old "Bug" received a life sentence. Workman was paroled in 1964 and permitted to return to New York under parole supervision. He worked in the garment center for several years until age and illness overcame him. He was placed in a Long Island nursing home to finish out his days. Weiss was electrocuted in 1944 for an unrelated murder.

Lepke Buchalter

On the syndicate "commission" in New York, it was Louis Buchalter—known as the "Judge"—who "vetoed" the murder of Thomas E. Dewey (Turkus and

On October 23, 1935, top enforcers working for Lepke Buchalter entered the Palace Chop House in Newark and gunned down Dutch Schultz and three aides. "The Dutchman" survived for almost a day. His deathbed ravings ranged from million-dollar deals to moralistic admonitions such as "Mother is the best bet" and "Don't let Satan draw you too fast."

Feder 1951), a decision that he probably lived to regret. "Lepkeleh" (an affectionate Yiddish expression for "Little Louis") was born on New York's Lower East Side on February 6, 1897. His father died when Lepke was thirteen, and his destitute mother sent him to live with his older sister. He had three brothers: one became a rabbi, another a pharmacist, and the third a dentist, but Lepke took a different route. He was arrested and imprisoned for burglary several times. After being released from Sing Sing Prison in 1922, he teamed up with Jacob ("Gurrah") Shapiro, and the two began working as strong-arms for labor-industrial racketeer "Little Augie" Orgen, who worked for Arnold Rothstein.

In 1927 a labor dispute erupted in the painting trade, and the head of the painters' trade association gave Little Augie $50,000 to end the strike. Without consulting his lieutenants, Augie ordered the union to stop the walkout. The brother of one of Augie's top lieutenants, however, was a friend of a painter's union official, who had asked that the mob remain neutral. Augie's men demanded that he return the $50,000 retainer, but instead, Augie contracted with Legs Diamond for help in breaking the strike.

> At 8:30 P.M., on October 15, 1927, Li'l Augie and his new associate were walking along a lower Manhattan street. A black sedan picked its way through the pushcarts. Behind the wheel was Lepke. Next to him, pistol in hand, sat Gurrah.
> . . . Gurrah hit the sidewalk yelling, "Move over Diamond!" Legs fell back instinctively against the building. Li'l Augie, transfixed, was killed. Diamond got a bullet through his shoulder—for butting in. If he hadn't drawn his gun, he would not have been touched. (Turkus and Feder 1951: 336–37)

After taking over the Orgen organization, Lepke and Gurrah revolutionized industrial racketeering (Berger 1944: 30): "Instead of using his sluggers and gunmen to terrorize labor unions during strike periods, Lepke worked them directly into the unions. By threat and by violence they controlled one local after another." Meyer Berger (1944: 30) points out that manufacturers who hired Lepke to deal with the unions "soon found themselves wriggling helplessly in the grip of Lepke's smooth but deadly organization. He moved in on them as he had on the unions."

Until 1940, Lepke was the head of an organization that extorted wealth from the garment, leather, fur, baking, and trucking industries in New York. Burton Turkus (Turkus and Feder 1951) estimated that his income was between $5 million and $10 million annually—and this was during the Depression. Berger (1940: 30) notes: "All through the Prohibition era, when other mobsters were splashing headily in alcoholic wealth and getting their names in headlines with a series of competitive killings that strewed urban and suburban landscapes with untidy corpses, Lepke went his quiet way."

A slightly different picture of Buchalter's operations is presented by Alan Block (1975). He notes that while Lepke and Gurrah had their share of successes, they also experienced dramatic setbacks. In 1932, for example, Buchalter and Shapiro were invited into the fur industry, where the Protective Fur Dressers Corporation was attempting to put an end to cutthroat competition that was hurting the business owners. Lepke and Gurrah were notified when dealers, dressers, or manufacturers were not "cooperating." Bombings, assaults, acid, and arson were the responses. However, the duo had a great deal of difficulty dealing with the fur union, and this led to their sudden exit from

Thomas Dewey (right) was a crusader against organized crime. Here he and his assistant Murray T. Gurfein arrive at the County Court House in New York City in 1935 for a grand jury indictment of a racketeer demanding a five-dollar monthly retainer for "protecting" a merchant.

the fur industry. On April 24, 1933, Buchalter and Shapiro had their thugs stage an attack on the headquarters of the fur workers' union, where a membership meeting was taking place. Although heavily armed, the Lepke thugs met fierce resistance and were driven out into the street by the irate workers. There they were joined by other workers as news of the attack spread throughout the fur district. A number of men were killed, and several gangsters were severely beaten. Seven were convicted of felonious assault, and this ended Buchalter's activities in the fur industry.

Special prosecutor Thomas E. Dewey began to move against Buchalter and Shapiro, and by 1937 both were in hiding, leaving day-to-day operations to Mendy Weiss. Shapiro surrendered the following year and was tried and convicted for extortion in the bakery industry (Joselit 1983). Lepke remained in hiding. In an effort to remove all possible witnesses, he ordered a murder rampage. The number of killings at his direction is estimated at between sixty and eighty (Berger 1940). Despite his violent reputation, Lepke was a shy, slender man of about five feet, seven inches. In contrast to many of his more flamboyant colleagues, Buchalter preferred to spend most of his non-working time at home with his English wife and stepson, occasionally playing a round of golf or basking on the Miami beach (Tully 1958).

Turkus (Turkus and Feder 1951) reports that the murder binge backfired; the reign of terror turned loyal Lepke men into terrified informers seeking police protection. Law enforcement pressure against organized crime intensified in an effort to "smoke" Lepke out of hiding, particularly after one of his gunmen mistakenly killed an innocent music publisher. There was also a $50,000 reward on his head. On August 24, 1939, Lepke surrendered to J. Edgar Hoover and columnist Walter Winchell according to a prearranged plan. Buchalter had been misled into believing that a deal had been arranged with the authorities, that he would only have to stand trial for federal (drug) and not state (murder) charges. On January 2, 1940, Buchalter was convicted in federal court of antitrust and narcotic law violations and sentenced to fourteen years. Block (1975) reports that Buchalter's involvement in narcotics was limited to declaring himself in for half of the profits of a lucrative narcotics-smuggling business—simple extortion—but Andrew Tully (1958) reports a more extensive involvement.

To Buchalter's dismay, he was subsequently turned over to New York authorities and prosecuted by Dewey for extortion, for which he received a sentence of thirty years to life. Then, in 1941, he was prosecuted by Burton Turkus for murder in Brooklyn, along with Mendy Weiss and Louis Capone (of "Murder, Inc."). The three were convicted and, after a protracted legal battle, electrocuted on March 4, 1944. Buchalter has the dubious distinction of being the only major organized crime figure to be executed by the state.

Meyer Lansky and Benjamin Siegel

Lansky was born Maier Suchowljansky in either 1902 or 1904 in Grodno, Byelorussia, one of the fifteen republics of the former Soviet Union. Meyer Lansky, his brother Jacob, and his sister were brought to the United States by their parents in 1911. Meyer attended school in Brownsville, Brooklyn, and then Public School 34 on the Lower East Side, where he completed the eighth grade. At age seventeen (Lacey [1991] says he was fifteen), Meyer left school for a job as a tool and die maker (McFadden 1983). His first recorded arrest was on October 24, 1918. Until that time, various popular sources report, Meyer was an honest and hardworking apprentice craftsman, although another source refers to Lansky's early skill at crap games (Lacey 1991). On that date he was arrested for assaulting Lucky Luciano with a crowbar. According to Hank Messick (1973), Lansky was returning home from work, tools in his hand, when he came upon Luciano beating a woman in an alley while the young (age twelve) Ben Siegel feebly attempted to stop him. Meyer and his crowbar succeeded. They were all arrested, and Lansky was fined two dollars for disorderly conduct. The judge is reported to have stated to Siegel and Lansky: "You boys have bugs in your heads," and Messick notes that Siegel not only kept the nickname, but lived up to it. No one, however, called Ben Siegel "Bugsy" to his face a second time.

Robert Lacey (1991) presents a different version of the first encounter between Lansky and Luciano. The young Sicilian, head of a gang that preyed on Jewish youth, encountered the physically unimpressive Lansky. Surrounded and subjected to threats and demands for money, Lansky reportedly told them to commit a physically impossible sex act. His pluck apparently provided the basis for a lifelong friendship.

Benjamin Siegel was born on February 28, 1906, and raised in the Williamsburg section of Brooklyn (just across the Williamsburg bridge from the Lower East Side). He had four sisters and a brother, Maurice. Maurice became a respected Beverly Hills physician. Ben grew into a handsome and powerfully built young man who was quick to violence (Jennings 1967). The diminutive Lansky (five feet, four inches, 135 pounds) and his friend Ben Siegel were part of a gang of Jewish young men. Lansky was the brains, Siegel represented the brawn. (Their partnership is reminiscent of the ties between Johnny Torrio and Al Capone, discussed in chapter 4.)

In addition to his legitimate shop work, Lansky accepted assignments as a labor union strong-arm and protector of crap games (Lacey 1991). He and Siegel organized their own dice games. As they grew successful, the duo surrounded themselves with *starkers* (Yiddish for "tough guys"), men such as Phil ("Little Farvel") Kovolick, described as a "hulking brute" (Nash 1975: 195). At the onset of Prohibition, Meyer Lansky and Ben Siegel were primed to take advantage of the new opportunities that would present themselves, and they found one such opening in the transportation business. Lansky became an automobile mechanic. His reputation and mechanical ability soon led to servicing and "souping up" stolen vehicles for use by bootleggers. Hauling whiskey, however, was a very risky business, and the "Bug and Meyer Gang" was soon providing the *starkers* necessary to ensure those valuable shipments from the likes of Legs Diamond, who became a liquor hijacker.

In addition to their transportation and bootlegging activities, Lansky and Siegel continued their gambling operations. This eventually attracted the attention of Italian crime boss Joe Masseria, whose men tried to "muscle in." At this point, Luciano intervened—he was working for Masseria—and reconciled the differences between the Jewish and Italian gangsters. Throughout his career, Luciano was apparently able to act as an intermediary between Jewish and Italian gangsters, a position that enabled him to gain important stature in organized crime. The duo, often in partnership with Luciano, also initiated their own bootlegging business. By the end of Prohibition, Lansky and Siegel were major powers in organized crime.

In 1936 or 1937, Siegel left New York for the West Coast. Turkus (Turkus and Feder 1951) reports that he was sent by eastern gang leaders who were interested in exploiting opportunities in California. Syndicate units in Cleveland, Chicago, and New York sent men to join the Siegel operation on the West Coast. One of them was notorious ex-boxer Mickey Cohen. Cohen in his

(1975) autobiography confirms that he was sent to California by Lou Rothkopf, one of the leaders of the Cleveland syndicate: "When I was told to come out here and that Benny was out there, I actually wasn't told that I was *fully* under Benny's arm" (1975: 35). Dean Jennings (1967), in his biography of Siegel, asserts that Ben went to California not at the behest of organized crime bosses but for personal reasons—he was partial to the glamour that it afforded and to a French actress who had left New York for Hollywood. Mickey Cohen (1975: 41) reports that Jack Dragna (b. 1891 in Corleone, Sicily), crime boss in southern California, was not running things too well: "The organization had to pour money on to help Dragna at all times. So Benny came out here to get things moving good."[4]

Siegel "got things moving good." Ed Reid and Ovid Demaris (1964) report that he organized a coalition of the big crime bosses in California, with himself at the top and crime boss Jack Dragna his top lieutenant. His thugs forced bookmakers in California and Arizona to subscribe to the syndicate-backed Trans-America Wire Service (which reported racing results throughout the country). He muscled in on gambling operations throughout the state, set up a narcotics pipeline through Mexico, and organized prostitution from Seattle to San Diego. Siegel also established off-shore gambling on ships anchored beyond the three-mile limit, gained control of the union that represented movie extras, and extorted money from the movie industry. He was also the (hidden) owner of the California Metals Company in Los Angeles, which handled salvage metals during the Second World War.

Although he established himself in a host of rackets, Siegel is best remembered for his activities in Las Vegas. Beginning in 1946, with financial backing from Nevada-based gamblers and eastern gang leaders, Siegel built the first of the grand-style Las Vegas gambling casino hotels, the Flamingo. Upon opening, however, the not-quite-finished luxury hotel became a money-loser—a combination of bad luck, incompetent help, and a business downturn. Siegel reached out for more financing, and his activities apparently took on a streak of independence that alienated him from Lansky and the other gang leaders. He would not, for example, dissolve the Trans-America Wire Service, even though the syndicate had taken over the rival service by murdering its owner, James M. Ragen. At midnight, June 20, 1947, Siegel was hit by a "fusillade of bullets fired through the living room of a Beverly Hills house [home of Virginia Hill] where he was staying" ("Siegel, Gangster Is Slain on Coast" 1947: 1). Lacey (1991) states that it was Siegel's Las Vegas partners, Gus Greenbaum, Moe Sedway, Davie Berman, Morris Rosen, and Willie Alderman, who were behind his murder. In any event, they took over the Flamingo upon Siegel's demise.

---

4. By the end of the Second World War, Mickey Cohen was well-established (and notorious) in suburban Los Angeles, where he ran a large gambling operation. Jack Dragna had a number of Cohen associates killed, and also attempted to kill Cohen in a secret but unsuccessful attempt to take over his gambling operations (Demaris 1981).

During the 1930s, Lansky was able to arrange with the Cuban dictator Fulgencio Batista for the syndicate to control gambling in Havana. This domination was interrupted by the Second World War and Batista's U.S. post-war exile. A coup in 1952 brought him back to power, and Meyer Lansky returned to Cuba. Until he assumed dominance in Havana gambling, the industry had been crippled by dishonesty and publicity about cheated tourists. Lansky put an end to this and turned the city into a gambling mecca, which did not come to an end until Fidel Castro booted both Batista and the syndicate out of Cuba (Lacey 1991). Lansky moved his gambling interests into the Bahamas and Haiti.

Lansky was known as a thinker and a reader—Lansky belonged to the Book-of-the-Month Club—features of his personality that apparently brought kudos from his colleagues. His extensive gambling enterprises, many in partnership with Vincent ("Jimmy Blue Eyes") Alo, a boyhood friend from the Lower East Side and a partner of Lucky Luciano, reached from upstate New York to Fort Worth, Texas. Alo, a captain in the Genovese crime Family, provided the muscle for Lansky's operations (Lacey 1991). Lansky became known as the premier "money mover" for organized crime, "washing" illegitimate funds and investing them in legitimate enterprises such as the jukebox business.

During World War II Lansky registered for the Selective Service but was never called—he was above the draft age. In 1953, he served a brief jail term for running a gambling operation at the Arrowhead Inn in Saratoga Springs, New York (just north of Albany). Afterward, Lansky moved to Florida and concentrated on investments in the southern part of that state. His operations were so lucrative that he is reputed to have kept a former bootlegger associate, Jack Pullman, in Switzerland as his full-time money manager (McFadden 1983).[5] In 1970, fearing an indictment for income-tax evasion, Lansky fled to Israel, where he touched off a twenty-six month legal fight. Lansky claimed citizenship as a Jew under Israel's "Law of Return." He also reported that his efforts before the 1948 War of Independence resulted in badly needed munitions being smuggled out of East Coast ports to the Jewish underground in Palestine. The United States pressured for his return—Lansky was a dangerous criminal. The case went to Israel's highest court, which ruled in 1972 that he was not entitled to citizenship because his past made him a "danger to public safety" (McFadden 1983: 21).

When Lansky returned to Miami, he was immediately arrested and posted a cash bail of $250,000. He was ultimately cleared of, or ruled too ill to stand trial on, all the tax evasion, conspiracy, and Las Vegas "skimming" charges against him. Lansky spent his last years in seclusion in a Miami Beach

---

5. John ("Jack") Pullman was born in Russia in 1903. He was an associate of Meyer Lansky during Prohibition. In 1931 Pullman served a fifteen-month sentence for bootlegging. He lived in Chicago, emigrated to Canada, and finally settled in Switzerland in 1960 (Petacque and Hough 1983).

condominium with his second wife. His first marriage in 1929 had ended in a 1946 divorce. The couple had two sons and a daughter. In 1948, Lansky married his second wife, a manicurist at a Manhattan hotel. He died of cancer on January 15, 1983 (McFadden 1983). One of Lansky's two sons, Paul, is a graduate of West Point, a pilot with a master's degree in engineering who served a tour in Vietnam (Lacey 1991).

ITALIAN ORGANIZED CRIME IN NEW YORK

In order to understand and appreciate the development of Italian-American organized crime in New York (and elsewhere), it is necessary to refer back to the history of southern Italy discussed in chapter 1. Most Italians who came to the United States did so during the years 1875–1920, and 80 to 90 percent were from the poorest part of their country, the *Mezzogiorno*, southern Italy. These poor immigrants encountered an economy shaped by the Astors, the Morgans, and the Vanderbilts, in which powerless people had little opportunity. They faced enormous social and economic hardship exacerbated by ethnic prejudice.

Like earlier generations of immigrants, a small number of Italians sought to succeed by bending and breaking both moral and legal codes. Being relative latecomers, they could not imitate the scions of earlier generations who had already, by "hook or crook," secured a place in society. Instead, they adapted their southern Italian culture to the American experience. In order to understand the type of organized crime that resulted, we have to understand southern Italy and the phenomena of Mafia, Camorra, and 'Ndrangheta that were discussed in chapter 1.

Southern Italians in New York

Between 1891 and 1920, 4 million Italians entered America, the overwhelming majority coming from southern Italy. They were poor and uneducated (Gallo 1981: 33): "It has been estimated that the average Italian immigrant who arrived in New York in 1910 had a total of $17 in his possession." They "found work in the city's construction crews, laboring as ditch diggers, hod carriers, and stone cutters. As long as they had strong arms, it did not matter if they could not speak English or operate a complex machine" (1981: 44). They experienced nativist prejudice and discrimination from employers, organized labor, and public officials. Arthur Train (1912: 83), a former assistant district attorney, wrote that "the Italians from the extreme south of the peninsula have fewer of these [American characteristics than the northern Italian], and are apt to be ignorant, lazy, destitute, and superstitious. A considerable percentage, especially those from the cities, are criminal." Ironically, in 1912, gambling and prostitution in Manhattan were well organized under the able leadership of Tammany Hall; southern Italians were not part of this Irish-Jewish cabal.

The Mafia is mentioned in a *New York Times* article on October 21, 1888, which quoted New York police inspector Thomas Byrnes (a notoriously corrupt official). Byrnes stated that he had discovered the murderer of one Antonio Flaccomio to be "an Italian fruit dealer and a member of a *secret society* to which Flaccomio also belonged." Inspector Byrnes went on to report that the *secret society* was known as the Mafia, and the persons involved in the killings were fugitives from Sicily: "There are two principal headquarters of this society in this country—one is in this city and the other in New Orleans[6]—so that members of the society who commit a serious crime in this city find refuge among friends in the South and vice versa" ("By Order of the Mafia" 1888: 8; emphasis added). David Chandler (1975) agrees that the Flaccomio murder was a Mafia killing, although it appears that Flaccomio was actually killed because of an altercation over a card game. According to follow-up stories in the *Times*, no evidence was ever presented linking either the deceased or the accused to the Mafia.

The Black Hand

Whether or not New York had a Mafia is subject to one's definition of the phenomenon. However, without any doubt, New York did have *La Mano Nero*, the Black Hand, which is the subject of a great deal of controversy. Francis Ianni (1972: 52) states that "Black Hand activities were the work of individual extortionists or small gangs, and there is no evidence which suggests that there was any higher level of organization or any tie with the *Mafia* in Sicily, or the Camorra in Naples." Thomas Pitkin and Francesco Cordasco (1977) present a different version: leaders of a prominent Black Hand group in New York, Ignazio Saietto ("Lupo the Wolf"; lupo means "wolf" in Italian) and Giuseppe Morello, maintained affiliations with Mafia chieftains back in Sicily. When Morello was arrested in 1909 by agents of the United States Secret Service (he and Saietto were also counterfeiters), correspondence was found linking him with Vito Cascio Ferro, a prominent *capomafioso*. It is believed that Ferro spent some time in the United States at the turn of the century.

According to Train (1922), Camorra and Mafia were never transferred to the United States, and many immigrants who were involved with these groups in Italy became quite honest and respectable in the United States. He points out, however, that there were Mafia and Camorra gangs in New York, and each was headed by a *capo*: "Each *capo maestra* works for himself with his own handful of followers, who may or may not enjoy his confidence, and each gang has its own territory held sacred by the others" (1922: 287). Train points out that these gangs rarely attempted blackmail or terrorized anyone but Italians. Occasionally an important *capomafioso* from Sicily arrived and local

---

6. In New Orleans, two Italian factions, Sicilian and Neapolitan, fought for control of the stevedoring business. During the struggle David Hennessey, the chief of police, was murdered. It was blamed on the "Mafia." A number of Italians were tried for murder. After their acquittal, a mob stormed the prison, and eleven of the defendants were lynched on March 15, 1891. (See Gambino 1974 for a discussion of this incident.)

amici had to "get busy for a month or so, raising money for the boys at home and knowing they will reap their reward if they ever go back" (1922: 288). The most popular method of collecting the money was to hold a banquet that all *amici* were required to attend: "No one cares to be conspicuous by reason of his absence and the hero returns to Italy with a large-sized draft on Naples or Palermo" (1922: 301).

In 1895, Giuseppe Petrosino, a New York City police officer, was put in charge of a special squad of Italian detectives and assigned the task of investigating "Italian crime," in particular Black Hand extortion. The latter flourished in Italian ghettos until Prohibition began to offer greater criminal opportunities. Italian families with varying amounts of wealth would receive a crude letter "signed" with a skull or black-inked hand. The letter "requested" money, offering dire threats as an alternative. These threats, usually bombings, were sometimes carried out. Petrosino and his squad were quite successful in their work, and he was sent to Italy to check judicial records for lists of criminals about to be released or recently released from Italian prisons so that these men could be picked up and deported if they arrived in the United States. Petrosino left New York secretly on February 9, 1909; on March 12, 1909, he was shot down on a street in Palermo. No one was ever apprehended for the murder, but the *campomafioso* Vito Ferro boasted that he had personally killed the officer (Petacco 1974).

Unione Siciliana

By early 1900 there were about 500,000 (mostly southern) Italians in New York City, living in the most deprived social and economic circumstances. The Italian immigration "made fortunes for speculators and landlords, but it also transformed the neighborhood into a kind of human antheap in which suffering, crime, ignorance and filth were the dominant elements" (Petacco 1974: 16). The Italian immigrant provided the cheap labor vital to the expanding capitalism of that era. "Functional deficiencies of the official structure," notes Robert Merton (1967: 127), generate an alternative (unofficial) structure to fulfill existing needs somewhat more effectively." Randall Collins (1975: 463) adds that "where legitimate careers are blocked and resources available for careers in crime, individuals would be expected to move in that direction." Thus, Collins notes, the prominence of Italians in organized crime "is related to the coincidence of several historical factors: the arrival of large numbers of European immigrants from peasant backgrounds who demanded cultural services that the dominant Anglo-Protestant society made illegal; the availability of a patrimonial form of military organization that could be applied to protecting such services; and the relatively late arrival of the Italians in comparison with other ethnic groups (e.g., the Irish) who had acquired control of legitimate channels of political and related economic mobility." Luigi Barzini (1965: 273) adds: "In order to beat rival organizations, criminals of Sicilian descent reproduced the kind of illegal groups they had belonged to in the old country and employed the same rules to make them invincible." Richard Gambino (1974: 304) concludes that, although southern Italian characteristics do not predispose people toward crime, "where the mode of life has been impressed onto organized crime it has made it difficult to combat effectively the criminal activity." He argues that Italian criminals "totally corrupted and perverted traditional codes of *la famiglia* and vendetta" (1974: 297).

There were Mafia gangs in every American city that had a sizable Sicilian population, notes Humbert Nelli (1976: 136), "feeding off the common laborer's honest toil and claiming to serve as a means of easing adjustment to American society." Eric Hobsbawm (1969: 686) states that the Mafia "was imported by Sicilian immigrants, who reproduced it in the cities in which they settled, as a ritual brotherhood consisting of loosely linked but otherwise independent and uncoordinated 'families' organized hierarchically." Nelli points out that Mafia organizations "served important social as well as financial functions. The group produced a sense of belonging and of security in numbers. This function was at least in part through the use of initiation ceremonies, passwords and rituals, and rules of conduct with which members must abide" (1976: 138). These groups of *mafiosi* were involved in the manufacture of low cost, high proof, untaxed alcohol, a business that prepared them well for Prohibition.

One of Ianni's informants describes a Mafia gang operating in Brooklyn in 1928:

All the old Sicilian "moustaches" used to get together in the backroom of the club—it was a *fratallanze* [brotherhood] and they used to call it *Unione Siciliana*. They spent a lot of time talking about the old country, drinking wine and playing cards. But these were tough guys too, and they were alky cookers [bootleggers] and pretty much ran things in the neighborhood. They had all of the businesses locked up and they got a piece of everything that was sold.

The *Unione Siciliana* is described by James Inciardi (1975: 115):

L'Unione siciliana emerged in the late nineteenth-century New York as a lawful fraternal society designed to advance the interests of Sicilian immigrants. The *Unione* provided its members with life insurance and additional social benefits, and was energetic in the eradication of crime within Sicilian-American communities. . . . Additional branches of *L'Unione siciliana* were chartered wherever new colonies of Sicilians expanded.

The respectability and benevolence of the *Unione* declined as Prohibition approached. First in New York and later in distant city branches, cadres of gangsters began to infiltrate and pervert the association. *L'Unione siciliana* acquired a dual character: it was open and involved in good works among needy Sicilians, yet it was hidden and malevolent, dealing in theft, murder and vice. With an expanding criminal front, leaders of this "society" became natural catalysts for any racketeers seeking to widen their influence and profit potentials. *L'Unione* membership included old and clannish *Mafia* types who stressed the maintenance of the cultural traditions of the Sicilian *Società onorata*. To these were added the younger Americanized factions that were anxious to increase their operations through cooperative agreements with a greater variety of criminal groups, even with those not of their blood. The *Unione* of the 1920s became the object of power struggles, with both orientations contending at local, regional, and national levels for more advantageous posts. This struggle terminated in 1931 in the Castellammarese war.

The Castellammarese War

In 1930, there were two major factions in Italian organized crime in New York, one headed by Giuseppe ("Joe the Boss") Masseria and the other by Salvatore Maranzano. Prohibition had enabled the Mafia gangs to break out of the bounds of "Little Italy" and operate in the wider society; booze-hungry Americans were not fussy about the source of their liquor. The struggle for domination of Italian-American OC in New York became known as the Castellammarese War because Maranzano and many of his supporters came from the small Sicilian coastal town of Castellammare del Golfo. The Maranzano group consisted mainly of Sicilians, especially the "moustaches," Old World types, many of whom had fled from Mussolini's prosecution of *mafiosi*. Maranzano had helped to smuggle many of his compatriots into the United States and they supported their *padrone*. The Masseria group had both Sicilian and non-Sicilian members, including Lucky Luciano (a Sicilian), Vito Genovese (a Neapolitan born in 1897), and Frank Costello (born Francesco Castiglia in Lauropoli, Calabria, 1893). They were allied with non-Italians such as Meyer Lansky and Ben Siegel. As the war turned against Masseria—the Maranzano forces were reinforced by a continuing supply of Sicilian exiles—five of his leading men, Luciano, Genovese, Ciro Terranova, Frank Livorsi, and Joseph ("Stretch") Stracci, went over to the other side, and they failed to notify Joe the Boss.

On April 15, 1931, Masseria drove his steel-armored sedan, a massive car with plate glass an inch thick in all of its windows, to a garage near the Nuova Villa Tammaro at 2715 West Fifteenth Street in the Coney Island section of Brooklyn. He then walked to the restaurant for a meal and a card game with Luciano. It was Masseria's last meal ("Racket Chief Slain by Gangster Gunfire" 1931). Luciano excused himself and went to the washroom: "Joe the Boss was shot as he sat at the table. Five bullets hit him, and some fifteen were sprayed around for good measure. As Masseria died, he still clutched the ace of diamonds, and that, in years to come, became a symbol of impending death to all good Mafia members" (Messick 1973: 54). Virgil Peterson (1983a) states that six bullets out of twenty hit Masseria. According to Hank Messick (1973), the shooters were Vito Genovese, Albert Anastasia, Joe ("Adonis") Doto, and Ben Siegel. Peterson adds that the driver was an important *capomafioso*, Ciro

Terranova, the "Artichoke King." In any event, the Castellammarese War was over.

It did not take long for Maranzano to irritate many of his followers, particularly the more Americanized gangsters such as Luciano. Joseph Bonanno, who was born in Castellammarese del Golfo, was a staunch ally of Maranzano. In his autobiography (1983: 137–38), however, Bonanno points out that the new Mafia boss was out of step with the times: "Maranzano was old-world Sicilian in temperament and style. But he didn't live in Sicily anymore. In New York he was advisor not only to Sicilians but to American-Italians. Maranzano represented a style that often clashed with that of the Americanized

New York Organized Crime Families from the end of the Castellammarese War to 1968

Maranzano Family

Reina Family

Joseph Bonanno

Gaetano Gagliano

Thomas Lucchese

Masseria Family

Charles Luciano

Frank Costello

Vito Genovese

New York Organized Crime Families, continued

Profaci Family

Joseph Profaci

Joseph Magliocco

Joseph Colombo

Mineo Family

Frank Scalise

Lawrence Mangano

Albert Anastasia

Carlo Gambino

men who surrounded him after the war. It was difficult, for example, for Maranzano even to communicate effectively with many of these men, for they only understood American street cant."

On September 10, 1931, four men carrying pistols entered a suite at 230 Park Avenue, the Grand Central Building, in New York City. "One of them ordered the seven men and Miss Frances Samuels, a secretary, to line up against the wall. The others stalked into the private office of Salvatore Maranzano. There was a sound of voices raised in angry dispute; blows, struggling, and finally pistol shots, and the four men dashed out of the suite." Maranzano was found with "his body riddled with bullets and punctured with knife wounds" ("Gang Kills Suspect in Alien Smuggling" 1931: 1). The killers are believed to have been Jews (whom Maranzano and his bodyguards would not recognize) sent by Meyer Lansky at the behest of Luciano. Because the killers flashed badges, Maranzano and his bodyguards apparently believed them to be federal immigration agents who had visited him before as part of an investigation into the smuggling of Sicilians into the country. They attempted to kill him silently with knives, and when Maranzano fought back to save his life, they shot him.

In the aftermath of the Castellammarese War, five Italian-American crime Families emerged, and they continue to maintain distinct identities.

Luciano/Genovese Family

Luciano was born in Lercara Friddi, a sulfur-mining area in western Sicily, in 1897. He arrived in New York with his parents, Antonio and Rosalia Lucania, early in 1907, and the family settled on Manhattan's Lower East Side. Nelli (1976) reports that although Luciano's conduct in school was satisfactory, his academic record was poor and made worse by chronic truancy. He left school when he reached the age of fourteen and secured employment as a shipping boy in a hat factory with a Jewish owner. The young Luciano became a member of the Five Points Gang and a heroin user and seller. On June 26, 1916, at age eighteen, he was found guilty of possessing narcotics and sent to a reformatory for six or eight months (Nelli 1976; Lacey 1991).

With the advent of Prohibition, Luciano emerged as a leader in the Masseria crime Family. During the Castellammarese War he was kidnapped, badly beaten, and left for dead—his survival has often been given (incorrectly) as the source of his nickname "Lucky." (Articles in the *New York Times* refer to Lucania as "Lucky" prior to this incident. The nickname is apparently derived from a shortening of Lucania to "Luc" and then "Lucky.") With the death of Masseria and Maranzano, Luciano became the most important Italian organized crime figure in New York, a status he would enjoy until 1935. In that year, investigators for Thomas E. Dewey discovered an extensive prostitution network which, although independent at one time, had been taken over by Luciano henchmen headed by David ("Little Davey") Betillo. In a single raid, Dewey's investigators arrested prostitutes, madams, and "bookers" (pimps).

They were pressured and cajoled into testifying against Luciano, who protested that he had no knowledge of or involvement in Betillo's activities. Dewey charged that Betillo had acted on behalf of Luciano to "organize" two hundred bordellos and three thousand prostitutes into a $12 million-a-year business. Luciano chose to take the stand in his own defense—a bad decision as it turned out. Although there was scant evidence, Dewey was able to trap him in lies about his criminal record. On June 7, 1936, Luciano was found guilty of sixty-one counts of compulsory prostitution and sentenced to a term of thirty to sixty years in prison (R.N. Smith 1982). Luciano was actually convicted of being "notorious" (Nelli 1976).

Luciano languished in Clinton State Prison at Dannemora, New York, while war raged in Europe and the Pacific. By May 1942, German submarines operating in American coastal waters had sunk 272 U.S. ships. It was suspected that information on American shipping was being leaked to the Germans by people employed in eastern ports. It was also suspected, incorrectly, that German submarines were receiving supplies from American fishing boats. The specter of sabotage was raised when the luxury liner *Normandie*, which had been refitted as a naval vessel, rolled over in flames while harbored in the Hudson River. (In fact, renamed the U.S.S. Lafayette, the *Normandie* was accidentally set on fire by workers using acetylene torches.)

With the help of Frank Hogan, Dewey's successor as Manhattan district attorney, Naval intelligence officials met with Joseph ("Socks") Lanza, the vicious criminal "czar" of the Fulton Fish Market, who was under indictment for conspiracy and extortion.[7] Lanza agreed to help, but noted that his influence was limited; he suggested the man to see was Lucky Luciano. Luciano was transferred to Great Meadow Prison, which is closer to New York City, and there he met with Naval intelligence officers. Through Meyer Lansky the word went out. According to Rodney Campbell (1977), in addition to ordering port workers and fishermen to "keep alert," crime figures helped to place intelligence operatives in key areas by supplying them with union cards and securing positions for them on the waterfront, on fishing boats, and in waterfront bars, restaurants, and hotels. They also provided another important service. At the request of Naval officials they prevented strikes and other forms of labor unrest that could interrupt wartime shipping.

While Campbell provides documentation of Luciano's domestic role during the war, his data on Luciano's role in the invasion of Sicily are tenuous. According to Campbell, Luciano sent word to Sicilian *capomafiosi* to assist the Allied landing. However, *mafiosi* did not need encouragement from Luciano—their desire to rid the island of Mussolini's iron hand was incentive enough. In fact, notes Barzini (1972: 282), when Luciano arrived in Palermo after being deported from the United States, local *mafiosi* swindled him out of fifteen million lire. "Thus was the mastermind of the American underworld treated in his native island by the real Mafia." According to Tommaso Buscetta,

---

7. Socks Lanza is discussed in chapter 8.

a Sicilian *capomafioso*-turned-informer, Luciano was greatly respected among Sicilian *mafiosi* (Shawcross and Young 1987). R.N. Smith (1982: 572) presents a more modest claim with respect to Luciano's help: "Sicilians expelled by Mussolini proved willing to help devise maps of possible landing sites. The island coastline and the contour of land off the coast were assessed with the help of underworld informants."

In 1945, Governor Thomas E. Dewey received a petition for executive clemency on behalf of Luciano, citing his efforts during the war. On January 3, 1946, the governor announced that Luciano would be released from prison and deported to Italy. Luciano left the United States on February 9, 1946. Before the end of the year, however, he was in Havana holding court with the elite of New York's crime leaders. The following year, U.S. pressure on Fulgencio Batista compelled Luciano to return to Italy, where he died of a heart attack in 1962. Buscetta revealed that in 1957 he and several other important *mafiosi* met with Luciano and Joseph Bonanno in a Palermo restaurant. The two American gang leaders, Buscetta recalled, recommended the formation of a Mafia commission for Sicily fashioned along the lines established by Luciano in the United States, and a commission was formed in Sicily (Shawcross and Young 1987).

Frank Costello

With Luciano in prison and then deported to Italy, leadership of his crime Family was assumed by Frank Costello. Christened Francesco Castiglia, Costello was born on January 26, 1891, in Calabria. Like several other Italian criminals, he affected an Irish surname, something that was certainly no hindrance in New York, where the Irish dominated Tammany and Tammany dominated the city. In 1915 he served a ten-month sentence for carrying a concealed firearm. By 1923 Costello was a successful bootlegger working for Bill Dwyer, an ex-longshoreman turned rumrunner, who brought liquor from Canada across the Great Lakes in armored speedboats (Talese 1965). Costello moved into gambling and eventually became a successful (and legitimate) real estate dealer.

Known as the "King of the Slots," Costello operated an extensive network of "one-armed bandits"[8] in New York City until Mayor Fiorello La Guardia went on a highly publicized campaign to rid the city of "that bum." Many sources report that Costello was then invited to bring his slot machines to New Orleans by the political boss of Louisiana, United States Senator Huey P. Long. The "Kingfish's" biographer, T. Harry Williams (1969), questions Long's connection to Costello. Costello informed a federal grand jury that Senator Long had invited him into New Orleans to set up a thousand slot machines for

---

8. The slot machines dispensed candy mints as well as tokens that were redeemable for money. "The purpose of this arrangement was to make it arguable before friendly judges that the one-armed bandits were actually vending machines" (Peterson 1983a: 183).

a fee of thirty dollars per machine. However, Williams argues that such a setup would require police protection in a city that in 1935 was controlled by Semmes Walmsley, a bitter enemy of the Kingfish. In any event, Costello moved his slots into New Orleans and placed Philip ("Dandy Phil") Kastel in charge. (Suffering from cancer and apparently fearing blindness, in 1962 Kastel committed suicide in his New Orleans apartment.)

Costello was known for his political influence. In one widely reported incident, a telephone wiretap in 1943 revealed that Thomas A. Aurelio called Costello to thank him for securing the Democratic nomination for judge of the New York Supreme Court (a court of general, not appellate, jurisdiction) from Manhattan. "When I tell you something is in the bag," Costello replied, "you can rest assured." To which Aurelio responded by assuring Costello of his "loyalty for all you have done. It's undying" (Reid 1953: 212–13). Despite a grand jury probe, Aurelio was elected and served with distinction, without any hint of favoritism toward organized crime. Costello, it appears, was motivated more by ethnic than criminal interests. He had broken Irish domination over judicial appointments in Manhattan. The Irish had been very slow to share patronage with other ethnic groups. In the 1940s, however, "Tammany's aging Irish chieftains turned to the Italian-controlled underworld for desperately needed funding." This "Mafia Plan" was not without risk: Frank Costello and his colleagues "decided to install their own Italian district leaders in Tammany clubhouses" (Erie 1988: 122).

In 1949, Costello was asked to serve as vice chairman of a Salvation Army fund-raising drive. He gladly accepted and held a fund-raising party at the Copacabana, inviting judges and other leading political figures. The party netted $3,500 and Costello added another $6,500 of his own, sending the Salvation Army a check for $10,000. However, newspapers found out about the party, and the public reaction was one of indignation (Talese 1965).

In 1951, Costello appeared before the Kefauver Committee (discussed in chapter 10) and was exposed on national television as a major crime figure. For the television viewers, however, only Costello's hands could be seen; his lawyer had insisted that Costello not be televised. The crime boss's evasive responses, coupled with a dramatic walkout, eventually led to an eighteen-month prison term for contempt of the Senate. In 1952, the government moved against him for income-tax evasion, for which in 1954 Costello received a sentence of five years' imprisonment. In 1956 his attorney, noted criminal lawyer Edward Bennett Williams, proved that the conviction had been based on illegal wiretaps, and Costello was freed. Even while he was in prison, Costello's power continued unabated. In fact, while on a prison visit, attorney Williams mentioned to Costello that he wanted, but had been unable to purchase, tickets for the Broadway musical hit *My Fair Lady*. Later that same day, Williams reported, his doorbell at home rang: "A broad-shouldered man thrust an envelope in his hands and disappeared"; it contained four tickets for that evening's "sold out" performance ("Frank Costello Dies of Coronary at 82" 1972: 21).

By refusing to be seen on camera during the televised Kefauver committee hearings, Frank Costello unwittingly created far more publicity for himself. Millions of viewers were spellbound by the crime boss's evasive responses and his nervous, fidgety hands.

Costello routinely travelled without any bodyguards. On May 2, 1957, he had an appointment to meet Anthony ("Tony Bender") Strollo, Family *caporegime* in charge of Greenwich Village. The meeting, at Chandler's Restaurant on East 49th Street, had been arranged by Vito Genovese, Family underboss. At the restaurant with Bender was Vincent Mauro (also known as Vincent Bruno). Mauro left but monitored Costello's movements by telephone. He spoke to someone on a pay phone, outside of which a double-parked car was waiting for word that Costello was on his way home to his Central Park West apartment. As Costello rushed to catch the elevator in his luxury apartment building, he ran by a large man wearing a fedora. The man yelled, "This is for you, Frank." As Costello turned, the man fired a revolver at Costello's face from a distance of six to ten feet. The bullet hit Costello in the head but caused only superficial damage. When questioned by the authorities, Costello insisted he did not recognize his assailant, the easily recognizable Vincent ("The Chin") Gigante, an obese ex-pugilist and Genovese gunman (who in 1985 would become boss of the crime Family). Several months later, in what is believed to have been a related incident, Albert Anastasia, Costello's close ally and boss of the Mineo crime Family, was murdered, and Costello retired, leaving Vito Genovese as boss of the Luciano Family (Katz 1973).

Vito Genovese

The man who allegedly ordered the bungled attempt on Costello was born near Naples on November 27, 1897. At age fifteen he arrived in New York and lived with his family in the Little Italy of downtown Manhattan. Beginning as a street thief, Genovese graduated to working as a collector for the Italian lottery and eventually became an associate of Lucky Luciano. When his first wife died of tuberculosis in 1931, Genovese announced his intention to marry Anna Petillo—but she was already married. Twelve days later, Mr. Petillo was strangled to death and Genovese married the widow Petillo. After twelve years of marriage, Anna Genovese sued him for support and denounced Vito in court as a racketeer with a huge income. The much-feared crime boss did nothing. Nicholas Gage (1972) reports that Genovese was too much in love with her to have her killed.

During the 1930s Genovese was already a power in organized crime, making huge profits in narcotics. In 1934, however, he was involved in the bungled murder of Ferdinand ("The Shadow") Boccia, and Genovese was forced to flee to Italy in order to avoid prosecution; he took $750,000 with him. In Italy he is reputed to have become a confidant of Benito Mussolini. In 1943, Carlo Tresca, a stridently anti-fascist Italian newspaper editor in New York, was shot to death "gangland style." The contract for this murder has been linked to Genovese's friendship with Mussolini (Peterson 1983a). During the American invasion, Genovese was able to gain the confidence of American military authorities, for whom he acted as an interpreter. This position enabled him to become a major black marketeer, until he was identified as an American fugitive and returned to the United States to stand trial. While he was awaiting trial, a key witness was poisoned while in protective custody, and Genovese went free.

On April 14, 1959, Genovese, along with fourteen others, was convicted of conspiracy to violate narcotics laws and received a fifteen-year sentence. Ralph Salerno, a former New York City detective, says about the conviction:

> Oddly enough, several Bosses have gone to jail on evidence that knowledge-able people find questionable. One such case is that of Vito Genovese, a powerful New York family boss who went to prison in April 1959 on a federal narcotics conviction. Genovese's family had indeed been involved in narcot-ics, but Nelson Cantellops, a narcotics courier, swore in court that he had personally met and talked with Genovese about details of the business. To anyone who understands the protocol and insulation procedures of Cosa Nostra, this testimony is almost unbelievable. (1969: 157)

141

Chuck Giancana (1922) states that Genovese was framed with the connivance of other crime bosses, and that Cantellops was part of the plot.

On February 14, 1969, while serving his fifteen-year sentence, Genovese died of a heart ailment. However, the group that he headed is still referred to as the *Genovese Family*, despite numerous changes in leadership. Its operations extend into New Jersey, Connecticut, and parts of Massachusetts and upstate New York.

Mineo/Gambino Family

Al Mineo (born Manfredi) was a close ally of Joseph Masseria and also a victim of the Castellammarese War—he was murdered in 1930. After the death of Masseria, Frank Scalise, who had defected from the Mineo Family early in the war, was made boss of that same Family. He became a close confidant of Maranzano, and after Maranzano's death was replaced by Vincent Mangano. Mangano disappeared—presumably murdered at the direction of Family underboss Albert Anastasia, who then became Family boss. Frank Scalise, known as "Don Cheech," made his peace with Luciano and eventually emerged as the underboss of the Family headed by Albert Anastasia. On June 17, 1957, at age sixty-three, Scalise was shot to death in the Bronx. Joseph Valachi (Maas 1968) says that Scalise was selling memberships—people were paying him up to $50,000 to be "made." This activity apparently infuriated Anastasia, who ordered Scalise's murder. Scalise's brother Joseph publicly swore vengeance and soon disappeared forever (Mustain and Capeci 1992).

Albert Anastasia

Albert Anastasia was born Umberto Anastasio in Tropea, Italy, on September 26, 1902. He entered the United States in 1919 and reportedly changed his name to save his family some embarrassment as a result of his 1921 arrest for murdering a fellow longshoreman (Freeman 1957). His brother Anthony ("Tough Tony") Anastasio became the official ruler of the Brooklyn waterfront as head of Local 1814 of the International Longshoremen's Union (ILA). Albert became the unofficial ruler of these same docks. (A third brother, Salvatore, became a priest.) Albert was widely feared even among his associates and reportedly enjoyed the title "Executioner" (Berger 1957)—he issued the "contract hits" for Murder, Inc. (discussed in chapter 2).

In 1923, Anastasia was sentenced to two years of imprisonment for possessing a firearm, although this did not prevent him from serving stateside in the United States Army during the Second World War. In 1955, he served a one-year sentence for income-tax evasion. Anastasia lived in a home along the Palisades in Fort Lee, New Jersey—a home with a seven-foot barbed wire fence, Doberman pinschers, and bodyguards. On October 25, 1957, he was getting his hair cut (some sources say he was getting a shave), when his bodyguard conveniently absented himself. Two gunmen entered, and the "Executioner" was executed. (The barbershop was located in the Park Sheraton, which in 1928 was known as the Park Central, the hotel where Arnold Rothstein was shot.) The killers are believed to have been from the Gallo brothers' faction of the Profaci Family, acting on Profaci's orders. Underboss Carlo Gambino, believed to have been in league with Vito Genovese and Joseph Profaci, became boss of the crime Family.

Carlo Gambino

Born in Palermo on August 24, 1902, Gambino arrived in the United States (an illegal alien) in 1921 and never became a citizen. He resided in Brooklyn, assisted by numerous relatives who had arrived earlier. In turn, he helped his brothers Paolo (Paul), born in 1904, and Giuseppe (Joseph), born in 1908, when they arrived in the United States. His boyhood friend from Palermo, Gaetano Lucchese, was already in the United States and rising in the ranks of organized crime, first under Masseria and then, as a defector, under Maranzano. Gambino's son Thomas married Lucchese's daughter. Although nominally on the side of "Joe the Boss," Gambino appears not to have actively participated in the Castellammarese War. He followed Lucchese into the Maranzano camp and after Maranzano's death moved into the ranks of the Mineo Family, eventually becoming a *caporegime* under Vincent Mangano.

After Prohibition, Gambino continued in the bootlegging business. In 1939, he received a twenty-two-month sentence for conspiracy to defraud the United States of liquor taxes. Eight months later, the conviction was thrown out because evidence was based on illegal wiretaps. The Second World War served to make Gambino a millionaire; it also prevented him from being deported to Italy. Joseph Valachi testified before a Senate committee that Gambino "made over a million dollars from ration stamps during the war. The stamps came out of the O.P.A.'s [Office of Price Administration] offices. First Carlo's boys would steal them. Then, when the government started hiding them in banks, Carlo made contact and the O.P.A. men sold him the stamps" (Gage 1975: 26). Meskil (1973: 58) points out that "Wartime rationing of gasoline, meat, and groceries opened a nationwide black market that the American public patronized as eagerly as it had once bought bootleg booze."

When Albert Anastasia became Family boss, he made Gambino the *sottocapo*. After Anastasia's murder in 1957, Carlo became the boss of reputedly the largest and most influential crime Family in the country. A strong family man, Gambino had one daughter and two sons who operated trucking firms—Consolidated Carriers—in the garment center. Gambino's wife died in 1971. On October 15, 1976, Gambino died of a heart attack in his Massapequa, Long Island, home. His place was taken by Gambino's first cousin and brother-in-law, a powerful Brooklyn *caporegime*, Paul ("Big Paul") Castellano.

Castellano was born in Brooklyn in 1915, the only son of Sicilian immigrants. He dropped out of school after the eighth grade. After five years at the helm of the Gambino Family, Castellano withdrew from many of the day-to-day activities, preferring to spend most of his time with a mistress at his Staten Island mansion. The mansion was bugged by the FBI for almost five months in 1983. In 1984, Castellano was indicted because of the activities of a murderous Gambino crew in Brooklyn (see Mustain and Capeci 1992). The following year he was hit with more indictments, this time the "commission case" (discussed in chapter 1). On December 16, 1985, Castellano and his underboss, Thomas Bilotti, were heading to a meeting at Spark's Steak House in midtown Manhattan:

> Three men in trench coats, tipped off to Castellano's expected arrival by a confidant-turned-traitor named Frankie De Ciccio,[9] loitered in the urban shadows of the early Christmas-season dusk. Thomas Bilotti turned his boss's black Lincoln onto Forty-sixth Street, and parked it directly in front of a No Parking sign; the car had a Patrolmen's Benevolent Association sticker on the windshield. As the two victims emerged, the assassins approached them, producing semiautomatic weapons from under their coats and loosing a barrage of bullets at close range. Castellano and Bilotti were each shot six times in the head and torso.... [O]ne of the killers then crouched over Castellano's body and delivered a coup de gràce through the skull. (O'Brien and Kurins 1991: 11)

Two weeks later, at a meeting of Gambino Family captains, John Gotti was elected boss (Gotti trial tapes).

John Gotti

John Gotti is a career criminal whose media coverage has eclipsed all previous crime figures. He has been the subject of cover stories in *Time, People, New York,* the *New York Times Magazine,* and numerous television specials. As with Al Capone, also a man of Neapolitan heritage, notoriety aided in his downfall.

John ("Johnny Boy") Joseph Gotti, Jr., was born in the South Bronx on October 27, 1940, to poor Neapolitan immigrants. He was one of thirteen siblings, seven boys and six girls, two of whom died in infancy, and four of whom became part of OC. John Gotti was raised in the East New York-Brownsville section of Brooklyn, and became a member of the Fulton-Rockaway Boys, a neighborhood gang. He dropped out of high school at age sixteen and began working for Angelo Bruno, a soldier in the Gambino Family. Later he became part of the East New York crew, which was headed by Carmine ("Charley Wagons") Fatico, a hijacker and Gambino *caporegime*. Gotti moved to Queens when his crew boss set up headquarters at the Bergin Hunt and Fish Social Club, two storefronts in Ozone Park, a quiet, working-class neighborhood. Gotti, strong-arm and ex-convict (for a hijacking conviction), subsequently became a confidant of Aniello ("Neil") Dellacroce, Gambino Family underboss. When Fatico came under intense federal investigation and became inactive, Gotti, despite his lackluster performance as an "earner"—his

---

9. For his aid in killing Castellano, John Gotti named *caporegime* Frank De Ciccio as his underboss. On April 13, 1986, De Ciccio was the victim of a car bombing on a Brooklyn street, reputedly a response to his treachery by Gambino-Castellano kin.

wife once sued him for nonsupport—was placed in charge of the Fatico crew by Dellacroce.

In 1973, in a poorly executed murder, Gotti and his close friend Angelo Ruggiero—a Dellacroce nephew—gunned down the head of an Irish gang from Hell's Kitchen, one of the kidnap-murderers of Carlo Gambino's nephew, Manny Gambino. In a plea bargain, Gotti and Ruggiero received sentences with four-year maximums. Carlo Gambino died in 1976, and succession should have gone to Dellacroce. Instead, before his death, Gambino chose Paul Castellano to succeed him. At year's end, Dellacroce and Castellano met at a private home in Brooklyn and a deal was struck: Castellano would become boss and, in order to appease the Dellacroce faction, Castellano would keep Dellacroce as underboss, just as Gambino had appointed Dellacroce underboss to placate Anastasia stalwarts. The loyal Dellacroce opposed any efforts to move against Castellano.

But the Family now had two factions, one headed by Castellano, the other by Dellacroce. The more sophisticated Castellano faction was immersed in labor and business racketeering, while the more predatory Dellacroce group engaged in hijacking, extortion, loansharking, gambling, and, in a violation of a Castellano edict, drugs. In 1989, Gotti's brother Gene, forty-two, was convicted of drug violations and sentenced to fifty years imprisonment. In fact, before becoming Family boss, drugs were the primary source of John Gotti's income. When one of his crew, Angelo Ruggiero, was indicted for drug trafficking, Gotti feared he and Ruggiero would be killed by Castellano. Soon afterward his mentor, Dellacroce, died of cancer at age seventy-one. Castellano, awaiting trial, failed to attend the funeral and replaced Dellacroce with a loyal aide who lacked real stature—Thomas Bilotti, a vicious forty-five-year-old enforcer. Two weeks later, both were dead. As boss, Gotti's finances changed considerably. His underboss gave him more than $100,000 a month as his percentage of Gambino Family income (Fried 1993). Gotti, a compulsive gambler, lived in a modest home in Howard Beach, Queens—a *defended neighborhood*.

John Gotti represents a distinctly different type of mob boss than his Gambino Family predecessors. A flashy dresser with a high public profile, Gotti has been featured in news stories throughout the world and appears to take delight in his notoriety. This "Capone-like" trait made him an especially attractive target for federal prosecutors. On December 12, 1990, Gotti was indicted for racketeering and murder. He had previously been acquitted at three separate trials in five years, earning the sobriquet "The Teflon Don." This dexterity at avoiding conviction appears to have been aided by several factors: competition between Justice Department officials (Dannen 1992a), a detective on the New York City Police Department's Intelligence Unit who in 1993 pled guilty to selling secrets, and jury tampering (Lubasch 1992)—one juror was convicted of selling his vote (1993). On April 2, 1992, Gotti was found guilty of forty-three federal charges, including six murders, one being that of Paul Castellano. His acting underboss, Frank Locascio, age fifty-nine, was found guilty of racketeering and murder conspiracy charges. On June 23, 1992, both were sentenced to life imprisonment.

Gotti was betrayed by his handpicked underboss, Salvatore ("Sammy Bull") Gravano of Bensonhurst, and his own careless communications. Although he suspected that his conversations were being intercepted, Gotti engaged in incriminating conversations on the telephone and other bugged locations. He was even taped warning others to be guarded in their conversations. Bugs were placed in his headquarters at the Ravenite Social Club, 247 Mulberry Street, in Manhattan's Little Italy. Gravano, born March 12, 1945, is a former stickup man and Army veteran who dropped out of school in the eighth grade. He admitted to participating in nineteen murders, and testified that the Castellano murder had been planned for months after getting informal consent from the Lucchese, Colombo, and Bonanno—but not the Genovese—Families. Gotti's son John, Jr., age twenty-eight in 1992, a captain in the crime Family, has reportedly been acting on his father's behalf during Gotti's imprisonment.

Despite the changes in leadership, the crime group is still referred to as the *Gambino Family*. Its operations extend into upstate New York, New Jersey, and parts of New England.

Reina/Lucchese Family

Gaetano ("Tommy") Reina headed one of the five Families in New York City that "formed spontaneously as Sicilian immigrants settled there" (Bonanno 1983: 84). Bonanno reports that because of the power of Masseria, Reina had to be careful not to offend him, "and generally toed the Masseria line" (1983: 85). At the start of the Castellammarese War, however, Reina began talking (privately) against Masseria: "An informant within Reina's Family relayed these sentiments to Reina's *paesano* from Corleone, Peter Morello. And Morello reported it to Masseria" (Bonanno 1983: 106). On February 26, 1930, Reina was killed by the blast of a sawed-off shotgun. According to Bonanno, Masseria backed one of his own supporters, Joe Pinzola, to head the Reina Family. However, Gaetano Gagliano formed a splinter group and was joined by Thomas Lucchese, who became the underboss of the newly formed Gagliano Family. Gagliano emerged on the side of the victorious Salvatore Maranzano. His leadership of the crime Family lasted until his death in 1953, at which time Lucchese became boss.

Lucchese was born in Palermo, Sicily, in 1900 and came to the United States in 1911. In 1919 he lost his right index finger in a machine-shop accident. His obituary in the *New York Times* stated that the accident "apparently soured him on the workingman's life and steered him into a life of crime" (July 14, 1967: 31). As a result of the accident and his first arrest in 1921 for car theft, Lucchese was nicknamed "Three-Finger Brown"—the policeman who fingerprinted Lucchese was a fan of Mordechi ("Three-Finger") Brown, a pitcher for the Chicago Cubs, and wrote that name down under the alias section of the fingerprint card. Despite the 1921 conviction, he became a

Anthony Accetturo plants a kiss of gratitude on the cheek of defense attorney Michael Critchley following his acquittal on federal racketeering charges.

naturalized citizen in 1943, and in 1949, on the recommendation of the Republican leader of the New York State Senate (Reid and Demaris 1953), Lucchese received a "certificate of good conduct" that restored his right to vote.

Lucchese was active in gambling, particularly numbers and bookmaking in Queens, New York. One of the principal members of his crime Family (and subsequent Family boss himself), Anthony ("Tony Ducks") Corallo,[10] was a major labor racketeer. "Police officials listed eight dress firms in New York City in which Lucchese was a part owner and he had similar holdings in Scranton, Pennsylvania." His firms in New York City were nonunion and, Peterson

---

10. Anthony Corallo received the nickname "Ducks" because of his ability to escape ("duck") assassinations and convictions. During the 1960s this "ability" apparently failed. In 1961 he tried to bribe both a New York State Supreme Court judge and the chief assistant United States attorney for the Eastern District of New York. He received a two-year sentence for his efforts. The case he was trying to fix involved James Marcus, commissioner of the New York City Department of Water, Gas and Electricity, and Carmine De Sapio, head of Tammany Hall.

(1983a: 403) notes, "strangely free from labor troubles." On November 18, 1935, Lucchese was arrested for vagrancy, his last arrest.

Lucchese lived in a luxurious yellow brick ranch house that he constructed in Lido Beach, Long Island. Married in 1927, Lucchese's son Robert is a graduate of the United States Air Force Academy and an Air Force officer. Lucchese's daughter Frances went to Vassar College and later married the son of Carlo Gambino. Lucchese died of natural causes on July 13, 1967.

In recent years, the Lucchese Family has been racked by betrayal, rebellion, and prosecution. When Family boss Vittorio ("Little Vic") Amuso (age fifty-six in 1993) lost control of the New Jersey faction—a crew of about fifteen members headed by Anthony ("Tumac") Accetturo and his son, Tony, Jr.—he declared them outlaws and ordered their execution. Some, including the Accetturos, fled, while others were accepted back into the fold after pledging fealty. In 1993, Accetturo, Sr., and five other members of the New Jersey faction were convicted of murder and racketeering.

By 1990, Amuso was a fugitive. His handpicked acting boss, Alphonse

ANTHONY SALVATORE "GASPIPE" CASSO

Born May 21, 1940, Casso's nickname stems from an earlier career in safecracking. His criminal history dates back to his adolescence in the waterfront section of Red Hook, Brooklyn, where he developed a reputation as a marksman and vicious street brawler. By age twenty-one, Casso was an enforcer on the Brooklyn docks. A close associate of Vic Amuso, Casso subsequently became his underboss. Known for a lavish life-style that included a $500,000 diamond ring and a $1 million house in the Mill Basin section of Brooklyn, Casso is alleged to have had the architect killed rather than pay him a $40,000 fee. He bought $2,000 suits by the dozen, and restaurant tabs of $1000 were not uncommon.

With Amuso's imprisonment in 1991, Casso became acting boss, despite the fact that he was a fugitive from racketeering and murder charges at the time. He was tipped off about an impending indictment in 1990 from a source within law enforcement. After being at large for thirty-two months, Casso was captured without a struggle by FBI agents at his hideaway, a home in suburban Mount Olive, New Jersey. At the home, the FBI found $340,000 in cash and internal FBI documents. During his time as a fugitive, Casso is reported to have ordered the murder of at least eleven persons.

Sources: Selwyn Raab, "'Most Dangerous Mafioso' Left at Helm of Lucchese Crime Family." *New York Times*, November 28, 1992: 14; "FBI Arrests a Mafia Boss in New Jersey." *New York Times*, January 20, 1993: B1, B6; Murray Weiss and Jim Nolan, "Scrub Out! Top Mobster Nabbed in the Shower." *New York Times*, January 20, 1993: 7.

D'Arco, subsequently became a government witness (Marriott 1992). In 1992, Amuso was found guilty on fifty-four counts, including nine murders, and was sentenced to life imprisonment. In what is becoming a pattern in traditional organized crime, leadership was assumed by a most violent capo, Anthony Casso. Despite changes in leadership, the crime Family is still referred to as the *Lucchese Family*.

Profaci/Colombo Family

Joseph Profaci was born in Palermo on October 2, 1897. An ex-convict, he came to the United States in 1922, when Mussolini was chasing *mafiosi*. In the United States, Profaci never served a prison sentence, a remarkable feat for a man who had a crime Family named after him. He did, however, manage to owe the United States $1.5 million in income taxes. And he became the only mob boss to be arrested at OC conclaves both in Cleveland in 1928 and in Apalachin, New York in 1957 (discussed below; Neff 1989).

Profaci owned numerous (at least twenty) legitimate businesses and as the "Olive Oil King" was at one time the largest single importer of olive oil into the United States. In addition to his modest Brooklyn home, he owned a luxurious home in Miami Beach and a hunting lodge ("Profaci Dies of Cancer, Led Feuding Brooklyn Mob" 1962). Bonanno (1983) reports that at the outbreak of the Castellammarese War, Profaci was the boss of his own crime Family. While he sided with Maranzano, his Family did not participate in the conflict: "Maranzano urged Profaci to remain officially neutral and to act as an intermediary with other groups" (1983: 85). His daughter Rosalie married the son of Joseph Bonanno, Salvatore ("Bill").

Although clean shaven, Profaci was clearly a "moustache," faithful to Old World traditions. He was a devoted family man, devoid of any apparent extramarital interests. His profession notwithstanding, Profaci was a faithful churchgoer, a friend of the pastor, and a large contributor to church charities. One of the churches in the Bensonhurst-Bath Beach section of Brooklyn, where he lived, had a statue adorned with a crown of jewels worth several thousand dollars. Some reports indicate that Profaci had been the contributor of the crown. In any event, James ("Bucky") Ammino decided to steal the crown—an outrage that Profaci ordered "corrected." Although the crown was returned, Bucky failed to restore three missing diamonds. His body was subsequently found, and lest the meaning of his demise be misinterpreted, a set of rosary beads was wrapped around his neck (Martin 1963).

The Gallo Brothers

Profaci's traditionalism was viewed as despotic by some members of his crime Family. He apparently demanded a big percentage of all their illegal profits, and he placed "blood" and old friendships above business: relatives and old friends received larger shares of Family opportunities than younger men in his

149

ranks. In 1959, a numbers operator, Frank ("Frankie Shots") Abbatemarco, was murdered on orders from Profaci. The contract was carried out by Joseph ("Joe Jelly") Gioiello, a short, rotund, vicious killer. Gioiello was part of the Gallo brothers crew of the Profaci Family, based in Red Hook, Brooklyn. The Gallo brothers, Larry, Albert ("Kid Blast"), and Joe ("Crazy Joe," b. 1929), expected to receive a large share of Abbatemarco's gambling operations. Instead, Profaci divided it up among friends and relatives. The Gallo crew fumed until February, 1961. Then, in one twenty-four-hour period, they abducted four of Profaci's closest associates, but the boss himself evaded capture. What transpired afterward would rival the Roman plots in the days of the Caesars.

Profaci agreed to be more generous with the Gallo crew. However, several Gallo men secretly went over to the Profaci side, and on August 20, 1961, they lured Larry Gallo to the Sahara Lounge in Brooklyn. At an early hour in the morning, before the lounge had opened for business, Carmine ("The Snake") Persico (who, in 1972, became boss of the Family) and another man placed a rope around Larry's neck and slowly began to squeeze the life out of him. A police sergeant came into lounge apparently only minutes before the victim was about to expire—Larry Gallo had already lost control of his bowels and bladder. The officer noticed Larry's feet sticking out behind the bar, and he saw two men dash from the darkened room out a side door. A patrolman waiting outside attempted to stop the two men and was shot in the face, suffering a wound in the right cheek. Larry survived the ordeal, his neck badly scarred.

Later that day Joe Jelly was "put to sleep with the fishes"—his coat was dumped near the Gallos' South Brooklyn headquarters wrapped around several fresh fish. The "war" was on, but it was a rather one-sided affair; at least twelve men were killed, mostly Gallo loyalists. The Gallo group "took to the mattresses"—that is, they took refuge in their Red Hook headquarters at 49–51 President Street, a block away from the Union Street Seventy-Sixth Police Precinct House. A special squad of New York City detectives headed by Raymond V. Martin (whose book on the subject was published in 1963) was assigned to maintain surveillance of the area. The police probably saved the Gallos from being completely wiped out by Profaci gunmen. During this period, the Gallos were responsible for saving several neighborhood youngsters from a building fire; they joked to television reporters that the police would probably arrest them for arson. In any event the Gallo boys became neighborhood heroes and the news media reported extensively on their exploits.

Gang wars are expensive. It is difficult to earn money if one is in hiding, or spending most of one's time seeking out the enemy while avoiding being killed. The financial condition of the Gallos grew worse. On May 11, 1961, in an effort to replenish income that was dwindling, Joey Gallo attempted to extort money from the owner of several bars. The victim refused to pay, so "Crazy Joe" performed his best "Richard Widmark," explaining to the businessman that he could meet with an "unfortunate accident." It was no accident that two detectives were in the bar and Gallo received a lengthy prison sentence. In 1968, Larry Gallo died of cancer.

Joseph Colombo

In 1962, Profaci died of natural causes, and his place was taken by Joseph Magliocco, his brother-in-law. Magliocco died of natural causes at the end of 1963, and his place was taken by Joseph Colombo, Sr. A truce was finally arranged with the Gallo faction in 1966. Ralph Salerno (Salerno and Tompkins 1969) reports that one condition of the truce was that several top Gallo men were "made," inducted as members of the Colombo Family.

While in prison, Crazy Joe continued to "raise hell." He so annoyed some of his fellow inmates in Attica that several of them threw him off a tier. Transferred to another prison, Joey befriended many black inmates, several of whom he recruited for his Brooklyn organization. In May 1971, Gallo was released from prison, and the intrigue reached new heights.

There appears to be general agreement on how Joseph Colombo was chosen to succeed Magliocco as boss of the Profaci Family. A plot was afoot to kill two crime Family chieftains—Carlo Gambino and Thomas Lucchese—and Colombo informed Gambino of the plot. Some accounts say that the person who was supposed to effect the murders was Colombo, on behalf of Joseph Bonanno, boss of his own crime Family. Salerno (Salerno and Tompkins 1969) reports that Bonanno and Joseph Magliocco, underboss of the Profaci Family, were behind the plot. Gay Talese (1971) places responsibility on Magliocco, and Bonanno (1983) denies any involvement. Instead he blames his cousin, Buffalo crime boss Stefano Magaddino, for "disseminating the story that Joe Bonanno wanted to kill Gambino and Lucchese" (1983: 235). In any event, Magliocco died, and Joseph Colombo was chosen by the "commission" to head the Profaci Family (Bonanno 1983).

In 1970, Colombo founded the Italian-American Civil Rights League and led in the daily picketing of New York FBI headquarters, generating a great deal of media coverage. The league soon became a vehicle for protesting about discrimination against, and negative stereotyping of, Italian-Americans. Colombo and the league succeeded in having all references to the "Mafia" or "Cosa Nostra" deleted from the script of *The Godfather* as well as the television series *The FBI*. Attorney General John Mitchell and Governor Nelson Rockefeller ordered their employees to refrain from using such references.

The league raised large sums of money through dues and testimonial dinners, and held an "Annual Unity Day" rally, which in 1970 drew about 50,000 persons to Columbus Circle in Manhattan. Nicholas Gage (1972: 172) notes that the "rally conspicuously closed stores in neighborhoods controlled by the Mafia: New York's waterfront was virtually shut down . . . and almost every politician in the city joined" the 1970 celebration. There were articles in newspapers and magazines about Colombo and the league, and the boss began to portray himself as a civil rights leader who was simply misunderstood by the police.

Reports state that other crime Family bosses, particularly Carlo Gambino, did not look favorably on the activities of Colombo and the league, either because Colombo failed to share the financial fruits or because they resented

151

the publicity—or both. At the second Annual Unity Day rally on June 28, 1971, only an estimated 10,000 persons were in attendance. While reporters and news photographers crowded around the podium, a lone black man wearing a camera and apparently presenting himself as a newsman approached Colombo, pulled out a gun, and shot him in the head and neck. The gunman, twenty-four-year-old Jerome A. Johnson, was immediately shot to death: "Johnson's killer escaped as professionally as he had carried out his mission, shooting Johnson three times even as police clustered around" (Gage 1972: 171). Colombo remained paralyzed until his death in 1978.

Interest focused on Jerome Johnson. He was never connected to organized crime, although he had a criminal record and was known as a violent person. Suspicion immediately centered on Joey Gallo; he had reason to dislike the Family boss and was known to have as his associates black criminals. The day after Colombo was shot, the *New York Times* (Gage 1971b: 21) stated: "When Joseph Gallo was released in May from prison he was reported to have complained that the lot of his faction within the family had not improved much in his absence. He was also said to have questioned Colombo's involvement in the Italian-Civil Rights League as drawing undue attention to the family."

With Colombo out of the way, and acting boss Carmine Persico in prison, Gallo men began moving in on Colombo activities and completely took over the South Brooklyn waterfront (Goddard 1974). On April 7, 1972, Joey Gallo was celebrating his birthday with a late-night stop at Umberton's Clam House in Lower Manhattan, territory of the Genovese and Colombo Families. The restaurant was owned by Mattie ("The Horse") Ianniello of the Genovese Family. With Joey was his new bride, her daughter, bodyguard Pete ("The Greek") Diapoulos, Pete's girlfriend, and Joey's sister. Three Colombo gunmen entered the restaurant and opened fire, killing Joey and wounding his body-guard, who sought to return the fire (Diapoulos and Linakis 1976; Goddard 1974).[11]

Despite the death of Joseph Colombo, the group he headed is still referred to as the *Colombo Family*, and intra-familial violence has continued. Persico, who is in prison serving combined sentences of one hundred years, attempted to engineer a shift in leadership to his son Alphonse. Victor J. Orena, who had been handpicked by Persico to head the Family, refused to step aside. Since 1991 the two factions have been shooting at the other's partisans. On November 3, 1992, for example, shortly after 7:00 P.M., in Queens, New York, four to six men wearing masks jumped from a stolen van and opened fire with shotguns and semiautomatic weapons into a 1992 Lincoln Town Car. They killed the fifty-one-year-old driver and wounded his two passengers, ages forty-seven and fifty-one. The victims were carpenter union officials associated with the Orena faction. On December 21, 1992, the then-fifty-eight-year-old Orena was

---

11. Tourists reportedly descended on Umberto's as a result of its notoriety. In 1986, Matty Ianniello was imprisoned for skimming the restaurant's profits (Hampson 1993).

convicted in Brooklyn federal court of RICO violations and murder. He received a life sentence. Nine days later, Gregory Scarpa, a *caporegime* and Persico loyalist (who is suffering from AIDS, the result of hernia surgery) was ambushed near his Brooklyn home, receiving wounds in the face and left eye. Two associates were also wounded in the attack (Raab 1992c). More than a dozen people have been slain, including Joseph Scopo, age forty-seven, under-boss of the Orena faction. In 1993, he was gunned down by automatic weapons in front of his Ozone Park home (James 1993). Clearly, while many report the impending demise of traditional organized crime, there are still persons willing to kill for its favors.

Bonanno Family

We know more about Joseph ("Don Peppino") Bonanno than most other crime figures because he was the subject of the biography by Gay Talese (1971) and authored his own autobiography (Bonanno and Lalli 1983). Bonanno states that his father, Salvatore ("Don Turridu"), was the head of the Bonanno clan in Castellammarese del Golfo and a "man of honor" (*mafioso*). Salvatore left Sicily for the United States with his wife and three-year-old son, Giuseppe, in 1908 to avoid prosecution (Bonanno does not say for what crime). In 1911, at the request of his brothers in Castellammarese, Don Turridu returned home with his wife and child. He died in 1915 of a heart attack.

Bonanno states that he was attending the nautical preparatory school in Trapani when Mussolini came to power. He claims that his anti-Fascist activities forced him to leave, and he entered the United States in 1924. Bonanno quickly found help and refuge among friends and family from Castellammarese. His cousin Stefano Magaddino was already a criminal power in Buffalo, and Bonanno eventually became involved in bootlegging with the Castellammarese clan in Brooklyn under Salvatore Maranzano. During the Masseria-Maranzano conflict, Bonanno became an aide to Maranzano and was seen as a leader of the Castellammarese group arrayed against Joe the Boss. After Maranzano's murder, a meeting of Family members was held, and Bonanno was elected "Father" (a term he uses for "boss") of what became known as the Bonanno Family. Bonanno successfully parlayed income received as boss into legitimate enterprises such as garment and cheese manufacturing.

Although he was arrested numerous times, Bonanno did not serve a prison term until 1983. In 1945 he was convicted of violating rent-control laws and paid a $450 fine. In 1959, a federal grand jury indicted him for conspiracy to obstruct justice in the aftermath of the (in)famous meeting of crime bosses in Apalachin, New York, in 1957. In that year, events such as the attempt on the life of Frank Costello and the murder of Albert Anastasia sparked a top-level conference, held at Apalachin, New York.

In 1963 came the alleged plot against Gambino and Lucchese, and Bonanno sought, and was denied, Canadian citizenship. In February 1964, while Bonanno was still in Canada, crime Family *capiregime* chose his son Bill

THE APALACHIN CRIME CONFERENCE

In November of 1957, New York state police sergeant Edgar Croswell became suspicious of the activities at the home of Joseph M. Barbara, Sr., whom he knew was an "organized crime figure" —actually boss of the Northeastern Pennsylvania crime Family. Barbara was from Castellammarese del Golfo and had become the wealthy owner of a soda-pop distributing business and a bottling plant outside of Endicott, New York. His estate in Apalachin was about six miles away. While investigating a bad-check case at a hotel in the area, the sergeant discovered Barbara's son making room reservations. He later noted a number of expensive automobiles with out-of-state license plates parked at the Barbara estate. "There was nothing Croswell could legally do about Barbara's visitors, but by Saturday, November 14, 1957, with what he figured to be as many as seventy guests assembled, Croswell could no longer stifle his curiosity. He organized what few deputies he had and conducted a raid on Barbara's house, one merely, as he explained later, to see if anything criminal was going on or if Barbara's guests were wanted on any outstanding warrants" (Brashler 1977: 144). Salerno (Salerno and Tompkins 1969: 298) states that "within minutes dozens of well-dressed men ran out of the house and across the fields in all directions." Using roadblocks and reinforcements, the police reportedly took sixty-three men into custody, although this figure is disputed. Bonanno was reported to have been at the meeting, and his driver's license was confiscated. However, he claims not to have been there, but to have been attending a private meeting in a nearby motel. Frederic Sondern (1959: 36) reports: "One by one they were summoned to Sergeant Croswell's office, gave their names and addresses, took off their shoes, emptied their pockets as troopers searched and watched." Those arrested included Joseph Profaci, Carlo Gambino, Paul Castellano, Vito Genovese, Philadelphia crime boss Joseph Ida and his underboss, Dominick Olivetto, and Russell Bufalino. (Russell Bufalino, born in Sicily in 1903, became Joseph Barbara's underboss. When Barbara died in 1959, Bufalino became boss of the Northeastern Pennsylvania Family. According to the Pennsylvania Crime Commission, Bufalino retired. His Family is no longer active.)

In 1959, Bonanno and twenty-six other leading OC figures, after refusing to answer questions as to the purpose of the meeting in Apalachin, were indicted for conspiracy and obstruction of justice. Bonanno's case was separated from the others when he suffered a heart attack. After a three-week trial, a jury found twenty defendants guilty of conspiracy. The verdict, however, was overturned in 1960 by the U.S. Court of Appeals; the court concluded that the people at the Barbara estate had been taken into custody, detained, and searched without probable cause that a crime had or was being committed: "[I]n America we still respect the dignity of the individual, and even an unsavory character is not to be imprisoned except on definite proof of specific crime" (*United States v. Bufalino* et al. 285 F.2d. 408).

Sources: William Brashler, *The Don: The Life and Death of Sam Giancana*. New York: Harper and Row, 1977; Ralph Salerno and John S. Tompkins, *The Crime Confederation*. Garden City, NY: Doubleday, 1969.

consigliere. The elevation of the young Bonanno was opposed from within and without the Bonanno Family. This act, coupled with the plot against Gambino and Lucchese, resulted in a "summons" for Joseph Bonanno to appear before the "commission," of which he was one of the nine members; Bonanno declined. On October 21, 1964, Bonanno and his attorney were standing in front of a luxury apartment house in Manhattan, where they had sought shelter from the rain. Bonanno describes what followed (1983: 260): "Two men grabbed me from behind by each arm and immediately forced me toward the nearby street corner. . . . 'Come on, Joe, my boss wants you.' . . . As they rushed toward the corner, I heard Maloney [Bonanno's attorney] shouting after us. He was saying something about my being his client and they couldn't take me away like that. A pistol shot pinged the sidewalk. Maloney retreated."

Bonanno reports that he was kidnapped by two of his cousins, the son and brother of Stefano Magaddino, and held in a rural farmhouse for more than six weeks. Federal officials called it a hoax, an effort by Bonanno to avoid appearing before a grand jury investigating organized crime. Bonanno states that following his release, he remained in hiding in his Tucson home for more than a year. In the meantime, a revolt broke out within the Bonanno Family, led by *caporegime* Gasper DiGregorio, Bill Bonanno's godfather and best man at the wedding of Fay and Joseph Bonanno.

On January 28, 1966, in an effort to reestablish unity, Bill Bonanno and several Family members loyal to his father went to Troutman Street in Brooklyn to meet with DiGregorio. The unity meeting turned out to be an ambush, and the young Bonanno narrowly escaped in an exchange of gunfire. On May 18, 1966, Joseph Bonanno reappeared and the revolt (dubbed the "Banana War") raged on. DiGregorio eventually withdrew, and the commission turned the Family over to Paul Sciacca. Joseph Bonanno retired to his Tucson home, leaving a three-man committee to fill the leadership until the "loyalists" could select a new boss. In the early 1970s, Philip Rastelli, who was subsequently convicted of labor racketeering, became boss. In 1991, at age seventy-three, Rastelli died of cancer.

In 1979, a federal grand jury indicted Bonanno and a commodities dealer for obstructing justice. During the fourteen-week nonjury trial in 1980, the prosecutor maintained that Bonanno and his codefendant worked together to keep the records of several businesses from the grand jury. The FBI collected evidence by tapping Bonanno's telephone and retrieving his garbage for four years. The defense objected to the introduction of notes in Sicilian fished out of Bonanno's garbage, contending that their translation into English was in doubt because there are no English equivalents to many of the terms used. Nevertheless, Bonanno was found guilty and sentenced to a term of one year. He entered the federal prison at Terminal Island at the end of 1983.

Despite Bonanno's retirement, the crime Family he headed is still referred to as the Bonanno Family, something which Bonanno decried: "It is improper for people to still refer to this Family as the Bonanno Family. It stopped being

THE FIVE FAMILIES

While the crime Families of New York have been subjected to intense investigation and successful prosecution, they have successfully recruited new members. Precision with respect to the number of "made" members is difficult, but these approximations reveal the relative strength of each.

Gambino: 400–500
Genovese: 300–400
Lucchese: 125
Colombo: 100
Bonanno: 75

the Bonanno Family when I retired. In Sicily, a Family is sometimes likened to a *cosca*—an artichoke. The Family members are like the artichoke leaves and the Family is like the central stem on which they all hang. Remove the central stem and all you have is a lot of separate leaves. When I left New York to retire, all the separate leaves had to find themselves another stem."

Organized crime in New York remains unique—it is the only city with numerous traditional crime Families operating. In the next chapter we will examine the history of organized crime in Chicago and Philadelphia.

REVIEW QUESTIONS

1. Why is it difficult to present an accurate history of organized crime?
2. What was the relationship between Tammany Hall, the police, and vice entrepreneurs?
3. What was the relationship between Tammany Hall and the gangs of New York?
4. How did Prohibition change the relationship between Tammany, the vice entrepreneurs, and the gangs?
5. Why was Arnold Rothstein so important for the development of organized crime in New York?
6. What was the broker role that enabled Lucky Luciano to gain important stature in organized crime?
7. What was the "Black Hand"?
8. What factors led to the prominence of Italians in organized crime in New York?
9. What was it that permitted the small Mafia gangs of New York to operate outside of their ghetto neighborhoods and in the wider society?
10. What was the outcome of the Castellammarese War?

4

The History of
Organized Crime:
Part Two

Traditional organized crime in the United States has been considerably weakened by prosecutions and a declining applicant pool—an issue that will be discussed at the end of this chapter, along with ethnic succession. Outside of New York, there remain several centers of strength; in particular, Chicago and Philadelphia.

CHICAGO

When Chicago was incorporated as a town on August 5, 1833, it was little more than an Indian trading post. The following month a peace treaty led to the voluntary removal of the Chippewa, Ottawa, and Potawatomi Indians from the region, and large-scale immigration into Chicago began. Immigration, usually by steamship, increased with the breaking of ground for the Lake Michigan-Illinois River Canal in 1836. Land speculation was rampant. The population boom led the Illinois legislature to pass an act incorporating Chicago as a city in 1837, and extending its corporate limits to about ten square miles. A census that same year revealed a population of 4,170. In the spring of 1837, however, a depression and banking panic led the real estate market to drop, and the state of Illinois went bankrupt. It was not until 1845 that the city of Chicago began to boom again. The canal opened in 1848, and by 1852 the first railroad had rolled into Chicago. By 1855 it was the terminus of ten railroad trunk lines and eleven branch lines, and was the country's greatest meat-packing center and grain port (Asbury 1942).

The boom naturally attracted adventurers, gamblers, pimps, prostitutes, and other undesirables—pickpockets, burglars, and hold-up men. A vice district known as The Sands developed north of the city along the lake. It was raided and destroyed by Mayor "Long" John Wentworth (he stood six feet, seven inches) in 1857. "Judging from the frequency of the raids which the police made on brothels during the following six months," noted John Flinn in 1877, "it appears plain that the immediate effect of the [Wentworth] raid was to scatter the former denizens of the sandy lake shore throughout the city, and the newspapers commented upon the result at the time in anything but complimentary terms" (1973: 83). The Civil War brought prosperity to Chicago, but it also brought thousands of soldiers and the gambling establishments and brothels that were patronized by large numbers of unattached young men on military leave. At this time, Chicago became known as "the wickedest city in the United States" (Asbury 1942: 61). Even the great Chicago fire in 1871 would not change this. But it was not until Mike McDonald became established that vice in Chicago could be said to be truly *organized*.

Mike McDonald

Humbert Nelli (1969) traces the origins of organized crime in Chicago to the election of 1873, in which Michael Cassius McDonald backed Harvey D. Colvin for mayor. "In the mayoralty election of 1873, Mike McDonald, the gambling boss of Chicago, demonstrated that under effective leadership the gamblers, liquor interests, and brothel keepers could be welded into a formidable political power" (Peterson 1963: 31). At the time there were three thousand saloons in the city (Asbury 1942), and the election pitted the "reformers" of the Law and Order Party, who insisted on the enforcement of Sunday closing "blue laws," against the People's Party, organized by McDonald, whose ranks were swelled by Irish and German immigrants (Flinn 1973).

"King Mike," as he became known, was born in Niagara Falls, New York, around 1840 and left for Detroit when he was about fifteen. He held a number of menial jobs and spent a great deal of time gambling, working the trains between New Orleans and Chicago. At the outbreak of the Civil War, McDonald organized a gang of bounty hunters who "recruited" men for the various Union regiments. In 1867 he opened a gambling den on Dearborn Street, which was destroyed in the fire of 1871. Early in 1872, McDonald bought a bar in the heart of downtown Chicago. "Our Store" (better known as "The Store") became the city's largest liquor and gambling house. In the lower floors, Mexican onyx formed the wainscotting in the barrooms. One huge bar was made of genuine mahogany, and the floor was a Roman mosaic. It was frequented by politicians who utilized McDonald as a "bagman," an intermediary for the collection of bribes (Klatt 1983).

Wayne Klatt (1983: 30) points out that "until McDonald opened shop, gambling had been rather unorganized in Chicago—and so were politics. The city was fairly evenly divided between Democrats and Republicans; mayoral elections were every two years; and everything was a mess. The Democrats were interested only in winning aldermanic seats and let the mayor be damned.

The history of gambling and politics in late nineteenth-century Chicago is largely the history of Mike McDonald. Here, "King Mike" feeds Chicago's young Tammany cub from bottles labeled "Political Pap" and "Corruption Tonic."

McDonald changed this by backing gambler Harvey D. Colvin. "When Colvin won the election," notes June Sawyers (1988a: 10), "McDonald had Chicago in his back pocket." From then on until his death in 1907, McDonald controlled mayors, congressmen, and senators. His newspaper, the *Globe*, often influenced the outcome of elections, and he also owned the elevated railroad line in Chicago (Wendt and Kogan 1974).

The history of gambling and politics in Chicago from the great fire until the middle 1890s, notes Herbert Asbury (1942: 142), is largely the history of Mike McDonald: "McDonald, bounty-broker, saloon and gambling-house keeper, eminent politician, and dispenser of cheating privileges; any gambler or swindler who wished to operate outside of the red-light districts had to 'see Mike' and arrange to pay over a large proportion of his stealings for division among the police, various city officials, and the members of McDonald's syndicate. As a close friend and chief advisor of Harvey D. Colvin and later [Mayor] Carter Harrison, Sr., and as a leader of the Cook County Democracy for a dozen years, Mike McDonald was the boss of Chicago."

Reform hit Chicago in 1893 at a time when a rich and powerful McDonald had lost interest in maintaining his vast empire. His personal life had deteriorated. His wife, Mary Noonan, shot and wounded a police officer who was snooping around the Store's third floor living quarters. She was acquitted, ran off with a minstrel singer, and then took up with a Catholic priest whom McDonald had designated as her personal chaplain (Sawyers 1988a). In 1898, at age sixty-six, McDonald renounced his Catholic faith and secured a divorce to marry Dora Feldman, a twenty-three-year-old divorcee. He built a mansion for his bride and they lived together until 1907, when she shot her lover, fifteen years her junior, during a heated argument. Dora told the police of her affection for the deceased and her dislike of her husband. McDonald never recovered from the shock of her revelations, and the gambling-political empire he ruled over fell apart. His political mantle was picked up by Michael Kenna and John Coughlin; gambling went to Mont Tennes. McDonald died on August 9, 1907; Dora was tried and acquitted in 1908 (Asbury 1942; Sawyers 1988a).

Michael "Hinky Dink" Kenna and "Bathhouse" John Coughlin

McDonald's Store was located in the Levee District of Chicago's notorious First Ward. With his backing, a "Mutt and Jeff" team became the political "Lords of the Levee": John ("Bathhouse," or simply "The Bath") Coughlin, a powerfully built six-footer, and Michael ("Hinky Dink") Kenna, a diminutive organizational genius. Born in the First Ward to Irish immigrant parents in 1860, Coughlin began his political career as a rubber in the exclusive Palmer Baths, where he met wealthy and powerful politicians and businessmen. These contacts helped him when he opened his own bathhouse, and the others that soon followed. Among his customers were important politicians, and "The Bath" (a nickname he enjoyed) quickly became a Democratic precinct captain and president of the First Ward Democratic Club.

On April 5, 1892, Coughlin was elected alderman from the First Ward, one of the thirty-five city wards. The First Ward, in addition to the Levee, contained the city's central business district, "The Loop" (so-called because of the elevated train line circling the area). The city council that Coughlin entered was literally selling out the city of Chicago. The "boodles," schemes through which city privileges were sold, made the three-dollar-a-meeting alderman's position quite lucrative. "The irksome aspect of the boodling," note Lloyd Wendt and Herman Kogan (1974: 34), "was not only that the vicious system corrupted the whole of Chicago politics but that the city gained from the passage of boodle ordinances hardly a cent in compensation. Even the grafting aldermen . . . actually were being paid only a small fraction of the real worth of the privileges they were selling. Big business was the beneficiary of this system, for it needed such favors to expand and grow rich."

Michael Kenna was born in the First Ward in 1858. His nickname, "Hinky Dink," may have been a reference to his small stature or, some maintain, may allude to a water-hole in which he swam as a young boy. After working as a newsboy for the *Chicago Tribune*, Kenna went to a booming mining town in Colorado where he worked for two years as a circulation manager. When he returned home, Kenna became a successful saloonkeeper (despite being a teetotaler) and, of course, a politician. He worked hard in First Ward Democratic politics as a saloon-based precinct captain, and eventually became friendly with John "The Bath" Coughlin. With Kenna as the mastermind, the two men organized the vice entrepreneurs of the First Ward, established a legal fund, and forged an alliance with Mayor Carter Harrison. Eventually, they "found themselves in possession of a thriving little syndicate" (Wendt and Kogan 1974: 81).

After Mayor Harrison was murdered by a disgruntled job seeker, "The Bath" and "The Hink" provided his successor, John Hopkins, with his margin of victory. When a depression swept the country in the winter of 1893, Kenna provided care for 8,000 homeless and destitute men who did not forget this kindness. They registered in the First Ward and were brought back for each election. Coughlin and Kenna were also assisted by the police of the ward and the Quincy Street Boys, who included some of the toughest and most feared hoodlums of the First Ward. In fact, notes John Landesco writing in 1929, the use of street gangs in politics became widespread in Chicago (1968: 184–85): "The young of the immigrant group, beginning with the child at play in the street, were assimilated uncritically into all of the traditions of the neighborhoods in which they lived. Street gangs were their heritage, conflict between races and nationalities often made them necessary—conflict and assimilation went on together. The politician paid close attention to them, nurturing them with favors and using them for his own purposes. Gang history always emphasizes this political nurture. Gangs often became political clubs."

The ability of Coughlin and Kenna to deliver the vote was their key to power. Majorities in the First Ward were so overwhelming that they could affect city, county, and even state elections. As their power grew, it became necessary to be "licensed" by Kenna and Coughlin to do business in the First Ward. But reform was also making headway. In time, many of the boodlers were defeated, and the Republicans became a majority in the council. In fact, when the council was expanded to two aldermen per ward, Kenna ran for the second slot, but the Republicans beat him in his first run for public office. Undaunted, Kenna and Coughlin responded by organizing the Annual First Ward Democratic Ball. Solicitors from the organization visited each saloon, gambling house, and bordello selling tickets, and the affair netted the pair $25,000 for their political war chest. But the ball was outrageous, even for the First Ward. It was held in an armory, and all of the denizens of the underworld attended. Prostitutes dressed in their most outrageous outfits mingled with policemen and politicians. Each year the balls grew bawdier until 1910; in that year "the Roman Catholic archbishop threatened to denounce the ball from the pulpits of Catholic churches, [and] Mayor Fred Busse finally issued a ban against it" (Sawyers, 1987: 7).

In 1897, Kenna and Coughlin skillfully engineered the Democratic nomination of Carter Henry Harrison (the younger), son of the murdered mayor. In the First Ward, they delivered a vote of five to one, and Kenna was elected to the city council, defeating the Republican incumbent 4,374 to 1,181. That year Tammany boss Richard Croker recruited Kenna to help elect Robert A. Van Wyck mayor. The Hink travelled to New York, and Van Wyck overwhelmed his opposition. In 1901 Kenna was reelected to the council 6,191 to 502 (split among three opponents). When Harrison was reelected in a close contest, the First Ward supplied more than half of his margin of victory. When Harrison decided not to stand for reelection in 1904, the Democrats, with wholehearted support from the First Ward, elected Judge Edward F. Dunne, and Kenna was reelected 6,006 to 656 (split among three opponents). Coughlin and Kenna, however, broke with Dunne and attempted to engineer the nomination for Carter Harrison. Dunne was renominated nevertheless, only to go down in defeat with the delayed backing of the First Ward, where he barely received a plurality of 751 votes. Republican Fred Busse became mayor.

Busse did not prove to be much of a reformer, at least not as far as the First Ward was concerned. He acted only after being placed under considerable pressure by the Women's Christian Temperance Union and the Church Federation. But Coughlin and Kenna were busy planning the political return of Carter Harrison. He defeated the former mayor, Dunne, in the Democratic primary by a citywide margin of only 1,556—his majority in the First Ward was 2,424—and went on to defeat Republican Charles Merriam. Merriam, an alderman and professor at the University of Chicago, wrote some years later (1929: 21) that Harrison, while not a leader of reform, "on the whole prevented the drift of the city into the hands of the spoilsmen of the worst type." In fact, Harrison, to the consternation of Coughlin and Kenna, began to ally himself with reformers and moved against the Levee. Citizen vice-crusaders invaded the area, and the Republican state's attorney, denied renomination, moved relentlessly against gambling houses and brothels of the Levee. This encouraged Harrison to become even more vigorous, which cost the mayor vital support of the First Ward.

In the Democratic primary of 1915, Harrison was opposed by Robert M. Sweitzer, the county clerk, who was backed by the Democratic organization including The Bath and The Hink. Sweitzer won the First Ward 6,105 to 1,098 and swept the rest of the city. He was opposed in the general election by Republican William Hale Thompson.

William Hale Thompson

William Hale ("Big Bill") Thompson began his political career as a reformer, backed by the nonpartisan Municipal Voters' League in a successful race for alderman from the Second Ward in 1900. He was "a towering athlete with a snaggled front tooth who had brought glory to the Chicago Athletic Association in half a dozen sports" (Kobler 1971: 55). His father was a wealthy real estate dealer, but the young Thompson (born 1865) preferred the life of a cowboy and spent much of his youth out West—as mayor he often sported cowboy hats. Thompson was a gifted orator—to call him demagogic would not be an exaggeration—who vilified real and imagined enemies such as the British and the king of England. Such attacks gained him the support of German and Irish voters. In 1902 he was elected to the Cook County Board of Commissioners. His victory over Sweitzer in 1915 was based on his demagogic appeal. In German neighborhoods he attacked the British; in German-hating Polish neighborhoods he attacked the Germans; in Irish areas he attacked the British; and when addressing Protestant audiences he warned that a vote for Sweitzer was a vote for the pope. He promised the reformers strict enforcement of the gambling laws, and he promised the gamblers an open town. Thompson received strong support in the black wards, and many Harrison Democrats deserted the party to support the Republican.

Merriam (1929: 22) notes that with the election of Thompson, "The spoils system swept over the city like a noxious blight, and city hall became a symbol for corruption and incompetence." Asbury (1942: 309) points out that "during the last few months of Mayor Harrison's final term Chicago was probably as free from organized vice as at any time in its history." This would change dramatically with the election of Big Bill Thompson. John Kobler (1971: 57) notes that "within six months he had violated every campaign promise but one. He did keep Chicago wide open." Despite these excesses, Big Bill was reelected in 1919 (Nash 1981: 242): "His 1919 campaign was all banner and slogan. Thompson organized the Chicago Boosters Club which put up huge posters everywhere reading: 'A booster is better than a knocker.' He extorted more than $1 million from business leaders for his war chest—he said it was 'to help publicize Chicago'—by threatening not to renew their licenses. He led dozens of marches down the main streets while his paid henchmen gave out the roaring chant, 'All hats off to our mayor, Big Bill the Builder.' "

In 1923, with Prohibition in full swing, and despite the support of Al Capone, Thompson was defeated by reform-minded William E. Dever, a judge and "by Chicago standards a decent man" (Royko 1971: 34). In 1927, running on a pledge to let the liquor flow again in Chicago, Big Bill was swept back into office for a third term. Mike Royko (1971: 35) states: "As much as Chicagoans wanted reform, they wanted their bootleg gin more, so after four years of Dever, they returned Thompson to power." In 1931, Thompson was defeated by Anton J. Cermak, the founder of what has since been called the Chicago "machine."

Mont Tennes

Mont Tennes inherited much of the gambling empire left by Mike McDonald. Writing in 1929, John Landesco, an investigator for the Illinois Association for Criminal Justice, stated (1968: 45): "The complete life history of one man, were it known in every detail, would disclose practically all there is to know about syndicated gambling as a phase of organized crime in Chicago in the last quarter century. That man is *Mont Tennes*." By 1901 Tennes dominated gambling on the city's North Side, and by 1904 he appeared as the backer of several hundred handbooks, becoming the major operator in Chicago racetrack betting (Asbury 1942). In 1907 he secured control of the wire service that transmitted the results of horse races throughout the country. Every bookmaker was dependent on the service. The wire service utilized operatives with

ANTON CERMAK

Anton Cermak was born in Kladno, Czechoslovakia, in 1873, and was brought to the United States when he was a year old. Like his father, he worked as a coal miner before moving to Chicago in 1889, where he obtained a job as a railroad brakeman. Cermak became a member of a saloon-centered gang of young Bohemians and excelled in the group's two major interests—drinking and fighting. He later opened his own business and prospered, becoming a Democratic precinct captain and head of the "United Societies," a group representing liquor interests who were opposed to Sunday closing laws. In 1902 he was elected to the state assembly, and in 1921 became president of the Cook County Board of Commissioners and a wealthy man. Mike Royko (1971: 36) notes that Cermak "had sense to count up all the Irish votes, then he counted all the Italians, Jews, Germans, Poles and Bohemians." Cermak concluded that Irish domination of the Cook County Democratic Party did not make numerical sense. He organized instead an ethnically balanced slate of candidates and put together "the most powerful political machine in Chicago history." That machine ended the political career of Bill Thompson.

Harold Gosnell (1977) reports that Cermak was deeply involved with bootlegging interests, and Kenneth Allsop (1968: 217) states that while Thompson's organization was corrupt, Cermak "systematized grand larceny." Fletcher Dobyns (1932: ix) reported that Cermak reached his position of wealth and power by joining with a group of men who "organized the denizens of the underworld and their patrons, political job holders and their dependents and friends, those seeking privileges and immunities, and grafters of every type." Alex Gottfried (1962), on the other hand, in his extensive biography of Cermak, portrays him as a dynamic and hardworking public figure: an honest man who literally went from "rags to riches" and power in accord with the American tradition of Horatio Alger.

On February 15, 1933, before a large crowd gathered in Miami's Bayfront Park to greet President-elect Franklin D. Roosevelt, Cermak, who was sitting next to Roosevelt, was shot by Guiseppe Zangara, an Italian immigrant residing in Hackensack, New Jersey. Shortly after he was arrested, Zangara was quoted as saying, "I'd kill every president." In his pockets he had several local newspaper clippings announcing Roosevelt's visit to Miami (Hagerty 1933: 1).

Sources: Mike Royko, *Boss: Richard J. Daley of Chicago*. New York: Dutton, 1971; Kenneth Allsop: *The Bootleggers: The Story of Prohibition*. New Rochelle, NY: Arlington House, 1968; Fletcher Dobyns, *The Underworld of American Politics*. New York: Fletcher Dobyns, 1932; Alex Gottfried, *Boss Cermak of Chicago*. Seattle: University of Washington Press, 1962; James A. Hagerty, "Assassin Fires into Roosevelt Party at Miami; President-elect Uninjured; Mayor Cermak and 4 Others Wounded." *New York Times*, February 16, 1933: 1; Harold Gosnell, *Machine Politics: The Chicago Model*. Chicago: University of Chicago Press, 1977 [1937].

Chicago Organized Crime Figures

Mike McDonald

John Coughlin

Michael Kenna

William Thompson

Anton Cermak

James Colosimo

Johnny Torrio

Chicago Organized Crime Figures

Al Capone

Jack Guzik

Edward O'Donnell

Frankie Yale

Bugs Moran

Frank Nitti

Anthony Accardo

Sam Giancana

binoculars whose instant reports on races were transmitted over phone and telegraph lines. Without the wire service, a bookmaker was vulnerable to "past-posting"—the act of placing a bet after the race was already over and the winner determined. The swindler would set up a relay system to a confederate, who quickly placed a bet on a horse that had already won. The bookmaker would accept the bet because regular channels had not informed him that the race had even started.

When some bookmakers balked at paying Tennes for the service, he instigated an outbreak of violence and police raids. In retaliation, while walking with his wife, Tennes was attacked and badly beaten. Tennes responded with stepped-up police raids and bombings. By 1909, he had absolute control over racetrack gambling in Chicago. "The Tennes ring at this time established systematic exclusion. Anyone wishing to enter the gambling business had to apply to the ring. The man and the location would be investigated, the leading gamblers in the city would be asked to approve the applicant, and if disapproved he would be placed upon the 'dead list'" (Landesco 1968: 54). Tennes paid the Payne Telegraphy Service of Cincinnati, politicians, and the police; gamblers who paid Tennes received race results immediately and protection from police raids. The Tennes syndicate paid half of the money lost to betters who won from bookmakers, and received 50 percent of net receipts after racing sheets were balanced each day. Tennes' agents made rounds of subscribers checking betting sheets.

Tennes eventually established his own wire service, the General News Bureau, and a struggle ensued with the older Payne News Service. Disclosures resulting from the feud revealed that Tennes "had risen from king of Chicago gamblers to czar of all the race track gambling in the United States and Canada." His combine had a grip on the police in twenty American cities and enforced its dictates with dynamite. Cities from New York to San Francisco, and from Detroit to San Antonio paid for the Tennes wire service, which involved eighteen telephone and telegraph companies (Landesco 1968: 59).

With the advent of Prohibition, the level of violence in organized crime increased dramatically. Tennes sold his service to both George ("Bugs"—for his sudden rages) Moran and his rival, Al Capone. In the end, Tennes became an associate of Jimmie Mondi, the Capone organization manager for gambling operations. Tennes withdrew from this "shotgun marriage" and retired about 1927, a millionaire (A. Smith 1962).

From Colosimo to Torrio to Capone

Like Mont Tennes, John Coughlin and Michael Kenna would soon feel the power of gangsterism in the First Ward. With William Hale Thompson in charge of city hall, the power of The Bath and Hinky Dink was reduced considerably. Political-police protection now had to be negotiated directly from "the hall"—individual Democratic aldermen had little or no influence with Big Bill. One of their precinct captains, a man who had aided Coughlin and

Kenna in capturing the growing Italian vote of the First Ward, began to assert control over the Levee; that man was James Colosimo.

James ("Big Jim" or "Diamond Jim") Colosimo was ten years old when his father brought him to the United States from Calabria, Italy. He spent all but three years of the rest of his life in the Levee district of Chicago. Beginning as a newsboy and bootblack, by the time he was eighteen Colosimo was an accomplished pickpocket and pimp. For a year or two, states Asbury (1942), Colosimo was a successful "Black Hand" extortionist. In the late 1890s, after several close brushes with the law, he obtained a job as a street cleaner, and by 1902 had been promoted to foreman. Known as the "white wings" because of their white uniforms, sweepers were organized by Colosimo into a social and athletic club that later became a labor union under the notorious "Dago Mike" Carrozzo. Kenna appointed Colosimo a precinct captain in return for delivering the votes of his club, a position that brought with it virtual immunity from arrest.

In 1902, Colosimo married Victoria Moresco, a brothel keeper, and he began to manage her business. In 1903, with Maurice Van Bever, he organized a gang of "white slavers," an operation that brought girls from many American and European cities, often as young as fourteen—turnover was good for business (Asbury 1942). Some were willing entrants to the business of house prostitution, but most were lured by false promises of domestic employment and other duplicity, e.g., promises of marriage. Once in Chicago, the recruiters turned them over to specialists who would drug, rape and humiliate the girls for days. After being thus "broken in," the girls were sold as chattel to brothel keepers who would restrict their contacts with the outside world. (The activities of white slavers led to the enactment of the Mann Act in 1910, making it a federal crime to transport females interstate for "immoral purposes.") Colosimo opened several brothels and a string of gambling houses. He also owned a nationally famous restaurant, Colosimo's Cafe, which attracted luminaries from society, opera, and the theater—such persons as George M. Cohan and Enrico Caruso (Nelli 1969). "By the middle of 1915 Colosimo was the acknowledged overlord of prostitution on the South Side, and because of his political power was almost as important in other sections of the city" (Asbury 1942: 314).

Colosimo flaunted his success: "He wore a diamond ring on every finger, diamond studs gleamed in his shirt front, a huge diamond horseshoe was pinned to his vest, diamond links joined the cuffs, and his belt and suspender buckles were set with diamonds" (Asbury 1942: 312). All this attracted attention, some of it unwelcome. In 1909, Colosimo, like many other successful Italians, became the target of Black Hand extortion threats. In response, he brought Johnny Torrio to Chicago. Some sources (Irey 1948; Kobler 1971) refer to Torrio as Colosimo's nephew, while Jack McPhaul (1970) reports that he was a distant cousin of Colosimo's wife Victoria.

Torrio was born near Naples in 1882 (Schoenberg 1992), and his parents settled on New York's Lower East Side. Using brains rather than brawn, Torrio

169

became leader of the James Street Boys, which was allied with Paul Kelly's Five Points Gang. He later moved operations to Brooklyn and entered into a partnership with Frankie (Uale) Yale, a member of the Five Points Gang who became a notorious gang leader in Coney Island. According to Robert Schoenberg, Yale was born in Calabria in 1893, while other sources (Asbury 1942; Turkus and Feder 1951; Kobler 1971) report that he was a Sicilian who held high office in the *Unione Siciliana*. While Torrio, a happily married man, did not smoke, drink, or consort with women, he was the right man for the job. Shortly after arriving in Chicago, Torrio lured three Black Handers into an ambush where gunmen shot them to death. His Chicago career was underway.

Torrio's usefulness extended to overseeing brothels and gambling operations for Colosimo. He encountered trouble when a white-slave victim agreed to testify against him under the recently passed Mann Act. The potential witness against Torrio was in federal custody when she was mysteriously murdered (McPhaul 1970). In 1912, when public opinion in Chicago turned against the red-light district of the Levee, Mayor Carter Harrison ordered the police to close down the brothels and gambling houses. In response, Torrio moved the Colosimo operations into Burnham, a south suburban township of a few thousand persons. There he put Johnny Patton, the "The Boy Mayor" (he was elected while still a teenager), and the chief of police on his payroll. Torrio was able to open a series of roadside brothels in rural Cook County by bribing public officials and residents where the brothels and gambling houses were located. He bought a four-story building a block away from Colosimo's Cafe, which became known as the Four Deuces because of its address, 2222 Wabash Avenue. The first floor had a saloon and Torrio's office, protected by a steel-barred gate. The second and third floors had gambling rooms with solid steel doors; the fourth floor housed a bordello.

Back in New York, Frankie Yale hired a heavy-fisted member of the Five Points Gang to deal with obstreperous customers in his saloon. On one occasion, however, the young bouncer made an offensive remark to a young girl in the saloon, which led to a four-inch scar courtesy of her irate brother and his pocketknife. The young Five Pointer was prone to be overly exuberant in carrying out his responsibilities. He was a suspect in two murders, and his third victim was on the critical list when Yale thought it best that Alphonse ("Scarface") Capone leave for Chicago.

Al Capone

Capone's birthplace is the subject of some debate; in addition to Brooklyn, various parts of Italy are mentioned (Albini 1971). Allsop maintains that he was born in Castel Amara, near Rome, on January 6, 1895. The *New York Times* states that he was born in Naples on January 17, 1899 ("Capone Dead at 48; Dry Era Gang Chief" 1947). Robert Schoenberg (1992) states that the Capones entered the United States from the Naples area in 1893 and were living in the Greenpoint-Williamsburg section of Brooklyn when Alphonse was born in

1899. A chronic truant, Alphonse left school in the sixth grade at age fourteen. As a teenager he held a variety of unskilled jobs and was a member of various youth gangs that proliferated in the area.

Capone arrived in Chicago at a fortuitous time—in 1919, the year before Prohibition would go into effect. He went to work as a bouncer for Johnny Torrio at the Four Deuces. Meanwhile, Colosimo fell in love with a young musical comedy singer. He divorced Victoria and three weeks later, on April 17, 1920, married Dale Winter. His young wife took much of Colosimo's time, and he left Torrio in charge of operations. Torrio began to give Capone important responsibilities (McPhaul 1970). Then came Prohibition.

PROHIBITION

With the coming of Prohibition, "the personnel of organized vice took the lead in the systematic organization of this new and profitable field of exploitation. All the experience gained by years of struggle against reformers and concealed agreements with politicians was brought into service in the organizing and distribution of beer and whiskey" (Landesco 1968: 43). Colosimo, however, was fearful of federal enforcement efforts and wanted to stay away from bootlegging (McPhaul 1970). Torrio and Capone chafed at this reluctance; not only would it deny access to untold wealth, but it would also enable competing racketeers to grow rich and powerful. On May 11, 1920, Diamond Jim was found in the vestibule of Colosimo's Cafe—he had been shot to death. The murderers and the reason for his murder remain unknown. Speculation about who was responsible for his murder centers on Frankie Yale, who was in Chicago on business for the *Unione Siciliana*. Infatuation with his young bride made Colosimo neglect business, and his murder has been ascribed to a reluctance to take full advantage of the new areas of profit offered by Prohibition. A second possibility concerns his ex-wife, who may have been bitter about the divorce. McPhaul (1970) reports, however, that Victoria had remarried and at the time of Colosimo's murder was in Los Angeles visiting her new in-laws. Colosimo was denied a Catholic burial—he had been divorced and remarried. Nevertheless, five thousand persons attended the funeral, including one thousand members of the First Ward Democratic Club, aldermen, judges and other politicians, white-slavers, and the dredges of the underworld.

"After Colosimo's death," Nelli (1969: 386) notes, "John Torrio succeeded to the first ward based Italian 'syndicate' throne, which he occupied until his retirement in 1925. An able and effective leader, Torrio excelled as a master strategist and organizer and quickly built up an empire which far exceeded that of his predecessor in wealth, power, and influence." This power is highlighted by an incident in 1921, when Torrio was arrested as a result of the white-slavery activities of his aide, Jake ("Greasy Thumb") Guzik. Guzik had advertised for a housemaid, whom he subsequently had imprisoned, raped, and forced into a brothel. She was able to contact her brothers, who rescued her, and Guzik and Torrio were prosecuted. Before a verdict could be reached, however, the two

JAKE GUZIK

Jacob Guzik, sometimes spelled Cusik, grew up in Chicago's Maxwell Street area, then a predominantly Jewish neighborhood. He started out as a waiter in a brothel, went on to run brothels with his wife, and eventually became the financial genius of the Capone organization. In 1924, Capone decided to teach some etiquette to someone who had slapped, kicked, and otherwise insulted Guzik, then an important but physically unimposing Torrio aide. Temerity turned to outright stupidity—the man also insulted Capone, who responded with six shots fired in front of witnesses. The witnesses to the killing subsequently experienced memory problems (Kobler 1971).

Guzik ran a twenty-five person auditing office for Capone that was once raided by the police. They found a list of customers, police officers, and public officials on the Capone payroll, leading reform Mayor William E. Dever to announce: "We got the goods this time." The next day a judge impounded the lists, and they were returned to Capone. In 1932, Guzik was convicted of income-tax evasion and served a forty-one month sentence at Leavenworth.

When he was arrested in 1946, Guzik told a policeman: "I've got more cash than Rockefeller, and there's twenty of us with more than I have." Until his death in 1956, at age sixty-nine, Guzik helped the Outfit run gambling operations. At his funeral, Rabbi Noah Ganze of the Loop Synagogue eulogized Guzik as a man who performed quiet charities and gave contributions to the synagogue (Bowman 1983b).

Sources: John Kobler, *Capone: The Life and World of Al Capone*. Greenwich, CT: Fawcett, 1971; Jim Bowman, " 'Greasy Thumb' Guzik: From Brothel to Bookkeeper for Al Capone's Gang." *Chicago Tribune Magazine*, March 8, 1983: 10.

were pardoned by Governor Len Small. Small himself had been indicted shortly after taking office, only to be saved by a Torrio enforcer who bribed and intimidated the jurors. The governor's pardon was a reward for Small's acquittal (Kobler 1971).

"As an organizer and administrator of underworld affairs," states Asbury (1942: 320–21), "Johnny Torrio is unsurpassed in the annals of American crime."

> He conducted his evil enterprises as if they had been legitimate business. In the morning he kissed his wife good-by and motored to his magnificently furnished offices on the second floor of the Four Deuces. There he bought and sold women, conferred with the managers of his brothels and gambling dens, issued instructions to his rum-runners and bootleggers, arranged for the corruption of police and city officials, and sent his gun squads out to slaughter rival gangsters who might be interfering with his schemes.

When the day's work was done, Torrio returned to his Michigan Avenue apartment and, except on rare occasions when he attended the theater or a concert, spent the evening at home in slippers and smoking jacket, playing cards with his wife or listening to phonograph records.

As in New York, Prohibition enabled men who had been street thugs to become crime overlords. Outside of the First Ward, various gangs ruled over sections of Chicago, where they pushed aside the local aldermen and parlayed crime and politics into wealth and power. On the Northeast Side, the gang headed by Dion O'Banion controlled the Forty-second and Forty-third Wards. O'Banion controlled the Irish vote much as Colosimo controlled the Italian vote in the First Ward. Despite his sordid background, including several shootings in public view, a banquet was held in O'Banion's honor by the Chicago Democratic organization in 1924. It seems that O'Banion had decided to switch his loyalty to the Republicans, because Democratic Mayor Dever had insisted that laws against many of O'Banion's activities be enforced. Democratic officials made speeches in his honor and even presented O'Banion with a platinum watch—all to no avail. O'Banion and the votes of the Forty-second and Forty-third Wards went to the Republicans. O'Banion was a regular churchgoer and loved flowers. This led him to purchase a florist shop and become gangland's favorite florist.

The O'Banion gang, Landesco (1968) notes, lacked the ethnic cohesion that bound together the dominant element in the Torrio-Capone organization. Important members of O'Banion's gang included Samuel ("Nails") Morton (born Markowitz), a Jew; Vincent Drucci, an Italian; Earl Wajciechowski (better known as Hymie Weiss), a Pole; and Louis Alterie (born Leland Verain), of French descent. In contrast, an estimated 80 percent of the Torrio-Capone organization were Italians (Asbury 1942). Other parts of Chicago also had their gangs. William ("Klondike") O'Donnell and his brothers Myles and Bernard were on the West Side. On the South Side was another group of O'Donnells: Steve, Walter, Thomas, and Edward ("Spike"). On the West Side was the Druggan-Lake or Valley (a tenement neighborhood southwest of the Loop) Gang, headed by Terry Druggan and Frankie Lake. On the Southwest Side, the Saltis-McErlane gang held sway, headed by Joe Saltis (born in Hungary) and Frank McErlane, a notorious killer. Saltis is noted for having introduced the Thompson submachine gun ("Tommy gun") into Chicago gang warfare. Until the 1920s, the Tommy gun could be freely purchased by mail or in sporting-goods stores.

On the South Side were Ragen's Colts, selected by Landesco (1968: 169) as examples of "the genuine popularity of the gangster, home-grown in the neighborhood gang, idealized in the morality of the neighborhood." The gang began as a baseball team with Frank and Mike Ragen as star players. As the Morgan Athletic Club, they participated in amateur football, baseball, and rugby and stood high in their respective leagues. Many of the neighborhood's social events centered around their activities: picnics, dances, and an annual

CHICAGO RACE RIOTS

A rock-throwing group during the 1919 Chicago race riots.

The beach along the South Side of Lake Michigan was segregated at Twenty-ninth Street; blacks used one part of it and whites the other. On Sunday afternoon, July 27, 1919, some blacks crossed the unmarked boundary that separated the two groups and were chased away by whites. A rock-throwing battle ensued. When a homemade raft with five black youngsters aboard floated into the white section, a seventeen-year-old was hit by a rock and drowned in the fifteen-foot water. A black policeman attempted to arrest the alleged rock thrower, but was thwarted by a white policeman. Word of the officer's actions resulted in a gathering of several hundred blacks near the beach. One of them fired into a group of policemen who were attempting to disperse the crowd. The police fired back and hit the man, and the riot was on. It was joined by a number of white gangs, most notably Ragen's Colts. During the week of violence, thirty-eight people died; seven blacks (but no whites) were shot by the police.

Source: Jim Bowman, "The Long Hot Summer When Chicago Erupted in Violence." *Chicago Tribune Magazine*, August 29, 1984: 7.

ball supported by businesses and professional men throughout the neighborhood. In 1908, the club's name was changed to the Ragen Athletic Association and Frank Ragen remained president. He became a respected public figure and county commissioner, and eventually announced his separation from the club. In 1917, the club's New Year's Eve party was attended by more than five thousand persons. The group prided itself on patriotism, and five hundred members went into the armed forces during the First World War. Ragen's Colts were also active in the racial violence of 1919, which began when a black youngster drowned after being subjected to a rock-throwing crowd at a white beach.

The Colts became "election specialists" during the years of Prohibition and

ALDERMAN'S WAR IN THE NINETEENTH WARD

John ("Johnny de Pow") Powers had been the ruler of the Nineteenth Ward since 1888, when the ward was predominantly Irish. The influx of Italian immigrants changed the ethnic makeup of the ward, and by 1916 Italians held a majority of votes. In that year, Anthony D'Andrea announced that he would oppose Alderman James Bowler, a protégé of Johnny Powers. D'Andrea had been educated at the University of Palermo and was an accomplished linguist. According to Schoenberg (1992), he was also a convicted counterfeiter. D'Andrea served as president of the International Hod Carriers' Union and was later business agent for the Macaroni Manufacturers' Union. He was also head of the Chicago branch of the *Unione Siciliana*. On February 21, 1916, the campaign began, and a ward boss for Powers, Frank Lombardi, was shot to death in a Taylor Street saloon (the Gennas were suspected). D'Andrea, however, lost the election to Bowler and the Powers organization, but the war for the Nineteenth Ward had begun.

In March 1920, in an effort to secure Italian support and placate D'Andrea, Powers had D'Andrea elected in his place as Democratic committeeman from the Nineteenth Ward. The Illinois Supreme Court, however, voided the election, and Powers retained the post. D'Andrea cried "foul," and on September 28, 1920, a bomb exploded on the porch of Powers' house. In 1921, D'Andrea announced that he was a candidate for the aldermanic seat held by Johnny Powers, and things heated up. Numerous bombings and killings followed as sluggers and gunmen from both camps patrolled the streets. In the end, Powers defeated D'Andrea by only 435 votes, and the violence continued. On March 9, 1921, a Powers supporter was murdered, and another was murdered a short time later. The "Bloody Nineteenth" remained an armed camp. D'Andrea announced his withdrawal from "politics," but it was too late. On May 11, 1921, he was shotgunned to death (Landesco 1968; Kobler 1971).

Sources: Robert J. Schoenberg, *Mr. Capone*. New York: William Morrow, 1992; John Landesco, *Organized Crime in Chicago*. Chicago: University of Chicago Press, 1968; John Kobler, *Capone: The Life and World of Al Capone*. Greenwich, CT: Fawcett, 1971.

were used for strong-arm work throughout Chicago (Landesco 1968: 170): "In the days before machine-gun politics, the knuckles of the club members made themselves felt so that, in the words of a member, 'When we dropped into a polling place everyone else dropped out.' The club was credited with settling the political fate of many candidates for the city council and the state legislature." At their height, the Colts had two thousand members, but they eventually split into various factions during Prohibition. Members joined opposing beer-running gangs that were then at war in Chicago. On August 4, 1927, the twelve remaining members met and voted to disband their club headquarters (Landesco 1968).

In the "Little Italy" of the South Side's Taylor Street neighborhood were the "Terrible Gennas," six brothers known for their brutality but, like Dion O'Banion, were regular churchgoers. Prohibition enabled them to become quite prosperous—they organized the Italian home stills that proliferated and were encouraged by the Gennas in the neighborhood, and distributed the spirits with police and political protection (Kobler 1971). It was not always clear where politics ended and crime began in Chicago, as the history of the Nineteenth Ward highlights.

The Torrio Organization

Late in the summer of 1920, Johnny Torrio held long conferences with the major gang leaders in Cook County:

> [He] persuaded them to abandon bank robbery, burglary, and banditry, for the time being at least, in favor of bootlegging and rumrunning. . . . Torrio exercised general supervision over every phase of the liquor traffic, but to facilitate operations the city and county were divided into spheres of influence, in each of which an allied gang chieftain was supreme, with sub-chiefs working under his direction. A few of these leaders themselves owned and operated breweries and distilleries, but in the main they received their supplies from Torrio and were principally concerned with selling, making deliveries, protecting shipments, terrorizing saloon-keepers who refused to buy from the syndicate, and furnishing gunmen for punitive expeditions against hi-jackers and independents who attempted to encroach upon Torrio territory. (Asbury 1942: 324–25)

Torrio also moved to extend the suburbanization of his business, and by 1923 had expanded beer and bordello operations well beyond his South Side stronghold into towns west and southwest of Chicago. He toured the Cook County suburbs, and when a location was decided upon, the neighborhood people were canvassed. If they were agreeable, Torrio agents would provide rewards: a new car, a house redecorated or painted, a new furnace, mortgage payments. The local authorities were then approached and terms negotiated (Allsop 1968). Most of this was accomplished peacefully; but then there was Cicero.

WHEN YOU SMELL GUNPOWDER, YOU'RE IN CICERO

Adjacent to Chicago's Far West Side, in the suburban city of Cicero (current population about 55,000), the saloons were associated with Klondike O'Donnell. The only gambling was slot machines owned by a local politician. At the time, the O'Donnells were opposed to prostitution, so when Torrio opened a brothel in Cicero, it was promptly raided by the police. Torrio opened another brothel, and it too was raided. Two days later, at Torrio's direction, a posse of deputy sheriffs entered Cicero and confiscated the slot machines—no whores, no slots. The outcome was an arrangement whereby the slot machines were returned, the O'Donnells continued to handle bootlegging, and Torrio was allowed to operate his bordellos and gambling houses (Allsop 1968).

In 1923, reform hit Chicago and the mayoralty went to Democrat William E. Dever. He ordered the police to move against the rampant vice in Chicago, but corruption was too deeply ingrained to be easily pushed aside. Allsop (1968: 201) states that "sporadically and trivially" Dever harassed some liquor deliveries and effected an occasional police raid. Although he was not corrupt, Dever accomplished very little. However, with the Democrats in control of Chicago, the Republicans were fearful of a reform wave that ould loosen their control of the suburban areas of Cook County. As a result, a local Republican leader made a deal with Al Capone while Torrio was on vacation in Italy. In return for helping the Republicans maintain control in Cicero, Torrio would be given a free hand in that city (Allsop 1968).

In the election of April 1924, the Capone brothers, Al and Salvatore (usually called "Frank"), led a group of two hundred Chicago thugs into Cicero. They intimidated, beat, and even killed Democrats who sought to oppose the Republican candidates. Some outraged Cicero officials responded by having a county judge deputize seventy volun-

teer Chicago police officers who entered Cicero and engaged the Capone gangsters. In one incident, Chicago police saw the Capone brothers, Charley Fischetti (a Capone cousin), and a Capone gunman standing by the polls with guns in their hands ushering voters inside. In the ensuing exchange of gunfire, during which the police were probably mistaken for rival gunmen (Schoenberg 1992), Frank Capone was killed. In spite of this, the Capone candidate, Joseph Z. Klenha, was overwhelmingly reelected mayor of Cicero (Kobler 1971).

Capone moved his headquarters from Chicago to Cicero, where he took over the Hawthorne Inn with a little help from his friends, Myles O'Donnell and gunman James J. Doherty. They opened fire at the owner "while shopping housewives and local tradesmen threw themselves behind cars and into doorways in the horizontal position that was becoming an identifiable posture of Cicero citizens" (Allsop 1968: 62–63). At the Hawthorne Inn, Capone ruled with an iron hand. When Mayor Klenha failed to carry out one of his orders, Capone went to city hall, where he personally knocked "his honor" down the steps and kicked him repeatedly as a policeman strolled by (Allsop 1968). Mike Royko states that since the Capone organization took over Cicero, it has never completely let go: "It still has its strip of bars where gambling and whoring are unnoticed. The only thing they won't tolerate in Cicero are Negroes" (1971: 34).

In 1965, Dr. Martin Luther King, Jr., highlighted his Chicago campaign for "open housing" by a march into Cicero. After becoming painfully aware of the futility of such a gesture, he stated: "We can walk in outer space, but we can't walk the streets of Cicero without the National Guard."

(continued on next page)

177

Jim Bishop, noting that shortly after entering Cicero the National Guard retreated, stated: "It was worse. Blacks couldn't march in Cicero *with* the National Guard" (1971: 444).

Sources: Kenneth Allsop, *The Bootleggers: The Story of Prohibition*. New Rochelle, NY: Arlington House, 1968; Robert J. Schoenberg, *Mr. Capone*. New York: William Morrow, 1992; John Kobler, *Capone: The Life and World of Al Capone*. Greenwich, CT: Fawcett, 1971; Mike Royko, *Boss: Richard J. Daley of Chicago*. New York: Dutton, 1971; Jim Bishop, *The Days of Martin Luther King, Jr.* New York: Putnam's, 1971.

Among a number of localities, the Torrio organization expanded its suburban operations into Stickney, Posen, Burr Oaks, Blue Island, Steger, and Chicago Heights. In Forest View, a small town of about a thousand persons south of Cicero, Torrio gunmen intimidated town officials into leaving. With their own chief of police in control, the Torrio organization turned Forest View into one large brothel and gang headquarters (Kobler 1971). Chicago Heights continues to suffer from corruption problems. Numerous public officials, including the mayor, members of the city council, and police officers, have been convicted of criminal activity (O'Connor 1993a; 1993b).

The Chicago Wars

The election of a reform mayor in Chicago had unexpected consequences. It created an unstable situation and encouraged competitive moves by various ganglords. When Thompson lost to Dever in 1923, the system of protection broke down, and in the ensuing confusion Chicago became a battleground.

South Side Beer War

The head of the South Side O'Donnell clan, Spike, was in prison for bank robbery when Johnny Torrio allocated territory. Spike's group had to be satisfied with "crumbs." Spike was known to have shot a half a dozen men during his long criminal career. In the year Dever was elected, Spike O'Donnell was paroled by Governor Len Small at the request of six state senators, five state representatives, and one criminal court judge. Within months of his return to Chicago, O'Donnell men began hijacking Torrio beer shipments and terrorizing saloon-keepers into buying his beer (Asbury 1942).

On September 7, 1923, O'Donnell sluggers entered Joe Kepka's saloon and began threatening him. The lights went out, shots rang out, and by the time the police arrived, the O'Donnells were short one young tough. Ten days later two more O'Donnell men were dispatched, and Spike stopped bothering Torrio (Landesco 1968). Instead, the O'Donnells began to move into the territory of the McErlane-Saltis gang, but they didn't fare much better. In the *South Side Beer War* that resulted, the "take 'em for a ride" technique was inaugurated by McErlane-Saltis gunmen, and Frank McErlane used his Tommy gun for the first time against human targets—but the shots went wild and Spike escaped. The war continued into 1928. " 'I've got a mob of blue-eyed Irish boys who are with me to stay,' O'Donnell told police in 1928. 'No Saltis is going to run us out.' But Saltis had his Irishmen too, in the person of Lefty Paddy

Gangland funerals in Prohibition Chicago were ostentatious affairs, complete with police escorts, lavish floral tributes, and aldermen and judges in attendance. Black tie was *de rigueur* for the cortege of Angelo Genna, one of the "Terrible Gennas" slain during the city's West Side Beer Wars.

Sullivan, a former Chicago police sergeant who reportedly joined his boss and two others in a blistering machine-gun attack on O'Donnell from a moving auto . . . on October 9, 1928. O'Donnell survived, returning their fire with his pistol and in the confusion shooting a policeman by mistake" (Bowman 1983a: 8).

The murder score stood at seven to two, and Spike had been wounded twice in ten assassination attempts when he left Chicago. He returned in a year or so and reached an accommodation with Capone. The O'Donnells resumed their bootlegging operations on a smaller scale than before (Asbury 1942). Spike died of a heart attack in 1962, a few years after Joe Saltis, who also died of natural causes.

West Side Beer War

Gang warfare on the West Side of Chicago began in 1924, when O'Banion forces began to feud with the Genna brothers. Allsop (1968) reports that the Gennas moved in on O'Banion territory, while Kobler (1971) says that it was O'Banion who was selling liquor in Genna territory. Asbury (1942) states that the Gennas had moved in on the O'Banions, but O'Banion had also made moves against Torrio interests. When his complaints about the Gennas were ignored by Torrio, O'Banion hijacked a load of Genna liquor. The Gennas bristled, but Torrio restrained them and attempted to negotiate a peaceful settlement. In that same year, O'Banion swindled Torrio and Capone out of $500,000 by selling them his share in the Sieben brewery,[1] which he knew was going to be raided by the police. This indicated that Torrio had lost control of the police under Mayor Dever. Emboldened by the lack of a response from Torrio, and apparently mistaking caution for fear, O'Banion went around boasting about how he had "taken" Torrio. "To hell with them Sicilians," was a phrase O'Banion gunmen quoted when they told the story in underworld circles (Asbury 1942). This was a serious violation of *rispetto* and the response was inevitable.

On November 10, 1924, Mike Genna and two Sicilian immigrants who worked for the Gennas, Albert Anselmi and John Scalise, entered the O'Banion flower shop at 738 North State Street. O'Banion was busy preparing flower arrangements for the funeral of Mike Merlo, president of the *Unione Siciliana*, who had died of natural causes a few days earlier. What the florist didn't know was that Merlo had been exerting his influence to keep the Gennas and Torrio from moving against O'Banion. Kobler (1971) reports that Merlo abhorred violence and also got along very well with O'Banion—but now he was dead. "Hello, boys, you want Merlo's flowers?" a black porter told the police he heard O'Banion say to the three men. Torrio had placed an order for $10,000

---

1. Sieben's North River Brewery was opened by Mike Sieben, a German immigrant, in 1865. After the raid it closed until Prohibition ended in 1933. It continued to operate until 1967, when competition from major brewers caused it to shut operations. In 1987, a group of investors reopened the brewery to produce four kinds of German beer (Kamin 1987).

worth of assorted flowers and Capone had ordered $8,000 worth of roses. While shaking O'Banion's hand, Mike Genna suddenly jerked him forward and seized his arms. Before he could wriggle free and reach for any of the three guns he always carried, O'Banion was hit by five bullets. A sixth, the coup de grâce, was fired into his head after he fell to the floor. The war that followed lasted more than four years and ended on St. Valentine's Day, 1929 (Asbury 1942; Kobler 1971; Allsop 1968).

The O'Banion forces, under the leadership of Hymie Weiss, struck back. Torrio left Chicago one step ahead of Weiss gunmen. On January 12, 1925, Capone's car was raked with machine-gun fire; his driver was wounded, but Capone and his bodyguards were not hit. Capone began travelling in a specially built armored Cadillac limousine. That same year, twelve days after Torrio's return to Chicago to serve a nine-month sentence for bootlegging (Torrio pled guilty in an apparent effort to avoid the warfare), Torrio was critically wounded while shopping with his wife in the Loop. Torrio eventually served his sentence in Waukegan, a quiet suburban community north of Chicago. In the fall of 1925, he left Chicago for a visit to Italy, leaving his organization to Capone (Landesco 1968). As far as it is known, Johnny Torrio never returned to Chicago.

Sam and Chuck Giancana (1992), godson and brother of Chicago crime boss Sam Giancana, report that Torrio was shot on orders from Al Capone—Sam being one of the shooters—in order to get him to leave Chicago. In any event, Torrio emerged as part of organized crime in New York, where he apparently received some type of senior advisory status. He worked in partnership with a number of leading New York OC figures, including Dutch Schultz, with whom he was a partner in the bail bond business, and Frank Costello (Peterson 1983a). He later received a two-and-a-half year sentence for income tax evasion (Irey 1948). Some sources (for example, Messick 1967; Turkus and Feder 1951) credit Torrio with inspiring the formation of a national crime syndicate in 1934. Torrio suffered a heart attack while in a barber's chair in Brooklyn, and died on April 16, 1957. His death went unnoticed by the media until May 8, when the New York Times ran a story: "Johnny Torrio, Ex-Public Enemy 1, Dies; Made Al Capone Boss of the Underworld." Torrio was described as a real estate dealer at the time of his death.

As the West Side Beer War continued, four of the Genna brothers were killed, three by rival gunmen and one by the police. The two remaining brothers fled Chicago. Sam and Chuck Giancana (1992) maintain that Capone was actually behind the attacks on the Gennas—he wanted their lucrative income for himself. Schoenberg (1992) states that the Gennas had moved against Capone and simply suffered the consequences. While Capone was busy fighting with the O'Banion forces under Hymie Weiss, the West Side O'Donnells (Klondike, Myles, and Bernard) and their all-Irish gang began to move in on Capone operations in Cicero. On April 27, 1926, William H. McSwiggin, a twenty-six-year-old assistant state's attorney, was in front of a Cicero saloon with Klondike and Myles O'Donnell and several members of their West Side gang.

A car drove by and its occupants machine-gunned McSwiggin and two others to death. The murderers were never identified, but Capone was suspected. Known as the "hangman prosecutor," McSwiggin had obtained seven death penalties in eight months. He was unsuccessful, however, in his prosecution of Myles O'Donnell for murder. His reason for being in front of a Cicero saloon with Myles and other O'Donnell gangsters has never been determined (Landesco 1968; Sawyers 1988b). McSwiggin's murder resulted in a public outcry and raids on Capone's suburban empire by both police and vigilante groups. Capone became a fugitive from a federal grand jury, although he eventually surrendered and avoided prosecution.

The Weiss gunmen of the North Side made a dozen attempts to kill Capone, and they nearly succeeded on September 20, 1926. The street in front of Capone's Cicero headquarters was filled with a lunch-hour crowd, and Capone was eating at a restaurant next door, when "eleven automobiles filled with Weiss gangsters drove slowly past the Hawthorne Inn and poured slugs from machine-guns, automatic pistols, and shotguns. After the roar of the attack had subsided, bullet holes were found in thirty-five automobiles parked at the curb. Inside the hotel, woodwork and doors had been splintered, windows shattered, plaster ripped from walls, and furniture wrecked in the office and lobby." Capone, however, was uninjured, although one of his bodyguards was hit in the shoulder and a woman sitting with her infant son was struck thirty times. Capone paid the physicians who saved her sight (Asbury 1942: 358–59).

On October 11, two gunmen armed with submachine guns, who had been waiting for three days, opened fire on Hymie Weiss and his four companions as they approached their headquarters above the O'Banion flower shop. Weiss was hit ten times. He and one of his companions died; the others survived. Weiss, at age twenty-eight, reportedly left an estate worth $1.3 million (Allsop 1968).

AL CAPONE'S CHICAGO

Gang wars are "bad for business," so in the middle of the mayhem and murder, a truce was called. The principals met at a Chicago hotel—there is some disagreement over the date and place. Kobler states that the meeting occurred on October 21, 1926, at the Morrison Hotel; Landesco (1968), writing in 1929, concurs. Allsop (1968) states that the principals met at the Hotel Sherman on October 20. Asbury says there were actually two meetings. The first took place at the Hotel Sherman in late September, and it included only representatives of Capone and Weiss. A second meeting took place on October 21 at the Morrison Hotel and was attended by the major gang leaders in Cook County. At the time, Weiss was dead, and the O'Banion forces were led by George ("Bugs") Moran and Vincent Drucci. Allsop and Kobler agree that the meeting was initiated by Joe Saltis, who had pledged his loyalty to Capone but who was secretly allied with Moran and Drucci. Capone had apparently discovered this treachery, but wanted peace more than he wanted revenge.

THE PINEAPPLE PRIMARY

In 1927, supported by Capone and other criminal interests, Big Bill Thompson ran on a pledge to let the liquor flow again in Chicago and was swept back into office. The following year, in the Republican primary campaign for Cook County state's attorney, there was so much violence that it became known as the "Pineapple Primary" (named after the exploding device—hand grenade—of similar appearance). Fletcher Dobyns (1932: 1–4) describes what happened after the primary:

> "Scarface Al" Capone sat in his grand headquarters in Chicago [at the Lexington Hotel]. The doors opened and past heavily armed guards moved the venerable figure of Frank J. Loesch, counsel for the Pennsylvania Railroad Company, president of the Chicago Crime Commission, and member of the National Commission on Law Observance and Enforcement [Wickersham Commission]. He had come by appointment and secretly to present to the all-powerful chief a humble petition that the people of Chicago be permitted to select their own State's Attorney—the official whose first and most imperative duty would be to hang Capone and every member of his gang.

Capone agreed to help, and "it turned out to be the squarest and most successful election day in forty years. There was not one complaint, not one election fraud and not one threat of trouble all day."

> That the president of that [Chicago Crime] Commission knew that it would be useless to appeal to the Mayor, the Chief of Police, the State's Attorney, or the Sheriff to prevent "hoodlums and cutthroats" from controlling the election of a State's Attorney shows that these officials were dominated by the criminal elements of the city. . . .
>
> The orderly election and the success of the candidate in whom Mr. Loesch was interested created not a ripple of excitement in Chicago's gangland. It was understood that whatever his intentions might be, he would be powerless. Capone knew this when he agreed to permit the people to elect him.

Source: Fletcher Dobyns, *The Underworld of American Politics*. New York: Fletcher Dobyns, 1932.

The assembled gang chieftains divided up the city and the county, with the largest shares going to the Capone organization and the Moran-Drucci gang. (Drucci was later killed on election day, April 4, 1927, by the police as they were driving him to the station house for "questioning.") Also receiving shares were representatives of the McErlane-Saltis gang (both men were in jail) and the gang headed by Ralph Sheldon, now allied with Capone. The initial truce lasted seventy days, until a member of the Sheldon gang was killed on orders from Joe Saltis. Sheldon complained to Capone, and two Saltis men were shot to death in their car. Peace once again prevailed (Allsop 1968).

In 1928, Capone clashed with Frankie Yale. Kobler (1971) states that Capone had discovered that Yale—his onetime Brooklyn boss, *Unione Siciliana* leader, and the person responsible for protecting Capone's liquor shipments as they were trucked west to Chicago—was actually behind a series of hijackings. According to Kobler (see also Schoenberg 1992), Yale had become friends with Capone's enemies, the Aiellos (Joseph and his eight brothers and numerous cousins), Sicilians who took over from the Genna brothers in the Little Italy of the Taylor Street neighborhood. Joe Aiello was aligned with the O'Banion gang (and in 1927 Capone gunmen had killed five Aiello men). McPhaul (1970) provides a different version. He reports that Capone had been cheating some New York gangsters, especially Yale, over his beer shipments. Both Kobler and McPhaul agree that Yale was responsible for killing a Capone aide, James De Amato, who had been sent to New York to spy on Yale. On July 1, 1928, two weeks after De Amato's murder, a black sedan followed Yale's new Lincoln as it moved down a Brooklyn street. As the sedan drew near, shots were fired, and Yale sped off with the sedan in pursuit. The end came with a devastating blast of gunfire that filled Yale's head with bullets and buckshot ("Gangster Shot in Daylight Attack" 1928). Yale was thirty-five years old.

During the first few months of 1929, while a peace agreement was in effect (at least in theory), Bugs Moran had been hijacking Capone's liquor, owned jointly by Capone and the (predominantly Jewish) Purple Gang of Detroit. Then Pasqualino Lalardo, "a harmless old codger," who with Capone's efforts had been elected president of the *Unione Siciliana*, was murdered by the Aiellos—Joseph Aiello coveted the top office for himself (McPhaul 1970). Aiello finally won the presidency and held it for almost one year—until October 23, 1930, when he was struck down by a barrage of machine-gun fire.

Capone gave the orders and went off to enjoy the Florida sun in his fourteen-room palatial home on Miami's Palm Island. The house, shaded by a dozen palm trees, had been built in 1922 for Clarence M. Busch, the St. Louis brewer. Capone bought it a few years later. The house had a dock that could accommodate four vessels, one of which was Capone's plush six-stateroom yacht, the *Reomar II*, built in 1924 for auto magnate R. E. Olds and acquired by Capone a few years later. On February 14, 1929, St. Valentine's Day, Capone entertained more than one hundred guests on Palm Island: gangsters, politicians, sports writers, and show-business personalities. They all enjoyed a hearty buffet and an endless supply of champagne (Galvan 1982).

Meanwhile, back in Chicago, six of Bugs Moran's men and Reinhart Schwimmer, an optometrist who liked to associate with gangsters, were waiting at a warehouse at the S.M.C. Cartage Co., 2122 North Clark Street, to unload a shipment of hijacked liquor from Detroit. They had been "set up." A Cadillac touring car with a large gong on the running board, similar to those used by detectives, stopped outside, and five men, two wearing police uniforms, entered the warehouse. Once inside, they lined up the seven men against the warehouse wall and systematically executed them with machine guns. One of the victims, Frank Gusenerg, lived nearly three hours with fourteen bullets in him, but refused to tell the police who was responsible for the shooting. Bugs Moran was not in the warehouse at the time, even though the "St. Valentine's Day Massacre" had been arranged in his honor. He arrived late, and seeing the "police car," left. It was later learned that the killers thought Moran was among the victims. Lookouts had mistaken one of the seven for the gang's leader (Koziol and Estep 1983).[2] The killers were never caught; it was suspected that they were brought in from Detroit or St. Louis (where Capone had ties with "Eagan's Rats"). The affair was apparently arranged by South Side hit man and Capone bodyguard, James Gebardi (some sources say his real name was Vincenzo DeMora), better known as "Machine-Gun Jack McGurn."[3] For a long time it was generally believed that *real* policemen were the actual killers (Kobler 1971).

While the wrath of Bugs Moran continued, his gang withered. Jack Zuta, who handled brothels and "immoral cabarets" for Moran, was gunned down on August 1, 1930. Less than three months later, Joe Aiello met the same fate. Moran eventually returned to more conventional crime. In 1946 he was sent to prison for robbing a tavern employee of $10,000 near Dayton, Ohio. After ten years he was released from prison, and a few days later was arrested for bank robbery. On February 26, 1957, the *New York Times* reported that Moran died while serving his sentence in the federal penitentiary in Leavenworth, Kansas ("Bugs Moran Dies in Federal Prison" 1957: 59).

In May of 1929, after attending a national crime conclave in Atlantic City, Capone decided to go to jail to avoid the wrath of Bugs Moran and any number of Sicilians who had vowed to kill him to avenge the beating deaths of John Scalise, Albert Anselmi (who had murdered Dion O'Banion), and Joe Giunta, each of whom Capone suspected of disloyalty. He arranged to be arrested by a friendly detective in Philadelphia on a firearms violation. Although the maximum sentence was one year, Capone anticipated a sentence of about ninety days, enough time to let things cool down in Chicago. His arrest, however, generated a great deal of media attention, and the judge imposed the maximum sentence. Capone was released on March 17, 1930, two months early for "good

---

2. The warehouse on Clark Street was torn down in 1967 as part of a redevelopment project. An entrepreneur from Vancouver, British Columbia, bought the wall from the company that demolished the building. He rebuilt the wall, brick by bullet-riddled brick, in the men's room of a "Roaring Twenties" banjo sing-along bar (Kozial and Estep 1983).

3. The Moran gang had twice tried to kill McGurn, and on one occasion he was seriously wounded. On the eve of Valentine's Day seven years later, McGurn was himself machine-gunned to death in a Chicago bowling alley. The two killers left a comic Valentine card next to his ruined body. McGurn, who is believed responsible for killing at least twenty-two people, used to place a nickel in the hands of his victims. He was responsible for the 1927 attack on comedian Joe E. Lewis during which his vocal cords were slashed and his tongue lacerated. Lewis, then a nightclub singer, had left McGurn's club for employment at another speakeasy. The Lewis story was told in the Frank Sinatra motion picture *The Joker Is Wild*.

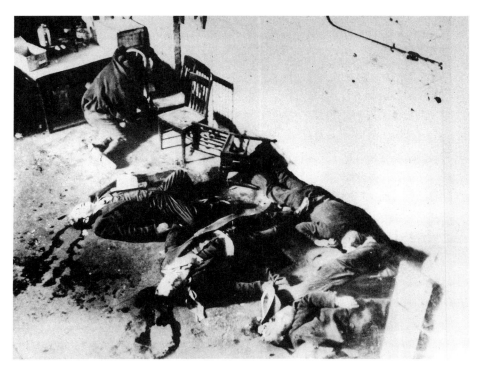

Seven men lay dead in a North Clark Street warehouse following the St. Valentine's Day Massacre in 1929. The killers were never caught.

behavior." While he continued to live with his family in a modest red-brick, two-flat house at 7244 South Prairie Avenue, the former saloon bouncer from Brooklyn was now the most powerful person in Chicago, thanks to Prohibition.

Bathhouse John Coughlin and Michael Hinky Dink Kenna maintained their political dominance of the First Ward, but only with the sufferance of Al Capone. "Had he wished," note Wendt and Kogan (1974: 344), "Capone could have ousted either or both from politics." But he chose not to, and "Capone's obvious friendship rather increased their political stature in the day when many politicians were fawning upon the gangster" (1974: 345).[4] Prohibition enabled Al Capone to rise from the ranks of common thugs to a place in the *Guiness*

---

4. In 1923 the legislature passed a redistricting bill that reduced representation in the city council to one alderman per ward. Kenna dropped out in favor of Coughlin, but he continued in the position of Democratic ward committeeman and, thus, the dispenser of patronage and other favors. While Kenna was a rich man, Coughlin had lost his money on bad business investments, horse racing, and women. On November 8, 1938, he died a poor man. Kenna, in order to maintain political peace—turmoil had broken out over who would replace Coughlin—reluctantly filed petitions for the alderman's seat and, although he did not campaign, won the election. He was eighty

Book of World Records for the highest gross income ever achieved by a private citizen in a single year: $105 million in 1927.[5] During the Great Depression, Capone used some of this money to open "soup kitchens" where he fed thousands of needy people daily. But, notes Mark Haller (1974: 11), the leadership of the "Capone Organization"

> can best be described *not* as a hierarchy directed by Al Capone but rather as a senior partnership involving four men, who in turn entered into a variety of partnerships to run specific enterprises. The senior partners were Al Capone; his brother Ralph; Al's boyhood friend, Frank Nitti; and Jack Guzik, who was Jewish. As senior partners, each received one-sixth of the income that they derived from their various enterprises. The remaining one-third probably went toward the maintenance of their central headquarters with its clerks, gunmen, chauffeurs, and hangers-on. The senior partners, in turn, invested money and, when possible, provided political protection for an expanding and diverse group of enterprises.

Business and Labor Racketeering

During Prohibition, numerous forms of racketeering flourished in Chicago. Haller (1971–72: 225–26) describes one facet:

> The small businesses of the city were generally marginal and intensely competitive. To avoid cutthroat competition, businessmen formed associations to make and enforce regulations illegally limiting competition. The Master Barbers Association, . . . dairies, auto parts dealers, garage owners, candy jobbers, butcher stores, fish wholesalers and retailers, cleaners and dyers, and junk dealers. Many of the associations were controlled, or even organized by, racketeers who levied dues upon association members and controlled the treasuries; they then used a system of fines and violence to insure that all businessmen in the trade joined the association and abided by the regulations [designed to keep prices uniform and high].

The Depression severely reduced the income of the Capone organization. New areas of profit were sought by the chieftains of organized crime, who had

---

years old and his sight was failing—this would be Hinky Dink's last term (Wendt and Kogan 1974).

5. When it comes to organized crime, however, the *Guiness Book of Records* is not reliable, as evidenced by the perpetuation of the myth surrounding the death of Salvatore Maranzano and "40 allies" (discussed in chapter 3). *Guiness* also reports that the Mafia got its start in the United States in New Orleans in 1869. This assertion is probably based on a feud between two factions, Sicilian and Neapolitan, for control of stevedoring business in New Orleans. During the struggle David Hennessey, the chief of police, who was apparently siding with one faction, was murdered. A number of Italians were tried for the murder, and after their acquittal, a mob stormed the jail and eleven of the defendants were lynched on March 14, 1891 (Gambino 1977).

grown wealthy in gambling and bootlegging. Harold Seidman (1938) points out that until 1929, business and labor racketeering was only a sideline for most top gangsters such as Capone. However, as the sale of liquor fell off with the onset of the Depression, gang leaders were faced with a restless army of young and violent men whom they were committed to paying anywhere from $100 to $500 per week. McPhaul (1970) states that Capone also recognized by 1928 that Prohibition would probably only last a few more years; new sources of income would be needed. Capone moved into racketeering on a grand scale. He took over many rackets then prevalent in Chicago: extortion from Jewish butchers, fish stores, the construction industry, garage owners, bakeries, laundries, beauty parlors, dry cleaners, theaters, sports arenas, even bootblacks. In 1928, the state's attorney of Cook County listed ninety-one Chicago unions and business associations under gangster control, and these gradually came under the control of the Capone organization (Kobler 1971). Seidman (1938) points out that the gangsters who controlled racketeering in Chicago proved no match for the Capone forces. (It was the same in other cities; in Detroit, for example, the Purple Gang took over labor racketeering through a reign of terror.)

The Capone organization

controlled a score of labor unions, most of them officered by ex-convicts, and as many protective associations. To build up this phase of the Capone syndicate operations, and to hold in line the businesses already conquered, bands of gunmen and sluggers hi-jacked and destroyed truckloads of merchandise, bombed stores and manufacturing plants or wrecked them with axes and crowbars, put acid into laundry vats, poured corrosives onto clothing hanging in cleaning and dyeing shops, blackjacked workers and employers, and killed when necessary to enforce their demands or break down opposition. (Asbury 1942: 366–67)

Capone's Downfall

Not only did the Depression severely reduce the income of the Capone organization but also a special team of federal investigators, headed by Eliot Ness and dubbed "The Untouchables," began to move against Capone distilleries, breweries, and liquor shipments. The most important event for Capone, however, was a U.S. Supreme Court decision (*United States v. Sullivan* 274 U.S. 259), that was handed down in 1927. That decision upheld the Internal Revenue Service's contention that even *unlawful* income was subject to income taxes, the Fifth Amendment guarantee against self-incrimination notwithstanding. The tax evasion case against Capone was begun in 1929 by the Special Intelligence Unit of the Treasury Department headed by Elmer Lincoln Irey. It was a low-key agency that avoided publicity. In 1929, Secretary of the Treasury Andrew Mellon, acting under pressure from President Herbert Hoover, directed Irey to investigate Capone. J. Edgar Hoover and his FBI were apparently unwilling to take on Capone because the risk of failure was too high (Spiering

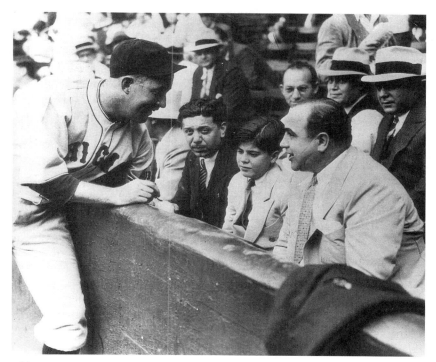

Gabby Hartnett of the Chicago Cubs autographs a ball for Al Capone, Jr. This picture was probably taken without the subjects' knowledge—"Scarface" Al rarely allowed himself to be photographed from the left side.

1976). Frank Wilson, a nearsighted special agent who never carried a firearm, was put in charge of the investigation: he brought Capone down with a pencil.

Treasury agents engaged in an intensive investigation, interviewing hundreds of persons, scanning bank records (Capone did not have a personal account) and Western Union records. The latter revealed that, while in Florida, Capone received regular payments from Jake Guzik. "Some of the more daring investigators actually joined gangs controlled by Capone in Chicago, Cicero, and elsewhere" (Horne 1932: 1). Wilson also had an informant in the Capone organization, Edward J. O'Hare, a businessman who was involved with Capone in dog racetracks. O'Hare owned the rights to the mechanical rabbit.[6]

---

6. On November 9, 1939, Edward O'Hare was shotgunned to death in Chicago. In return for his father's service to the Treasury Department, Edward ("Butch") O'Hare, Jr., received an appointment to the Naval Academy at Annapolis. As a fighter pilot, on February 20, 1942, Butch shot down five Japanese bombers and was awarded the Congressional Medal of Honor. A year later, he was killed while pioneering night radar flights in the Pacific (Spiering 1976). Chicago's O'Hare Airport is named in his honor.

Capone stood trial for having a net income of $1,038,654 during the years 1924 to 1929, for which he failed to pay income tax. On October 17, 1931, he was found guilty of income-tax evasion and received sentences totaling eleven years. On May 3, 1932, his appeals exhausted, Capone entered the federal prison in Atlanta. He was transferred to Alcatraz in 1934 and found to be suffering from syphilis. For several years he refused treatment. Early in 1938, he began showing symptoms of paresis and was transferred out of Alcatraz. Capone was released in 1939, his sentence shortened for good behavior, and by then he was suffering from an advanced case of syphilis. After living for many years as an invalid, Capone died in 1947 at his Florida villa of pneumonia following a stroke. He was buried in Mt. Olivet Cemetery on Chicago's Far South Side, but his family subsequently had his remains transferred to Mt. Carmel Cemetery in the west suburb of Hillside. In 1972, the simple stone that marked Capone's grave was stolen, and the family decided not to have it replaced ("Who Took the Stone of Alphonse Capone?" 1981). Al Capone had six brothers and two sisters. When his father, Gabriel, died, Capone brought his mother, sisters, and three brothers to Chicago. They lived in a house that Al bought in 1923 on Chicago's far South Side. His wife and mother continued to live there until 1953. When his mother died, the family sold it.

The federal government was also able to convict other members of the Capone organization for income-tax evasion. Ralph ("Bottles") Capone, Al's older brother, received a three-year sentence; Frank ("The Enforcer") Nitti received eighteen months; Sam Guzik received one year, while brother Jake was sentenced to a term of five years (Horne 1932).

Al Capone was the subject of a great deal of public adulation and even hero worship. He emphasized the "service" aspect of his activities, proclaiming: "All I do is to satisfy a public demand" (Nelli 1969: 389). Kobler (1971: 292) said of Capone: "Ordinary citizens throughout the country tended to accept his own estimate of his activities." Allsop (1968: 244) concludes that the enormity of the piracy by public officials and businessmen in Chicago placed the bootlegger and gangster "in a state of relative grace." Michael Woodiwiss (1987: 8) argues that "Capone became the world's most famous criminal because he was the first of the racket bosses to attract saturation treatment in the Press, and not because of his criminal success":

> In fact, in relative terms Capone was not a success; his power and freedom in Chicago were short-lived. His downfall was a direct result of receiving too much publicity. The federal administration of President Herbert Hoover was committed to a show of effective liquor-law enforcement and someone had to pay the price. Capone's national notoriety ensured that only he could fit the bill properly.

ORGANIZED CRIME IN CHICAGO AFTER CAPONE

With Prohibition at an end and Capone in prison, Frank Nitti assumed control of what remained of the post-Prohibition "Capone Organization," the "Outfit," which he ran with the help of Capone's brothers, Ralph and Matt, Capone's cousins Charles and Rocco Fischetti, as well as Anthony Capezio, Paul de Lucia (better known as Paul "The Waiter" Ricca), Anthony ("Joe Batters") Accardo, Jake Guzik, and Murray Humphreys.[7] The Chicago Crime Commission points out that the Outfit "has been somewhat unique in its willingness to deal with and, indeed, grant considerable responsibility to non-Italians. For many years, the outfit's chief political fixer and trouble shooter was Murray 'The Camel' Humphreys, a Welshman, and he was succeeded by Gus Alex, who is of Greek ancestry" ("Spotlight" 1981: 8).

Frank Nitti was born in Sicily in 1889 and brought to the United States at age two. Known as "The Enforcer" for his role in dealing with internal discipline and external enemies of the Capone organization, Nitti began his career as a barber fencing stolen goods on the side. Although physically unimposing, he had Capone's confidence and became his second in command (Schoenberg 1992). In 1943, Nitti, who had been in poor health, feared prosecution for a nationwide extortion scheme involving the motion picture industry (Demaris 1969), discussed below. On the day an indictment was handed down by a New York grand jury, Nitti committed suicide with a .32 revolver along a railroad embankment. He was not thrown off the roof of a building by Eliot Ness, as portrayed in Brian De Palma's *The Untouchables* (Koziol and Baumann 1987).

The Willie Bioff Episode

Willie Bioff was a Chicago racketeer who specialized in shakedowns of kosher butchers. He went into partnership with George Browne, a local official of the International Alliance of Theatrical Stage Employees (IATSE), whose members also included motion picture projectionists and other movie theater employees. The two began extorting money from theater chains under the threat of "labor trouble." Frank Nitti soon "muscled in" on the scheme, first as a 50 percent and eventually as a 75 percent partner. In 1932, Browne unsuccessfully ran for the presidency of the international union. In 1934, Nitti arranged for Browne to gain the support of Lucky Luciano, Lepke Buchalter, and Longie Zwillman, and he was elected president of the IATSE (Nelli 1976). The convention that elected Browne, notes Malcolm Johnson (1972: 329), was pervaded with "such an atmosphere of intimidation that opposition wilted." Browne appointed Bioff to a union position, and the two increased their extortion activities, this time on a nationwide scale. They were able to extort money from Hollywood film studios such as RKO and Twentieth Century-Fox under the threat of closing down theaters throughout the country (Johnson 1972).

The scheme came to an end in 1941. Joseph M. Schenck, the brother of Twentieth Century-Fox chairman of the board Nicholas Schenck, was indicted for income-tax evasion. In exchange for leniency, he disclosed the activities of

---

7. For a journalistic biography of Murray Humphreys, see Morgan 1985.

Bioff and Browne. Bioff was eventually sentenced to ten years, Browe to eight. But as a result of their cooperation, members of the Outfit, including Nitti, were indicted in 1943 and subsequently convicted. Three years later all were paroled in a scandal that rocked the administration of President Harry Truman. Senator Estes Kefauver (1951b: 148) had this to say:

> The three mobsters [Paul Ricca, Louis "Little New York" Campagna, and Charles "Cherry Nose" Gioe] were released on parole after serving a minimum period of imprisonment although they were known to be vicious gangsters. A prominent member of the Missouri bar presented their parole applications to the parole board, which granted parole against the recommendations of the prosecuting attorney and of the judge who had presided at their trial. In the opinion of this committee, this early release from imprisonment of three dangerous mobsters is a shocking abuse of parole powers.

Bioff, using the name William Nelson, emerged as a friend of Senator Barry Goldwater of Arizona—Bioff was living in Phoenix. In October 1955, Bioff returned from Las Vegas (where he was employed at a gambling casino) in Goldwater's private plane with the senator and Mrs. Goldwater and Mrs. Bioff. At the Riviera Casino, Bioff was spotted by a Chicago gangster, Marshall Caifano (Giancana and Giancana 1992). Two weeks later, on November 4, 1955, Bioff left his Phoenix home and entered his pickup truck. A moment later Bioff and the truck went up in a tremendous explosion—a dynamite bomb had been wired to the starter. Reid and Demaris state that when Goldwater was questioned by reporters, he replied that he did not know William Nelson was the notorious Willie Bioff. "Later, the Senator changed his story. Bioff, he said, was helping him in his study of American labor, giving him special insight into union racketeering" (1964: 42–43).

Paul Ricca

With the death of Nitti, Paul Ricca, born in Naples in 1897, became head of the Outfit. (Giancana and Giancana 1992 maintain that Ricca was the head all along, and that Nitti was simply a figurehead.) Ricca arrived in New York in 1920, fleeing prosecution for murder, and eventually settled in Chicago. There he secured employment with "Diamond Joe" Esposito, a major bootlegger and political power. He also worked in Esposito's restaurant, earning the nickname "Paul the Waiter." Ricca left Esposito to manage a theater in "Little Italy," and was hired by Capone to manage his World Playhouse Corporation. This theater background provided the knowledge needed to engineer the Browne-Bioff extortion scam. With the imprisonment of Capone, Ricca emerged the major power in Chicago organized crime. When Ricca was imprisoned for his role in the theater scheme, Tony Accardo emerged as leader of the Outfit.

Tony (Antonio Leonardo) Accardo

Tony Accardo was born in Chicago in 1906, one of six children, to Sicilian parents. His father was a shoemaker. Raised in the tough Grand Avenue neighborhood, an Italian ghetto on Chicago's Near West Side, Accardo dropped out of school at age fourteen. He subsequently became a member of the Circus Cafe Gang (named after the site of its headquarters), a truckdriver in the bootleg trade, and an enforcer and bodyguard for Al Capone. While his arrest record dates back to 1922, and although he had been arrested about thirty times and was a suspect in at least two murders—including that of Joe Aiello—Accardo could boast that he had never spent a night in jail. In 1955, the Internal Revenue Service expressed dissatisfaction with his tax returns. Since 1940, Accardo had reported over 43 percent of his income as coming from "gambling and miscellaneous sources." The IRS considered this too vague, and prosecution was initiated for income-tax violations. He was eventually convicted and sentenced to six years imprisonment, but the conviction was reversed on appeal. Fearing further federal prosecution as head of the Outfit, Accardo and his aging partner, Paul Ricca, looked for someone to take over the day-to-day operations of the Outfit (Peterson 1962; Brashler 1977). They turned to Sam Giancana.

A resident of suburban River Forest, where he once owned a twenty-two room mansion and later a modest condominium, Accardo spent his winters at a home in Palm Springs, California. During the summer, he often stayed at the home of his son-in-law, Ernest Kumerow, president of Laborers Union Local 1001. In 1978, while in California, Accardo's mansion was burglarized. It appears that the burglars originally stole jewels from the shop of an Accardo friend, and the gang boss ordered them returned. They were in a safe at Accardo's home when the thieves apparently had a change of heart and retrieved their booty, raising the ire of a dangerous man. Within a month, all five were dead. On May 27, 1992, Tony Accardo, the Outfit's elder statesman, died of natural causes, survived by his wife (née Clarice Porter), two sons, two daughters, and six grandchildren (Koziol and O'Brien 1992).

Sam Giancana

Sam Giancana was born Gilormo Giangona in Chicago on May 24, 1908, to Sicilian immigrants. He was called "Mo," "Momo," and "Mooney" by law-enforcement officials and fellow criminals, an apparent reference to his "crazy" behavior as a young man. Raised in the notorious "Patch" of the Taylor Street neighborhood, Giancana was abused as a child and dropped out of school at age fourteen. Living mostly in the streets, he became a member of the "42 Gang," a group that even other criminals of that day viewed as "crazy" (Giancana and Giancana 1992). Fellow members of the 42s, such as Sam ("Teets") Battaglia, Felix ("Milwaukee Phil") Alderisio, Marshall Caifano (legally changed to John M. Marshal), Sam ("Mad Dog") DeStefano, Fiore

Buccieri, and Joe DiVarco, would also gain prominence in the Outfit. While the gang was periodically involved in politics and union organizing as "muscle," its primary activity centered around conventional and often reckless criminality. Deaths, via the police or rival criminals, and imprisonment eventually brought an end to the 42s (Brashler 1977).

His younger brother, Chuck Giancana, and godson, Sam Giancana (1992), report that as an adolescent, Momo Giancana served as a gunman for Al Capone and ran sugar shipments for Joe Esposito. He was arrested thirteen times in 1926, fifteen times in 1927, and twenty-two times in 1928. Many of these arrests resulted in felony indictments, but not a single case reached the trial stage, due to "sympathetic judges." In one murder indictment, the prosecution witness was murdered before trial. In 1928, Esposito was gunned down, reportedly by Giancana on orders from Capone (Giancana and Giancana 1992). In 1929, however, Momo's "luck" finally ran out: he was sentenced to one to five years for burglary. Drafted by the army in 1943, Giancana was rejected for being a "constitutional psychopath" with an "inadequate personality and strong anti-social trends" (Demaris 1969: 8).

Giancana's specialty for the 42s was being a "wheelman"—driving a getaway car. This eventually earned him a position as chauffeur for "Machine Gun" Jack McGurn and, later, Paul Ricca. His Outfit connection, however, was no advantage in rural Garden Prairie, where Giancana was convicted of bootlegging in 1939. (The Outfit continued in the alcohol business after Prohibition, selling backwoods-still whiskey bottled as imported or quality domestic brands to saloon-keepers eager to improve their profits.) Giancana served three years in the federal prison at Terre Haute, Indiana, where he met Eddie Jones, a wealthy black numbers operator. Jones and his brothers were major gambling and political figures in the city's black areas. Eddie had pled guilty to income-tax evasion in 1939 (Haller 1990b). Jones told Giancana about the large amount of money he and his brother George had made in this enterprise, something that had been dismissed by leading white gangsters as "penny ante." Since Prohibition, blacks had dominated the numbers business in Chicago (Haller 1990b). When Giancana was released from prison in 1942, Jones financed his entry into the jukebox racket and became his partner in a variety of gambling enterprises centered in the black areas of the city's South Side.

Giancana repaid his benefactor by advising Tony Accardo of the lucrative black numbers operation, and requested permission to take it over using his crew of 42s (Brashler 1977). After Jones's release from Terre Haute in 1946, he was kidnapped and held for ransom in Giancana's new suburban home in Oak Park. After a payment of $100,000 (according to Giancana and Giancana 1992, the price was $250,000) was made by his family, Jones was released and fled to Mexico with his brother, leaving Teddy Roe in charge of the business. Roe did quite well for six years, his income-tax returns indicating an income of more than $1 million a year, but he was feeling heat from Giancana. After a campaign of intimidation, murder, beatings, and bombings, Roe became the last holdout from Giancana's takeover of the South Side numbers racket. Aiding Giancana's efforts were the police, who raided Roe's policy wheels. In June 1951, three Giancana men tried to kidnap Roe. In the ensuing gun battle, Marshall Caifano's brother, Leonard ("Fat Lenny"), was killed, but Roe escaped. Finally, on August 4, 1952, Roe was ambushed and cut down by a shotgun blast. Sam Giancana had become a principal player in Chicago organized crime (Brashler 1977; Giancana and Giancana 1992).

Money from the numbers enabled Giancana to branch out into other enterprises, and his organizational skills and murderous crew allowed him to prosper. In 1955, Tony Accardo and Paul Ricca, fearful of federal investigations, placed Giancana in charge of the Outfit's day-to-day operations. William Brashler (1977: 258) points out that the "Chicago outfit had always been run more like a corporation than like a family." In fact, the organization inherited from Al Capone more closely resembles the corporate/bureaucratic model of OC discussed in chapter 1, than do the New York crime families. Many powerful figures in the Outfit have been non-Italians: Gus Alex, Greek; Murray

LEONARD PATRICK

Leonard Patrick (1913–   ) was born in England (or possibly in Chicago of English parents—Jews who had somehow acquired an Irish surname) on October 6. He grew up in the Jewish community on Chicago's West Side. His criminal record includes a conviction (as "Joe Cohen") and a seven-year sentence for a 1933 Indiana bank robbery. He has admitted to committing two murders and ordering four others, all during the 1930s and 1940s. During the 1950s, Patrick ran a West Side restaurant that was a center for bookmaking. In 1975, he was sentenced to four years for criminal contempt after refusing to testify in federal court. He has been closely associated with Gus Alex. With a crew of vicious enforcers, Patrick was responsible for gambling and loansharking operations on the city's North Side and northern suburbs. He also controlled several legitimate industrial laundering companies that rent towels, linens, and uniforms.

In 1992, after being accused of extortion from numerous legitimate firms—restaurants, car dealers, theaters—and illegal gambling operators, Patrick pled guilty and agreed to become a government witness. As a result of his testimony, Gus Alex and the crew's main enforcer, Nick Gio, were found guilty of extortion. Patrick and other members of the crew, Mario Rainone and James LaValley, had already pled guilty. In 1993, Gio, at age twenty-six, a thug who reputedly enjoyed beating people, received an eleven-and-a-half-year sentence; Alex, at age seventy-six, was sentenced to fifteen years. In return for his assistance to the prosecution, Patrick received a six-year term, becoming eligible for release in two years.

Sources: Chicago Crime Commission and various articles in the *Chicago Tribune*.

Humphreys, Welsh; and Jews such as Jake Guzik, Dave Yaras, and Lenny Patrick.

Giancana lived a high profile social life, something that had become anathema for the now modernized leaders of organized crime. He had a widely publicized romance with Phyllis McGuire (of the singing McGuire sisters) and a public friendship with Frank Sinatra. He even shared a girlfriend with President John F. Kennedy. Giancana generated a great deal of publicity when he secured an injunction against the FBI's intensive surveillance of his activities. He was imprisoned for contempt from July 1, 1965, until May 31, 1966, for refusing to testify before a federal grand jury, after being granted immunity from prosecution (Peterson 1969). Following his release, Giancana went into exile in Mexico. His daughter states that he was forced into exile by Ricca and Accardo (Giancana and Renner 1985). Giancana remained in Mexico until 1974:

> On July 21, 1974, Mexican immigration agents had literally kidnapped Sam from his San Cristóbal home as he was administering to his plants, clad only in pajamas and a robe. They had dragged him to a waiting car, driven him 150 miles to Juarez, and pushed him across the border of El Paso, Texas, into the waiting arms of U.S. Customs and FBI agents. He was then brought to Chicago for grand jury investigations and for questioning in the murder of Richard Cain (Scalzetti), who had been killed on December 20, 1973, by two shotgun-armed killers. (Giancana and Renner 1985: 349)

Although he was secretly a member of the Outfit, Richard Cain had been appointed head of Cook County Sheriff Richard B. Ogilvie's Special Investigations Unit; the SIU was formed to investigate organized crime. In 1964 Cain was convicted of perjury, but the conviction was reversed on appeal. Fluent in Spanish, Cain went with Giancana to Mexico. He subsequently returned to the United States to stand trial for withholding evidence in a mob murder and was sentenced to four years. Released in 1971, Cain returned to Giancana in Mexico; he was subsequently murdered in 1973 on a visit to Chicago (Giancana and Renner 1985).

The organization was running smoothly without Giancana—Accardo had apparently resumed active control—and his subsequent return to Chicago was apparently not welcomed by the Outfit leadership. On June 19, 1975, Giancana was shot to death at close range in his suburban Chicago home by someone he apparently knew and obviously trusted. Even in death controversy about Giancana continued. It was disclosed that in 1960 the Central Intelligence Agency had contacted John Roselli, a Giancana lieutenant, to secure syndicate help in assassinating Fidel Castro. As noted in chapter 3, Meyer Lansky had arranged for syndicate leaders to establish gambling operations in Havana. When Castro came to power this all ended, costing these men a lucrative income. Syndicate leaders had reason to kill Castro, and they also had contacts in Cuba and among exiles in south Florida. The plot apparently never materialized, and in 1976, Roselli's body was found in an oil drum floating in Miami's Biscayne Bay.

In 1986, top leaders of the Outfit were convicted of skimming $2 million from gambling casinos in Las Vegas, except Accardo, who had assumed senior/semi-retired status. The leaders received long prison sentences: Outfit boss Joseph J. Aiuppa (b. 1907); his second in command, John P. Cerone (b. 1914); Joseph Lombardo (b. 1929); Angelo LaPietra (b. 1920). Also convicted were Milwaukee crime boss Frank Balistrieri, who died in 1993 at age seventy-four; Carl DeLuna, then fifty-eight, a capo in the Kansas City Family; and Milton ("Maishe") Rockman, then seventy-three, brother-in-law of Cleveland crime boss John Scalish and business brains of the Cleveland Family. A key witness at the trial was Angelo Lonardo, the head of organized crime in Cleveland who was seeking leniency on a drug trafficking charge.

Leadership was assumed by Joseph ("Joe Nagal") Ferriola, the former Outfit enforcer who is alleged to have permitted members to involve themselves in drug trafficking, something that had heretofore been off limits. Ferriola died of natural causes in 1989 and leadership was assumed by Sam Carlisi (b. 1921)—who was convicted of racketeering in 1993—and John ("No-Nose") DiFronzo (b. 1928). In 1993, DiFronzo and Donald Angelini, age sixty-six, were found guilty of attempting to infiltrate an Indian reservation gambling operation in California for illegal purposes and were sentenced to 37 months and fined $10,000 and $5,000 respectively. On November 13, 1992, Joseph Lombardo was released from prison and, unlike other mob leaders who live in the suburbs, resumed his residence on the city's West Side.

The size of the Outfit today is markedly smaller than the version once

THE FIRST WARD

From the 1870s to 1990, Chicago's First Ward remained a seemingly untouchable political link to organized crime. That changed in 1990, when indictments were announced against First Ward politicians and gangsters, most of whom were subsequently found guilty: Harry Aleman (b. 1939), a feared Outfit hitman who, as the result of a fix, beat a murder charge in spite of the testimony of two eyewitnesses that he killed a Teamster Union official; Fred Roti, alderman of the First Ward; state senator John D'Arco, Jr., son of the First Ward Democratic Committeeman; D'Arco's law partner; and a former Cook County judge. The case against Pat Marcy (born Pasquale Marchone), secretary of the First Ward Democratic Club and a notorious fixer, was postponed because of his health. In 1993, at age seventy-nine, he died of a heart attack. The First Ward case was developed by the FBI through the use of a corrupt lawyer acting as a mole, and the placing of an electronic bug in a restaurant frequented by First Ward politicians.

ruled by Al Capone. Estimates of membership range from as low as thirty to as high as one hundred and thirty, revealing that it is still hard to determine who is and who is not a "member." Many important Outfit personages are not of Italian heritage, such as Frankie ("The German") Schweihs (b. 1930), a feared enforcer. Nevertheless, outside of predominantly black and Hispanic neighborhoods, the Outfit has been able to maintain hegemony over gambling and related activities in an area that ranges from southern Wisconsin to northern Indiana.

PHILADELPHIA

While New York and Chicago contain the strongest traditional OC groups, there are Italian-American groups operating in other cities, particularly Philadelphia, where there has been a great deal of violence in recent years for domination of that city's OC group.

The Early Days

As one of America's oldest cities, the intertwining of politics, immigration, the saloon, and street gangs was an early part of Philadelphia's history. Unlike New York and Chicago, the Republican Party dominated Philadelphia until the 1950s. As in other urban areas, the outlawing of alcoholic beverages in 1920 provided the outlaws of Philadelphia with unparalleled opportunity:

> While the Volstead Act restricted the manufacture of alcohol for beverage purposes, alcohol was used in a variety of industrial processes and was a normal component of such diverse products as hair oil, lotions, and rubbing alcohol. Federal law required that alcohol manufactured for non-beverage purposes be "denatured"—that is, that poisons be added to the alcohol to prevent its use in products for human consumption. Because the Delaware Valley [New Jersey-Pennsylvania-Delaware] was a major center for the American chemical industry, including the manufacture of industrial alcohol, the area was a center for diversion by bootleggers. (Haller 1985b: 218)

Prohibition rationalized crime to an extraordinary degree. Saloon-keeper Max ("Boo Boo") Hoff and Charles Schwartz emerged as the leading bootleggers. Their cabal consisted of Irish, Jewish, and Italian gangs, although leading assassins often bore Anglo-Saxon names. The Hoff-Schwartz cabal ran gambling houses, one of which fronted as a Fifth Ward political club. Their Industrial Alcohol Company produced millions of gallons, which they distributed to cities as far away as Chicago and Minneapolis (Haller 1985b; Fox 1989).

In 1926, the relative calm between various bootlegging factions began to fall apart, leading to a series of gang wars between the Hoff group and the gang headed by the Haim brothers, Charles and Irving. The struggle took many lives—in one three-day period, fourteen gangsters died. Public pressure eventually led to the impaneling of an extraordinary grand jury. The violence subsided, and Nig Rosen entered the picture.

Nig Rosen

Born Harry Stromberg in Russia in 1903, but better known as Nig Rosen, the future crime leader was raised on New York's Lower East Side and appears to have been associated with the "Bug and Meyer" gang. His arrest record goes back to Prohibition and includes burglary and robbery. Rosen apparently moved to Philadelphia as part of an effort by New York's leading gangsters to draw local syndicates into a wider Jewish-Italian cabal known as the "Big Seven." Rosen formed his own organization in Philadelphia, pushed Hoff aside (Hoff wound up running a dancehall and committed suicide at age forty-eight), and eventually became the most powerful crime figure in the city—but not without considerable violence (Jenkins and Potter 1985; Fox 1989).

After Prohibition ended, Rosen moved into gambling. By 1939, he dominated the numbers racket in Philadelphia, described by Senator Kefauver (1951b: 46):

> The numbers game in Philadelphia has achieved the size of a big industry and, like big industry, it appears to be organized on a highly efficient scale. It operates through tight control, manipulated by a politico-gambler-police tie-up that makes it impossible for any intruder to edge his way in from the outside. The city is organized into a number of geographical territories, each with its own bank, in turn affiliated with sufficient political connections to be able to operate without too much fear of molestation.

Success in gambling did not prevent Rosen from involvement in drugs, and in 1958 he was sentenced to five years for his role in a French Connection heroin conspiracy. Rosen subsequently retired to Florida, where he had gambling interests and close friends, particularly Meyer Lansky (Lacey 1991). He later moved to Israel. His chief lieutenant, Willie Weisberg, continued to be a power in the rackets, working with other criminals, including Angelo Bruno.

The Bruno Family

In 1911, Salvatore Sabella (b. 1881), a Sicilian fugitive from a murder charge, fled the island for the United States. Despite his illegal alien status, Sabella became a crime boss in the South Philadelphia Italian community. In a 1927 incident, two of his rivals were murdered and four others wounded. Sabella was charged with murder. Although acquitted, publicity surrounding the case led to his deportation. John Joseph ("Nazone") Avena took over from Sabella and remained boss until his murder in 1936 at the hands of a rival Italian faction—the six Lanzetti brothers, former bootleggers who had been enforcers for Nig Rosen. Joseph Bruno ("Giuseppe Dovi"), no relation to Angelo,

199

became boss of this group, ruling from Bristol, Pennsylvania, and Trenton, New Jersey, until his death of natural causes in 1946. He was succeeded by underboss Joseph Ida. Ida and his underboss, Dominick Olivetto of Camden, New Jersey, were arrested at the 1957 meeting of crime bosses in Apalachin, New York (discussed in chapter 3). Fearing deportation, Ida moved back to Italy, and Olivetto declined to assume control of the Family (Pennsylvania Crime Commission 1990).

The Philadelphia crime Family, composed of Sicilian and Calabrian factions, became locked in a power struggle between Antonio Dominick Pollino, a Calabrian, and Angelo Bruno (Annaloro), born in Villalba, Sicily, in 1911. Angelo's father ran a grocery store in South Philadelphia and Angelo married in 1932. His two children, a son and daughter, are not involved in organized crime. Bruno was sponsored by Michael Maggio. In addition to his criminal activities, Maggio owned a cheese company—Bruno appeared on the books as a salesman. In 1934, Bruno became a partner in a land deal with New York crime Family boss-to-be Carlo Gambino (Friel and Gunther 1990). Pollino reportedly plotted against Bruno, and the latter learned of the plot. With backing from fellow Sicilian Carlo Gambino, Bruno moved against Pollino. Instead of killing him, however—and thereby risking a Sicilian-Calabrian rift—Bruno permitted his rival to flee Philadelphia. In 1958, with Gambino's backing, Bruno became Family boss. By this time, the era of the Jewish gangster had been eclipsed by those of Italian heritage.

For more than twenty years Bruno ran his small Philadelphia crime Family rather quietly and efficiently, earning him the sobriquet "the quiet don." (For a discussion of the economics of the Bruno Family, see Haller 1991.) He dressed simply, and when a *caporegime* bought a new Lincoln, Bruno reportedly ordered him to trade it for a less ostentatious car (Salerno and Rivele 1990). His relationship with bookmakers, loansharks, and racketeers was symbiotic—based on their need for his assistance, particularly financing—and not coercive. He permitted *caporegime* Harry ("Hunchback") Riccobene (b. Sicily, 1910) to run his crew without interference and, except for a handsome Christmas offering, without sharing his profits. By 1980, this manner of rule was in trouble (Anastasia 1991).

The younger members of his fifty- to sixty-member Family were disturbed by Bruno's nonchalance with respect to the lucrative opportunities afforded by legalized gambling in Atlantic City and his somewhat hypocritical attitude about drug trafficking. Bruno's employers of record for tax purposes, Raymond ("Long John") Martorano and his brother John, owners of a vending machine company, were major methampetamine ("speed") dealers. While Bruno and the Martoranos made a considerable profit from Atlantic City, these were not shared with other Family members, who operated behind their boss's back to deal in drugs. Also, Frank Friel and John Gunther (1990) state that Bruno knowingly made money—albeit indirectly—from heroin. On March 21, 1980, as Bruno sat in a car in front of his modest South Philadelphia home talking to driver John Stanfa, he became the victim of a shotgun blast. A month later, the body of the man believed to be behind the murder, Family *consigliere* Antonio ("Tony Bananas") Caponigro of Newark, was found stuffed in a car trunk in the Bronx. He had been tortured, strangled, stabbed, and finally shot, and several hundred dollars in twenty dollar bills were found in various parts of his naked body. Caponigro's murder was reportedly ordered by commission members for the unauthorized killing of a fellow boss (Anastasia 1991; Pennsylvania Crime Commission 1990).

Nicky Scarfo

Underboss Philip ("Chicken Man"—he owned a chicken restaurant) Testa became boss of the Bruno Family. He chose Nicholas ("Little Nicky") Scarfo (b. 1929), a man of small stature (five feet, five inches, 130 pounds) with a reputation as a violent hothead, as *consigliere*. Scarfo became a member of the Family during the late 1950s, sponsored by one of his uncles, a *caporegime*. In fact, four of his uncles were Family members. In 1963, during an argument in a diner, Scarfo stabbed a man to death, for which he received a two-year sentence, but served only three months. Bruno wanted to rid himself of this Calabrian troublemaker, and did it in his own inimitable manner. Scarfo was promoted to *caporegime*, but was "exiled" to Atlantic City, which was at that time a beach resort in serious decline. There Scarfo assembled a group of violent young men who worked at whatever illegal activities could be found. In 1972, he was imprisoned for two years after refusing to testify before the New Jersey State Commission of Investigation. Bruno was also incarcerated at the time for the same "offense." By the time of Bruno's murder, however, casino gambling had turned Atlantic City into a mob gold mine, buoying the fortunes of Scarfo and his crew.

In the wake of Bruno's death, Testa and Scarfo quickly cleaned house, killing those suspected of involvement in the plot against Bruno. They "opened the books" to new members, including Testa's son Salvatore ("Salvie"; b. 1956) and Scarfo's nephew, Philip ("Crazy Phil") Leonetti (b. 1953), a man with a murderous reputation. The quiet, relatively peaceful ways of Bruno were history. For example, despite warnings from Testa and Scarfo, Philadelphia union boss John McCullough attempted to organize workers in Atlantic City, at the expense of Scarfo-backed Local 54 of the International Hotel and Restaurant Employees Union. He received a Christmas delivery of poinsettia plants:

> The deliveryman placed two plants on the table and said he had to bring several more in from his truck. . . . Moments later the deliveryman, wearing a ski cap, heavy jacket, and thick rubber glovers, returned with more plants. He headed straight for the kitchen, put the flowers on the table, then pulled out a .22 caliber pistol and pumped six bullets into the head and neck of the union boss. (Anastasia 1991: 99)

On March 15, 1981, as Phil Testa put a key into the door of his home, a powerful remote-controlled bomb filled with nails and explosives detonated under Testa's porch, ending his short reign as Philadelphia crime boss. His

201

Philadelphia Organized Crime Figures

Max Hoff

Nig Rosen

Joseph Bruno

Nicodemo Scarfo

underboss, Peter Casella, was suspected of the crime. When his gambit for becoming boss failed, Casella retired from Philadelphia one step ahead of Scarfo's expected vengeance. He died of natural causes two years later. Apparently with the approval of the New York bosses, Nicky Scarfo became boss. He maintained a high profile—Rolls Royce, cabin cruiser, travel with an entourage. His regime became noted for a dramatic expansion of money-making activities—and violence. Real and imagined enemies were killed. Vicious young enforcers imposed a street tax ("the elbow") on any illegal entrepreneurs who could be located—bookmakers, loansharks, drug dealers—and Scarfo got half of all they collected. (An exception were outlaw motorcycle clubs, which were not approached.) Then there was the matter of Hunchback Riccobene.

When Scarfo insisted on his share of the Riccobene profits, the *caporegime* balked. Attempts on his life proved fruitless. The aging Riccobene—he was nearly seventy—struck back: Scarfo's *consigliere* was ambushed and killed in 1982. Later that year Riccobene was ambushed twice: once he was shot five times; the shooter missed on the second occasion. In the midst of the war, Scarfo served a seventeen-month federal prison term for an old gun possession charge. Meanwhile, Scarfo enforcers stalked Riccobene and his men. While they failed to get the Hunchback, they killed his brother Robert at the end of 1983. The Riccobene faction finally sued for peace, and their operations were divided up among the Scarfo group. In 1984, Scarfo was released from prison.

The Philadelphia Family was now filled with violent young men who had been recruited for this very trait. Scarfo appointed an underboss (Salvatore "Chuckie" Merlino, b. 1939) with alcohol problems, and opened membership to inexperienced men under thirty. Fearful that his leadership would be challenged, and growing increasingly violent, erratic, and paranoic, Scarfo had his loyal *caporegime* and chief enforcer, Salvie Testa—Phil's son—murdered. The young, newly initiated Family members intimidated and abused neighborhood people who had once been cultivated with favors by the older criminals. Scarfo moved back and forth between Atlantic City and South Florida, running the Family from afar.

While street taxes provided substantial income, especially shakedowns of drug dealers, there was also a more sophisticated aspect of the Scarfo Family enterprise. He established his own cement company, Scarf, Inc., reaping profits from the building craze resulting from legalized gambling in Atlantic City. In 1982, Scarfo helped engineer the election of Atlantic City's mayor. There were also real estate and construction deals, through which Scarfo sought to control all building in Philadelphia. This "sophistication" eventually proved the undoing of the Scarfo Family. An FBI undercover construction industry sting incriminated a member of the city council, along with Nicholas ("Crow") Caramandi (b. 1935), a Family member who reported directly to Scarfo. Left unaided by a resentful Scarfo, and believing he would be killed by his erratic boss, Caramandi became a government witness. His testimony, and that of five other Family turncoats—including his own underboss and nephew, Philip

Leonetti—brought an end to the Scarfo regime. Between 1987 and 1989, every ranking member and dozens of top associates were convicted and sentenced to long prison terms. Scarfo received sentences of fourteen years, fifty-five years, and life. An attempt by Scarfo to run his Family from prison through his son, Nicky, Jr., failed; indeed, there was an attempt on Nicky, Jr.'s life in 1989.

The dismantling of the Bruno/Scarfo Family did not bring traditional organized crime in Philadelphia (and Southern New Jersey, where the Family held sway) to an end. John Stanfa moved to the front. If Stanfa is successful in asserting control over the Bruno Family, it will represent the completion of a historical circle. Stanfa was born in Sicily in 1940. He arrived in New York in 1964, and eventually was sent to Philadelphia by the Gambino Family. Stanfa was the driver for Angelo Bruno on the night of his assassination and served almost six years in prison for perjury connected to that murder. While Scarfo was boss, Stanfa was *persona non grata* in Philadelphia, and only his connection to the Gambino Family kept him alive. His two brothers and brother-in-law are members of the Sicilian Mafia and, as boss, Stanfa has brought Sicilians into the Philadelphia Family (Pennsylvania Crime Commission 1991). In the style of old-time crime bosses, the balding, bearded Stanfa keeps a low profile, driving the same Chevrolet in which Bruno was killed back in 1980 (Anastasia and Hollman 1992). He is able to draw upon fellow Sicilians as well as a core of young South Philadelphia Italian-Americans who aspire to be part of "the life" (Mallowe 1993). But Stanfa's leadership has been challenged by remnants of the Scarfo group, reinforced by other young, violent men, and warfare has broken out between the two factions.

ORGANIZED CRIME: THE FUTURE

During the decades following the Second World War, organized crime underwent considerable change. It became increasingly clear that OC was dominated mainly by Italians—the Irish, except for small pockets in New York and Boston, were no longer involved. And while the sons of Jewish immigrants played a vital role in organized crime, by the third generation the Jews had moved out. Jackson Toby (1958: 548) explains:

> Jews and Italians came to the United States in large numbers at about the same time—the turn of the century—and both settled in urban areas. There was, however, a very different attitude toward intellectual accomplishments in the two cultures. Jews from Eastern Europe regarded study as the most important activity for an adult male. The rabbi enjoyed great prestige because he was a scholar, a teacher, a logician. He advised the community on the application of the Written and Oral Law. Life in America gave a secular emphasis to the Jewish reverence for learning. Material success is a more important motive than salvation for American youngsters, Jewish as well as Christian, and secular education is better training for business and professional careers than Talmudic exegesis. Nevertheless, intellectual achievement continued to be valued by Jews—and to have measurable effects. Second generation

Jewish students did homework diligently, got high grades, went to college in disproportionate numbers, and scored high on intelligence tests. Two thousand years of preparation lay behind them.

Immigrants from Southern Italy, on the other hand, tended to regard formal education either as a frill or as a source of dangerous ideas from which the minds of the young should be protected. They remembered Sicily, where a child who attended school regularly was a rarity. There, youngsters were needed not [sic] only to help on the farm. Equally important was the fact that hard-working peasants could not understand why their children should learn classical Italian (which they would not speak at home) or geography (when they would not travel in their lifetimes more than a few miles from their birthplace). Sicilian parents suspected that education was an attempt on the part of Roman officials to subvert the authority of the family. In the United States, many Southern Italian immigrants maintained the same attitudes. They resented compulsory school attendance laws and prodded their children to go to work and become economic assets as soon as possible. They encouraged neglect of schoolwork and even truancy. They did not realize that education has more importance in an urban-industrial society than in a semi-feudal one. With supportive motivation from home lacking, the second-generation Italian boys did not make the effort of Jewish contemporaries. Their teachers tried to stuff the curriculum into their heads in vain. Their lack of interest was reflected not only in low marks, retardation, truancy, and early school leaving; it even resulted in poor scores on intelligence tests. They accepted their parents' conception of the school as worthless and thereby lost their best opportunity for social ascent.

The pool of available candidates for membership in organized crime dwindled in Jewish communities. In Italian communities it remained adequate enough; the large-scale organizations needed to profit from Prohibition were no longer necessary. In Chicago, for example, during the height of Prohibition, Al Capone is reputed to have employed seven hundred gunmen for an organization that involved thousands of persons, while contemporary estimates of the size of the Chicago Outfit have ranged only as high as one hundred and thirty. The largest of the crime Families, the Gambino Family, is estimated to have about four hundred members. These core members, however, have associates, and the total number of criminal actors participating directly or indirectly in a crime group's enterprises is many times the size of the core membership at any given time.

Noting the small size of Italian-American crime groups and the absence of armed retainers, Peter Reuter (1983: xi) has concluded: "My analysis suggests that the Mafia may be a paper tiger, rationally reaping the returns from its reputation while no longer maintaining the forces that generated the reputation." He theorizes that having established a dominant position, an unchallenged monopoly of force, the Mafia can depend on its fearsome reputation, an asset that can be substituted for personnel costs that would be incurred by maintaining armed forces. Reuter states that challenges to Mafia power in black and Hispanic communities have not "generated any effort by the Mafia to assert control through superior violence" (1983: 136). Reuter further theorizes that this may be based upon the lack of available force, or simply the result of a cost-benefit analysis that mitigates against its use—excessive force attracts law-enforcement attention and is bad for business in general.

Reuter notes that challenges to the Mafia outside of black and Hispanic communities have not been noticeable. The structure of Italian-American OC groups provides an explanation. Business activities are typically decentralized, often franchised, while violence is not. The Mafia is often "invisible"; that is, members usually avoid directly operating illegal enterprises such as gambling or marginal businesses such as "topless bars" or "strip joints." Instead, they often finance or "license" such enterprises, sometimes receiving payments for restricting entry or competition, sometimes providing no service—simple extortion. How would a competing group set out to deal with this operation? The most obvious method would be a direct attack on its members. But they do not reside, meet, or otherwise assemble in significant numbers, and they may be unknown to anyone except persons intimately involved in the local criminal underworld. The decentralized nature of the organization would render a frontal assault unproductive. While a number of members and associates could be killed here and there, the net effect would be analogous to punching an empty bag.

Any group with the temerity to undertake this challenge would require the resources necessary to sustain an "army in the field" for an indefinite period of time. Elderly members would probably head for condominiums in south Florida and Palm Springs, California, but remaining behind would be a cadre of assassins whose sole function would be the murder of those mounting the challenge to the group's supremacy. They could be reinforced by executioners from other groups. In addition, as Reuter (1983: 133) notes: "Large numbers of young men in major American cities are willing to accept paid employment as violence disputants." Rational criminals with martial skill would be inclined to side with an organization with proven staying power—the Mafia—rather than take a chance with a seemingly reckless new group.

Summing Up: Ethnic Succession and the Future of Organized Crime

Nicholas Gage (1971: 113) points out in *The Mafia Is Not an Equal Opportunity Employer* that "no door is more firmly locked to blacks than the one that leads to the halls of power in organized crime." He states that Irish, Jewish, and Italian mobsters have tended to recruit and promote from within their own ethnic groups, while cooperating with one another. Organized crime is no less stratified than the wider "legitimate" society, and the dominant groups in both have always been white. This leads to the issue of *ethnic succession* in organized crime.

Daniel Bell (1964) refers to crime as an American way of life, "A Queer Ladder of Social Mobility." He points out that the "jungle quality of the American business community, particularly at the turn of the century, was reflected in the mode of 'business' practiced by the coarse gangster elements, most of them from new immigrant families, who were 'getting ahead' just as Horatio Alger had urged" (1964: 116). Francis Ianni (1974: 13–14) notes that this "queer ladder" had organized crime as its first few rungs:

> The Irish came first, and early in this century they dominated crime as well as big-city political machinations. As they came to control the political machinery of large cities they won wealth, power and respectability through subsequent control of construction, trucking, public utilities and the waterfront. By the 1920s and the period of prohibition and speculation in the money markets and real estate, the Irish were succeeded in organized crime by the Jews, and Arnold Rothstein, Lepke Buchalter and Gurrah Shapiro dominated gambling and labor racketeering for over a decade. The Jews quickly moved into the world of business and the professions as more legitimate avenues to economic and social mobility. The Italians came next. . . .

According to this thesis, each successive immigrant group experienced *strain* (see chapter 2) to which some members reacted by *innovating* in accord with a tradition that had been established by earlier American entrepreneurs—the "robber barons" discussed in chapter 2. Ethnic succession results when a group experiences success in crime and legitimate opportunities become more readily available. Strain subsides, and the group moves out of organized crime, creating an opportunity for innovation for the succeeding immigrant group. According to this thesis, persons involved in organized crime are not committed to a deviant subculture, but are merely using available, albeit illegal, opportunity to achieve economic success.

Ianni states that ethnic succession is continuing, that "the Italians are leaving or being pushed out of organized crime [and] they are being replaced by the next wave of migrants to the city: blacks and Puerto Ricans." While the succession may not have been obvious to Ianni when he was conducting his research in New York during the early 1970s, today we would have to add other ethnic groups: Mexicans, Cubans, Colombians, Dominicans, Chinese, and Vietnamese, all of whom will be discussed in chapter 5. According to the ethnic succession thesis, involvement in organized crime is simply a rational response to economic conditions. Other theorists reject this one-dimensional view; organized crime, they argue, provides important psychic rewards and meaningful social structures.

New York has experienced the rise of a notorious gang of Italian-American hoodlums dubbed the "Purple Gang" (apparently after the murderous Detroit Jewish mob of Prohibition Days) in the Pleasant Avenue section of Harlem, a syndicate stronghold. They have reportedly been used as "muscle" and executioners in many gangland murders, and their reputation for violence has made them very useful to the leadership of traditional organized crime. The Purple Gang has been involved in numerous rackets, particularly drug trafficking, which is facilitated by their contacts with young men of other ethnic backgrounds who have access to importation quantities of heroin and cocaine. In his study of some members of the Purple Gang, Peter Lupsha (1983) found that they tend to have been born between 1946 and 1951, third-generation Italian-Americans who are related by blood and marriage. While they come from the Pleasant Avenue neighborhood, most reside in the Bronx or suburban Westchester County. "They are now, like many New York suburbanite businessmen, commuters to the old neighborhood for work, money, and visiting rather than residents" (1983: 76). The leadership of the Purple Gang has reportedly been "made"—inducted into membership of traditional OC Families in New York. Similar groups have been identified as part of other OC families. In 1992, for example, the head of an enforcement crew in the Bonanno family, Thomas ("Tommy Karate") Pitera, age thirty-seven, was accused of dealing drugs, torturing victims, and killing seven people. The martial arts devotee, owner of a Brooklyn bar and disco, had no prior criminal record (Lubasch 1992a). After a seven-week trial, Pitera was convicted of six murders and sentenced to life without parole.

Entry into organized crime, states Lupsha (1981: 22), is not based on blocked aspirations; that is, anomie or strain. Rather, it "is a rational choice, rooted in one perverse aspect of our values; namely, that only 'suckers' work, and that in our society, one is at liberty to take 'suckers' and seek easy money." In fact, the term for a member of traditional OC, "wiseguy," exemplifies such an attitude. Nicholas Pileggi (1985: 20) presents Paul ("Paulie") Vario, a powerful *caporegime* in the Lucchese crime family, as an example. Henry Hill stated:

> Paulie was always asking me for stolen credit cards whenever he and his wife, Phyllis, were going out for the night. Paulie called stolen credit cards "Muldoons," and he always said that liquor tastes better on a Muldoon. The fact that a guy like Paul Vario, a *capo* in the Lucchese crime family, would even consider going out on a social occasion with his wife and run the risk of getting caught using a stolen credit card might surprise some people. But if you knew wiseguys you would know right away that the best part of the night for Paulie came from the fact that he was getting over on somebody.

With a great deal of insight, Pileggi (1985: 36) captures the wiseguy attitude toward society: "They lived in an environment awash in crime, and those who did not partake were simply viewed as prey. To live otherwise was foolish. Anyone who stood waiting his turn on the American pay line was beneath contempt." According to this view, OC comprises a deviant subculture to which members have a commitment that is not mitigated by the absence of strain. As one Gambino crime Family member told a reporter: "[W]e don't want to be part of your world. We don't want to belong to country clubs" (Brenner 1990: 181). Benjamin ("Lefty") Ruggiero of the Bonanno Family explained: "As a wiseguy you can lie, you can cheat, you can steal, you can kill people—*legitimately.* You can do any goddamn thing you want, and nobody can say anything about it. Who wouldn't want to be a wiseguy?" (Pistone 1987: 330).

There is an additional dimension to OC that explains the ability to recruit young men into its ranks, even in the absence of sense of *strain*. Certain persons find the notion of being part of the "mob" or the Outfit, being a wiseguy or goodfella, as alluring as other youths might find being part of a popular college fraternity. There are romantic notions about OC, often reinforced by media portrayals—life imitating art. Such young men have been exposed to discussions of OC among relatives or friends, although the latter may not be involved in any criminal activity. For such young men, if they have the necessary connections—a relative friendly with an OC figure, for example— organized crime can take on the dimension of an attractive career choice.

In Chicago, where the writer has been conducting research into organized crime, this phenomenon has been referred to as the "suburbanization of the Mob": young men who have only known middle-class economic conditions becoming part of organized crime. Like the member of an outlaw motorcycle club (discussed in chapter 5), these young men are attracted to a lifestyle, not necessarily by the potential financial rewards offered by organized crime. For example, Salvatore ("Solly D.") DeLaurentis (b. 1938), who was raised in the Taylor Street neighborhood in Chicago, aspired to be a "gangster"—a term he uses to describe himself—since his earliest days. Once his family moved out to suburban Lake County, Solly D. found himself cut off from his career path—Lake County lacked the critical mass of older criminals and their young associates/wannabees. So DeLaurentis gradually made connections back in the old neighborhood and eventually became a member of the Infelice crew (discussed in chapter 1).

But while such young men appear to enjoy playing the wiseguy role—often outfitted with large pinkie rings and gold chains—many are neither bright nor tough. The long, neighborhood-based apprenticeships through which OC chooses the cream of the "wannabees" are history. Those accepted into membership are often not the street-smart, stand-up kids of yesteryear, but social failures and potential informants quick to play "I've got a secret"—turn on their closest associates to avoid incarceration. As one knowledgeable Chicago detective explains, the Outfit lacks "quality control." In fact, he notes, the lack of adequate resources for violence has caused a greater reliance on nonmember associates and even outlaw bikers to carry out murders.

But in New York, young men raised in comfortable middle-class circumstances have advanced into organized crime in a most violent way. Roy DeMeo of Brooklyn, a second generation American of Neapolitan heritage, became a loanshark while still in his teens. His uncle was a star prosecutor in the Brooklyn District Attorney's Office. But at age thirty-two, in order to protect an extortion scheme run with his partner, a member of the Gambino Family, Roy committed his first murder—a solo job using a silencer-equipped pistol. He subsequently put together a crew of active criminals from the Carnarsie section of Brooklyn. Their initial murder victim, a car dealer who was testifying against them before a Brooklyn grand jury, was kidnapped, stabbed repeatedly, and dismembered. The medical examiner who handled the case, Dr. Dominick

ETHNIC SUCCESSION?

Peter Lupsha (1981: 22) questions the "ethnic succession" thesis. He argues that despite Francis Ianni's (1972; 1974) limited findings, Italian OC figures who have gained economic status are not leaving organized crime and, in many instances, their progeny have followed them into the "life." This view certainly has some empirical support. For example:

Joseph Doto, Jr., son of Prohibition racketeer and New Jersey gambling boss Giuseppe ("Joe Adonis") Doto

Michael Franzese, the stepson of Colombo Family *caporegime* John ("Sonny") Franzese*

Salvatore ("Bill") and Joseph Bonanno, Jr., sons of crime boss Joe Bonanno

Michael Bolino, son of Colombo Family soldier John Bolino

Raymond Patriarca, Jr., son of New England crime boss Raymond Patriarca

Jason Angiulo, son of New England underboss Gennaro Angiulo

Anthony, Joseph, and Vincent Colombo, sons of crime boss Joseph Colombo

Armond Dellacroce and Angelo Ruggiero, the son and nephew of Gambino Family underboss Aniello Dellacroce

Alphonse Persico, Jr., son of Colombo Family boss Carmine Persico

Anthony Zerrilli, Jr., son of Detroit crime boss Anthony Zerrilli

Louis ("The Mooch") Eboli, son of Genovese Family crime boss Thomas ("Tommy Ryan") Eboli

Jimmy Eppolito and his son Jimmy, Jr., both members of the Gambino Family

Thomas and Joseph Gambino, sons of crime boss Carlo Gambino

Anthony Indelicato, son of Bonanno Family *caporegime* Alphonse ("Sonny Red") Indelicato

Paul Vario, Jr., son of Lucchese *caporegime* Paul Vario

Peter Mosca, son of Ralph Mosca, a *caporegime* in the Gambino Family

John Gotti, Jr., son of imprisoned crime boss John Gotti

DiMaio, did not know that his cousin Roy DeMeo—his branch of the family spelled the name differently—was responsible for the murder. DeMeo was initiated into the Gambino Family, and his crew eventually killed an estimated seventy-five persons (most of the bodies were never found). In fact, contrary to mob custom, Roy DeMeo added murder-for-hire to his repertoire, and against the edict of the Gambino Family boss, dealt in cocaine. One of DeMeo's leading assassins was arrested and began providing evidence against the Gambino Family. Soon afterward, in January 1983, Roy DeMeo was the victim of a volley of shots fired into his head at close range. He was forty-two years old (Mustain and Capeci 1992).

Ianni (1972: 193) describes the "Lupollos," the Italian OC Family he studied, whose core members are all related by blood or marriage. In the fourth

Joseph D'Arco, son of Lucchese Family underboss Alponse D'Arco

Anthony Accetturo, Jr., son of New Jersey Lucchese Family captain Anthony ("Tumac") Accetturo

Giacomo ("Jackie") DiNorscio, son of Dominick ("Tommy Adams") DiNorscio, a member of the Bruno family

James Carmine Galente, nephew of former Bonanno Family boss Carmine Galente

Joseph Scopo, son of Ralph Scopo, a *caporegime* in the Colombo family.

Joseph Carl Gallo, son of Gambino Family *caporegime* Joe N. Gallo

Joseph and John Balistrieri, (both lawyers and) sons of Milwaukee crime boss Frank Balistrieri

In Philadelphia: Philip and Frank, Jr., sons of caporegime Frank ("Chickie") Narducci; the three sons of *caporegime* Michael Ciancaglini; Vincent Iannece, son of member Charles Iannece; Joseph Merlino, son of underboss Salvatore Merlino; Salvatore Testa, son of boss Philip Testa.

Sources: Peter A. Lupsha, "Individual Choice, Material Culture, and Organized Crime." *Criminology* 19: 3–24, 1981; Francis A. J. Ianni, *A Family Business: Kinship and Social Control in Organized Crime*. New York: Russell Sage Foundation, 1972; Francis A. J. Ianni, *The Black Mafia: Ethnic Succession in Organized Crime*. New York: Simon and Schuster, 1974.

----

* In 1986, Michael Franzese, then thirty-five, pleaded guilty to a massive swindle to sell gasoline without paying taxes. He received a ten-year sentence and was released in 1989 to pay the government back more than $14 million—which was never paid. That year, under a grant of immunity, Franzese admitted that he was a member of organized crime and testified in Chicago federal court that he provided credibility for threats against sports figures and entertainers who balked at doing business with World Sports and Entertainment, Inc. He also dealt with club owners who did not want to book acts represented by the firm. Franzese, who had a financial interest in World Sports, provided testimony against its owners in order to gain government leniency. The owners of World Sports, Norby Walters and Lloyd Bloom, were convicted of racketeering and fraud. Franzese produced low-budget movies and wrote a book in which he portrayed himself as the "yuppie Don." In 1991, he received a four-year sentence for probation violation. For Michael Franzese's version of these and other events surrounding his life, see Franzese and Matera (1992).

generation, "only four out of twenty-seven males are involved in the family business organization. The rest are doctors, lawyers, college teachers, or run their own businesses." Ianni argues that ethnic succession continues (1974: 12): "We shall witness over the next decade the systematic development of what is now a scattered and loosely organized pattern of emerging black control in organized crime into the Black Mafia." Gus Tyler (1975: 178) does not find Ianni convincing, claiming that Ianni's evidence "consists of a pimp with a stable of seven hookers, a dope pusher, a fence who dabbles in loan sharking and gambling, a con man who gets phony insurance policies for gypsy cabs, and a numbers racketeer, etc." Tyler points out that, although these activities are "organized," they are not in a class with white organized crime either qualitatively or quantitatively. Indeed, early in his (1974) book, Ianni reports that the brother and partner of the aforementioned "dope pusher," actually a large-scale heroin dealer in Paterson, New Jersey, was found without his genitals—a "message" from the "White Mafia." As for blacks and Hispanics replacing Italians in OC, Lupsha (1981) argues that black and Hispanic groups have only succeeded in controlling markets that Italian-American groups have discarded because of poor risk-to-profit ratios.

A development affecting ethnic succession in OC is the arrival of relatively large numbers of southern Italian immigrants into the New York metropolitan area during the 1960s. According to the President's Commission, many of these immigrants are *mafiosi* fleeing intense pressure from Italian law enforcement and a murderous factional conflict between competing Mafia groups in Sicily. "Their entry into the United States was made particularly easy by the reversal of a restrictive immigration statute that had discriminated against southern and eastern Europeans" (PCOC 1986a: 53). Any number of these southern Italians—from the city of Naples, the surrounding Campania area, and the Province of Calabria, in addition to Sicily—are related to members of traditional OC groups in New York. According to police sources in New York City, some of these "zips" have been admitted to membership in traditional OC Families, while many more are operating in their own associations independent of, but in cooperation with, the traditional crime groups. They have been particularly active in heroin trafficking. ("Zips" will be discussed in chapter 5.)

While *strain* can help explain why some persons in disadvantaged groups become involved in organized crime, it fails to provide a satisfying explanation for the continued existence of traditional organized crime. In other words, while poverty and limited economic opportunity can certainly impel one toward innovative activities, they do not explain why middle-class youngsters become involved in organized crime, or why crimes by the wealthy and the powerful—for example, securities fraud, insider trading, collusive agreements— continue to be a problem in the United States. Perhaps the mind-set we are referring to as "wiseguy" transcends socioeconomic boundaries. In fact, organized criminal activity on a rather outrageous scale, not necessarily connected to conditions of *strain*, has been an important part of American history.

In recent years, however, the ranks of organized crime have been thinned by successful federal prosecutions using the RICO statute (to be discussed in chapter 9)—particularly the long, double-digit sentences typically handed down. Whether or not the Italian-American community will be able to provide sufficient replacement to keep traditional organized crime viable in the years to come remains an open question. In the meantime, new criminal groups are emerging that may prove to be more powerful and difficult to combat than those of traditional organized crime. These nontraditional crime groups are the subject of chapter 5.

REVIEW QUESTIONS

1. What was the connection between corrupt politicians in Chicago, vice entrepreneurs, and big business?
2. What was the importance of the family in the development of organized crime in Chicago?
3. What was the effect of Prohibition on Chicago politics, politicians, and vice entrepreneurs?
4. What effect did the election of a reform mayor have on Chicago during Prohibition?
5. How did the onset of the Depression and the end of Prohibition affect organized crime?
6. What happened to the Capone organization after the imprisonment and subsequent death of Al Capone?
7. How does organized crime in Chicago differ from that in New York?
8. How did politics in Philadelphia differ from that of most other cities with organized crime?
9. How did the geographic location of Philadelphia allow criminals to take advantage of profits from Prohibition?
10. How is the continued participation of Italians, and the absence of Jews, in organized crime explained?
11. Why would it be difficult for a new criminal group to challenge traditional organized crime?
12. What is meant by "ethnic succession" in organized crime?
13. What are the nonfinancial dimensions that attract persons to organized crime?

5

Nontraditional Organized Crime

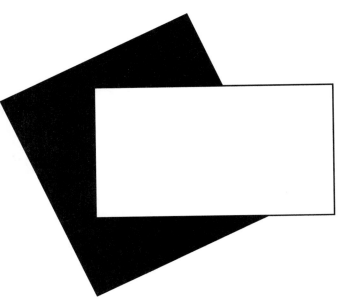

One element that characterizes nontraditional criminal organizations discussed in this chapter is drug trafficking. Francis Ianni (1974: 320) notes that this sector of organized crime activity seems to offer some possibility for black and Hispanic innovators to expand beyond the confines of the ghetto: "Narcotics and drug traffic have the same pattern of relationship which surrounded alcohol and bootlegging during the Prohibition era." David Durk, a New York City police officer and former partner of Frank Serpico, states that if anything positive can be said for the drug business, it is that it has become *an equal opportunity employer* (Durk and Silverman 1976).

Some of these organizations are native to the United States, some were formed by recent immigrants, and others are headquartered in countries such as Mexico and Colombia. These criminal organizations are developing in the United States in the absence of the corrupt political machines that provided a protective incubator for the Irish, Jewish, and Italian criminal organizations of an earlier era. The first groups to be discussed in this chapter originated in southern Italy—the *Nuovo Mafia* and *Nuovo Camorra Organizzata*.

NUOVO MAFIA

The second World War had negative consequences for southern Italy, blocking the northward migration of excess labor (Catanzaro 1992). The end of the war brought a Mafia renaissance in Sicily. A vacuum in local leadership was filled by former *capomafiosi*: "Not only were they respected local figures, but as victims of Mori's operation against the mafia, they were also in a good position to pose as anti-Fascists" (Finley, Smith, and Duggan 1987: 214). Many *mafiosi* became town mayors under the Allied military government (Catanzaro 1992). There was a brief flirtation with Separatism, seceding from the mainland in favor of affiliation with the United States. That idea was discarded when the government in Rome announced Sicilian autonomy in 1946. In return, the most important *capomafioso*, Calogero Vizzini ("Don Calo"), the illiterate son of a peasant father, pledged support for the Christian Democratic Party. Born in 1877, Don Calo had been imprisoned by Mussolini, although he spent only a few days in prison before being released through the intervention of a young Fascist he had befriended. Vizzini was now a *gabelloto* and mayor of Villalba. He "would hold court each morning in the small plaza of Villalba. People would approach him for favors, such as help with a bank loan or assistance with a court case—indeed anything in which 'authority' could be useful" (Duggan 1989: 67). As an "anti-Fascist," he possessed a special business license from the Allied military government. This allowed him to head up a flourishing black market in olive oil. In this endeavor, Vizzini worked with American expatriate Vito Genovese (Lewis 1964).

When Don Calo died of natural causes in 1954, he left an estate worth several million dollars (Pantaleone 1966). He was the last of the old-style *capomafiosi*, characterized by modesty in both speech and dress: "The old Mafia chief was a rural animal, holding sway over the countryside, dressed in shirt-sleeves and baggy pants: a multi-millionaire who chose to look like a peasant" (Servadio 1974: 21). In fact, notes Pino Arlacchi (1986), the behavior of the old *mafioso* had power—*rispetto*—as its primary goal. The modern *mafioso*, however, is a materialist for whom power is simply a means to achieve wealth; he exudes conspicuous consumption. The "New Mafia" is centered in Palermo and its urban environs. The "new" *mafioso* is not bound by the traditions of the rural *cosca*. He dresses like a successful businessman, sometimes a bit flashy, like the American gangster whose pattern he seems to have adopted—cross-fertilization. According to Norman Lewis (1964: 273), the New Mafia has a distinctly American tint, the result of American gangsters being deported to Sicily "where they immediately assumed leading positions in the Mafia hierarchy of the island."

The New Mafia resorted to robbery and kidnapping to accumulate the capital necessary to be a player in legal endeavors such as the construction industry and also illicit heroin and cocaine marketplaces. The New Mafia also continued the *pizzo*, protection money extorted from large and small businesses (Cowell 1992f). Financial considerations play a secondary role in this enterprise—it is primarily the Mafia way of maintaining territorial domination (Stille 1993).

The contrast between the "Two Mafias"—rural and urban—is evidenced by a conflict between the *capomafiosi* of Corleone in the immediate postwar years. Michele Navarra was a medical doctor and a representative of the old Mafia. Luciano Liggio (sometimes spelled Leggio) represented the New Mafia. Born in 1925, at the age of nineteen, Liggio was the youngest *gabelloto* in the history of Sicily—his predecessor was murdered. Navarra was the Inspector of Health for the area, head of the town's only hospital—his predecessor was mysteriously murdered. In the tradition of Don Calo, Navarra also trafficked in stolen beef and served as chair of the local branch of the Christian Democratic Party. Luciano Liggio was his most violent assistant. Liggio murdered a trade unionist who was a threat to Navarra's power, and the murder was witnessed by a shepherd boy. In a state of shock after telling his story, the boy fainted and was taken to the hospital. There, an injection from Dr. Navarra ended the boy's life (Servadio 1976).

With his followers, Liggio began to develop activities of his own, but they "had nothing in common with the organization presided over by Don Calo but its iron laws of secrecy and the vendetta" (Lewis 1964: 123). Liggio chose to control the supply of meat to the Palermo market rather than raising livestock. He drove out all of the tenant farmers on the estate under his protection, burning down their houses, and replaced them with day laborers. He recruited gunmen, and when anybody crossed him they were summarily shot. From 1953 to 1958 there were 153 recorded Mafia murders (Servadio 1976). According to Jerre Mangione (1985: 147), Liggio was connected to organized crime in the United States and "had been a key contact man working closely with Joseph Profaci of the American Mafia."

The Old Mafia benefitted from feudal conditions, living off its control of the land and cheap labor. When a dam was proposed for the town of Corleone to harness the river water going into the ocean, Dr. Navarra vetoed it—he made money from the water pumped from artesian wells. The New Mafia, oriented toward capitalistic change, recognized the profits that could be earned from control over building projects, although this dam has yet to be built. While Navarra and his followers were living in the nineteenth century, Liggio was a man of the times. With Navarra in control, Lewis (1964) notes, nothing would change, and the New Mafia recognized this reality. In 1958, fifteen of Liggio's men ambushed Dr. Navarra's car; there were 210 bullets found in his body. One by one, the remaining followers of Navarra were murdered (Servadio 1976). Liggio, who once marched a peasant leader through the crowded sidewalks of Corleone and hanged him from a tree without anyone doing anything about it, became the undisputed *capomafioso* of the Corleonesi *cosca*.

During the 1960s the emerging *cosche* engaged in a bitter struggle for dominance. This led to the trial of 114 *mafiosi* in 1967, and Luciano Liggio emerged as the most powerful *capomafioso* (Shawcross and Young 1987). In 1974 Liggio was convicted for the murder of Dr. Navarra (Schmetzer 1987; 1988a). In 1993, he died of a heart attack while serving a life sentence. Liggio's right-hand man, Salvatore ("Toto") Riina, became the head of the Corleone *cosca*. Possessing only a grammar school education, Riina is called "The Beast" for allegedly ordering mass killings and personally participating in some of them. He formed private alliances with rising members of many *cosche*, planted his own men in others, and then with a reign of terror came to dominate the Mafia—at a cost of nearly one thousand lives (Stille 1993).

After being tried in absentia and sentenced to life imprisonment for murder and drug trafficking, Riina became the most wanted man in Italy. He was able to avoid authorities for more than twenty-three years—his photographs were out-of-date. While living as a fugitive, Riina was married by a Mafia priest (who was eventually defrocked), honeymooned in Venice, sired four children, and continued to oversee the activities of his Mafia clan. (In Corleone most people deny the existence of a Mafia, which serves to keep this town of 12,000 safe from crime.)

The violence that gained the *capomafioso* his nickname, however, also drove *mafiosi* to the authorities seeking protection from the Beast (Cowell 1992e; 1992h). Their cooperation is believed to be behind the capture of the sixty-two-year-old Don Toto, arrested in his car on a Palermo street on January 16, 1993. He and his driver were unarmed. Later that year, he was ordered imprisoned for life by a Palermo court.

One of the victims of Riina's campaign was *capomafioso* Tommaso Buscetta. He lost ten relatives, including two sons, a brother, a nephew, a son-in-law, and two brothers-in-law. In 1983 Buscetta, who had escaped to Brazil, was arrested on an international warrant. He attempted to commit suicide with a strychnine pill. When he came out of the coma, Buscetta agreed to cooperate with American and Italian authorities. In 1987, with the help of Buscetta and other informants, the Italian government convicted 338 *mafiosi* in the largest mass trial (452 defendants) of its kind ever held in Italy. Michele Greco and his brother Salvatore, leaders of the Ciaculli *cosca* and allies of the Corleone *cosca*, were sentenced to life imprisonment for ordering the murder of a senior anti-Mafia magistrate and seventy-seven other persons. Buscetta also revealed ties between leading government figures, industrialists, and the Mafia, part of an unprecedented scandal that rocked Italy at the beginning of 1992 and continues (Cowell 1993b).

Despite the convictions—or perhaps because of them—a Mafia campaign of murder and terror ensued in 1988. Eighteen people were slain in a two-week period. The victims included a retired prosecutor, although many of the others were informers or relatives of informers. The anti-Mafia mayor of Palermo, who had all public contracts transferred to Rome and out of the hands of *mafiosi*, is protected by a police squad on a twenty-four hour basis (Schmetzer 1988b). On September 27, 1988, the judge who sentenced the Greco brothers, Antonio Saetta, and his son, were killed by men wielding submachine guns on a Sicilian country road. By 1988, only 112 of those sentenced remained incarcerated—the rest had been released on "legal technicalities" (Schmetzer 1988). In November of 1992, in yet another highly publicized "Mafia roundup," the police arrested Giuseppe Greco, Michele's son. And the crackdown continued throughout 1993: Benedetto ("Nitto") Santapaola, Riina's heir apparent, who had been a fugitive for eleven years, was captured near Messina in Eastern Sicily; the head of the Camorra and 'Ndrangheta and hundreds of their followers were arrested (Cowell 1993c).

The ruling Christian Democratic Party was able to coopt Mafia power through a reorganization of the party apparatus in the south, the judicious use of the police and new detention laws, and control of expanded opportunities for political patronage divorced from clientelistic Mafia power brokers (Arlacchi 1986). Party officials replaced *mafiosi* as power brokers (Catanzaro 1992). To the extent that *mafiosi* remained politically active, it was as an integral part of the Christian Democrats, and not as an adjunct and independent source of power. In their new role, notes Arlacchi, the many *cosca*-clans have become a political power more directly involved with government than the old rural Mafia. They forge alliances with one another, and the *cosche* run their own candidates for office. The advantage of this new role is that it "simplifies the problem of relations with official power, obviating the need to negotiate agreements and alliances with politicians from outside the mafia family itself" (1986: 174). Across southern Italy, the government has dissolved dozens of town councils because of their corrupt relationships with Mafia clans (Cowell 1992f).

Vast government spending in the *Mezzogiorno*, often on useless building projects that provide patronage opportunities, had become a vehicle for Mafia infiltration. "By corruption and physical intimidation," notes Alexander Stille (1993: 63), "Mafia-controlled firms took their share of public contracts, either directly or through subcontracts and dummy companies." This approach has aided the spread of the Mafia phenomenon beyond its traditional areas, "to towns and provinces that had once been free of organized crime. In many areas, democracy as we know it ceased to exist." The *Nuova Mafia* is quite capable of killing politicians: On March 12, 1992, they murdered the Sicilian head of the Christian Democratic Party in a Palermo suburb. It was his job to keep peace between the party and the Mafia—"This was the Mafia's way of announcing that it was 'renegotiating' its arrangement with the Prime Minister" (Kramer 1992: 112; Cowell 1992b).

As their political role changed, so too did their ability to act as brokers between peasant and officialdom. The *mafioso* was no longer *un uomo di rispetto*, but simply an urban gangster in the American tradition; that is, a predatory criminal without popular roots or popular backing. The New Mafia, notes Arlacchi (1986: 60), reflects the emerging *Mezzogiorno*. The south is changing: modernization, fed by government-sponsored public works, is slowly encroaching on feudal ways. Above all, the mark of respect has more to do with one's wealth than with one's name or reputation. It was power, not wealth, that the traditional *mafioso* pursued: "The possession of wealth, regarded by the traditional *mafioso* as one among the proofs and results of a man's capacity to make himself respected, becomes, in the 1960s and 1970s, meritorious in itself." Family wealth, not family honor, were the reasons for violence: "Wealth, in a word, becomes intrinsically honourable and confers honour on its possessors."

As the Mafia was reduced to a marginal role in society, many *mafiosi* reacted in a similar fashion as other marginalized persons such as Jews during the early days of capitalism. They pursued wealth as the only way back to honor and power (Arlacchi 1986). The New Mafia jumped into capitalism and showed a willingness to use violence as a tool for achieving economic ends. To that extent, the Mafia entrepreneur has a distinct advantage over non-Mafia competitors. The result has been a tremendous escalation of Mafia violence (Chubb 1982). Mafia violence as a result of economic competition serves to pollute the Sicilian political system (Catanzaro 1992).

The *mafioso*-entrepreneur is the outcome of an astonishing cultural mutation, in which many old-established individual qualities are put to fresh use. A taste for risky undertakings, lack of scruple, the ability to close his eyes to the immediate consequences of his actions—all these typical characteristics of the old man of honour are found again, appropriately modified, in this figure. In consequence, the *mafioso* is not held back by the legal and cultural checks that restrain his fellow entrepreneurs: for him, even more than for them, personal considerations count for little when it comes to business. (Arlacchi 1986: 87–88)

Since 1971, the New Mafia has assassinated investigative, judicial, and political officials, something that was anathema to the Old Mafia: "Offenses against symbols of authority were foreign to the methods of a Mafia that, considering itself an authority and surrogate for the state, wanted to preserve and respect certain values" (Kamm 1982a: E3). Raimondo Catanzaro (1992: 24) reports that "the mafioso customarily collaborated with the justice system. In fact, he would often appear before those who accused him of illicit activities as an honest citizen who helped bring the true outlaws to justice, claiming it was to his credit that order reigned in his community." On May 23, 1992, the prosecutor who helped gather evidence for the massive Mafia trial, Judge Giovanni Falcone, was killed, along with his wife and three bodyguards, when a half ton of TNT was detonated by remote control on a road near Palermo. The killer(s) obviously had inside information about Falcone's movements. His murder led to an anti-Mafia demonstration by about 40,000 persons in Palermo, a remarkable occurrence for that city (Cowell 1992c). But it did not prevent the Mafia from striking again. On July 20, 1992, Paolo Borsellino, Falcone's replacement as Palermo's chief public prosecutor and head of a new anti-Mafia superagency, was killed along with five police bodyguards. One hundred and seventy-five pounds of a Czech-made plastic explosive placed under a car were detonated while Borsellino was walking outside an apartment building where his mother and sister live (Cowell 1992d). The government responded by dispatching 7,000 troops to Sicily in a highly publicized anti-Mafia campaign. The move failed to impress law enforcement officials, who wondered how the military could provide the type of investigative services required to deal with the Mafia. The Mafia was apparently similarly unimpressed: on July 28, 1992, four assassins on motorcycles killed a senior Mafia investigator, Inspector Giovanni Lizzio, as he drove home from work.

As a result of the assassination of government officials, the New Mafia has lost the support of important elements of Italian society. In 1982, Salvatore Cardinal Pappalardo, the Sicilian-born archbishop of Palermo, led Sicilian priests "in a vocal campaign against the Mafia, reversing decades of church indifference toward and even tolerance of local dons" (Withers 1982: 5). Later that year, in November 1982, while on a visit to the island of Sicily, Pope John Paul II issued an attack on the Mafia. Even the Christian Democratic party took an official stance against the Mafia, a move that cost the party heavily at the polls in Sicily (Colombo 1983), where at least 500,000 persons (out of a population of five million) are directly tied to the Mafia (Cowell 1992b). In 1993, the Mafia struck back at its critics in the Catholic church: Giuseppe Puglisi, age fifty-six, a priest who spoke out against the Mafia, was shot in the neck and killed in front of his rectory in a Palermo slum.

There is some dispute over the degree of organization in the New Mafia. There are an estimated five to seven thousand members—each with his own network and a circle of dozens of relatives, friends, associates, and employees—divided into about 150 *cosche* (Stille 1993). According to Arlacchi (1986), the New Mafia consists of *cosche* throughout Sicily and Calabria (where it is sometimes referred to as *'ndrangheta*), each held together by a core of blood relatives and encompassing a membership of about thirty persons (Arlacchi 1986). Within each *cosca* there are important ties and relationships, but an absence of formal structures (Hoffman 1983). *Capomafioso*-turned-informer Tommaso Buscetta describes the *cosca* as hierarchical, with elected leaders and precise decision-making processes. Catanzaro discounts the "electoral procedure" since it is not used to decide between two or more contenders, but simply to confirm the single contender for leadership—a "rubber stamp." Each *cosca* is linked to other *cosche* by a twelve-man commission (*cupola*) under Michele Greco, known as "The Pope of the Ciaculli *cosca*." The New Mafia, Catanzaro contends, like its older predecessor, is not formally structured like a bureaucratic organization. Similarities between the Mafia and formal associations, he argues, are largely superficial.

The murders and the Italian government's apparent disarray "alarm both Italian and American officials, who suspect that the Mafia's heroin trade to the New York area is passing unimpeded through new conduits and that Sicilian drug traffickers are forming a potentially dangerous alliance with Colombia's cocaine lords" to supply cocaine to European consumers (Suro 1988: 1). According to one report, on Valentine's Day, 1989, a meeting took place in Nice, France, between representatives of the Mafia, 'Ndrangheta, Camorra, Venezuelan, and Colombian cartels: "The outcome of the meeting was an alliance and a carving up of the trade bringing heroin from the East and cocaine from South America. By and large, the Sicilians kept the heroin routes and a foothold in the white-powder trade, the Calabrians won a lucrative client role in heroin, and the Camorra emerged as the specialists in cocaine" (Vulliamy 1992: 13).

By 1992, the Latin American connection was becoming more apparent—six hundred kilograms of cocaine were shipped directly from Colombia to Sicily (Cowell 1992a). That same year, authorities from the United States, Colombia, and Italy reported the arrest of 165 persons for money laundering that involved Sicilian *mafiosi* and the Cali cocaine cartel. The money represented the considerable profits from Mafia distribution of Colombian cocaine in Europe—more than $40 million was transferred to Colombia through accounts at commercial banks in the United States (Pear 1992; Moseley 1992).

The greater political and economic unity that emerged with the formation of the European Community and the breakup of the Communist bloc provides new opportunities for Mafia, Camorra, and 'Ndrangheta clans to move drugs, firearms, extortionate practices, and laundered money into northern Italy and across national boundaries. "Drug money," states Jane Kramer, (1992: 112) "has put the Mafia all over Italy." The Corleone cosca, for example, "has what amounts to an official Milan [Italy's industrial and commercial heartland] branch." The profits generated from its illegal business, particularly drugs, cannot easily be reinvested in these same enterprises. These cash-rich criminals have spread their investments throughout Europe. For example, fourteen Camorra members were arrested for using drug money to purchase restaurants and supermarkets in Germany and Spain, while others invested in casinos and real estate in France. "There is hardly a European city without mob representatives who have forged profitable ties with local criminals" ("Mafia Poised for East Europe" 1992: 7). As if to emphasize this point, in November 1992, Italy issued arrest warrants for fugitive Mafia suspects in the Netherlands, France, and Germany (Cowell 1992g). There are even reports of mafiosi forming ties with criminal groups in Eastern Europe (Moseley 1992).

THE "ZIPS"

The connection between the Nuovo Mafia, Nuova Camorra Organizzata, and American organized crime is heroin and, more recently, cocaine. The Old Mafia was "hampered by the cult of honour, which obligated them to squander their time and resources in gaining supremacy over their rivals, and by the fact that their income was drawn from parasitic activities: in consequence, they were unable to amass the large cash sums needed to get involved at the highest levels of the world drugs import-export circuit" (Arlacchi 1986: 203). The New Mafia is under no such cultural constraints, and activities in the construction industry allowed New Mafia firms to amass the money necessary to invest in large-scale drug trafficking.

Among Italian-American crime groups in the United States there has been a demand for what Arlacchi (1986: 221) refers to as "criminal labour," particularly in the highly rewarding but dangerous enterprise of drug trafficking. Southern Italy has provided a vast labor market for Italian-American drug trafficking organizations. "In southern Italy, mafia and camorra groups can rely on a 'reserve army' of individuals prepared to endanger their own—and other people's—lives in the execution of especially risky and violent tasks, because the problem of inner-city environment and youth unemployment are growing continually worse in the Mezzogiorno, so that the supply of criminal labour is continually increasing" (Arlacchi 1986: 194). In Naples and the surrounding Campania area, the Nuova Camorra Organizzata of Raffaele Cutolo has recruited young boys, most under fourteen—the Italian penal code exempts them from punishment—to commit murders and deliver heroin. Uli Schmetzer (1985: 4) points out that "for a child growing up in the slums of Naples, amid daily violence and where only the strong and cunning are admired, the

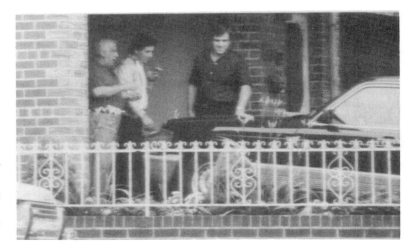

The "Pizza Connection" under FBI surveillance. Benny Zito (center), heroin buyer, and brother-in-law Sal Finazzo (in black shirt), meet with Giuseppe Ganci, heroin supplier, at Ganci's house on June 20, 1983.

Café owner Anthony Aiello (left), go-between, visits Ganci on June 23, and in the garage takes out a brown paper bag from the trunk of Ganci's Mercedes.

Aiello (left) confers with Ganci before departing. Aiello's pizza parlor in Brooklyn was a suspected heroin dispensary.

Aiello departs with the bag. The principals in these drug buys use code names related to restaurants. Before this pickup, FBI wiretaps revealed Ganci saying he was going to get the "rolls."

Aiello carries the bag of "rolls" to his Mercedes.

Another pickup. Salvatore Mazzurco (left), go-between, and Ganci meet at Ganci's garage on June 30. Mazzurco's telephone beeper bypasses lines that could be wiretapped.

Left. Moments later, Ganci takes a wad of bills from Mazzurco. *Right.* Mazzurco leaves Ganci's with a Fiuggi mineral water carton that he deposits in his Mercedes. This exchange occurs after a conversation in a restaurant between the two men about "cleaning tables" with "water."

On July 10, Cesare Bonventre arrives at Ganci's carrying a man's purse—big enough to hold a considerable amount of money.

Salvatore Catalano takes the purse to his bakery around the corner and returns with it, apparently empty, to Ganci's house.

Ganci (left) and Catalano hold a discussion, with the purse between them on the railing.

Bonventre joins the group. The purse is still on the railing.

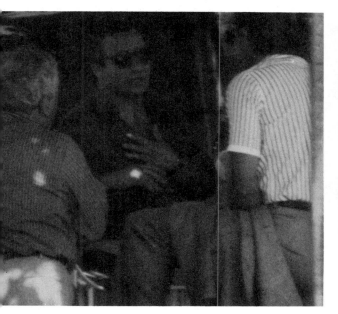

Ritual kisses signal the departure of Bonventre, to whom Catalano has returned the purse. A prominent New Jersey contractor looks on.

On July 23, 1983, Giuseppe Ganci leaves his New Jersey pizzeria carrying a plastic bag with unknown contents.

227

Camorra bosses grow to idol stature." Members of this "criminal labor" who have entered the United States are collectively referred to (by criminals and law enforcement alike) as "Zips," reputedly because of their ability to speak Italian or the Sicilian dialect rapidly.

In the early 1960s, southern Italian criminal organizations came under intense pressure, the result of a murderous factional conflict discussed earlier. As a result of this conflict, which eventually became known as *La Grande Guerra*, "The Great War," a number of *mafiosi* fled to the United States. The struggle flared up again during the 1980s, and between 1980 and 1983 cost the lives of more than five hundred *nuovo mafiosi*. Scores of members were arrested and held for trial, and in a pattern reminiscent of the early years under Mussolini, many *mafiosi* fled southern Italy. "Their entry to the United States was made particularly easy by the reversal of a restrictive immigration statute that had discriminated against southern and eastern Europeans" (PCOC 1986a: 53). The escalating violence and mass trials of Mafia suspects, combined with a need for criminal labor in the United States, served to increase immigration. "Law enforcement experts naturally assumed that the new arrivals would be absorbed into existing families in the United States as others before them had been assimilated. However, these expatriates remained loyal to their original families in Sicily and formed the nucleus of an independent *La Cosa Nostra* group in the United States" (PCOC 1986a: 53).

Ties between traditional organized crime and the *Nuovo Mafia* were highlighted during the "Pizza Connection" case, which was concluded in 1987. Tommaso Buscetta was a prosecution witness at the drug trial of twenty-two defendants. (For an exciting journalistic look at the "Pizza Connection" investigation, see Blumenthal 1988a; also Alexander 1988.) A Mafia group of Gaetano Badalamenti, then sixty-four, an ousted *capomafioso* from Cinisi, Sicily, was found to have supplied heroin with a total value in excess of $1.6 billion to a group headed by Salvatore ("Toto") Catalano, then forty-six, a captain in the Bonanno crime Family of New York. Catalano arrived in the United States from Sicily in 1961 and headed a crew of Zips in the Knickerbocker Avenue section of Brooklyn. The Sicilian defendants purchased morphine base in Turkey and processed it in Sicily. Pizza parlors in the United States owned by the defendants were used to facilitate the drug trafficking. Testimony revealed that southern Italian criminal organizations, in addition to cooperating with their American counterparts, were engaging in totally independent heroin operations. Two men implicated in the case were with Carmine Galente in a Brooklyn restaurant when he was shot down in 1977: Baldo Amato (b. 1952) and Cesare Bonventre (b. 1951). Both men were Sicilians, Bonanno cousins, and members of his crime Family. They helped set up Galente's murder on behalf of Bonanno boss Phil Rastelli. (On April 6, 1984, the body of Bonventre was found stuffed into two barrels in a Garfield, New Jersey, warehouse.)

One of the important Zip drug organizations was led by several Gambino cousins and headquartered in Cherry Hill, New Jersey. Gary D. Liming of the Drug Enforcement Administration (DEA) states:

Although related to the late Carlo Gambino family of New York, the New Jersey Gambino drug operations are independent from the New York family. There are direct lines of communication and influence based on actual blood ties between the New Jersey Gambinos and other traditional organized crime families in New York. Gambino family members own significant interests in the pizza industry in South Jersey and parts of Pennsylvania. These businesses have been used for concealing illegal immigrants, for laundering money, and for storing drugs. They are known to have employed illegal aliens and other nonfamily members who were more experienced in drug trafficking to smuggle heroin into and transport it within the United States. (Permanent Subcommittee on Investigations 1983: 134)

In 1988, during a follow-up to the Pizza Connection case investigation, fifty-two persons, many of them Zips, were arrested in the United States and charged with trafficking in heroin and cocaine. Among those arrested were several "Cherry Hill Gambinos," including the brothers Giuseppe (Joseph) and Giovanni (John) Gambino. Giovanni was a fugitive from an Italian conviction for heroin trafficking and a *caporegime* in the Gambino Family under John Gotti; Giuseppe is a soldier in that Family. A third brother, Rosario, is serving a sentence for a 1984 drug conviction in New Jersey (Blumenthal 1988b; Lubasch 1993). Rosario and Giuseppe operated pizza shops, restaurants, and a disco in Philadelphia. On October 23, 1984, after a six-week trial, four Gambino relatives including Rosario were convicted in a Newark federal court of marketing heroin in South Jersey. Rosario was sentenced to forty-five years; Erasmo received thirty-four years; Antonio received thirty years; and Antonio Spatola received thirty-four years. In 1993, the trial of Giuseppe and Giovanni Gambino and two of their associates resulted in a mistrial. The two were convicted of bail jumping.

The Zips and their American counterparts "share similar customs, criminal philosophies and a common heritage. The prototype of the crime Family is identical in each system" (PCOC 1986a: 53). In criminal and law enforcement circles, however, their "Old World" ways have earned them more fear and respect than their American counterparts. Just how many Zips are in the United States is not clear, but they are believed to be concentrated in the Northeast particularly in the New York City area. According to the President's Commission (1986a), other groups are known to be located in Boston, Buffalo, Chicago, Philadelphia, Houston, and Dallas. In 1988, Carmine Esposito, then thirty-two, a Camorra leader who entered the country illegally in 1984, was discovered working as a chef in an upscale restaurant of which he was part owner, on Chicago's North Side. He was arrested by federal officials on Italian warrants alleging involvement in twelve murders. The Italian authorities subsequently declined to extradite Esposito because a "speedy trial" deadline had expired (Koziol 1988), but in 1989 he was ordered deported by a U.S. immigration judge.

These recent additions to the organized crime scene have confounded the theory of "ethnic succession" (discussed in chapter 4) in which older ethnic groups move out of organized crime, to be followed and replaced by newer groups.

LATINO ORGANIZED CRIME

Most Latino organized crime groups import their criminal organizations along with the drugs they sell. Most active among them are groups based in Mexico and Colombia, Cuban exiles, and more recently, Dominicans.

The Herrera Family

The major Mexican trafficking organizations supplying heroin to the United States

> are generally extended familial organizations, but loyal workers sometimes are given the status of "quasi-family" [compadres] members of the groups. The organizations work to eliminate competition and to control as completely as possible all aspects of the heroin trade. Members act as opium cultivators, village middlemen, and heroin brokers and distributors. In the United States, the organization typically controls distribution from the wholesaler to the retail distributor, but has little or no involvement in street distribution. This is seen as an unnecessarily risky and low-profit aspect of the business, and is left to outsiders. (PCOC 1986: 108–109)

Much of the trafficking in Mexican heroin has been dominated by one group, the Herrera Family, whose operations began shortly after World War II. From their first laboratory in Mexico, the Herreras shipped heroin to relatives who had moved to Chicago. Actually a cartel of six interrelated family groupings, the Herrera Family has been headed by the sometimes imprisoned Jaime ("Don Jaime") Herrera-Nevarez (born 1924 or 1927), a former Mexican state judicial police officer. (The judicial police are similar to the Canadian Royal Mounted Police in jurisdiction.) Headquartered in Durango, a city of about 200,000 in the state of Durango (with a population of about 1 million), the organization is estimated to have around five thousand members, about two thousand of whom are related by blood or marriage. Despite the 1978 conviction and incarceration of ("Don") Jaime Herrera-Nevarez and several key Family members, the organization remains active.

Since most members are tied by blood, marriage, or fictional kinship, the group has proven to be very difficult to infiltrate on both sides of the border. In the United States the Family operates out of Chicago. From Chicago, Mexican heroin is wholesaled to groups in New York, Philadelphia, Boston, Detroit, and Louisville. "Efficient organizational management is maintained by some twenty-six executive-level directors, and a vast array of 'field representatives' in a number of American cities. This network is held together through the Herrera organization's Chicago 'offices' and through constant communications and trips back to the organization's headquarters in Durango" (Lupsha and Schlegel 1980: 7). Elaine Shannon (1988: 59) reports that Don Jaime lives the life of a *padrone*, giving to the poor, befriending the rich, and playing godfather at weddings and baptisms. "In the village of Santiago Papasquiaro, where many of the opium farmers lived, the clan built the water system, installed streetlights, and created a town square. Three hospitals benefited from the clan's philanthropy." The Herreras did not buy off the power structure in Durango—they *are* the power structure.

By the 1980s, the Herrera family had established cocaine contacts throughout Latin America. In fact, Colombians have now married into the Herrera Family. In 1985 Federal Judicial Police arrested Don Jaime's son for cocaine trafficking. His case was subsequently transferred from Mexico City to Durango, where he was ordered released by a local judge for lack of evidence. In July 1985, 135 persons comprising eight separate Herrera-related distribution rings were indicted in Chicago. By 1987 the Herrera Family was reeling under a continuing federal investigation in the Chicago area that resulted in more than eighty convictions, and dozens more became fugitives. By the end of 1988, however, those who had been convicted and those who were fugitives had been replaced. Herrera Family operations in both heroin and cocaine surged.

Cubans

Until 1976, Cuban criminal organizations arranged for the importation and distribution of cocaine from Colombia. When Fidel Castro overthrew the corrupt dictatorial regime of Fulgencia Batista early in 1959, he expelled American gangsters who operated gambling casinos in Havana. Many of their Cuban associates fled to the United States along with *narcotraficantes* who had distributed cocaine in Cuba. They settled primarily in the New York-New Jersey and Miami areas and began to look for new sources of income. Many Cubans who fled with, or soon after, the Batista loyalists were organized and trained by the Central Intelligence Agency in an effort to dislodge Castro. After the Bay of Pigs debacle in 1961, members of the CIA-organized Cuban exile army were supposed to disband and go into a lawful business. However, as Donald Goddard (1978: 44) points out, "they had no lawful business." Elements of these exile groups (they often overlapped) began to enter the cocaine business. At first they imported only enough cocaine to satisfy members of their own community, but by the mid-1960s the market had expanded way beyond the Cuban community, so they began to import the substance in greater quantities.

Until the early 1970s, the importation of marijuana, counterfeit Quaaludes, and cocaine into the United States was largely a Cuban operation; the suppliers were Colombians. During the latter half of the 1960s Colombians began emigrating to the United States in numbers sufficient to establish communities in New York, Miami, Chicago, and Los Angeles. Many were illegal immigrants who entered the United States through the Bahamas. They carried false documents—phony Puerto Rican birth certificates or forged immigration papers of high quality. The Colombian traffickers became highly organized both in the United States and at home. By 1973, independent foreign nationals could no longer "deal drugs" in Colombia. In 1976 the Colombians became dissatisfied with their Cuban agents in the United States who were reportedly making most of the profits and shortchanging the Colombians. Enforcers, often young men from Colombia's version of the "wild west," the Guajira Peninsula, or Barrio Antioquia, the slums of Medellín, were sent in. Cubans were systematically executed in Miami and New York. By 1978, Cubans remaining in the cocaine business had become subordinate to the Colombians. Then the cocaine wars began between rival Colombian gangs, bringing terror to south Florida.

Colombians

Control of most of the cocaine industry remains in the hands of a cartel of Colombian dealers, although some Colombian traffickers have set up laboratories in other Latin American countries and even in the United States: "Reasons for this trend include increased law enforcement in Colombia and the increasing cost of ether and acetone in Colombia. [While acetone has wide industrial use in Colombia, ether does not, and each kilo of cocaine requires seventeen liters of ether.] The cost of these chemicals has increased as a result of controls imposed by the Colombian government on their importation and sale and a concerted effort by the U.S. Drug Enforcement Administration to disrupt the supply of chemicals esssential in the cocaine refinement process. . . . Further, acetone and ether are widely available for commercial purposes in the United States, making control of their illicit use much more difficult than it has been in South America" (PCOC 1986C: 32). Increasingly, Colombian traffickers are moving over their western border into neighboring Venezuela.

Colombia, a nation of about 26 million, is the only South American country with both Pacific and Caribbean coastlines. It is a nation that has been torn by political strife, with civil wars in 1902 and 1948. On April 9, 1948, the leftist mayor of Bogotá was assassinated in the street before thousands of his supporters. The assassin was immediately lynched and three days of rioting ensued, setting the stage for a civil war. *La Violencia*, as the civil war of 1948–58 is known, cost the lives of about 300,000 persons (Riding 1987a). It ended when the Liberals and the Conservatives formed the National Front, but several Marxist insurgencies continue to threaten the stability of the central government. Not only was murder frequent, but the methods used were often sadistic, such as the *corte de corbata*—the infamous "Colombian necktie"—in which the throat is cut longitudinally and the tongue pulled through to hang like a tie. Another practice, *no dejar la semilla* (do not leave the seed), includes the castration of male victims and the execution of women and children (Wolfgang and Ferracuti 1967).

Kathleen Romoli (1941: 37) notes: "At the root of Colombia's easy violence is an extraordinary indifference toward death." The homicide rate is 68 per 100,000—eight times higher than that of the United States. Murder is the leading cause of death for Colombian males aged fifteen to forty-four (Marx 1991b; Riding 1987a). Romoli points out that since "death has small significance, human life has little importance" (1941: 37). An example can be found in the battle to control Colombia's lucrative emerald industry. In 1989 about fifty men stormed the luxury ranch of Gilberto Molina, the "Emerald King," who was also suspected of involvement in the drug trade. The attackers took over the ranch and systematically executed Molina and sixteen of his body-guards and friends.

In this socio-political atmosphere bandits have roamed freely, engaging in a combination of brigandage, terrorism, and revolution. In the northern cities of Barranquilla and Santa Marta, and in La Guajira, smuggling (*contrabandista*) groups have operated for decades. Bandits, *contrabandistas*, and Guajiran Indians, often backed and financed by businessmen in Bogotá, have emerged as crime Families or the *narcomafia*. Members are often related by blood, marriage, or *compardrazgo* (fictional kinship), and in many important respects the core groups resemble those of the Sicilian Mafia. In a country where drug barons act as a state within a state, George de Lama (1988b: 5) reports that an estimated 120 armed paramilitary groups "ply their murderous trade in the cities and countryside, sometimes selling themselves to the highest bidder as outmanned and intimidated judges and government officials feel helpless to stop them."

The President's Commission on Organized Crime (1986c: 78–79) points out that the Colombians have been able to control the cocaine market for a number of reasons:

> Geographically, Colombia is well-positioned both to receive coca from Peru and Bolivia and to export the processed drug to the United States by air or by sea. In addition, the country's vast central forests effectively conceal clandestine processing laboratories and air strips, which facilitate the traffic. Perhaps most importantly, the Colombians have a momentum by benefit of their early involvement in the cocaine trade. They have evolved from small, disassociated groups into compartmentalized organizations and are sophisticated and systematized in their approach to trafficking cocaine in the United States. Further, groups in the Colombian population in the U.S. provide traffickers access to this country and often serve as a distribution network for Colombian cocaine. And, there is a Colombian reputation for violence that serves to maintain discipline and intimidate would-be competitors.

Enforcers (*sicarios*) are well trained in their craft (Mowatt 1991) and are known to torture and mutilate their targets and members of his family—women and children and even pets—are not spared. Thus, in 1982 when a thirty-two-year-old Colombian dealer was murdered in his new Mercedes on the Grand Central Parkway in Queens, New York, authorities also found the bodies of his wife, their eighteen-month-old-daughter, and four-month-old son. The police

Figure 5.1. Typical Colombian Cocaine Organization

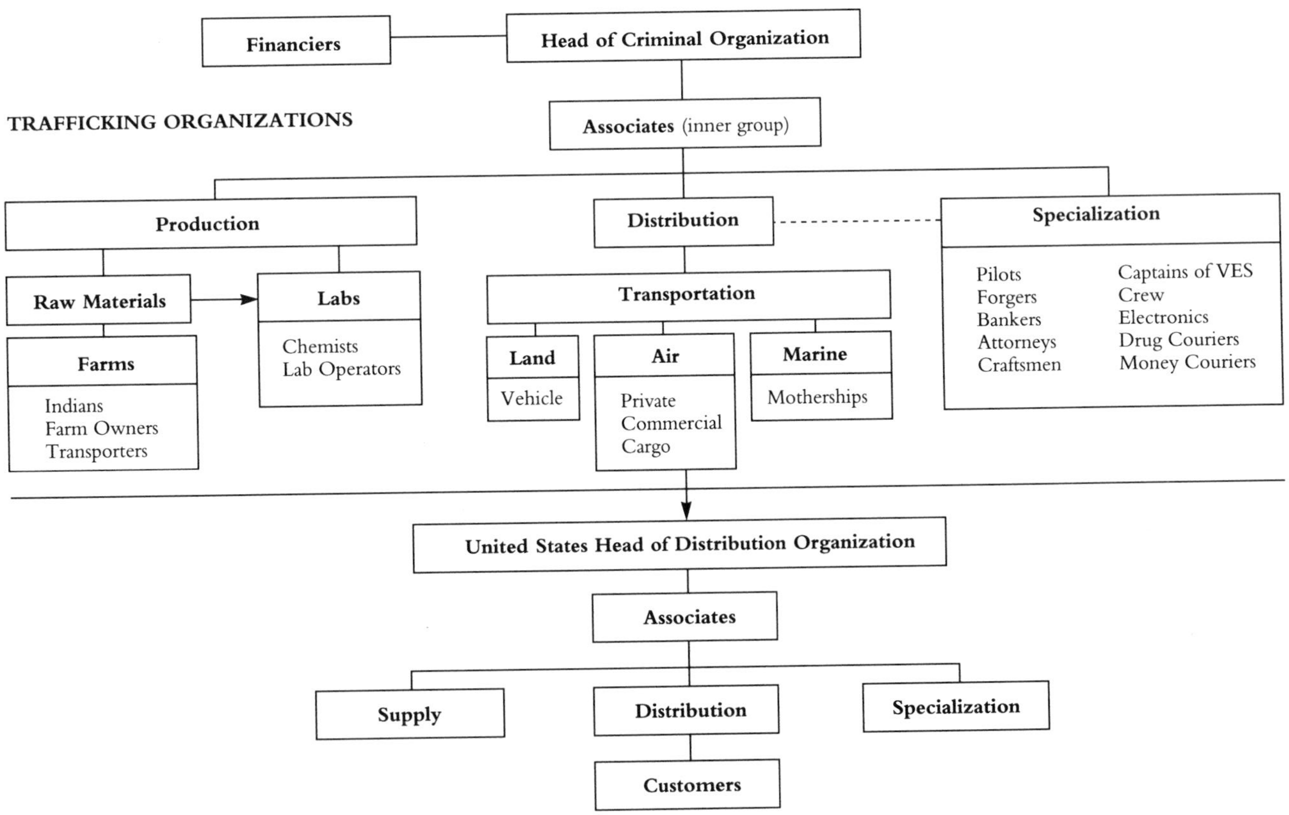

TRAFFICKING ORGANIZATIONS

Financiers

Head of Criminal Organization

Associates (inner group)

Distribution

Specialization

Pilots   Captains of VES
Forgers   Crew
Bankers   Electronics
Attorneys   Drug Couriers
Craftsmen   Money Couriers

Transportation

Land   Air   Marine

Vehicle   Private   Motherships
        Commercial
        Cargo

Production

Raw Materials   Labs

Farms   Chemists
          Lab Operators

Indians
Farm Owners
Transporters

United States Head of Distribution Organization

Supply   Associates   Specialization

Distribution

Customers

Source: Drug Enforcement Administration.

found an arsenal of weapons, 140 pounds of cocaine, and nearly $1 million in cash in his apartment (Pileggi 1982). In 1975, when DEA agents entered the house of Oscar Toro, one of their Colombian informants, in Jackson Heights, Queens, they found

> Susan Toro, aged five, had been hanged by the neck from a ceiling support with a four-foot length of gaudy nylon cord left over from wrapping the family's Christmas presents. She had been stabbed four times in the chest and abdomen. There was no sign of Oscar Toro, Jr., aged ten, or the baby-sitter. (Goddard 1988: 307)
>
> . . . . Oscar Toro, Jr., Susan's ten-year-old brother, was found hanged in an abandoned post office. . . . Dangling from another beam, thirty feet away, was the body of the seventeen-year-old mother's helper, Liliana Bustamonte. Before being hanged, she had been raped repeatedly. (Goddard 1988: 313)

The President's Commission (1984a: 562) reports that the major Colombian trafficking organizations are structured to control each intermediate step required in processing and exporting cocaine. Thus, "each of the trafficking groups in Medellín, Bogotá, and Cali contain various sections, each with a separate function, such as manufacturing, transportation, distribution, finance and security." Not only does this bureaucratic structure promote greater efficiency, it also serves to protect the organization: "Few members of one section are aware of the others involved, and the loss of one member or even a whole section does not threaten the stability of the entire organization." In fact, at the lower levels of organization there are many workers who move between one organization and another, and are often unaware of which organization they are working for at any given time. At the highest levels, members are well-insulated from the physical operations of their organizations. U.S. distribution is the responsibility of six- to eight-person teams operating independently, selling cocaine to mid-level wholesalers. Team members are low-profile entrepreneurs who use legitimate businesses as fronts and employ lawyers and accountants.

> The money generated by the wholesale cocaine transaction is maintained for the organization by financial experts familiar with international banking and investing drug profits, and for assuring that a portion of the drug profit is returned to Colombia for reinvestment in the organization's cocaine enterprise. The cartel's own financial experts are supported by a complement of bankers, lawyers and other professionals in the United States who play a crucial role in facilitating these transactions. (PCOC 1986c: 82)

In the United States, cocaine cartel representatives act as brokers to coordinate deliveries, usually one hundred kilos at a time, to the various drug networks. The number of Colombian cocaine distribution networks is unknown because most "are informally structured and operate in a fluid, transactional manner. Often, a network will develop solely to distribute a single shipment of cocaine. The network may operate from six months to one year and then dissolve" (Comptroller General 1989: 13–14). While structurally independent of the cartels, these distribution networks are symbiotic and in regular contact with their cartel sources:

> While the main organizers are hand-picked by the Colombian traffickers, individual members of the same network seldom know one another and usually deal with one another on a single occasion. Each drug transaction is conducted separately and each part of the network is compartmentalized. Inventories are stored in hidden locations. After raids or arrests, the cartels conduct internal investigations to assure that their employees were loyal, security measures were followed, and lessons were learned to improve the operation. (Comptroller General 1989: 14)

The sheer volume of Colombian drug transactions makes them vulnerable to sophisticated law enforcement efforts:

> While most drug traffickers conduct financial transactions in cash, the volume of business conducted by the Colombian traffickers requires sophisticated record-keeping to track expenses and sales. Modern methods of monitoring inventories and deliveries are used; advanced communication centers arrange for the arrival of smuggled drugs, their distribution, the movement of cash proceeds, and other logistical matters. Distributors are instructed to keep accurate records, and many use facsimile machines to keep track of sales and to relay information to Colombia. (Comptroller General 1989: 19)
>
> However, infiltrating a Colombian group is near impossible: A prospective wholesale buyer must establish his bona fides at an audience with top management in Cali. If he is approved, he is not required to pay cash up front. He will send the cartel payment after he resells the drugs to middlemen. The wholesale buyer must put up collateral, cash or deeds to real property as insurance if he is caught. He must also provide human collateral in the form of his family in Colombia, who will pay with their lives if he ever turns informer. (Shannon 1991: 32)

Although commonly referred to as cartels, Colombian drug organizations are not tightly integrated monopolies. They "are in fact simply loose trade associations, assisting shifting coalitions of traffickers to more efficiently produce, market, transport, and distribute their products" (Lupsha 1990: 7). Relatively decentralized and amorphous, the cartels "are not bureaucracies in the Weberian sense, but rather coalitions or confederations with fluid boundaries. No single heart or head drives these syndicates." Their activities "are dispersed among many trafficking groups that seemingly are held together through an intricate system of contractors, subcontractors, codes of honor, and family bonds" (Lee 1992: 98). The most notorious are those centered in Medellín and Cali.

The Medellín Cartel

There are about twenty major cocaine groups in Colombia and, although independent, they often work cooperatively. Three of the largest drug organizations operate out of Medellín, an Andean industrial and tourist city of about 1.5 million persons in the province of Antioquia. Antioquia and neighboring provinces bore the brunt of the civil war violence of 1948–1958. Long before cocaine emerged as an important commodity, Medellín had a long-standing reputation for smuggling and a school for pickpockets. It is known as a place where assassins are trained in such techniques as the *asesino de la moto*: a passenger on a motorbike uses an automatic weapon—usually a .45 caliber machine pistol. The murder rate in Medellín is nearly nine times that of New York City. It is virtually free of any American diplomatic personnel; the small U.S. Drug Enforcement Administration office had to be closed because of the danger (Uhlig 1989b). The city serves as the headquarters for the organizations of Carlos Lehder-Rivas, the Ochoa family, and Pablo Escobar Gaviria, known in Colombia as *Los Grandes Mafiosos*, and in the United States as the *Medellín Cartel*.

Carlos Lehder-Rivas. Lehder-Rivas was born in Colombia in 1949 to a Colombian mother and German engineer who had emigrated to Colombia in 1922. At age fourteen his parents separated and Carlos' mother took him to live in Detroit, where he was homosexually abused. Lehder-Rivas became involved with a band of car thieves, and in 1973 was charged with interstate transportation of stolen vehicles. He subsequently skipped bail and was arrested in Miami three months later for possessing 237 pounds of marijuana. Lehder-Rivas served time in the federal prison at Danbury, Connecticut, with George Jung, an ex-student radical and small-time marijuana dealer who had been supplying pot to persons in the film and record industries. In 1975, Lehder-Rivas was released from Danbury and deported. Two years later, he reentered the United States using a stolen New York driver's license. He teamed up with fellow ex-inmate George Jung: Lehder-Rivas bought cocaine in Colombia and, using mules with suitcases, smuggled it into the United States, where Jung distributed it in California (Eddy, Sabogal, and Walden 1988).

Business was so good that by 1977 they were bringing in planeloads of cocaine, including 250 kilos provided by Pablo Escobar. Lehder-Rivas and Jung became millionaires. A year later, however, Lehder-Rivas ended his partnership with Jung to become president of an aircraft company in the Bahamas. He purchased a luxurious home in Norman's Cay, a small Bahamian island near Florida; a hotel, marina and yacht club; and land for an airstrip. Lehder-Rivas brought in forty Colombian and German employees who terrorized the residents into leaving. He then constructed an airport to facilitate smuggling operations. Among a host of minor and major officials, he is alleged to have paid off the Bahamian Prime Minister, Lynden O. Pindling—a charge Pindling vehemently denies. Lehder-Rivas' transport service was also used by Pablo

In 1988, Colombian drug kingpin Carlos Lehder-Rivas was convicted of smuggling 3.3 tons of cocaine into the United States. Lehder-Rivas, one of the country's *Grandes Mafiosos*, is now serving a term of life without parole, but the Medellín Cartel has wasted no time in filling the vacuum created by his capture.

Escobar and Jorge Ochoa. "The close relationship between Ochoa, Escobar, and Lehder provided the nucleus of a coalition that would rule the cocaine trade during its period of greatest expansion" (Gugliotta and Leen 1989: 50).

On September 14, 1979, a raid was launched by Bahamian authorities, but Lehder-Rivas was able to escape in his powerboat, empty cocaine into the bay, and return to Norman's Cay. He was arrested upon his return, but when no drugs were discovered, he was released. Thirty others were arrested for possession of firearms and dynamite, including Lehder-Rivas' mistress, but eventually they were freed—substantial bribes are suspected. Cocaine smuggling continued unabated. There were two more raids on Norman's Cay, but each time Lehder-Rivas was tipped off well in advance. He began building a luxury resort, but pressure from the United States on the Pindling government was increasing. In 1981 a Jacksonville, Florida, federal grand jury indicted him for drug trafficking and income-tax evasion, and in 1983 the United States requested his extradition. Lehder-Rivas went underground, emerging back in Medellín and denouncing the United States for imperialism.

Obsessed with a dream of political power, anti-American sentiment and a love of Hitler, Lehder-Rivas founded the *Movimiento Latino Nacional* (National Latin Civic Movement), which has run successful candidates for local offices in regional elections. He also founded and financed a youth movement—*Los Lenadores* (The woodcutters)—patterned after the Hitler Youth of Nazi Germany. In 1985, while a fugitive, Lehder-Rivas appeared on Colombian television to appeal to revolutionary organizations to participate in the "cocaine bonanza" in an effort to fight United States imperialism: "This is about political action and cocaine has become and marijuana has become, a revolutionary weapon in the struggle against North American imperialism." He threatened to join forces with the Marxist revolutionary group known as M-19. His party newspaper—*Quinidio Libre*—printed articles condemning the United States and the Drug Enforcement Administration's efforts to curtail cocaine trafficking in Colombia. The weekly was distributed nationally by Lehder-Rivas' fleet of planes.

In a 1987 shoot-out, Lehder-Rivas was arrested by Colombian authorities and extradited to the United States. He was apparently betrayed, perhaps by fellow members of the Medellín Cartel (Eddy, Sabogal, and Walden 1988). The

THE BELOVED GONZALO RODRIGUEZ GACHA

Born in 1947, Gonzalo Rodriguez Gacha was a native of Pacho, a village of about 15,000, fifty miles from Bogotá. The son of poor parents, he worked as a shoeshine boy, pig farmer, and bartender before hiring out as a gunman to gangsters attempting to control Colombian emerald mines. With other leaders of the Medellín cartel, Gacha went on to become one of the world's richest men: he owned more than one hundred ranches, a top Colombian soccer team, and hundreds of prized walking horses. At his ranch in Pacho, he built a Wild West-style saloon, a two-room home for his favorite horse, a private bedroom lounge shaped like a space shuttle, pathways covered with Astroturf, an equestrian center, Turkish baths, a helicopter pad, and a private zoo.

But he shared his wealth: According to the mayor of Pacho, almost all of the village benefitted from Gacha's patronage. He paid triple the prevailing wage, gave out cash to the poor, and provided money and supplies to the church. Although his dozens of bodyguards drove customized Jeeps, carried automatic weapons, and used road signs for target practice, to the people of Pacho, Gacha was a revered benefactor. Reportedly killed along with his son by the police in 1989, many people in Pacho claim he is still alive.

Source: Gary Marx, "Drug Lord, or Ghost, Stalks Colombian Town," *Chicago Tribune*, July 28, 1991: 4.

following year Lehder-Rivas was convicted of shipping 3.3 tons of cocaine to Florida and Georgia in 1979 and 1980 via Norman's Cay. On July 20, 1988, Carlos Lehder-Rivas, age thirty-eight, was sentenced to life without parole in a Jacksonville, Florida, federal court. His place in the Medellín Cartel was quickly filled by Jose Gonzalo Rodriguez Gacha of Bogotá. In 1991, Lehder-Rivas appeared as a U.S. government witness in the trial of General Manuel Noriega, who he stated provided enormous help to—and sometimes double crossed—the cartel. Lehder-Rivas alleged that Noriega had sold the cartel an arsenal of Uzi submachine guns and photographs and addresses of DEA agents; but had also seized their cocaine and, after being praised by the DEA, sold it back to the traffickers (Rohter 1991a).

The Ochoa Family. The *paterfamilias* of the Ochoa clan, Fabio Ochoa Restrepo, rarely travels without a contingent of a dozen bodyguards. He owns a country estate with herds of cattle and horses, *La Finca la Loma* ("The Ranch on the Hill") in Medellín. Nearby is a bullring in which he has invested; his family business is inextricably tied to bullfighting. Don Fabio, as he is known locally, heads a wealthy and close-knit clan of old-line cattle breeders and landowners. They claim to have descended from the second wave of settlers to Colombia from the Basque region of Spain who founded Medellín in 1616. These Spaniards enslaved and annihilated the native Indians they found. During the early 1970s, Fabio Ochoa experienced financial difficulties that forced him to sell off some horses in Venezuela. At the time, his middle son, Jorge Ochoa Vasquez, lived in Miami where he headed the Sea-8 Trading Corporation, an import-export firm. The firm imported cocaine for Jorge's uncle, Fabio Restrepo Ochoa. A narrow escape from the DEA caused Jorge to flee to Medellín, where he informed his father, Don Fabio, of the demand for cocaine in the United States (Eddy, Sabogal, and Walden 1988). Fabio Restrepo Ochoa was mysteriously murdered in Miami shortly after his nephew Jorge's return to Colombia (Gugliotta and Leen 1989).

Jorge Ochoa Vasquez, born in 1949, owns large tracts of land in Medellín, where he raises horses for bullfighting and owns a horse-breeding farm near Bogotá and a bullfighting arena near Cartagena. He was a frequent traveler to Panama, where his assets are in secret accounts, to Brazil, where he has important investments, and to Spain. In 1984, Jorge Ochoa and his associate Rodriguez Orejuela, of the Cali cartel, were arrested while living under assumed names in Spain; they were reportedly setting up a Colombian cocaine network in Europe. After two years in a Spanish prison awaiting extradition to the United States, they were instead extradited to Colombia. Meanwhile, Spain has emerged as a major consumer and transshipment point for cocaine (Delaney 1988).

In Colombia, Jorge Ochoa was convicted of illegally importing bulls—it turned out that they had hoof-and-mouth disease and had to be destroyed. Although serious drug charges and a U.S. extradition request were outstanding, Ochoa was released pending appeal. Six months later more cocaine was reportedly flowing out of Colombia than ever before (Riding 1987b). While the judge who released Ochoa lost his job, he remains alive and rumored to be quite wealthy. Orejuela was tried in 1987 and acquitted of all charges: Paul Eddy, Hugo Sabogal, and Sara Walden (1988: 328) refer to his trial as a "farce." The Colombian extradition treaty with the United States was subsequently declared unconstitutional. Later that year Jorge Ochoa was arrested and once again released by judicial order.

In response to the 1986 release of Jorge Ochoa, the U.S. Customs Service increased inspections of all cargo, passenger luggage, and passengers arriving from Colombia. Even the more than 1,400 passengers on the luxury ocean liner Queen Elizabeth II, which had stopped briefly in Cartagena, Colombia, were subjected to a search taking several hours. This scrutiny led to the discovery of 422 pounds of cocaine in a shipment of cut flowers on an Avianca cargo plane (the national airline of Colombia) in Miami. The airline agreed to discontinue all cargo shipments into the United States. Reprisals, however, have caused strong feelings of nationalism and generated anti-U.S. sentiment that is exploited by Colombian left-wing political groups who often denounce the United States as "imperialistic." Colombian officials chide the United States for not providing enough material support for Colombian efforts against the *narcotraficantes*, and for not doing enough about the demand for cocaine in the United States.

Pablo Escobar Gaviria. Born in 1949, Pablo Escobar had a fair start in life: his father was a farmer, his mother a school teacher. Young Pablo received a high school education. Too poor to attend college, he embarked upon a career in petty crime, later rising to bodyguard-enforcer for an electronics smuggler. In the mid-1960s Escobar entered the United States illegally and saw firsthand the potential American market for cocaine (Eddy, Sabogal, and Walden 1988; Gugliotta and Leen 1989 state, however, that Escobar had no U.S. experience). He returned to Colombia in the early 1970s and continued a life of crime, mostly as a car thief, but occasionally as a courier smuggling coca paste and coca base in trucks from Peru back into Medellín. His first known arrest was in 1974 for car theft. By 1976 Escobar headed a small group of "mules" who transported the raw paste and base from the south into Colombia, where it was processed into cocaine. In that year he was arrested with five other men and charged with attempted bribery—they had attempted to smuggle a thirty-nine-pound shipment of cocaine inside a spare tire. After three months the case was dropped on a technicality. The records of the case subsequently disappeared, and the two officers who had arrested Escobar were murdered.

As the market for cocaine in the United States increased dramatically, Escobar invested much of his profits in a fleet of planes. He was then able to deal directly with source countries for his coca paste and coca base, and to ship the finished cocaine directly to the United States. As his wealth grew, his lifestyle changed accordingly. Escobar purchased several large ranches, houses, and apartments in and around Medellín, and he invested in legitimate businesses, including a bicycle factory. *Hacienda Napoles*, his favorite residence, several hours from Medellín, includes a private zoo with a variety of exotic wildlife, twenty-four artificial lakes, and a network of some sixty miles of roads. It also houses a life-sized statue of Escobar's favorite prostitute by one of Colombia's most renowned sculptors (Eddy, Sabogal, and Walden 1988). In 1980 he purchased a $762,500 Miami Beach mansion, and the following year, the King's Harbour Apartments in Plantation, north of Miami, for $8.03 million.

In 1982, Escobar was elected as an alternate Colombian representative in Envigado, a barrio outside of Medellín. There he cultivated a Robin Hood image, building five hundred small houses for slum squatters and financing the construction of eighty soccer fields for the young men. His newspaper, *Medellín Civico*, was a public relations piece that promoted Escobar as an up-from-the-slums statesman. As a representative he enjoyed immunity from arrest until this was removed by the government of Colombia, and a warrant was issued for his arrest for having smuggled an assortment of African wildlife into the country for his own personal zoo (Eddy, Sabogal, and Walden 1988; Gugliotta and Leen 1989).

Political contributions and executive bribery have gained a substantial amount of immunity for the *narcotraficantes* of Colombia. As noted in figure 5.2, the Ochoa organization lists the police and military as special subdivisions of its enforcement section. Where this has failed, violence becomes the tool to neutralize enforcement—hundreds of police officers have been killed. They are frequently offered a choice: *plata o ploma* ("lead or silver"), a bullet or a bribe. A 1989 U.S. Department of State report stated that Colombian *narcotraficantes* have so intimidated and corrupted the criminal justice system of that country that it is virtually impossible to arrest and convict them or significantly damage their organizations. According to local experts on Colombian politics, more than half of the members of Congress and a smaller number of senators have had their election campaigns underwritten by the *narcomafia* (Uhlig 1989c). Colombia responded to the threat against its judges by implementing legislation allowing for judicial anonymity. The identity of a judge is kept confidential from all but his or her immediate supervisor, and they preside over cases from one side of a two-way mirror, speaking over an intercom through a voice distorter (*New York Times*, October 13, 1991: 4). In April of 1990, Pablo Escobar offered a bounty of $4,200 for each police officer killed. In the following month, forty-two police officers were murdered (Brooke 1990a). Journalists have been tortured and killed, and hundreds more have been threatened or forced into exile. Articles in Colombian newspapers on cocaine are unsigned as a matter of policy. Editors travel with bodyguards, to protect them not only from the *narcotraficantes*, but also from right and left wing terrorists (Uhlig 1989a).

In 1987 the Colombian Supreme Court ruled against the extradition treaty with the United States. Throughout 1987, notes Alan Riding (1988a: 1), "judicial decisions favorable to cocaine mobsters confirmed that organized crime had succeeded in either bribing or intimidating many key judges."

IMMUNITY FROM EXTRADITION

Pablo Escobar escaped in 1992 from his custom-built prison cell. The cell possessed all the comforts of home and office, and the government paid the bill. Right, Escobar attending a 1983 soccer game.

In response to the terror waged by the Medellín cartel, at the end of 1990 the Colombian government offered traffickers immunity from extradition to the United States and shorter prison terms if they surrendered and confessed to one or more crimes. Shortly afterward, three Ochoa brothers, Fabio (in December), Jorge Luis (in January) and Juan David (in February) surrendered to authorities. Although under indictment in Florida, they await legal action in Colombia while enjoying home-cooked meals and watching television via a private cable hookup at a high-security jail in the suburbs of Medellín.

In 1991, ten hours after the constitutional assembly voted to ban extraditions, Pablo Escobar, then forty-one, surrendered to the authorities. He was accompanied by a popular television priest who had helped to negotiate the surrender. Escobar was placed in a specially built jail overlooking his hometown of Envigado, just south of Medellín. It was in Envigado that Escobar assisted in the construction of a hospital and sports stadium and endeared himself to the people with jobs and lavish gifts. The jail was a converted mountaintop

(continued on next page)

IMMUNITY FROM EXTRADITION (*Continued*)

ranch with many amenities—a Jacuzzi, waterbed, bar, wood-burning fireplace, sophisticated electronic equipment that included a computer with a modem, sixty-inch television, and cellular telephone. The guards were assigned by Envigado's mayor, and several aides to Escobar also surrendered to provide him with companionship and security while he awaited further legal action. He apparently also enjoyed female companionship. On July 22, 1992, the Colombian government attempted to transfer Escobar to a more secure prison, a site where he would (in theory at least) be unable to continue overseeing the drug trade. The result was a furious gunfight during which Escobar and nine of his aides escaped. Seven have since surrendered.

Even while awaiting trial, Escobar continued to inspire fear. Cartel gunmen assassinated the recently returned Colombian ambassador to Switzerland, a former minister of justice. Within hours after announcing his intention to testify against Escobar, a right-wing death squad leader was kidnapped; two days later his badly disfigured body was found with a sign reading, "Traitor." The drug kingpin refused to be photographed by the police who, out of fear, acquiesced. The investigating magistrate in his case conducted interviews at the jail behind a one-way mirror. His or her voice was distorted to prevent identification. This attempt at anonymity

failed Judge Miriam Rocio Valez, age thirty-eight. The judge was shot and killed by Escobar gunmen after his escape. In addition to Judge Valez, twenty police officers were murdered in one month on Escobar's orders ("21 Killings Ridicule Talk of Surrender by Escobar" 1992).

Escobar's chief executioner, Pablo Daniel Muñoz Mosquera, was able to walk out of a Bogotá prison in 1991 after paying bribes in excess of $500,000. It was his second successful attempt to elude prison. He was subsequently arrested by federal agents in Jackson Heights, New York.

On December 2, 1993, Escobar was killed in a rooftop shootout with police and soldiers while attempting to elude capture. His whereabouts had been determined by the use of telephone tracking equipment—he made a cellular call to his family—contributed by the United States.

Sources: Various media reports; James Brooke, "Trafficker is Still Feared in Colombia." *New York Times*, January 21, 1992: 5; James Brooke, "How Escobar, a Rare Jailbird, Lined His Nest." *New York Times*, August 5, 1992: 1, 2; Joseph B. Treaster, "U.S. Seizes Suspect in New York in 40 Colombian Drug Slayings." *New York Times*, September 27, 1991: 1,7; Shirley Christian, "Why Indulge Drug Lord? Colombia Pressed to Tell." *New York Times*, July 29, 1992: 3.

The war on the drug cartels is tying up 85 percent of Colombia's police forces and 60 percent of its military. Nevertheless, Colombian judges began ordering the return of seized ranches and estates, while eighty suspected Medellín gunmen were released because witnesses were too frightened to testify against them (Brooke 1990c). The murder and kidnapping of journalists has likewise served to intimidate the press.

Members of the Medellín cartel regularly exchange personnel and equipment to maximize efficiency and profit. Their individual wealth is estimated to be in the billions of dollars. Law enforcement agents confiscated a chart from a mid-level trafficker that diagrammed the responsibilities of each group (see figure 5.2). The Ochoa organization employed its own air transport service, "Air America," which between 1981 and 1984 flew nearly ten tons of cocaine into the United States (Rice 1988). This cooperation apparently dates back to November 1981 when Lehder-Rivas was kidnapped and escaped, but not before being wounded—the Marxist revolutionary group, 19th of April, known as M-19, was blamed (Gugliotta and Leen 1989). That same month M-19 kidnapped Jorge Ochoa's twenty-eight-year-old sister, Marta Nieves, from the campus of the University of Antioquia in Medellín and demanded a ransom of $1 million. In response, the Ochoa family called a meeting of traffickers—223 attended. Leaflets later announced that each had contributed $33,000 to a common fund to establish a special enforcement section, *Muerte a Secuestradores* ("Death to the Kidnappers"—MAS), for the "immediate execution of all those involved in kidnappings." The leaflets warned that those who escaped would simply leave their families and friends liable for retribution. Soon afterward, dozens of persons believed connected to M-19 were tortured and murdered (Kerr 1988c):

> Ten M-19 guerrillas were kidnapped and tortured, and two of them—who were on the Colombian army's "most wanted" list—were handed over to the military commanders amidst widespread publicity. In Medellín, MAS invaded homes and shot suspected guerrillas—but also trade unionists, old ladies, young children, horses, pigs, and chickens. Mere sympathizers of M-19 were abducted from the university, tortured, and, if they were lucky, sent home in their underwear. After a few weeks of this... Marta Nieves was released unharmed. (Eddy, Sabogal, and Walden 1988: 289)

Guy Gugliotta and Jeff Leen (1989) report that Ochoa negotiated with M-19 and paid a reduced ransom for Marta Nieves. Max Mermelstein (1990) denies that any ransom was paid. In 1990, M-19 disarmed its fighters and formed a political party whose leader was appointed the Colombian minister of health.

Conflict between leftist guerrillas and the *narcotraficantes* has intensified, notes Riding (1988b: 1), as the drug barons continue to purchase huge tracts of land, an estimated 2.5 million acres of fertile countryside. "In the process, they are also emerging as a powerful political force in the countryside where, backed by private armies of gunmen, they are trying to put an end to the kidnappings and extortion, traditionally carried out by rural guerilla groups." For the traffickers, a Marxist government would bring an end to their lucrative business, if not their lives. In fact, guerilla activity, particularly extortion, has left many cattlemen eager to sell their ranches, often to the *narcotraficantes* who are the most willing buyers and whose private armies are able to keep the guerrillas at bay (Weisman 1989). The rancher-traffickers invested their resources in organized peasant bands that were turned into fighting units. A U.S. congressional

Figure 5.2. A Cocaine Collaboration: The Ochoa/Escobar Joint Venture

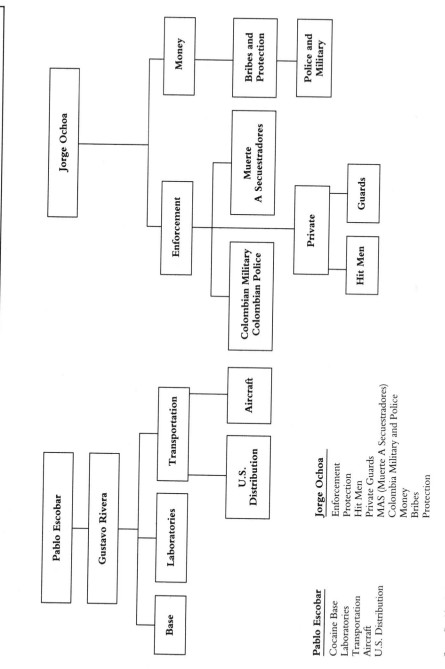

Pablo Escobar

Cocaine Base
Laboratories
Transportation
Aircraft
U.S. Distribution

Jorge Ochoa

Enforcement
Protection
Hit Men
Private Guards
MAS (Muerte A Secuestradores)
Colombia Military and Police
Money
Bribes
Protection

Source: President's Commission on Organized Crime.

committee revealed that the private armies of Rodriguez Gacha had been trained by British and Israeli mercenaries under the guise of helping Colombian ranchers fend off leftist guerrillas. This relationship reportedly soured when Pablo Escobar began recruiting leftist guerrillas for his own use. Meanwhile, most of the rebel organizations have reached a political accommodation with the Colombian government and have ceased their military activity.

Subsequently, right wing "death squads" formerly allied with the cartel made their peace with the government and began a war against the traffickers. On February 14, 1993, a paramilitary unit in Medellín known by the Spanish acronym *Pepes*—People Persecuted by Pablo Escobar—set fire to Escobar's collection of expensive limousines, which included six Rolls Royces. According to Colombian authorities, this group has pledged to respond to each of the drug baron's attacks by seeking vengeance on his family and associates. They have already murdered thirty-seven Escobar associates. The core of the *Pepes* appears to be remnants of two gangs, formerly part of Escobar's organization, with whom he had a falling out over $20 million in stolen drug profits (Brooke 1993).

The Medellín cartel uses Mexican connections and the heroin-smuggling networks established by the Mexican-based Herrera family. Intermarriages between the two groups have been reported. Cocaine is also moved through Mexico by the organization headed by Angel Félix Gallardo, a former Sinaloa state police officer. Although imprisoned, Gallardo has been able to keep in touch with his operatives by cellular telephone and fax machines (Golden 1993). Another ominous sign of Medellín cartel activity is its apparent connection to Sicilian *mafiosi*. This connection was unveiled in a 1989 federal indictment in Miami, which alleged that Sicilian *mafiosi* residing in New York and Miami purchased more than 1,300 pounds of cocaine from members of the cartel in Miami and Colombia for distribution in European markets.

The Cali Cartel

The drug boom in Colombia inspired a competing cartel from Cali, a city of 1.5 million persons located about 250 miles south of Medellín. It is second only to Spain in the number of Spanish books it publishes each year; advanced printing technology has made the city a center of counterfeiting, mostly of U.S. currency (Brooke 1991a). The Cali cartel is a loose alliance of about fifteen trafficking groups. Preeminence is shared by the kinship crime Families of Jose Santacruz Londoño ("Don Chepe"), forty-nine in 1993, and Gilberto Rodriguez Orejuela ("The Chess Player"), fifty-four in 1993. Members of the Cali cartel have typically favored bribery over violence. They take a percentage of the profits from shipments by smaller organizations, in return providing transportation, distribution, and enforcement services.

These groups are organized in a patriarchal manner, with a stress on discipline and loyalty. The leaders operate compartmentalized organizations so that the loss of any one section does not destroy the enterprise. In Cali, there is a chief executive officer whose executives are responsible for acquisition, production, transportation, sales, finance, and enforcement (Shannon 1991). There are dozens of overseas branches. In New York, five independent groups are each headed by a chief. Each chief has two assistants who are responsible for seventy to one hundred persons. In 1991, the chief of one group, Ramiro Herrera Buitrago, was arrested at his ranch-style house in the exclusive suburb of Great Neck; forty-one other members were also arrested, including the group's accountant. She was found with numerous computer discs containing details of the group's transactions—$50 million a month (Treaster 1991a).

Cali operations in the United States are headquartered in the Elmhurst-Jackson Heights area of Queens, home to about 30,000 Colombians. It was there that in 1992, a Colombian journalist who had written articles about the Cali cartel, was shot to death. The gunman, wearing a hooded sweater, walked calmly into a restaurant and fired two shots from a 9-millimeter pistol into the brain of Manual de Dios Unanue; the gunman was sixteen years old (Treaster and Myers 1993a). The neighborhood houses an excess of travel agencies and wire services that facilitate the movement of drug money to Colombia—very little is invested in legitimate businesses in the United States (Fisher 1993).

Gilberto Orejuela and his brother, an attorney, own several banks, a national chain of 150 drugstores, television stations, and a leading soccer team (Treaster 1989a; Lupsha 1990). His seven children have been educated at American and European universities (Moody 1991). Santacruz Londoño was trained as an engineer; when he was refused membership in a local club, Londono had a replica built in an exclusive suburban neighborhood (Brooke 1991b). In 1991 Orejuela and forty-two others were indicted in the United States for allegedly laundering $65 million a year in drug profits from Miami, New York, and Los Angeles. He has no charges pending against him in Colombia and cannot be extradited.

While the Medellín cartel has generally used air transport, the Cali group prefers freighter cargo containers (Brooke 1991b). While the Medellín cartel has been dominant in south Florida, Cali operations have been centered in New York. In 1989, however, twenty-nine Colombians, consisting of four families from Cali, were indicted in Chicago for operating a multimillion dollar cocaine ring that sold 440 pounds a month. They were suspected of having ties to the Herrera Family. The ring operated out of four jewelry stores on the city's North Side. There is evidence that the Cali group has been working with elements of New York's Mafia Families. During the 1980s, the Cali cartel entered the European market, which they now dominate.

Until 1987, the Medellín and Cali groups often cooperated. But the glut of cocaine reaching the U.S. market caused a reduction in price, and elements in the Medellín group began to aggressively expand their small operations in New York. According to Gugliotta and Leen (1989: 337), Rodriguez Gacha "traveled to New York in a bid to take over the Cali group's longtime distribution network there." This led to an outbreak of violence, with dozens of murders in Colombia, New York, and Florida. Most of the murders occurred in Colombia, and most victims were from the Cali group (Kerr 1988a). Early in 1988, the

Cali group bombed an exclusive eight-story apartment house owned by Pablo Escobar. He was not at home but two watchmen were killed. Escobar responded with twenty-two bombing attacks against a nationwide chain of pharmacies owned by the head of the Cali cartel. According to Gugliotta and Leen (1989) the Ochoas stayed out of the fray. The Cali cartel struck back: On March 20, 1989, a bomb was thrown at a ground-level food shop in Medellín, destroying a three-story building, killing five people, and injuring eleven others. It was the third attack in a week against businesses owned by the Medellín cartel (Associated Press, March 21, 1989).

The Cali group hired British mercenaries in an abortive attempt to kill Pablo Escobar (Treaster 1989a). In 1990 a series of bombs in and around Cali killed dozens of people as Escobar struck back. On July 28, 1991, seven to ten gunmen dressed in black stormed a crowded bar in Cali and began firing with automatic weapons; fifteen persons were slain in the attack (Associated Press).

According to the DEA, crackdowns on the Medellín traffickers have left the Cali group with 70 percent of the U.S. and 90 percent of the European cocaine market (Shannon 1991). The Cali cartel members are intricately intertwined with the wider society, reportedly paying for police posts that flourish in the city's middle-class neighborhoods in an effort to curtail street crime (Brooke 1991c). In the United States, both groups operate out of South Florida and have regional headquarters in the Jackson Heights section of the borough of Queens.

Since 1984, acres of poppy plants have also been discovered in Colombia, and there are reports of Colombian cartel interest in cultivating the plant and testing market demand for heroin (Drug Enforcement Administration 1991a). At the end of 1991, police raids in Colombia disclosed thousands of acres of poppy plants, indicating that the cartels may have moved beyond the experimental stage ("Colombian Heroin May Be Increasing" 1991). At the end of 1992, Ivan Urdinola, then thirty-two, leader of the North Valley faction of the Cali cartel, was sentenced to seventeen-and-a-half years, a sentence likely to be reduced to seven years. Urdinola is believed to be the mastermind behind the cartel's entry into poppy cultivation.

Dominicans

The Dominican Republic occupies about two-thirds of the Caribbean island of Hispaniola which is shared by Haiti. The island lies roughly between Colombia and Florida, making it an ideal transshipment point. While the Dominican Republic is not as depressed as Haiti, in the mid-1960s political unrest and economic upheavals caused many residents to seek their fortunes by going north. In New York City, Dominicans who legally entered the United States number about 350,000; thousands more are illegal aliens. Some of these immigrants, legal and illegal, have entered the drug trade. Known as Dominican-Yorks, the traffickers keep a low profile in the United States, returning their profits to cities in the Dominican Republic such as San Francisco de Marcoris, a city conspicuous for its wealth in a country where the per capita income is less than $900 a year (French 1991).

Dominicans have demonstrated the necessary talent for moving large amounts of heroin and crack cocaine at the street level. They purchase directly from Asian and Colombian importers, sharing a common language and entrepreneurial values with the latter. Dominicans have apparently applied their well-known skills as tradesmen and merchants to become New York City's top traffickers and have captured markets in Pennsylvania (Pennsylvania Crime Commission 1990). They also control a significant portion of the cocaine trafficking in New England (Drug Enforcement Administration 1991b). Dominicans generally provide top quality, uncut drugs at competitive prices, avoiding the common practice of diluting the product as it passes through the distribution chain. Often operating out of grocery stores, bars, and restaurants in Hispanic neighborhoods, they employ any variety of marketing gimmicks to move their product. In Philadelphia they sold heroin packets with lottery tickets attached that a winner could use to claim an additional twelve packets (Pennsylvania Crime Commission 1990).

The structure of Dominican drug trafficking organizations is based on familial or regional loyalties.

In the Dominican Republic, a country with a per capita income of less than $900 a year, the city of San Francisco de Macoris is an oasis of conspicuous prosperity, dotted with sumptuous villas with satellite dishes. These signs of prosperity are due to the "Dominican-Yorks," young people from the town who have gone to live in New York and succeeded in drug trafficking, specifically cocaine. In San Francisco de Macoris, most Dominican-Yorks lead quiet lives at home with their families.

The organizations are *vertically integrated*, with the family maintaining control over several consecutive stages of the operation. They obtain uncut heroin and cocaine from Colombian and Chinese sources on the supply end in New York and then distribute the drug to street-level dealers who may be Dominican, Black, Puerto Rican, white, or someone of other ethnic origin. Activities of the group are directed by the leader through a number of "lieutenants," who may include brothers, sisters, cousins, and friends from home. Lower level workers—largely Dominican nationals, and often illegal aliens—will travel a circuit taking them between New York City and various communities in Eastern and Central Pennsylvania (and sometimes New Jersey), performing various specialized tasks as they are directed, serving as couriers, security for stash houses, cutters and packagers, lookouts, street dealers, and enforcers. Women often serve as "mules" or couriers, carrying kilo packages on their person. When riding public transportation, these women may appear to be unaccompanied. Actually they are being shadowed by a group member who can provide protection if needed (Pennsylvania Crime Commission 1990: 267–68, edited)

The Dominicans prefer to avoid violence and show a willingness to cooperate with other crime groups. They have developed a reputation as reliable dealers who promptly pay their suppliers. While they are prepared for violence when necessary, Dominicans typically avoid its use to muscle in on others or maintain exclusive control of a particular market. Instead, they compete on the basis of efficiency and pricing, which allows them to avoid high-profile violence (Pennsylvania Crime Commission 1990).

ASIAN ORGANIZED CRIME

A number of unrelated Asian groups are involved in organized crime. Some, such as the Yakuza, are more of a problem in Japan, although there is a potential for expansion overseas. Others, such as the Triads, have been an international problem for many years.

Yakuza

Most Americans have heard of the Mafia—Lucky Luciano, Al Capone, and their "soldiers"—but what about the Yamaguchi-gumi—Kazuo Taoka, Hideomi Oda, and their *yakuza*? The Yamaguchi-gumi (*gumi* means "group") is a criminal organization that dominates the industrialized, densely populated region extending from Kyoto through Osaka to Kobe, as well as Tokyo and most other major centers in Japan. They are the largest *boryokudan*, organizations that constitute Japanese organized crime, with a membership of 30,000 in 1992. These organizations have been in existence for about three hundred years and date back to the Tokugawa period, when Japan was united under a central system of government. With the end of Japanese feudalism, many *samurai* or knights lost their role in life (Rome 1975). The *yakuza* were

Yakuza relaxing at a bath. Note the missing fingers of both hands of the man holding a newspaper.

originally a mixture of outcast *samurai*, unscrupulous itinerant peddlers, professional gamblers, and criminals. Under the leadership of their *kumi-cho* (boss), they are able to exert control over sections of Japan's urban areas. They are the most loyal consumers of American automobiles, particularly Cadillacs.

Present-day *yakuza* view themselves as modern *samurai* and maintain exotic rituals, including extensive tattooing that virtually covers their entire body from neck to ankles and clipped fingers that have been self-amputated with a short sword in a ritual that serves as a sign of contrition for mistakes. The amputated top of the smallest digit is placed in alcohol in a small bottle with the person's name written on it; it is sent to whoever one is asking forgiveness from. While not obligatory, the tattooing indicates the ability to withstand pain and commitment to the *yakuza* life. Resignation or expulsion is accomplished with a *homojo* or "red letter" to all members of the *boryokudan*, which signals that the person is no longer a member (PCOC 1984b). There are almost 90,000 identified *yakuza* members in more than 3,000 gangs in Japan who are affiliated with the three largest syndicates.

The term *yakuza*, notes Clyde Haberman (1985: 6), "is derived from an old card game . . . whose object was to draw three cards adding up as close as possible to 19 without exceeding it," similar to our game of "21" or blackjack. "Ya-ku-za represents the Japanese words for 8, 9, 3, which total 20, a useless number. Basically, yakuza means 'good for nothing'." Like many of their American counterparts, the *yakuza* "were born into poverty and graduated from juvenile delinquency into organized crime" (Kirk 1976: 93). The Al Capone of Japan, Kazuo Taoka, was, like Capone, born into a poor family. He began his criminal career as a bouncer in Kobe, much as Capone filled this capacity in Brooklyn before going to Chicago. Taoka, like Capone, played a major role in the gang conflicts of the day, and both men rose to prominence because of their penchant for violence and talent with organization. In 1981, Taoka, sixty-eight, died of a heart attack. His funeral in Kobe (a city about 275 miles southwest of Tokyo) was attended by more than 1,200 *yakuza*. "Taoka's friendships and contacts extended to the highest levels of government, with two former prime ministers . . . among his friends. That kind of relationship reflected not only Taoka's personal success but also historic ties between gangsters and prominent government figures" (Kirk 1981: 17).

Similar ties were forged by Susumu Ishii, boss of Japan's second largest crime group, the 8,200 member Inagawa-kai. Before he died of natural causes in 1991, Ishii was involved with the world's largest brokerage houses. He had invested heavily in real estate and stocks; his portfolio was estimated to be worth in excess of $1 billion. Four thousand persons attended his funeral. In 1992 it was revealed that one of the most powerful figures in Japan, a high-ranking governing (Liberal Democrat) party official, had business and political ties to Ishii; the politician's parliamentary colleague is an admitted former *yakuza* member (Sanger 1992; Sterngold 1992b). Executives of Japan's most profitable retailer paid gangsters to insure that the firm's stockholders meetings would not be disturbed—this is a standard, albeit now illegal, practice in Japan (Sterngold 1992c).

The *yakuza* are ultra-nationalistic and conservative on matters of foreign policy. They are vigorously anticommunist. This has endeared them to many right-wing politicians, and *yakuza* are intimately involved in the politics of Japan. David Kaplan and Alec Dubro (1986) argue that the relatively low rate of "street crime" in Japan is in large part the result of a symbiotic relationship between the *yakuza* and the police. The police share the political views of the *yakuza* and do little against the *yakuza*—police raids are often a publicity sham. The *yakuza* reciprocate by keeping *disorganized* crime under control. They are also concerned about their public image: when famed Japanese film director Juzo Itami—*Tampopo, A Taxing Woman*—portrayed them in an unflattering manner, he became the victim of a knife attack by assailants who slashed his neck and face (Goozner 1992; Sterngold 1992a).

Japan, however, does have a serious drug problem, particularly the abuse of amphetamines, which the *yakuza* produce in clandestine laboratories in Japan, the Philippines, and Korea (many *yakuza* are of Korean heritage). More recently they have been linked to the importation of cocaine, which is growing

253

in popularity in Japan. The *yakuza* are also at the center of an international trade in sexual slavery: women, often children, are bought and sold throughout Third World countries. They helped to popularize the Southeast Asian "sex tours" (*Kisaeng* parties) favored by Japanese businessmen. Rounding out their criminal activities are extortion from both legitimate and illegitimate entrepreneurs and intimidation and eviction of people from their homes on the behalf of real estate developers. Automobile accident victims will sometimes hire *yakuza* to retrieve damage payments on a contingency basis (Weisman 1991).

The *boryokudans* "form closed societies in their individual groups, but the groups are inter-linked through a widespread underworld syndicate" (Takahashi and Becker 1985: 3). Sadahiko Takahashi and Gary Becker (1985: 4) outline the structure of the Yamaguchi-gumi:

> It includes 578 sub-groups and [in 1982] 13,063 members, divided into 51 lineal "family" (staff) organizations. Each of these 51 "family" bosses had their own groups with one to eleven subordinate bosses (called "grandchildren"), and some of these subordinate bosses in turn have gang bosses under them. Thus the Yamaguchi mafia headquarters has 51 staff groups under it, which in turn control 149 "grandchildren" gang bosses, and there are another 11 "great-grandchildren" bosses on a level under them, forming a total of 211 "recognized" (dues-paying) groups.
>
> All 211 groups pay dues . . . to the Yamaguchi headquarters, and additional fees determined by headquarters. . . ; they are passed vertically up through their respective channels until they reach the staff at headquarters. When the members of a given local group cannot collect the money which their boss owes, the boss often pays the dues from his own private sources. This in turn places his group members in debt to him, which they must repay by becoming assassins, scapegoats.

Boryokudans distinguish between members (*kumiin*) and associates (*jun-kumiin*) who have not been initiated into the secrets of the organization by way of an elaborate sake ceremony, and are therefore at the bottom of the *yakuza* world. Rising in the ranks depends on the amount of money sent up to superiors in the organization. One's share of the profits is in order of rank, with the boss getting about half. There are a variety of ranks and titles in the various *yakuza* groups; these "establish the status and power hierarchy and the order of authority within the family group" (Iwai 1986: 216). "On occasion when a follower reaches a certain status in the hierarchy, he is given permission to train his own followers and become a small boss. He announces the name of his own family and, in accordance with his prestige, he is permitted to call himself either the boss of 'a branch of the family' or boss of 'a whole family'" (Iwai 1986: 217).

The self-image of the *yakuza* stands in contrast to their American counterparts. The Yamaguchi-gumi, for example, is listed in the telephone book and publishes a membership newsletter, and their headquarters are clearly marked for all to see. They typically wear lapel pins that designate their *boryokudan*.

The logo of the Yamaguchi-gumi, for example, a golden diamond-shaped design, appears on their headquarters building in Kobe, on lapel pins, and on members' business cards. Movies that portray *yakuza* as noble gangsters are very popular in Japan, and the *yakuza* are very influential in the Japanese movie industry. In 1981, when Masahisa Takenaka was installed as the head of the Yamaguchi-gumi, the event was seen on national television. His funeral in 1985 was also telecast. (Takenaka was gunned down by rival members of his *boryokudan*.) When a rival for leadership, Hiroshi Yamamoto, seceded from the clan, he announced it at a news conference at one of Kobe's leading restaurants (Haberman 1985). With eighteen top lieutenants, he formed the 3,000 member Ichiwa-Kai.

The rebellion of the Ichiwa-kai against the mainstream Yamaguchi-gumi resulted in a great deal of violence, and it made headlines in Hawaii. While the Yamaguchi-gumi loyalists had numerical superiority, the Ichiwa-kai had seized most of the organization's arsenal. Desperate for firepower, Masashi Takenaka (brother of the slain leader and his replacement as head of the Yamaguchi-gumi) and two of his ranking officers attempted to exchange large quantities of amphetamines for military arms in Honolulu, but they were caught in a Drug Enforcement Administration undercover sting. A DEA agent told Takenaka that the weapons would be delivered to Japan aboard a U.S. Air Force plane in order to avoid scrutiny by Japanese authorities—Japan has very strict gun-control laws (Yates 1985). By the end of 1988, the gang war had left twenty-five dead and seventy injured and led to a significant increase in Yamaguchi-gumi membership. According to Japanese law enforcement officials, tough police crackdowns "may have worked to the syndicate's benefit, putting many smaller gangs out of business or forcing them to seek Yamaguchi-gumi protection" (Talmadge 1988: 2).

At times the *yakuza* have been big news in Hawaii, the result of alleged involvement in drug trafficking, gambling, and prostitution on the islands. There have also been news stories tying the *yakuza* to crime on the West Coast and Las Vegas, some of it taking on racist overtones: Japanese criminals "invading" America.

Triads, Tongs, and Chinese Street Gangs

Secret societies have a long history in China (Fong 1981; Chin 1990). Martin Booth (1990) dates them back to the beginning of the common era. An important part of these societies are the Triads and their American offshoots, tongs and street gangs.

Triads

The term "triad" refers to the Chinese societies' common symbol: an equilateral triangle representing the three basic Chinese concepts of heaven, earth, and man. Triads members are assigned numbers based on their position. For example, enforcers or "Red Poles" are assigned number 426; an ordinary member is a 48; a leader or "Hill Chief" is 489. Assigned numbers always begin with a 4, based on ancient occult numerology (Booth 1990). These groups, based in Hong Kong and Taiwan, engage in highly ritualized behavior and dress—secret hand signs, passwords, and blood oaths are used in elaborate initiation ceremonies. The initiation ceremony includes the recital of the Triads' thirty-six oaths, each of which ends with the death penalty for its violation. For example, number eighteen: "If I am arrested after committing an offense, I must accept my punishment and not try to place blame on my sworn brothers. If I do so, I will be killed by five thunderbolts" (Carter 1991b). The ceremony may take as long as six or seven hours (Booth 1990).

The Triad phenomenon is believed to have originated in opposition to the Ch'ing dynasty established by the conquering Manchus in 1644 (Fong 1981). The Ch'ing dynasty ended in 1911 with the success of Sun Yat-sen (1866–1925), who had been a Triad member. Many Triad members then turned to criminal activities: gambling, loansharking, extortion, and trafficking in opium from the Golden Triangle of Southeast Asia. This trade was strengthened considerably by the activities of Chinese Nationalist forces in the Golden Triangle (discussed in chapter 7). Chiang Kai-shek, himself a Triad member, is reputed to have used Triads in his war against the Communists and labor unions. Triads were suppressed with a great deal of violence on the mainland by Mao Tse-tung when his Communist forces defeated Chiang's Nationalist Army in 1949. Ko-lin Chin (1990) reports that Triad members who fled to Taiwan with Chiang Kai-shek were tightly controlled by the Kuomintang, the Nationalist Party, and unable to expand their criminal operations on the island.

Thousands of other Triad members fled into the British colony of Hong Kong, which already had locally organized Triads that dated back to the early twentieth century. The indigenous Hong Kong Triads began as guilds and benevolent societies, extended into criminal activities, and actively collaborated with the Japanese during their World War II occupation of the colony. In the postwar era, they emerged as powerful criminal societies (Chin 1990). There is fear of an exodus of Triad members to other parts of the world in anticipation of the return of Hong Kong to Chinese rule in 1997. There are reports, however, that the relationship between the Communist regime and Triads is not necessarily adversarial (Schmetzer 1993). Indeed, in 1993, China's top law enforcement officer acknowledged police links with Triads (Kristof 1993).

The drug trafficking Triads expanded their operations during the Vietnam War, when thousands of GIs were attracted to the potent heroin of Southeast Asia. When the Americans withdrew from Vietnam, the Triads followed the market and internationalized their drug operations. Since many soldiers were stationed in Europe, a major Triad marketplace developed there, with operations headquartered in Amsterdam. There are about fifty Triads operating out of Hong Kong, the most powerful being the 14K Society which, according to Gerald Posner (1988), has as many as 30,000 members, although Barbara Basler (1988) reports that there are approximately fifteen active Triads in Hong Kong with about 20,000 members. (The colony has a population of 5.6

Triad Society members were discovered at a meeting by Hong Kong police officers.

million.) Membership requires a sponsor who is a ranking official of the society. Many of the younger members are involved in the martial arts, and martial arts schools are often controlled by Triads. In Hong Kong, membership in a Triad is a criminal offense. In addition to drug trafficking activities, Triads are involved in extortion from legitimate businesses, gambling, loansharking, and prostitution (Basler 1988).

Fenton Bresler, testifying before the President's Commission (1984b: 42–43), points out that:

> Each specific organization operating within its own territory has its own flag. If I want to become a new Triad head, I have to ask the original guy back in Hong Kong or Taiwan to give me a flag which means I can bring it over and that means this is my territory. The flag is a triangular flag. It authorizes . . . me to go to the new town and organize my branch.
>
> Theoretically, there is no control over me from the original base: once I have my own flag, I become independent. I am a 489 [symbolic number indicating a boss] but really I am only semi-independent. Spiritually I am linked with the old country.

The typical structure of Triad lodges is presented by Martin Booth. Each has a hierarchy that determines its activities (1990: 33–35, edited):

> The leader is called the Shan Chu, and there is a deputy leader, the Fu Shan Chu, to assist. Below them come the Heung Chu, or Incense Master, and the Fin Fung, or Vanguard. These two officers administer the lodge rituals and

have the power to invest, initiate, and order retribution against the members. Beneath them are a number of departmental heads responsible for the everyday running of the society and of any sub-branches, each of the latter having an internal structure similar to that of the main lodge except for the Incense Master and Vanguard. These are only found in principal lodges and their presence is a sign that a lodge has reached maturity and achieved power in its own right. Sub-branches are controlled by a leader, the Chu Chi, and his deputy, the Fu Chu Chi. Some lodges also have a treasurer, but this is comparatively rare. All Triad officers are appointed for fixed periods and are elected by lodge members.

Initiate members are required to pay an entrance fee. They must also obtain a sponsor, to whom further fee is payable—often far in excess of the entrance fee. This is a private arrangement and is only reached after the initiate's credentials have been thoroughly checked by the Incense Master and Vanguard. A sponsor must also be found, and paid for, when a member seeks promotion within the lodge. All monies earned by an individual society, from whatever source, are deposited in the central lodge fund. Embezzlement is not uncommon and has caused major rifts in some societies sometimes leading to violence.

Within each society there are four ranks of officials. The first is the Hung Kwan, or Red Pole, who is a fighter and is responsible for discipline. The Paz Tsz Sin is also known as the White Paper Fan and occupies a position similar to the *consigliere* in the Mafia. The Cho-Hai or Messenger is a liaison officer who acts as a go-between in lodge affairs and as a representative in its dealings with the outside world or with other lodges.

Tongs

The term "tong" means "hall" or "gathering place." Some Chinese immigrants, like Sicilian immigrants who had been *mafiosi*, were Triad members at home. In the United States they engaged in organized criminal activities, particularly opium trafficking, prostitution, gambling, and extortion. Many of these men became part of the tongs, benevolent associations that—in a pattern similar to the *Unione Siciliana* discussed in chapter 3—have been able to transcend the worlds of legitimate business and crime. At the turn of the century, "fighting tongs" controlled large-scale vice operations—gambling and prostitution—in urban areas with significant Chinese populations.

While most tongs were business, fraternal, or political in character, Ivan Light (1977: 472) notes that the "fighting tongs" licensed illegal businesses and were part of a tight-knit nationwide alliance. A purely local dispute between fighting tongs, therefore, "could and often did precipitate a fight between affiliates in every U.S. Chinatown." During the last decade of the nineteenth century and the first two decades of the twentieth, tong wars occurred on the East and West Coasts. In New York in 1909, a "tong war" between the On Leongs and Hip Sings claimed an estimated 350 lives (Sante 1991). As the importance of gambling and house prostitution in Chinatowns declined following the First World War, vice entrepreneurs discovered the profitability of tourist enterprises, and restaurants replaced the brothels and gambling halls.

Contemporary tongs such as the Hip Sing and the On Leong have dropped the term from their names because of its association with "tong wars" (Chin 1990).

Nevertheless, these tongs continue to be associated with illegal gambling. In 1988, for example, federal agents raided the Chicago headquarters of the On Leong where they found evidence of extensive commercial gambling, including more than $320,000 in cash, and records indicating extortion from local Chinese merchants. A 1990 indictment accused the Chicago On Leong and affiliates in New York and Houston of being a key part of a gambling operation that netted $11.5 million. Gambling, in particular Pai Gow, an ancient Chinese domino game, was available from 9:30 P.M. to 7:00 A.M. seven nights a week at the On Leong headquarters (Hayner 1990).

Chinese Street Gangs

Many contemporary tongs are national in scope, particularly the Hip Sing, On Leong, and Tsung Tsin, and some are connected to Chinatown street gangs such as the Ghost Shadows and the Flying Dragons in New York, Chicago, Boston, and San Francisco. The gangs date back to 1965, the year new immigration laws resulted in a large influx of youths from Hong Kong. Their arrival led to an upsurge of violent street crime in communities that heretofore had been relatively crime free. Gangs began to form and engage in robbery, kidnapping, extortion, prostitution, and loansharking. Youths involved in these gangs are sometimes as young as thirteen years, although established gang leaders would normally be in their thirties. Each gang typically has twenty to fifty members. As opposed to outlaw motorcycle clubs (discussed below) and traditional crime groups (discussed in chapter 1), Chinese street gangs make great efforts to attract potential members and sometimes coerce others into joining. "Once a youth decides to join the gang, he goes through an initiation ceremony that is a simplified version of the Chinese secret societies' recruiting rituals. The youth takes his oath, burns yellow paper, and drinks wine mixed with blood in front of the gang leaders and the altar of General Kwan, a heroic figure of the Triad subculture" (Chin 1990: 124).

Members dress in black outfits and sport exotic tattoos—dragons, serpents, tigers, and eagles. The gang becomes a substitute for the member's family. "They are not youth gangs in the usual sense but, rather, a young form of organized crime" (Dannen 1992b: 77).

Some of these gangs form around a tong member, typically a martial arts master who helps to train the members (Chin 1990), and they may be used by the tongs to provide security for gambling operations: "The On Leong Merchants Association utilizes the services of the Ghost Shadows street gang; the Hip Sing Tong is allied with the Flying Dragons; and the Tsung Tsin Association is connected to a gang called the 'Tung On Boys'" (Pennsylvania Crime Commission 1988: 22). Many gang members join tongs. While they have little to say about tong operations, gang members "act as protectors of the gambling places operated by tong members, are involved in demanding protection money from the stores that are located within the tong's vicinity, guard the territory from invasion by other gangs, and lay a hand on almost all illegal activities that are carried out within the territory" (Chin 1990: 59). In a study of Chinese/Vietnamese street gang members in San Francisco, Karen Joe (1992: 10) found that "a majority of the nine groups knew little or nothing about the tongs and triads," and ties that existed between the two groups were based on associations between individuals, not organizations: that is, gang members connected to particular tong members. But Calvin Toy (1992: 655) points out that certain tongs needed gang members "to ensure the smooth operation of the gambling houses; they needed guards, escorts for gamblers with large sums of money, lookouts for police raids, and especially people to collect gambling debts." The tongs, he points out, "do not have direct control of gangs nor are the arrangements permanent. Tong members often use certain respectable gang leaders as liaisons between the tong and the gangs in order to carry out specific criminal activities. More often that not, the average gang member is not aware of the particulars of this connection" (1992: 656).

While these gangs draw upon the traditions of the Triads, particularly the ceremonial aspects of initiation, they have many members who are Vietnamese (of Chinese ancestry); the latter are apparently favored because of their reputed ability with firearms. There are also mixed gangs of Vietnamese and Chinese-Vietnamese, who are usually heavily armed. They operate mainly in California, but also reach into Vietnamese and Chinese communities in other locales. The Born to Kill gang—the name was adopted by Vietnamese from a slogan that often appeared on the helmets of American GIs—was based in Queens, New York, with members in Boston, Houston, and Los Angeles. Unaffiliated with any tong, the gang was known for easy resort to violence, lack of discipline, and activities centering around extortion from, and home invasions of, Vietnamese immigrants (Lorch 1990). Members were tattooed with "BTK," a coffin, and three candles, signifying that they do not fear death. Successful prosecutions of the gang's leadership have severely disrupted the group. The Vietnamese avoid the territoriality that characterizes other similar crime groups, a lesson they learned from Vietcong who routinely changed their unit designations to confuse American intelligence (Okada 1992).

The Green Dragons, a Chinese gang that was also based in Queens, were enemies of the Born to Kill gang. Their leader, Taiwan-born Chen L. Chung—the *dai lo* or big brother—was barely out of his teens. The Green Dragons had a clearly defined hierarchy that exacted complete obedience from subordinates. An order to kill would be carried out even in the absence of an explanation. Without any ties to the tongs, and with only about two dozen members, the Green Dragons successfully moved the extortion practices of Chinatown into Queens. They were a particularly vicious group of criminals, murdering rivals and innocents alike. A joint police-FBI investigation using wiretaps led to arrests of the gang leadership in 1990. They were prosecuted at the same time and in the same federal courthouse in Brooklyn as the Born to Kill defendants. On another floor, John Gotti was being tried; his trial garnered the media attention. Like Gotti, Chung and six of his Green Dragons received life without parole (Dannen 1992b).

Special Agent John Feehan of the Drug Enforcement Administration testified before the President's Commission that he did not see "a direct connection between the Triads based in Hong Kong and our Chinese criminals here in New York City" (1984b: 99). Taken from an historical perspective, the relationship between tongs and Triads appears to parallel that of the *Unione Siciliana* and Sicilian criminals during the late 1920s and early 1930s (see chapter 3). According to testimony before the President's Commission, ties between Chinese criminals and Mafia groups in New York are as much the result of geographic proximity as shared mutual interests—Chinatown adjoins and overlaps the Mafia stronghold in the Mulberry Street area of New York's Lower East Side (PCOC 1986a).

A trial in 1986 of members of the Taiwan-based Triad United Bamboo revealed a criminal organization with some 15,000 members worldwide. Formed in Taiwan in 1957, the United Bamboo emerged in the United States in 1979, engaging in gambling, prostitution, and drug trafficking. As with Triads, the United Bamboo has an elaborate secret ceremony for inducting members (Lubasch 1986). Members of the United Bamboo were implicated in the 1984 murder of Chinese-American journalist Henry Liu in suburban San Francisco; Liu had written a book critical of Taiwan's president. For his murder, two leaders of United Bamboo were convicted by a court in Taiwan and sentenced to life imprisonment in 1985. United Bamboo was believed to have killed the journalist on orders from high-ranking government officials in Taiwan (Lohr 1985).

As with almost all organized criminal groups prior to the onset of Prohibition, Asian criminal organizations have typically exploited only their own countrymen and were therefore able to avoid serious law enforcement efforts. In more recent years, however, the extensive heroin networks of Chinese organizations have drawn intensive investigative efforts, particularly by the Drug Enforcement Administration. In 1989, for example, Johnny ("Onionhead") Eng, head of the Flying Dragons, was arrested in Hong Kong and extradited to the United States for masterminding the importation of four hundred pounds of heroin. At the end of 1992 Eng was convicted in Brooklyn federal court, and in 1993 he was sentenced to twenty-four years in prison and fined $3.5 million. The efforts of the DEA, however, have been hampered by a lack of Chinese-speaking agents. In New York, Chinese organizations—not necessarily tied to Triads or tongs—have supplanted Italian-American crime Families as the main importers of heroin, selling their highly potent Southeast Asian "China White" directly to wholesalers from black and Hispanic groups. In 1993, as a result of the seizure of a steamer with almost three hundred Chinese aboard, it was revealed that the Fuk Ching gang is a major player in the smuggling of illegal aliens. The leader of the Fuk Ching, Guo Liang Chi ("Ah Kay"), twenty-seven, often relayed orders to New York by telephone from his fortresslike

261

headquarters in China's Fujian province. He was eventually arrested in Hong Kong as a fugutive from a murder charge in the United States (Treaster 1993; Faison 1993).

BLACK ORGANIZED CRIME

A variety of black criminal groups exist throughout the United States; some are home grown, such as the El Rukns; others such as Nigerians and Jamaicans, are imported. There are important black criminal organizations in the heroin business, particularly in New York, Detroit, Chicago, Philadelphia, and Washington, D.C. While blacks have traditionally been locked out of many activities associated with organized crime (labor racketeering and loansharking, for example) by prejudice, *dope is an equal opportunity employer.* African American criminal groups made important strides in the heroin business when the Vietnam War exposed many black soldiers to the heroin markets of the Golden Triangle—previously black groups were dependent on Mafia Families for their heroin. As a result of their overseas experience, black organizations were able to bypass the Mafia and buy directly from suppliers in Thailand. We will review the better known of these groups.

Nigerians

West African countries, Nigeria in particular, have become important transshipment centers for Golden Crescent heroin: "Nigerian couriers based in Lagos travel to Pakistan to obtain heroin, then continue on commercial flights to their final destinations, or return to Nigeria to repackage the narcotics into smaller amounts for smuggling to the West" (PCOC 1986c: 124). Nigerian students or poor residents of Lagos are used as "mules"; they receive about two thousand dollars a trip for bringing in one hundred grams, usually by swallowing heroin-filled condoms ("The Nigerian Connection" 1991). At home, most Nigerians earn about three hundred dollars a year, and the country is infamous for its level of official corruption. In the capital of Lagos, multimillionaire drug barons rule vast organizations, at the bottom of which are the drug couriers who take most of the actual risks (Treaster 1992a). Customs officials use x-rays of the digestive tract to discover the drugs. In 1991, a Nigerian-Chicago connection was uncovered that used the Philippines as a transshipment point. Asian women transported heroin from Bangkok to Manila, where Caucasian American women received the drugs for transportation to the United States. This elaborate setup was designed to reduce the suspicion that would accompany Asian women flying from Thailand to the United States. Couriers carried between 4.5 and 6.5 pounds of heroin and were paid $20,000 plus expenses (Schmetzer 1991a). Nigerian nationals are reputed to dominate the heroin business in the Washington, D.C. area.

El Rukns

The best-known black organized crime group in Chicago is the El Rukns headed by Jeff Fort. Born in 1947 in Mississippi, Fort was brought to Chicago by his mother in 1955. They settled in the poverty-stricken Woodlawn neighborhood. Fort left school after the fourth grade and remained functionally illiterate. Nevertheless, he emerged as leader of Woodlawn's notorious Blackstone Rangers, named after the intersection of 65th Street and Blackstone Avenue. With Fort at its head, the Blackstone Rangers fought a long and bloody gang war with a rival group. In 1965, the charismatic leader organized a coalition of twenty-one gangs into the Black P. Stone Nation, governed by a commission of gang leaders known as the "main 21," with Fort as the head. Through the efforts of some white clergymen and community activists who were seeking to channel gang violence into more constructive pursuits, the Black P. Stone Nation was given a federal grant of $1 million from the Office of Economic Opportunity for an elaborate grass-roots learning program. Mayor Richard J. Daley was outraged, and in 1968 and 1969 the grant was the subject of a United States Senate Investigation. In response to a subpoena, Fort appeared before the Senate Permanent Subcommittee on Investigations, introduced himself, and then walked out. In 1972, he was imprisoned for contempt of Congress and embezzlement of $7,500 in federal funds.

While in prison, Fort founded the El Rukns, a "Moorish" religious organization, and dubbed himself Prince Malik. The Blackstone P. Nation headquarters at 3949 S. Drexel, a former theater, became the Grand Major Temple. After serving two years of a five-year sentence, Fort was paroled and his organization began to dominate large areas of the black community. He purchased a home in Milwaukee for his wife and children but spent most of his time in Chicago's South Side riding in a chauffeured limousine with several bodyguards. Fort, who was a thin teenager, grew into a physically imposing adult with a beard, braids, fur coats, and Chinese coolie-type triangular hats. He granted no interviews and rarely spoke to anyone who wasn't part of his organization. In 1982, Fort was convicted of participation in a cocaine conspiracy and sentenced to thirteen years imprisonment. In 1987, Fort and four members of the El Rukns were convicted of plotting terrorist acts on behalf of Moammar Gadhafi of Libya; Fort was sentenced to eighty years. In 1988, Fort and three other El Rukns were convicted of the 1981 murder of a rival gang member. (Willie "Dollar Bill" Bibbs, of the Titanic Stones, had failed to heed the El Rukn warning to share the proceeds of his drug dealings.)

In 1969, referring to the Black P. Stone as a community group, President Richard Nixon invited Fort to his inauguration. In the 1983 mayoral race, the Cook County Democratic organization paid the El Rukns $10,000 to campaign in black wards and serve as poll watchers for Mayor Jane M. Byrne. In 1984, the Reverend Jesse Jackson publicly praised them for their role in a voter registration drive on behalf of his presidential campaign (Shipp 1985a). But by the end of the 1980s, the fortunes of the group took a decided turn downward:

Jeff Fort was in prison, the gang's headquarters were forfeited and destroyed, and a series of indictments and convictions occurred. In 1989, sixty-five El Rukns were indicted, and by 1991, nineteen had been convicted of drug- and murder-related offenses. In 1992, numerous El Rukn generals who had held the highest rank under Jeff Fort, all in their thirties and forties, received long prison sentences. In 1993, charges of prosecutorial misconduct had serious results: the convictions of many El Rukn defendants were thrown out, and new trials were ordered.

Jamaican Posses

The introduction of crack cocaine (discussed in chapter 7) has led to changes in consumer demographics and thus in the domestic drug market. Although they first developed in Jamaica as informal mechanisms for social control, some Jamaican groups have become key players in the U.S. crack market. About forty Jamaican criminal groups, commonly known as posses—the term is derived from the Western movies popular with Jamaicans—have an estimated membership of between ten and twenty thousand and operate in at least seventeen U.S. cities (McGuire 1988: 22):

> The Jamaican posses currently active in the United States can be traced to specific neighborhoods in Jamaica. Key members formed their associations based on geographical and political ties in Jamaica. . . . The majority of posse members are convicted felons and/or illegal aliens. [They] differ from other narcotics trafficking cartels in that their members are importers, wholesalers and distributors. Therefore, their profit margin is higher than traffickers who utilize middlemen. A posse that controls 50 crack houses in one city can make $9 million a month. Other major importers of illegal narcotics, such as the Colombians and Cubans, are usually only wholesalers. They will turn a profit on only one sale. The Jamaicans, on the other hand, never exchange any money until the narcotics are sold at the street level by members of the organization. The money is then funneled back up to the leaders.

In other words, posses

> exhibit a strong vertical structure and maintain control over the product from acquisition of the cocaine powder close to the source; through cutting, manufacture, and distribution to street sales. Most significantly they exercise control over money from the street back up to the leader. No division of money takes place until it has all been returned to the leader. (Pennsylvania Crime Commission 1990: 241)

The Pennsylvania Crime Commission (1990: 240) outlines the structure:

> At the national level, posses have one or more top leaders, sometimes called "generals." The Shower Posse has one leader in Jamaica and one leader in the United States. The first region of the country in which a posse operates may

evolve into "headquarters" or base of operations from which the subsequent expansion of operations is directed. From this headquarters, posse leaders may send "captains" or "lieutenants" to establish operations in new regions. These representatives of the national leadership are responsible for recruiting supervisors to manage workers, the latter are frequently illegal aliens smuggled from Jamaica into the United States.

In Kansas City, notes Ronald Koziol (1988), a group of Jamaicans from the Waterhouse section of Kingston established fifty-five dope and crack houses and launched a wave of violence early in 1986 that took at least twenty-two lives in an eighteen-month period. Leaders of the posse insulated themselves by using Jamaicans living in New York and Miami to transport cocaine and staff retail outlets in the fifty-five houses. The workers were paid on a commission basis: five dollars for every thirty dollar bag sold. A CBS television report (*West 57th Street*, March 19, 1988) stated that posse drug profits have been used to ship automatic weapons to Jamaica and to support rival political parties in that island nation, where election campaigns have often been marked by violence.

The posses are characterized by an extreme predilection toward violence. The most notorious, the five thousand member "Shower posse," reportedly got its name for engaging in frenzied shootouts—*showering* gunfire (Witkin 1991). In Jamaica, the Shower posse has been linked to the Jamaica Labor Party and has engaged in bloody warfare with posses aligned with other political parties, including the ruling People's National Party (French 1992). Posses often move into neighborhoods where black street gangs are active, touching off competitive violence. In 1990 federal agents arrested seventeen members of the Gulleymen—named after a neighborhood in Kingston, Jamaica—a posse that allegedly controls crack houses in Brooklyn and Dallas and has been linked to at least thirty murders. As part of their business operations, the Gulleymen sell franchises to street-level dealers, providing them with crack and protection (McKinley 1990). Posse members have a fascination with firearms, particularly high caliber weapons, and prefer to always be armed. Therefore, they avoid the use of commercial airplanes.

Other Black Organizations

Haitians and a variety of black street gangs have been expanding their operations and drug markets interstate, in particular the Crips and the Bloods of Los Angeles. The Crips, whose membership is reputed to number 15,000, have moved into Seattle, Denver, Minneapolis, Oklahoma City, St. Louis, and Kansas City, as well as smaller cities throughout California (Egan 1988). Along with the Bloods, a smaller gang, members have been slowly moving east, establishing drug distribution networks, particularly crack, as far as Omaha; Crips have been noted in Baltimore and Washington, D.C.

Bloods and Crips are heavily armed and quick to use violence. They have depressed prices for crack by flooding the market (Robbins 1988). The Drug

Gang members on a street corner in Omaha, one of many cities where the Los Angeles-based Bloods and Crips gangs have set up drug networks.

Enforcement Administration (1988: 11) points out, however, that outside of Los Angeles the Crips are "splinter groups composed of former gang members, ranging in age from their low to upper twenties, who utilize the gang names as a means of identifying their organization. These subgroups are independent entities, often operating in competition with one another." Nevertheless, these subgroups are highly organized and extremely violent: "Neither gang is rigidly hierarchial. Both are broken up into loosely affiliated neighborhood groups called 'sets,' each with 30 to 100 members. Many gang members initially left Southern California to evade police. Others simply expanded the reach of crack by setting up branch operations in places where they visited friends or family members and discovered that the market was ripe" (Witkin 1991: 51). In 1992, it was reported that the Crips, or perhaps older former members of the gang, had developed direct ties with the Medellín cartel ("FBI Says Los Angeles Gang Has Drug Cartel Ties" 1992).

In many areas of the country, particularly in New York and Los Angeles, the relatively stable neighborhood criminal organizations that dominated the heroin and cocaine trade found new competitors: youthful crack dealers. Requiring only a small investment to enter the trade, street gangs or groups of friends and relatives have entered the market, often touching off an explosive level of competitive violence that frequently involves the use of high-powered handguns and automatic weapons. In New York, crack dealers have set booby traps for the police; electrified doorknobs, for example. In the South Jamaica section of Queens, one of New York's five boroughs, crack dealers executed a New York State parole officer in 1987 and a New York City police officer in 1988. A feature story in *Newsweek* ("The Drug Gangs" 1988: 20) concluded: "The crack trade, built on the enormous influx of cocaine from Latin America, is now transforming some of the country's toughest street gangs into ghetto-based drug trafficking organizations" The article notes that some gangs have established direct connections to major Colombian traffickers.

Jerome Skolnick and his colleagues (1990) distinguish between two gang types. *Cultural gangs* are strongly grounded in a neighborhood identity, and members may be involved in crime, including drug trafficking. *Entrepreneurial gangs* are organized for the express purpose of distribution of drugs. The first type is maintained by loyalty to the gang and the neighborhood; the second is based on continuing economic opportunity. In the cultural gang, involvement in drug use and dealing can serve as membership requirements; stature in the group can be linked to success in the drug trade. Unlike the entrepreneurial gangs, these groups define themselves in terms of brotherhood, are highly protective of their turf, and engage in nonutilitarian violence with other gangs. While the cultural gang is not organized expressly to sell drugs, "the gang organization facilitates that activity" (1990: 7). This can also be said of outlaw motorcycle clubs (discussed below). However, the low level of cohesiveness, loose organization, high member turnover, and unstable leadership typical of most street gangs mitigates against their being effective drug entrepreneurs (Klein, Maxson, and Cunningham 1991).

A number of other black criminal groups operate in urban areas throughout the country, for example, the Junior Black Mafia of Philadelphia and the Vice Lords of Chicago, but they have a limited degree of organization and longevity. Whether or not they will emerge as a "black mafia" is a question to be answered in the future. In comparison with traditional organized crime, black groups have an inherent weakness: confinement to the inner city,

> which stymies the development of symbiotic community relationships that contribute to the survival of indigenous crime organizations. LCN Crime Families traditionally have generated "goodwill" by providing certain community services, and by keeping the more predatory kinds of crime (e.g., drugs, prostitution) out of their own neighborhoods even while organizing it elsewhere in the city. . . . Black numbers operators cultivated considerable goodwill, but Black drug operations prey almost exclusively on their own people and thereby generate organized opposition from within their own community. (Pennsylvania Crime Commission 1990: 233).

New laws, particularly RICO, and effective law enforcement mitigate against the development and expansion of upstart criminals into self-perpetuating criminal organizations.

267

IRISH ORGANIZED CRIME

The Irish presence in organized crime can be seen in the Boston area, where three gangs, whose membership is predominantly Irish, operate. In 1961, a murderous war erupted between two of these gangs—the McCleans of Winterhill and the McLaughlins of Charlestown—and lasted for several years. In 1964, Raymond Patriarca, boss of the New England crime Family, intervened in an attempt to broker a settlement. The attempt failed, and Patriarca "declared war" on the McLaughlins, a move that brought the conflict to an end in 1966 (Teresa 1973).

According to the President's Commission, the three Irish gangs have divided Boston into territories: "The [Howard] Winter gang controls the docks in Boston and Local 25 of the International Brotherhood of Teamsters. Apparently, all trucks that service the docks must pay protection money to the Winter gang; stores, restaurants, and other dockside businesses also are reported to pay extortion money. Permission to operate a criminal enterprise in the territories comes from [James] Bolger, [Steven] Flemmi, and Winter; it is estimated that independent drug dealers pay a 'street tax' of 25 percent to the Irish leaders" (1986a: 121). The Irish groups also have a working relationship with the traditional OC group, the Patriarca Family (known as the "Office").

The Westies

New York City's Hell's Kitchen stretches from the shows and restaurants of the theater district and Times Square to the docks of the Hudson River, home of the infamous "Pistol Local" of the International Longshoremen's Association. It continues to house one of the last vestiges of the Tammany Hall political machine, the McManus Democratic Club (Roberts 1992). In an earlier era, Hell's Kitchen was home to Owney Madden and his Gopher gang (discussed in chapter 3). Men from this West Side gang continued in the rackets long after Madden retired to Hot Springs. John ("Cockeye") Dunn, who was electrocuted for murder, and his partner Eddie McGrath, who eventually retired to Florida, ran the docks and other neighborhood rackets with the man who eventually succeeded them, Hughie Mulligan. Mickey Spillane took over when Mulligan was imprisoned (he died in 1974). Spillane began kidnapping "wiseguys," killing one victim after the Gambino Family had paid a $100,000 ransom. The outcome was predictable: on May 13, 1977, Spillane's corpse was found between two cars in front of his house, stabbed and shot to death (Coffey and Schmetterer 1991). According to Gene Mustain and Jerry Capeci (1992), Spillane's murder was the work of the DeMeo crew (discussed in chapter 4) as a favor to Westies member James Coonan.

Spillane's operations and organized criminal activities on the West Side were taken over by a group dubbed (by police and press) "The Westies." Their founder, Jimmy Coonan is a high school drop-out and ex-convict whose father is a certified public accountant. Coonan put together a lucrative loansharking operation and a murderous crew of followers, in particular, Mickey Featherstone and James McElroy. By the late 1970s they controlled criminal activities in Hell's Kitchen.

The Westies have a reputation for being extremely violent: one victim was killed over a $1,250 debt; another for "badmouthing" Coonan's brother; a fight over a pinball game ended the life of another; the head and penis of one victim were kept in a bag and bottle and displayed by members in neighborhood bars. Nevertheless, or perhaps because of, their violence, the Westies developed important ties to the Gambino crime Family. They have been implicated in at least thirty murders, some on behalf of the Gambino Family, including that of Vincent Leoni, a Gambino *caporegime* suspected of skimming loansharking profits from Paul Castellano (Johnson 1986). In return, the Westies shared in some Gambino Family operations on Manhattan's West Side. According to Mickey Featherstone, he and Jimmy Coonan met with Paul Castellano and ranking members of the Gambino Family in 1978 at a Bay Ridge, Brooklyn, Italian restaurant. Castellano told Coonan:

> Alright Jimmy, this is our position. From now on, you boys are going to be with us. Which means you got to stop acting like cowboys and wild men. If anybody is to be removed, you have to clear it with my people. *Capisch?* Everything goes through Nino [Gaggi, a *caporegime*] or Roy [DeMeo, a member discussed in chapter 4]. You'll have our permission to use the family name in your business dealings on the West Side. But whatever monies you make, you will cut us in 10 percent. Except, of course, for the shylocking. That you'll work out with Roy. (English 1990: 174)

"For the most part," notes James Traub (1987: 44), "the Westies bore little resemblance to their new partners. Unlike the Mafia, they have never had the sophistication or manpower to run legitimate businesses. The core of the gang rarely numbered more than a dozen men. Most gang members and associates hold union cards, either from one of the construction trade unions, or one of the theatrical unions." The Westies also have influence on the declining docks of the West Side. Some members have received money for "no show" jobs through Local 1909 of the International Longshoremen's Association (Raab 1987). "Some law enforcement authorities say that while the Westies' overall impact on New York organized crime is insignificant, its influence is considerable in the entertainment industry. Once a major power on the New York docks, the Westies now control many theatrical unions, giving them a foothold in television studios, exhibition halls, and convention centers" (PCOC 1986a: 121).

Coonan's closest associate, Francis T. ("Mickey") Featherstone, a high school drop-out and Vietnam veteran (he was a supply clerk), was diagnosed as a paranoid schizophrenic—following his second homicide. After his discharge from a Veteran's Affairs psychiatric hospital, Featherstone killed a third victim and wound up back in the hospital. In 1986, facing a murder charge for which he had been framed by his colleagues, Featherstone decided to become an informant. At the same time, Hell's Kitchen, in its new name, Clinton, was undergoing gentrification. Featherstone and demographics placed the Westies on the extinction list (English 1990): Coonan received a sixty-five year term; McElroy sixty years. Featherstone is in the Witness Protection Program (Coffey and Schmetterer 1991).

OUTLAW MOTORCYCLE CLUBS

There is one facet of OC in which ethnic identity is unimportant: the biker subculture, although it is overwhelmingly white and working class (Wolf 1991). The outlaw motorcycle club is a uniquely American derivation, although several of them now have chapters in countries throughout the world. They date from the years after World War II, when many combat veterans, particularly those residing in California, sought new outlets for feelings of hostility and alienation. Some found release in the motorcycle and association with others in motorcycle clubs such as the "Booze Fighters" and "Market Street Commandos." These clubs became a means of continued quasi-military comradery among the members. At the same time, the motorcycle became a symbol of freedom from accepted social responsibilities and restraints. Soon these new groups became a nuisance, if not a threat, to local communities in southern California.

Shortly after World War II, a group of California veterans formed a motorcycle club and called themselves the POBOBs, an acronym for "Pissed Off Bastards of Bloomington." Bloomington is a small southern California town between San Bernadino and Riverside. By some accounts the POBOBs were dedicated to mocking social values and conventional society through acts of vandalism and general lawlessness. Over Independence Day weekend, 1947, following the arrest of a POBOB member for fighting in Hollister (south of Oakland), a reported 750 motorcyclists descended on the small town and demanded his release. When local authorities refused, the cyclists literally tore up the small community, a scene that was later depicted in the 1954 Marlon Brando film *The Wild One*. The movie also featured Lee Marvin and helped to spread the outlaw motorcycle phenomenon.

Hunter Thompson (1966) reports a different version of this incident, which he states grew out of a July Fourth celebration that included motorcycle races sanctioned by the American Motorcycle Association (AMA). Around three thousand cyclists participated. The cyclists grew unruly, and the seven-man police force was unable to handle the ensuing disorder. After marshalling additional officers, the unruly cyclists were easily controlled—the actual riot was timid compared to the film version. Daniel Wolf (1991: 4) states that about five hundred unaffiliated bikers disrupted the AMA-sponsored event "by drinking and racing in the streets of the host town of Hollister. The ineffective efforts of a numerically insufficient seven-man police force, in conjunction with the sometimes provocative vigilante tactics of indignant local residents, caused the

THE OUTLAW CREDO

Outlaw bikers view themselves as nothing less than frontier heroes, living out the "freedom ethic" that they feel the rest of society has largely abandoned. They acknowledge that they are antisocial, but only to the extent that they seek to gain their own unique experiences and express their individuality through their motorcycles. Their "hogs" become personal charms against the regimented world of the "citizen." They view their club as collective leverage that they can use against an establishment that threatens to crush those who find conventional society inhibiting and destructive of individual character. (Wolf 1991: 9)

Members of outlaw motorcycle gangs refer to themselves as "one-percenters," in reference to an esti-mate advanced some years ago by the American Motorcycle Association that outlaw motorcyclists comprised less than one per cent of the motorcycling population. Outlaw gangs immediately seized on the figure as a reflection of their belief that they are rebels, operating outside society's laws and mores. (PCOC 1986a: 61)

Sources: Daniel R. Wolf, *The Rebels: A Brotherhood of Outlaw Bikers*. Toronto: University of Toronto Press, 1991; PCOC, *The Impact: Organized Crime Today*. Washington, D.C.: U.S. Government Printing Office, 1986

motorcyclists to coalesce as a mob." Bikers rode motorcycles into bars and broke windows with beer bottles. This unruly behavior ended thirty-six hours later, after the arrival of additional police.

The term "outlaw" was first used by the sheriff of Riverside to distinguish southern California bikers such as the POBOBs from those motorcycle enthusiasts affiliated with the mainstream AMA. The Hollister incident gave rise to an important outlaw biker tradition—the annual July Fourth run. Another run is traditionally held over Labor Day Weekend. The lifestyles and traditions of the outlaw biker are promoted by a handful of magazines that cater to both the hard-core outlaw subculture and the "wannabe" outlaw. Biker magazines, notes Wolf (1991: 37), "make it possible for a man to construct a biker identify and develop a sense of loyalty to that image without having met another biker."

In 1947 several members of the POBOBs organized a group in San Bernardino. In Fontana on March 17, 1948, these dedicated outlaws adopted a name favored by World War II fighter plane pilots—*Hells Angels*. "A seamstress [sewed] their crests: a grinning, winged death's head wearing a leather aviator's helmet. The chapter name [was] shortened to 'Berdoo' to fit on the bottom of the rocker on the back of the jacket" (Lavigne 1987: 23).

In 1957, a nineteen-year-old former infantry veteran joined the Hells

Angels. Ralph Hubert ("Sonny") Barger, Jr., had dropped out of the tenth grade to join the army. He completed basic training and advanced infantry training before being discharged for being too young. The five foot, ten inch tall, one hundred and forty-five pound novice quickly rose in the biker ranks to become president of the club. He moved its headquarters to Oakland. This became the "mother club." In 1967, Barger appeared in a film with Jack Nicholson, *Hell's Angels on Wheels*—it did not win an Academy Award, but added greatly to the outlaw motorcycle club mystique.

According to Thompson (1966), by 1965 police harassment of the Hells Angels in California had thinned their ranks to fewer than one hundred members. The original Berdoo Chapter was reduced to only a handful of diehards. Yves Lavigne (1987) reports that in the early 1960s police harassment and legal fees left them on the brink of extinction. The Hells Angels, however, had been exposed to the drug subculture through a tenuous relationship with the counterculture movement—the "hippies" and "flower children." Needing money to survive, they turned to a one-shot deal involving the sale of methamphetamine—"speed." The outlaw bikers eventually broke with the counterculture over the Vietnam War—the former military veterans were rabid hawks. But the easy money they had found in drugs eventually moved the Hells Angels beyond the biker subculture and into organized crime.

Until 1965, the Hells Angels were virtually unknown outside of California. In that year the state's attorney general unwittingly helped them score a publicity coup. In his annual report he exaggerated their violent activities;

THE OUTLAW MOTORCYCLE CLUB AND OC

In many ways all outlaw clubs are pre-adapted as vehicles of organized crime. Paramilitary organization lies at the core of their tightknit secret society. It is a society capable of enforcing internal discipline, including an iron-clad code of silence.... Uncompromising commitments of brotherhood generate cohesion, mutual dependence, and a sense of a shared common fate. The lengthy socialization required to become a legitimate "biker" and the two years of proving oneself as a striker in order to become a member make the infiltration of a club by the police a virtual impossibility. The political structure of the club, the anti-Establishment attitudes and high-risk nature of the individuals involved, and the marginal social environment in which they operate have the potential to produce a clubhouse of crime.

Source: Daniel R. Wolf, *The Rebels: A Brotherhood of Outlaw Bikers.* Toronto: University of Toronto Press, 1991: 226.

then, the California correspondent for the *New York Times* hyped the report for readers of "All the News That's Fit to Print." The result was a spate of articles on the Hells Angels in the national media, including *Time, Newsweek,* and the *Saturday Evening Post.* These articles led to radio and television appearances by club members. This exposure fueled interest in the Hells Angels and other outlaw motorcycle clubs and helped to swell their ranks. At the time, Thompson states, most of the Angels were lawfully employed, and the publicity caused many of them to lose their jobs. In 1966 the Hells Angels were still confined to California, but massive publicity and the Vietnam War soon changed this.

During the late 1960s and early 1970s, interest and membership in outlaw motorcycle clubs swelled due to the return of disgruntled veterans from the Vietnam War (Lavigne 1987). In some instances, entire outlaw motorcycle clubs were issued charters as Hells Angels. The organization became national and then international in scope, with about sixty-four chapters in thirteen countries. In 1973, Sonny Barger was convicted and imprisoned for possession and sale of heroin, marijuana, and other drugs. He was released in 1977, but other indictments against Barger and the Hells Angels soon followed.

The development of the POBOB from an outlaw motorcycle club (OMC) to a criminal organization was a model for other groups who emulated the Hells Angels. According to Allen ("Rod") McMillan, an expert on OMC from Central Washington University, these groups moved through four stages (personal correspondence):

1. Rebellious and antisocial activity is random and nonutilitarian.
2. A police response causes less committed members to drop out; members of weaker clubs either disperse or join stronger clubs.
3. The remaining clubs are better able to exercise discipline and control over their membership, particularly control over violence, which now changes from random and nonutilitarian to instrumental.
4. The leadership uses organizational skills and the ability to intimidate for utilitarian criminal pursuits, and the group becomes a fully committed criminal organization.

From the fun-loving and hell-raising clubs of the immediate post-World War II era, a number of outlaw motorcycle clubs have developed into self-perpetuating, highly structured, and disciplined organizations whose major source of income is from criminal activity. Not all of the estimated five hundred outlaw motorcycle clubs are sophisticated criminal organizations. Only four, according to law enforcement officials, fit the definition of organized crime: The "Big Four" are (1) Hells Angels, (2) Outlaws, (3) Pagans, and (4) Bandidos.

Hells Angels chapters are centered in California and the East Coast; the mother club is in Oakland. The Outlaws were founded in 1959 in Chicago, and chapters are scattered in Michigan, Illinois, western New York, Ohio, western Pennsylvania, parts of Oklahoma, Arkansas, Kentucky, North Carolina, Georgia, and Florida. The mother club was moved from Chicago to Detroit in

1984. The Pagans were founded in 1959 in Prince George's County, Maryland; chapters are centered on the East Coast. Although there are chapters in West Virginia and New Orleans, most Pagan chapters are located in Pennsylvania. The mother club, which has no fixed location and often changes whenever a new national president is elected, has moved from Maryland, to Pennsylvania, to Suffolk County, New York. It is the only one of the "Big Four" that does not have international chapters, although there are ties to outlaw bikers in Canada. The Bandidos were founded in 1966 in Houston. Chapters are centered in the far Northwest and the South, particularly in Texas where the "mother club" is located in Corpus Christi. Together, these four groups have a combined membership of about three to four thousand. All members are white and male. The Bandidos have been closely allied with the Outlaws, while the Hells Angels and the Outlaws have been at war since 1974.

Structure

Consistent with their founders' background as military veterans, the Hells Angels and outlaw clubs that have copied them exhibit a bureaucratic structure. Each has a written constitution and bylaws. While there are some minor variations, the Outlaws, Bandidos, and Pagans have a "mother club" that serves as the (inter)national headquarters. The Bandidos' mother club consists of a president and four regional vice presidents. The national president has final authority over all club activities. The Outlaws have a similar structure. The United States is divided into four regions; each has a regional president who reports to the mother club, which is ruled by the national president. According to Lavigne (1987), the Pagan national president—head of the "Pagan Nation"—is not a supreme commander. Instead, club activities are directed by a mother club of thirteen to twenty former chapter presidents who wear the number 13 on the back of their colors, in deference to the original thirteen founding members (Pennsylvania Crime Commission 1990). Membership in the mother club is a promotion based on skill and competence. Each member of the Pagans' mother club has authority over chapters in specific regions. This includes making decisions on all problems that the local chapters are unable to resolve and seeing to it that each chapter generates income, from which the regional head receives a portion.

The Hells Angels, reports Lavigne (1987: 66), do not have a national president or national officers to give the club direction, Sonny Barger, despite law enforcement reports that describe him as national president, is simply a highly respected member who is often consulted on crucial club business. But he does not exert control over the individual chapters. Instead, the club is divided into East and West Coast factions, with Omaha, Nebraska, as the dividing line.

East Coast Officers' Meetings (ECOMS) and West Coast Officers' Meetings (WCOMS) are held every three months in different chapters' areas. The

Figure 5.3. National Organization Structure of the Pagans, the Outlaws, and the Bandidos

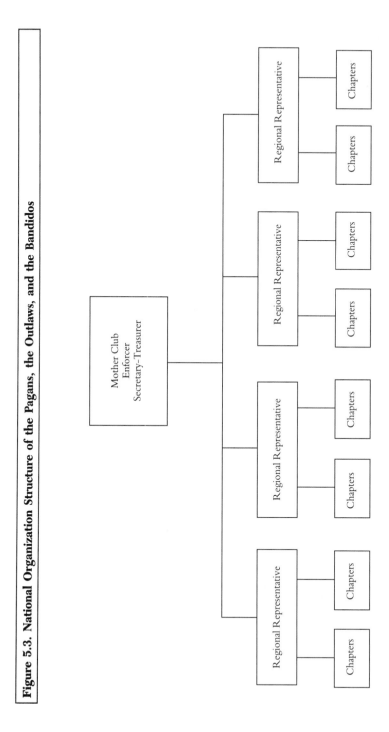

faction officers and the president or vice-president from every chapter in the faction discuss only club business at the quarterly meetings: how to financially assist a chapter; should a new chapter be admitted; how individual chapters perform; how many new patches should be ordered; should the club issue a press release on the latest arrests of members. Drug deals and other crimes are not discussed.

The East Coast and West Coast factions also hold a meeting before their annual "USA Run" that each faction hosts in alternate years. The host faction president presides, and criminal activities are not discussed. In addition, special president's meetings may occasionally be called as needed.

Any problems that involve a national outlaw club as a whole will usually be submitted to the mother club. The national secretary-treasurer is responsible for the club's finances, makes revisions in the club bylaws, and records and maintains the minutes and other club records. The national enforcer answers directly to the national president or to the mother club and may act as the president's bodyguard. In addition, he handles all special situations involving violations of club rules. There are some standard functional positions. Each of the four clubs has a national enforcement unit. Hells Angels enforcers are adorned with Nazi storm trooper-like lightning bolts tattooed underneath the words "Filthy Few"; the Outlaws have their "SS Death Squad"; the Pagans have the "Black T-Shirt Squad"; and the Bandidos have their "Nomad Chapter." John David (1988: 17) reports that the outlaw clubs also have at least one member responsible for "security/intelligence." He often travels under a variety of names, does not wear his colors, and is rarely if ever seen near the clubhouse.

> [He] compiles photographs, descriptions, addresses, phone numbers, personal and financial information, vehicle descriptions, not only on rival gang members, but on police officers, reporters, lawyers, judges, public officials and witnesses. Dossiers include names and addresses of relatives, girlfriends and boyfriends. Many of the newer members of the various outlaw motorcycle gangs have learned their intelligence skills in the military, where they also acquired the talent to use weapons and make bombs.

Each "Big Four" chapter has a president, vice president, secretary-treasurer, enforcer, and sergeant-at-arms (see figure 5.4). The sergeant-at-arms is usually the toughest member and may also serve as an enforcer and executioner. There is also the road captain. He fulfills the role of logistician and security chief for club-sponsored "runs" or motorcycle outings. The road captain maps out routes; arranges for refueling, food, and maintenance stops en route; and establishes "strong points" along the route to protect the main body from police harassment or rival motorcycle clubs. Outlaw motorcycle clubs have several mandatory runs a year, and all members not otherwise incapacitated—hospitalized or imprisoned—must participate with motorcycle (only large Harley Davidson models are acceptable) and full colors.

Figure 5.4. Chapter Organizational Structure, Outlaw Motorcycle Clubs

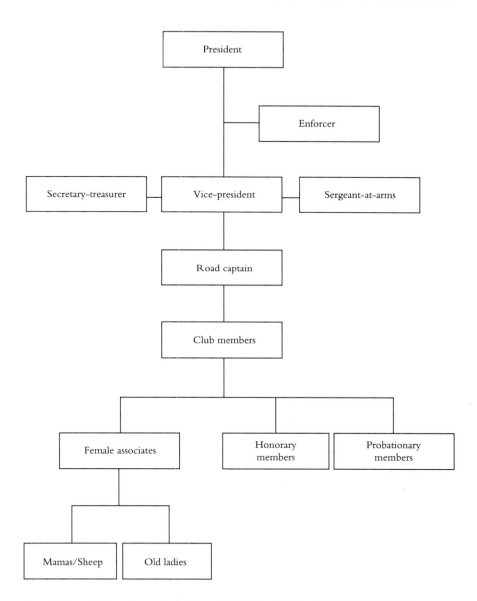

Source: Permanent Subcommittee on Investigations, *Profile of Organized Crime: Mid-Atlantic Region* (Washington, D.C.: U.S. Government Printing Office, 1983).

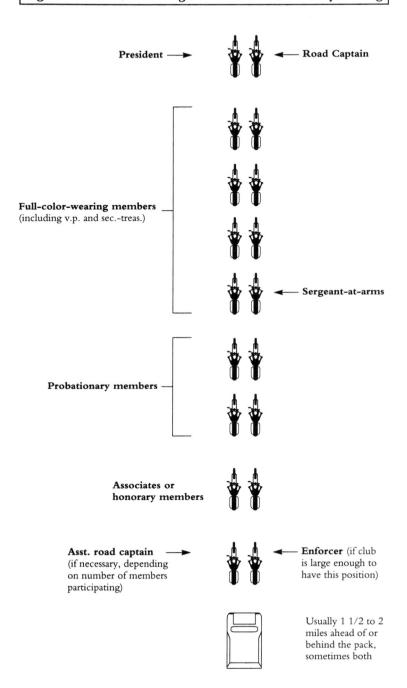

Figure 5.5. Formation during a Run of an Outlaw Motorcycle Gang

President ⟶ ⟵ Road Captain

Full-color-wearing members
(including v.p. and sec.-treas.)

⟵ Sergeant-at-arms

Probationary members

Associates or
honorary members

Asst. road captain ⟶
(if necessary, depending
on number of members
participating)

⟵ Enforcer (if club
is large enough to
have this position)

Usually 1 1/2 to 2
miles ahead of or
behind the pack,
sometimes both

"Colors" are the official club insignia. A member wears colors on the back of a denim jacket with sleeves cut off. The insignia consists of three separate sections or "rockers." The top rocker carries the club name; the center is the club emblem; and the bottom rocker designates the club location or territory. Colors may also be worn as a tattoo—mandatory for Hells Angels. Loss of colors can bring sanctions including expulsion from the club (Wolf 1991). Also sewed or pinned on the jacket are all other "authorized" patches, which are usually quite offensive to conventional society; for example, swastikas, 666 (sign of Satan), FTW ("Fuck the World"), and 1%. Consistent with a military orientation, various offenses can result in the "pulling of patches." The clubs practice precision riding, and club runs are accomplished in a military-style formation (see figure 5.5).

Outlaw clubs limit membership. Each chapter has prospective members ("strikers") who spend from one month to one year (striking period) on probationary status. Each prospective member has a sponsoring member, who is responsible for his striker. During this time strikers must prove themselves worthy of membership by following orders and committing felony crimes—this helps keep law-enforcement agents from infiltrating the organization. "Gang members do extensive background checks on prospective members, often using female associates who have been placed in positions with public utilities, government services, and law enforcement agencies to assist them" (PCOC 1986a: 65).

Probationers must be nominated by a member and receive a unanimous vote for acceptance into provisional status. They carry out menial jobs at the clubhouse and for other members. Initiation ceremonies are frequently degrading and may involve felony crimes, acts that enhance solidarity while serving to keep out undercover law-enforcement officers. When a man is admitted to membership, he is allowed to wear the club's colors—the proudest possession of any outlaw club member and clearly parallel to being "made" in traditional organized crime. The death's head emblem of the Hells Angels, for example, is copyrighted, although, notes Lavigne (1987: 75), violations rarely get into litigation: "The Hells Angels like to settle out of court." A member's death's head tattoo must be crossed out if he leaves the group. A Hells Angels member who retires under "honorable" circumstances is permitted to keep the tattoo by adding the date of his separation from the club."

While most outlaw biker chapters have headquarters, the Bandidos instead meet in members' homes that, like clubhouses, are usually heavily fortified and guarded by attack dogs. Motorcyclists in general, but outlaw clubs in particular, also have their own version of a rally every August in the Black Hills (Sturgis) of South Dakota. Drawing in excess of 250,000 persons, the outlaw clubs "profile"—the motorcycle equivalent of cruising. The potential for violence has required the active presence of shotgun-wielding state police officers (Worthington 1990). In more recent years, smaller outlaw clubs have frequently disbanded, their members becoming part of the "Big Four."

Figure 5.6. Pagans' Motorcycle Club Constitution

Club Organization
The Pagan motorcycle club is run by the Mother Club. The Mother Club has last and final say so on all club matters. Any violation of the constitution will be dealt with by the Mother Club.

Chapter Organization
Six (6) members needed to start a chapter. No new chapter may be started without approval of the Mother Club.

President
Runs chapter under the direction of the Mother Club. Keeps chapter organized, makes sure chapter business is carried out, inspects all bikes before runs and makes President meetings.

Sergent-at-Arms
Makes sure President's orders are carried out.

Vice-President
Takes over all President's duties when the President is not there.

Secretary-Treasurer
In charge of minutes of meetings and treasury. No members may change chapters without the Mother Club members permission in his area. All present chapter debts are paid and is approved by the president of the new chapter he wishes to change to. If a member has a snival, he must use chain of command, in other words, (1) His Chapter President, (2) Mother Club member in area, (3) President of Club.

Meetings
1. Chapters must have one organized meeting per week.
2. Chapter meetings are attended by members only,
3. Members must be of sound mind (straight) when attending meetings.
4. If a Mother Club member attends a meeting and a member is fouled-up, he will be fined by the Mother Club member.
5. Miss three (3) meetings in a row, and you're out of the club.
6. Members must attend meeting to leave club and turn in his colors and everything that has the name PAGANS on it. (T-shirts, Wrist Bands, Mugs, Etc.)
7. If a member is thrown out of the club or quits without attending meeting, he loses his colors, motorcycle, and anything that says PAGANS on it, and probably an ass kicking.
8. When a member is traveling, he must attend meeting of the area he is traveling in.
9. If a vote is taken at a meeting and member is not there, his vote is void.
10. Members must have colors with him when attending meeting.

Bikes
1. All members must have a Harley Davidson 750-1200 CC.
2. If a member is not of sound mind or too fouled-up to ride his motorcycle in the opinion of another member, his riding privilege may be pulled by said member until he has his head together.
3. All bikes must be on the road April 30th, or otherwise directed by the Mother Club.
4. All members must have a motorcycle license.

Mandatories
Two (2) mandatories, July 4, and Labor Day, Mother Club may call additional mandatories if need be.

Funerals
1. If a member dies in a chapter, it is necessary for all members in his chapter to attend funeral.
2. Chapter is in charge of taking care of all funeral arrangements, parties, police, procession, etc.

Parties
Pagan parties are Pagan parties only. Each chapter must throw (1) party or run per year.

Respect
1. Respect is to be shown to all Mother Club members, officer members, member's personal property, Bike, Old Lady, House, Job, etc. In other words, if it's not yours, "Don't Mess With It."

Figure 5.6. Pagans' Motorcycle Club Constitution (*Cont'd*)

2. No fighting among each other is allowed, any punches to be thrown will be done by the Sgt.–at–Arms or a Mother Club Member.
3. No stealing from members.
4. Respect your Colors.

Colors

1. President gets colors from Mother Club member in area when new member is voted in.
2. When a member leaves club, the president of his chapter turns over his colors to the Mother Club member in his area.
3. Respect your Colors, don't let anyone take them from you except the president of your chapter or a Mother Club member.
4. No colors are worn in a cage, except during funerals and loading or unloading a bike from a truck.
5. Nothing will be worn on the back of your jacket except your colors, Diamond, 13 patch.
6. No Hippie shit on the front.
7. Colors are to be put on cut off denim jackets only.
8. The only member who may keep his colors if he leaves the club is a Mother Club Member.

Old Ladies

1. Members are responsible for their Old Ladies.
2. Members may have more than one (1) Old Lady.
3. Members may not discuss club business with their Old Lady.
4. No Old Ladies allowed at meetings.
5. No property patch is worn on an Old Lady. So if you see a chick you better ask before you leap.

Prospects

1. Prospect must be at least 18 years old.
2. Prospect must be sponsored by one member who has known him at least one year.
3. Sponsor is responsible for prospect.
4. Prospect must have motorcycle.
5. Prospect must ride his bike to meeting at time of being voted into club.
6. Prospect can not do any drugs.
7. Prospects can not carry weapons at meetings and Pagan functions, unless otherwise directed by the President.
8. No stealing from Prospects.
9. Prospects must attend all meetings and club functions.
10. Prospect must do anything another member tells him to, that a member has done or would be willing to do himself.
11. Prospect must be voted in by all members of the chapter and Three (3) Mother Club Members.
12. Prospect must pay for his colors before receiving them.
13. Prospects period is determined by Mother Blub Member.
14. Pagan's M.C. is a motorcycle club and a non-profit organization.

Activities

Outlaw motorcycle clubs usually exhibit racist attitudes, and in the United States no known black males hold membership in the Big Four. However, there are predominantly black clubs with white members. Hells Angels has Jewish members. Women associated with the group are treated as playthings—objects to be used, traded, and sold. "Old ladies" are the wives or steady girlfriends of club members. Sexual and other demands for their services can only be made by their husbands or boyfriends. "Mamas" and "sheep" belong to the gang at large and are expected to consent to the sexual whims of any club member. While women are not permitted to wear club colors, they may wear denim jackets with the inscription "Property of [club's name]." Women often carry the gang's weapons and engage in prostitution or drug trafficking. Because of the freewheeling image of the outlaw clubs, teenage girls are often attracted to them. The girls are frequently gang raped, which bikers refer to as "training" or "pulling a train." They may also be photographed for blackmail purposes or transported to other states for employment in sex-oriented establishments, go-go bars and club-owned massage parlors.

The outlaw clubs are involved in distributing automatic weapons, explosives, stolen motorcycles, and motorcycle parts; providing exotic dancers and prostitutes for various sex-oriented establishments; trafficking in LSD, PCP, and cocaine, and methamphetamine. They have been particularly successful in exerting control over the methamphetamine market. George Wethern (Wethern and Colnett 1978), a former ranking member of the Hells Angels in Oakland, California, states that because of their reputation for violence and anti-establishment attitudes, the Hells Angels are perfect middlemen for drug dealers. The wholesalers sell to the Angels, who then act as distributors for street-level operators. Using violence, they are able to restrict market entry and monopolize the trade in parts of California. Other outlaw clubs have done the same elsewhere.

Members of outlaw clubs have reportedly been involved in activities with traditional organized crime, providing "muscle," firearms, bombs, or drugs. In Philadelphia, there was a great deal of friction between the Bruno crime Family and the Pagans. On one occasion Pagan member James DiGregorio, thirty-four, attempted to shoot Harry ("Hunchback") Riccobene over a drug deal. DiGregorio missed and wounded Victor DeLuca, a former bodyguard for murdered Philadelphia crime boss Phil Testa (Pennsylvania Crime Commission 1989). Afterward, relations between the Philadelphia crime Family and the Pagans improved and led to a variety of partnerships in the biker's most lucrative activity: the manufacture and distribution of methamphetamine and phencyclidine (PCP or "angel dust"). In recent years, cocaine has been added to the repertoire. While most bikers operate along the lines of short-term hedonism, some profits have been invested in a vast array of legitimate businesses, often for profit and sometimes as fronts for illegal activities. The outlaw clubs have a reliable pipeline of members and chapters for the flow of illicit goods, and the members are highly mobile—they can find support and safety in any city that has a club charter.

The basic element shared by all members of outlaw motorcycle clubs is a penchant for violence, and violence pervades the world of outlaw bikers. Rationally utilized, violence may be for the purpose of maintaining organizational discipline or to defend hegemony. William Costello, president of the Baltimore chapter of the Pagans, who eventually became a government witness, testified before a Senate committee:

> In 1972 or 1973, Satan [Pagan national president] directly ordered 40 armed Pagans, including myself to Richmond to end, with whatever means necessary, an attempt by Hell's Angels to move into Richmond, considered Pagan territory. At that time, Pagan territory included Virginia, Maryland, Delaware, and part of Pennsylvania, New Jersey, and New York. The Hell's Angels, a competing national gang, were negotiating with the Confederate Angels, a local Richmond group, for territory and power in and around Richmond. Although local gangs such as the Confederate Angels were tolerated within Pagan territory, Satan would never allow the entry of another national club into the Pagan area.
>
> We went to the Confederate Angels' clubhouse in Richmond where Satan's order was enforced with Pagan violence: one individual was shot to death, at least one crippled for life, and at least two others injured. Such violence was by no means foreign to Pagan activities. On another occasion, one Pagan member, who had crossed other Pagans, was welded inside of a drum which was then shot full of holes and tossed into the bay. Again fear was a constant reality within Pagan clubs. (Permanent Subcommittee on Investigations 1983c: 118)

According to the President's Commission, if the outlaw motorcycle club has a discernable weakness, it is that members are easily identified by their colors. "However, there are growing reports that members are abandoning their outlaw image, wearing business suits and driving luxury cars; in essence, becoming an outlaw motorcycle gang without motorcycles. If so, that would complete the evolution that has been under way for more than 20 years, a period during which the Hell's Angels developed from a collection of rowdy rebels into a genuine organized crime group" (PCOC 1986a: 65). In fact, the leadership of these outlaw clubs has become more conventional in appearance, leaving the more overtly subcultural dimensions to underlings.

As we have seen, the outlaw motorcycle club exhibits a number of characteristics that are bureaucratic. Given the military background of the founders and many members of the outlaw biker subculture, this is to be expected. There is a rather elaborate hierarchy, specialization, advancement based on skill, and extensive rules and regulations that are in written form. There is general uniformity in style of dress—colors—and motorcycle, which must be large Harley-Davidsons. Minutes of meetings are recorded, and dues are collected and maintained by a secretary-treasurer. Each member contributes weekly dues to the chapter, and the chapter pays into the national treasury. Lavigne (1987) reports that the Hells Angels also maintain a multimillion-dollar fund to which members and chapters are occasionally asked to contribute. The fund goes for legal expenses and to help support the families of imprisoned members.

As noted in chapter 1 with respect to traditional organized crime, a criminal organization can exhibit a formal structure, while its economic activities may

---

Figure 5.7. Hells Angels California Bylaws

1. All patches will be the same on the back, nothing will show on the back except the HELLS ANGELS patch. City patch is optional for each chapter. 1 patch and 1 membership card per member. Member may keep original patch if made into a banner. Prospects will wear California rocker on back and prospect patch left from where top of pocket is on a Levi jacket.
   FINE: $100 for breaking above by-law.
2. No hypes. No use of Heroin in any form. Anyone using a needle for any reason other than having a doctor use it on you will be considered a hype.
   FINE: Automatic kick-out from club.
3. No explosives of any kind will be thrown into the fire where there is one or more HELLS ANGELS in the area.
   FINE: Ass-whipping and/or subject to California President's decision.
4. Guns on CA runs will not be displayed after 6 PM. They will be fired from dawn until 6 PM in a predetermined area only. Rule does not apply to anyone with a gun in a shoulder holster or belt that is seen by another member if it is not being shot or displayed.
   FINE: $100 for breaking above by-law.
5. Brothers shall not fight with each other with weapons; when any HELLS ANGELS fights another HELLS ANGELS, it is one on one; prospects same as members. If members are from different chapters, fine goes to CA Treasurer.
   FINE: $100 for breaking above by-law or possible loss of patch.
6. No narcotics burns. When making deals, persons get what they are promised or the deal is called off.
   FINE: Automatic kick-out from club.
7. All HELLS ANGELS fines will be paid within 30 days. Fines will be paid to that chapter's treasurer to be held for the next CA run.
8. One vote per chapter at CA officer's meetings. For CA 2 no votes instead of a majority to kill a new charter and a charter goes below 6 they must freeze or dissolve on the decision of CA Officers' Meeting.
9. If kicked out, must stay out 1 year then back to original chapter. HELLS ANGEL tattoo will have an in-date and out-date when the menber quits. If kicked out, HELL ANGELS tattoo will be completely covered with a 1/2 X through the tattoo.
10. Runs are on the holidays; 3 mandatory runs are Memorial day, July 4th, and Labor Day.
11. No leave period except hospital, medical or jail.

---

actually involve small firms or partnerships among members that can also include non-member associates. This is often the case with outlaw motorcycle clubs. Each member of the "Big Four" is reputed to have about ten associates, each with his own network of friends. For business purposes, each member is at the center of an action group which, although tied to every other member through the structure of the club, operates independently or in partnership arrangements. In other words, the formal structure of the motorcycle club is not necessarily the same as its economic structure. While there is a relatively clear hierarchy within each of the four outlaw clubs, its income-generating activities involve several smaller operationally independent units.

PRISON GANGS

In the last twenty years, notes the President's Commission (1986a: 73), some prison groups "have evolved into self-perpetuating criminal gangs. Several operate both in and out of prison and have taken on the characteristics of true organized crime associations." These groups typically engage in extortion and drug and weapons trafficking. "Many prison gangs have a 'blood-in-blood-out' policy, meaning that an inmate may become a member only after killing or assaulting another prisoner or staffer and that his blood will be spilled before he is allowed to quit the gang." In a pattern reminiscent of the Neapolitan Camorra (discussed in chapter 1) members released from prison remain in the gang, providing support and enforcement services for the organization outside. Income generated by outside members is shared with those remaining in prison. The Department of Justice has identified 114 different gangs, with greatly varying structures. Four of these gangs "appear to meet the criteria of an organized crime group: the Mexican Mafia, Aryan Brotherhood, Black Guerilla Family, and Texas Syndicate." Some sources add La Nuestra Familia. In all five, "either murder or the drawing of blood are prerequisites for membership" (PCOC 1986a: 75).

Mexican Mafia

Reputed to be the most powerful of the prison-organized groups, the Mexican Mafia—MEXIKANEMI (Soldiers of Aztlan)—is comprised primarily of Mexican-American convicts and ex-convicts from the barrios of East Los Angeles. Its origins are traced to the Deuel Vocational Institute in Tracy, California, where in 1957 twenty young Mexican-Americans from the Maravilla area of East Los Angeles formed a self-protective group. But, notes the President's Commission, they soon "began to control such illicit activities as homosexual prostitution, gambling, and narcotics. They called themselves the Mexican Mafia out of admiration for *La Cosa Nostra*" (1986a: 73). Attempts by the Department of Corrections to diminish gang power by transferring members to other institutions only helped to spread their influence.

Vigorous recruiting from among the most violent Mexican-American inmates, particularly those housed in adjustment centers for the most dangerous and incorrigible, has resulted in a membership of about six to seven hundred. Entry into the gang is relatively easy. It is granted to any Hispanic inmate who meets the "homeboy connection"— he is known by an active member as a childhood friend—and receives a majority vote, which accounts for the relatively large number of members (Fong 1990). The hierarchy is composed of a president, vice president, regional generals, lieutenants, sergeants, and soldiers (Fong 1990; see figure 5.8). Members are required to kill without question, which gives the gang a constant pool of potential contract killers. The penalty for failing to carry out a contract is death.

By the mid-1960s the Mexican Mafia had assumed control over prison heroin trafficking and numerous other inmate activities. In 1966 they started to move their operations outside of the prison. By 1967 their influence and reliance on wholesale violence increased, and in that year they attacked the first Mexican-American outside of their group. This attack on an inmate from rural

---

Figure 5.8. Mexican Mafia Structure

President
(system-wide)

Vice-President
(system-wide)

Generals
(regional level)

Lieutenants
(unit level)

Sergeants
(unit level)

Soldiers ———————————————————————*Associates*

Source: Robert S. Fong, "The Organizational Structure of Prison Gangs: A Texas Case Study." *Federal Probation*, Vol. 54, March 1990: 36–43.

---

northern California led to the formation of a second Mexican-American gang, *La Nuestra Familia*. The two groups have been feuding since 1968. The Mexican Mafia is also at war with the Texas Syndicate.

La Nuestra Familia

"Originally founded in 1967 as a Latin cultural organization in Soledad Prison, *La Nuestra Familia* began to sell protection to others who had been victimized by the Mexican Mafia," and the two groups have been feuding ever since. "Soon the group moved into the extortion rackets that their rivals had monopolized. In 1975, the gang began establishing 'regiments' outside prison, using Fresno County, California, as a home base" (PCOC 1986a: 77). The group's constitution regulates prison and nonprison members, most of whom are Mexican-Americans from rural areas in California. It has a total member-ship of about eight hundred. The gang is headed by a single "general" with supreme power. Under the general are captains, lieutenants, and *soldados*. "Rank is usually achieved by the number of 'hits' in which a member is involved" (1986a: 77). In its struggle with the Mexican Mafia, La Nuestra Familia has been allied with the white supremacist group known as the Aryan Brotherhood, and the Black Guerilla Family.

Texas Syndicate

This major Mexican-American prison gang originated in California's Folsom Prison, although the founders were all from Texas. They banded together for

MEXICAN MAFIA CONSTITUTION

1. Membership is for life—"blood in, blood out."
2. Every member must be prepared to sacrifice his life or take a life at any time when necessary.
3. Every member shall strive to overcome his weakness to achieve discipline within the MEXIKANEMI brotherhood.
4. Never let the MEXIKANEMI down.
5. The sponsoring member is totally responsible for the behavior of the new recruit. If the new recruit turns out to be a traitor, it is the sponsoring member's responsibility to eliminate the recruit.
6. When disrespected by a stranger or a group, all members of the MEXIKANEMI will unite to destroy the person or the other group completely.
7. Always maintain a high level of integrity.
8. Never release MEXIKANEMI business to others.
9. Every member has the right to express opinions, ideas, contradictions, and constructive criticisms.
10. Every member has the right to organize, educate, arm, and defend the MEXIKANEMI.
11. Every member has the right to wear the tattoo of the MEXIKANEMI symbol.
12. The MEXIKANEMI is a criminal organization and therefore will participate in all aspects of criminal interest for monetary benefits.

Source: Robert S. Fong, "The Organizational Structure of Prison Gangs: A Texas Case Study." *Federal Probation*, Vol. 54, March 1990: 36–43.

---

mutual protection and soon became known for their swift retaliation against any opposition. As gang members were released from prison they returned from California to their home state. Many were soon rearrested and imprisoned in Texas. With about two hundred members, the Texas Syndicate is reputed to be the largest gang in that state's prison system.

In California prisons, the Texas Syndicate is reputed to be the most feared gang. In Texas and California, members participate in drug trafficking, contract assaults and murders, and extortion. Members take a life oath, and the group is more secretive than most prison gangs. Members are known to be exceptionally violent, frequently assaulting or killing nonmembers and prison staff. The chain of command is similar to that of most prison gangs.

Aryan Brotherhood

The Aryan Brotherhood originated in the early 1960s in San Quentin Prison. Known as the "Diamond Tooth Gang"—members had a piece of glass embedded in one of their front teeth—the gang developed into a Nazi-oriented, white-supremacist group dominated by members and associates of outlaw motorcycle gangs. The present name dates back to 1968. The gang has branches in prisons around the country, but is particularly active in California, Arizona, Wisconsin, Idaho, and the federal prison system. The gang insignia is a three-leaf shamrock, three sixes (666), and the letters "AB."

The Aryan Brotherhood, which engages in extortion and protection schemes, is ruled by a commission and a governing council. Members advance in the ranks through acts of violence. A commission of three members plays a leadership role, but gang members as a group do not usually relate to any one leader. Internal discipline and control is lax, and there is a great deal of internal conflict and violence within the Aryan Brotherhood. From a membership as high as 500 in 1986, the gang is believed to be declining. Upon leaving prison, members often became part of outlaw motorcycle clubs or street gangs.

Black Guerilla Family

The Black Guerilla Family was established by George Jackson of the Black Panther Party when he was in San Quentin in 1966. In accord with its founder's ideals, it is the most politically oriented of the five major prison gangs, generally following a Maoist philosophy. Many of its members were formerly part of the Black Liberation Army and various street gangs. The motivation of its membership—political action and pecuniary profit—has led to a split between those favoring one or the other goal. The ruling structure consists of a single leader known as the Chairman or Supreme Commander, a central committee, and a very loose ranking of soldiers (PCOC 1986a: 79).

THE *MAFIYA*: RUSSIAN ORGANIZED CRIME

In 1988, Soviet officials revealed that organized crime groups with as many as two hundred members were operating throughout the country. Referred to as the *Mafiya*, it was reported that they were involved primarily in extortion and were protected through corrupt relationships with Soviet authorities. Many were influenced by portrayals of organized crime in such movies as "The Godfather," via smuggled videotapes (Schodolski 1988). With the breakup of the Soviet Union, organized criminal activity has emerged on a much larger scale. Nascent capitalism, a relaxation of the totalitarian law enforcement apparatus, and liberalization of travel have provided a fertile environment for criminals who were schooled in a Soviet system ripe with corruption and an underground economy.

Organized crime and government are frequently symbiotic in the former Soviet Union. Criminals and bureaucrats form a network "that is highly organized, stratified, meticulous in planning, highly efficient in execution and well disciplined" (Serio 1992a: 130). Organized crime infests economic and political systems from the local level to the pinnacle of power. This includes government ministers in Moscow who control the supply of raw materials, and criminal clans in the republics who control trade and transportation. They have proven to be very violent. Machine-gun fire, daytime assassinations, and onlookers who remember nothing have become common (Handelman 1993; Bohlen 1993).

Russian criminal groups have excelled at restraining trade and controlling pricing in a variety of arenas including airport taxis and farmer's markets. They extort from both legitimate and illegitimate entrepreneurs. Russian gangsters have been involved in extensive drug trafficking, particularly the production and sale of methadone and similar synthetic narcotics. Another activity is ransom kidnappings. "Some of the gangs in the Russian mafia are local, others span the entire former Soviet Union and more and more are establishing links abroad" (Elliot 1992: 52). There are dozens of criminal gangs operating in Moscow, where they have divided the city into spheres of influence for collecting protection money (Shapiro 1993), and more than three thousand across the country. Police resources have been inadequate to deal with this menace. Many officers are on gang payrolls, while others have left the service to work for the gangs full time (Gallagher 1992a). Members of various ethnic groups have moved into organized criminal activity. Organized around feudal-like clan and tribal relationships, literally "crime families," these groups are well-suited to take advantage of dislocations in post-Soviet society.

One of these groups originated in the Central Asian region of the Caucasus Mountains. The Chechen national homeland is located due north of the Georgian Republic, on the western shores of the Caspian Sea. Largely Muslim and legendary warriors, the Chechens were subjected to massive deportations by Stalin, who accused them of collaborating with the Nazis during the Second World War. They returned to the region in 1957 and currently number about 700,000. Chechen crime groups operate in many areas of the former Soviet Union, including Moscow, where there are about 1,500 active members. Joseph Serio (1992b: 5) reports that "the group is more structured than most. Most important for them is the strict hierarchical arrangement of their clan relationships. It is a closed organization, recruiting only from among their own people. Chechens actively recruit juveniles from the Chechen regions where unemployment is high. This ensures a degree of 'purity' in the membership, making it difficult for law enforcement agencies lacking personnel that speak Chechen to infiltrate the group. . . . Each group has a clear structure: leader, senior advisors, soldiers, and associated members."

The Chechen gangs are quite violent and much feared. Protection rackets, enforcing restraint of trade agreements, narcotics, and weapons trafficking are all part of the Chechen crime repertoire. In 1993, a group of well-armed gangsters drove to a building across the Moscow River from the Kremlin to extort money from a local businessman. They were met by the businessman's protectors, Chechens, who opened fire, killing the gangster boss and four of his men (LeVine, McKay, and Lebedeva 1993). Members of the Chechen groups have been found throughout Eastern and Western Europe, and have sent members to New York to set up operations. Some have entered the United

Evsei Agron, a reputed killer, extortionist, and thief, was shot to death in Brooklyn in 1985. Agron was a member of an organized crime group originating in Leningrad and operating in New York City. According to the director of the FBI's New York office, the Russians follow in many ways the pattern of other ethnic organized crime groups in America, preying first on their own and then, when they feel strong enough to evade the law, spreading out to victimize others.

States for contract crimes—murder, extortion, fraud—after which they return home before authorities can detect and apprehend them.

Emigrés from what was the Soviet Union have taken advantage of the easing of travel restrictions to return to their homeland for criminal purposes. In the United States, these Russian groups are typically fluid and are comprised of five to twenty persons. This pattern has been compared to that involving the Zips (Mitchell 1992). In a number of U.S. cities where Russian immigrants have settled, there are Russian OC groups—Philadelphia, Cleveland, Chicago, Dallas, Portland, Boston, San Francisco, and New York—known by their fellow Russians as the *organizatsiya* (the organization).

There are more than a dozen Russian organized crime groups in New York with a total strength of about five hundred members. They are loosely structured, without formal hierarchy, and typically formed on the basis of regional backgrounds. One gang may be comprised mainly of immigrants from Kiev, while another consists mainly of those from Soviet Georgia. Gang members themselves are usually professional criminals. After the experiences of criminal life in the Soviet Union, where police were feared and treatment of lawbreakers harsh, they view the United States as a "thieves' haven." These gangs engage in extortion, insurance fraud, con games, counterfeiting, tax fraud, and narcotics trafficking. In 1993, a ton of cocaine was seized by officials near St. Petersburg, Russia, possibly revealing a tie between Russian criminals and Colombian cartels (Hanley 1993).

Many of the new criminals are Jews. Others have forged identity papers that allowed them to leave the former Soviet union and enter the United States as legitimate immigrants. Unlike Jewish immigrant groups who made up organized crime in the past, the Russians are relatively well-educated and adept at exploiting weaknesses in American society. There have been reports of business connections between some Russian criminals and traditional organized crime groups in Brooklyn, particularly the Lucchese and Colombo Families (Mitchell 1992). Jewish emigrés from the former Soviet union have settled in the Brighton Beach section of Brooklyn, and the New York City Police Department has been handicapped in dealing with the protection rackets and loansharking activities in the community by a lack of Russian-speaking officers (Blumenthal and Bohlen 1989). As with the Zips discussed at the beginning of this chapter, these Jewish immigrants have added a dimension to the ethnic succession thesis. Or as Yogi Berra might say, "It's deja vu all over again."

Now that we have completed our examination of traditional and emerging criminal organizations, the next two chapters will look at the "business" of organized crime.

REVIEW QUESTIONS

1. What do the nontraditional organized crime groups have in common?
2. How does the "New Mafia" differ from the "Old Mafia"?
3. How have the "Zips" confounded the theory of "ethnic succession"?
4. How does the Herrera Family operate?
5. What is the relationship between Cuban exiles, Colombians, and cocaine trafficking?
6. What variables account for the Colombian success in the cocaine business?
7. Why has it been so difficult for Colombia to eradicate their cocaine trafficking organizations?
8. Why has it been difficult for the United States to respond to the Colombian cocaine trafficking organizations?
9. What is the relationship between cocaine trafficking and politics in Colombia?
10. Who are the yakuza, and how are they organized?
11. What are Triads and how do they operate?
12. Why have the Triads had a great deal of success in international heroin trafficking?
13. What led to the success of black criminal groups of the 1960s in the heroin trade?
14. Why has the introduction of crack touched off a new level of criminal violence?

15. What are the Jamaican posses? How do they differ from other large drug trafficking organizations?
16. What is the "Westies" phenomenon?
17. What led to the development of the original outlaw motorcycle clubs?
18. What explains the rather bureaucratic structure adopted by outlaw motorcycle clubs?
19. In the organizational structure of outlaw motorcycle clubs, what are the functions of the "mother club"?
20. What aspects of outlaw motorcycle clubs are bureaucratic?
21. What are the similarities and differences between traditional organized crime and outlaw motorcycle clubs?
22. What are the basic qualifications for membership in an outlaw motorcycle club?
23. How are the prison gangs similar to the Neapolitan Camorra?
24. What are the characteristics of Russian organized crime groups that make them resemble the Zips?

6

The Business of Organized Crime: Gambling, Loansharking, Theft, Fencing, and Sex

The business of organized crime has been described as providing *goods and services* that happen to be illegal. According to the Task Force on Organized Crime, "the core of organized crime activity is the supplying of illegal goods and services—gambling, loansharking, narcotics, and other forms of vice—to countless numbers of citizen customers" (1967: 1). Herbert Packer (1968: 279) points out:

> Regardless of what we think we are trying to do, when we make it illegal to traffic in commodities for which there is an inelastic demand, the effect is to secure a kind of monopoly profit to the entrepreneur who is willing to break the law. In effect, we say to him: "We will set up a barrier to entry into this line of commerce by making it illegal and, therefore, risky; if you are willing to take the risk, you will be sheltered from the competition of those unwilling to do so."

Thus, translating morality into a statute backed by legal sanctions does not provide for greater morality; it merely widens the scope of the law and creates both temptation and opportunity for a particular set of social actors. As in any business, the better organized are usually the more successful, and organized crime is basically a business enterprise.

But the business of organized crime often includes activities that are neither "goods" nor "services," but are clearly *parasitic*. Thomas Schelling (1971) states that organized crime has a relationship with the purveyors of illegal goods and services that is extortionate. The business of organized crime is extortion, and those criminals who provide goods and services are its victims. Thus, Schelling points out, a bookmaker operating in an area dominated by an OC unit will be required to pay for the "privilege" of doing business—or suffer from violence (or perhaps a raid by corrupt police). The OC unit merely "licenses" the business, and the bookmaker or other criminal purchases a "license" through the payment of "street taxes" to avoid being beaten or killed (or subjected to police harassment). Edward D. Hegarty, former special agent in charge of the Chicago office of the FBI, points out that while persons in organized crime do not get involved in the theft of automobiles, they extort money from those who do:

> They get involved to the extent that they extort the lower level organized crime groups that are continually involved in the theft of automobiles and the chopping up of automobiles [for their parts], and they impose upon them a street tax.
>
> Many of the murders which have been committed in the Chicago area in recent years arose from automobile theft and chop shop activity. Generally these murders resulted from a failure, inability, or cheating by lower level organized crime figures on their La Cosa Nostra superiors. They were cheating on the street tax which is imposed on criminal cartels of the lower strength, the lower power base, that you have in and around the Chicago area. (Permanent Subcommittee on Investigations 1983b: 33–34)

During the 1970s, the Outfit began "taking over" (collecting regular street taxes) from the owners of chop shops around Chicago and into Lake County, Indiana. About fourteen of those who resisted were killed (O'Brien 1988). A 1990 federal indictment revealed the Outfit's response when their hegemony over gambling was challenged. Three men from the street crew of Sam Carlisi forced their way into a Chicago apartment at gunpoint and took money and jewelry from the persons running a high-stakes card game. There were threats of physical harm and a demand for $2,000 from each. Subsequently, the operators agreed to turn over 50 percent of the game's profits to Carlisi, who subsequently became the head of OC in the Chicagoland area. Games in Cicero were similarly raided because the operators had not been paying street taxes. In New York, four of that city's five OC Families muscled in on a ring of gasoline wholesalers who were keeping the federal tax of nine cents a gallon, a scheme that netted the dealers about $1 billion a year. The wholesalers were forced to pay members of the Gambino, Lucchese, Genovese, and Colombo Families a tribute of a one cent a gallon, which was later increased to two cents a gallon. When OC suspected—correctly—that one of the dealers was cooperating with the government, he was strangled to death (Raab 1989).

The boundary between providing a good or a service and being parasitic is not clearly delineated. For example, while professional gamblers may be required to pay "street taxes" to operate in a particular area, in return the OC group may limit market entry—competition—and provide collection and/or arbitration services that are vital in such enterprises. Jonathan Rubinstein and Peter Reuter (1978a: 64) note that a distinctive service provided by Italian-American OC is arbitration: "In an economy without conventional written contracts, there is obviously room for frequent disagreements. These are hard to resolve. Many bookmakers make payments to 'wise-guys' to ensure that when disputes arise they have effective representation." As noted in chapter 1, traditional OC operates as a shadow government, providing policing and judicial services to a vast underworld, thereby increasing efficiency and coordination in an otherwise anarchic and Hobbesian environment.

According to the New York State Organized Crime Task Force (1988: 73), the effectiveness of traditional organized crime is "grounded in its power to provide illegal services to its own members and, for a price, to other racketeers and legitimate businessmen. Among the more valuable services are mediation of disputes with other criminals, criminal enterprises and ventures; allocating turf to Cosa Nostra and other criminal groups; fending off incursions by others into these territories; providing financing, muscle, or a corrupt contact wherever necessary to the success of a criminal venture."

The concept of *rispetto* enables a made-guy to act as an arbitrator. If, at the request of an aggrieved party, an *uomo di rispetto* is asked for assistance, he can summon the accused to a "sitdown" or "table," an informal hearing over which he presides. Robin Moore (Moore and Fuca 1977: 64) points out that "anyone in the community, mob-connected or not, who had a legitimate complaint against someone else was entitled to ask for a Table hearing" and "any ranking Mafioso or man of respect could be prevailed upon to preside at a Table." To refuse to appear or to disregard a decision made at a table would indicate disrespect with attendant life-threatening consequences. In Chicago, crime boss Joey ("The Clown") Lombardo reveled in his role as an arbitrator for all types of neighborhood disputes. As noted by Reuter (1983) and Abadinsky (1983), the arbitrator receives a fee for this service when the disputants are criminals.

In 1985 a successful bookmaker in New York stated that he always kept a "wise-guy" on the payroll at a cost of between $200 to 300 per week. This was insurance—it prevented other criminals from placing bets and then refusing to pay, using their status as "made-guys" to protect them. It also kept other criminals from trying to "shake-down" the bookmaker. The "wise-guy" can also assist in the collecting of debts. The amount he keeps as a "commission" varies, but it can be as high as 50 to 100 percent. In northwestern Indiana, Ken ("Tokyo Joe") Eto, the lottery kingpin, paid thousands of dollars a month in street taxes to the Outfit in order to remain in business. On one occasion, an Eto lieutenant was beaten up by a syndicate thug. Eto complained to his Outfit overseer, Ross Prio, and the man was executed (O'Brien 1983).

Eto (born in 1920 of Japanese ancestry) was convicted on January 18, 1983, for operating an illegal lottery business that grossed nearly $6 million between May 4, 1980, and August 20, 1980. While facing imprisonment, Eto met with his boss, Vincent Solano, head of Laborer's Union Local 1 and Outfit boss of Chicago's North Side. Eto assured Solano that he could be trusted to be a "stand up guy," but the boss was apparently not convinced. On February 10, 1983, Tokyo Joe was taken for a ride, shot three times in the back of the head, and left for dead by Jasper Campise and John Gattuso—the latter a Cook County deputy sheriff. But Eto survived. On July 12, 1983, the bodies of Campise and Gattuso were found in the trunk of a car with multiple stab wounds—apparently the Outfit's penalty for botching a murder. Eto went into the federal witness protection program.

Organized crime needs victims who cannot easily hide, states Schelling (1971: 648), persons with fixed places of business: "Even if one can find and recognize an embezzler or jewel thief, one would have a hard time going shares with him, because the embezzler can fool the extortionist if he can fool the firm he embezzles from, and the jewel thief needn't put his best prizes on display."

Schelling underestimates members of organized crime—they spend a great deal of time on the prowl for information and opportunity. Bartenders, fences, prostitutes, and a host of legitimate and illegitimate persons are often eager to provide the "wise-guy" with information, to be on his "good side." They may owe him favors or money, or simply seek to ingratiate themselves for any number of reasons. Salvatore ("Sally Crash") Panico of the Genovese crime Family found out about brothels operating in the area he controlled (the Upper East Side to the lower end of Manhattan) by perusing sex-oriented publications in which the owners usually advertised. The owner was then visited by Panico and his men, and guns, threats, and robbery soon brought the brothel into line. The scheme ended when Panico appeared on closed-circuit television threatening an FBI agent who was playing the role of bordello manager (Post 1981).

Albert Seedman (1974: 70–74), former chief of detectives in New York City, taped a conversation between "Woody," who had swindled $500,000 from Mays Department Store in Brooklyn, and Carmine ("The Snake") Persico, an enforcer for the Profaci Family and subsequently boss of the Colombo Family. In this edited conversation, Woody wants to know why he is being "asked" to pay a rather large share of the money he had stolen to Persico, who had played no part in the scheme:

> *Persico:* When you get a job with the telephone company, or maybe even Mays Department Store, they take something out of every paycheck for taxes, right?
>
> *Woody:* Right.
>
> *Persico:* Now why, you may ask, does the government have the right to make you pay taxes? The answer to that question, Woody, is that you pay taxes for the right to live and work and make money at a legit business. Well, it's the exact same situation—you did a crooked job in Brooklyn [in the territory of the Profaci crime Family]. You worked hard and earned a lot of money. Now you have to pay your taxes just like in the straight world. Why? Because *we* let you do it. We're the government.

The jewel thief deals in expensive merchandise, and he needs a fence who can provide large sums of cash on very short notice. Some jewel thieves fence their jewels the same night they are stolen (Abadinsky 1983). A fence connected to organized crime can be relied upon to have, or be able to raise, large amounts of cash on short notice. Dealing with a "connected" fence also provides insurance for the thief. It guarantees that he will not be "ripped off" by other criminals (since this would indicate a lack of *rispetto* and raise the ire of the crime unit). Thus, dealing with a traditional OC unit can provide an umbrella of protection to independent criminals who might otherwise be at risk from other criminals. Marilyn Walsh (1977) notes that although fencing is basically a sideline for the OC entrepreneur, the organized crime connection "is particularly helpful to the vulnerable good burglar who needs a somewhat amorphous affiliation with the criminal superstructure to protect him from some of its less genteel elements" (1977: 132). She provides an example:

> Greg and his three associates had successfully executed a residence burglary, netting a substantial amount of expensive jewelry, one item in particular being an $8,000 bracelet watch. A few days after the theft the following series of events evolved.
>
> A local enforcer in the area decided he wanted the bracelet. Determining who had stolen it, he and two associates proceeded to the apartment of the youngest of the thieves involved and took him "for a ride," explaining that the thieves and the bracelet would be expected to appear the following day at a private club in the city so that he might bargain for the purchase of the bracelet. When the thief returned from his ride, he called Greg and explained the situation. Smelling a shake-down, Greg got in touch with the bodyguard of one of the big syndicate men in the city. He offered to sell [the] bracelet to the latter individual at an extremely low price and asked for help. It was given.
>
> The next morning only the bodyguard and Greg made the appointment at the private club. On entering it was obvious that Greg's evaluation of the situation had been accurate. There sat the enforcer with nearly ten others waiting for the burglars. The appearance of the bodyguard startled them. This latter individual said only three words, "Joe's getting it," and the whole charade was over. (1977: 108–109)

Because of the extensive network that is traditional organized crime, a connection can provide a professional criminal, such as Chicago's Frank Hohimer, with invaluable information (1975: xvii–xviii):

> The outfit knows them all: Palm Springs, Beverly Hills, Shaker Heights. . . . You name the state and the Mob will give you not only the names of the millionaires and their addresses, but how many people are in the house, a list of their valuables, and where they keep them and when they wear them. . . . Their information is precise, there is no guess work. It comes from insurance executives, jewelry salesmen, auctioneers of estates. The same guy who sold you the diamond may be on the corner pay-phone before you get home.

Information of value to conventional criminals operating in and around Kennedy Airport in New York comes from cargo handlers and persons holding similar positions. In one instance, a cargo supervisor in debt to OC-connected gamblers provided information to a Lucchese Family crew that led to the largest cash robbery in U.S. history—$6 million from Lufthansa Airlines: "He had methodically worked out the details: how many men would be needed, the best time for the heist, how to bypass the elaborate security and alarm system" (Pileggi 1985: 203).

For Vincent Teresa (Teresa and Renner 1973), an associate of the New England crime Family of Raymond Patriarca, what started out as a "service" ended up as an extortion scheme. Joseph ("The Animal") Barboza, a vicious ex-fighter of Portuguese ancestry, was an unaffiliated criminal operating in Massachusetts with his own band of thugs. One evening, they were at the Ebbtide, a legitimate nightclub in the Boston suburb of Revere. They beat up the owners and threatened to return and kill everybody. The owners went to Teresa for help, and he went to Patriarca's underboss who agreed to help—for a price. On behalf of underboss Henry Tameleo, Teresa found Barboza: "Henry Tameleo wants to see you." When Barboza hesitated, Teresa explained: "You want to come, fine. You don't want to come, you don't have to, but he'll send someone else to see you" (Teresa and Renner 1973: 123). After being "called in," Barboza agreed not to bother the Ebbtide—it was now a "protected" club. This gave Teresa an idea: "We sent Barboza and his animals to more than twenty nightclubs. They would go into these places and tear the joints apart. . . . These people would come running to us to complain about Barboza, to ask for protection" (1973: 123–124). Barboza eventually became the top executioner for Patriarca. In 1967, feeling betrayed, he became a federal witness, testifying against Patriarca and ranking Family members. In 1976, after serving a five-year term for murder in California, Barboza was shot to death in San Francisco.

When it comes to "goods and services," then, the picture is mixed. Many of those who provide gambling and other goods and services such as loansharking have a relationship with organized crime that is forced upon them. Others find the OC connection useful to their enterprise, and sometimes the made-guy is a bookmaker, numbers operator, or (more frequently) a loanshark.

With this in mind let us review the "goods and services" of organized crime. In this chapter we will examine several services—gambling, loansharking, theft/fencing, commercial sex—that are part of the business of organized crime. In chapter 7 we will look at the business of drugs, and in chapter 8 we will examine organized crime in labor and business.

GAMBLING

Gambling includes an array of games of chance and sporting events on which wagers are made. Some of these are legal, for example, betting at state-licensed horse and dog racing tracks, government-operated off-track betting parlors, state lotteries, casino gambling in Nevada, Atlantic City, New Jersey, on riverboats in Illinois, on Indian reservations, and licensed gambling clubs and casinos in California, which are restricted to poker and similar card games. State, county, and municipal governments earn a great deal of money from these authorized gambling activities. At the same time, there are unauthorized (illegal) gambling operations whose control is the responsibility of those same governments. In such an ambiguous environment, it is easy to understand why gambling enforcement may not generate a great deal of public support.

The low priority given to gambling enforcement adds to its attractiveness to organized crime. While profits from drug trafficking are quite substantial, so are enforcement activities and penalties; sentences for illegal gambling are minimal. In fact, arrests for illegal gambling have declined significantly during the 1990s, particularly in urban centers (McMahon 1992). Lack of enforcement resources due to competing demands for police services, combined with advanced telephonic communications—for example, the mobile phone—explain why enforcement has declined. There is currently no public pressure to improve gambling enforcement.

Bookmaking

Horsebooks became popular during the 1870s when racetracks licensed individuals (usually for a daily fee of $100) to take bets at a particular facility. The bookmakers subsequently began operating off-track betting parlors in urban areas to accommodate bettors unable to attend the races at the track. Thus, the wire service developed as a vital aspect of off-track betting (Commission on the Review of the National Policy Toward Gambling 1976; hereafter, Gambling Commission).

Bookmakers "book" bets on two types of events—horse and sometimes dog races and sporting events such as football, basketball, baseball, and boxing. In earlier days "horse parlors" or "wire rooms," neighborhood outlets, were often set up in back of a legitimate business. Results coming in over the wire service were posted on a large chalkboard for waiting bettors. Today, most bets are placed by telephone directly, or through a roving "handbook," "runner," or "sheetwriter," who transmits the bet to the bookmaker. To maintain security, some bookmakers change locations frequently, often monthly, and/or they may use cellular telephones. Many use a "call back" system. The bettor calls an answering service or answering machine and leaves his or her number. The bookmaker returns the call and the bet is placed.

Bets are usually written down and may also be tape recorded by a machine attached to the phone. This helps to avoid any discrepancies over what arrangements were actually made over the phone. The bookmaker usually employs clerks and handbooks, runners, or sheetwriters. The clerks handle the telephone, record the bets, and figure out the daily finances. The runners call the clerks and are given the day's totals for the bets they booked. Based on this information, they either collect or pay off. The runners receive a portion of the winnings, usually half, and they must also share in the losses. Rubinstein and Reuter explain how (1977: 10):

> [I]f his customers win the first week a total of $1000, then the bookmaker will give the sheetwriter $1000 to pay them. This will give the sheetwriter a "red

figure" of $1000. In the next week, let us assume that the sheetwriter's customers lose $400; then the red figure will be reduced by that amount, to $600. In the next week assume the customers lose $2000. The sheetwriter will pay the bookmaker the remaining $600 of the red figure plus half of the $1,400 which represents the net winnings, a total of $1300. His risks are the same as the bookmaker's but he invests no money.

Horse-Race Wagering[1]

The oldest of the major bookmaking activities, illegal horse-race wagering ranks behind sports wagering. This discrepancy has increased with the advent of legalized off-track betting in places such as New York, Connecticut, and Illinois. The typical bettor is middle-aged or older, and wagers are usually modest. Information on the horses running at each track on a given day may be obtained from a local newspaper, a "scratch sheet" (such as the *Armstrong Daily News Review, Turf and Sports Mirror*, or *Illinois Sports Journal*), or the *Daily Racing Form*. Voluminous data are available in the *Daily Racing Form*, and the scratch sheets provide information on the time and nature of each race, the jockeys, the post positions, the weights carried, the probable odds, and the handicapper's estimates of horses' finishing position. This information, especially what is gleaned from the scratch sheet, is the basic data needed by the bookmaker in handling wagers.

Payoffs at the track are the basis for the bookmaker's profits (a net of between 10 and 15 percent), except where a bookmaker's limits are reached. The bookie's cut is obtained in the following manner: before the track makes a payoff under the parimutuel system (in which the track acts as a broker to pay the winners from the money it collects from the losers), it deducts for taxes and operational expenses. The bookmaker, by keeping wagers roughly equal to the track's, realizes a profit from that portion which, at the track, goes to expenses and taxes. Since this deduction is generally from 15 to 20 percent, there is comfortable room for maneuvering. A bookmaker who has booked too much money on one horse, vis-à-vis the track, lays off the excess. This layoff process continues wherever a lack of balance exists until it reaches the top layoff operation, which has its agents stationed near major tracks. Upon being given their orders, the agents make an ultimate layoff by placing large wagers at the track's parimutuel window. In the event that the wager is a winning one, money to assist in making payoffs comes from the track winnings. Also by placing large wagers at the track, the track's payoff, and consequently the bookmaker's, is reduced because the odds are determined by the amount of money bet on each entry.

The bookmaker cannot, of course, know precisely what percentage of money will be wagered on each horse at the track. However, information supplied by the scratch sheet or the *Daily Racing Form* is generally an

---

1. Unless otherwise cited, material in this section has been edited from Boyd (1977).

Off-track betting was legalized in New York City in 1971. Here, an elderly woman leaves a betting parlor in Queens on its opening day, after placing her bet.

acceptable guide. In the event of a high track payoff, the bookmaker invokes limits: generally 15 or 20 to 1 for a "win" bet, 6 or 8 to 1 for a "place" bet, and 3 or 4 to 1 for "show"; for multi-horse events such as the "daily double," it will usually be 50 to 1.

Wagers shown in figure 6.1 are commonly recorded by a bookmaker. The information includes the bettor's identity (often in code), the racetrack, the identity of the horse, the type of wager, and the amount of the wager. The name of the track is almost always abbreviated (either by name or location). The identity of the horse may be written out fully or represented by its post position or the handicapper's number as found on the scratch sheet.

Sports Wagering

"From a gross dollar volume standpoint," notes Kier Boyd (1977: 13), "sports wagering is the king of bookmaking," although the net profit for the bookmaker is typically less than 5 percent. Boyd notes that, as in other forms of bookmaking, the sports bookmaker seeks to act as a broker, not a gambler. "In order to achieve equality between teams, one which the bookmaker hopes will

---

Figure 6.1. Common Wagers as Recorded by a Bookmaker

Win–choose the horse which will finish first.

> (First race, New York (e.g., Aqueduct), $2 to win on Joey Boy) (Sixth race, Laurel horse with post position or handicap number 8, $5 to win)

Place–choose the horse which will finish first or second

> (Fourth race, Gulfstream, $10 to place on Mary Mary)

Show–choose the horse which will finish first, second, or third.

> (Ninth race, Santa Anita, horse #6, $5 to show)

Combo (Across-the-Board)–a single bet encompassing equal amounts for win, place, and show.

> (Sixth race, Bowie, horse #2, $2 to win, $2 to place, $2 to show)

---

attract like sums of money on each contestant, a 'handicapping' process takes place" through the use of a line. R. Phillip Harker explains how the line works (1977: 2):

> The line theoretically functions as a handicap to balance relative strengths of the opposing teams. It consists of points either added to the underdog teams' final scores or subtracted from the favorite teams' final scores. Then again, theoretically having balanced the relative strengths of the teams, wagers are accepted by bookmakers usually at eleven to ten odds. Thus, for instance, if a bettor desires to bet $500 on the Washington Redskins at −6 (meaning Washington is favored by 6 points and, thus, 6 points are subtracted from Washington's final score to determine the result of the wager), he would actually risk $550 to the bookmakers $500.
>
> The line is only theoretically a balancing of the strengths of the teams. However, as a practical matter, the line is really a number of points, either added to the underdogs' scores or subtracted from the favorites' scores, which the bookmakers feel will tend to attract relatively even amounts of wagering on both sides of the contest. If the bookmaker achieves an even balance of wagering on a game and he has no gamble or risk, his profit is assured of being 10 percent, the "juice" or "vigorish" of the losing wagers.

Harker explains how the line is derived (1977: 3–5):

> To a great extent the line is developed in Las Vegas, Nev. Not only may the line be formulated legally there and posted publicly in legal bookmaking establishments, but Las Vegas is the recognized hub of wagering and the clearinghouse for much of the intelligence information used to develop the

303

Figure 6.2. Sports Betting Lines

Chicago Tribune

College basketball odds

Latest line

Favorite	Points	Underdog

Syracuse 16 over RUTGERS: W Virginia 1 over MARYLAND: SMU 18 1/2 over Cornell; ECAC Holiday Festival (at New York)–Ohio St. 7 1/2 over Florida; ST JOHN'S 10 over FORDHAM; Lobo invitational (at Albuquerque–Wake Forest 8 1/2 over Fairfield; NEW MEXICO 17 over Geo Washington; Rainbow Classic (at Honolulu)–Purdue 14 over Southern Cal; HAWAII 15 over Yale.

Home team in CAPS, © 1988 Tribune Media Service, Inc.

NFL playoff odds

Latest line

Favorite	Points	Underdog

Saturday
CINCINNATI 6 over Seattle
Sunday
BUFFALO 3 1/2 over Houston

Home team in CAPS © 1988 Tribune Media Services, Inc.

Chicago Sun-Times

GLANTZ-CULVER LINE

NFL

SATURDAY

NFC Divison Playoff

FAVORITE	LINE	UNDERDOG
CHICAGO	5	Philadelphia

AFC Divisional Playoff

FAVORITE	LINE	UNDERDOG
CINCINNATI	6 1/2	Seattle

SUNDAY

NFC Divisional Playoff

FAVORITE	LINE	UNDERDOG
SAN FRANCISCO	3	Minnesota

AFC Divisional Playoffs

FAVORITE	LINE	UNDERDOG
BUFFALO	3 1/2	Houston

NBA

WEDNESDAY

FAVORITE	LINE	UNDERDOG
CLEVELAND	15	Charlotte
NEW JERSEY	6 1/2	Indiana
DETROIT	10 1/2	Phoenix
UTAH	14 1/2	Sacramento
LA. LAKERS	10	Philadelphia

NCAA

WEDNESDAY

FAVORITE	LINE	UNDERDOG
MISSOURI	16	Arkansas
CALIFORNIA	8	American U
Ucla	13	CAL-IRVINE

Palm Beach Classic

FAVORITE	LINE	UNDERDOG
Miami-Fla	4	Pennsylvania
Wichita St.	11	Washington

Volunteer Classic

FAVORITE	LINE	UNDERDOG
Memphis St.	10	Illinois St.
TENNESSEE	10 1/2	Miami, Ohio

Red Lobster Classic
at Orlando, Fla.

FAVORITE	LINE	UNDERDOG
Villanova	3	Auburn

Connecticut Mutual Classic

FAVORITE	LINE	UNDERDOG
Connecticut	25	Harvard

Hoosier Classic

FAVORITE	LINE	UNDERDOG
INDIANA	22	St. Bonaventure
Utah St.	7 1/2	Detroit

Super Bowl Classic

FAVORITE	LINE	UNDERDOG
Seton Hall	6	Virginia
DePaul	5	Mississippi St.

Kactus Klassic
at Tempe, Ariz.

FAVORITE	LINE	UNDERDOG
Cal-Santa Barbara	2 1/2	Iowa St.

Utah Classic

FAVORITE	LINE	UNDERDOG
UTAH	7	Holy Cross

Fiesta Bowl Classic

FAVORITE	LINE	UNDERDOG
Pittsburgh	5	Northwestern
ARIZONA	22	Loyola

Far West Classic

FAVORITE	LINE	UNDERDOG
Oregon St.	11 1/2	St. Joseph's
Michigan St.	3 1/2	Colorado

Rainbow Classic
at Honolulu, Hawaii

FAVORITE	LINE	UNDERDOG
Illinois	18	Tulsa
Georgia Tech	1 1/2	Houston

NHL

TUESDAY

FAVORITE	GOALS	UNDERDOG
HAWKS	1/2-1	Minnesota
QUEBEC	1/2-1	Hartford
BUFFALO	1/2-1	Detroit
WINNIPEG	1/2-1	St. Louis

COLLEGE FOOTBALL

BOWL GAMES

FAVORITE	LINE	UNDERDOG

Dec.. 28
Liberty Bowl at Memphis, Tenn.

Indiana	2 1/2	So. Carolina

Dec.. 29
All-American Bowl at Birmingham, Ala.

Florida	5 1/2	Illinois

Freedom Bowl at Anaheim, Calif.

Colorado		Brigham Young

Dec.. 30
Holiday Bowl at San Diego

Oklahoma St.	3	Wyoming

Dec.. 31
Peach Bowl at Atlanta

N. Carolina St.	1	Iowa

Jan. 1
Gator Bowl at Jacksonville, Fla.

Georgia	4	Michigan St.

Jan. 2
Hall of Fame Bowl at Tampa, Fla.

Syracuse	2	LSU

Florida Citrus Bowl at Orlando, Flo.

Clemson	1	Oklahoma

Cotton Bowl at Dallas

UCLA	5	Arkansas

Fiesta Bowl at Tempe, Ariz.

Notre Dame	4 1/2	Virginia

Rose Bowl at Pasadena, Calif.

USC	6 1/2	Michigan

Orange Bowl at Miama, Fla.

MIAMI	6 1/2	Nebraska

Super Bowl at New Orleans

Florida St.	5 1/2	Auburn

Home team in CAPS

Figure 6.2. Sports Betting Lines Cont'd.

New York Post

SUPER BOWL LINE

Sunday, Jan. 31
At Pasadena

Favorite	Points	Underdog
Cowboys	7(44½)	Bills

(Over/Under in Parentheses)
WAGERING REPORT: In case you are not familiar with how the money line works: you would put up $170 to win back $100 on the Cowboys, or, put up $100 to win back $130 on the Bills. All wagers are based on an imaginary $100 unit.

NBA LINE

Favorite	Points	Underdog
KNICKS	7½	Hornets
CELTICS	8	Hawks

CAVALIERS	4	Suns
HEAT	4	76ers
Trail Blazers	7	T'WOLVES
WARRIORS	3	Jazz
SuperSonics	3	LAKERS

NHL LINE

Favorite	Goals	Underdog
CANADIENS	1-1½	Devils

(Home Team in CAPS)

COLLEGE HOOP LINE

Favorite	Points	Underdog
BOST. COLL.	5	Pittsburgh
Florida St.	3½	CLEMSON
FLORIDA	14	S. Carolina

Evansville	6	DAYTON
E. MICHIGAN	5	Kent
RICHMOND	7½	William & Mary
x-ALA.-BIRM.	1	DePaul
Michigan	4	MINNESOTA
AUBURN	Pk.	Tennessee
IOWA	23	Northwestern
BOWL GREEN	22	Ball St.
Miami, Ohio	9	C. MICHIGAN
OHIO U.	7	W. Michigan
TOLEDO	1	Akron
WISCONSIN	Pk.	Ohio St.
VANDERBILT	3	Arkansas
Miss. St.	1	MISSISSIPPI
ILLINOIS ST.	9½	Loyola, IL.
RICE	9	Texas Tech
Southern Meth.	6½	TCU
N.CAROLINA	15	Virginia
Arizona	4	ARIZONA ST.

x-at Jefferson Civic Center
(Home Team in CAPS)

SPORTS LINE

NBA

Favorite	Today Pts.	Underdog
ATLANTA	12	Minnesota
INDIANA	6	Charlotte
NEW JERSEY	11	Milwaukee
PHILADELPHIA	12 1/2	Dallas
SAN ANTONIO	9	Orlando
CHICAGO	15	Washington
UTAH	3	Seattle
PHOENIX	10 1/2	Detroit
LA. LAKERS	4	Boston
PORTLAND	2 1/2	Houston
SACRAMENTO	3 1/2	Golden State

NCAA tournament

First round

Today
EAST
At Winston-Salem, N.C.

Favorite	Pts.	Underdog
Nebraska	11/2	New Mex. St.
Virginia	7	Manhattan

Massachusetts	9	Pennsylvania
Cincinnati	19	Coppin St.

SOUTHWEST
At Orlando, Fla.

Iowa	8 1/2	NE Louisiana
Kentucky	27	Rider
Utah	Pick	Pittsburgh
Wake Forest	13	Tenn.-Chattanooga

MIDWEST
At Chicago

Oklahoma St.	4	Marquette
Indiana	21	Wright St.
New Orleans	3	Xavier, Ohio
Louisville	13	Delaware

WEST
At Salt Lake City

Iowa St.	4	UCLA
Michigan	21	C. Carolina
New Mexico	3	G. Washington
Ga. Tech	13	Southern

NIT
First round

Favorite	Pts.	Underdog
CONNECTICUT	13	Jackson State

UTEP	2	Houston
UC SANTA BARB.	8 1/2	Pepperdine

NHL

Favorite	Today Pts.	Underdog
RANGERS	3-2 1/2	San Jose
WASHINGTON	2-1 1/2	Hartford

HOW TO READ THE HOCKEY LINE: The odds always appear to the right of the favored team. The figure to the right of the dash (the lower number) is the number of goals one would get for taking the underdog. The figure to the left of the dash (the higher number) is the number of goals one would have to give for taking the favored team.

Copyright 1993 World Features Syndicate Inc.

line. Persons there, who are instrumental in line development, have vast sources of information about the games, as well as knowledge of major trends or "moves" in game wagering, especially by the so-called "smart" or knowledgeable bettors. Each week in Las Vegas, the football line is developed, legally printed, and published. Thereafter, line information is disseminated almost instantaneously, usually via telephone, to various persons throughout the country. . . .

When the bookmaker obtains *the* line, he then often adjusts it to suit his needs or makes up *his* line. He may well know his usual bettors and be able to anticipate what volume on various games he can expect. If the line he receives is 4 and he knows that his bettors are likely to bet heavily on the underdog (the hometown favorite, perhaps), he might decide to use 3 or 3½ as his line. Then, as wagering progresses during the wagering period, such as often from Tuesday until Sunday on professional football games, he may vary his line upwards or downwards one-half point at a time to tend to attract betting, or conversely, to discourage betting on the other side, in order to balance the betting. . . .

The bookmaker must know not only the Las Vegas opening line, but he must get frequent updates on the line. A change in the Las Vegas line does not mean that Las Vegas has changed its collective mind as to the anticipated final score (as if the line were a true power rating); it means that there has been an influx of wise money on the game. The bookmaker must be wary of the same influx. Also the Las Vegas books may either "scratch" a game or "circle" it. To scratch a game means to eliminate further betting or to take it off the board. To circle it means literally to draw a circle around the game on the line sheet, resulting in a limitation of wagering on the game. Bookmakers may take no betting on a circled game or may accept only a limited amount of wagers on it, such as a maximum of $100. In either case, scratching or circling arises because of some unusual factors developing after the opening of betting. These factors include critical injuries, rumors of a fix in the game, or extremely unusual patterns of wagering. This type of information is of vital importance to every bookmaker because by the time he learns of the scratching or circling, he frequently will have been besieged with bets by bettors who have also been privy to the information. . . .

Because of the use of the point spread (line) in illegal (except in Nevada) sports gambling, when there are attempts to "fix" the outcome of sporting events, the approach is to have key players "shave points." That is, their play will reflect the need to keep the score within the point spread favored by the fixers. The National Football League has been extremely outspoken in its opposition to the legalization of sports betting. Pete Rozelle, speaking for the NFL, stated (quoted in Tuite 1978: B21): "The league believes legalized gambling on professional sports will dramatically change the character of the fan interests in the sports. No longer will sports fans identify their interests with the success or failure of their favorite teams, but with the effect of their team's performance in the winning or losing of bets." The NFL's real fear, of course, is that "legalized gambling will greatly multiply the security problems confronting all professional sports" (Tuite 1978: B21).

When the state of Delaware experimented very briefly with football wagering in 1976, the NFL sued the state but lost the suit. The league's chief security officer explained why the suit was brought: "We are not naive. We are not unaware of the fact that there is a great deal of gambling going on, but we don't think that the state or any governmental authority rightfully should come in and impose a gambling situation on our game" (Marshall 1978: 21). Delaware gave up football wagering "after it found out that state officials were less adept at setting odds than the underworld. Professional gamblers realized they could take advantage of Delaware's inexperience in bookmaking and collect a lot of easy money" (Marshall 1978: 21). (For an inside look at the effect of gambling on college basketball, see Rosen 1978; Cohen 1977; Hill 1981.)

Organized Crime and Bookmaking

In an earlier period, bookmaking was an important source of income for organized crime. OC units ran the operation directly or "licensed" syndicate bookmakers. As we have seen in chapter 4, the wire service was an important source of organized crime control over bookmaking. However, most illegal wagering today involves sports, as opposed to horse racing, and bets are made by telephone. Payoffs are made the day after the event, so the prompt results provided by the wire service are no longer relevant. The almost exclusive use of the telephone provides greater security and has reduced the need for police protection, often an important syndicate service. Allegedly, the nation's biggest bookmaker, Ron Socko, has set up bookmaking operations in the Dominican Republic where gambling is legal; an 800-number provides a link to bettors in the United States. Rubinstein and Reuter (1978a, 1978b) report that their research in New York City revealed very little syndicate involvement in bookmaking. However, this is certainly not the case in Chicago, where bookmakers do not operate without the Outfit's approval—and this control has been routinely enforced by murder.

Lotteries/Numbers

The American colonies were floated with lotteries, notes Henry Chafetz (1960). In 1612, King James I authorized a lottery to promote the colony of Virginia. The colonies themselves used lotteries, and such outstanding men as George Washington bought and sold lottery tickets (1960: 20–21). The lottery was used (unsuccessfully) to help finance the Revolutionary War. Many of America's outstanding institutions of higher learning were supported through the use of lotteries—Rhode Island College (now Brown), Columbia, Harvard, University of North Carolina, William and Mary, and Yale (Chafetz 1960).

During the nineteenth century, lotteries under state license or control were found throughout the United States. Because of the negative publicity surrounding problems with the Louisiana Lottery, in 1890 the United States enacted legislation prohibiting lotteries from using the mails and even prohibited newspapers that carried lottery advertisements from using the mails (Chafetz 1960). This prohibition opened the way for the illegal exploitation of the desire to bet on lotteries through such devices as "numbers" or "policy" betting.

Policy and Numbers

Policy is based on drawing numbers from 1 to 78 by spinning a wheel; twelve to fifteen numbers are drawn and players bet that from one to four numbers in various sequences will be among those drawn. Bets are typically small, but when a policy operation is controlled by a syndicate, the total profits can be quite large. In the past, bets were placed in "policy shops" or, in more contemporary times, through "runners." "Dream books" are sold to help players choose their lucky numbers. During the 1920s, numbers were introduced in competition to policy, and it is now the prevailing form of illegal lottery (Gambling Commission 1976).

In numbers (sometimes called "policy") a player selects one, two, or three digits from 0 to 9 with the odds of winning running from 10 to 1, 100 to 1, and 1,000 to 1. For a single digit ("single action") play, the payoff is 6 or 7 to 1; for two digits ("double action") the payoff is between 50 and 64 to 1; for three digits the payoff is between 550 and 600 to 1. On certain popular combinations, for example, 711, the payoff may be reduced to 500 to 1 or even lower. A player can also "box" numbers—bet all the possible three-digit combinations. While this increases the chances of winning, it also lowers the payoff to about 100 to 1.

In the past there were a variety of elaborate schemes for determining the winning numbers, often using the amounts for win, place, and show of the first race at a particular racetrack, or the last three digits of the racetrack's "handle" (total gross receipts)—figures that are readily available in the daily newspapers. In some games the numbers are selected before an audience of bettors at a central location. An example is the game of *bolita* in Asheville, North Carolina, in which the winner is paid odds of 80 to 1 for selecting a single number:

> The winning number is determined on a daily basis at a designated time in the following manner: several subjects stand at various locations in close relation to one another; at this time a bag is passed around which contains small balls numbered 1 through 100. When this bag is passed to a designated person, he or she grasps one ball from the outside of the bag and it is tied off. The rest of the balls are removed from the bag. The number on the ball remaining in the grasp of the designated person represents the winning number. (From an Asheville, NC Police Department affidavit in support of a search warrant)

Today, in states having a legal lottery, the illegal lottery will use the same numbers as the state lottery, although the odds in the illegal lottery may be higher than that offered by the state. Furthermore, the illegal lottery will often accept bets over the phone, on credit, and without reporting earnings to the

Internal Revenue Service. They may also accept bets in amounts smaller than that needed to purchase a state lottery ticket.

Numbers organizational structure.

At the bottom of the hierarchical totem pole is the person who accepts wagers directly from the bettors. These are known as writers, runners, sellers, etc., and generally are individuals with ready access to the public (e.g, elevator operators, shoeshine boys, newspaper vendors, bartenders, waitresses). Customarily they are paid a percentage of the wagers they write (unlike sports bookmaking, numbers wagering is done on a cash basis), usually from 15 to 30 percent, and frequently they are given a 10 percent tip from bettors receiving payment for hits. In only a very few places do writers furnish their customers with a written record of the wager.

The number writer is strictly a salesman and assumes no financial burden for the numbers he writes. It is essential, therefore, that his wagers reach trusted hands before the winning number or any part of it is known. Sometimes this is done by telephone; other times the wager records (commonly known as work, action, business, etc.) are physically forwarded to a higher echelon by a pickup man (frequently a taxi driver, vending machine serviceman, etc.).

In a small operation the wagers may go directly to the central processing office (commonly called the bank, clearinghouse, countinghouse). More often, in large enterprises they are given to management's field representative (known as the field man, controller, etc.), who may be responsible for making a quick tally to determine the existence of any heavily played numbers which should be laid off. At such levels of operation one frequently finds charts consisting of 1,000 spaces numbered 000 to 999 where tallies can be made for all wagers or only for certain wagers meeting a minimum dollar value.

Near the top of the totem pole is the bank, the place where all transactions are handled. During the collection process the bank will be making decisions as to whether or not to lay off certain heavily played numbers. After the winning number is known the bank will meticulously process the paperwork to determine how much action has been written, how many hits are present, and the controllers and/or writers involved. Provision will be made for the payment of hits. Frequently, if the hits are small the payment will be made directly by the writer and deducted from the amount he owes the bank. In other cases, particularly large hits, payment will first be made to the writer by the bank or the controller.

Numbers wagers produce a large volume of records, hence the bank will seldom keep the recorded wagers for much longer than a week. Some retention is necessary in case of claims arising by bettors or writers. Not infrequently a winning number may be missed by the bank's clerical personnel, resulting in a claim for an "overlook."

Behind the bank and at the top of the totem pole is the financial backer who may or may not be associated with the day-to-day operations. He will frequently provide the funds to furnish bond and legal counsel to employees who are arrested.

309

Settlement with the writers may be on a daily basis, but more frequently it is done on a weekly basis. The bank will prepare a "tape," i.e., adding machine tape showing the gross action written, deductions for the writer's commission plus any payment for hits he has made from his own funds, and ending with the amount due from the writer to the bank advising the writer how much to pay the collector, controller, or other person who represents the bank. (Boyd 1977)

The paper used to record bets may be deliberately treated with chemicals so that it is quite flammable and thus easily destroyed in order to avoid arrest and prosecution. Records of bets may be made on metal strips which can be swallowed and later retrieved; in New York's Chinatown, bets are recorded on rice paper which can be easily swallowed, or on water-soluble paper.

Sports pools. The *sports pool* has several versions, but the essentials are the same. A series of "tips" are placed on a "tip-board" or in some container. Each tip bears two three-digit numbers; the last two digits of each number represents a team. Players purchase a tip, which they select blindly; if this tip bears the two numbers representing the two teams which scored the most runs (points, goals, etc.) that day, they are winners. In a baseball pool, for example, there are 153 different combinations (tips), and the payoff is usually 120 times the amount wagered.

In this form of lottery the seller receives about 10 percent of the wagers he or she collects, while payoffs come from the bank through the seller. Between the bank and the seller is often a tip-board salesperson, someone who does not solicit bets but who sells the tip-boards for the bank and receives a 10 percent commission.

Several aspects of lotteries help to enhance the game. Desmond Cartey points out that the writer often provides valuable information to the player on matters ranging from vacant apartments for rent to securing stolen merchandise at discount prices (1970: 35).

Casino Gambling and Related Activities

Casino gambling (with a wide array of games of chance including roulette, chuck-a-luck, blackjack, and craps) requires a great deal of planning, space, personnel, equipment, and financing. In the past, casino gambling was available in "wide-open towns" such as Newport, Kentucky,[2] and Phenix City,

2. Newport was run by the Cleveland syndicate, headed by Moe Dalitz, Morris Kleinman, Sam Tucker, and Louis Rothkopf. Located in Kentucky's Campbell County, just across the Ohio River from Cincinnati, Newport is a city of only 1.5 square miles with a population of about 25,000. As part of a reform effort in 1961, George Ratterman, a former professional football player, agreed to run for sheriff of Campbell County. In a famous incident, Ratterman was drugged and, with the cooperation of the Newport police, was arrested with a striptease dancer and taken to police headquarters

Alabama,[3] and on a more discreet level in Saratoga Springs, New York, and Hot Springs Arkansas. In some cities there is a tradition of holding "Las Vegas Nights." These events are often run under the auspices of or with the approval and protection of an organized crime unit, utilizing the legitimate front of a religious or charitable organization. The operators provide gambling devices, personnel, and financing, and they share some of the profits with the sponsoring organization.

Organized crime operatives may also organize or sponsor card or dice games, taking a cut out of every pot for their services. These may be in a permanent location, for example, a social club or veteran's hall, or for security reasons may "float" from place to place. The games may be operated in the home of a person in debt to a loanshark as a form of paying off the loan. In certain cities, gambling activities not operated under OC protection, "outlaw games," run the risk of being raided by the police or being held up by independent criminals or robbery teams sponsored by an OC unit. Vincent Siciliano (1970: 50), an armed robber with OC connections, reports: "The organization knows there is this game and when some friend in the police needs an arrest, to earn his keep as a protector of the people against the bad gamblers, the organization guy tells the police and off they go with sirens wailing." During the raid, Siciliano notes, the police can also help themselves to much of the game's proceeds. He points out that even the dumbest thief knows which are syndicate games and recognizes the consequences of disregarding the OC connection. Norman Greenberg (1981: 93) quotes one armed robber who expressed concern with the possibility of "knocking over" a "connected" operation: "I don't think the Mafia'd read me my rights and let me go consult with an attorney. And I said [to my partners], 'Is this thing connected?' I said, 'Look, if this is the Mafia's money I don't want any part of it. I don't want some guys to come gunnin' for me.'"

The Las Vegas Connection

In 1931, the state of Nevada, desperate for tax revenue during the Great Depression, legalized gambling and established licensing procedures for those wishing to operate gambling establishments. Ed Reid and Ovid Demaris (1964: 12) point out that Las Vegas "served principally as a comfort station for tourists fleeing across the desert heat." Then came Bugsy Siegel, the first important criminal to recognize the potential from legalized gambling in Nevada. Operating out of California "from about 1942 until the time of his death,

---

wearing only a bedspread. The ploy failed; Ratterman was elected and the town was "closed" (Messick 1967).

3. On June 15, 1954, Albert L. Patterson, a Phenix City reformer who had been nominated Alabama attorney general, was murdered. His son was subsequently elected governor of Alabama, and Gordon Patterson declared martial law in Phenix City and sent in the National Guard to "close it down." These events inspired the movie *The Phenix City Story* (Wright 1979).

With help from a cadre of ex-bootleggers, Bugsy Siegel built the Flamingo Hotel, the first of Las Vegas's elaborate hotel-casinos.

Siegel controlled the wire-service in Las Vegas through Moe Sedway, an ex-convict, gambler, and long-time associate of many New York mobsters, who Siegel brought to Las Vegas. Through control of the wire service, Siegel controlled the operations of all handbooks operating in Las Vegas. He refused wire service to any book unless he or his agents operated and managed it" (Kefauver 1951a: 91).

With financing from OC leaders throughout the country, including Frank Costello, Meyer Lansky, Moe Dalitz of the Cleveland syndicate, Tony Accardo of the Chicago Outfit, and Longie Zwillman of New Jersey, Siegel built the Flamingo Hotel, the first of the elaborate Las Vegas gambling establishments. Up until then, gambling consisted of a "few ancient one-armed bandits and a couple of homemade crap tables," and most of the action was at the poker table (Reid and Demaris 1964: 12). The former bootleggers were ideally suited to exploit Las Vegas: they had available capital that they were used to pooling, expertise in gambling, and business acumen developed during Prohibition. "Without the ex-bootleggers to found and staff the first generation of hotel casinos," argues Mark Haller (1985a: 152), "Las Vegas might not have been possible."

Since Siegel's murder in 1947, the Flamingo and a number of plush hotels were controlled (through hidden interests) by OC units. Typically, funds were "skimmed" before being counted for tax purposes, and the money was distributed to OC bosses in proportion to their amount of (hidden) ownership. According to federal officials, from 1973 to 1983 at least $14 million was skimmed from just one hotel, the Stardust. In 1983, several Stardust employees were prosecuted and the owners (of record) were forced to sell the hotel. The Stardust was originally licensed to Moe Dalitz, a leader of the Cleveland syndicate, who sold it to Howard Hughes in 1967. In 1983, two Kansas City, Missouri, OC figures and an executive of the Tropicana Hotel-Casino were sentenced to long prison terms for skimming operations (Turner 1984). As noted in chapter 4, the top leaders of organized crime in Chicago, Kansas City, Cleveland, and Milwaukee were sentenced to prison in 1986 for skimming the profits of Las Vegas casinos.

Gambling in Atlantic City

The second state to authorize casino gambling, New Jersey, made intensive efforts to keep organized crime out of Atlantic City casinos. The New Jersey State Police, which has extensive experience in dealing with OC, along with the New Jersey Casino Control Commission, were put in charge of overseeing casino operations to prevent OC infiltration. While there has been no information linking OC to any casino hotel in Atlantic City, OC has been able to influence the purchase of goods and services through control over key unions, particularly Local 54 of the Hotel Employees and Restaurant Employees Union. Local 54, which represents 22,000 casino hotel employees, has long been dominated by the Bruno Family of Philadelphia. In 1990, the federal government, under provisions of the Racketeer Influenced and Corrupt Organizations (RICO) statute, sued to have Local 54 placed in receivership. In 1991, the government reached an agreement with the union and Local 54 was placed into receivership. Its leaders accepted voluntary "banishment" (Sullivan 1991).

Other Gambling

Bingo is legal in forty-six states. Although it is played purportedly to raise funds for charitable causes, bingo is also a source of profits for organized crime. Crime groups may run the operations for the front (charity) or merely be connected through "licensure." Gary Bowdach, an enforcer and executioner for OC groups, explained to a U.S. Senate Committee how OC members took over a bingo operation in Florida (Permanent Subcommittee on Investigations 1978: 157–58):

> *Mr. Bowdach:* The operation was owned by a gentleman, I don't know his name. I met him on one occasion. He was a little old Jewish fellow who was moved in on by the organization run by Carlo

DiPietro [member of the Genovese Family] and the organization run by Eddie Coco [*caporegime* in the Lucchese Family]. They had cut themselves into this operation.

Senator [Lawton] Chiles [D-FL]: Was he legitimate at the time he was running the organization and the mob moved in on him? How did that work?

Mr. Bowdach: What happened is that the Coco organization moved in on him first for a certain percentage of his receipts. They started getting a little bit out of hand. They wanted more and more and he went out to seek help, and ended up with the help of Carlo DiPietro, and losing the bigger end of it, had he had [sic] given it to Eddie Coco.

Senator Chiles: When you say somebody moved in on him, do you mean they just kind of went to see him and said, "We would like to buy part of your business?" How does "moved in" work?

Mr. Bowdach: You move in, you tell him you are going to protect his operation from anybody else moving in, the bingo operation in Florida has grown to a pretty good sized business today. So they offer protection. If they don't take, the place is burned down or bombed.

The Pennsylvania Crime Commission (1992) documented the extensive involvement of crime Families in that state's bingo operations.

In a number of localities, coin-operated video poker machines are very popular, often a staple in many bars or taverns. In areas where organized crime groups are able to assert hegemony, the placement of these devices is under their control. The machines ostensibly dispense candy to those who win, but the actual attraction is the cash rewards dispensed by the bartender. Net profits from the poker machines are typically split fifty-fifty between the distributors of the machine and the bar owner, and each machine can generate $2,000 per week.

USURY/LOANSHARKING

The generally negative view of money lending is highlighted in the Bible, which on three separate occasions cautions against charging interest—*neshek* (literally to "bite"): "If thou lend money to any of My people, even to the poor with thee, thou shalt not be to him as a creditor; neither shall ye lay upon him interest" (Exodus 22: 24); "And if thy brother be waxen poor . . . Thou shalt not give him thy money upon interest nor give him thy victals for increase" (Leviticus 25: 36–37). However, "Unto a foreigner thou mayest lend upon interest [for business investment purposes]; but upon thy brother thou shalt not lend upon interest." Thus, the Hebrew could not charge interest on a loan to another Hebrew. Later, the Christian Church adopted a similar interpretation: Christians could not charge interest on a loan to another Christian. This prohibition created problems for commercial enterprises and led to a paradoxical situation.

Within organized Jewish communities, the Hebrew Free Loan Society developed to lend money to Jews without interest. Laws and regulations restricting their ability to purchase land and enter guilds resulted in Jews becoming moneylenders to Christians. William Shakespeare's Shylock in *The Merchant of Venice* (1596) is based on this historical irony. Shakespeare depicted the unsavory Shylock as a money-lending Jew who demanded a pound of flesh from a desperate borrower as repayment for a delinquent loan. At the time Shakespeare was writing, there were no Jewish moneylenders in England—all Jews had been expelled from that country in 1290. The name "Shylock" reportedly became slurred by illiterate criminals into "shark," and the word "loanshark" was born. As noted, the Hebrew term for interest is "neshek," to bite, something for which sharks are noted.

Between 1880 and 1915 a practice known as "salary lending" thrived in the United States. This quasi-legal business provided loans to salaried workers at usurious rates. The collection of debts was ensured by having the borrower sign a variety of complicated legal documents that subjected him or her to the real possibility of being sued and losing employment. Through the efforts of the Russell Sage Foundation, states began enacting small-loan acts to combat this practice (Massachusetts was the first in 1911). These laws, which licensed small lenders and set ceilings on interest, eventually led to an end of salary lending; credit unions, savings banks, and similar institutions began to offer small loans. However, it also led to the wholesale entry of organized crime into the illicit credit business (Goldstock and Coenen 1978).

Ronald Goldstock and Dan Coenen (1978: 2) note that loansharking embodies two central features: "the assessment of exorbitant interest rates in extending credit and the use of threats and violence in collecting debts." As noted in chapters 3 and 4, as Prohibition was drawing to a close, and with the onset of the Great Depression, persons in organized crime began searching for new areas of profit. These criminals found themselves in the enviable position of having a great deal of excess cash in a cash-starved economy, and this gave them an important source of continued income. Goldstock and Coenen (1978: 4) point out that "contemporary loansharking is marked by the dominance of organized crime. This pervasive influence is hardly surprising. Syndicate access to rich stores of capital allows the underworld to pour substantial amounts of cash into the credit market. The strength and reputation of organized operations lends credence to threats of reprisals, thus augmenting the aura of fear critical to success in the loansharking business. Moreover, organized crime's aversion to competition militates strongly against successful independent operations."

Persons in organized crime often insulate themselves from direct involvement in loansharking by using nonmember associates. For example, Gambino Family soldier Tony Plate (Piatta) employed—actually funded—his associate Charles ("The Bear") Calise. Calise, in turn, employed others as lenders and collectors. The connection with Tony Plate gave the whole operation an umbrella of protection from other criminals and credibility to debtors. Without this connection, a borrower who is a "made-guy" or associate of a crime Family could very easily avoid paying back the loan; and violence used to collect the debt would bring retaliation from the Family.

Many loansharks provide loans to other criminals. Rubinstein and Reuter (1978b: Appendices 3-5) report that "there is strong evidence for specialization by loansharks. Some deal with legitimate businessmen only, some with illegal entrepreneurs. One medium level loanshark specialized in fur dealers, though he might make loans to other small businessmen. Some specialize in lending to gambling operators." Joseph Valachi (Maas 1968) worked as a loanshark and reported that most of his customers were themselves involved in illegal activities such as numbers and bookmaking. Rubinstein and Reuter (1978b: 53) report that loansharks "frequently provide capital for a bookmaker who is in financial difficulty."

Individual gamblers may also borrow from a loanshark who stays around card and dice games or accepts "referrals" from a bookmaker. In one case, a young gambler borrowed from a loanshark to pay his bookmaker. He continued to gamble and borrow and eventually was unable to pay his loanshark. As a result, he embarked on a series of illegal activities that eventually led to a prison term. He ran high-stakes poker games, at which his wife played hostess, and secured fraudulent loans from numerous banks. On one occasion, he decided to use some of this money to continue gambling and missed his loanshark payment. He was severely beaten in a parking lot, leaving him with two black eyes and a broken nose. The loanshark obviously has methods of collection not typically employed by other lending institutions.

However, loansharks are not in the "muscle" business; they are in the credit business and, thus, "they lend money to customers whom they expect will pay off and eventually return as customers again. The loanshark is not attempting to gain control of the customer's business" (Rubinstein and Reuter 1978b: Appendices 3–4). A loanshark obviously has the money to be in a legitimate business. Loansharking, however, requires very little time and can be engaged in by those with limited intelligence and ability. While some persons in organized crime are obviously very bright, many others would lose in an argument with a fire hydrant.

But sometimes a loanshark finds himself involved in a debtor's business. Joseph Valachi lent money to a legitimate businessman, the owner of a dress and negligee company, and became a partner when the loan could not be repaid. With Valachi's financial backing, however, and his ability to keep labor unions from organizing the factory, the business prospered (Maas 1968). As Rubinstein and Reuter (1978b: Appendix 4) report, their research in New York revealed that

collection very rarely involves violence, or even the threat of violence. Loansharks are interested in making credit assessments in the manner of legitimate lenders. Often they secure collateral for the loan, though it may be in an illiquid form. Sometimes a borrower will have to produce a guarantee. In many cases the loan is very short term, less than a month, and collection is

Joseph Valachi testifying before a Senate investigation subcommittee in Washington, against his former boss, Vito Genovese.

simply not an issue. Repeat business is the backbone of those operations we have studied. A good faith effort to make payments will probably guarantee the borrower against harassment, particularly if he has made substantial payment of interest before he starts to have repayment problems.

There are two basic types of usurious loan: the *knockdown* and the *vig*. The knockdown requires a specified schedule of repayment including both principal and interest—for example, $1,000 might be repaid in fourteen weekly installments of $100. The vig is a "six-for-five" loan: for every $5 borrowed on Monday, $6 is due on the following Monday. The $1 interest is called "vigorish" or "juice," and loansharking is frequently referred to as the "juice racket." If total repayment of the vig loan, principal plus interest, is not forthcoming on the date due, the borrower must pay the interest, and the interest is compounded for the following week. Thus, for example, a loan of $100 requires repayment of $120 seven days later. If this is not possible, the borrower must pay the vig, $20, and this does not count against the principal or the next week's interest. The debt on an original loan of $100 will increase to $120 after one week; to $144 after two weeks; to $172.80 after three weeks; to $207.36 after four weeks, and so on.

The insidious nature of the vig loan is that the borrower must keep paying interest until the principal plus the accumulated interest is repaid at one time.

It is quite easy for the original loan to be repaid many times without actually decreasing the principal owed. The loanshark is primarily interested in a steady income and is quite willing to let the principal remain outstanding for an indefinite period.

THEFT AND FENCING

Members of organized crime do not usually engage directly in theft, burglary, or robbery, although many have a criminal record for such activities that typically precedes their entry into organized crime. However, members of organized crime will provide information and financing, arrange for necessary firearms or stolen cars, and help to link up criminals to carry out more predatory crimes such as payroll robberies, large-scale commercial burglaries, hijackings, and thefts of stocks and bonds. They will finance frauds, swindles, and any conventional criminal activity that can bring in a profit substantial enough to make the effort worthwhile. They will help to market stolen merchandise such as securities, checks, and credit cards. Members of organized crime are in a unique position to provide these services. Their widespread connections to both legitimate and illegitimate outlets provide a link between conventional criminals and the business world. Organized crime serves as a catalyst for a great deal of "disorganized" crime.

Stolen Securities

During the late 1960s and early 1970s there was a dramatic increase in the volume of securities being traded, and this provided a lucrative source of income for organized crime. Because of the large volume of stocks, bonds, and other securities being traded, security grew lax. Paperwork began to back up, and brokerage houses and banks were frequently totally unaware that hundreds of thousands of dollars worth of securities were taken from their vaults. Thus, they were not even reported as missing for several months. The securities industry employs a great many persons—clerks, runners—whose pay is relatively low. Such persons with gambling or loanshark debts, or merely seeking to supplement their incomes, found a ready market for such "paper." All that was needed was an OC connection. In some cases, armed robbery or "give ups" (faked robberies) of messengers were utilized.

There are three basic methods for converting stolen (or counterfeit) securities into cash:

1. The securities are moved out of the United States to a country whose secrecy laws protect such transactions, for example, Panama. The securities are deposited in a bank, which issues a letter of credit. The letter of credit is used to secure loans or to purchase legitimate securities, which are then sold for cash.
2. The securities are used as collateral for bank loans. An operative presents them at a bank, usually to a "cooperative" loan official, and secures a loan, which is subsequently defaulted.

Figure 6.3. Conversion of Stolen Securities

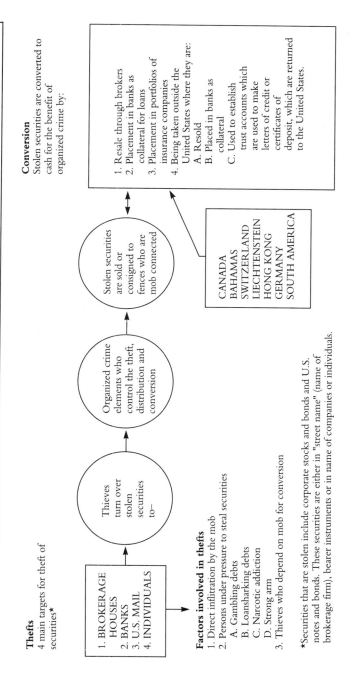

Thefts

4 main targets for theft of securities*

1. BROKERAGE HOUSES
2. BANKS
3. U.S. MAIL
4. INDIVIDUALS

Thieves turn over stolen securities to—

Organized crime elements who control the theft, distribution and conversion

Stolen securities are sold or consigned to fences who are mob connected

CANADA
BAHAMAS
SWITZERLAND
LIECHTENSTEIN
HONG KONG
GERMANY
SOUTH AMERICA

Conversion

Stolen securities are converted to cash for the benefit of organized crime by:

1. Resale through brokers
2. Placement in banks as collateral for loans
3. Placement in portfolios of insurance companies
4. Being taken outside the United States where they are:
   A. Resold
   B. Placed in banks as collateral
   C. Used to establish trust accounts which are used to make letters of credit or certificates of deposit, which are returned to the United States.

Factors involved in thefts

1. Direct infiltration by the mob
2. Persons under pressure to steal securities
   A. Gambling debts
   B. Loansharking debts
   C. Narcotic addiction
   D. Strong arm
3. Thieves who depend on mob for conversion

*Securities that are stolen include corporate stocks and bonds and U.S. notes and bonds. These securities are either in "street name" (name of brokerage firm), bearer instruments or in name of companies or individuals.

Source: Permanent Subcommittee on Investigations, 1971.

3. The securities may be "rented," as Murray J. Gross, an assistant District Attorney in Manhattan, explained to the Permanent Subcommittee on Investigations (1971: 75, edited):

> A legitimate businessman who finds himself temporarily short of capital after exhausting his available credit with legitimate institutions, may seek out a loanshark. Most often he will receive money; however, sometimes the loanshark has an alternative proposition to suggest. He may "rent" stolen securities to the businessman who then uses them as collateral for a loan. The securities become a reusable stock-in-trade which may be "rented" repeatedly.
>
> The borrower, on the other hand, is less apt to be compromised since he is then a legitimate businessman with a longstanding relationship with the bank or supplier.
>
> It should be borne in mind that the intention of the parties is that the loan be repaid. Nevertheless, the element of risk of exposure still exists for the businessman; if he were unable to repay the loan, the true status of the collateral would become known and immediately traceable to him.
>
> A still more conservative method has been evolved. The "rented" securities may instead be used to bolster a sagging financial profile. The businessman calls in a reputable accounting firm, and presents his assets—the "rented" securities. He obtains a certified statement of his apparently sound business, and on the basis of that statement is able to obtain a line of credit. Although many people may have access to valuable securities, few can put stolen securities into immediate use. . . . Organized crime groups serve as the intermediate link in the criminal enterprise. Bookmakers and loansharks who may have exerted the pressure that induced the thief to take the securities frequently serve as the conduit by which the stolen securities get into the hands of other organized crime figures. Passing through the network of organized crime, the stolen securities will eventually reach the hands of someone who does have the expertise, the capital, and the personnel to effect a profitable disposition.

Fencing

The fence provides a readily available outlet for marketing stolen ("hot") merchandise. He thus provides an incentive for thieves and may also organize, finance, and direct their operations. In her research on fences, Walsh (1977: 13) found that about 13 percent of the fences she studied were part of organized crime: "For these individuals fencing appeared to be just another enterprise in a varied and totally illegal business portfolio." In addition to fencing, she notes, these persons were active in loansharking and gambling, and some were enforcers. In the Genovese Family, for example, Anthony ("Figgy") Ficcorata (or Ficcarata) forced jewel thieves to deal only with certain fences, from whom Ficcorata would receive a commission. In Chicago, eight "independent" burglars "were murdered for refusing to dispose of their loot through syndicate-connected fences" (Nicodemus and Petacque 1981: 5). Because of his connection with criminals (and otherwise) legitimate businessmen, the OC member is in a unique position to arrange for the disposition of stolen goods.

THE BUSINESS OF SEX

Organized crime's involvement in sex as a money-maker has changed with the times. House prostitution (whorehouses or bordellos) was an important social phenomenon during the days of large-scale immigration. Immigrants were most often unattached males, single or travelling without their wives (Light 1977). Commercial sex, usually confined to infamous ("red light") vice districts in urban areas, was a target of social and religious reformers. The campaign against this activity became known as the war on the "white slavery" trade, which at the turn of the century was an international problem. In a book entitled "White Slavery" (Bell 1909: 48) Edwin W. Sims, U.S. attorney for Chicago, states (in a run-on sentence): "The recent examination of more than two hundred 'white slaves' by the office of the United States district attorney at Chicago has brought to light the fact that literally thousands of innocent girls from the country districts are every year entrapped into a life of hopeless slavery and degradation because parents in the country do not understand conditions as they exist and how to protect their daughters from the 'white slave' traders who have reduced the art of ruining young girls to a national and international system."

On May 18, 1904, an international treaty was signed in Paris by the governments of Germany, Belgium, Denmark, Spain, France, Great Britain, Italy, the Netherlands, Portugal, Russia, Sweden, Norway, and Switzerland. The respective governments, as the treaty preamble states, were "desirous to assure to women who have attained their majority and are subjected to deception or constraint, as well as minor women and girls, an efficacious protection against the criminal traffic known under the name of trade in white women ('Traite des Blanches')." The treaty was ratified by the U.S. Senate in 1908. In 1910, the "White Slave Act," called the Mann Act after its sponsor, Congressman James R. Mann of Illinois, prohibited the interstate transportation of women "for the purpose of prostitution, or debauchery or for any other immoral purpose." Nevertheless, the practice flourished.

There was an elaborate system for procuring and transporting women between New York, Milwaukee, St. Louis, and Chicago (Landesco 1968). The constant transfer of women provided "new faces" and was good for business. The syndicates that dominated the trade included one headed by Big Jim Colosimo and Johnny Torrio in Chicago. Madams opened brothels, attracted prostitutes and customers, and secured protection from the police. The most famous of these establishments was owned and operated by the Everleigh sisters, who left their brutal husbands in Kentucky and travelled to the Windy City at the turn of the century. The two sisters opened the lavish "Everleigh Club" in the downtown area in 1900. Despite the high cost of political protection, the establishment netted $10,000 a month. The club was closed in

Prostitution and the white slave trade flourished in several cities at the turn of the century, but nowhere as profitably as in Chicago. The Everleigh Club, the city's most famous brothel, netted $10,000 a month before it closed in 1911.

a flush of reform in 1911 (Washburn 1934). The madam also acted as a "housemother," preventing quarrels and providing advice; she was both friend and employer: "Her work made it almost inevitable that she would assume traditionally maternal functions" (Winick and Kinsie 1971: 98).

Organized crime's interest in prostitution waned during Prohibition—money could be made more easily in bootlegging. With Prohibition drawing to a close, and with the advent of the Great Depression, OC groups began looking for new areas of income. In many cities they "organized" independent brothels; the madams were forced to pay OC middlemen for protection from the police and from violence. Gangsters such as David ("Little Davey") Betillo, a member of the Luciano crime Family, organized previously independent brothels in

New York, which eventually resulted in Luciano's imprisonment. The normalization of the gender ratio (immigrants were predominantly male), and changes in sexual mores, led to a reduction in the importance of prostitution. Charles Winick and Paul Kinsie (1971) note that the brothel industry reached its peak in 1939. During World War II, and more significantly after 1945, the importance of brothels as a source of income for OC steadily declined but did not entirely disappear. OC members may be involved in an extortionate relationship with the proprietors of commercial sex establishments ranging from brothels to bars that feature sexually explicit entertainment. In some of the Chicago suburbs, such establishments pay "street taxes" to the Outfit for the privilege of operating. There is also pornography.

The OC pornography business, like prostitution, apparently suffers from a great deal of "amateur" involvement. Pornography, which at one time was under the exclusive control of organized crime, is widely available throughout the United States. Liberal court decisions have virtually legalized pornography, and legitimate entrepreneurs have entered the market. OC involvement today may simply be parasitic—extorting "protection" money. In Los Angeles, for example, the entire hierarchy of the Dragna crime Family was convicted of, among other crimes, extorting money from the owners of porno shops, Since

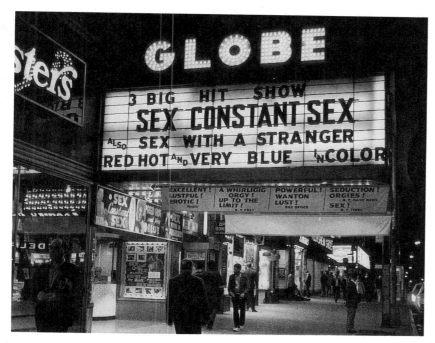

Pornography, at one time a product of organized crime, is widely available throughout the United States.

they were no longer illegitimate entrepreneurs, porno operators in Los Angeles were able to go to the authorities and complain about the extortion attempt. In Chicago, however, the porno business is reputedly under the domination of the Outfit—a domination achieved by violence. Warehouses have been fire-bombed, and men wearing ski masks have smashed peep machines and dumped paint over books and magazines. In the early 1970s the Apache Film Corporation, owned by Harry Goodman, was the major distributor of pornographic films in the Chicago area. A rival firm was established by Patrick Riciardi, a reputed Outfit loanshark. Goodman sold out to Riciardi—but only after his home was bombed four times in two years (Kogan and Ginnetti 1982a, 1982b). In 1988, Frank ("The German") Schweihs, then fifty-eight, a feared Outfit executioner, and Anthony Daddino, then fifty-nine, another Outfit figure, were videotaped by the FBI extorting money from the owner of a Chicago pornographic video store.

While there have been allegations of OC involvement in the wholesale pornography industry (Attorney General's Commission on Pornography 1986), conclusive evidence has not been forthcoming. In a study of the retail pornography business in Philadelphia, Gary Potter (1989) found no evidence of ties to organized crime, although some of the porno shops employed members of the Pagans Motorcycle Club. Potter notes, however, that these business outlets are the focal point of a great deal of illegal activity, including drugs, gambling, and prostitution, which could attract OC interest.

REVIEW QUESTIONS

1. In addition to providing "goods and services" that happen to be illegal, what important criminal activity is part of the business of organized crime? How does this activity operate?
2. How does the concept of *rispetto* enable a member of organized crime to act as an arbitrator?
3. Why is it often important for a professional criminal to have ties to organized crime?
4. How can traditional organized crime act as a catalyst for a great deal of conventional crime?
5. What are the various roles of organized crime in bookmaking?
6. What was the role of organized crime in Las Vegas?
7. What factors led to the heavy involvement of organized crime in loansharking?
8. Why has OC involvement in the sex industry waned in recent years?

7

The Business of
Organized Crime:
Drugs

In order to fully appreciate the relationship between drug trafficking and organized crime, it is necessary to examine the history of how drug trafficking, like bootlegging during the Prohibition era, became an important criminal enterprise. Since concern over opium products, morphine and heroin, led to the most important piece of drug legislation, the Harrison Act, our historical review will center on that substance.

HISTORICAL BACKGROUND

The earliest "war against drugs" (other than Prohibition) in the United States was in response to opium. Opium is a depressant and an analgesic (pain reliever). Its source is the *papaver somniferum*, or opium poppy, of which there are many species. There is some dispute as to when opium was first used. Wherever the plant is found, the young leaves of the poppy have been used as potherbs and in salads. Its small, oily seeds are high in nutritional value. The seeds can be eaten, pressed into an edible oil, baked into poppycakes, ground into poppy flour, or used as lamp oil. As a source of fat, "the seed oil could have been a major factor attracting early human groups to the opium poppy" (Merlin 1984: 89).

There is disagreement about where the opium poppy originated. A great deal of debate surrounds its initial use as a drug, which may date back about two million years to the Old Stone Age. Opium was probably used medically and in religious ceremonies in western Asia and the eastern Mediterranean prior to the year 2,000 B.C.E.. Some researchers believe that it was introduced into Europe from Asia as early as the late Bronze Age, around 3,500 B.C.E. (Merlin 1984). Scientists have discovered ancient art relics depicting opium use in Egyptian religious rituals as early as 3,500 B.C.E. (Inverarity, Lauderdale, and Feld 1983). By the sixteenth century B.C.E., the Egyptians had discovered the uses of opium, "listing it as an analgesic in the giant reference work called the *Ebers Papyrus*" (Burkholz 1987: 17). Its use spread from Egypt to Greece (O'Brien and Cohen 1984).

Opium is mentioned by Homer in *The Odyssey* (circa 700 B.C.E.). The term "opium" is derived from the Greek word *opion*, meaning juice of the poppy (Bresler 1980). Alexander the Great may have brought it to Persia and India about 330 B.C.E. Opium was brought to East Asia by Arab merchants around the year 300 of the Common Era. As Islam, which prohibits the use of alcohol, spread during the seventh century, "opium became widely used as a 'safer' recreational agent" (Snyder 1989: 30). "Its notorious endemic use in the Orient," however, "didn't begin until the 1700s, when industrious European mercantilists turned a modest native herb trade into the most profitable big business in the history of commerce up to that time" (Latimer and Goldberg 1981: 16). Wherever it was found, opium was used both medicinally and recreationally. During the eighteenth and nineteenth centuries, recreational use was popularized by English intellectuals such as Samuel Taylor Coleridge (1772–1834) and Thomas De Quincey (1952 [1821]: 6) who referred to the "divine luxuries" of opium eating and opium drinking.

Charles Terry and Mildred Pellens explain the popularity of opium (1928: 58): "When we realize that the chief end of medicine up to the beginning of the last century was to relieve pain, that therapeutic agents were directed at symptoms rather than cause, it is not difficult to understand the wide popularity of a drug which either singly or combined so eminently was suited to the needs of so many medical situations." At a time when the practice of medicine was quite primitive, opium became the essential ingredient in innumerable remedies dispensed in Europe and America for the treatment of diarrhea, dysentery, asthma, rheumatism, diabetes, malaria, cholera, fevers, bronchitis, insomnia, and pain of any kind (Fay 1975). In the early sixteenth century, the physician Paracelsus created a tincture of opium—powdered opium dissolved in alcohol—that he called laudanum, which proved to be a popular medication until the end of the nineteenth century (O'Brien and Cohen 1984). De Quincey noted that opium was often cheaper than alcohol.

Opium is a labor-intensive product. Production of an appreciable quantity requires repeated incisions of a great number of poppy capsules. About 18,000 capsules—one acre of poppies—yield twenty pounds of opium (Fay 1975). Accordingly, supplies of opium in Europe were limited until the eighteenth century, when improvements in plantation farming increased opium production. Attempts to produce domestic opium in the United States were not successful. While the poppy could be grown in many sections of the United States, particularly the South, Southwest, and California, labor costs and an opium gum that was low in morphine led to a reliance on imported opium (Morgan 1981).

As the primary ingredient in many patent medicines—actually secret formulas that carried no patent at all—opiates were readily available in the United States until 1914. Doctors and quacks prescribed them for general symptoms as well as for specific diseases: "Patent medicine promoters listed dozens of such symptoms, some of which indeed might occur in a person not really sick at all. . . . All this had the most disastrous consequences. People who were not really sick were frightened into the medicine habit" (Young 1961: 68). The medicines often contained opium, which gave the truly sick patient the false impression that he or she was on the road to recovery. Since scientific medical treatment was often absent for even the mildest of diseases, a feeling of well-being was at least psychologically, and perhaps by extension physiologically, beneficial. However, babies born to opiate-using mothers were often small and suffered the distress of withdrawal. Harried mothers often responded by relieving them with infant remedies that contained opium.

The smoking of opium was popularized by Chinese immigrants, who brought the habit with them to California, which in 1848 became part of the United States. During the latter part of the nineteenth and early twentieth centuries they also operated commercial "opium dens," which often attracted the attention of the police, "not because of the use of narcotics but because they became gathering places for thieves, footpads and gangsters." In fact, "opium dens were regarded as in a class with saloons and, for many years, were no more illegal" (Katcher 1959: 287).

Morphine and Heroin

Around the turn of the eighteenth century, Frederich W. Serturner, a German pharmacist, poured liquid ammonia over opium and obtained an alkaloid, a white powder he found to be many times more powerful than opium. Serturner named the substance *morphium* after Morpheus, the Greek god of sleep and dreams. Ten parts of opium can be refined into one part of morphine (Bresler 1980). It was not until 1817, however, that the publication of articles in scientific journals popularized the new drug, resulting in widespread use by doctors. Quite incorrectly, as it turned out, the medical profession viewed morphine as an opiate without negative side effects.

By the 1850s, morphine tablets and a variety of morphine products were readily available without prescription. In 1856 the hypodermic method of injecting morphine directly into the bloodstream was introduced to American medicine. The popularity of morphine rose dramatically during the Civil War, when it was used intravenously in an indiscriminate manner to treat battlefield casualties (Terry and Pellens 1928). Following the war, the increase in morphine use was so marked among ex-soldiers as to give rise to the term "army disease." "Medical journals were replete with glowing descriptions of the effectiveness of the drug during wartime and its obvious advantages for peacetime medical practice" (Cloyd 1982: 21). Hypodermic kits became widely available, and the use of unsterile needles by many doctors and laypersons led to abscesses or disease (Morgan 1981). However, David Musto (1973) argues that the Civil War actually had very little impact on the popularity of opium. He notes that the importation of opium continued to increase from 1840 to the end of the century, with per capita importation reaching a peak in 1896.

In the 1870s, morphine was exceedingly cheap, cheaper than alcohol. Pharmacies and general stores carried preparations that appealed to a wide segment of the population. Physicians commonly prescribed morphine for any complaint, from a toothache to consumption (Latimer and Goldberg 1981), and widely abused the substances themselves. Until the late 1870s, the concept of addiction was not widely known or understood (Morgan 1981). While it eventually became associated with the underworld elements of urban America, morphine abuse in the latter part of the nineteenth century was apparently most prevalent in rural areas (Terry and Pellens 1928).

In 1874, a British chemist experimenting with morphine synthesized diacetyl-morphine, creating the most powerful of opiates: "Commercial promotion of the new drug had to wait until 1898 when the highly respectable German pharmaceutical combine Bayer, in perfectly good faith but perhaps without sufficient prior care, launched upon an unsuspecting world public this new substance, for which they coined the tradename 'heroin' and which they marketed as—of all things—a 'sedative for coughs'" (Bresler 1980: 11). Jack Nelson and his colleagues (1982) state that heroin was isolated from morphine in Germany by Heinrich Dreser in 1898. Dreser was searching for a non-habit-forming analgesic to take the place of morphine. Dreser named it after the German word *heroisch*, meaning large and powerful (Nelson et al. 1982).

Opiates, including morphine and heroin, were readily available in the United States until 1914. In 1900 alone, 628,177 pounds of opiates were imported into the United States (Bonnie and Whitebread 1970). The President's Commission on Organized Crime (1986c) notes that between the Civil War and 1914, there was a substantial increase in the number of persons using opiates, the result of a number of factors;

1. The practice of smoking opium spread from Chinese immigrants into the wider community;
2. An increase in morphine addiction resulted from its indiscriminate use to treat battlefield wounds during the Civil War;
3. The hypodermic syringe was introduced as a method of administering morphine;
4. Opium derivatives were widely used by the American patent medicine industry;
5. Beginning in 1898, heroin was marketed as a safe, powerful, and nonaddictive substitute for the opium derivatives morphine and codeine.

Heroin was "put out as a safe preparation free from addiction-forming properties, possessing many of the virtues and none of the dangers of morphine and codeine, and recommended even as an agent of value in the treatment of chronic intoxication to these drugs" (Terry and Pellens 1928: 76).

The Pure Food and Drug Act

National efforts against opiates (and cocaine) were part of a larger campaign to regulate drugs and ingredients of food substances. In 1879, a bill was introduced in Congress to accomplish national food and drug regulation. These efforts were opposed by the Proprietary Association of America, which represented the patent medicine industry. The American medical profession was more interested in solving the problem of quacks within the profession than of patent medicines. The American Pharmaceutical Association had mixed feelings about patent medicines. Its members, in addition to being scientists, were also merchants who "found the sale of proprietary remedies bulking large in [their] gross income" (Young 1961: 208). Toward the end of the nineteenth century, the campaign for drug regulation was assisted by agricultural chemists, who decried the use of chemicals to defraud consumers into buying spoiled canned and packaged food. In 1884, state-employed chemists formed the Association of Official Agricultural Chemists to combat this widespread practice. They began to expand their efforts into nonfoodstuffs, including patent medicines.

The nation's newspapers and magazines made a considerable amount of revenue from patent medicine advertisements. Toward the turn of the century, however, a few periodicals, in particular *Ladies Home Journal* and *Collier's*, vigorously investigated and denounced patent medicines. The American Medical Association (AMA, founded in 1847), which was a rather weak organization at the close of the nineteenth century (Musto 1973), eventually began to campaign in earnest for drug regulation. The U.S. Senate hearings on the pure food issue gained a great deal of newspaper coverage and aroused the public (Young 1961). The most dramatic accomplishment, however, and the event that quickly led to the adoption of the Pure Food and Drug Act, was the 1906 publication of Upton Sinclair's *The Jungle*. Sinclair exposed the filthy, unsanitary, and unsafe conditions under which food reached the American consumer in a fictionalized description of the Chicago meat-packing industry. The sale of meat fell by almost 50 percent, and President Theodore Roosevelt dispatched two investigators to Chicago to check on Sinclair's charges. Their "report not only confirmed Sinclair's allegations, but added additional ones. Congress was forced by public opinion to consider a strong bill" (Ihde 1982: 42). The Pure Food and Drug Act passed later that year, requires medicines to list their ingredients and the amount of psychoactive substances contained, including alcohol and opiates.

China and the Opium Wars

Since the American response to drugs in the twentieth century is directly related to international affairs and trade with China, we need to review China's opium problem before returning to drugs as a domestic issue. China's historical experience with the West, particularly Britain, has been generally negative. The first British ship appeared on the coast of China in 1626, and its captain bombarded the city of Canton to impose his will. In the wake of the Napoleonic Wars, Great Britain possessed the most formidable naval fleet in the world, while the Chinese had virtually no national navy. In response to the danger posed by British ships, the emperor opened the city of Canton to trade.

The British East India Company enjoyed a government-granted monopoly over the China trade. Shipments of tea to England were particularly important. By the 1820s, a trade imbalance existed between England and China. While the British consumer had an insatiable appetite for Chinese tea, few English goods were desired by the Chinese—the exception was opium (Beeching 1975). Poppy cultivation was an important source of revenue for the Moghul emperors (Muslim rulers of India, 1526–1857). When the Moghul empire fell apart, the British East India Company salvaged and improved upon the system of state control of opium. In addition to controlling the domestic market, the British supplied Indian opium to China.

Opium was first prohibited by the Chinese government in 1729, a time when only small amounts of the substance were reaching China. Ninety years earlier, tobacco had been similarly banned as a pernicious foreign good. Opium use was strongly condemned in China as a violation of Confucian principles, and for many years, the Imperial decree against opium was supported by the population (Beeching 1975). In 1782, an attempt by a British merchant ship to sell 1,601 chests of opium resulted in a total loss, for no purchasers could be found. By 1799, however, a growing traffic in opium led to an imperial decree condemning the trade. Dean Latimer and Jeff Goldberg (1981) doubt that opium addiction was extensive or particularly harmful to China as a whole. The poorer classes, the authors note, could afford only adulterated opium, which was unlikely to produce addiction. "Just why the Chinese chose to obtain their supplies from India," states Peter Fay (1975: 11-12), "is no clearer than why, having obtained it, they smoked it instead of ate it." In the end, he notes, the Chinese came to prefer the Indian product to their own. However, since the Chinese preferred to smoke opium, it had to be specially prepared by boiling the substance in water, filtering the solution and boiling it again until it reached the consistency of molasses, thereby becoming "smoking opium."

Like the ban on tobacco, the one on opium was not successful. Official corruption was endemic in China. As consumption of imported opium increased and the method of ingestion shifted from eating to smoking, official declarations against opium increased, as did smuggling. "When opium left Calcutta, stored in the holds of country ships and consigned to agents in Canton, it was an entirely legitimate article. It remained an entirely legitimate article all the way up to the China Sea. But the instant it reached the coast of China, it became something different. It became contraband" (Fay 1975: 45). The actual shipping of opium to China was accomplished by independent merchants, British or Parsie. Thus, notes Beeching, "the Honourable East India Company was able to wash its hands of all formal responsibility for the illegal drug trade" (1975: 26).

Opium provided the British with the silver needed to buy tea. Since opium was illegal in China, however, its importation—smuggling—brought China no tariff revenue. Prior to 1830, opium was transported to the coast of China, where it was offloaded and smuggled inland by the Chinese themselves. The outlawing of opium by the Chinese government led to the development of an organized underworld. Gangs became secret societies—Triads—which still smuggle heroin out of Hong Kong and Singapore to destinations all over the world (Latimer and Goldberg 1981). The armed British opium ships were safe from Chinese government intervention, and the British were able to remain aloof from the actual smuggling.

In the 1830s, the shippers grew bolder, entering Chinese territorial waters with their opium cargo. The British East India Company, now in competition with other opium merchants, sought to flood China with cheap opium and drive out the competition (Beeching 1975). In 1837, the emperor ordered his officials to move against opium smugglers, but the campaign was a failure and the smugglers grew even bolder. The following year, the emperor changed his strategy and moved against Chinese traffickers and drug abusers, helping to dry up the market for opium. As a result, the price fell drastically (Fay 1975).

In 1839, in a dramatic move, Chinese authorities laid siege to the port city of Canton, confiscating and destroying all opium awaiting offloading from foreign ships. The merchants agreed to stop importing opium into China, and the siege was lifted. The British merchants petitioned the Crown for compensation and retribution. The reigning parliamentary Whig majority, however, was very weak, and compensating opium merchants was not politically or financially feasible. Instead, the cabinet, without Parliament's approval, decided to wage a war that would result in the seizure of Chinese property (Fay 1975).

British troops capture the city of Chin-Keang-Fo in 1842 during the Chinese Opium Wars.

In 1840, a British expedition attacked the poorly armed and organized Chinese forces. The emperor was forced to pay $6 million for the opium his officials had seized, and $12 million as compensation for the war. Hong Kong became a crown colony, and the ports of Canton, Amoy, Foochow, Ningpo, and Shanghai were opened to British trade. Opium was not mentioned in the peace (surrender) treaty, but the trade resumed with new vigor. In a remarkable reversal of the balance of trade, by the mid-1840s China had a significant opium debt (Latimer and Goldberg 1981). In the wake of the First Opium War, China was laid open to extensive missionary efforts by Protestant evangelicals who, although they opposed the opium trade, viewed saving souls as their primary goal. Christianity, they believed, would save China from opium (Fay 1975). Unfortunately, morphine, in the form of "antiopium pills," was actively promoted by Catholic and Protestant missionaries as an agent for detoxifying opium addicts (Latimer and Goldberg 1981).

The Second Opium War began in 1856, when the balance of payments once again favored China. A minor incident between the British and Chinese governments was used as an excuse to force China into making further treaty concessions. This time, the foreign powers seeking to exploit a militarily weak China included the Russians, the Americans, and particularly the French, who were jealous of Britain's success. Canton was sacked, and a combined fleet of British and French warships sailed right up the Grand Canal to Peking and proceeded to sack and burn the Imperial summer palace. The emperor was forced to indemnify the British more than enough to offset the balance of trade that had actually caused the war. A commission was appointed to legalize and regulate the opium trade (Latimer and Goldberg 1981), which increased from less than 59,000 chests a year in 1860 to more than 105,000 by 1880 (Beeching 1975). Until 1946, the British permitted the use of opiates in its crown colony of Hong Kong, first under an official monopoly, and after 1913 directly by the government (Lamour and Lambert 1974). The colony continues to contain a large addict population.

The "Chinese Problem" and the American Response

Chinese workers were originally encouraged to emigrate to the United States in 1848 to labor in the gold mines, doing the dangerous work refused by most white men such as blasting shafts, putting beams in place, and laying track lines in the mines. Chinese immigrants also helped to build the Western railroad lines at pay few whites would accept—"coolie wages." After their work was completed, the Chinese were often banned from the rural counties. By the 1860s, they were clustered in cities on the Pacific coast, where they established Chinatowns—and smoked opium.

In the 1870s, the British opium monopoly in China was challenged by opium imported from Persia and cultivated in China itself. Because British colonial authorities were heavily dependent on a profitable opium trade, they increased the output of Indian opium. This caused a decline in prices, driving the competition out of business. This oversupply resulted in an increase in the amount of opium entering the United States for the Chinese population.

Beginning in 1875, there was an economic depression in California, and the first significant piece of prohibitionary drug legislation in the United States was enacted by the city of San Francisco. "The primary event that precipitated the campaign against the Chinese and against opium was the sudden onset of economic depression, high unemployment levels, and the disintegration of working-class standards of living" (Helmer 1975: 32). The San Francisco ordinance prohibited the operation of opium dens, commercial establishments for the smoking of opium, "not because of health concerns as such, but because it was believed that the drug stimulated coolies into working harder than non-smoking whites" (Latimer and Goldberg 1981: 208).

Depressed economic conditions and xenophobia led one western state after another to follow San Francisco's lead and enact anti-Chinese legislation that often included the prohibition of smoking opium. The anti-Chinese nature of the legislation was noted in some early court decisions. In 1886, an Oregon district court responded to a petition for *habeas corpus* filed by Yung Jon, who had been convicted of opium violations:

> Smoking opium is not our vice, and therefore it may be that this legislation proceeds more from a desire to vex and annoy the "Heathen Chinese" in this respect, than to protect the people from the evil habit. But the motives of legislators cannot be the subject of judicial investigation for the purpose of affecting the validity of their acts. (Bonnie and Whitebread 1970: 997)

"After 1870 a new type of addict began to emerge, the white opium smoker drawn primarily from the underworld of pimps and prostitutes, gamblers, and thieves" (Courtwright 1982: 64). In Chicago during the 1890s, Chinatown was located in the notorious First Ward (see chapter 4). Alderman John "Bathhouse" Coughlin "couldn't stomach" opium smokers, however, and threatened to raid the dens himself if necessary. There was constant police harassment, and in 1894 the city enacted an anti-opium ordinance. By 1895, the last of the dens had been raided out of business (Sawyers 1988a).

Anti-Chinese efforts were supported and advanced by Samuel Gompers (1850–1924) as part of his effort to establish the American Federation of Labor. The Chinese served as a scapegoat for organized labor, who accused the "yellow devils" of undercutting wages and breaking strikes. Anti-opium legislation was also fostered by stories of Chinese men seducing white women into prostitution—"white slavery"—through the use of opium. In 1882 the Chinese Exclusion Act banned the entry of Chinese laborers into the United States. Not until 1943, when the United States was allied with China against Japan in World War II, were citizenship rights extended to Chinese immigrants. China was then permitted an annual immigration of 105 persons.

In 1883, Congress raised the tariff on the importation of smoking opium. In 1887, Congress responded to obligations imposed on the United States by a

Chinese-American commercial treaty negotiated in 1880 that became effective in 1887 by banning the importation of smoking opium by Chinese subjects. Americans were still permitted to import the substance, and many did so, selling it to both Chinese and U.S. citizens (PCOC 1986c). The typical American opiate addict during the nineteenth century, notes Courtwright (1982), was a middle-aged white woman of the middle or upper class. As opposed to the Chinese, however, this addict did not smoke opium, but ingested it as a result of poor medical advice. The Tariff Act of 1890 increased the price of smoking opium to $12 per pound. This resulted in a substantial increase in smuggling and in diversion of medicinal opium for manufacture into smoking opium. In response, the tariff was reduced to $6 per pound in 1897 (PCOC 1986c).

During the nineteenth century, opiates were not associated in the public mind with crime. While opium use may have been frowned upon by some as immoral,

> Employees were not fired for addiction. Wives did not divorce their addicted husbands, or husbands their addicted wives. Children were not taken from their homes and lodged in foster homes or institutions because one or both parents were addicted. Addicts continued to participate fully in the life of the community. Addicted children and young people continued to go to school, Sunday School, and college. Thus, the nineteenth century avoided one of the most disastrous effects of current narcotic laws and attitudes—the rise of a deviant addict subculture, cut off from respectable society and without a "road back" to respectability. (Brecher 1972: 6–7)

The Twentieth Century

In an effort to increase American influence in China, and thus improve its trade position, the United States supported efforts of the International Reform Bureau (IRB). A temperance organization representing over thirty missionary societies in the Far East, the IRB sought a ban on opiates. In 1901 Congress enacted the Native Races Act, which prohibited the sale of alcohol and opium to "aboriginal tribes and uncivilized races." The provisions of the act were later expanded to include "uncivilized elements" in the United States proper: Indians, Eskimos, and Chinese (Latimer and Goldberg 1981).

In 1898, the Philippines were ceded to the United States as a result of the Spanish-American War. At the time of Spanish colonialism, opium smoking was widespread among Chinese workers on the islands. Canadian-born Reverend Charles Henry Brent (1862–1929), a supporter of the IRB, arrived in the Philippines as the Episcopal bishop. His arrival coincided with a cholera epidemic that began in 1902 and reportedly led to an increase in the use of opium. As a result of his efforts, in 1905 Congress enacted a ban against the sale of opium to Filipino natives except for medicinal purposes, and three years later banned sales to all Philippines residents. The legislation was ineffective, and smoking opium remained widely available (Musto 1973). "Reformers attributed to drugs much of the appalling poverty, ignorance, and debilitation they encountered in the orient. Opium was strongly identified with the problems afflicting an apparently moribund China. Eradication of drug abuse was part of America's white man's burden and a way to demonstrate the New World's superiority" (Morgan 1974: 32).

Reverend Brent proposed the formation of an international opium commission to meet in Shanghai in 1909. This plan was supported by President Theodore Roosevelt, who saw it as a way to assuage Chinese anger at the passage of the Chinese Exclusionary Act (Latimer and Goldberg 1981). The International Opium Commission, chaired by Brent and consisting of representatives from thirteen nations, convened in Shanghai on February 1. Brent successfully rallied the conferees around the American position that opium was evil and had no use outside of medical applications. The commission unanimously adopted a number of vague resolutions (Terry and Pellens 1928):

1. Each government should take action to suppress the smoking of opium at home and in overseas possessions and settlements.
2. Opium has no use outside of medicine and, accordingly, each country should move toward increasingly stringent regulations concerning opiates.
3. Measures should be taken to prevent the exporting of opium and its derivatives to countries which prohibit its importation.

Only the United States and China, however, were eager for future conferences, and strong anti-opium legislative efforts in the United States following the conference were generally unsuccessful. Southerners distrusted federal enforcement, and the drug industry was opposed to any new regulations. Efforts to gain Southern support for anti-drug legislation focused on the alleged abuse of cocaine by blacks, which reputedly made them uncontrollable. On February 14, 1914, a *New York Times* headline declared: "Negro Cocaine 'Fiends' Are a New Southern Menace." This caused many Southern police departments to change from .32 caliber revolvers to more powerful .38 caliber revolvers (Kinder 1992).

While tariff legislation with respect to opium already existed, Terry and Pellens note that its purpose was to generate income. In 1909, federal legislation to control the domestic use of opium was passed as a result of the Shanghai conference. "An Act to prohibit the importation and use of opium for other than medicinal purposes" failed to regulate domestic opium production and manufacture, nor did it control the interstate shipment of opium products, which continued to be widely available through retail and mail-order outlets (PCOC 1986c).

A second conference was held in the Hague in 1912, with representatives of the United States, Turkey, Great Britain, France, Portugal, Japan, Russia, Italy, Germany, Persia, the Netherlands, and China in attendance. A number of problems stood in the way of an international agreement. Germany wished to protect her burgeoning pharmaceutical industry and insisted on a unanimous vote before any action could be agreed upon. Portugal insisted on retaining the Macao opium trade. The Dutch demanded to maintain their opium trade in the West Indies. Persia and Russia wanted to continue growing opium poppies. Righteous American appeals to the delegates were rebuffed with allusions to domestic usage and the lack of laws in the United States (Latimer and Goldberg 1981). Nevertheless, the conference resulted in a patchwork of agreements known as the International Opium Convention, which was ratified by Congress on October 18, 1913. The signatories committed themselves to enacting laws designed to suppress the abuse of opium, morphine, and cocaine, as well as any drugs prepared or derived from these substances (PCOC 1986c). On December 17, 1914, the Harrison Act was approved by President Woodrow Wilson, representing the U.S. attempt to carry out the provisions of the Hague Convention.

The Harrison Act

The Harrison Act provided that persons in the business of dealing in drugs covered by the act—including opium derivatives and cocaine— were required to register yearly and to pay a special annual tax of $1. The statute made it illegal to sell or give away opium or opium derivatives and coca or its derivatives without a written order on a form issued by the Commissioner of Internal Revenue. Persons who were not registered were prohibited from engaging in interstate drug trafficking, and anyone who possessed drugs without first registering and paying the tax faced a penalty of up to five years imprisonment and a fine of up to $2,000. Rules promulgated by the Treasury Department permitted only medical professionals to register, and they had to maintain records of the drugs they dispensed. Within the first year, more than 200,000 medical professionals registered, and the small staff of treasury agents could not scrutinize all the prescription records generated (Musto 1973).

Concern over federalism—constitutional limitations on the police powers of the central government—led Congress to use the taxing rather than the police authority of the federal government to respond to the problem of drug control. At the turn of the century, federal authority to regulate narcotics and the prescription practices of physicians was generally thought to be unconstitutional (Musto 1973). In 1919 the use of taxing authority to regulate drugs was upheld by the Supreme Court (*United States v. Doremus* 249 U.S. 86):

> If the legislation enacted has some reasonable relation to the exercise of the taxing authority conferred by the Constitution, it cannot be invalidated because of the supposed motives which induced it. . . . The Act may not be declared unconstitutional because its effect may be to accomplish another purpose as well as the raising of revenue. If the legislation is within the taxing authority of Congress—that is sufficient to sustain it.

The Harrison Act was supported by the AMA, which by that time "was well on its way to consolidation of American medical practitioners" (Musto 1973: 56), and by the American Pharmaceutical Association which, like the AMA, had grown more powerful and influential in the first two decades of the twentieth century. The medical profession had been granted a monopoly over the dispensing of opiates and cocaine. The Harrison Act also effectively imposed a stamp of illegitimacy on most narcotics use, fostering an image of the degenerate "dope fiend" with immoral proclivities (Bonnie and Whitebread 1970). At this time, according to Courtwright's (1982) estimates, there were about 300,000 opiate addicts in the United States.

But the addict population was already changing. The medical profession had, by and large, abandoned its liberal use of opiates. Imports of medicinal opiates declined dramatically during the first decade of the twentieth century. The public mind came to associate heroin with urban vice and crime. Unlike the often female, "respectable" opiate addicts of the nineteenth century, opiate users of the twentieth century were increasingly male habitués of pool halls and bowling alleys, denizens of the underworld. As in the case of minority groups, this marginal population was an easy target of drug laws and drug law enforcement.

The Commissioner of Internal Revenue was in charge of upholding the Harrison Act. In 1915, 162 collectors and agents of the Miscellaneous Division of the Internal Revenue Service were given the responsibility for enforcing drug laws. In 1919, a narcotics division was created within the Bureau of Prohibition, with a staff of 170 agents and an appropriation of $270,000. The narcotics division, however, suffered from its association with the notoriously inept and corrupt Prohibition Bureau and from a corruption scandal of its own: "[There was] public dissatisfaction with the activities of the Narcotics Division, which was tainted by its association with the country's anti-liquor laws" (PCOC 1986c: 204).

In 1916 the Court ruled in favor of a physician (Dr. Jin Fuey Moy) who had provided maintenance doses of morphine to an addict (*United States v. Jin Fuey Moy* 241 U.S. 394). Three years later, however, the Court ruled (*Webb v. United States* 249 U.S. 96) that a prescription for morphine issued to an habitual user who was not under a physician's care, and that was intended not to cure but to maintain the habit, was not a prescription and thus violated the Harrison Act. Private physicians found it impossible to handle the sudden upsurge in their drug clientele. They could do nothing "more than sign prescriptions" (Duster 1970: 16). In the *United States v. Behrman* (258 U.S. 280, 289, 1922), the Court ruled that a physician was not entitled to prescribe large doses of proscribed drugs for self-administration *even* if the addict was under the physician's care. The Court stated that "prescriptions in the regular course of practice did not include the indiscriminate doling out of narcotics in such quantity as charged in the indictments." In 1925 the Court limited the application of *Behrman* when it found that a physician who had prescribed small doses of drugs for the relief of an addict did not violate the Harrison Act

(*Linder v. United States* 268 U.S. 5). In reversing the physician's conviction, the Court distinguished between *Linder* and the excesses shown in the case of *Behrman*:

> The enormous quantities of drugs ordered, considered in connection with the recipient's character, without explanation, seemed enough to show prohibited sales and to exclude the idea of *bona fide* professional activity. The opinion [in *Behrman*] cannot be accepted as authority for holding that a physician, who acts *bona fide* and according to fair medical standards, may never give an addict moderate amounts of drugs for self-administration in order to relieve conditions incident to addiction. Enforcement of the tax demands no such drastic rule, and if the Act had such scope it would certainly encounter grave constitutional guarantees.

The powers of the narcotics division were clear and limited to the enforcement of registration and record-keeping regulations. "The large number of addicts who secured their drugs from physicians were excluded from the Division's jurisdiction. Furthermore, the public's attitude toward drug use," notes Donald Dickson (1977: 39), "had not much changed with the passage of the Act—there was some opposition to drug use, some support of it, and a great many who did not care one way or the other. The Harrison Act was actually passed with very little publicity or news coverage." Richard Bonnie and Charles Whitebread (1970: 976) note the similarities between the temperance and anti-narcotics movements. "Both were first directed against the evils of large scale use and only later against all use. Most of the rhetoric was the same: These euphoriants produced crime, pauperism and insanity." However, "the temperance movement was a matter of vigorous public debate; the anti-narcotics movement was not. Temperance legislation was the product of a highly organized nationwide lobby; narcotics legislation was largely ad hoc. Temperance legislation was designed to eradicate known evils resulting from alcohol abuse: narcotics legislation was largely anticipatory."

Wayne Morgan (1981) notes that until the nature of addiction became clear, comparisons between alcohol and opiates often favored opium. Public sentiment did not lead to anti-drug legislation; instead antidrug legislation created an increasing public perception of the dangers of certain drugs (Bonnie and Whitebread 1970). As we will see, this perception was later spread by officials of the federal drug enforcement agency.

Writing in 1916, Pearce Bailey (1974: 173–74) noted that the passage of the act "spread dismay among the heroin takers":

> They saw in advance the increased difficulty and expense of obtaining heroin as a result of this law; then the drug stores shut down, and the purveyors who sell heroin on the street corners and in doorways became terrified, and for a time illicit trade in the drug almost ceased. . . . Once the law was established the traffic was resumed, but under very different circumstances. The price of heroin soared [900 percent, and was sold in adulterated form]. This put it

beyond the easy reach of the majority of adherents, most of whom do not earn more than twelve or fourteen dollars a week. Being no longer able to procure it with any money that they could lay their hands on honestly, many were forced to apply for treatment for illness brought about by result of arrest for violation of the law.

Beginning in 1918, narcotic clinics opened in almost every major city. Information about them is sketchy (Duster 1970), and there is a great deal of controversy surrounding their operations. While they were never very popular with the general public, most clinics were well-run under medical supervision (Morgan 1981). While some clinics were guilty of various abuses, the good ones enabled addicts to continue their normal lives without being drawn into the black market (Duster 1970). Troubled clinics such as those in New York City, where the number of patients overwhelmed the medical staff, generated a great deal of newspaper coverage and created public outrage.

Following the First World War and the Bolshevik Revolution, xenophobia and prohibitionism began to sweep the nation. The United States severely restricted foreign immigration, and alcohol and drug use were increasingly associated with an alien population. In 1922 federal narcotic agents closed the drug clinics and began to arrest physicians and pharmacists who provided drugs for maintenance. At issue was section eight of the Harrison Act, which permitted the possession of controlled substances if prescribed "in good faith" by a registered physician, dentist, or veterinarian in accord with "professional practice." The law did not define "good faith" or "professional practice." Under a policy developed by the federal narcotic agency, thousands of persons, including many physicians, were charged with violations: "Whether conviction followed or not mattered little as the effects of press publicity dealing with what were supposedly willful violations of a beneficent law were most disastrous to those concerned" (Terry and Pellens 1928: 90). "After this initial burst of arrest activity directed against registrants, the Narcotics Division turned its attention to closing clinics that had been established to conduct research and treat large numbers of addicts who could not afford private care" (PCOC 1986c: 202). They were declared illegal by the drug agency and were closed down (Terry and Pellens 1928).

The medical profession stopped dispensing drugs to addicts, forcing them to look to illicit sources and giving rise to an enormous illegal drug business. Those persons addicted to opium smoking eventually found their favorite drug unavailable—the bulky smoking opium was difficult to smuggle—and they turned to the more readily available heroin, which was prepared for intravenous use (Courtwright 1982). The criminal syndicates that resulted from Prohibition added heroin trafficking to their business portfolios. When Prohibition was repealed in 1933, profits from bootlegging disappeared accordingly, and drug trafficking remained an important source of revenue for organized criminal groups.

The actions of the federal government toward drug use must be understood within the context of the times. The years immediately following World War I were characterized by pervasive attitudes of nationalism and nativism and by fear of anarchy and communism. The Bolshevik Revolution in Russia, a police strike in Boston (see Russell 1975), and widespread labor unrest and violence were the backdrop for the infamous "Palmer Raids" of 1919. Attorney General A. Mitchell Palmer, disregarding a host of constitutional protections, ordered the arrest of thousands of "radicals." That same year, the Prohibition Amendment was ratified, and legislation was soon enacted to stop the "huddled masses yearning to breathe free" from entering the United States—large-scale legal immigration had ended. Drug addiction—morphinism/heroinism—was added to the un-American "isms" of alcoholism, anarchism, and communism (Musto 1973). In 1918 there were only 888 federal arrests for narcotics-law violations; in 1920, there were 3,477. In 1925, the year the clinics closed, there were 10,297 (Cloyd 1982).

Legislation was introduced in 1923 to curtail the importation of opium for the manufacture of heroin, virtually banning heroin in the United States. (It wasn't until 1956 that Congress declared all heroin to be contraband.) The few witnesses who testified before Congress supported the legislation. The AMA had already condemned the use of heroin by physicians, and the substance was described as the most dangerous of all habit-forming drugs. Some witnesses argued that the psychological effects of heroin use were a stimulus to crime. Much of the medical testimony, in light of what is now known about heroin, was erroneous, but the law won easy passage in 1924 (Musto 1973). A pamphlet published the same year by the prestigious Foreign Policy Association summarized contemporary thinking about heroin use (cited in Trebach 1982: 48): Heroin

1. is unnecessary in the practice of medicine;
2. destroys all sense of moral responsibility;
3. is the drug of the criminal; and
4. recruits its army from youth.

The use of opiates was now thoroughly criminalized except for narrow medical purposes, both in law and in practice. The law defined drug users as criminals, and the public viewed heroin use as the behavior of a deviant criminal class. The federal government had shaped vague and conflicting court decisions into definitive pronouncements reflecting the drug enforcement agency's own version of its proper role: "American administrative regulations took on the force of ruling law" (Trebach 1982: 132). The drug agency also embarked on a vigorous campaign to convince the public and Congress of the dangers of drugs and, thereby, to justify its approach to the problem of drug abuse. According to Bonnie and Whitebread (1970: 990), the existence of a separate federal narcotics bureau "anxious to fulfill its role as crusader against the evils of narcotics" has been *the* single major factor in the legislative history of drug control in the United States since 1930.

341

Public dissatisfaction with the narcotics division intensified because of a scandal involving falsification of arrest records and charges relating to payoffs by, and collusion with, drug dealers (PCOC 1986c: 204). In 1930, Congress responded by withdrawing drug enforcement responsibilities from the Bureau of Prohibition and establishing the Federal Bureau of Narcotics (FBN), a separate agency within the Department of the Treasury. "Although the FBN was primarily responsible for the enforcement of the Harrison Act and related drug laws, the task of preventing and interdicting the illegal importation and smuggling of drugs remained with the Bureau of Customs" (PCOC 1986: 205).

The Uniform Drug Act

Until 1930, efforts against drugs were concentrated primarily at the federal level. Only a few states had drug-control statutes, and these were generally ineffective (Musto 1973). At the urging of federal authorities, many states enacted their own anti-drug legislation. By 1931, every state restricted the sale of cocaine and all but two opiates. However, there was a considerable lack of uniformity among state statutes and a weakness in state enforcement procedures. This, combined with the growing hysteria about dope fiends and criminality, resulted in several requests for a uniform state narcotic law as early as 1927 (Bonnie and Whitebread 1970). A recognition of the need for greater uniformity in state statutes dates back to the first half of the nineteenth century, when a prominent New York attorney, David Dudley Field (1805–1894), campaigned for a uniform code of procedure for both civil and criminal matters. During the 1890s, the American Bar Association set up the National Conference of Commissioners on Uniform State Laws, which included representatives from each state. This resulted in the adoption of uniform codes by virtually all American jurisdictions (Abadinsky 1991).

A uniform drug act for the states was the goal of the Committee on the Uniform Narcotic Act, and also of representatives of the American Medical Association—doctors wanted uniformity for legal obligations. The committee's first two drafts copied a 1927 New York statute that listed coca, opium, and cannabis products as habit-forming drugs to be regulated or prohibited. Many opposed the inclusion of cannabis on the habit-forming list, so it was dropped from later drafts with a note indicating that each state was free to include cannabis in its own legislation without affecting the rest of the statute. The final draft was also modelled after the 1927 New York statute and included suggestions from the newly appointed Commissioner of the Federal Bureau of Narcotics, Harry Anslinger. It was adopted overwhelmingly by the National Conference of Commissioners on Uniform State Laws. By 1937, thirty-five states had enacted the Uniform Act, and every state had enacted statutes relating to marijuana. Despite propagandizing efforts by the FBN, "the laws went unnoticed by legal commentators, the press and the public at large" (Bonnie and Whitebread 1970: 1034).

The lack of public concern over the act is related to the demographics of drug abuse, which was concentrated in minority, lower-class areas, and the criminal subculture. Prior to the Harrison Act, "estimates of distribution reported considerable use of habit-forming drugs in rural areas" (Morgan 1981: 32). This pattern reemerged during the 1990s when drug use became a problem in more rural areas of the country, particularly in the South (see Covington 1992). The South used more opiates than any other part of the country, because drugs were often substituted for alcohol in dry areas. After the Harrison Act, addicts in rural America were quietly attended to by sympathetic doctors. After the passage of the Harrison Act and its vigorous enforcement by the FBN, heroin users continued to be concentrated in impoverished urban areas. In New York City during the early decades of the twentieth century, for example, heroin use was heaviest in the Jewish and Italian neighborhoods of the Lower East Side. As these two groups climbed the economic ladder and moved out, they were replaced by blacks looking for affordable housing, who became the addict population (Helmer 1975). The demographics intensified the problem— blacks had a higher birth rate than Jews or Italians, and an extraordinary number of youngsters at the age of highest risk for addiction, sixteen. John Helmer (1975) argues it was the Vietnam War—fought in an area of the world noted for opium production—that changed the demographics of heroin use, with increasing numbers of white ex-servicemen joining the abuser population.

Pointing to the similarities between the prohibition of alcohol and of other drugs, David Courtwright (1982: 144) asks why the public withdrew its support for one and increased its support for the other.

> One factor (in addition to economic and political considerations) must have been that alcohol use was relatively widespread and cut across class lines. It seemed unreasonable for the government to deny a broad spectrum of otherwise normal persons access to drink. By 1930 opiate addiction, by contrast, was perceived to be concentrated in a small criminal subculture; it did not seem unreasonable for that same government to deny the morbid cravings of a deviant group.

World War II had a dramatic impact on the supply of heroin in the United States. The Japanese invasion of China interrupted supplies from that country, while the disruption of shipping routes by German submarines and attack battleships reduced the amount of heroin moving from Turkey to Marseilles to the United States. When the United States entered the war, security measures "designed to prevent infiltration of foreign spies and sabotage to naval installa-tions made smuggling into the United States virtually impossible." As a result, "at the end of World War II, there was an excellent chance that heroin addiction could be eliminated in the United States" (McCoy 1972: 15). Obviously, this did not happen, According to Alfred McCoy, "the reasons for the revival of the illicit narcotics trade lie with the conduct of U.S. foreign policy and its covert action arm [the CIA]" (1991: 18). "During the forty years

343

of the cold war several of the CIA's covert allies were to play a significant role in sustaining a global narcotics industry that supplied the United States" (1991: 25).

HEROIN

The opium poppy requires a hot, dry climate and very careful cultivation (Wishart 1974). Poppy seeds are scattered across the surface of freshly cultivated fields. Three months later, the poppy is mature, the green stem topped by a brightly colored flower. Gradually the flower petals fall off, leaving a seedpod about the size of a small egg. Incisions are made in the pod just after the petals have fallen but before it is fully ripe. A milky-white fluid oozes out and hardens overnight on the surface into a dark brown gum—raw opium. The raw opium is collected by scraping the pod with a flat, dull knife—a labor-intensive process. "Because the yield per acre is small and because laborious care is required in collecting the juice, it can only be grown profitably where both land and labor are cheap" (Ausubel 1978: 9).

The raw opium is dissolved in drums of hot water, and lime fertilizer (calcium oxide) is added, drawing out organic wastes and leaving morphine suspended near the surface. The residual waste is removed, and the morphine is transferred to other drums, where it is heated and mixed with concentrated ammonia. The morphine solidifies, falls to the bottom of the drum, and is filtered out in the form of chunky white kernels. The morphine is dried, and then weighs about one-tenth as much as the original raw opium. To produce 10 kilograms (hereafter kilos) of almost pure heroin, the chemist mixes 10 kilos of morphine and 10 kilos of acetic anhydride and heats the mixture to exactly 185°F for six hours, producing an impure form of heroin. While this step is not complex, it can be dangerous: "If the proportion of morphine to acetic acid is incorrect or the temperature too high or too low, the laboratory may be blown up." Acetic acid is also highly corrosive, attacking both skin and lungs (Lamour and Lamberti 1974: 17).

Next, the solution is treated with water and chloroform until the impurities precipitate out. The heroin is drained off into another container, and sodium carbonate is added until crude heroin particles solidify and drop to the bottom. The particles are filtered out and purified in a solution of alcohol and activated charcoal. This mixture is heated until the alcohol begins to evaporate, leaving almost pure granules of heroin at the bottom. This is known as *No. 3 heroin*. In the final step, the granules are dissolved in alcohol and ether, and hydrochloric acid is added to the solution. Tiny white flakes form and are filtered out under pressure and dried in a special process; the result is a powder of between 80 and 99 percent purity known as *No. 4 heroin*. While anyone with a basic knowledge of chemistry could go through the rather simple operations to produce No. 3, the production of No. 4 heroin requires a great deal of skill. "In the hands of a careless chemist, the volatile ether gas may ignite and produce a violent explosion that could level the clandestine laboratory" (McCoy 1972: 13).

Opium growers harvest their crop in northwest Pakistan. The opium poppy requires a hot, dry climate and careful cultivation.

For street sale, the white crystalline powder (the Mexican product contains impurities that give it a brown, black tar color) is diluted ("stepped on") with any powdery substance that dissolves when heated, such as lactose, quinine, flour, or cornstarch. Heroin prepared for intravenous use typically has a purity level of less than 5 percent. In more recent years, however, supply has increased dramatically, with competition resulting in purity levels of well over 50 percent, making the substance ideal for snorting (which is a safer but less efficient manner of ingestion than intravenous use). In equivalent doses, heroin is about two-and-a-half times as potent as morphine since it penetrates the blood-brain barrier more easily. Once heroin reaches the brain, however, it is converted back into morphine.

Heroin is typically ingested intravenously, although some users inject it just under the skin, a process called "skinpopping." Powdered heroin is placed in a "cooker" (a spoon or bottle cap), a small amount of water is added, and the mixture is heated with a match or lighter until the heroin is dissolved. The mixture is drawn up into a hypodermic needle and inserted into a vein that is distended as a result of being tied with a tourniquet. The user may bring blood back into the hypodermic where it can mix with the heroin, a process known as "booting." Powdered heroin can also be sniffed like cocaine and even smoked. When smoked—"chasing the dragon"—heroin powder is heated and the fumes are inhaled, usually through a small tube. This method of ingestion has become popular in England, and may develop a following in the United States. This may cause the heroin-using population to expand much like crack has expanded the ranks of cocaine users. Many persons are reluctant, if not unwilling, to subject themselves to injections; for them, smoking or sniffing may present a tempting method of ingestion. Recently, heroin mixed with barbiturates has been found in some urban areas—the substance, known as *karachi*, is prepared for smoking.

Heroin has analgesic and euphoric properties. While sharp, localized pain is poorly relieved by opiates, duller, chronic and less localized pain is effectively relieved (Snyder 1977). Heroin appears to reduce anxiety and distress, creating a detachment to psychological pain. The continued use of heroin produces *tolerance*— "a progressive increase in the ability of the body to adapt to the effects of a drug that is used at regular and frequent intervals. It is manifested in two ways: (1) progressively larger doses must be administered to produce the same effects; and (2) eventually as much as ten or more times the original lethal dose can be safely taken" (Ausubel 1978: 14).

Heroin impairs the normal functions of the body's systems. There is a slight decrease in body temperature, although dilation of blood vessels provides the user with a feeling of warmth. The body retains bodily fluids; there is a decrease in the secretion of digestive fluids, a depression of bowel activity, and the user suffers from constipation. Heroin also causes a constriction of the pupils of the eyes—addicts may frequently be seen wearing sunglasses. At relatively high doses, the sedating effects cause a semistuperous, lethargic, and dreamy state—"nodding"—in which there is a feeling of extreme contentment. As opposed to alcohol, heroin depresses aggression, and also stimulates the brain area controlling nausea and vomiting. Instead of euphoria, some initial users experience nausea and vomiting. A very dangerous side effect of heroin is that it depresses the respiratory centers in the brain, so an overdose can result in respiratory arrest. Heroin is addicting, and addiction requires regular use.

Most of the heroin smuggled into the United States originates in those areas of the world in which the opium poppy thrives: parts of Asia known as the Golden Triangle and the Golden Crescent, and Mexico.

Figure 7.1. Major Asian Opium Regions

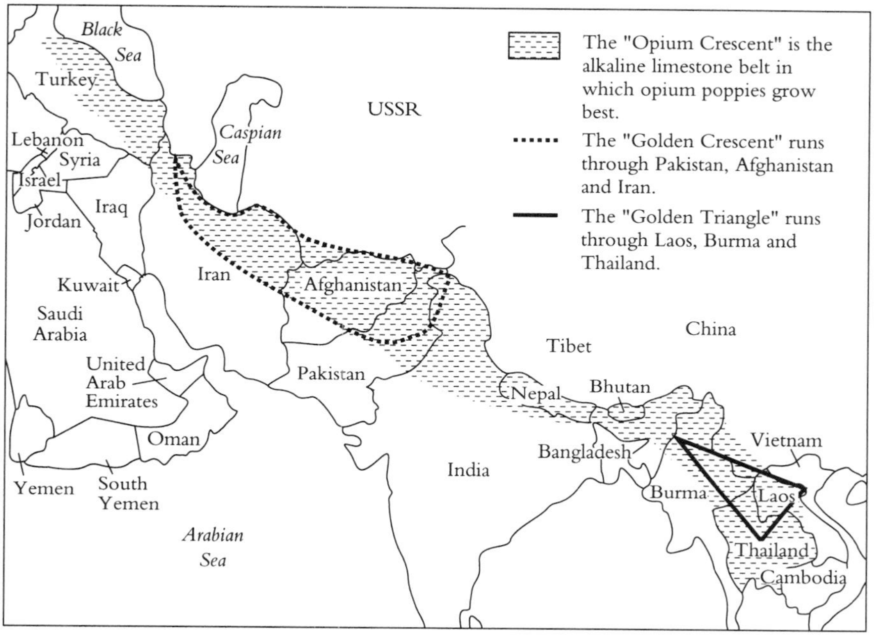

The "Opium Crescent" is the alkaline limestone belt in which opium poppies grow best.

The "Golden Crescent" runs through Pakistan, Afghanistan and Iran.

The "Golden Triangle" runs through Laos, Burma and Thailand.

Source: Levins, 1980: 115.

The Golden Triangle

The Golden Triangle of Southeast Asia encompasses approximately 150,000 square miles of forested highlands including the western fringe of Laos, the four northern provinces of Thailand, and the northeastern parts of Burma. These countries emerged from British and French colonial rule with relatively weak central governments. Their rural areas were inhabited by bandits and paramilitary organizations such as the Shan United Army and the Kuomintang. Colonial officials, particularly the French, used these organizations and indigenous tribes in their efforts against various insurgent groups, particularly those following a Marxist ideology. As support for overseas colonies dwindled at home, French officials in Southeast Asia used the drug trade to finance their efforts. Golden Triangle opium was shipped to Marseilles, where the Corsican underworld processed it into heroin for distribution in the United States. The French withdrew from Southeast Asia in 1955. Several years later the United States took up the struggle against Marxist groups—the Vietnam War is part of this legacy. The U.S. Central Intelligence Agency waged its own clandestine war; again heroin played a role, for many of the indigenous tribal groups organized by the CIA cultivated opium. In Laos and South Vietnam, corrupt governments were heavily involved in heroin trafficking, making the substance easily available to American GIs (McCoy 1972: 1991). This longstanding tradition of using drugs to help finance military efforts continues in this part of the world today.

The Shan States

The Shan States, an area somewhat larger than England, lie on a rugged hilly plateau in eastern central Burma, flanking the western border of China's Yunan Province. The Shan States contain an array of tribal and linguistic groupings. The largest group is the Shans, who speak Thai and thus have more in common with their neighbors in Thailand than Burma. The Shans are lowland rice cultivators, but hill tribes cultivate opium on the mountain ridges around them. During the period of British colonial rule (1886–1948), the Shan States were administered independently from Burma, and the Shan princes enjoyed a great deal of autonomy. Burma won independence in 1948; the Shans, with great misgivings, agreed to join the Union of Burma in return for statehood and guarantees of a number of ministry posts. As a final incentive, the Shans were given the right to secede after 1957. Since a coup in 1962, Burma has been dominated by a repressive military dictatorship. In 1989, the country changed its name to Myanmar. Brutality against ethnic minorities and collaboration with drug trafficking continues.

The Burmese government's heavy-handed approach to the Shan States set the stage for revolution. Official Burmese financial policies were devastating to many hill farmers, who turned more and more to poppy cultivation as a cash crop outside of central government control (Delaney 1977). Shan princes (known as *sawbwas*) "had been encouraged to introduce the opium poppy to their fiefdoms by the British as far back as 1866 and opium shops had been opened throughout Burma to retail the narcotics to licensed addicts" (Bresler 1980: 67). McCoy (1972) notes, however, that in later years, the British made a number of efforts to abolish opium cultivation in the Shan States, although they were never completely successful. In any event, many Shans blamed their princes for accommodating the central government, and traditional systems of authority deteriorated. Into this amorphous situation stepped the Kuomintang.

The Kuomintang

After the defeat of the Chinese Nationalist forces in 1949, the Third and Fifth Armies of Chiang Kai-shek which were stationed in the remote southern province of Yunan, escaped over the mountainous frontier into the Shan States. While some members of this army dispersed and became integrated with the local population, "more than six thousand of them remained together as a military entity, their numbers being swollen by indigenous tribesmen" (Lamour and Lamberti 1974: 94). By 1952, the Kuomintang (KMT) numbering about twelve thousand, became the *de facto* power in the eastern part of the Shan States. In 1951 and 1952, with support from the United States, the KMT was rearmed and resupplied. Along with additional troops from Taiwan and recruits from the Hmong hill tribesmen—poppy cultivators—the KMT attempted to invade China. When the attempts failed, U.S. interest and support waned, and the KMT settled permanently in Burma. For several years the Burmese military attempted to evict the armed KMT intruders and finally succeeded in 1954, forcibly escorting them to the Thai border. The Nationalist government evacuated about six thousand troops to Formosa. Nevertheless, the strength of the KMT grew, either through secret reinforcements from Taiwan and/or through recruitment among indigenous tribes, to about ten thousand troops. In Mae Salong, Thailand, KMT General Tuan Whi-wen ruled a heroin empire, collected taxes, and drafted boys as young as thirteen into his army. The general died in 1980.

In 1961 a resentful government in Rangoon, perhaps with assistance from the People's Republic of China, finally drove the KMT into the Thai portion of the Golden Triangle (Lamour and Lamberti 1974). There, the KMT sold its military skills to a joint Central Intelligence Agency-Thai Army command fighting communist insurgents in the Shan States. This force aimed to prevent the Laotian Pathet Lao from linking up with local insurgents. In 1961 and 1969, there were U.S.-backed airlifts of KMT troops to Taiwan. These airlifts were the last official contacts between the KMT remnants on the mainland and Chiang Kai-shek's government, but Lamour and Lamberti (1974) report that unofficial ties remained strong. The remaining troops, about four thousand strong, became known as the Chinese Irregular Forces (CIF). While the KMT had always dabbled in opium, it now became the sole support of the CIF. Despite this fact, the CIF has been tolerated on the Thai border as a barrier against communist insurgents. During the 1970s, the Thai government supplied the CIF with arms and uniforms in its efforts against Marxist insurgents among Hmong tribesmen (Lamour and Lamberti 1974). The ranks of the CIF forces have been replenished by local tribesmen and young Chinese living in the Thai-Burma area. Its current strength is about two thousand troops.

Burmese Communist Party

Until 1989, another formidable private army in the Golden Triangle served the Burmese Communist Party (BCP). The BCP force had received support from the People's Republic of China in the past. After Beijing cut off this aid in order to improve relations with Burma, the BCP, following a long-established precedent in the region, went into the opium business. The BCP controlled much of the poppy-producing areas. The BCP received opium as a form of tax and tribute from local farmers, then refined it into heroin in its own laboratories. In 1989 its ethnic rank and file, primitive Wa tribesmen, rebelled, and the BCP folded as an armed force (Haley 1990). It was replaced by the Wa National Army and the United Wa States Army.

Shan United Army

The Shan United Army (SUA) resorted to opium trafficking in order to purchase arms and to support its independence movement (Delaney 1977). In

1965 an opium war broke out between the SUA and the CIF, and the latter drove SUA leader Khun Sa (born Chang Chi-fu in 1934) into Laos. Khun returned, defeating the remnants of the CIF in 1981. The town of Mae Salong was subsequently tamed by the Thai government and is now full of old CIF soldiers; the town even pays taxes to Thailand. The SUA came to dominate the opium trade along the Thai-Burma border, where about 400,000 hill tribesmen have no source of income other than heroin (Permanent Subcommittee on Investigations 1981a). The SUA was able to control both the shipments of opium and the production of heroin in SUA laboratories.

In the 1980s the Thai government succeeded in driving the SUA out of Thailand and back into Burma, but the group continued to dominate the opium traffic, collecting taxes from drug caravans crossing their territory. In 1990 the Shans suffered significant setbacks. Khun Sa was indicted for drug trafficking by a federal grand jury in the United States, and his Shan United Army suffered defeats by the Wa, the powerful tribe that was the backbone of the old BCP (Schmetzer 1990). Nevertheless, the 15,000-member SUA army under Khun Sa continues to dominate the heroin trade in the Golden Triangle (Carter 1991a), and has opened some processing laboratories in Laos.

Kachin Independence Army

In 1961 the Burmese premier, U Nu, declared Buddhism the official state religion. Most Kachins are Animists or Christians who live in the mountains of northern Burma, the heart of the poppy-growing region of the Golden Triangle. That same year, the Kachin Independence Army (KIA) was formed to seek independence for the Kachin State, and it used drug trafficking to support these efforts. Reputed to have eight thousand members, the KIA has taken a leading role among rebel minority groups in the Golden Triangle that form the Democratic Alliance of Burma. *Newsweek* (November 11, 1991: 8) reports that the rebels have responded to a Chinese plea to curtail drug trafficking in the region. China is concerned about the amount of heroin entering the country from the Kachin area. The rebels have reportedly substituted potatoes for opium and in return are surreptitiously receiving weapons from the People's Republic.

Thailand

Whether the source is the CIF, the BCP, the SUA, the Wa, or the KIA, opium in the form of morphine base or of almost pure heroin is usually brokered in Thailand. That nation of 50 million persons is almost as large as France. A staunch anti-Communist ally of the United States, Thailand sent troops to fight alongside American soldiers in Korea and Vietnam. In addition to its role in drug trafficking, Thailand has a reputation of being the "world's biggest whorehouse"—an estimated 50,000 brothels are active (Schmetzer 1991b). At Mai Sai, the northernmost border town in Thailand, "Word of a potential customer spreads quickly around the dusty little town. A middleman sets up negotiations in an innocent-looking place, such as a bus station. The buyer pays in advance, depositing the money in a joint account with the seller at one of the five local bank branches. Only then can the purchaser pick up the merchandise, often at a Burmese village a few hours away by foot" (Kraar 1988: 38). In 1991, a military coup—one of seventeen since 1932—overthrew the democratically elected Thai government.

At the center of much of this drug trafficking are ethnic Chinese organizations such as the Triads discussed in chapter 5. They have come to dominate a major part of the world heroin market. Posner (1988: 66) points out that "in Southeast Asia, not only did the British and French opium monopolies create massive addict populations, but they also inadvertently formed a smuggling network that was crucial to the post-World War II heroin epidemic. Although the colonial administrations reaped huge profits, they never became involved in the drug's distribution and sale. That work was left to each colony's licensed opium merchant. Invariably they were Chinese."

Bangkok has a large population of Thai-born Chinese, called *Haw*, who are known by Thai names but maintain close ties with compatriots in Hong Kong, Yunnan Province (where the Chinese government has not succeeded in wiping out the drug business), Amsterdam, and British Columbia. From Bangkok, Chinese criminal organizations have flooded their "China White" into major cities of Europe, Canada, and the United States. In New York, for example, the Drug Enforcement Administration estimates that more than half of the heroin sold is supplied by Chinese criminal organizations (Kerr 1988b). One group from Fujian has been reinforced by recent Chinese immigrants and dominates a large part of the drug trade in New York. "The groups usually send the heroin to New York hidden in cargo shipments. Often they return the profits to Asia disguised as the cash transfers of international trading companies" (Kerr 1987b: 16). Chinese criminals are aided by an underground banking system operating through gold shops, trading companies, commodity houses, travel agencies, and money changers in many countries, orchestrated by the same Chinese family: "The method of moving money is the *chop*, which is in effect a negotiable instrument. A chop can be cashed in Chinese gold shops or trading houses in many countries. The value and identity of the holder of the chop is a secret between the parties. The form of chop varies from transaction to transaction and is difficult to identify. In effect, the chop system allows money to be transferred from country to country instantaneously and anonymously" (Chaiken 1991: 495). For example, cash to finance a heroin deal is deposited in a Chinatown gold shop in return for a chop. The chop is sent by courier to Hong Kong and is cashed. The owner of the chop receives his money from the original issuer, who is fronting for the drug deal.

On February 20–21, 1989, federal agents and police officers seized eight hundred pounds of Southeast Asian heroin in two homes in Queens, New York. The drugs had been shipped from Hong Kong to Los Angeles in small, hollow, rubber cart wheels and driven in rental trucks to New York; it was the largest heroin seizure in U.S. history. Thirty-one persons associated with a

Figure 7.2. Southeast Asian Heroin

Selling Prices for the Equivalent of One Kilogram of Southwest Asian Heroin at Successive Stages of Trafficking.

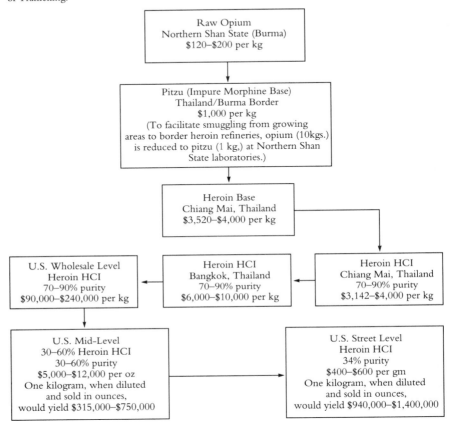

The change in price levels as opiates move from source to the street primarily reflects the profit motive of dealers at each level of distribution. Factors such as geographic distance from the source (and hence replacement), increased refinement and portability through laboratory processing, and greater risk of seizure at borders and in distribution systems also affect the cost.

Southeast Asian opiates, from opium to heroin, are produced in Burma, Laos, and Thailand. Heroin from these laboratories is usually the injectable type (No.4) and averages from 70 to 90 percent in purity. Heroin base is smuggled into Malaysia for further processing. The smoking heroin (No.3, with a purity of 20 to 40 percent) produced in these locations is primarily for local consumption.

Source: Drug Enforcement Administration, 1992.

Chinese drug ring were arrested in Canada, Hong Kong, and several U.S. cities. The ring's leader was identified as a New York businessman, Fok Leung ("Peter") Woo, who was active in the Chinatown Democratic Party. Another member of the ring, a seventy-year-old Chicago Chinatown resident, was arrested for playing a role in the delivery of thirty kilograms of cocaine from Peter Woo.

The Golden Crescent

The Golden Crescent of Southwest Asia includes parts of Iran, Afghanistan, and Pakistan. The region has the limestone-rich soil, climate and altitude ideal for poppy cultivation, and like the Golden Triangle, it has a ready abundance of cheap labor for the labor-intensive production of opium. Afghanistan is second only to the Golden Triangle as a source of opium. "Most of the opium is processed in laboratories in the rebel areas, or shipped—generally aboard donkeys, but sometimes aboard jeeps bought with United States funds—to processing plants in Pakistan" (Burns 1990: 28). In Pakistan the typical poppy farmer lives in semiautonomous northern tribal areas outside of the direct control of the central government in Islamabad. "The Pakistani authorities have little control in these areas," notes Terry Atlas (1988: 6), and must appeal to tribal leaders to move against the region's dozens of illegal processing laboratories.

In northwest Pakistan's Karakorum Mountains, one acre of poppies yields about a dozen kilos of opium gum; ten kilos of opium gum can be converted into a kilo of base morphine. The wholesaling is accomplished in lawless border towns such as Landi Kotal, which is about three miles from the Afghan border, Jonathan Broder (1984: 12) describes his visit to a heroin merchant in the bazaar town of Bara, Pakistan (edited):

> He carefully unfolded a small brown paper packet to reveal the off-white heroin powder that he was eager to sell. "Taste it," he encouraged. "By the prophet's beard, it is nearly 100 percent pure. I don't lie. I have made the pilgrimage to Mecca twice. Allah has made me rich because I don't lie. Go ahead and taste it."
>
> He didn't lie. A fingernail dab of this heroin, more than 90 percent pure, packed enough wallop to dull the senses and induce vomiting for hours. He was rich too. His fortresslike stone house, surrounded by hard dirt fields, was the size of a small school. In one large room, brown bales of raw opium were stacked to the ceiling. Another room was cluttered with bottles of chemicals and plastic bowls for converting opium into heroin.

Unlike Southeast Asia, Afghanistan's rugged terrain and the martial tradition of its tribes kept it free of colonialism. Western interest in the country was limited until the Soviet invasion. The Pathans or Pushtun, a tribe that populates Pakistan's Northwest Frontier Province, comprise more than half of the inhabitants of Afghanistan. Known as exceptional warriors, the Pathans are the major drug traffickers in the region, although they generally leave the job of transporting the drug to nomadic tribesmen such as the Kuchi (Kurtis 1980). Along with other Islamic groups, many Pathans fought a guerilla war against the Soviet-backed regime in Kabul.

> In late 1979, the Soviets rolled their tanks into the opium provinces of the Pashtun and Baluchi peoples. Suddenly, the tribes which had spent the last decade maneuvering their heavily armed drug caravans past the increasingly troublesome patrols of the U.S. Drug Enforcement Administration's agents found themselves flung into the limelight as the new anti-Communist "crusaders." (Levins 1980: 201)

U.S. anti-Soviet efforts in Afghanistan were orchestrated by the CIA, who adopted a benign attitude toward drug trafficking. As the conflict wound down, the U.S. became increasingly concerned with rebel drug activity. There is some dispute over the level of drug trafficking by the Islamic *mujahedin* (holy warriors) who fought the Soviet-backed Afghan government. However, opium is the cash crop that has traditionally enabled feuding tribes in Afghanistan and in Pakistan's Northwest Frontier Province to purchase weapons and ammunition. In fact, the leading trafficker in the region is a rebel commander. In 1991, U.S. officials announced that they would no longer provide military assistance to Afghan rebels. Prior to its disintegration, the Soviet Union also agreed to stop aiding the Afghan government. On April 25, 1992, *mujahedin* forces entered Kabul without encountering resistance and the war officially ended, although conflict between rebel groups—and drug trafficking—continues.

The United States has pressured Pakistan to move against poppy cultivation (Crossette 1990), but the infusion of more than 200,000 Afghan tribesmen into the area has made this difficult, if not impossible. Tribesmen in Pakistan are now armed with rocket-propelled grenade launchers and automatic weapons to protect miles of poppy plants, pledging to die fighting rather than give up their best cash crop (Associated Press May 20, 1993). Furthermore, there is a growing domestic market for heroin in Pakistan. While most poppies now grow on the Afghan side of the border and are shipped to Europe and America in the form of powdered heroin, Pakistan's heroin-smoking population has grown to between 400,000 and 1 million users (Kamm 1988). In 1990 heroin traffickers from tribal areas were chosen as members of parliament (National Assembly) and sworn in, despite their backgrounds (Crossette 1990).

At the time of the Soviet invasion of Afghanistan in December 1979, heroin from the Afghanistan-Pakistan region accounted for almost half of all heroin entering the United States. For a while, the Soviet invasion disrupted normal drug-trade routes into Iran and Turkey. As a result, morphine base was moved out of Afghanistan into Pakistan through the Khyber Pass. Once in Pakistan, the morphine base was smuggled from the city of Peshawar, near the Khyber Pass, to the port city of Karachi, or to Delhi or Bombay. India, with

DRUGS AND POLITICS

In the Khyber Pass, Pakistan, a forty-acre estate boasts marble buildings, fountains, an Olympic-sized pool, an apple orchard, and luxuriously furnished guest rooms, all surrounded by a twenty-five-foot high brick wall. Guards carry automatic weapons, and the estate contains mortar launchers and other artillery pieces. It is the home of a member of the National Assembly—a major heroin trafficker.

Source: Steve Le Vine, "Alleged Drug Kingpin's Election Sends a Signal to Pakistan." *Chicago Tribune*, January 2, 1990: 6.

borders on both the Golden Triangle and the Golden Crescent, has became a major transshipment center for heroin entering Europe and the United States. In addition to receiving heroin, Indian criminal groups ship the precursor chemical acetic anhydride to drug cartels in Afghanistan, Pakistan, and Burma/ Myanamar (Hazarika 1993).

Turkey continues to serve as a land bridge to markets in the West for heroin from the Golden Crescent. Turkish criminal groups (*babas*) have important connections in the western drug market; they move heroin across the highways of Turkey and into Europe. From there, other criminal organizations, in particular Mafia and Camorra groups, distribute the drug throughout the European market and into Canada and the United States. The explosion of heroin entering Europe from the Golden Crescent is in part due to Kurdish separatists in eastern Turkey, who use the drug business as a source of funding for their military efforts against the Turkish government. Morphine base is frequently transported by ship through the Suez Canal into Turkey. Balkan overland routes, disrupted by war in the former Yugoslavia, have now shifted to Bulgaria, Romania, and Czechoslovakia (Cowell 1993).

Morphine base is also delivered to mobile processing laboratories in Lebanon's Syrian-controlled Bekaa Valley. Along with domestic opium, the smuggled morphine base is converted into heroin for shipment to Arab groups in Europe, Canada, and the United States. More than 30 percent of the farmers in the Bekaa cultivate the opium poppy (Kelly 1990). In fact, Lebanon has a long history of involvement in the heroin trade (McCoy 1991). Also connected to this Middle East traffic are a variety of terrorist groups, including the Palestine Liberation Organization (Ehrenfeld 1990; Sterling 1990), and the Lebanese militias (Hijazi 1991), for whom drugs provide a source of funds or are exchanged for arms.

355

Figure 7.3. Southwest Asian Heroin

Selling Prices for the Equivalent of One Kilogram of Southwest Asian Heroin at Successive Stages of Trafficking.

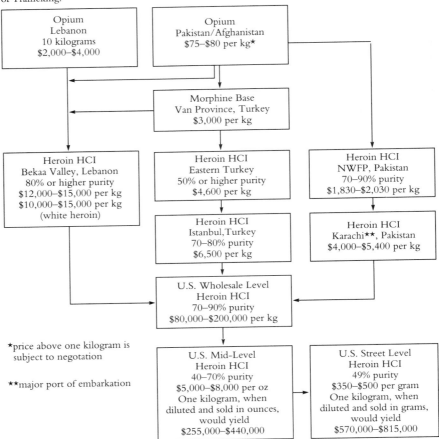

*price above one kilogram is subject to negotiation

**major port of embarkation

The change in price levels as opiates move from source to the street reflects primarily the profit motive of dealers at each level of distribution. Factors such as geographic distance from source (and hence replacement), increased refinement and portability through laboratory processing, and greater risk of seizure at borders and in distribution systems also affect the cost.

Southwest Asian heroin is produced in laboratories in Pakistan, Afghanistan, Iran, and several Middle Eastern countries. The morphine base used in these laboratories comes from Pakistan and Afghanistan, which also are opium source areas.

Source: Drug Enforcement Administration, 1992.

THE VALLEY OF DRUGS

"I have myself seen hashish-laden lorries, trundle down Bekaa Valley's single main road, undisturbed by Syrian troops. Traffickers with passes signed by Syrian generals move about freely. Heroin dealers entertain Syrian officers in the grandiose mansions that house their laboratories. One trafficking family brought in Colombians to show them how to grow coca leaves." (Haden-Guest 1990: 92) On August 9, 1991, federal authorities in Boston seized 6,393 pounds of high-grade hashish from the Bekaa Valley. The shipment was destined for Canada.

Source: Anthony Haden-Guest, "Medellin East," *Vanity Fair*, May 1990: 82–92.

Mexico

Mexico is the source of "brown heroin," which got a foothold in the American drug market after the demise of the "French Connection." "In the five years after the collapse of the French connection, Mexico became the major source of U.S. heroin. Mexico's rise was logical: the country contains extensive regions suitable for both opium cultivation and refining and shares a lightly guarded 2,000 mile border with the United States. Mexicans could manufacture heroin and smuggle it into the United States with little risk of detection. This simplified trafficking system resulted in increased Mexican heroin availability in the United States" (PCOC 1986c: 107). In more recent years, Mexico has been the source of "black tar" heroin, a less refined but more potent—and very popular—form of the substance. Its widespread use has caused a sharp increase in heroin-related hospital emergencies (Comptroller General 1988).

The poppy is not native to Mexico but was brought into the country at the turn of the century by Chinese laborers who were helping to build the railroad system. Chinese immigrants dominated heroin trafficking until anti-Chinese riots and property confiscations during the 1930s caused the trade to pass into Mexican hands (Lupsha 1991). Roughly 90 percent of the Mexican poppy crop is harvested between September and April; harvests peak in November and March. Poppy fields are generally small and difficult to detect, although larger fields cultivated by more sophisticated growers have been discovered. The poppies are grown in remote areas of the Sierra Madre states of Durango, Sinaloa, and Chihuahua, as well as Sonora (the Mexican state just south of Arizona); opium gum is then transported to nearby villages. *Acaparadores*, or gatherers, travel around the countryside buying large quantities of opium gum,

357

BLACK TAR HEROIN

"The conversion of the opium gum to black tar [No. 3] heroin is more convenient and requires only simple equipment which can be readily dismantled if law enforcement is detected in the area. In addition, almost anyone can be trained to perform the conversion process making it unnecessary to pay the higher salary which would most certainly be demanded by legitimate chemists. The process is more rapid and more economical than that required to produce the higher purity [No. 4] white heroin."

Source: Drug Enforcement Administration, *Worldwide Heroin Situation*. Washington, DC: DEA, 1991.

which is flown to secret laboratories owned and operated by major heroin organizations. The major trafficking organization in Sinaloa is headed by Angel Felix Gallardo, who also finances and arranges for the shipment of cocaine from the Colombian cartels (Golden 1993).

The conversion process for Mexican heroin takes about three days (although with special equipment and trained personnel it can be accomplished in one day). While white heroin from the Golden Triangle and the Golden Crescent can approach 100 percent purity, Mexican brown generally ranges from 65 to 85 percent pure. Once the chemists are finished, the heroin is moved to large populations centers ("Mexico: A Profile" 1985). From there, Mexican couriers transport the heroin to members of the trafficking organization in the United States (PCOC 1986c).

The drug trade is big business in poverty-wracked Mexico. Large traffickers such as the Herrera Family (discussed in chapter 5) have traditionally received protection from the highest levels of government and law enforcement. Indeed, some important traffickers have backgrounds in law enforcement. As Peter Lupsha notes, "for some of Mexico's top enforcement officials entrance into drug trafficking has simply been a lateral transfer" (1990: 12). This ugly facet of the drug trade was dramatically revealed when several Mexican law enforcement officers were implicated in the torture-murder of a U.S. drug agent. They were acting on orders from drug kingpin Rafael Caro Quintero. When Quintero and other members of his Guadalajara cartel were arrested, they were carrying credentials identifying them as agents of the *Direccion Federal de Seguridad*, the Mexican FBI. Sicilia Falcon, another leading Mexican trafficker, carried similar credentials (Lupsha 1991). In Rafael's hometown of Sinaloa, just south of Arizona, he and other members of the Caro Quintero

Figure 7.4. The Border Between Mexico and the United States

The border between Mexico and the United States has virtually no fences or barricades. Patrolling the border is difficult. Heroin is easily transported from Mexico into California, Texas, Arizona, and New Mexico.

clan are revered and are even the subjects of songs and legends (Bowden 1991).

The 1,933-mile border between Mexico and the United States has virtually no fences or barricades. The vast and remote border makes patrolling very difficult and facilitates the transportation of heroin into Texas, California, Arizona, and New Mexico. Heroin is also secreted in a variety of motor vehicles and smuggled past official border entry points. Private aircraft make use of hundreds of small airstrips that dot the U.S.-Mexican border and dozens of larger airstrips on the Yucatan Peninsula to move heroin north.

In 1984, Mexican traffickers introduced poppy seeds into northwestern Guatemala; the final product is processed in Mexico for transport to the United States. Since then, several thousand acres in Guatemala have come under cultivation, and the poorly equipped police and armed forces, which are besieged by guerilla insurgencies, usually avoid confronting the well-armed

Figure 7.5. Mexican Heroin

Selling Prices for the Equivalent of One Kilogram of Mexican Heroin at Successive Stages of Trafficking.

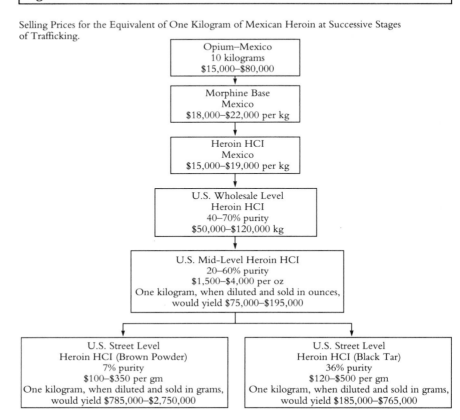

Although many small, independent traffickers now smuggle heroin within Mexico and across the border into the United States, some large organizations remain which direct virtually all aspects of heroin trafficking to include opium poppy cultivation, the refining process, and the movement of the heroin within Mexico. These same organizations may also control the smuggling of the heroin into the United States and its eventual sale at both the wholesale and retail levels.

Colombia has emerged as a source country for heroin distributed in the United States. Due to the trade's rapid development, however, information on prices at successive stages is limited.

In early 1992, a kilogram of Colombian opium ranged in price from $1,100 to $1,900. By June 1992, opium gum had saturated local markets causing prices to drop to $670–$770 per kilogram in some areas. A kilogram of morphine base reportedly cost $18,000.

The kilogram price of Colombian-produced heroin ranges from $40,000 to $100,000 in Colombia depending on purity and place of delivery. In the United States, prices are generally comparable to those for Southeast and Southwest Asian heroin. Wholesale kilogram prices range from $80,000–$180,000 varying with purity and point of delivery.

Source: Drug Enforcement Administration, 1992.

drug traffickers. Guatemala also serves as a transshipment point for cocaine, and many Colombian traffickers reside in the country (Gruson 1990). U.S. Drug Enforcement Administration agents, and pilots under contract with the State Department, have searched out and sprayed fields of opium poppies in Guatemala (Christian 1991).

The Mafia

Enormous profits accrue at each level of the heroin business (Figures 7.2, 7.3 and 7.5). The criminal organizations of Italy have grown wealthy from the drug trade. Some Mafia groups entered the heroin business when the demise of Prohibition in 1933 created a need for new sources of profits. The onset of the Second World War led to the demise of this lucrative business, but after 1945 these groups came to dominate the heroin trade by reestablishing lines of supply that had been disrupted by the war. They imported most of the substance from refineries controlled by Mafia groups in Southern Italy and later from Corsicans in Marseilles, France. Alfred McCoy (1972) argues that this was accomplished with the assistance of the U.S. Office of Strategic Services (OSS) and later its successor, the Central Intelligence Agency (CIA). With the aid of the OSS/CIA, Mafia and Corsican criminal groups that had been badly weakened during the war were able to reassert their authority in an effort to combat what was perceived as a greater evil—the growth of Communist political parties and leftist labor groups in Sicily and Marseilles.

According to the President's Commission on Organized Crime (1986c: 106–107):

> When the Italian government banned the manufacture of heroin in the early 1950s, *La Cosa Nostra* traffickers were forced to look for other sources. A new system was quickly devised, by which Turkish morphine base was refined to heroin in Marseilles, then shipped to Montreal or Sicily. Organized crime groups located in these transshipment points then sent the heroin directly to the United States. This arrangement, popularly known as the "French Connection," allowed *La Cosa Nostra* to monopolize the heroin trade from the 1950s through the early 1970s. During the peak French Connection years, the LCN controlled an estimated 95 percent of all heroin entering New York City, as well as most of the heroin distributed throughout the United States. The *La Cosa Nostra* heroin monopoly lasted until 1972, when under diplomatic pressure from the United States, Turkey banned opium production and the French connection collapsed. Amsterdam replaced Marseilles as the center of European heroin traffic, and Chicago, Los Angeles and Miami joined New York City as major U.S. distribution centers. Other trafficking groups rose to compete with the LCN for heroin dollars in New York City and throughout the country.

As noted in chapter 5, the Mafia and related groups in southern Italy have reemerged as important players in the heroin trade; their compatriots in the United States ("Zips") have assumed a leading role in wholesale trafficking.

Distribution

The organizers who arrange for the importation and wholesale distribution of heroin typically avoid physical possession. The actual smugglers ("mules") take much of the risk. David Durk (1976: 49), a New York City detective (and partner of Frank Serpico), points out: "The key figures in the Italian heroin establishment never touched heroin. Guys who were in the business for twenty years and had made millions off it had never seen it. After all, does a commodities trader on Wall Street have to see hog bellies and platinum bars?" Importation often entails little or no risk of arrest—heroin or cocaine can be secreted in a variety of imported goods, and possession cannot be proven. Furthermore, while a single shipment may be detected and confiscated, smugglers often divide their supplies so that other shipments arrive unimpeded. (Colombian cocaine cartels often insure their shipments through a joint arrangement; the cost of insurance is passed on to the import buyer who is then financially protected in the event of interdiction by American authorities.)

After importation, the drugs are sold in 10 to 50 kilo quantities to wholesalers—"kilo connections." Heroin is then "stepped on" or diluted several times. The wholesaler, basically a facilitator, arranges for the cutting (diluting) of the almost pure heroin. The actual work is often done by women brought together for the task. Between ten and twenty women cut from 10 to 50 kilos in an apartment rented for this purpose. Under guard, often working without any clothes on (as a precaution against theft of the precious powder), wearing surgical masks to avoid inhaling heroin dust, they mix the heroin with quinine, lactose, and dextrose, usually four or five parts of the dilutant to one part of heroin. They work through the night and receive several thousand dollars each, making the risk and embarrassment worthwhile.

When the cutting is complete, jobbers—"weight dealers"—who have been waiting for a telephone call arrive with the necessary cash, which they exchange for 2 to 5 kilos of the cut heroin. The jobbers move it to wholesalers, who cut it again. From there it moves to street wholesalers, then to street retailers, and finally to consumers. At each step of the process profits accrue as the kilo of pure heroin increases in bulk, the result of further cutting.

The enormous profits that accrue in the business of heroin are part of a criminal underworld where violence is always an attendant reality. Heroin transactions must be accomplished without recourse to the formal mechanisms of dispute resolution that are usually available in the world of legitimate business. This reality leads to the creation of private mechanisms of enforcement. The drug world is filled with heavily armed and dangerous persons in the employ of the large cartels, although even street-level operatives are often armed. These private resources for violence serve to limit market entry, to ward off competitors and predatory criminals, and to maintain internal discipline and security within an organization. In the drug business, an employee is not usually fired—more likely, he is fired upon!

COCAINE

Spanish explorers observed indigenous people chewing coca leaves during their colonization of South America, although they did not adopt the practice. In the middle of the nineteenth century, scientists began experimenting with the substance, noting that it showed promise as a local anesthetic and had an effect opposite that of morphine. At first, cocaine was used to treat morphine addiction, but the result was often a morphine addict who also became dependent on cocaine (Van Dyke and Byck 1982). "Throughout the late nineteenth century, both coca itself (that is, an extract from the leaf including all its alkaloids) and the pure chemical cocaine were used as medicines and for pleasure—the distinction was not always made—in an enormous variety of ways" (Grinspoon 1976: 19).

"By the late 1880s, a feel-good pharmacology based on the coca plant and its derivative cocaine, was hawked for everything from headaches to hysteria. Catarrh powders for sinus trouble and headaches—a few were nearly pure cocaine—introduced the concept of snorting" (Gomez 1984: 58). Cocaine was particularly popular in literary and intellectual circles (Grinspoon 1976). One very popular product was coca-wine, *Vin Mariani*, which contained two ounces of fresh coca leaves in a pint of Bordeaux wine; It received the praise of

The nation's only legal commercial importer of coca leaves is this Stepan laboratory in Maywood, New Jersey. It obtains them mainly from Peru and processes the leaves into a flavoring sold exclusively to the Coca-Cola Company. Stepan also extracts cocaine, which is then sold to a St. Louis pharmaceutical manufacturer, Mallinckrodt Inc., the only company in the United States licensed to purify the product for medicinal use.

prominent persons such as Sarah Bernhardt and John Philip Sousa, as well as three popes and sixteen heads of state. *Peruvian Wine of Coca* was available for $1 a bottle through the Sears, Roebuck catalog in 1902. The most famous beverage containing coca, however, was first bottled in 1894. According to Linda Gomez (1984), cocaine was removed from Coca-Cola in 1903 after a presidential commission criticized the use of habit-forming drugs in soft drinks. However, an advertisement for Coca-Cola in the *Scientific American* in 1906 publicized the use of coca as an important tonic in this "healthful drink" (May 1988: 29). In 1908, a government report listed over forty brands of soft drinks containing cocaine (Helmer 1975). (Coca-Cola continues to use nonpsychoactive residue from the coca plant for flavoring.)

After the first flush of enthusiasm for cocaine in the 1880s, there was a decline in its use. While it continued to be used in a variety of notions and tonics, cocaine did not develop a separate appeal as did morphine and heroin (Morgan 1981). Indeed, it gained a reputation for inducing bizarre and unpredictable behavior. After the turn of the century, cocaine, like heroin, became identified with the urban underworld. From 1930 until the 1960s there was limited demand for cocaine and, accordingly, only limited supply. Cocaine use was associated with deviants—jazz musicians and the denizens of underworld—and supplies were typically diverted from medical sources.

During the later 1960s and early 1970s, attitudes toward recreational drug use became more relaxed, a spinoff of the wide acceptance of marijuana. Cocaine was no longer associated with deviants and, note Donald Wesson and David Smith (1985: 193), the media played a significant role in shaping public attitudes:

> By publicizing and glamorizing the lifestyle of affluent, upper class drug dealers and the use of cocaine by celebrities and athletes, all forms of mass media created an effective advertising campaign for cocaine, and many people were taught to perceive cocaine as chic, exclusive, daring, and nonaddicting. In television specials about cocaine abuse, scientists talked about the intense euphoria produced by cocaine and the compulsive craving that people (and animals) develop for it. Thus, an image of cocaine as being extraordinarily powerful, and a (therefore desirable) euphoriant was promoted.

Cocaine soon became associated with a privileged elite, and the new demand was sufficient to generate new sources, refining and marketing networks outside of medical channels (Grinspoon and Bakalar 1976), and the development of the international cocaine organizations discussed in chapter 5. This led to greater availability of cocaine with a corresponding increase in use, and the spiral continues. Enormous profits accrue at each level of the cocaine business (figure 7.6). These profits have proven so alluring that criminal organizations that have traditionally avoided direct involvement in drug trafficking, such as the Chicago Outfit, have become increasingly involved in the cocaine business.

Figure 7.6. Cocaine

Selling Prices for Cocaine at Successive Stages of Trafficking.★

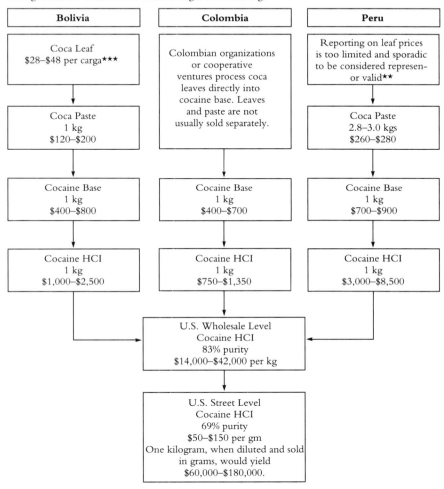

★All source country prices are in terms of undiluted products.

★★The majority of Peruvian coca growers now process the leaves directly into paste, thereby reducing the bulk of the product transported to buyers.

★★★One carga equals 100 lbs.

Source: Drug Enforcement Administration, 1992.

Cocaine is an alkaloid found in significant quantities only in the leaves of two species of coca shrub. One species grows in the Andes of Ecuador, Peru, and Bolivia; and the other is found in the mountainous regions of Colombia, along the Caribbean coast of South America, on the northern coast of Peru, and in the dry valley of the Marañón River in northeastern Peru. Coca leaves have been chewed by Indians in Peru for at least twenty centuries. The leaves are used as a poultice for wounds and to brew a tea, *mate de coca*, said to cure the headaches of tourists bothered by the 12,000-foot altitude of La Paz. Most cash crops raised on the mountain slopes of Peru require a great deal of care, because the nutrient-poor soil needs continuous fertilization. However, coca is a hardy jungle plant with abundant seeds that needs little or no fertilizer. "Once a coca field is planted, it will yield four to five crops a year for thirty to forty years, needing little in return but seasonal weeding" (Morales 1989: xvi).

Bolivia is South America's poorest nation, with a per capita annual income of $600. Coca is grown legally, and its leaves are sold openly at street markets. Until the 1970s, small amounts of coca paste were shipped from Bolivia into Argentina, Brazil, and Chile, where it was combined with tobacco to make *pitillos* (cigarettes). During the early 1970s, the industry changed dramatically when the demand for cocaine mushroomed in the United States. Numerous kitchen laboratories sprang up in response to the market. Later in the decade, wealthy and influential cattle ranchers in the Benji region, powerful ranchers, farmers, and businesspeople in the Santa Cruz area, and some senior officers in the Bolivian military began to organize the industry on a large scale. Military involvement increased, leading to a "cocaine coup" in 1980: a number of traffickers were freed from prison, and the U.S. Drug Enforcement Agency pulled out of Bolivia (Henkel 1986). In 1982, the military leaders were replaced by a civilian government. Nevertheless, the country's leading trafficker, Roberto Suarez Gomez, a member of the landed gentry, continued to reside at his remote El Sujo ranch even though he had been sentenced to fifteen years imprisonment in 1988. On July 20, 1988, anti-drug police arrested him and two bodyguards at his cattle ranch and flew him to La Paz. Although he is also under indictment in Miami, Bolivia's interior minister stated that Suarez Gomez would not be extradited to the United States. He is currently serving a fifteen-year prison sentence in La Paz. In 1990 his son, Roberto Suarez Levy, was killed by police officers in Santa Cruz. Later that year, his nephew, Roca Suarez, and Roca's wife were arrested at their nineteen-room estate in San Marino, California, on cocaine conspiracy charges.

Cocaine supports not only those directly involved in drug trafficking but also their dependents and the legitimate businesses that depend on their patronage. U.S. dollars brought into poor Latin American countries help keep the *narcomafia* in luxury and also provide benefits for poorer elements of society. In the coca-growing regions of Peru and Bolivia, the *coqueros* provide a level of income that would otherwise be unavailable to the peasants who cultivate and process the leaves for the illegal market. Government attempts to curtail coca cultivation always meet with opposition, which is often violent. In

Women from the Shining Path rebel group in Peru stand in formation shouting in support of their leader.

order to improve desperate economic conditions, the Bolivian government is attempting to amend the 1961 United Nations treaty that labels coca leaf as a harmful substance and bans its export worldwide. Boliva is interested in exporting its *mate de coca* and other coca-derived products, which is opposed by the United States (Marx 1992).

In Peru, any government that moves to eradicate coca risks gaining the enmity of peasant voters and their elected representatives and strengthening the Marxist insurgencies, such as *Sendero Luminosa* ("Shining Path"). The Shining Path guerillas, followers of a radical Maoist brand of communism, have reportedly entered into an alliance with drug dealers in the Upper Huallaga River Valley, a dense jungle area about the size of West Virginia along the eastern slopes of the Andes. The valley is the world's greatest source of coca—an estimated 250,000 acres are covered with the crop. Shining Path's involvement is designed to help finance acquisition of sophisticated weaponry. In areas that it controls, Shining Path charges drug traffickers up to $15,000 for "landing rights" for each planeload of cocaine paste and levies a tax of 5 to 10 percent on drug earnings (Massing 1990).

The guerillas have reputedly assisted leading traffickers in battles with rival groups. The traffickers, in return, have assisted the guerillas in battles with the pro-Cuban *Tupac Amaru* revolutionary movement (Trujillo 1992a). In 1990, the Drug Enforcement Administration set up a base in the valley to launch raids on laboratories and clandestine airfields. The base has come under attack from Shining Path, and U.S. civilian helicopter pilots under government contract have engaged in firefights with the guerillas (Brooke 1990f). One of these helicopters was brought down on January 12, 1992, reportedly by a guerilla surface-to-air missile, killing three Americans (Krauss 1992).

The Revolutionary Armed Forces of Colombia (FARC) has collected taxes from and permitted the traffickers to operate in jungle areas. More symbiotic ties have been established: the FARC guerillas provide protection for cocaine-processing operations of the traffickers in the territory they share (Westrate 1985; also "Drug Smugglers Used Cuban Base" 1988). There have also been allegations that officials of the Sandinista government in Nicaragua trafficked in cocaine (Ehrenfeld 1990) and that the anti-Sandinista forces—the "contras"— have done the same (see Cockburn 1987; Engelberg 1988; Scott and Marshall 1991; Harmon 1993). Late in 1975, members of the Medellín cartel met with the Cuban ambassador in Bogotá and negotiated an arrangement for Cuban assistance with efforts to smuggle cocaine into Florida (Ehrenfeld 1990).

In the past, coca-leaf was usually converted to cocaine base in Bolivia and Peru and smuggled by small aircraft or boat into Colombia or Brazil where it was refined into cocaine in jungle laboratories. In more recent years, laboratories have relocated to cities far from cultivation sites to be closer to sources of precursor chemicals and also because improved law-enforcement methods facilitate the detection of jungle laboratories. The number of laboratories has grown in northwestern Argentina and even in Buenos Aires (Christian 1988a). Precursor chemicals are usually manufactured in the United States and Germany, and Panama and Mexico serve as major transit sources. Colombian cartels, using dummy companies and multiple suppliers, pay up to ten times the normal prices for these chemicals (Rohter 1990).

Because of crackdowns in Colombia, the Bolivian organization of Suarez Gomez, which is run by his nephews, has bypassed the Colombians. The Bolivians produce finished cocaine hydrochloride in the jungles and ranges of the northern part of the Santa Cruz and Benji regions, and deal directly with importers from Brazil, Mexico, Europe, and the United States (Christian 1988b). Bolivian traffickers usually make deliveries of cocaine in Bolivia, leaving the shipping and smuggling to other organizations—usually Colombians (Levine 1990). A new drug trafficking elite has emerged in the Santa Cruz area. Crackdowns in Colombia have led some Colombians to settle in Bolivia (Lupsha 1990). These crackdowns have also caused traffickers to relocate their laboratories to Peru. As a result, the primitive coca agricultural business has been transformed: cartels have formed and violence is increasing (Nash 1991b). Increased law enforcement activity, the result of United States pressure, has expanded the problem throughout much of Latin America ("Widening the Drug War" 1991). Ecuador, Chile, and Venezuela have become major cocaine transshipment locations, with the accompanying problem of official corruption (Brooke 1992b; Nash 1992; Brooke 1992f). A customs union between Colombia and Venezuela has led to open borders, which is attractive to Colombian cartels who move cocaine and heroin through Venezuela for shipment to the United

States. Three Sicilian brothers, Pasquale, Paolo, and Gaspare Cuntrera, twenty-year residents of Venezuela, were deported in 1992. They were the suppliers for the "French Connection" and "Pizza Connection" heroin cases in New York (discussed in chapter 5) and were also major cocaine dealers (Brooke 1992f). Drugs, cocaine and heroin, from Colombia are dropped into the waters off Puerto Rico where they are picked up by waiting boats. Small boats built to avoid radar also move drugs from Colombia to Puerto Rico; it is then shipped to mainland cities. This is facilitated by Puerto Rico's commonwealth status: travelers do not pass through customs (Treaster 1993b).

According to then-president George Bush, when U.S. troops invaded Panama in 1989, the reason was "to combat drug trafficking." Since the ouster of Manuel Noriega, however, most observers believe the drug problem has grown considerably worse: "In most of the world, drug smuggling is a sneaky nighttime affair. But in Panama . . . traffickers are boldly hauling drugs at all hours" (Treaster 1991b: 1). Panama has emerged as a major transshipment and laboratory source for cocaine. Its geographic location, a long border with Colombia consisting of a dense, sparsely populated jungle province, and inadequate law enforcement allow the trafficking to thrive (Uhlig 1990; Robinson 1991; Jolidon 1992). In fact, law enforcement has been so inadequate that a dozen major drug traffickers captured by the Panamanian police have escaped from custody (Sheppard 1990b). Colombian traffickers have relocated to Panama, where they enjoy virtual immunity from overworked, underfunded, and by many accounts corrupt law enforcement (Sheppard 1991a, 1992). When the traffickers fell victim to the general lawlessness that has overtaken Panama, cartel gunmen hunted down and shot some armed robbers as an example to others (Sheppard 1991a, 1991b). At the end of 1992, Panama's attorney general was suspended because of charges that he released about $38 million in frozen bank assets belonging to members of the Cali cartel. A building boom of luxury housing in Panama City that has reduced high unemployment is reputedly financed by drug money (Sheppard 1993).

Law enforcement pressure has also led to the "invasion" of Surinam, a Dutch protectorate in northern South America, by Colombian traffickers who are using it as a transshipment point to European and U.S. markets. Greater surveillance of the Mexican-Southwest border and the Caribbean has led to increased use of Canada as a transshipment point. Aircraft originating in Colombia offload their cargo in Canada; it is then transported by land across the Maine border and subsequently into New York City (Drug Enforcement Administration 1991b).

Cocaine Pharmacology

Coca is a flowering bush or shrub that in cultivation stands three to six feet tall. Each shrub yields at most four ounces of waxy, elliptical leaves that are about 1 percent cocaine by weight. Pulverized leaves of the coca bush are soaked and shaken in a mixture of alcohol and benzol (a petroleum derivative). The liquid is then drained, sulfuric acid is added, and the solution is again shaken. Sodium carbonate is added, forming a precipitate, which is washed with kerosene and chilled, leaving behind crystals of crude cocaine known as coca paste. Between 200 and 500 kilos of leaves yield 1 kilo of paste; 2.5 kilos of coca paste are converted into 1 kilo of cocaine base—a malodorous, grainy, greenish-yellow powder of more than 66 percent purity. Cocaine base is converted into cocaine hydrochloride by being treated with ether, acetone, and hydrochloric acid. One kilo of cocaine base is synthesized into 1 kilo of cocaine hydrochloride, a white crystalline powder that is about 95 percent pure.

In the United States cocaine hydrochloride is cut for street sale by adding sugars such as lactose, inositol, mannitol, or talcum powder, borax, or other neutral substances, and local anesthetics such as procaine hydrochloride (Novacaine) or lidocaine hydrochloride. (Novacaine is sometimes mixed with mannitol or lactose and sold as "cocaine.") After cutting, the cocaine typically has a consumer sale purity of less than 20 percent. More recently, however, huge increases in the availability of cocaine has resulted in consumer sale purity levels as high as 50 percent—and a concomitant increase in the number of emergency room admissions for cocaine overdoses.

The most common method of using cocaine is "snorting"—inhaling it into the nostrils through a straw or rolled paper or from a "coke spoon." Some abusers take it intravenously, which is the only way to ingest 100 percent of the drug. When the drug is inhaled, its effects peak in fifteen to twenty minutes, and disappear in sixty to ninety minutes. Intravenous use results in an intense feeling of euphoria that crests in three to five minutes and wanes in thirty to forty minutes. Cocaine causes the release of the natural substance adrenaline: "In essence the cocaine-stimulated reactions in the body are mimicking a natural physiological stress response." The body prepares for "fight" or "flight," but the brain sends the message that everything is better than fine (Gold et al. 1986: 38).

In small doses, cocaine will bring about a sensation of extreme euphoria and indifference to pain, along with illusions of increased mental and sensory alertness and physical strength: "A few hundredths of a gram of cocaine hydrochloride, chopped finely and arranged on a smooth surface into several lines, or rows of powder, can be snorted into the nose through a rolled piece of paper in a few seconds. The inhalation shortly gives rise to feelings of elation and a sense of clarity or power of thought, feelings that pass away for most people in about half an hour" (Van Dyke and Byck 1982: 128). At higher doses, however, the drug has the potential "to produce megalomania and feelings of omnipotence in most individuals" (Gold et al. 1986: 44).

Cocaine has limited medical use. It constricts blood vessels when applied topically, the only local anesthetic that has this effect. Because of this quality, cocaine is used in surgery of the mucous membranes of the ear, nose, and throat, and for procedures that require the passage of a tube through the nose or throat (Van Dyke and Byck 1982).

Crack

While cocaine hydrochloride cannot easily be smoked, freeing the alkaloid from the hydrochloride attachment produces purified crystals of cocaine base that can be crushed and smoked in a special glass pipe or sprinkled on a tobacco or marijuana product. This form of cocaine is often referred to as *crack*. "The availability of crack was first reported in Los Angeles, San Diego and Houston in 1981. This form of cocaine abuse," notes the Drug Enforcement Administration (1988: 1), "was considered a localized phenomenon until late 1985, when crack became a serious problem in New York City. Crack cocaine literally exploded on the drug scene during 1986 and was reported available in 28 states and the District of Columbia."

This form of cocaine has proven particularly alluring to young men and women, ages seventeen to twenty-five. The drug is relatively cheap, $5 to $10 a "rock," although the per gram price is twice as expensive as cocaine hydrochloride (Gold 1984). According to one study (Frank et al. 1987), crack users in New York who are "hooked" report spending between $100 and $200 a day on the substance. It is generally sold on the street in small glass vials. The nickname "crack" comes from the crackling sound the drug makes when it is smoked (Gold 1984). Crack is typically smoked in a glass pipe about five inches long and a quarter-inch in diameter with a metal screen at the top to hold a small clump of the substance. When lit, the substance melts and clings to the screen; some of it oozes down inside the stem where it dries and forms a hard residue that can later be scraped off and smoked.

Cocaine hydrochloride powder is easily converted into crack by cooking it in a mixture of sodium bicarbonate (baking soda) and water, then removing the water. The soaplike substance is then cut into bars or chips, sometimes called "quarter rocks," and smoked. Haitian groups traffic in crack in the form of small rectangular strips, called "French Fry" crack, that range in length from one-half inch to one inch. They are often cut with Benzocaine and retail for $50 a strip (Drug Enforcement Administration 1988). Smoking crack produces a short but very powerful euphoria that lasts from ten to fifteen minutes. Since crack is inhaled directly into the lungs, bypassing much of the circulatory system en route to the brain, it takes about five seconds to take effect—even faster than intravenous ingestion.

> [Crack] produces an immediate euphoria (the "rush"), which is soon followed by a dysphoric withdrawal (the "crash"). After smoking crack repeatedly, the user develops an intense craving for more. This craving is often uncontrollable, and the crack user will lie, steal, or even commit acts of violence in order to obtain more of the drug. Although it can take months or even years for a nasal cocaine user to progress from recreational to compulsive use, this can happen within days to weeks with crack. (Rosecan, Spitz, and Gross 1987: 299)

Crack is distributed by a number of groups, some of whom were previously involved in street-level heroin trafficking. As noted in chapter 5, some emerging criminal organizations such as the Jamaican posses and prison gangs have been trafficking in crack. The level of competitive violence seems to rival that of the Prohibition era.

STREET-LEVEL HEROIN AND COCAINE BUSINESS

Below the wholesale level, cocaine or heroin is an easy-entry business, requiring only a source, clientele, and funds. A variety of groups deal heroin, including street gangs in many urban areas. In several areas of the country, particularly New York City and Los Angeles, the relatively stable neighborhood criminal organizations who dominate the heroin and cocaine trade have found new competitors: youthful crack dealers. Crack requires only a small investment for entry to the trade. Street gangs or groups of friends and relatives have entered the market, often touching off explosive competitive violence that frequently involves the use of high-powered handguns and automatic weapons.

Ko-lin Chin and Jeffrey Fagan (1990b: 25) state that this violence occurs for two reasons:

> First, crack selling was concentrated in neighborhoods where social controls had been weakened by intensified social and economic dislocations in the decade preceding the emergence of crack. Second, the rapid development of new drug-selling groups following the introduction of crack brought with it competition. Accordingly, violence within new selling groups *internally* to maintain control and violence *externally* to maintain selling territory (product quality) was more likely to characterize the unstable crack markets than the more established drug markets and distribution systems.

As noted in chapter 5, some gangs have established direct connections to major Colombian traffickers and have expanded their organizations and drug markets interstate.

Thomas Mieczkowski (1986) studied the activities of a loosely organized retail heroin group in Detroit—"The Young Boys, Inc." At the center of their activities is a *crew boss*, who receives his supply of heroin from a drug-syndicate lieutenant. The crew boss provides a consignment of heroin to each of his seven to twenty *runners*, young (sixteen to twenty-three-year-old) black males whom he recruits. Afterward, each runner takes his station on a street adjacent to a public roadway, which facilitates purchases from vehicles. To avoid rip-offs and robberies, each crew is guarded by armed men, including the crew boss himself. Runners reportedly earn about $160 for a ten-and-a-half hour workday.

Participants in these drug networks tend to be serious delinquents:

> [They] are frequently hired by adult or older adolescent street drug sellers as runners. Loosely organized into crews of 3 to 12, each boy generally handles small quantities of drugs—for example, two or three packets or bags of heroin. They receive these units "on credit," "up front," or "on loan" from a supplier and are expected to return about 50 to 70 percent of the drug's street value.

In addition to distributing drugs, these youngsters may act as lookouts, recruit customers, and guard street sellers from customer-robbers. They typically are users of marijuana and cocaine, but not heroin. Moreover, in some cities, dealers and suppliers prefer to hire distributors who do not "get high" during an operation. But their employment as runners is not generally steady; it is interspersed with other crimes including robbery, burglary, and theft.

A relatively small number of youngsters who sell drugs develop excellent entrepreneurial skills. Their older contacts come to trust them, and they parlay this trust to advance in the drug business. By the time they are 18 or 19 they can have several years of experience in drug sales, be bosses of their own crews, and handle more than $500,000 a year. (Chaiken and Johnson 1988: 12)

The sale of cocaine, crack, and heroin is carried out by thousands of small-time operators who dominate particular local markets—a public housing complex, a number of city blocks, or simply a street-corner location. Control is exercised through violence. For most participants at the street level, however, the net profits of heroin are rather modest. While dealers typically work long hours and subject themselves to substantial risk of violence and incarceration, their incomes generally range from $1,000 to $2,000 a month. Less successful participants eke out a living that rivals minimum wage. Many are involved to support their own drug habits, to supplement earnings from legitimate employment, or both. In the crack business young men often work for less than minimum wage—for example, $30 a day for acting as a lookout, or fifty cents for each vial of crack sold. They can expect to earn $100 to $200 per week for long hours under unpleasant conditions, and are without unemployment insurance, medical insurance, or any of the usual benefits of legitimate employment. A study in Washington, D.C., found that a majority of drug sellers in the sample did not sell drugs on a daily basis, and their median annual income was about $10,000. Those who sold daily earned about $3,600 per month (Reuter, MacCoun, and Murphy 1990).

The domestic business of cocaine requires only a connection to a Colombian, Peruvian, or Bolivian source and sufficient financing to initiate the first buy. A variety of persons are involved in the domestic cocaine business several steps removed from the Colombian source. Because the cocaine clientele is traditionally at least middle income, distributors likewise tend to come from the (otherwise) respectable middle class. (See Bowden 1987 for the story of a yuppie cocaine ring.) The popularity of crack, however, has dramatically altered the drug market at the consumer level. In particular, the age of many retailers has been affected. Experienced drug researchers James Inciardi and Anne Pottieger were shocked by the youthfulness of crack dealers compared to those traditionally found in the heroin business: "While both patterns ensnare youth in their formative years, crack dealers are astonishingly more involved in a drug-crime lifestyle at an alarmingly younger age" (1991: 269).

As with more conventional consumer items, heroin sold at the street level often carries a name and/or logo to promote "brand name" loyalty. As in other stages of the drug trade, the street-level business is filled with violence. Paul Goldstein (1985: 497) reports that violence in the drug trade is sometimes the result of brand deception.

> Dealers mark an inferior quality heroin with a currently popular brand name. Users purchase the good heroin, use it, then repackage the bag with milk sugar for resale. The popular brand is purchased, the bag is "tapped," and further diluted for resale.
>
> These practices get the real dealers of the popular brand very upset. Their heroin starts to get a bad reputation on the streets and they lose sales. Purchasers of the phony bags may accost the real dealers, complaining about the poor quality and demanding their money back. The real dealers then seek out the purveyors of the phony bags. Threats, assaults, and/or homicides may ensue.

In the drug business, Goldstein (1985) notes, norm violations—for example, a street-level dealer failing to return sufficient money to his superior in a drug network—often result in violence. Violence almost invariably accompanies the robbery of a drug dealer. No dealer who wishes to remain in the business can allow himself to be robbed without exacting vengeance. The punishment for a widespread norm violation—informing—is death. Violence and informing may be used to eliminate competition or extract vengeance for the sale of poor-quality dope, but informing is more often an effort to gain leniency from the criminal justice system. "Occasionally, distinct patterns of injury can be recognized: drug runners, young teenagers who carry drugs and money between sellers and buyers, are being seen in emergency rooms more frequently with gunshot wounds to the legs and knees; a more vicious style of drug-related injury has emerged in the western part of the United States. In this injury, known as 'pithing,' the victim's spinal cord is cut, and he or she is left alive, but paraplegic" (De La Rosa, Lambert, and Gropper 1990: 1–2).

The business of drugs includes substances other than cocaine and heroin. Most of these substances, such as PCP, LSD, amphetamines, and barbiturates are produced in domestic laboratories; marijuana is also grown in the United States. Except for the case of methamphetamine trafficking by outlaw motorcycle clubs (discussed in chapter 5), the persons and groups that manufacture and traffic in these substances are too varied for comprehensive coverage in this book, and they fit into no particular ethnic, geographic, or class pattern. There is little or no pattern to marijuana trafficking in the United States. It is easy to enter the business, and a number of relatives, friendship groups, and former military veterans have come together to "do marijuana."

CANNABIS

The biggest influence on marijuana legislation has been racism. State laws against marijuana were often part of a reaction to Mexican immigration

(Bonnie and Whitebread 1970). By 1930, sixteen states with relatively large Mexican populations had enacted anti-marijuana legislation. "Chicanos in the Southwest were believed to be incited to violence by smoking it" (Musto 1973: 65). However, Jerome Himmelstein (1983: 29) argues that the "crucial link between Mexicans and federal marihuana policy was not locally based political pressure from the Southwest, but a specific image of marihuana that emerged from the context of marihuana use by Mexicans and was used to justify antimarihuana legislation. Because Mexican laborers and other lower-class groups were identified as typical marihuana users, the drug was believed to cause the kinds of antisocial behavior associated with those groups, especially violent crime."

Because of marijuana's association with suspect marginal groups—Mexicans, artists, intellectuals, jazz musicians, bohemians, and petty criminals—it became an easy target for regulation (Morgan 1981). In the eastern United States, there was a mistaken belief that marijuana was addictive and would serve as a substitute for narcotics that were outlawed by the Harrison Act. The hysterical anti-marijuana literature produced during the 1930s often seems amusing. Rowell and Rowell (1939: 49) wrote that marijuana "seems to superimpose upon the user's character and personality a devilish form. He is one individual when normal, and an entirely different one after using marijuana," and that marijuana "has led to some of the most revolting cases of sadistic rape and murder of modern times." In 1936 the Federal Bureau of Narcotics presented a summary of cases that illustrate "the homicidal tendencies and the generally debasing effects which arise from the use of marijuana" (Uelmen and Haddox 1983: 1–11). The 1936 motion picture *Reefer Madness* presented a frightening portrait of the marijuana-user and "pusher."

By 1931 twenty-two states had marijuana legislation, often part of a general purpose statute against narcotics (Bonnie and Whitebread 1970). In 1937, Congress passed the Marijuana Tax Act, which put an end to lawful recreational use of the substance. Himmelstein (1983: 38) states that despite being outlawed, marijuana was never an important issue in the United States until the 1960s: "It hardly ever made headlines or became the subject of highly publicized hearings and reports. Few persons knew or cared about it, and marihuana laws were passed with minimal attention."

The source of marijuana, the hemp plant, grows wild throughout most of the tropic and temperate regions of the world, including parts of the United States. It has been cultivated for several useful products: the tough fiber of the stem is used to make rope; the seed is used in feed mixtures; and the oil as an ingredient in paint. The psychoactive part of the plant is a substance called Delta9THC, or simply THC, and is concentrated in the leaves and resinous flowering tops of the plant. The THC level of marijuana cigarettes varies considerably: domestic marijuana typically has had less than 0.5 percent, since the plants were originally introduced to produce hemp fiber. More recently developed strains, however, exhibit considerably higher levels, the result of careful cross-breeding by outlaw horticulturists. The domestic cultivation of

MARIJUANA GARDENING INDOORS

At the end of 1990 police officers discovered two elaborate underground marijuana farms in Southern California. One was a 6,000-plant operation situated in a bunker under a home in Lancaster (sixty miles northeast of Los Angeles); the other was a 4,000-plant farm under a house in Llano (about twenty miles from Lancaster). These multimillion-dollar operations were equipped with diesel-powered lights and ventilation systems.

marijuana has spawned a significant market in horticultural equipment. These suppliers advertise in *High Times,* a magazine devoted to marijuana use.

Jamaican, Colombian, and Mexican marijuana ranges from 0.5 to 4.0 percent THC. The most select product, sinsemilla (Spanish, *sin semilla,* "without seed"), is prepared from the unpollinated female cannabis plant. Sinsemilla has been found to have as much as 8.0 percent THC. Hashish, which is usually imported from the Middle East, contains the drug-rich resinous secretions of the cannabis plant, which are collected, dried, and then compressed into a variety of forms—balls, cakes, or sheets. It has a potency as high as 10 percent. Hashish is usually mixed with tobacco and smoked in a pipe. "Hashish oil" is a dark, viscous liquid, the result of repeated extractions of cannabis plant materials. It has a THC level as high as 20 percent. A drop or two on a cigarette has the effect of a single marijuana cigarette. Marijuana prepared for street sale may be diluted with oregano, catnip, or other ingredients, and may also contain psychoactive substances such as LSD. Marijuana from Vietnam often contains opium.

In the United States marijuana is usually rolled in paper and smoked. The user typically inhales the smoke deeply and holds it in his or her lungs for as long as possible. This tends to maximize the absorption of the active THC, about one-half of which is lost during smoking. The psychoactive reaction occurs in one to ten minutes and peaks in about ten to thirty minutes, with a total duration of three to four hours. The most important variables with respect to the drug's impact are the individual's experiences and expectations and the strength of the marijuana ingested. Thus, the first-time user may not experience any significant reaction. In general, low doses tend to induce restlessness and an increasing sense of well-being and gregariousness, followed by a dreamy state of relaxation; hunger, especially a craving for sweets, frequently accompanies marijuana use. Higher doses may induce changes in sensory perception—a more vivid sense of smell, sight, hearing, and taste—which may be accompanied by subtle alterations in thought formation and expression.

The negative short-term effects of marijuana seem quite limited: loss of inhibition, loss of self-confidence, aggressiveness, and even auditory hallucinations. High doses may affect short-term memory and reaction time, and significantly increase heart rate, but no more so than high doses of caffeine and nicotine. Casual use results in the same impairments that one would expect from equal amounts of alcohol (Abel 1978). The long-range effects are more controversial. Some researchers claim no significant physical or psychological damage, while others find the opposite.

The substance has some use in medicine—relieving pressure in the eyes of glaucoma patients and controlling the nausea and vomiting that accompanies cancer chemotherapy. Since 1982, there has been a legally available pharmaceutical for use in ophthalmology and cancer treatment. Called Marinol (dronabinol), it is 98.8 percent pure THC. There is some dispute as to whether or not THC administered orally is as effective as smoking marijuana.

There is little or no pattern to marijuana trafficking in the United States, although some geographical areas have apparently gotten hooked on the business. Until 1987, Garberville, California, was a boom town of 1,400 located in Humboldt County, two hundred miles north of San Francisco. The town's success was the result of an economic miracle performed by a single crop—marijuana. In the early 1970s, hippie growers began cultivating marijuana for themselves and their friends. The business soon expanded, and marijuana became a major agricultural product for the three-county "Emerald Triangle." A quarter-acre of plants could earn as much as $100,000 for its owner. At the same time, murders and other violent crimes soared, but so did the local economy. The growers in the valleys and hill slopes surrounding Garberville created an economic boom in this conservative rural town. Shopkeepers and motels catered to the traffickers; garden stores found new customers for irrigation equipment and organic fertilizer. In 1983 the Drug Enforcement Administration, the California Department of Justice, and local sheriffs began a successful campaign to eradicate the illegal harvest, to the chagrin of local businesspeople (Schneider 1988).

But these successful efforts were short-lived, and federal authorities sent in the military. In 1990, U.S. army personnel, the National Guard, federal agents, and sheriffs' deputies spent two weeks raiding clandestine marijuana gardens in the rugged terrain of the King Range National Conservation Area in Humboldt County. There were local protests against the military deployment, and some residents filed a lawsuit to bar the use of the military. The National Guard spent $400,000 on the operation, which succeeded in destroying 1,200 plants; no growers were arrested (Bishop 1990).

In Kentucky, reputedly the second largest marijuana-producing state in the nation, most cultivation takes place in the eastern region: the mountainous and inaccessible Appalachia. The impoverished region has an unemployment rate of 25 percent. Gary Potter, Larry Gaines, and Beth Holbrook (1990: 98–99)

Figure 7.7. Foreign Source Marijuana

Selling Prices for One Pound of Marijuana at Successive Levels of Trafficking

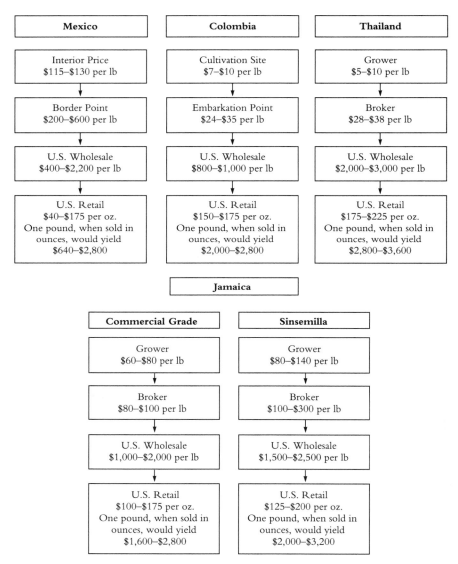

Mexico

| Interior Price |
| $115–$130 per lb |

↓

| Border Point |
| $200–$600 per lb |

↓

| U.S. Wholesale |
| $400–$2,200 per lb |

↓

| U.S. Retail |
| $40–$175 per oz. |
| One pound, when sold in |
| ounces, would yield |
| $640–$2,800 |

Colombia

| Cultivation Site |
| $7–$10 per lb |

↓

| Embarkation Point |
| $24–$35 per lb |

↓

| U.S. Wholesale |
| $800–$1,000 per lb |

↓

| U.S. Retail |
| $150–$175 per oz. |
| One pound, when sold in |
| ounces, would yield |
| $2,000–$2,800 |

Thailand

| Grower |
| $5–$10 per lb |

↓

| Broker |
| $28–$38 per lb |

↓

| U.S. Wholesale |
| $2,000–$3,000 per lb |

↓

| U.S. Retail |
| $175–$225 per oz. |
| One pound, when sold in |
| ounces, would yield |
| $2,800–$3,600 |

Jamaica

Commercial Grade

| Grower |
| $60–$80 per lb |

↓

| Broker |
| $80–$100 per lb |

↓

| U.S. Wholesale |
| $1,000–$2,000 per lb |

↓

| U.S. Retail |
| $100–$175 per oz. |
| One pound, when sold in |
| ounces, would yield |
| $1,600–$2,800 |

Sinsemilla

| Grower |
| $80–$140 per lb |

↓

| Broker |
| $100–$300 per lb |

↓

| U.S. Wholesale |
| $1,500–$2,500 per lb |

↓

| U.S. Retail |
| $125–$200 per oz. |
| One pound, when sold in |
| ounces, would yield |
| $2,000–$3,200 |

Source: Drug Enforcement Administration, 1993.

Figure 7.8. Domestic Marijuana

Selling Prices for One Pound of Marijuana at Successive Levels of Trafficking

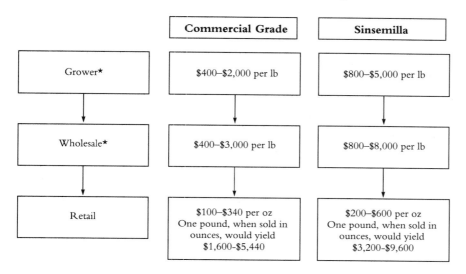

	Commercial Grade	Sinsemilla
Grower★	$400–$2,000 per lb	$800–$5,000 per lb
Wholesale★	$400–$3,000 per lb	$800–$8,000 per lb
Retail	$100–$340 per oz One pound, when sold in ounces, would yield $1,600-$5,440	$200–$600 per oz One pound, when sold in ounces, would yield $3,200-$9,600

★Grower and wholesale selling prices closely parallel
each other because growers often will act as wholesale level distributors.

Hashish

Since American cannabis users prefer marijuana,
there is limited trafficking in hashish. When
encountered, however, a pound of hashish at
the retail level sells for $1,600 to $6,000. The
probable sources of hashish available in the
United States are Pakistan/Afghanistan, Lebanon, and Morocco. (Lebanese hashish ranges in
price from $25 to $74 per kilogram in
Lebanon.)

Hashish Oil

Hashish oil is imported into the United States
generally from Jamaica for sale at the gram
level. Prices range from $35 to $55 per gram.

Source: Drug Enforcement Administration, 1992.

Horticulturalists in northern California de-leaf marijuana stalks. Domestic cultivation of the plant has grown significantly in recent years.

state that "with its long-standing history of crime and violence, no one should be surprised that the Appalachian region of Kentucky is now one of the leading marijuana-producing areas."

SYNTHETIC DRUGS

While all of the substances we have already discussed (except marijuana) are cultivated and processed outside of the United States, trafficking in synthetic drugs, products of the laboratory, is sometimes part of the business of organized crime.

Barbiturates

There are about 2,500 derivatives of barbituric acid and dozens of brand names for these derivatives. Lawfully produced barbiturates are found in tablet or capsule form. Illegal barbiturates may be found in liquid form for intravenous use since lawfully produced barbiturates are poorly soluble in water. "Barbiturates depress the sensory cortex, decrease motor activity, alter cerebralar function, and produce drowsiness, sedation, and hypnosis" (*Physicians' Desk Reference* 1987: 1163). They inhibit seizure activity and can induce unconsciousness in the form of sleep or surgical anesthesia. As opposed to opiates, barbiturates do not decrease one's sense of pain. They can produce a variety of mood alterations ranging from mild sedation to hypnosis and deep coma. A high dosage can induce anesthesia, and an overdose can be fatal. Barbiturates are used primarily as sedatives for the treatment of insomnia and as anticonvulsants (Mendelson 1980), although in some persons, they produce excitation (*Physicians' Desk Reference* 1988). The euphoria that follows barbiturate intake makes them appealing as intoxicants (Wesson and Smith 1977).

Barbiturates are classified according to the speed with which they are metabolized (broken down chemically) in the liver and eliminated by the kidneys: slow, intermediate, fast, and ultra-fast. The fast-acting forms are used to induce unconsciousness in a few minutes; the best known is sodium pentothal. At relatively high dosages they are used as anesthetics for minor surgery and to induce anaesthesia before the administration of slow-acting barbiturates. In low dosages, barbiturates may actually increase a person's reaction to painful stimuli. It is the fast-acting barbiturates, particularly Nembutal (sodium pentobarbital), Amytal (amobarbital sodium), Seconal (secobarbital sodium), and Tuinal (secobarbital sodium and amobarbital sodium combined) that are abuse risks (O'Brien and Cohen 1984).

There is no apparent pattern to the illegal market in barbiturates, and traffickers may sell them as part of their portfolio—many street dealers are "walking drug stores."

Methaqualone

Methaqualone was first synthesized in 1951 in India, where it was introduced as an antimalarial drug but found to be ineffective. At the same time its sedating effects resulted in its introduction in Great Britain as a safe, nonbarbiturate sleeping pill. The substance subsequently found its way into street abuse; a similar sequence of events occurred in Germany and Japan. In 1965, methaqualone was introduced into the United States as the prescription drugs Sopors and Quaalude. It was not listed as a scheduled (controlled) drug. By the early 1970s, "ludes" and "sopors" were part of the drug culture, and physicians overprescribed the drug for anxiety and insomnia, believing that it was safer than barbiturates. The supplies for street sales came primarily from diversions of legitimate sources.

Eight years after it was first introduced into the United States, the serious dangers of methaqualone became evident. The drug was placed on Schedule II in 1973. Although the drug is chemically unrelated to barbiturates, methaqualone intoxication is similar to barbiturate intoxication. Addiction develops rapidly, and an overdose can be fatal. However, while similar to barbiturates in its effects, methaqualone produces an even greater loss of motor coordination, which explains why it is sometimes referred to as a "wallbanger." Methaqualone is now illegally manufactured in Colombia and smuggled into the United States.

Amphetamines

"Among the commonly used psychoactive drugs," note Lester Grinspoon and Peter Hedblom (1975: 258), "the amphetamines have one of the most formidable potentials for psychological, physical, and social harm." Amphetamines are synthetic drugs, although their effects are similar to cocaine. They mimic the naturally occurring substance adrenaline and cause a biochemical arousal— being "turned on"—without the presence of sensory input that would cause such arousal. The body becomes physiologically activated, but it is a "false alarm." Because they ward off sleep, amphetamines have proven popular with college students cramming for exams and long-haul truckdrivers.

First synthesized in 1887, amphetamines were introduced into clinical use in the 1930s (Smith 1979) and eventually offered as a "cure-all" for just about every ailment. Between 1932 and 1946 there were thirty-nine generally accepted medical uses ranging from the treatment of schizophrenia and

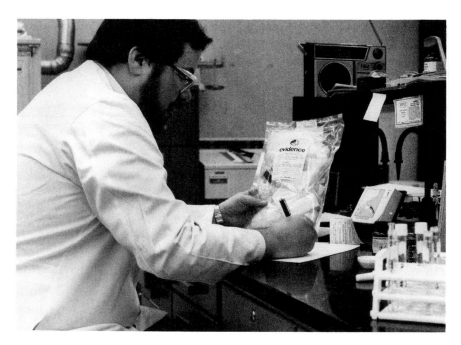

Roger Ely, a forensic chemist at the Drug Enforcement Administration laboratory in San Francisco, examines evidence obtained in a raid on a speed laboratory in Montana in 1988.

morphine addiction, to low blood pressure and caffeine and tobacco dependence. It was believed that the substance had no abuse potential (*Drug Abuse* 1987). Since amphetamines appear to act on the hypothalemus to suppress the appetite, at one time they were widely prescribed to treat obesity. As opposed to more natural forms of dieting, however, the appetite returns with greater intensity after withdrawal from the drug. Only as a "last resort" is methamphetamine hydrochloride (Desoxyn) used to treat obesity as one component of a weight-reduction regimen, and even then the treatment is limited to only a few weeks.

Legally produced amphetamine is taken in the form of tablets or capsules; some abusers crush the substance, dissolve it in water, and ingest it intravenously. Illegally produced amphetamines are often available in powdered form (called "ice") and are sometimes smoked. There are three basic types of amphetamine. Methyl-amphetamines have the greatest potential for abuse because they are fast acting and produce a "rush." Methamphetamine hydrochloride, one of the methyl group, is a widely abused drug known on the street simply as "meth"; in liquid form it is often referred to as "speed." As with cocaine, in small doses amphetamine will bring about a "rush," a sensation or euphoria often described in sexual terms, along with illusions of increased mental and sensory alertness, physical strength, and indifference to pain.

As noted in chapter 5, the distribution of amphetamines has been a main staple of outlaw bikers. In Philadelphia the Bruno crime Family, in association with the Pagan motorcycle club, were involved in the manufacture and distribution of methamphetamine. The production of amphetamines, particularly methamphetamine ("speed"), has blossomed in parts of rural America. In Texas, for example, authorities have seized more than 250 laboratories a year: "Most of the labs are located in rural areas and are reportedly set up and run by local residents. The predominant pattern for methamphetamine lab operations in the plains of West Texas and in heavily wooded East Texas is similar to the operation of small scale production and distribution of moonshine whiskey during the prohibition era; individually owned and operated, with networks of local users, but also with connections for export to urban population centers" (Spence 1989: 6). The main active ingredient in methamphetamine, phenyl-2-propanone, referred to as P2P, is widely available in Europe, and bulk shipments of P2P from Germany are often the source of illegal methamphetamine produced in the United States.

Phencyclidine (PCP)

Phencyclidine is reported to have received the name PCP—"peace pill"—on the streets of San Francisco. The drug was reputed to give illusions of everlasting peace. Frequently referred to as "angel dust," PCP was first synthesized in 1956 and found to be an effective surgical anesthetic when tested on monkeys. Experiments on humans were carried out in 1957; PCP proved to be an effective surgical anaesthetic, but there were serious side effects. Some patients experienced agitation, excitement, and disorientation during the recovery period. Some male surgical patients became violent, while some females appeared to experience simple intoxication (Linder, Lerner, and Burns 1981). "When PCP was subsequently given to normal volunteers in smaller doses, it induced a psychotic-like state resembling schizophrenia. Volunteers experienced body image changes, depersonalization, and feelings of loneliness, isolation, and dependency. Their thinking was observed to become progressively disorganized" (Lerner 1980: 14).

There are more than one hundred variations (analogs) of the substance. As opposed to other anesthetics, PCP increases respiration, heart rate, and blood pressure, qualities that make it useful for patients endangered by a depressed heart rate or low blood pressure. In the 1960s PCP became commercially available for use in veterinary medicine as an analgesic and anesthetic, but diversion to street use led the manufacturer to discontinue production in 1978. It is now produced easily and cheaply in clandestine laboratories in tablet, capsule, powder, and liquid form, and sometimes sold as LSD. Its color varies, and there is no such thing as a standard dose. As with any drug sold on the street, PCP is often mixed with other psychoactive substances. Most commonly, PCP is applied to a leafy vegetable, including marijuana, and smoked. Steven Lerner (1980: 15) notes that "street preparations of phencyclidine have continuously changed in name, physical form and purity."

A moderate amount of PCP produces a sense of detachment, distance, and estrangement from a person's surroundings within thirty to sixty minutes of ingestion; the effects last up to five hours. Numbness, slurred speech, and a loss of coordination also occurs. These symptoms are often accompanied by feelings of invulnerability. "A blank stare, rapid and involuntary eye movements, and an exaggerated gait are among the more common observable effects" ("Drugs of Abuse" 1979: 30). Users may also experience mood disorders, acute anxiety, paranoia, and violent behavior. Some reactions are similar to LSD intoxication: auditory hallucinations and image distortion similar to fun-house mirror images. "PCP is unique among popular drugs of abuse in its power to produce psychoses indistinguishable from schizophrenia" ("Drugs of Abuse" 1979: 30).

Like methamphetamine, PCP has been distributed by outlaw motorcycle clubs.

Lysergic Acid Diethylamide (LSD)

In 1949 LSD was introduced into the United States as an experimental drug for treating psychiatric illnesses, but until 1954 it remained relatively rare and expensive, since its ingredients were difficult to cultivate. In that year the Eli Lilly Company announced that they had succeeded in creating a totally synthetic version of LSD (Stevens 1987). LSD affects the body in a variety of ways. The visual effects range from blurring to a visual field filled with strange objects; three-dimensional space appears to contract and enlarge, and light appears to fluctuate in intensity. Auditory effects occur but to a lesser degree. All of these changes are episodic throughout the "trip." Temperature sensitivity is altered and the environment is perceived as being abnormally cold or hot. Body images are altered—out-of-body-experiences are common and body parts appear to float. Perceptions of time are affected; sometimes time is perceived as running rapidly forward or backward.

There are "good acid trips" and "bad acid trips"; this appears to be controlled by the attitude, mood, and expectations of the user and often depend on suggestions of others at the time of the trip. Favorable expectations produce "good trips," while excessive apprehension is likely to produce the opposite. Since the substance appears to intensify feelings, the user may feel a magnified sense of love, lust, and joy, or anger, terror, and despair: "The extraordinary sensations and feelings may bring on fear of losing control, paranoia, and panic, or they may cause euphoria and even bliss" (Grinspoon 1979: 13). Ingesting LSD unknowingly can result in a highly traumatic experience as the victim feels that he or she has suddenly "gone crazy" (Brecher 1972), and it only takes .01 milligram to have an effect. For those who knowingly ingest LSD, at this dose usually mild euphoria and a loosening of inhibitions occur (Grinspoon 1979). Illegally produced LSD may contain a variety of additives including amphetamines. Thus, laboratory studies in which volunteers ingest laboratory-produced (pure) drugs may not duplicate the experiences of street users. The addition of methamphetamine appears to increase the likelihood of a bad LSD experience (Ray 1978).

LSD is colorless, odorless and tasteless, and it is relatively easy to produce. One ounce contains about 300,000 human doses (Ray 1978). Although LSD has been used experimentally to treat a variety of psychological illnesses, it currently has no accepted medical use. It may be taken orally as a white powder, mixed with a number of other substances, or absorbed on paper ("blotter acid"), sugar, or gelatin sheets ("window panes"). A trip begins between thirty and sixty minutes after ingestion, peaks after two to six hours, and fades out after about twelve hours. There are no known physical dangers to long-term use, although psychosis has been reported in a few instances. A small number of users report recurring low-intensity trips—"flashbacks"—without ingesting the substance. Tolerance develops rapidly, and repeated doses may become completely ineffective after a few days of continuous use. Cross-tolerance to other hallucinogens also develops. LSD is not addicting—there are no physical withdrawal symptoms.

LSD was popular for a time during the 1960s, when it became part of the "hippie" culture. Current use appears limited, and distribution patterns are not well-known.

Analogs and Designer Drugs

There are many chemical variations, or analogs, of the drugs discussed in this chapter, and this has important implications for drug policy that will be discussed in chapter 10. For example, semi-synthetic opiates exist, such as hydromorphine, oxycodone, etorphine, and diprenorphine, as well as synthetic opiates such as pethidine, methadone, and propoxyphene (Darvon). The synthetic drug fentanyl citrate, which is often used intravenously in major surgery, works exactly like opiates: it kills pain, produces euphoria, and if abused leads to addiction. The substance is easily produced by persons skilled in chemistry. Fentanyl compounds are often sold as "China White," the street name for the finest Southeast Asian heroin, to addicts who cannot tell the difference. Those who know the difference may prefer fentanyl, notes Robert Roberton (1986), because it is usually cheaper than heroin, and more readily available, and some users believe it contains less adulterants than heroin. In fact, fentanyl compounds are quite potent and difficult for street dealers to cut properly, a situation that can lead to overdose and death. The newest derivative, notes Roberton (1986), 3-methyl fentanyl, is extremely potent (approximately 3,000 times as potent as morphine) and is thought to be responsible for an alarming number of recent overdose deaths in the San Francisco Bay area and in the Pittsburgh area ("Strong Synthetic Heroin Sold in Pittsburgh Area"

An assortment of paraphernalia associated with the psychedelic drug known as Ecstasy. Items include an X, a symbol of Ecstasy; a watch with an X; albums of "acid house" music; and a t-shirt that translates, "Acid house music + Ecstasy = happiness."

1988). Fentanyl has been used (illegally) to "dope" race horses since the substance is very difficult to detect in urine or blood.

Synthetic substances chemically similar to cocaine, such as lidocaine and procaine (Novocain), eliminate all feeling when applied topically—as dental patients recognize. Craig Van Dyke and Robert Byck (1982) report that single small doses of lidocaine, when taken intranasally by experienced cocaine users, produced the same euphoric response as cocaine—they could not distinguish between the two substances. Other tests indicate that laboratory animals will work as hard for procaine as they will for cocaine. Furthermore, researchers have found that their subjects could not distinguish between intravenously administered cocaine and amphetamine (Van Dyke and Byck 1982).

One analog, nicknamed "Ecstasy" (MDMA), received a great deal of public attention because of its purported ability to produce profound pleasurable effects: acute euphoria and long-lasting positive changes in attitude and self-confidence, but without the severe side effects typically associated with the analog's chemical relatives, amphetamines and mescaline. In 1985 MDMA was placed in Schedule I for control of drugs—high potential for abuse, no medically accepted use. In 1988, the *New York Times* (Foderaro 1988) reported that the drug has become quite popular among the New York nightclub set. Since the passage of the Anti-Drug Abuse Act of 1986, all analogs of controlled substances have themselves become controlled substances.

REVIEW QUESTIONS

1. Up until it was made illegal in the United States, why was opium/opiates so popular?
2. Why were attempts to produce domestic opium unsuccessful in the United States?
3. What was the real cause of the Opium Wars?
4. How did the Chinese opium problem impact on the United States?
5. What was the relationship between Chinese immigrants and the legislation against opium?
6. What was the relationship between the efforts against opiates and the Temperance Movement?
7. What was the direct cause of the passage of the Harrison Act?
8. How did the Supreme Court rule with respect to the Harrison Act?
9. How did the federal drug enforcement agency respond to the Harrison Act?
10. What are the similarities and differences between trafficking in alcohol during Prohibition and drug trafficking after the Harrison Act?
11. Why is it difficult, if not impossible, for an organized crime unit to control the drug market?
12. What elements are required to produce opium profitably?
13. What are the political elements that result in the enormous production of Golden Triangle heroin?

14. Why has it been difficult to curtail the cultivation of poppies and the manufacturing of heroin in the Golden Crescent?
15. What led to the widespread popularity of cocaine during the late 1960s and early 1970s?
16. What characteristics of the substance have made crack cocaine popular among young persons?
17. What are "designer drugs"?

8

Organized Crime in Labor and Business

"The United States has had the bloodiest and most violent labor history of any industrial nation in the world" (Taft and Ross 1969: 281). The rise of organized labor, and the subsequent reaction of American business, generated a conflict that provided fertile ground for the seeds of racketeering and organized crime. The leaders of organized crime provided mercenary armies to unions that were willing to use violence to organize workers and thwart strikebreakers. In the spirit of ideological neutrality, OC also provided private violence to business for use in its efforts against organized labor and also its dealings with the demanding competition of a capitalistic marketplace.

Barbara Newell (1961: 79) points out that an employer may be tempted into a corrupt relationship with labor unions for three reasons:

> First, he may hope that through a payment to the union officers he can persuade them not to organize his shop, thereby allowing for payment of less than the going union wage. Such an arrangement is particularly beneficial when his competitors are organized. Second, if he cannot stifle organization, he may at least be able to get a lenient "sweetheart" agreement with the union. Third, even if he cannot stop effective organization of his work force, the union itself can be used for the benefit of the employer through the limitation of competition. Competition can be limited by the union in several ways—either through the refusal to work on goods or by directly enforcing price agreements.

The employer may not have much of a choice. In 1992 it was revealed that members of the Bonanno Family threatened to disrupt operations of a major newspaper delivery company unless they were placed on the payroll. Like perishable products, daily newspapers have a limited shelf life, and delays in delivery can be quite costly. The "ghost employees" earned as much as $50,000 a year, each without ever going to work (Raab 1992a).

"Labor racketeering," notes the President's Commission on Organized

Crime (1986b: 9), "is the infiltration, domination, and use of a union for personal benefit by illegal, violent, and fraudulent means." Ronald Goldstock points out that the "sometimes bewildering array of labor rackets assume three basic forms: the sale of 'strike insurance' in which the union threatens a walkout and the employer pays to assure a steady supply of labor; the 'sweetheart deal' in which management pays the labor representative for contract terms unobtainable through arm's-length bargaining; and the direct or indirect siphoning of union funds" (PCOC 1985b: 658). Although labor racketeering can be conducted by anyone, the history of the labor movement shows that the most substantial corruption of unions is conducted by organized crime Families and syndicates.

ORGANIZED LABOR IN AMERICA

The Civil War led to the dramatic industrialization of America. War profiteers accumulated large amounts of capital enabling them to invest in the trusts: oil, coal, iron, steel, sugar, and railroads. Congress imposed protective tariffs and industry blossomed during the *Gilded Age* of the Robber Barons (discussed in chapter 2). "Within twenty-five years of the assassination of Abraham Lincoln," notes Thomas Brooks (1971: 39), "America had become the leading manufacturing nation in the world."

At the bottom of this industrial world was labor, which consisted of immigrants who spoke English with foreign accents, if they spoke English at all. Children of both sexes often labored twelve hours a day, six days a week, under conditions that threatened life and limb. Labor's struggle for better working conditions and wages resulted in what Sidney Lens calls *The Labor Wars* (1974: 4):

> The labor wars were a specific response to a specific set of injustices at a time when industrial and financial capitalism was establishing its predominance over American society. In a sense the battles were not different from the hundreds of other violent clashes against social injustices, as normal as the proverbial apple pie in the nation's annals.

During the first half of the nineteenth century until the Civil War, criminal conspiracy statutes were used against labor's efforts to organize and strike. This approach was replaced by the use of equity—a civil procedure—in the form of injunctions restraining unions from striking. The unions sought relief from Congress, but in 1908 the Supreme Court declared that Congress had no power with respect to union activities (*Adair v. United States* 208 U.S. 161). It was not until the Great Depression that Congress stripped the federal courts of their power to issue injunctions in labor disputes (1932 Norris-La Guardia Act). In 1935, the Wagner Act (National Labor Relations Act) gave explicit protection to the rights of workers to organize and engage in collective bargaining.

From the earliest days of our republic until the passage of the Wagner Act, labor's confrontations with employers often took on a particular scenario: company spies, often from the Pinkerton Private Detective Agency, would identify union leaders, who were then fired by management. The guard force would be increased and strikebreakers secured. Company lawyers would secure injunctions from friendly judges prohibiting a strike. The union would organize "flying squadrons" to guard against the influx of strikebreakers and plan for mass picketing. If the guard force proved inadequate, hired thugs, deputy sheriffs, policemen, National Guard, and even U.S. Army troops would be used to deal with strikers.

Labor Racketeering

In order to avoid the problem of company spies reporting to management, some unions employed the "walking delegate" or business agent, who was empowered to call a strike without any formal vote by the union membership. As an employee of the union, he was immune from management intimidation, and enabled the union to strike quickly and at the most opportune time. The men chosen for this position were usually tough, and it was this quality rather than intelligence, integrity, and commitment to labor that characterized business agents. Before long some of these men began abusing their power, calling needless strikes and engaging in extortionate practices (Seidman 1938). In 1928, for example, two racketeers set up the United Lathing Company and hired the Lathers Union walking delegate. He would appear at job sites and issue a strike order. When contractors asked for an explanation, he would refer them to the United Lathing Company where, for a fee, the strike would be called off (Nelli 1976). These type of racketeers, notes Newell (1961), intimidated union members but were usually not connected with a syndicate.

In the early days, labor unions provided their own "muscle" from the ranks of their membership to deal with Pinkerton agents and strikebreakers. In the first decade of the twentieth century, however, a need arose for a more systematic and professional approach. Enter Benjamin Fein (known as "Dopey Benny"—an adenoidal condition made him look sleepy). Fein became an integral part of the Jewish labor movement, notes Jenna Joselit (1983: 109). Whenever a strike was called under the auspices of the umbrella organization called United Hebrew Trades (UHT), "Dopey and his men were given union cards as pickets and union delegates." They protected fellow pickets against management goons—strongarm personnel who were employed by licensed detective agencies. Fein formed alliances with New York street gangs such as the Hudson Dusters, assigning territories and working out businesslike arrangements and patterns of operation. He also assisted the union in keeping its members in line. It soon became clear, however, that it was easier to hire gangsters than it was to fire them (Seidman 1938). Racketeers such as Lepke Buchalter and Gurrah Shapiro came to dominate many of the industries into which they were invited (see chapter 3). "The introduction of armed hoods as

FULTON FISH MARKET

At age fourteen, Joseph ("Socks") Lanza began working as a fish handler at the giant wholesale market on Fulton Street in lower Manhattan (which today handles close to 100 million pounds of seafood a year). He became a member of the crime Family of Lucky Luciano (now known as the Genovese Family), and in 1923 organized his fellow workers into Local 359 of the United Seafood Worker's Union. Because of the perishable nature of the product, seafood wholesalers depend on speed for display and delivery, which makes them vulnerable to threats of delay. As head of the local, and a *caporegime* in the Genovese Family, Lanza extorted money from every dealer in the market: "Lanza influenced the price of fish not only in New York but throughout much of the nation. The union served as the principal basis of Lanza's $20-million-a-year-racket" (Nelli 1976: 245). He and his brother Nunzio ("Harry") Lanza, also a Genovese captain, determined which businesses could operate in the market. Through his leadership of the union, Lanza asserted control over fishing boats—he could withhold the labor needed to unload the vessels. He also controlled the Fulton Market's Watchmen's Protective Association: "Dealers who visited the market and failed to have a Lanza watchman look after their vehicles usually found their tires slashed" (Peterson 1983a: 173).

Lanza was convicted of racketeering in 1938 (Carroll 1991). In 1943, he was convicted of extortion involving local Teamster union officials. Paroled in 1950, he was arrested as a parole violator seven years later in a case that touched off a scandal. New York State parole officers recommended returning Lanza to prison as a major racketeer, but the parole board member in charge of his case released the "Fish Market Czar." A subsequent investigation revealed that high-level political pressure had led to the release decision.

The parole board subsequently overruled the decision, and Lanza was returned to prison to finish out his unexpired term.

Lanza continued to control the Fulton Market until his death in 1968 (Nelli 1976). Domination of the market then passed into other hands, but the Genovese Family remained firmly in control. Despite the fact that the market operates on city property, government controls remain absent, creating a lawless atmosphere in which rules of operation were carved through violence and intimidation—an ideal atmosphere for organized crime (Carroll 1991). In 1988, as a result of a civil action brought by the U.S. Department of Justice, an outside administrator was appointed to monitor the market and rid it of illegal activities—U.S. Attorney Rudolph Giuliani convinced a federal judge that the market was dominated by the Genovese Family (Glaberson 1989). Two years later, however, the administrator stated that the market continues to operate "in a frontier atmosphere, in that the Fulton Fish Market is a sovereign entity where the laws of economic power and physical force, not the laws of New York City, prevail" (Raab 1990).

Sources: Humbert S. Nelli, *The Business of Crime*. New York: Oxford University Press, 1976; Virgil Peterson, *The Mob: 200 Years of Organized Crime in New York*. Ottawa, Il: Green Hill Publishers, 1983; Brian Carroll, "Combatting Racketeering in the Fulton Fish Market." In *Organized Crime and Its Containment*, edited by Cyrelle Fijnaut and James Jacobs. Deventer, Netherlands: Kluwer, 1991; Selwyn Raab, "Racketeering Held to Persist at New York's Fish Market," *New York Times*, August 9, 1990: B12.

'finks' (strikebreakers) or as 'nobles' (armed guards) by industry," notes Thomas Brooks (1971: 147), "facilitated the entry of the Arnold Rothsteins and Capones into the lucrative business of industrial racketeering."

When Max Bloch tried to organize a union, the Wholesale Butcher Drivers, and called a strike, he found himself meeting with some fearsome representatives of the meat packing houses: Harry ("Pittsburgh Phil") Strauss and his fellow partners in Murder, Inc. "Max the Butcher's" background as an ex-con and professional boxer allowed him to "sweet talk" the "Boys from Brooklyn," and he was left alone. "So the wholesalers couldn't break the strike. They'd gone to the toughest and lost. They saw they couldn't shake us, that nobody would go against us" (Bloch and Kenner 1982: 72). George McLane, the business agent for the Chicago local of the Bartenders International League (which later merged with the Hotel and Restaurant Employees Union), was not so lucky. In 1939, representatives of the Capone syndicate ordered him to step aside and appoint one of their men to the local's presidency: "McLane returned to his office and, after consultation with the other officers of the local, it was decided that McLane's life was worth more than resisting the syndicate." He resigned (Newell 1961: 87). James Neff (1989: 20) points out that labor racketeers "didn't target steel mills and auto factories and foundries, the giant pool of workers who truly needed the protection of a collective bargaining agreement." Instead, they "picked on small, vulnerable mom-and-pop operations such as dry cleaners, taverns, and bakeries."

Unions fought not only with management but also each other. In 1938, a number of industrial unions led by John L. Lewis broke with the American Federation of Labor (AFL) and formed the Congress of Industrial Organizations (CIO). During struggles over jurisdiction and representation between the AFL and the CIO, both sides resorted to "muscle" from organized crime. But whether labor or business, for whatever reason, whoever utilized OC was literally "playing with the devil." Many locals and some internationals were delivered into the hands of organized crime. Forty years later, a congressional committee concluded (Permanent Subcommittee on Investigations 1982: 5):

> At least four international unions are completely dominated by men who either have strong ties or are members of the organized crime syndicate. A majority of the locals in most major cities of the United States in the International Brotherhood of Teamsters (IBT), Hotel and Restaurant Employees Union (HRE), Laborers International Union of North America (Laborers), and International Longshoremen's Association (ILA) are completely dominated by organized crime.

Laborers International Union

Formed in 1903, the Laborers International Union of North America (LIUNA) is one of fifteen unions that belong to the Building Construction Trades Department of the AFL-CIO. It represents over 400,000 laborers in more than eight hundred locals in the United States and Canada. Members perform the dirtiest, most strenuous, and most dangerous work associated with building construction. Control over laborers provides control over many construction sites. Michael Kilian (Kilian et al. 1979: 247) notes that the Laborers Union

> is classic Chicago old-time unionism. It was headed for years by Peter Fosco,[1] an Italian immigrant whose association with Capone-era hoodlums did not prevent him from winning public office and once earning an Italian-American award at a dinner addressed by Richard Nixon.... The Laborers Union has always had a healthy treasury, kept brimming with hard-working workers' dues.

In Chicago, members of the Outfit have held important positions in the Laborers Union including Vincent Solano, president of Local 1 (until his death from natural causes in 1992), and Alfred Pilotta, president of Local 5 (until he was convicted in 1982 for his role in a kickback scheme involving the union's welfare benefit fund). Since 1981, the Chicago District Council of the Laborer's Union had been headed by Ernest Kumerow, who is married to the daughter of Tony Accardo. Until his death in 1992, Accardo spent winters in a coachhouse in the rear of Kumerow's home. In 1992, Dominick Palermo, age seventy-four, a veteran LIUNA official and Outfit boss in charge of the southern suburbs, was sentenced to thirty-two years for extorting money from bookmakers in northwest Indiana. A codefendant, Nick Guzzino, age fifty, a Laborer's Union field representative, received thirty-six years (Jackson 1990; O'Brien 1992).

In New York, several LIUNA locals are associated with "specific members of specific crime families operating in New York City; that [sic] Local 95 of the Laborers' is owned by Vincent, 'Vinnie the Chin,' Giganti [sic] of the Genovese family; that Local 1298 is owned by Paul Vario, a capo of the Lucchese family; that Local 731 is owned by Christopher Fornari, consigliere of the Lucchese family; Blasters Local 29 is owned and belongs to Samuel Cavalieri of the Lucchese family; Local 18-A of the Laborers in New York City is owned by Vinnie DiNapoli, a member of the Lucchese crime family" (PCOC 1985b: 75). The DeCavalcante Tapes[2] contain conversations involving New Jersey Family boss Sam DeCavalcante, during which he discussed how control of Laborers Union locals enabled him to "shake down" building contractors who wanted to avoid using expensive union labor.

---

1. Peter Fosco was succeeded by his son Angelo in 1975. Angelo was acquitted of union corruption charges and remained president of the LIUNA until his death in 1993 at age seventy-one.

2. During the 1960s, the FBI bugged the office of Sam ("The Plumber") DeCavalcante (sometimes spelled de Cavalcante), boss of a small New Jersey crime Family, for almost four years. On June 10, 1969, as a result of DeCavalcante's trial, some of the results of the bugging were made public. Known as the "DeCavalcante Tapes," the material is actually a document based on transcripts of conversations overheard by four microphones and summarized by FBI agents, with some verbatim transcriptions.

Hotel Employees and Restaurant Employees International Union (HEREIU)

The Hotel Employees and Restaurant Employees International Union was established in Chicago in 1891 (Permanent Subcommittee on Investigations 1982: 4):

> At first, only workers from pubs and restaurants were represented. Yet as America's cities began to grow, so did the international, and soon hotel workers as well as food and beverage workers were represented. Thwarted only by Prohibition in the 1920s, the international became the fastest growing union in the United States in the 1930s. By 1941, the international was the seventh largest union in North America.
>
> Today the international is the largest service union in the United States. Approximately 235 locals from 48 states and 8 provinces in Canada are affiliated with the international.

HEREIU charters often provided the basis for extortion from restaurants in Chicago, as U.S. Senator John L. McClellen explained (1962: 141–42):

> If an owner knew what was good for him, he agreed to have his place unionized upon the first visit of the organizer. The workers were not consulted in this organizing drive; they rarely knew it was going on. The restaurant owner was told that the union wasn't greedy, a compromise figure would always be accepted. If the owner had forty employees, then twenty memberships would be given to the union. The owner paid the initiation fees and the dues for twenty names that he gave the organizer. That arrangement usually continued for years. It didn't make any difference to anyone concerned in the deal that, after a period of time, possibly ten or more of the twenty union members may no longer be employees. . . . Dues continued to be collected for twenty names.

In return, there "were not sudden fires in the middle of the night, no beatings, no sugar poured into gas tanks, no tires slashed, no vandalism" (1962: 142). The restaurant owners did not have to worry about workers' salaries or working conditions, conditions of employment that are the concerns of legitimate unions.

Many of the HEREIU locals are reputed to be under the domination of organized crime. In 1935, for example, Local 450 in Chicago was chartered by Joey ("Doves") Aiuppa, a top leader of the Outfit. For forty years, the Outfit wielded power in the Chicago-area HEREIU locals and joint executive board. "Their actions took on national proportions when Edward Hanley, who began his career in Local 450 as a business agent in 1957, was elected to the HEREIU presidency in 1973" (PCOC 1986b: 73). In Chicago, the union has made significant political contributions.

Local 54 in New Jersey has about 15,000 members, most of whom are employed in the Atlantic City casino business. The local is reputedly controlled by the Philadelphia crime Family once headed by Angelo Bruno. As a result, Family members were able to force hotels in Atlantic City to buy supplies and provisions from companies they owned. In 1980, when the president of the Philadelphia Roofers Union Local 30 attempted to organize bartenders in Atlantic City away from Local 54, he was murdered at his home. Two union officials were convicted of ordering the murder and are serving life sentences. In 1981, the New Jersey Casino Control Commission concluded that Local 54 was controlled by Philadelphia crime boss Nicky Scarfo, and their legal action eventually forced the local's president to resign.

In New York, Locals 6 and 100 have been under the control of organized crime:

> HEREIU Locals 6 and 100 were used to dictate the way in which restaurants could do business in New York. In return for payoffs, restaurant owners could pay reduced wages and pension and welfare fund contributions, or buy a lease on a restaurant shut down because it owed money to the union, or hire and fire without regard to grievance procedures, or operate without regard to union work rules. (PCOC 1986b: 83–84)

At one point, there appeared to be a jurisdictional dispute between the two locals, something that is not unusual in organized labor. However, intercepted conversations between union officials and important OC figures revealed that the split was in fact, "a market allocation of New York's entire restaurant business between the Colombo and Gambino crime families" (PCOC 1986b: 84).

International Longshoremen's Association (ILA)

New York City's premier position as a commercial capital is due in large part to its deep water harbor, the finest in North America. The New York waterfront encompasses over 700 miles of wharves and shoreline and 1,900 piers. With government regulation absent, organized crime was able to assert control over this lucrative piece of geography.

With the able assistance of men such as Antonio Vaccarelli, better known as Paul Kelly, leader of the notorious Five Points Gang (discussed in chapter 3), the ILA was organized in the 1890s and gained complete control over the waterfront by 1914 (Nelli 1976). Before assuming his position as a vice president of the ILA, Kelly organized the ragpickers and served as their business agent and walking delegate, a position he used to extort money from real estate and property agents. Until the twentieth century, about 95 percent of the longshoremen in the New York City area were Irish. By 1912, Italians comprised about 35 percent, and by 1919 they accounted for about 75 percent of the area's longshoremen. The Irish controlled the notoriously violent West Side ("Hell's Kitchen") docks, while the Italians dominated the East Side, Brooklyn, and New Jersey docks.

For poorly educated and often illiterate immigrants, the waterfront provided attractive employment opportunities. It was also attractive to racketeers for its lucrative illegal opportunities. The "shape up," vividly portrayed in the

HARRY BRIDGES

Harry Bridges addresses longshoremen at a union meeting in 1965 in San Francisco.

On the West Coast, Australian-born Alfred Reuton ("Harry") Bridges withdrew from the ILA and organized the International Longshoremen and Warehousemen's Union (ILWU), which became part of the rival CIO. Bridges was born in 1901 and came to the United States as a merchant seaman in 1920. He went to work as a longshoreman in San Francisco. He reactivated a dormant ILA local in 1933 and led a successful strike in 1934, a strike that was opposed by ILA president Joe Ryan. Ryan attacked Bridges for his leftist views and close association with Communists (Lens 1974). During the 1940s, the House of Representative voted to have Bridges deported as an undesirable alien, an order that was overturned by the Supreme Court. In marked contrast to the ILA,

always a strongly anti-Communist union, the ILWU has been free of OC influence. Nevertheless, the ILWU was expelled from the CIO in 1950 for "following the Communist line." A variety of unions, including the Teamsters, unsuccessfully attempted to raid the ILWU membership (Kimeldorf 1988). Bridges headed the ILWU until his retirement in 1977. He died in 1990 (Saxon 1990).

Sources: Sidney Lens, *The Labor Wars*. Garden City, NY: Doubleday, 1974; Howard Kimeldorf, *Reds or Rackets? The Making of Radical and Conservative Unions on the Waterfront*. Berkeley, CA: University of California Press, 1988; Wolfgang Saxon, "Harry Bridges, Docks Leader, Dies at 88." *New York Times*, March 31, 1990: 11.

Academy Award-winning film *On the Waterfront*, provided corrupt officials with kickbacks from workers eager for a day's wage. Loansharking, large-scale pilfering, smuggling, and deals with employers eager for "labor peace" profited the criminals who dominated the waterfront. The President's Commission notes that the "necessity for speed, plus the lack of rail connections to the piers, gave rise to the coveted 'loading' racket, which involved moving cargo from the pier floor to waiting trucks. Since demand for cargo loading was inelastic and dependent upon immediate need when ships arrived, loading generated extraordinary profits, and was a principal incentive for organized crime to infiltrate the ILA" (1986b: 33). Whoever controls waterfront labor controls the waterfront.

While Paul Kelly led an influx of criminals to the waterfront, it was under Joseph P. Ryan that OC control of the waterfront became complete (Nelli 1976). Ryan—a strident anti-Communist—served as ILA president from 1927 to 1953.

"Once in control of the union," notes the President's Commission (1986b: 34–35), "the underworld found the shipping industry an attractive and easy target for the more traditional types of racketeering."

When a ship docks, it must be emptied quickly. The cargo may include perishable foodstuffs, and in any event, the owner gathers no return for his capital investment—the ship—while it is in port. Ship "turnaround" time is thus a crucial key to profitability. Besides direct evidence that individual pier bosses regularly shook down shippers by threatening walkouts, a pattern of payoffs at higher levels was suggested in 1948 when the international sanctioned a strike for the first time.

Time pressures also encouraged owners to maintain an oversupply of labor so that all ships, even on the busiest days, could be unloaded at once. The lucrative and commonly used "kick-back" racket also arose from time pressures. Because the number of ship arrivals fluctuated, the hiring boss (usually a union officer) selected the necessary number of workers from the surplus of men at the daily "shape up." The criterion for selection on many piers was the willingness, evidenced by a pre-arranged signal, such as a toothpick by the ear, to "kick-back" a part of the day's wages to the boss.

Other traditional rackets ran rampant on the ILA-controlled waterfront: gambling, loansharking, and cargo theft. OC-corrupted port employees provided "access to cargo shipments and storage areas, security for the movement of contraband, such as narcotics, falsification of invoices and shipping documents in insurance scams, and collusion in the expropriation of stolen property, such as luxury vehicles and construction equipment" (PCOC 1986b: 35).

On September 23, 1953, the AFL convention voted to revoke the ILA charter because of rampant corruption. In November, under indictment for misappropriating union funds, Ryan stepped down as president and was given a $10,000 annual pension. William V. Bradley was elected president. The AFL unsuccessfully attempted to wrest control of longshoremen from the ILA by setting up a rival union, the International Brotherhood of Longshoremen (IBL). In 1955, the AFL and CIO merged into the AFL-CIO. In 1959, after a series of often physical battles between the rival longshoremen's unions, the IBL and ILA were merged. Shortly afterward the ILA was admitted to the AFL-CIO. Bradley apparently failed to cooperate with OC, and taped conversations between leading waterfront racketeers indicate he "was visited by mob members who told him he'd have to give up his position to Teddy Gleason or he'd be killed" (Permanent Subcommittee on Investigations 1981b: 447). On July 17, 1963, after Bradley declined to run for reelection, Thomas W. ("Teddy") Gleason was unanimously elected president of the ILA. Gleason held the post until his retirement in 1987; he stepped down from leadership of the 110,000-member union at age eighty-seven because of poor health. (Gleason died of natural causes in 1992.) Without any opposition, the post went to his associate and ILA executive vice president, John Bowers.

In 1952 it was revealed that organized crime, using its control of the ILA, "had for years been levying the equivalent of a 5 percent tax on all general cargo moving in and out of the harbor" (Goddard 1980: 35). The outrage that was generated led to the establishment of the Waterfront Commission. In 1953, the states of New York and New Jersey passed legislation creating a bistate Waterfront Commission, which won the approval of Congress. The authorizing legislation was signed by President Dwight D. Eisenhower on August 12, 1953. The commission was empowered to license stevedoring concerns and regulate waterfront employees. Those with serious criminal records were banned from the docks. The commission was given subpoena power and investigative authority in New York and New Jersey. Thus began the movement to "clean up" the New York–New Jersey waterfront, an effort aided by federal investigations into the ILA. In 1953, Michael Clemente, president of ILA Local 856 in Manhattan and a member of the Genovese Family, was convicted of extorting money from waterfront employers and perjury before the New York State Crime Commission (PCOC 1986b).

Upon his release from prison, however, Clemente resumed his control of the Manhattan waterfront. Another Genovese Family member, Tino Fiumara, exercised similar control on the New Jersey side. In 1963, Anthony Scotto took over Local 1814 in Redhook, Brooklyn, when his father-in-law, Anthony ("Tough Tony") Anastasio, a member of the Gambino Family and brother of Albert Anastasia, died of natural causes. Scotto is reputed to be a *caporegime* in the Gambino crime Family.

As a result of more stringent law enforcement efforts in the port of New York and New Jersey, notes Donald Goddard (1980: 66), the ILA racketeers moved operations to Florida where they plundered the booming Port of Miami. The shape up was abolished by the Waterfront Commission in New York–New Jersey. The ILA shifted from exploiting its 90,000 members to "carving up the cargo traffic among the port's stevedores and 'taxing' them on their shares." The

ILA used its domination of the port to establish a system whereby competition among stevedoring companies (who hired longshoremen to unload ships) and other waterfront firms was significantly reduced. Goddard points out that shipowners, agents, stevedores, contractors, and service companies were caught up in a web of corrupt practices with the ILA—and few wanted to escape. "They only had to pay their 'rent' in order to enrich themselves with guaranteed profits." Then-special agent (now director) of the FBI Louis J. Freeh noted before a congressional committee (Permanent Subcommittee on Investigations 1981b: 183):

> You do not have extortion, you do not have threats, you do not have violence. What you have is a businessman who is as corrupt as the ILA official who he pays looking for additional business, looking for an advantage against his competitors and using his organized crime connection . . . to have that union official contact another businessman to extend an economic advantage.

The FBI's UNIRAC investigation (1975–79) was accomplished with the help of stevedore Joe Teitelbaum, who was approached by ILA officials for a $3,000 payoff as a down payment for continued business in Miami. When he declined to pay, shipping clients began to receive calls from the union officials indicating the stevedore was having labor problems and longshoremen could not be guaranteed when their cargo needed offloading in Miami. Teitelbaum went to the FBI and served in an undercover capacity. The investigation resulted in 117 convictions, including that of Tino Fiumara, Michael Clemente, and Anthony Scotto. (This did not stop Governor Hugh Carey, former mayors Robert Wagner and John Lindsey, and AFL-CIO Secretary-Treasurer Lane Kirkland from acting as character witnesses at Scotto's trial.)

The investigation revealed that ports along the East Coast from New York to Florida had been divided between the Genovese and Gambino Families into spheres of interest. Scotto and the others were convicted of a number of corrupt practices including:

1. Payoffs in lieu of employer contributions to ILA pension and welfare plans.
2. Payoffs to secure "labor peace" and avoid adhering to costly ILA rules that amounted to "featherbedding."
3. Payoffs by businessmen to secure union contracts that were necessary to qualify for maritime work in ports under ILA control.
4. Payoffs to help firms secure new business and to keep the business they had without competitive bidding.

The relationship between racketeers and employers has frequently been mutually beneficial: "convicted union officers have gone back to the ports working for industries closely associated with the port, thus enabling them to circumvent the provisions of the Landrum-Griffin Act" that bars them from holding union office (PCOC 1986b: 44). The President's Commission reports that despite the success of the FBI's UNIRAC investigation, there are still ILA locals in New York, New Jersey, and Miami under the control of the Genovese and Gambino Families, and "the Gambino family controls the international union" (1986b: 47). At the end of 1991, as the result of a federal RICO lawsuit (discussed in chapter 9), the top officers of Local 1814 agreed to step aside in favor of a government-appointed monitor.

International Brotherhood of Teamsters (IBT)

The IBT is the largest labor union in the United States, representing more than 1.5 million workers. In 1899, the Team Drivers International Union, headquartered in Detroit, received a charter from the AFL for its membership of 1,200 drivers. In 1902, Chicago members of the Team Drivers established a rival Teamsters National Union with 18,000 horse handlers. The following year Samuel Gompers, president of the AFL, arranged for a merger of the two, which became the IBT. The union was marked by violence from its very inception. When the Teamsters went on strike, the public suffered and therefore supported efforts against the drivers. Allen Friedman, IBT vice president and former strong-arm for the union, reports:

> [The Teamsters'] answer was to fight back, sending their own men to do battle with baseball bats, knives, guns, blackjacks, and any other weapon they owned or could make. They also teamed up with local gangsters who enjoyed being paid to break heads for either side.
>
> It was the influx of neighborhood gangsters that marked a major change in the Teamsters. Suddenly there were men involved who had neither loyalty nor ideology. They began changing the face of organized labor in many communities, taking control and becoming extortionists. (Friedman and Schwartz 1989: 9)

Although the Teamsters remained a relatively weak union, by 1933 they had about 125,000 members who were concentrated in industrial centers such as Detroit and Chicago. In 1907, Dan Tobin became IBT president and served without major scandal until 1952. He was succeeded by Dave Beck of Seattle, who controlled the Western Conference of Teamsters. Because of the support he received from Jimmy Hoffa, head of the Teamsters in Detroit, Beck awarded Hoffa with an IBT vice presidency. In 1957, Beck was convicted of embezzling union funds and income-tax violations and sentenced to five years imprisonment. At the 1957 IBT convention in Miami, James R. Hoffa, who had been accused of dozens of improper activities by the McClellan Committee,[3] was elected

---

3. The Senate Select Committee on Improper Activities in the Labor Management Field was established on January 31, 1957. A select committee is one appointed by the Senate to perform a particular task for a specific period of time. It goes out of existence when the task has been performed. After the Select Committee went out of existence, however, Senator McClellan continued Senate investigations into organized crime through his position as chairman of the Permanent Subcommittee on Investigations.

president. That same year the IBT was expelled from the AFL-CIO (Moldea 1978). In 1987, the AFL-CIO readmitted the 1.6 million member IBT to its ranks. At the time, the Teamsters were struggling against a Justice Department effort to place the international under the control of a court-appointed trustee under provisions of the Racketeer Influenced and Corrupt Organizations (RICO) statute.

Jimmy Hoffa

James Riddle Hoffa was born in Brazil, Indiana, on February 14, 1913, and moved to Detroit with his family in 1924. A high school dropout, Hoffa eventually became a warehouse worker and developed a reputation as a tough street fighter who always stood up for his fellow workers against management. Because of this, Hoffa was fired from his warehouse job. He was hired as an organizer for Local 299 of the IBT, a troubled local—misuse of funds, rigged elections—that had to be taken into receivership by the international. He and other IBT organizers battled management goons in their organizing efforts throughout Detroit. He also used OC connections to shake down an association of small grocery stores, leading to his first criminal conviction, for which Hoffa paid a fine. After he had risen to a leadership position in Local 299, Hoffa continued to work with OC in Detroit. For example, he used the threat of labor trouble to force businesses to use a mob-controlled overalls supply firm (Friedman and Schwarz 1989).

In 1941, Hoffa found himself in a battle with the CIO that began a "raid" to represent Detroit teamsters. The CIO action was backed by a small army of goons, and the IBT was literally being beaten in the streets of Detroit. Hoffa turned to his friends in the Detroit underworld and secured the assistance of the powerful Meli crime Family. Dan Moldea (1978: 38) notes: "The CIO raiders were defeated by the end of the year. And considering the new players on Hoffa's team, it was a miracle that the CIO survived at all in Detroit." Moldea (1978: 38) states that the victory was not without cost:

> The CIO's defeat, brought about by Hoffa's ringers, became the major factor in his rapid plunge from union reformer to labor racketeer. His pact with the underworld, no matter how tenuous at the time, took him out of the running as a potentially great leader of the Teamsters' rank and file.

Hoffa's road to power and the presidency of the IBT was strewn with scandal, for example, his alliance with Anthony ("Tony Pro") Provenzano:

> The Hoffa-Provenzano alliance was typical of the bargains Hoffa struck with gangsters around the country; they helped push him to the top, and he helped them use their union posts for a series of money-making schemes: extortion from employers, loan-sharking, pension-fund frauds, and anything else that control of union muscle and money offered. (Brill 1978: 125)

Tony Provenzano

Born in 1917, Anthony ("Tony Pro") Provenzano was one of six sons of Sicilian immigrants living on the lower East Side of New York. He dropped out of school at age fifteen (some sources indicate it was at age seventeen) to become a truck helper and later a driver in Hackensack, New Jersey. He had aspirations of becoming a professional boxer. His reputation for violence brought him to the attention of a next-door neighbor. Anthony ("Tony Bender") Strollo (b. 1899) was a *caporegime* in the Genovese Family and a powerful waterfront racketeer. As a result of Bender's patronage, Provenzano became a member of the Genovese Family and an organizer for IBT Local 560 in New Jersey. By 1941, Provenzano was a shop steward. In 1959, with the help of Jimmy Hoffa, Provenzano was elected president of the local. In 1960, Hoffa appointed Provenzano to fill a vacancy among IBT vice presidents. He also rose in the ranks of the Genovese Family, reportedly becoming a *caporegime* (McFadden 1988).

By 1963, Provenzano's union salaries totalled $113,000—at the time he was the highest paid union official in the world. That same year he was convicted of extorting $17,000 from the Dorn Trucking Company to end a discipline problem the firm was having with its union employees. During the four-and-a-half years he was in prison, and for the five years he was disqualified from holding union office (as per the 1959 Landrum-Griffin Act), his brothers Salvatore ("Sammy") and Nunzio headed the local, while Tony ran its affairs. Opponents of the Provenzanos in the union found themselves subjected to threats, beatings, or (in at least two instances) murder. In 1961 a rival, Anthony Castellito, was beaten and garroted with piano wire by mob executioners led by ex-heavyweight fighter Harold ("Kayo") Konigsberg. In 1963, another Provenzano rival was shot to death in Hoboken, New Jersey. In 1978, Tony Pro was convicted of the 1961 Castellio slaying and received a twenty-year sentence. There were additional convictions for racketeering in 1978 and 1979.

In 1981, Nunzio Provenzano, president of Local 560, was sentenced to ten years imprisonment. He was convicted on April 30 of accepting $187,000 from four interstate trucking companies to ensure "labor peace," and he permitted the companies to avoid contract rules for hiring Local 560 drivers. Brother "Sammy Pro" became president of Local 560. In 1984, Sammy Pro went to prison, and a close Provenzano aide, Michael Sciarra, became interim president; Josephine Provenzano, Tony Pro's daughter, became the secretary-treasurer at a salary of $71,000. That same year, the federal government invoked the civil racketeering provision of the Racketeering and Corrupt Organizations statute, and a federal judge in New Jersey removed Local 560's executive board and put the local into trusteeship "until such time as the membership can freely nominate and elect new officers" (PCOC 1986b: 123).

After more than two years under government trusteeship, the 7,800 members of Local 560 voted in the local's first contested election in twenty-five years. Michael Sciarra was barred from seeking his former position as the local's president after a federal judge released tapes indicating that Matthew

("Matty the Horse") Ianiello, a *caporegime* in the Genovese Family, wanted Sciarra to head the local. On December 7, 1988, the mailed ballots were counted and Danny Sciarra—running as a surrogate for his brother Michael— won by a vote of 2,842 to 1,535 (Sullivan 1988). On December 12, 1988, at age seventy-one, Anthony Provenzano died of a heart attack in a California hospital near the federal prison where he was incarcerated.

John Dioguardi and Anthony Corallo

Elections were scheduled to be held in 1956 to choose officers for the IBT's Joint Council 16 in New York City. If Jimmy Hoffa could affect the outcome of the Joint Council 16 elections, it would enable him to win control of the IBT presidency. Accordingly, in 1955, Hoffa had seven new Teamster charters issued to his friend John ("Johnny Dio") Dioguardi. Born on the Lower East Side on April 29, 1914, Dioguardi was the nephew of James Plumeri (better known as "Jimmy Doyle"), a *caporegime* in the Lucchese Family; Dioguardi became a member of that crime Family. He was first convicted in 1937 for extorting money from the trucking industry. In 1956 Dioguardi was indicted for the acid-throwing attack that blinded labor columnist Victor Reisel; the charges were dropped when a witness refused to testify. In 1967 Dioguardi received a five-year sentence for bankruptcy fraud ("scam"); when he finished that term he was convicted for stock fraud involving a car-leasing company. Johnny Dio died in prison on January 14, 1979 (Kihss 1979).

Along with Anthony ("Tony Ducks") Corallo, Dioguardi filled the IBT locals for which he had new charters with a number of gangsters who could then vote in the 1956 union election. Five of the seven locals did not have a single legitimate member—they were "paper locals." Corallo had already gained control of five other Teamster locals, although he held office in only one, Local 239; the president, Sam Goldstein, took orders from Corallo. Dioguardi and Corallo brought into the newly chartered locals forty men with an aggregate record of 178 arrests and seventy convictions. Corallo was described by Robert F. Kennedy (1960: 84) as "an underworld figure of great influence whose unusual nickname stems from his reputation for 'ducking' convictions in court cases in which he is arrested. Tony Ducks, whose police record includes drug and robbery charges and who is on the Treasury Department's narcotic list, lost only one bout with the law. In 1941 he was sentenced to six months for unlawful possession of narcotics." In 1962, Corallo received a two-year sentence for bribing a judge in a fraudulent bankruptcy case. In 1968 he was convicted for his part in a kickback scheme that involved James L. Marcus, a close confidant of New York City mayor John V. Lindsay and commissioner of the Department of Water Supply, Gas and Electricity. Marcus eventually cooperated with the prosecution and received a sentence of fifteen months; Corallo received a three-year sentence. He became boss of the Lucchese Family.

While Hoffa was interested in winning over the locals and their votes in his quest for the IBT presidency, Dioguardi and Corallo were interested in the financial rewards that control of the locals promised. The newly "elected" officers would approach various nonunion employers with an offer they could not easily refuse: pay the union initiation fees and membership dues for your employees (who usually did not even know they were members of a union) and you keep your business free of all labor problems, including demands by legitimate unions. Fail to pay, and labor problems, or worse, will result. By the time Hoffa gained control of the IBT in New York, twenty-five of the men Dio and Corallo had brought into their locals had already been convicted of crimes, including bribery, extortion, perjury, and forgery. Those convicted included Sam Goldstein and Harry Davidoff, the IBT boss of Kennedy International Airport's, Local 295 (Sheridan 1972; Brill 1978). According to the federal government, Lucchese crime Family control over IBT Local 295 continued into the 1990s. In 1992, a special trustee was appointed by a federal judge to monitor the local's activities (Fried 1992).

Allen Dorfman

An important part of the Hoffa Teamster legacy involves Allen Dorfman. Born in 1923, Dorfman was awarded the Silver Star during his World War II service with the Marine Corps. In 1948, he was a physical education teacher at the University of Illinois, earning $4,000 a year. By 1953 he was a millionaire.

Paul ("Red") Dorfman, Allen's stepfather, was a former professional boxer and close friend of Chicago Outfit boss Tony Accardo. In 1928 he was indicted for rigging election ballots and terrorist tactics in a local election, although there is no record of the disposition. In 1940 the founder and secretary-treasurer of the Chicago Waste Handlers Union was murdered. Red Dorfman, who had never been a member of the union or a waste handler, showed up at a union meeting, paid his dues, and on the same night became the new secretary-treasurer. In 1942 he was arrested as the result of a dispute with the chairman of the waste handlers employers' association—the two disagreed over wages to be paid to men in Dorfman's union. Using brass knuckles concealed in a glove, Dorfman severely beat the man in his office. The charges were dropped when the victim refused to prosecute. In 1949, Red Dorfman assisted Jimmy Hoffa by introducing him to important people in the Outfit and gaining their help in his organizing drive for the Teamsters (Brill 1978).

In 1949, Allen Dorfman formed an insurance agency:

> In 1950 and 1951, Hoffa successfully maneuvered the insurance business of the teamsters health and welfare funds to the Dorfmans. Hoffa entered into a collusive arrangement with the head of Union Casualty Company, and Paul and Allan [sic] Dorfman to assure the placing of Central States Insurance business with Union Casualty Company, with the understanding that Allan Dorfman would be named the broker on this lucrative account. Evidence indicated that Union Casualty placed its bid based on more favorable factors than those of its competitors, and when another company did offer a lower bid, it was rejected on baseless grounds. Subsequently, Allan, Paul, and Rose Dorfman, all of whom had absolutely no experience in the insurance field,

received more than $3 million in commissions and service fees on teamsters insurance over an eight year period. (Permanent Subcommittee on Investigations 1983b: 83)

In 1955, Hoffa negotiated the IBT's first pension plan in which each employer would contribute two dollars per week per Teamster employee. By June 1983, despite being subjected to a great deal of plundering, the Central States, Southeast and Southwest Areas Pension Fund and Health and Welfare Fund (usually referred to simply as the Central States Pension Fund) had assets of $4.7 billion (Wallace 1983).[4] Allen Dorfman was appointed as a consultant to the fund's board of trustees. He turned it into "a bank for the underworld and their cronies in the 1960s and early 1970s" (Frantz and Neubauer 1983: 1). Dorfman had the trustees lend millions of dollars to Las Vegas casinos, OC-connected resorts, and speculative hotel and land ventures, projects that conventional lending institutions would not finance. Investments in Las Vegas casinos were directed by OC bosses in Chicago, Kansas City, Milwaukee, and Cleveland, who were then able to skim casino profits.

In 1972, as a result of the FBI's PENDORF investigation, Dorfman was convicted of taking $55,000 in kickbacks to secure a $1.5 million loan from the pension fund, and he served ten months in federal prison. In 1974 he was indicted along with Irwin Weiner, an Outfit associate, Joseph ("Joey the Clown") Lombardo, and Anthony Spilotro, important members of the Outfit, on charges of fraud in connection with another pension fund loan. They were subsequently acquitted after the chief government witness was gunned down outside of his business establishment. In 1977, the federal government forced the trustees of the Central States Pension Fund to relinquish financial control to an independent management firm (Franz and Neubauer 1983).

On December 15, 1982, Dorfman, Lombardo, and Teamster president Roy L. Williams were found guilty of attempting to bribe U.S. Senator Howard Cannon of Nevada in return for his help in delaying legislation that would substantially deregulate the trucking industry. (In November 1982, Senator Cannon was defeated in his bid for a fifth term.) Dorfman, Lombardo, and Williams were scheduled for sentencing on February 10, 1983. On January 20, Dorfman was walking with Irwin Weiner in a parking lot of the suburban Lincolnwood Hyatt (now the Radisson) Hotel just outside of Chicago. Two men approached Dorfman from behind. One carried a sawed-off shotgun under his coat; the other drew a .22 caliber automatic with a silencer attached and fired five shots, point blank, into Dorfman's head. The two men then pulled on ski masks and fled in a car driven by a third person. The weapon and car plates were found several days later in a trash can. The plates had been stolen in

---

4. Union benefit funds, into which employers contribute amounts determined by collective bargaining, offer a tempting target. Since the Second World War the funds have grown dramatically. In 1986 there were more than 75,000 with cumulative assets in excess of $51 billion (PCOC 1986b).

August, and the .22 automatic was traced to a shop in Florida that had been out of business for two years. Williams received a ten-year sentence and was paroled in 1989.

Hoffa Versus Kennedy

During the 1950s, the activities of the Teamsters Union gained the attention of the U.S. Senate; in particular, the Permanent Subcommittee on Investigations, which for many years was chaired by John L. McClellan of Arkansas. The IBT officials, however, refused to cooperate with the committee.

> [They] would not produce records; they repeatedly challenged the jurisdiction of the Permanent Subcommittee to probe the inner workings of the union; they exerted considerable and constant pressure upon members of Congress in both houses to have Teamster activities rest in the traditionally gentle hands of the Senate's Labor Committee. (McClellan 1962: 14)

"The response of the Senate," notes Senator John McClellan (1962: 19), "was prompt and decisive." With a unanimous vote on January 30, 1957, an eight-member bipartisan Senate Select Committee on Improper Activities in the Labor or Management Field was established. The senator wrote of his experiences with the IBT in a 1962 book entitled *Crime Without Punishment*. Robert F. Kennedy, who was chief counsel to the committee, also authored a book on his experiences with the committee: *The Enemy Within* (1960). The first IBT target of the committee was its president, Dave Beck of Seattle. The committee spotlight shone very bright on Beck, and within months of his appearance he was convicted of embezzling union funds and income-tax violations. The spotlight then turned to James R. Hoffa.

Subpoenaed to appear before the Select Committee, Jimmy Hoffa was sometimes blunt, sometimes evasive in his testimony. In the following exchange Kennedy asked Hoffa about the vice president of IBT Local 239, Anthony Corallo (McClellan 1962: 50):

> *Kennedy*: He has been arrested twelve times, ranging from robbery, grand larceny, and narcotics. He was identified before the committee as an important figure in narcotics, and he was a close friend of Johnny Dioguardi. My question is, have you made any investigation of him? . . . Have you taken any steps against Mr. Tony Ducks Corallo?
>
> *Hoffa*: As of now, no.

At times the Teamster leader referred to Kennedy as "Bob" or "Bobby," and as "nothing but a rich man's kid." Law professor Monroe Freedman states: "From the day that James Hoffa told Robert Kennedy that he was nothing but a rich man's kid who never had to earn a nickel in his life, Hoffa was a marked man" (quoted in Navasky 1977: 395).

Teamster president Jimmy Hoffa spars with Robert Kennedy, chief counsel for the Senate Rackets Committee, during a recess in hearings. When Kennedy later became attorney general, he made the Labor and Racketeering Unit in the Department of Justice his personal "Get Hoffa Squad."

In 1957, FBI surveillance cameras recorded Hoffa giving $2,000 to John C. Cheasty, a New York attorney who was cooperating with the government, in exchange for confidential McClellan Committee documents. Hoffa had recruited Cheasty to serve as a plant on the committee. When FBI agents arrested Hoffa the following day, he had confidential committee reports on him. Nevertheless, Hoffa was acquitted in a jury trial. Kennedy (1960) describes the scenario carefully orchestrated by Hoffa's attorney, Edward Bennett Williams, which included an appearance by former boxing champ Joe Louis. He stayed in the courtroom for two days and publicly embraced Hoffa. During the trial, a full-page ad appeared in a black newspaper portraying Hoffa as a friend of the black race—the jury consisted of eight blacks and four whites. Kennedy adds, however, "in my estimation, it was not these tactics that won Hoffa his acquittal. It was rather, the work of Williams, his effective defense attorney, plus Hoffa's own strong testimony, together with the unpreparedness and ineffectiveness of the Government attorneys who prosecuted the case" (1960: 63).

In 1958, Hoffa was tried for illegally wiretapping the phones of some Teamster officials. The first trial resulted in a hung jury; the second in an acquittal. In 1960, John F. Kennedy was elected president of the United States and he appointed Robert Kennedy attorney general. The attorney general made the Labor and Racketeering Unit, a subdivision of the Organized Crime Section of the Criminal Division of the Department of Justice, his personal "Get Hoffa Squad." The unit was headed by former FBI Special Agent Walter Sheridan, who was actually on the attorney general's payroll as a "confidential assistant" (Navasky 1977). Sheridan wrote a book, *The Fall and Rise of Jimmy Hoffa*, on the IBT and the government's efforts to prosecute Hoffa.

Soon, federal grand juries across the country began investigating the IBT. Several important convictions were secured, including that of Anthony Provenzano. In 1962, Hoffa was charged with a conflict-of-interest violation of the Taft-Hartley Act—a misdemeanor. Victor Navasky (1977: 417) comments: "Never in history had the government devoted so much money, manpower, and top-level brainpower to a misdemeanor case." The trial lasted two months and ended in a hung jury—seven to five for acquittal. Hoffa was accused of trying to bribe jurors in the first trial, which was held in Nashville, Tennessee; the second trial was moved to Chattanooga on a defense motion for a change of venue based on adverse newspaper publicity. On March 4, 1964, Hoffa was convicted of jury tampering and sentenced to eight years' imprisonment.

On December 21, 1971, Hoffa was released from prison after President Richard Nixon approved his application for executive clemency (the IBT had supported Nixon for president). By 1975, Hoffa was actively seeking the Teamster presidency, and IBT officials loyal to him were holding fund-raising dinners to prepare for the campaign. Hoffa began attacking Frank Fitzsimmons, the man who had replaced him as IBT president. Ironically, Hoffa criticized Fitzsimmons as being the tool of organized crime. On July 30, 1975, Hoffa arrived at Machus Red Fox Restaurant to meet with several persons, including his friend Anthony ("Tony Jack") Giacalone, a *caporegime* in the Detroit crime Family, and Anthony Provenzano. Giacalone had arranged the meeting ostensibly to mediate differences between Provenzano and Hoffa over Hoffa's quest for the IBT presidency. None of the principals were at the Red Fox, however, and Hoffa has not been seen since. Fitzsimmons died of natural causes in 1981.

According to Eugene H. Methvin, a member of the President's Commission on Organized Crime, OC Families maneuvered behind the scenes to insure that Roy L. Williams of Kansas City, Missouri, would become the new IBT president. At the same time, "the Senate Permanent Subcommittee on Investigations rushed out a report spotlighting Williams' LCN ties. The senators revealed a portion of the Justice Department's evidence that Williams was getting kickbacks of cash skimmed from Las Vegas casinos bought with Teamster pension loans, kickbacks funnelled through Nick Civella's Kansas City Mafia family" (PCOC 1985b: 42). Nevertheless, the IBT executive board chose Williams to fill the unexpired term of Frank Fitzsimmons, and the Teamster convention subsequently elected him to a full term. After his 1982 conviction, Williams testified before the President's Commission on Organized Crime that his election had been engineered by OC bosses, and that he himself was under the control of Nick Civella. When Williams resigned, Jackie Presser

Jackie Presser's reports to
the Federal Bureau
of Investigation were
instrumental in the
Justice Department's 1989
racketeering case
against the teamsters.

of Cleveland was chosen to head the IBT, despite (or because of) his close ties
to organized crime. In 1984 the *Los Angeles Times* reported that Presser was an
FBI informant, which was supported by court documents unveiled in 1986.
After his death from cancer in 1988, the FBI confirmed that Presser had indeed
been a confidential informant; he continued to work for the FBI even after the
1984 newspaper report.

Jackie Presser

Born in Cleveland in 1926, Jackie Presser's future in organized labor was
established by his father. Bill Presser was a Teamster Union official and close
associate of the Cleveland crime Family. Large for his age, Jackie was an
unruly, brawling student. He dropped out of school at age sixteen and joined
the Navy; he was honorably discharged in 1947. As expected, Jackie went into
the union business, securing a position with the Restaurant Worker's Union
through his father's connections. He was joined by his uncle, an ex-convict
and loan collector, Allen Friedman. Jackie soon showed that he lacked the tact
necessary for successful labor racketeering: his threats, shakedowns, and
embezzlements attracted so much attention that he had to temporarily bow out
of union activities. Using IBT pension fund loans, Jackie opened up several

bowling alleys; they failed due to mismanagement, and the Teamster money was lost. Jackie's father Bill had a new IBT local chartered for him. Jackie teamed up with two relatives, Harold and Allen Friedman, both stalwart union organizers—also ex-convicts—to organize warehouse workers.

With Bill's help—he raided other IBT locals—Jackie's local prospered, moving beyond warehousemen and adding other workers to Local 507's membership. Part of Local 507's success was due to the sweetheart contract: employers fearful of other (legitimate) unions organizing their workers agreed to recognize the local and sign a contract with Jackie. A second factor contributing to the local's success was that although the local was headed by Jackie, it was actually run as a dictatorship by Harold Friedman. When Jimmy Hoffa went to prison and Frank Fitzsimmons became acting president, Bill Presser filled a vacancy on the IBT executive board, becoming a union vice president. Bill organized a political action committee called DRIVE to raise money and support political candidates, and Jackie was given a major role in DRIVE's efforts. Jackie Presser was astute enough to recognize the value of good public relations. He began a major effort to clean up the image of the IBT, hiring a PR firm and personal publicist. However, he continued to cheat his union members.

When Bill Presser fell seriously ill, Jackie replaced him as an IBT vice president. When IBT president Frank Fitzsimmons became terminally ill, Roy Williams became acting president with the strong support of Kansas City crime boss Nick Civella. Williams' conviction in the PENDORF case cleared the way for Jackie Presser to become IBT president; Jackie was supported by members of Cleveland's organized crime Family, represented by Maishe Rockman and Angelo Lonardo, who lobbied OC chieftains in Chicago and New York on Jackie's behalf (Neff 1989).

With Jackie's backing, DRIVE and the IBT supported Ronald Reagan's successful candidacy for president. After the election, Allen Friedman reports that his brother-in-law, Bill Presser,

> handed me a briefcase he said was filled with cash and told me to take it to [Attorney General] Edwin Meese in Washington. This was back in late November or early December after Ronald Reagan became president. I don't know how much was in that case; Bill knew I would never open it. But after Reagan got in, he named Bill's son, Jackie Presser, to his transition cabinet. Then he wanted to make Jackie under secretary of labor, though I guess cooler heads prevailed. Jackie's presence would have been just one more scandal for the administration. After all, though Jackie never did time in jail as Bill and I did, that was only because his father and I covered his ass, not because he was ever an honest man. (Friedman and Schwarz 1989: 3)

In 1989, as part of a RICO case against the IBT, court records revealed that Jackie Presser had been providing information to the FBI for nine years (Serrin 1989). According to the files:

- Exorbitant legal fees were paid to union-connected attorneys, sometimes for work that was not performed.
- Jackie Presser became IBT president because of the support of all of the East Coast OC Families.
- Two Chicago OC figures informed Anthony ("Fat Tony") Salerno, boss of the Genovese Family, that Presser was an informant, but Salerno refused to believe them.
- Presser provided information that helped to convict his predecessor, Roy Williams.
- All IBT favors had to be cleared through Milton ("Maishe") Rockman or John ("Peanuts") Tronolone, Cleveland OC figures, and they needed to be approved by Tony Salerno.

In 1989 the Department of Justice and IBT leaders reached a settlement in the government RICO suit against the union. In 1991, for the first time, the union's international officials were elected by the rank and file in a secret ballot supervised by the government. Previously they had been chosen at a national convention by delegates from the various locals. Under the settlement, three officials were appointed by the court to monitor corruption and act as chief administrators with limited powers to veto activities of the union if racketeering was detected. As a result of the electoral reforms, at the end of 1991 IBT members chose Ronald R. Carey, then fifty-five, as president. Carey heads the United Parcel Service local in Long Island City, New York, and is a longtime IBT dissident. Despite his reform credentials, in 1992 Carey was criticized by a federal judge overseeing the consent decree that helped elect him; the judge accused the IBT of dragging its feet on reforms. Fifteen months after taking office, Carey suspended six of the top officers of the 14,000-member IBT Local 705 in Chicago—the local has long been linked to organized crime (Franklin 1993).

BUSINESS RACKETEERING

As we have seen with respect to the waterfront, there is no hard-and-fast line separating labor racketeering from business racketeering—one is often an integral part of the other. In many schemes involving corrupt union officials, "legitimate" businessmen have willingly cooperated in order to derive benefits such as decreased labor costs, inflated prices, or increased business in the market (PCOC 1986b). Jonathan Kwitny (1979) describes the machinations of racketeer-extraordinaire Moses ("Moe") Steinman, who dominated the wholesale meat industry in New York City. Because of his connections with important OC figures such as John Dioguardi and Paul Castellano, Steinman was able to deal with racketeer-controlled unions and thus affect labor relations in the meat industry. This ability secured him a position as a supermarket-chain executive who led industry-wide negotiations with meat-industry unions. Utilizing under-the-table payments to the union leaders, Steinman determined from whom the supermarkets purchased their meat. Supermarket officials bought from firms recommended by Steinman, overpaying for their beef; they were rewarded with kickbacks. Steinman was paid handsome commission fees from the beef companies for these sales.

Steinman's greatest achievement was his relationship with Currier J. Holman, founder of Iowa Beef, the largest meat processing firm in the world. The patrician midwestern businessman and the hard-drinking, inarticulate New York racketeer had something in common—greed. In return for opening up New York markets for Iowa Beef and assisting the company with "labor relations," Iowa Beef gave millions of dollars to Steinman and his friends and relatives (Kwitny 1979). According to former FBI agents Joseph O'Brien and Andris Kurins (1991), a similar relationship existed between Gambino Family boss Paul Castellano and chicken tycoon Frank Perdue.

Collusion by otherwise legitimate business is often a vital ingredient in racketeering; labor leasing provides an example.

Labor Leasing

Eugene R. Boffa, Sr., controlled more than thirty labor leasing companies located in at least eleven states, Puerto Rico, and Canada. Boffa's companies had contracts with major U.S. corporations. A corporation would sign a contract with Boffa and then fire all of its union drivers, who were immediately hired by a Boffa company. The leasing company provided a buffer between management and labor. "Through each of these labor leasing companies, Eugene Boffa was the employer of truck drivers who he contracted with a major corporation to rent back to that corporation. These truck drivers were usually members of the International Brotherhood of Teamsters" (PCOC 1985b: 176). Corporations were often eager to participate in the arrangement in order to avoid labor problems that in some instances were instigated by members of Boffa's crew. They no longer had to deal with the IBT, and they realized net savings because drivers received less in salary and benefits than the IBT contract guaranteed, and safety considerations and seniority could be ignored without union problems.

Boffa's fee for this service was a percentage of the gross payroll, usually between 7 and 10 percent. He shared some of the profits with Russell Buffalino, crime boss of Pittston, Pennsylvania, who served as patron for the scheme, and also with corrupt Teamster officials. Everyone benefited, except of course the workers. If drivers complained they were fired or threatened with violence:

> Many courageous teamsters, unwilling to be exploited, did organize slow-downs or wildcat strikes. The affected company would alert Boffa, who would allow the company to terminate its contract with his labor-leasing company. (Neff 1989: 227)
>
> Just as soon as one Boffa company terminated its contract, another Boffa company under a new name would take its place on the scene. Usually the new labor leasing company would rehire the same drivers, except those drivers who had been deemed by the corporation management or by the Boffa

companies to be troublesome, usually worried about safety or in other ways a problem for the Boffa companies. (PCOC 1985a: 177)

The scheme eventually came apart when "several cars driven by LCN members and union officials in Detroit at the time of Jimmy Hoffa's disappearance were traced back to a leasing operation owned by Boffa. The cars were used as payoffs to favored union officials. Subsequent investigation uncovered Boffa's empire of companies" (PCOC 1986b: 135–36). Boffa and IBT officials were eventually convicted of a number of crimes, and in 1981 Boffa received a twenty-year sentence.

The Garment Center

As noted in chapter 3, extensive business racketeering in New York's garment industry dates back to the days of Lepke Buchalter. Its more contemporary manifestation centered on the ability of racketeers to control local trucking: whoever controls trucking controls the industry: "The fast paced nature of the fashion industry cannot countenance even short delays in shipping garments."

> In New York City, garment manufacturers do not, as a rule, actually cut cloth and sew it into a dress, shirt or other garment. They design clothes, order cloth and arrange for the cutting and sewing to be done in smaller shops, called contractors. As a result, cloth is constantly being shipped by truck from manufacturer to contractor, from contractor to contractor and from contractor back to manufacturer. (Mass 1991: 38–39)

Until 1992, control over garment-center shipping was held by the multimillionaire sons of Carlo Gambino, Thomas and Joseph, and a firm owned by a Lucchese Family member. They divided manufacturers and contractors among a limited number of truckers and assigned one to each shop. Manufacturers and contractors knew they were dealing with the Gambino brothers or the Lucchese Family member; this was usually enough to ensure compliance. Gambino Family *consigliere* Joseph N. Gallo was employed as a ("no show") labor relations representative for the Greater Blouse, Skirt, and Undergarment Association, which negotiates for about six hundred companies with the International Ladies Garment Worker's Union (O'Brien and Kurins 1991). In a 1992 plea bargain with the Manhattan district attorney's office, Joseph, then age fifty-five, and Thomas Gambino agreed to quit this competition-destroying aspect of trucking in the garment center (Blumenthal 1992).

Organized crime is not always a crucial element in labor racketeering. The pattern of racketeering may precede involvement of organized crime and would likely continue in its absence. The "Great Electrical Conspiracy," for example, was accomplished without organized crime. Executives of major corporations, including General Electric and Westinghouse, participated in a bid-rigging scheme (Smith 1961a, 1961b). The conspiracy began just before World War II

THE GAMBINO STING

New York's fashion industry is actually two worlds. The first is symbolized by long-legged models moving gracefully down a runway; the second is hidden among the cutting tables, sewing machines, and trucks of Manhattan's garment center. The fashion industry has traditionally attracted immigrant labor, ambitious businesspeople, and organized crime. Only a few miles away from the garment center is New York City's Lenox Hill neighborhood. An elegantly-dressed man in his early sixties resides at 6 East 68th Street, off Fifth Avenue, in an 1881 mansion once owned by a banking magnate. This is the home of the eldest son of Carlo Gambino, Thomas, who is married to Thomas Lucchese's daughter, Frances. He is a graduate of Manhattan College, known for his charitable contributions.

Tommy Gambino and his brother Joseph owned Consolidated Carriers, the major garment center cartage firm. Together with a trucking firm owned by a Lucchese Family member, the Gambino brothers divided manufacturers and contractors among a limited number of truckers and assigned one to each shop:

> None of these truckers will carry garments for a shop not assigned to him. If a shop uses a gypsy trucker and is caught, it is required to pay its regular trucker for the goods shipped, just as if the assigned trucker had carried them. Elaborate rules govern the trading of shops among the cartel members and the allocation of a trucker to a company leasing space that was formerly occupied by another company serviced by a cartel member. (Mass 1991: 39)

Because there was an absence of competition, trucking prices remained high, while service remained low. Some companies fled the garment center, and others refused to move in. The number of people employed in the industry declined substantially. This state of affairs impacted negatively on the New York City economy.

Evidence against the Gambinos was compiled through an elaborate sting operation orchestrated by investigators from the office of Manhattan District Attorney Robert M. Morgenthau. First, an undercover investigator using the name "David Chan" drove around Chinatown posing as a gypsy trucker soliciting business from companies that had been serviced by the Gambino cartel. He quickly found that no matter how competitive his prices, Chan could not secure any accounts. One manufacturer whispered the reason: "Mafia." Another undercover officer was hired by Consolidated Carriers. On October 31, 1989, investigators disguised as Con Edison workers broke into the Gambino trucking company headquarters and planted a court-authorized "bug." State police investigators opened up their own garment manufacturing firm called Chrystie Fashions, which was the ultimate weapon in the Gambino sting. In 1992, the Gambino brothers pled guilty to restraint of trade violations and agreed to quit New York City's garment center and pay a fine of $12 million in exchange for not being imprisoned. In 1993, at age sixty-four, Thomas Gambino was found guilty of racketeering stemming from his control of a Connecticut gambling operation and sentenced to five years' imprisonment.

Sources: Robert Mass, "Law Enforcement Approaches to Organized Crime Infiltration of Legitimate Industry." In *Organized Crime and Its Containment: A Transatlantic Initiative*, edited by Cyrelle Fijnaut and James Jacobs. Deventer, Netherlands: Kluwer, 1991; Ralph Blumenthal, "When the Mob Delivered the Goods." *New York Times Magazine*, July 26, 1992: 22–23, 31–34.

and climaxed in 1961. In that year, forty-five persons representing twenty-nine corporations were indicted. They were accused of price fixing by rigging bids and dividing the available market through a secret cartel that dealt with electrical equipment worth $1.7 billion annually. As part of the conspiracy, the defendants used secret codes and held clandestine meetings in hotel rooms. The defendants pleaded guilty: twenty-one were imprisoned for as much as *thirty days*. In 1980, thirty-seven manufacturers were accused of being part of an eighteen-year nationwide conspiracy to fix the prices of corrugated containers and sheets, a multibillion-dollar scheme. They settled out of court. In 1991, Pet, Inc., pled guilty to conspiring with other companies to rig bids on school milk contracts. Pet agreed to pay a $3.5 million fine (Associated Press, August 26, 1991). In 1993, it was revealed that in at least twenty states executives of the nation's largest dairy companies conspired, some for decades, to rig bids on milk products sold to schools and military bases. Dozens of dairy executives have already pleaded guilty (Henriques and Baquet 1993). From May 1983 through June 1992, the U.S. Department of Justice initiated 102 prosecutions for price fixing involving one hundred corporations: ninety-six pled guilty or were found guilty after trial (Ross 1992).

As discussed in chapter 6, organized crime is sometimes a provider of illegal goods and services—helping to arrange and enforce collusive bidding arrangements, for example—while at other times it is simply a predator imposing itself on those involved in such activities. With this in mind, we will examine business racketeering in the construction and private waste hauling industries.

Construction Industry

Construction is a lucrative and highly competitive industry. While competition is advantageous to the builder-client it necessarily reduces the profits of construction firms. Organized crime can play a crucial role in limiting competition by enforcing a system of collusive bidding. The President's Commission reports: "Participating construction contractors, with the guidance of union officials and LCN family members, allocate construction jobs among themselves and exclude non-cartel contractors whose entry into the New York market might threaten the stability, predictability, and control of construction work that the cartels offer their members. Under such a system, the participant companies are beneficiaries, not victims, since the benefits of the cartel may totally offset the increase costs it imposes" (PCOC 1986b: 219).

The construction industry in New York City is huge and fragmented, "with over one hundred thousand workers, many hundreds of specialty subcontractors, hundreds of general contractors, and dozens of major developers. There are also a large number of one-time or infrequent builders ranging from large corporations to small entrepreneurs" (New York State Organized Crime Task Force 1988: 3; hereafter NYSOCTF). The construction businesses range from those building private single-family dwellings to those putting up shopping centers and high-rise buildings. Construction workers are organized into approximately a hundred building trades local unions, who engage in collective bargaining with the approximately fifty employer associations formed by contractors in the same type of construction work.

"Traditionally, unions have had a great deal of leverage in high-rise construction because they have had a monopoly over the skilled workers needed to carry out this highly complex type of building" (NYSOCTF 1988: 44). Through collective bargaining agreements, construction unions typically control access to skilled labor: "Some pre-hire contracts contain clauses requiring contractors to hire all or part of their employees from union hiring halls. Even where there is no hiring hall provision, the union's designation as exclusive bargaining agent gives its elected officials control over who works for that contractor" (NYSOCTF 1988: 45–46). Through control over labor unions, racketeers are able to offer benefits to or impose prohibitive costs on contractors. The ability to assign (or not assign) workers to jobs is a powerful tool that can be used against union members who might wish to challenge racketeer leadership. There is also the very real threat of violence.

The New York State Organized Crime Task Force reports that the industry's structure creates fragmentation and fragility:

> An organized crime syndicate can use its network of relationships throughout the construction industry to reduce uncertainties and promote needed stability. For example, if more than one union has a jurisdictional claim over a particular construction task, an organized crime syndicate in return for a payoff can work out a reasonable arrangement between the contractor and the affected unions. In this role, the syndicate serves the same functions, albeit by criminal means, as a highly effective, legitimate labor consultant. (1988: 66)

According to the President's Commission,

> In New York City organized crime controls all construction contracts of a half-million dollars or more extending up to amounts of approximately $100 million.
>
> That the prime source of influence and the prime point of contact for organized crime are the 20 or so largest contractors in New York City who from time to time, through collusive bidding, decide among themselves who will get a particular project.
>
> The crucial point in time . . . is at the point of the winning of a construction bid. At that point in time, a bid having been submitted with the knowledge of the general contractor that he can count upon the influence of organized crime to ensure his profit and to ensure that the project will be completed on time in the way that it was bid in the first place.
>
> At that point, the point of winning of the bid, either an emissary of organized crime or a union official . . . approaches the contractor and tells the general contractor who his suppliers will be, who his subcontractors will be, from whom he will purchase materials and at what price those materials will be purchased, and, on occasion, designating to the general contractor which

unions he will use during the course of the construction of the building and other construction jobs in the New York City area. (PCOC 1985b: 71–72)

Ralph Scopo, a member of the Colombo Family and president of the Cement and Concrete Workers District Council of the Laborer's Union, was at the center of a "contractors club" that received payments for allocating bids on construction jobs. Jobs under $2 million required "one point" (1 percent), and "two points" were required for jobs over $2 million. In 1987, Scopo and Dominic ("Donny Shacks") Montemarano, a *caporegime* in the Colombo Family, were convicted of racketeering. (Scopo died in 1993 while serving a one hundred-year sentence.) On November 19, 1988, ten union officials and contractors were convicted in Brooklyn federal court for accepting or extorting payoffs from contractors in return for labor peace and rigging bids on projects to reward companies that paid bribes and to punish those that did not (Rangel 1988). In 1991, a federal jury convicted the *consiglieri* of the Genovese and Colombo Families for heading a twelve-year bid rigging scheme involving contracts for installing windows in New York City Housing Authority projects (Lubasch 1991b).

Payments to OC may be direct, or by making a racketeer (or one of his relatives) a business partner, or by employment of "ghost employees," names on a construction payroll who receive salaries but do not work. When two construction workers began complaining about ghost employees on the payroll of a contractor helping to build the World Trade Center in New York, one of the "ghosts," the boss of the Genovese Family, referred the problem to his private "police force":

Figgy [Anthony Ficarotta], Joey, Louie and me went over to the Twin Towers construction site. The building was up about eleven stories and there were no walls, just the frames and concrete floors. The elevator was in an open shaft, and that's how the workers got up and down. We went up to the top floor and Figgy [a former professional boxer] sees these two guys working. "Follow me," he says and we start walking around the floor. Figgy is telling the other workers: "Why don't youse go to lunch, go ahead." One of the workers says: "Who are you? We take our orders from Phillie." "Well I'm over Phillie," Figgy says, "so just go down and when you see him tell him who sent you—a short guy with the funny nose."

We walked around telling guys to go downstairs until we got to the two guys and they start to walk toward the elevator shaft. "You guys goin' to lunch?" Figgy asks. They are standing by the shaft for the lift to come back and Figgy picks up a two-by-four and pushes it under the chin of this guy. The guy grabs onto the shaft to keep from fallin' in: "So you want a fuckin' check too, huh? Well it's waitin' for you on the ground. I'm gonna see that you get it—in a hurry." The guy is hanging on for his life and Figgy keeps pushing him further into the shaft. The second guy doesn't know what to do—there's nowhere to run. Joe and Louie start backing him up—and there's nowhere to go except down eleven stories.

The guy with Figgy is yelling: "No, no, please, I don't want no check." "Why? You been bitchin' about some checks and I'm gonna send you down to get one." "Please no. I don't want no check." Joey and Louie back the other guy up to the edge and he yells out: "I don't want no check either." "Then just do your fuckin' work and shut the fuck up. Or we'll be back." Figgy threw the piece of wood down and we went onto the lift. There was no further trouble. (Abadinsky 1983: 131)

In New Jersey, firms owned by Philadelphia crime boss Nicky Scarfo and his one-time underboss Salvatore J. Merlino were able to gain lucrative construction contracts because of their influence over a few key labor unions, particularly Concrete Workers Local 33 and Ironworkers Local 350. Contractors subcontracting work to the Scarfo and Merlino firms were guaranteed labor peace and the two firms were able to underbid rivals by violating the union contract with respect to pension and other benefits (New Jersey State Commission of Investigation 1987). In fact, the construction industry is quite inefficient, characterized by various unions having overlapping jurisdictions and a great deal of featherbedding. "The existence of so much inefficiency provides a strong incentive to pay off union officials to not press their jurisdictional claims or to reach out to racketeers who can dictate accommodations between competing unions" (NYSOCTF 1988: 50).

Private Solid Waste Carting

If there is an industry that conjures up an image of organized crime, it is the private collection of solid waste. Back in 1931, Walter Lippman (1962: 61) noted that "racketeering in many of its most important forms tends to develop where an industry is subjected to exceedingly competitive conditions." Companies "faced with the constant threat of cutthroat competition are subject to easy temptation to pay gangsters for protection against competitors." Peter Reuter (1987) offers additional insight into an industry's attractiveness to OC. When the entrepreneurs have a low-status (e.g., limited education) background, enterprises are local, small, and family-based, the industry is vulnerable to OC infiltration. The solid waste collection industry meets these criteria. It is characterized by numerous, relatively small competing firms that are often family-based. It is an easy-entry enterprise, requiring only some trucks and a willingness to work hard. Competition for a customer's business drives down profits until, at some point, with or without help from OC, an association is formed. Association members divide up the industry, usually allocating geographic areas (territories) or specific customers. The members (illegally) agree not to compete for another member's business. Each is thereby free to charge whatever the market will bear for its services (see State Commission of Investigation 1989).

Organized crime may become involved if there is a need to police the (illegal) agreements. Peter Reuter (Reuter et al. 1983: 11) reports that in New York City:

Racketeers play a continuing role in the operation of this agreement. That role comes mainly through the need to constantly mediate the disputes that inevitably arise in a conspiracy that involves the allocation of over 100,000 customers between 30 carters. The "grievance committees" that settle these disputes, using the basic rule that whoever serviced the site first has continuing rights to any customer that occupies the site, include at least one Mafioso. While there is little evidence of either threats or actual violence, it seems reasonable to infer that the racketeers provide a credible continuing threat of violence that ensures compliance with the ruling of the committee.

Organized crime may become involved simply by using private resources for coercion and violence, something relatively easy to accomplish since the participants are operating outside of the law and cannot easily complain to the authorities. In New Jersey, for example, the organizer of a waste haulers association that had effectively restrained competition found himself being pushed out by an emissary from Gerardo ("Jerry") Catena, who ran New Jersey operations for the Genovese Family. The head of the association described his response: "I had a feeling, *fear*, that if I did not just put my tail between my legs and allow myself to be pushed out, they would find another way to get me out" (Abadinsky 1981: 30).

In 1986, Salvatore Avellino, Jr., a captain in the Lucchese Family, pled guilty to attempting to prevent an independent solid waste hauling firm owned by Robert Kubsecka and his family from doing business on Long Island. In 1989, Kubsecka and his brother-in-law were shot to death in their office (Lubasch 1992b). In 1992, the federal government accused Avellino, by then boss of the Lucchese Family, of maintaining a waste removal cartel on Long Island by "enforcing property rights through threats of labor unrest, property damage and violence." A federal court hearing a civil-racketeering/RICO case ordered Avellino, Anthony Corrollo, and Salvatore Santoro, former boss and underboss of the Lucchese Family, from any involvement in the waste haulers industry on Long Island. In 1993, Avellino was indicted for racketeering and murder. A week later, at age seventy-four, James Failla ("Jimmy Brown"—likes brown clothes), of the Gambino Family, for thirty years head of the Association of Trade Waste Removers of Greater New York, was indicted for his role in organizing and facilitating restraint of trade agreements and murder (Fried 1993b).

Organized Crime and Legitimate Business

In addition to the plethora of illegal business activities, persons involved in organized crime often own legitimate enterprises. One of the popular activities of government officials has been to decry the "infiltration" of organized crime into legitimate business. Michael Maltz (1976: 83) states that the "alternative to penetration of legitimate business is the reinvestment of the ill-gotten gains into some criminal enterprises, which may cause greater social harm." Annelise Anderson (1979: 77) points out, however, that funds from illegal business activities cannot easily "be profitably reinvested in illegal market enterprises without aggressive expansion of the territory controlled by the group." Thus, OC members have an oversupply of illegally derived funds that cannot be profitably used to expand illegal activities. Maltz (1976) concludes that the penetration of OC into legitimate business can be viewed as the equivalent of the legitimation of family fortunes by the robber barons discussed in chapter 2.

However, Mark Moore (1987: 51) points out that the features of the organized crime group, rather than the substantive offenses committed, make it a societal menace. Thus, "what is bad about organized crime is that the criminal groups seem resistant to law enforcement measures, that they seem to become rich as a result of their crimes, that they coolly calculate how best to make money without worrying about whether a planned enterprise is illegal and violent, and that they threaten additional criminal activity in the future even if their current conduct is tolerable." In other words, OC groups would pose a threat to society "even if they were engaged largely in legitimate activities and even if their criminal activities produced relatively insignificant levels and kinds of victimization" (1987: 52). Moore suggests that the OC group should be viewed as a business firm pursuing profit with a portfolio that encompasses illicit as well as licit enterprises, and that poses a serious societal threat.

Anderson provides six reasons for organized criminal involvement in legitimate business:

1. *Profit.* For persons in organized crime, profit provides motivation; not all members of OC are able to make a "respectable" income from illicit activities. In a conversation from the "DeCavalcante Tapes," Anthony Russo, an underboss in Long Branch, New Jersey, complained to Sam DeCavalcante that the *amici nostri* ("friends of ours"—OC members) could not even support themselves. In another incident, DeCavalcante arranged for the removal of a local union official, who was also a *caporegime* in his crime Family, because the official was not providing legitimate employment to the *amici nostri* as construction laborers. Jimmy Fratiano's 531-page autobiography, *The Last Mafioso* (Demaris 1981), contains very little discussion of his business activities. Indeed, it appears that Fratiano's most successful enterprise was a legitimate trucking firm he owned in California.
2. *Diversification.* A legitimate business provides the OC member with security of income. While it may be subject to market and other business conditions, a legitimate enterprise is usually not a target of law-enforcement efforts. (As will be discussed in chapter 9, since Anderson wrote her book in the late 1970s, federal and local governments have become increasingly active in the civil seizure of assets of criminals, including legitimate businesses.)
3. *Transfer.* Illegitimate enterprises are difficult, if not impossible, to transfer to dependents (particularly if they are female). Investing in legitimate enterprises, a business or real estate, for example, ensures that an estate can be legally inherited.
4. *Services.* An OC member with a legitimate business is in a position to act as a patron for persons in need of legitimate employment—for example, persons on probation or parole, or relatives he wants to shield from the stigma and risks associated with criminal enterprises.

5. *Front*. A legitimate business can provide a front or a base of operations for a host of illegal activities: loansharking, gambling, drug trafficking, to name a few.
6. *Taxes*. A legitimate business can provide a tax cover, thereby reducing the risk of being charged with income-tax evasion. Funds from an illegitimate enterprise can be mixed with those from the legitimate business, particularly if it is a "cash" business.

Obviously, these categories are not mutually exclusive. It is quite likely that OC involvement in legitimate business involves a combination of these six reasons. Persons in organized crime may also use a legitimate business as part of a scam.

The Scam

The scam is a bankruptcy fraud that victimizes wholesale providers of various goods, and sometimes insurance companies. The business used as the basis for a scam may be set up with that scheme as its purpose, or it may be an established business that has fallen into OC control as a result of gambling or loanshark debts. Scam operations are popular in industries with merchandise that has a high turnover potential, is readily transportable, and is not easy to trace. There are three basic variations (De Franco 1973: 5–7).

Three-step scam. A new corporation is formed, managed by a front man, or "pencil," who has no prior criminal or bankruptcy record. An initial large bank deposit, known as the "nut," is made to establish credit. (This money, plus other money subsequently deposited, is later withdrawn.) A large store is rented, and orders for merchandise are placed with as many companies as possible. The size of these orders appears to indicate a successful operation to the suppliers. Then the owners deal with suppliers in three steps:

1. Smaller orders are placed during the first month, and such orders are almost always paid for in full.
2. During the second month, larger orders are placed, and about a quarter of the balance due on such orders is paid.
3. During the third month, using the credit established as a result of payments made for the previous orders, very large orders are placed. Items easily converted into cash, such as jewelry and appliances, usually constitute a large proportion of these orders. Thereafter, merchandise is converted into cash through a fence or a surplus-property operator, normally one with a sufficiently large legitimate inventory to easily intermix the scam merchandise into the normal inventory. The company is then forced into bankruptcy by creditors since, according to plan, all cash has been appropriated by the scam operator.

One-step scam. Since the three-step scam requires several months for completion, the more rapid one-step scam is frequently used.

A successful business with good credit references is purchased. No notice of the change in management is provided to Dun and Bradstreet or other credit agencies, thus enabling the new management to trade on the previous owner's good credit reputation. Manufacturers are approached in person or at trade shows to arrange for the purchase of merchandise. The orders are usually of a large quantity, and suppliers who did not sell to the company previously are very politely informed by the scam operator that if they do not want to fill the order, some other company will be glad to do so. This technique is known as the "sketch." Orders often include many items not previously purchased by the company.

After the orders have been received, the merchandise is sold, as in the three-step scam. The money is milked from the business, and the company is forced into bankruptcy, just as the scam operator had planned.

Same-name scam. This is a variation of the one-step scam. A company is organized with a name deceptively similar, and often almost identical, to that of a successful company in the same area. Large orders are placed with suppliers who fill them, assuming the legitimacy of the company based on the similarity in firm names. The merchandise is then sold in the same fashion as with the other types of scam.

A popular time for the scam operator is just before a seasonal increase in the popularity of particular merchandise, when rush deliveries are commonplace and thorough credit checks often overlooked. In some scams, arson is the final step: the business is "torched" for the insurance instead of declaring bankruptcy.

Money Laundering

According to U.S. Attorney Robert W. Genzman, money laundering "means to knowingly engage in a financial transaction with the proceeds of some unlawful activity with the intent of promoting or carrying on that unlawful activity or to conceal or disguise the nature, location, source, ownership or control of these proceeds" (Genzman 1988). Ever since Al Capone was imprisoned for income-tax evasion, financially successful criminals have sought ways to "launder" their illegally secured "dirty" money. Some use a cash business, such as a vending machine firm, to mingle money from illegitimate sources with legally earned money. Some criminals have used casinos in New Jersey and Nevada for the same purpose. In New Jersey, one drug trafficking ring opened a casino account for $118,000 and stayed several days, but did not gamble. They then left the hotel with checks payable to third parties, who deposited the checks in a securities firm. The money was later withdrawn—"laundered" (PCOC 1984c). In 1991, several men from Lebanon and Argentina were convicted of laundering $1 billion in Colombian drug profits through the purchase and sale of gold, using jewelry companies in Houston, Miami, Los Angeles, and New York City as fronts.

In elaborate money-laundering schemes, the first step is to convert large quantities of cash into one or more cashier's checks. In addition to being easier to carry—450 bills weigh about one pound—they are difficult to trace since they do not bear the receiver's name or address. Transactions involving the proceeds of drug trafficking often consist of large amounts of cash in small denominations. In such instances, the first step is to convert the small bills into hundreds—$1 million in twenties weighs 110 pounds; in $100 bills, only twenty-two pounds. To avoid IRS reporting requirements under the Bank Secrecy Act, transfers of cash to cashier's checks or $100 bills must take place in amounts under $10,000 or through banking officials who agree not to fill out a Currency Transaction Report (CTR). A CTR is required for each deposit, withdrawal, or exchange of currency or monetary instruments in excess of $10,000. It must be submitted to the IRS within fifteen days of the transaction. In 1984, tax amendments extended the reporting requirements to anyone who receives more than $10,000 in cash in the course of a trade or business. A CMIR (Currency and Monetary Instrument Report) must be filed for cash or certain monetary instruments exceeding $10,000 in value that enter or leave the United States.

In 1985, it was revealed that the Bank of Boston, that city's oldest and biggest bank, had helped to launder money for the underboss of the Patriarca Family. From 1979 to 1983 Jerry Angiulo and his brothers would convert paper bags stuffed with tens of thousands of dollars in small bills into $100 bills and more than $7 million in cashier's checks. None of the transactions were reported to the IRS. Two real estate companies controlled by the Angiulos in the Italian neighborhood of Boston's North End had been placed on the "exempt" list, so their cash transactions in excess of $10,000 did not have to be reported to the IRS.[5] The only businesses legally entitled to such exemptions are retail outlets such as supermarkets that do a great deal of business in large amounts of cash on a daily basis. Money launderers may utilize car dealerships whose managers accept cash for automobile purchases and fail to file the required CTRs.

In recent years, currency exchanges (*casas de cambio*) have sprouted up along the Texas-Mexico border. These poorly regulated enterprises accept (illegally) large amounts of cash, which they then funnel into legitimate Texas banks. As a result of this activity, the Federal Reserve Bank in San Antonio reported more than $2 billion in surplus cash surging through the banking system of south Texas. Only Miami and Los Angeles have reported larger amounts (Weingarten 1989b).

---

5. Gennaro ("Jerry") Angiulo, born in 1919, grew up in Boston's North End, an Italian ghetto. He and his brothers were numbers operators and bookmakers who paid tribute to Raymond L.S. Patriarca for the privilege of running gambling operations in Boston. A decorated naval veteran and former truck driver before he entered gambling, Angiulo was initiated into the Patriarca Family because of his money-making abilities, not his muscle. Because he had never "made his bones" (had not been directly involved in a murder), Angiulo lacked the respect generally accorded other "made" guys. In 1986, Angiulo was convicted of RICO violations and sentenced to forty-five years. He was subsequently convicted on state charges for ordering a murder and sentenced to life without parole (O'Neil and Lehr 1989).

The *casas* pool many customers' funds in their own accounts in U.S. or foreign banks and keep their own records of the amounts owed to each customer. When a foreign drug trafficker wants to send money to his own country, the *casa* operator wires the funds from its bank to the trafficker's foreign account(s). Even when a U.S. bank completes a CTR, it names the *casa* as the owner of the funds, not the actual owner. In the Houston area, *giro* (wire) houses are found in addition to the *casas*. In general, the *giros* move drug money to Colombia, while the *casas* move Mexican drug money. (Webster and McCampbell 1992: 5)

Drug money has changed the face of Starr County, Texas, where smuggling— historically of cattle, liquor, and electronic equipment—has been a way of life. The area's remoteness and proximity to the Mexican border attract free-spending drug dealers. While very few of the more than 40,000 residents are involved in the drug business, many profit from it. Bank accounts and land values have soared, despite the county having the lowest per capita income in the United States. In the town of Roma, population 8,058, inflated property taxes helped build a new sixty-acre, $11.5 million high school campus with an indoor pool and tennis courts ("A Town That's Addicted to Illegal Drug Money" 1991).

Criminals use casinos to convert cash from small denominations to $100 bills. In some schemes money launderers use dozens of persons (called "smurfs") to convert cash into money orders and cashier's checks that do not specify payees or that are made out to fictitious persons. Each transaction is held to less than $10,000 to avoid the need for a CTR. One ring operating out of Forest Hills, New York, employed dozens of persons who used about thirty banks in New York and New Jersey to launder about $100 million a year for the Cali cartel. The checks were pasted between the pages of magazines and shipped to Cali; from there the money was transferred to banks in Panama. In 1989, the scheme resulted in the indictment of sixteen persons when one of the banks became suspicious of the unusual amount of cash transactions and reported them to federal authorities (Morgan 1989). "Smurfing" has now been made a federal crime, and increased bank scrutiny has made tellers suspicious of cash transactions just under $10,000. In response, smurfs have reduced transactions to as low as $5,000 and often make dozens of transactions in a day, typically in communities that do not usually have long lines in their banks (Walter 1990).

Money laundering has been greatly facilitated by advances in banking technology. It has become increasingly difficult for the government to effectively monitor banking transactions. "An alternative to physically removing money from the country is to deposit the cash, then transfer the funds electronically to other domestic and foreign banks, financial institutions, or securities accounts. Swiss law enforcement officials report that when money is transferred by wire to Switzerland, it seldom comes directly from the country of origin, rather it is 'prewashed' in a third country such as Panama, the Bahamas, the Cayman Islands, or Luxembourg," (Webster and McCampbell 1992: 4). The sheer

BANK OF CREDIT AND COMMERCE INTERNATIONAL

Sheik Kamal Adham, former director of Saudi Arabian intelligence, pleaded guilty in 1992 to a violation of New York banking laws. He was accused of acting as a front man on behalf of B.C.C.I. in its secret purchase of First American Bankshares in Washington. He has agreed to cooperate with American law enforcement officials, who believe he may be able to provide information on B.C.C.I. connections to intelligence communities around the world.

Sometimes referred to as the "bank of crooks and criminals international," BCCI was founded by Pakistanis and financed by Arabs. Incorporated in Luxembourg, a tiny nation known for its bank secrecy laws and lax regulation, BCCI became one of the largest private banks in the world, with offices in seventy-two countries. The bank later divided its headquarters between Luxembourg and the Cayman Islands, another location known for bank secrecy. The locations of its headquarters should have raised suspicions, but BCCI was able to wrap itself in a mantle of influence and respectability that included associations with former president Jimmy Carter and Washington lawyer and political insider Clark Clifford. In 1992, it was revealed that Orrin Hatch (R–Utah), a powerful senator and member of the Judiciary Committee,

was a behind-the-scenes mover to protect BCCI (Baquet and Gerth 1992). Because it "operated in nations that served as bases for terrorists and homes for drug factories, BCCI was, if nothing else, convenient—a sort of neighborhood bank in some of the world's worst neighborhoods" (Potts, Kochan, and Whittington 1992: 157).

BCCI became a full-service bank to drug traffickers and terrorists such as Abu Nidel, who maintained a $60 million account at a BCCI London branch, and the Iranian-backed terrorist group Hezbollah. The bank served to smuggle arms to Syria, Iran, and Libya, and to launder money for the Medellín cartel and Golden Triangle drug warlord Khun Sa (see chapter 7). In

(continued on next page)

BANK OF CREDIT AND COMMERCE INTERNATIONAL (*Continued*)

1988, the U.S. government accused BCCI of laundering $14 million for the Medellín cartel. Bank officials received cash from the traffickers and by wire placed it in certificates of deposit in BCCI branches in Europe, Panama (it was Manual Noriega's favorite bank), Uruguay, and the Bahamas. Using the certificates as collateral, the officials then created a loan at other branches and permitted the drug traffickers to withdraw the funds. The bank repaid the loan with the funds from the certificates of deposit. The scheme came to an end when federal undercover agents succeeded in convincing BCCI officials that they (the agents) were cocaine dealers seeking to launder money. In 1990, the bank pleaded guilty and paid a $15 million fine; two employees received twelve-year prison sentences. But this was only the tip of the iceberg. Billions of dollars had been moved electronically from one BCCI branch to another, further concealing its origins at each step.

In 1991, the activities of BCCI were brought to an end when bank regulators in England, the United States, and several other countries seized BCCI branches. It was revealed that, in addition to money-laundering activities, BCCI was actually a giant Ponzi scheme. Early investors were permitted to take out loans that they did not have to pay back, and shareholders continued to be provided with poorly or unsecured loans until the scheme was brought down by investigators. Many depositors from Third World countries took the loss. In 1992, Saudi Arabia's largest bank and its manager were charged by U.S. authorities with a multibillion-dollar fraud for its role in BCCI. The former head of Saudi intelligence pled guilty to U.S. charges related to the case.

Sources: Dean Baquet and Jeff Gerth, "Lawmaker's Defense of B.C.C.I. Went Beyond Speech in Senate." *New York Times*, August 26, 1992: 1, C2; Mark Potts, Nicholas Kochan, and Robert Whittington, *Dirty Money, BCCI: The Inside Story of the World's Sleaziest Bank*. Washington, DC: National Press Books, 1992; Dean Baquet, "Tips on B.C.C.I. Flowed Freely for Years." *New York Times*, August 27, 1992: C1, C2; Elaine Sciolino and Jeff Gerth, "Bank Charges Embarrass the Saudis." *New York Times*, August 2, 1992: 11.

volume of wire transfers makes accounting difficult—one major bank in New York handles about 40,000 wires each business day.

A customer can instruct his or her personal computer to direct a bank's computer to transfer money from an account to one in a foreign bank. The bank's computer then tells a banking clearing house that assists in the transfer—no person talks to another. While depositing more than $10,000 into an account requires the filing of a CTR, the government receives more than 7 million reports annually and is hopelessly behind in reviewing them. The daily average of American transactions is about $7 billion. On one day it actually amounted to $1.25 trillion (Labaton 1989b).

In 1989 a Panamanian bank pled guilty to money-laundering charges in the largest such case to end in a conviction. Although the bank (Banco de Occidente) has no operations in the United States, it held several accounts in Continental Illinois Bank's New York branch that were used to launder money. Drug dealers in New York, Miami, Houston, and Los Angeles distributed money from cocaine sales to bogus jewelry firms that acted as fronts. The cash was sent by Wells Fargo armored truck to other phony jewelry operations in Los Angeles, where it was counted by high-speed machines. The cash was then shipped by armored courier to Los Angeles banks, which were told it was being used to purchase gold bullion, something common in the jewelry business. The Los Angeles banks made an electronic transfer to New York, and from there it was electronically transferred to Europe or directly to Latin America, eventually winding up in Colombia. The operators were paid 7 percent of the funds they laundered. The scheme ended when Wells Fargo became suspicious and informed federal authorities of the unusually large amount of cash that was being deposited—$25 million in three months (Labaton 1989a).

At the beginning of 1989, federal agents seized $19,630,000 in cash—$5, $10, and $20 bills—that was being transported in a furniture truck in Queens, New York. The sum represented about two weeks' receipts for the Cali cartel. Six heavily armed Colombian aliens were in the truck when it was seized. The following month, thirty-three persons were charged with laundering more than $500 million on behalf of Colombian cocaine traffickers. The defendants, mostly family groups, packed money in boxes and shipped them between jewelry stores in New York, Los Angeles, and Houston. Two corporations, one in Hollywood, Florida, and the other in Los Angeles, were used to launder the money by creating false invoices for sales of huge quantities of gold. As part of the investigation into the ring, federal agents also seized 640 pounds of cocaine. In 1989 a laundering scandal erupted in Switzerland, which has an almost legendary reputation for bank secrecy—the "numbered account." Two Lebanese brothers used Swiss banks to launder more than $1.3 billion in drug profits from the United States, Turkey, and Colombia. As part of the scandal, the Swiss justice minister, whose husband's bank was the target of a laundering investigation, was forced to resign (Greenhouse 1989a).

As part of an overseas laundering scheme, a lawyer acting on behalf of a client creates a "paper" (or "boilerplate") company in any one of a number of countries that have strict privacy statutes, for example, Panama, which has over 200,000 companies registered. The funds to be laundered are transferred physically or wired to the company's account in a local bank. The company then transfers the money to the local branch of a large international bank. The paper company is then able to borrow money from the United States (or any other) branch of this bank, using the overseas deposit as security (Walter 1990). Or an employment contract is set up between the launderer and his or her "paper" company for an imaginary service for which payments are made to the launderer. In some cases, the lawyer may also establish a "boilerplate bank"— like the company, this is a shell. Not only does the criminal get his money

CAYMAN ISLANDS

Located south of Cuba, an easy flight from either Florida or Colombia, this small West Indian island is only one hundred miles square, with a population of 23,400—yet there are five hundred banks and twenty thousand registered companies on the Cayman Islands. The Georgetown financial district has the highest density of banks and fax machines in the world. Most banks are simply "plaques" or box offices—no vaults, tellers, or security guards—with transactions recorded by Cayman booking centers. In 1984, the United States and Great Britain signed an agreement that gives American officials investigating drug cases information about secret bank accounts in the Cayman Islands. The Caymans, which are administered by Britain, maintain secrecy in all other cases unless there is proof of an offense under their law. Virtually anyone can still

> establish his or her own shell company for a few thousand dollars in legal fees, open a local bank account and, because the required disclosure is minimal and business operates behind a wall of strict secrecy, no one need know about the company or what funds are stashed there. The few slips of paper that constitute the company records may be held in the office of a Cayman lawyer.

Source: Steve Lohr, "Where the Money Washes Up: Offshore Banking in the Cayman Islands." *New York Times Magazine*, March 29, 1992: 28.

laundered, but he also earns a tax write-off for the interest on the loan. Under the Bank Secrecy Act, however, wiring or physically transporting cash or other financial instruments out of the country in excess of $10,000 must be reported to the Customs Service. Once the funds are out of the United States, however, it may be impossible for the IRS to trace (Permanent Subcommittee on Investigations 1983a: 7).

Taking advantage of bank secrecy laws to avoid disclosure of ownership has drawbacks: it may be difficult, if not impossible, to pass on these assets to one's heirs.

In the next chapter we will examine laws and law enforcement efforts designed to combat organized crime.

REVIEW QUESTIONS

1. What are all of the possible advantages for an employer who enters into a corrupt relationship with a labor union?
2. How did "Dopey" Benny Fein rationalize labor's relationship with criminals?
3. What four international unions have reputedly been under the control of organized crime?

4. Why were waterfront firms often willing partners in corruption with organized labor?
5. What are "paper locals," and how were they used by labor racketeers?
6. How is labor leasing used by union racketeers?
7. How does business racketeering differ from labor racketeering?
8. What are the elements that make a particular industry, for example, private waste hauling, susceptible to racketeering?
9. What is a scam and how is it used by organized crime figures?
10. What are the various ways to accomplish "money laundering"?

9

Responding to Organized Crime: Laws and Law Enforcement

Before we examine the strategies and techniques used by law enforcement agencies to deal with organized crime, we will consider three constraints on law enforcement efforts in general and organized crime law enforcement in particular: constitutional restraints, jurisdictional limitations, and corruption.

CONSTITUTIONAL RESTRAINTS

Law enforcement in the United States operates under significant constitutional constraints. Important protections against government, while they protect individual liberty, also benefit the criminal population: the right to remain silent (Fifth Amendment); the right to counsel (Sixth Amendment); the right to be tried speedily by an impartial jury (Sixth Amendment); the right to confront witnesses (Sixth Amendment).

Particularly important for organized crime law enforcement are the Fourth Amendment and the exclusionary rule. The Fourth Amendment provides that "the right of the people to be secure in their persons, houses, papers and effects, against unreasonable searches and seizures shall not be violated, and no Warrants shall issue, but upon probable cause, supported by Oath or affirmation, and particularly describing the place to be searched, and the persons or things to be seized." In practice, information sufficient to justify a search warrant in organized crime cases is difficult to obtain. Unlike conventional crimes such as robbery and burglary, there is an absence of innocent victims to report the crime. The exclusionary rule provides that evidence obtained in violation of the Fourth Amendment cannot be entered as evidence in a criminal trial (*Weeks v. United States*, 232 U.S. 383, 1914; *Mapp v. Ohio*, 357 U.S. 643, 1961), although there are a number of exceptions that are beyond the scope of this book.

Intercepting confidential information is a prerequisite to moving against organized crime. However, the Fourth Amendment and Title III of the

Omnibus Crime Control and Safe Streets Act of 1968 (18 U.S.C. Section 2510–2520) place restraints on the manner in which the government can secure this information. In order to surreptitiously intercept conversations by wiretapping telephones or using electronic ("bugging") devices, a court order must be secured. Like a search warrant, it must be based upon information sufficient to prove the legal standard of probable cause. When an order to intercept electronic communications is secured (generally referred to as a "Title III"), it is quite limited, requires extensive documentation, and the persons who are monitored must be notified after the order expires. These requirements make electronic surveillance quite expensive (in terms of personnel hours expended), and difficult to accomplish.

Supervision of undercover law enforcement agents is difficult since they work without direct supervision. "Legal control over agents is problematic," note Jay Williams, Lawrence Redlinger, and Peter Manning (1979: 6), "and the circumstances of arrest are often such that there is a great temptation to perjury, violation of the exclusionary rule, misuse of informants, discretionary dropping, overlooking and altering charges, and other violations of procedural and/or legal rules." This is particularly true in drug law enforcement where pressure "to do something about drugs" is placed on the enforcers of the law, leading to the temptation to bypass due process in favor of unlawful (but often effective) shortcuts.

JURISDICTIONAL LIMITATIONS

The Constitution provides for a form of government in which powers are diffused horizontally and vertically. There are three branches of government: legislative, judicial, and executive; and four levels of government: federal, state, county, and municipal. Although each level of government has responsibilities for responding to organized criminal activities, there is little or no coordination between them—each level of government responds to the problem independent of the others. Federalism was part of a deliberate design to help protect us against tyranny; it also provides us with a level of inefficiency that significantly handicaps efforts to deal with organized crime.

On the federal level, a host of executive branch agencies, ranging from the military to the Federal Bureau of Investigation, have responsibility for combatting organized crime. There is also a separate federal judicial system that is responsible for trying OC cases and a legislative branch responsible for enacting OC legislation and allocating funds for federal enforcement efforts. The jurisdiction of many federal enforcement agencies overlaps, and efforts are often competitive rather than cooperative (see Dannen 1992a). At the local level, there are about 20,000 police agencies. Each state has state-level enforcement agents (state police or similar agency), and the state is responsible for operating prisons and the parole system (if one exists). County government usually has responsibility for prosecuting defendants, and a county-level agency, typically the sheriff, is usually responsible for operating jails. The county may also have a department with general policing responsibilities, independent of or part of the sheriff's office. Almost every municipality has a police department whose officers enforce laws involving organized criminal activity. Each of these levels of government has taxing authority and allocates resources with little or no consultation with other levels of government. The result is a degree of inefficiency that surpasses that of most democratic nations.

American efforts against drug trafficking are limited by national boundaries: cocaine and heroin originate where United States law enforcement has no jurisdiction. The Bureau of International Narcotics Matters, within the U.S. Department of State, is the primary agency responsible for coordinating international programs and gaining the cooperation of foreign governments in antidrug efforts. But the bureau has no authority to force governments to act in a manner most beneficial to U.S. efforts in dealing with cocaine or heroin. The State Department collects intelligence on policy-level international narcotics developments, while the Central Intelligence Agency collects strategic narcotics intelligence and is responsible for coordinating foreign intelligence on narcotics. The CIA, however, has often shielded drug traffickers who have provided foreign intelligence information useful to that agency. U.S. efforts against drug trafficking are often sacrificed for the benefit of foreign policy (Sciolino and Engelberg 1988). As noted in chapter 7, the U.S.-backed contras in Nicaragua trafficked in cocaine, allegedly with the knowledge if not the assistance of the Central Intelligence Agency (Harmon 1993).

CORRUPTION

Two basic strategies are available to law enforcement agencies—reactive and proactive—and many use a combination of both. *Reactive law enforcement* has its parallel with firefighting: firefighters remain in their stations, equipment at the ready, until a call for service is received. Reactive law enforcement encourages citizens to report crimes; the agency then responds. This type of law enforcement is used for dealing with conventional crimes such as murder, rape, assault, robbery, burglary, and theft—crimes that are likely to be reported to the police. (It should be noted, however, that with the exception of murder and auto theft, studies indicate that most of these crimes do not come to the attention of the police.) *Proactive law enforcement* requires officers/agents to seek out indications of criminal behavior, a necessity when the nature of the criminal violation includes victim participation: examples are gambling, prostitution, and drugs. These crimes are often referred to as "victimless"—although they clearly have victims, who are unlikely to report the crime to the police.

In order to seek out criminal activity in the most efficient manner possible, proactive law enforcement officers must conceal their identity and otherwise deceive the criminals they are stalking. James Q. Wilson (1978: 59) points out that both reactive and proactive law enforcement officers are exposed to opportunities for graft, but the latter are more severely tested. The reactive law enforcement officer, "were he to accept money or favors to act other than as his duty required, would have to conceal or alter information about a crime already known to his organization." The proactive enforcement agent, however, "can easily agree to overlook offenses known to him but to no one else or to participate in illegal transactions (buying or selling drugs) for his own rather than for the organization's advantage." Undercover officers pretending to be criminals are difficult to supervise; the agency for which they work often knows about their activities only to the extent that the agents inform them.

The "French Connection" heroin case provides an example; it was the subject of a best-selling book and of an Academy Award-winning film in 1971 for Best Picture. In 1962, detectives "Popeye" Eddie Egan (played in the movie by Gene Hackman in an Academy Award-winning role) and his partner Sonny Grosso (played by Roy Scheider) smashed an international drug ring that smuggled Turkish heroin into New York from Marseilles. That same year, the drugs seized in connection with the case, fifty-seven pounds of almost pure heroin, were vouchered with the police property clerk by detectives Egan and Grosso. In 1972 the Police Commissioner of the City of New York held a news conference: The French Connection heroin, he announced, had been stolen and replaced with white flour. Several days later, an inventory of the property clerk's office revealed that additional heroin was missing: a total of nearly four hundred pounds had been stolen—by police officers (Wallance 1982). During this period in New York, police corruption was endemic. For some officers, the move from the NYPD to organized crime was simply a lateral transfer (see Manca and Cosgrove 1991 for an example).

In 1988, it was revealed that more than five pounds of heroin had disappeared from the Los Angeles office of the Drug Enforcement Administration; DEA agents were accused of the thefts. In 1989, three former DEA agents at the Los Angeles office were indicted for dealing in large quantities of cocaine and heroin and stealing drugs from a DEA evidence vault. A 1986 article in the *New York Times* noted that in south Florida, "each passing week seems to bring another new drug-related charge against some local police officer as the rising tide of cocaine smuggling exposes more and more officers to bribes and payoffs" (Nordheimer 1986: 15). The pervasiveness of corruption in drug law enforcement was the subject of a *New York Times* feature story in which Philip Shenon (1988: 8) pointed out that drug enforcement corruption, which had heretofore been an urban phenomenon, is now reaching into rural America. Dozens of sheriffs in Tennessee and Georgia have been accused of involvement in drug trafficking. In Henry County, Georgia, for example, the sheriff was sentenced to thirty-five years for bribery in aid of drug smuggling. The sheriff in Dawson County, Georgia, was sentenced to thirty years for protecting a drug-smuggling ring (Coppola 1989). Local law enforcement officials have been convicted of allowing traffickers to land their aircraft at small airfields or on rural roads and offload drugs onto waiting trucks. "One small airfield in rural Morgan County, Georgia, became so popular among drug dealers that it was nicknamed Kennedy International by the state police."

There is also the problem of corruption in foreign countries that grow, process, or serve as transshipment stations for illegal substances. "The corrupt official," notes the President's Commission on Organized Crime (1986c: 178), "is the *sine qua non* of drug trafficking." The Commission concluded:

> Corruption linked to drug trafficking is a widespread phenomenon among political and military leaders, police and other authorities in virtually every country touched by the drug trade. The easily available and enormous amounts of money generated through drug transactions present a temptation too great for many in positions of authority to resist.

This was dramatically underscored in 1988 when a Los Angeles jury found a Mexican (Jalisco) state police officer guilty of the 1985 kidnapping and torture-murder of DEA agent Enrique Camarena Salazar (Shannon 1988). That same year, two Mexican police officers were arrested in New York for conspiring to import heroin into the United States. The following year, the Mexican government arrested Miguel Angel Felix Gallardo, head of a major international cocaine ring, for his reputed involvement in the murder of Camarena. Though wanted by both the Mexican and American governments, Gallardo was able to remain at large for more than a decade. At the same time, the entire police department of Culiacàn, Gallardo's hometown of 700,000 and the capital city of Sinaloa, was taken into custody by the Mexican army. Also

Miguel Angel Felix Gallardo stands before photographers in the attorney general's office detention center in downtown Mexico City after his capture in 1989. Gallardo was described by the attorney general as the "Number one narcotics trafficker in Mexico."

INFORMANTS IN LOS ANGELES

L.A. intelligence detective Mike Rothmiller was sharing an informant with a DEA agent. On one occasion he arranged to meet the DEA agent at the informant's home. When the detective walked in, he found the informant in the living room with at least a pound of cocaine on a glass table, dividing it up into sale packages as the DEA agent looked on. Rothmiller motioned the agent into another room:

"What's going on here?" he said. The federal agent explained that his infor-

mant was helping him take down some other dealers and that he also claimed to have information on a major hydroponic marijuana growing operation in Colorado. "You gotta do what you gotta do." The agent shrugged in apology.

Source: Mike Rothmiller and Ivan G. Goldman, L.A. *Secret Police: Inside the LAPD Elite Spy Network*. New York: Pocket Books, 1992: 89–90.

arrested was the assistant director of the anti-narcotics program in Sinaloa, who confessed to receiving $23,000 a month to keep Gallardo informed of police activities against him (Rohter 1989b). (For a discussion of the pervasive problem of corruption in Mexican law enforcement, see Shannon 1988.) In 1989, the government of Fidel Castro publicly acknowledged that high-ranking military officials had been cooperating with the Medellín cartel to ship cocaine into the United States through Cuba (Pear 1989a, 1989b).

Informants—"snitches" or CIs (confidential informants)—are another problem. Informants come in two basic categories—the "good citizen" and the "criminal." The former is so rare, particularly in OC law enforcement, that we will deal only with the criminal informant, an individual who provides help to law enforcement in order to further his or her own ends. These include vengeance, an effort to drive competition out of business, financial rewards, and most frequently "working off a beef"—securing leniency for criminal activities that have become known to the authorities.

Typically, "while serving as informers, suspects are unofficially allowed to engage in illegal activity" notes Joseph Goldstein (1982: 37). The more the informer is involved in criminal activity, the more useful is his or her assistance. This raises serious ethical and policy questions. Should the informant be given immunity from lawful punishment in exchange for cooperation? If so, who is to make that determination: the agent who becomes aware of the informant's activities; his or her supervisor; the prosecutor who is informed of the situation; or a trial judge? Should a murderer be permitted to remain free because he or she is of value to OC law enforcement efforts?

NICK MITOLA, JR.—INFORMANT

Raised in middle-class circumstances and college educated, Nick Mitola, Jr., became a career criminal at an early age. He moved from gambling, to credit card scams, to drugs; and, after being convicted for drug trafficking, to informer. In return for his freedom, Mitola worked for the FBI, developing evidence against a crew from the New Jersey branch of the Lucchese Family headed by *caporegime* Anthony ("Tumac") Accetturo. At the same time—without the knowledge of his FBI handler—Mitola continued in the drug business. In this capacity he began dealing with a DEA informant: "Not only was an undercover FBI informant dealing with an undercover DEA informant without either agency realizing that the other was an informant, but the DEA informant was cheating the DEA. In the spirit of true American entrepreneurs, the DEA informant claimed to be buying drugs from Mitola at a higher price than Mitola was actually selling them and, apparently, pocketing the difference."

Source: Robert Rudolph, *The Boys from New Jersey.* New York: Morrow, 1992: 341.

There are other dangers, note Paul Eddy, Hugo Sabogal, and Sara Walden (1988: 85). In south Florida, for example, given the number of law enforcement agencies and

given their heavy dependence on intelligence, it is inevitable that there are informants who inform on other informants, who are probably informing on them. A consequence of that is selective prosecution: arbitrary decisions made by police officers and agents as to who will go to jail and who will be allowed to remain on the street. Given the vast amounts of money at stake in the drug business, selective prosecution raises the specter of corruption.

This raises the problem of informant veracity. With strong incentives to produce information, how reliable is an informant? Journalist Jack Newfield (1979) quotes an FBI agent who specialized in OC cases:

I once had an informant who told me all sorts of stories. Later on I found out the guy was simultaneously an informant to the New York City Police Department, only I didn't know. What he was telling the police was completely different than what he was telling the bureau. And we were both paying him for his bullshit.

In 1989 an informant in Los Angeles admitted that he had committed perjury in several cases and suggested that some men may have gone to death row based, at least in part, on his false testimony. The informant said he received prison furloughs, a recommendation for parole, a reduction of bail, and $2,700 for his efforts ("Jail Informer's Admissions Spur Inquiry" 1989; Reinhold 1989).

Furthermore, working closely with informants is a potentially corrupting influence. The informant helps the agent enter an underworld filled with danger—and great financial rewards. Under such circumstances there is always concern that the law enforcement agent may become something else to the informer—a friend, an employee, an employer, or a partner. The rewards can be considerable: the agent can confiscate money and drugs, or receive payment for not arresting gamblers or traffickers and at the same time improve his or her work record by arresting competing or unaffiliated criminals. It is often only a small step from using criminals as informants to entering into business with them.

In 1968, for example, a number of federal agents in the New York office were in the business of selling heroin and protecting drug dealers; the bureau itself, notes Edward Epstein, "became a major source of supply and protection in the United States" (1977: 105). David Durk (Durk and Silverman 1976: 36) notes:

> By 1969, there were two major marketing operations of heroin in New York City. One operated out of Pleasant Avenue [an OC stronghold in Harlem]; the other operated out of the fourth floor of the First Precinct station house in lower Manhattan—the headquarters of the Special Investigations Unit of the police department's Narcotics Division.

These activities were popularized in books and motion pictures (*Serpico* and *Prince of the City*).

In 1982, FBI special agent Daniel A. Mitrione, an eleven-year veteran of the bureau, was assigned to an undercover operation involving drug trafficking. In his undercover role the agent began working with an informant, and Arnold Trebach (1987: 343) reports:

> In a familiar scenario that sometimes seems to flow naturally from the dynamics of the situation, one day the informer asked for the privilege of being a real dealer on the side while he was acting like one for the government. Agent Mitrione allowed the man to take a small load of cocaine to Miami and simply failed to tell his FBI supervisors about it. For this small initial courtesy, the appreciative informant-trafficker gave him $3,500 and a $9,000 Rolex watch.

Over the next few years, the agent received more than $850,000 and eventually a ten-year prison term.

Criminal informants who testify against former colleagues present problems for any prosecutor. These persons typically have serious criminal histories that may equal or surpass those of the defendants. They are almost invariably provided with significant incentives to provide testimony. Acquittals occur in such cases when the informant is a key to successful prosecution, and juries do not accept the credibility of the witness(es). An additional problem (well known in law enforcement circles) became public in Boston—*faking informants*. In 1989 it was disclosed that drug unit officers of the Boston Police Department invented informants for the purpose of securing search warrants (Gold 1989).

As noted in chapter 5, there is danger not only to the informants themselves, but also to innocent members of their families.

STATUTES

The business of organized crime involves the violation of numerous laws. Many of these statutes are routinely enforced by municipal police departments, for example, laws against gambling, drugs, prostitution, assault, and murder. The investigation and prosecution of organized crime per se, however, has largely been a responsibility of the federal government, which has a number of specialized statutes to carry out this purpose. Chief among them are the Internal Revenue Code, the Controlled Substances Act, the Hobbs Act, the Racketeer Influenced and Corrupt Organizations (RICO) statute, the Consumer Credit Protection Act, statutes against conspiracy, and the anti-money-laundering provision of Title 18.

Internal Revenue Code

In 1927 the U.S. Supreme Court decided the case of *United States v. Sullivan* (274 U.S. 259), which denied the claim of self-incrimination as an excuse for failure to file income tax on illegally gained earnings. This decision enabled the federal government to successfully prosecute Al Capone and members of his organization.

Because persons in organized crime have obligations as taxpayers, they can be prosecuted for several acts:

1. Failing to make required returns or maintain required business records.
2. Filing a false return or making a false statement about taxes.
3. Willful failure to pay federal income tax or concealment of assets with intent to defraud.
4. Assisting others to evade income taxes.
5. In gambling operations, failing to file a "Special Tax Return and Application for Registry-wagering."

"Acts which do not comprise a violation or attempt to violate any of these substantive sections may be punishable as part of a conspiracy 'to impair, defeat, and obstruct the functions of the Commissioner of Internal Revenue' by concealing matters relevant to collection of federal taxes" (Johnson 1963: 17). An employer can be prosecuted for not complying with social security withholding requirements relative to employees. Thus, the manager of an illegal enterprise, a gambling operation, for example, could be prosecuted for such evasions.

The Internal Revenue Service of the Department of the Treasury employs special agents in the Criminal Investigation Division (CID). While the primary role of the IRS is collection of revenue and compliance with tax codes, the CID seeks evidence of criminal violations for prosecution by the Department of Justice. In particular, the agents seek out information relative to income that has not been reported:

> Additional income for criminal purposes is established by both direct and indirect methods. The direct method consists of the identification of specific items of unreported taxable receipts, overstated costs and expenses (such as personal expenses charged to business, diversion of corporate income to office-stockholders, allocation of income or expense to incorrect year in order to lower tax, etc.), and improper claims for credit or exemption. The advantage of using this method is that the proof involved is easier for jurors and others to understand. (Committee on the Office of Attorney General 1974: 49–50)

Persons in organized crime have devised methods for successful evasion of taxes—dealing in cash, keeping minimal records, setting up fronts. This is countered by the indirect method known as the *net worth theory*: "The government establishes a taxpayer's net worth at the commencement of the taxing period [which requires substantial accuracy], deducts that from his or her net worth at the end of the period, and proves that the net gain in net worth exceeds the income reported by the taxpayer" (Johnson 1963: 17–19). In effect, the Internal Revenue Service reconstructs a person's total expenditures by examining the person's actual standard of living and comparing it with reported income. The government can then maintain that the taxpayer did not report his or her entire income. The government does not have to show a probable source of the excess unreported gain in net worth. Earl Johnson (1963: 18) points out that the Capone case taught many criminals a lesson: management-level persons in organized crime scrupulously report their income—at least the part of it that they spend.

The Internal Revenue Service explains its various investigative methods as follows (Committee on the Office of Attorney General 1974):

> The net worth method is an indirect method of computing income during a year by determining net worth increases and other outlays. Any change in net worth is adjusted to allow for non-taxable receipts and for reported income— the balance being unreported income. The formula here is: assets minus liabilities equals net worth; ending net worth minus beginning net worth equals net worth increase; net worth increase plus other expenditures plus (or minus) tax adjustments equals adjusted gross income; adjusted gross income minus deductions and exemptions equals corrected taxable income; and corrected taxable income minus reported taxable income equals additional taxable income.

Another indirect method is the expenditures method—related to net worth, but expressed differently. Funds are measured by their flow during the year, rather than by observing changes in net worth from the beginning to the end of the year. The formula here is: non-deductible applications of funds minus nontaxable sources equals adjusted gross income; from there, the formula is the same as for the net worth method. Note that the starting point for the beginning of the first year must be established in order to eliminate reasonable doubt that subsequent expenditures did not come from conversion of existing assets.

Another indirect method is the bank deposits method. This one is unlike the net worth and expenditures methods, which measure income at the point of its outflow—here, income is measured at the time of receipt. In this method, the three immediate dispositions of receipts for the year are determined: how much was deposited into banks; how much was spent without going through banks (cash expenditures); and how much was stored in other places (increases in cash on hand). The formula is: total deposits, plus cash expenditures, minus nonincome items, equals gross receipts. . . .

A special agent scrutinizes the tax returns for the years under investigation. A certificate of assessments and payments for the years involved in the investigation, and for prior years, if pertinent, is obtained. If returns were prepared by someone other than the principal, the person who prepared the return is interviewed concerning the circumstances surrounding the preparation of the returns. The books and records are reconciled with the returns, and differences are noted. Documents (invoices, canceled checks, receipted bills, etc.) supporting amounts shown on records and returns are examined, if available. The principal is questioned regarding his assets, liabilities, and personal expenditures. This information is of the utmost importance in a case where there are no books and records or where the records are incomplete or inadequate. . . .

If the taxpayer has not maintained adequate books and records, the agents may list and analyze all the canceled checks and classify them into business expenses, capital expenditures, personal items, and nondeductible expenditures. The agents may examine records of deposits to bank accounts.

During the course of the investigation information may be obtained from: banks; customers of the principal; other persons who have had business transactions with the principal; records of the principal; public records; and newspapers, etc., regarding sources of the principal's income. The agents may interview, and obtain records from, persons who have had, or have knowledge of, transactions with the principal to determine what payments the principal received and the purposes thereof. Transactions involving purchases or sales of property may be examined. Information relative to those matters may be obtained from the purchaser or seller, from real estate agencies, and from public records. Information regarding the principal's personal and financial history is obtained from the principal, from those who know him, and from documents. This includes determining whether or not the principal has a record of prior violation of federal, state, or local laws.

If the case is based on a net worth computation, evidence must be obtained to support the value of each item appearing in the net worth statement. The principal will be questioned regarding whether all assets and liabilities are included, especially in the beginning and ending computations of net worth. He also may be questioned about inheritances and gifts, both during the period under investigation and in prior years. Further questions will be asked about the taxpayer's assets and liabilities at the beginning and end of each year which is included in the investigation and of any prior year pertinent to the case. The principal will be given an opportunity to explain the alleged discrepancies, and his explanations will be verified to whatever extent is possible. In the examination of records and during interviews with witnesses, the special agent is constantly alert for any facts or circumstances that cast light on the principal's intent, that is, any conduct the likely effect of which would be to mislead or to conceal.

Where a violation involves a failure to file a return, the agent obtains from the District Director or Service Center a certificate stating that a search of the files failed to disclose a return in the name of the principal. The special agent also will question the principal concerning whether or not he filed a return and the reasons for his failure. If the principal alleges that he has filed a return, evidence is obtained to prove or disprove his statement. In other aspects the investigation of a failure to file a return proceeds in much the same manner as that of a case involving a willful attempt to evade or defeat income tax.

Controlled Substances Statutes

In 1914 the Harrison Act made it illegal to sell or give away opium or opium derivatives and coca or its derivatives without written order on a form issued by the Commissioner of Revenue. Persons who were not registered were prohibited from engaging in interstate traffic in the drugs, and no one could possess any of the drugs who had not registered and paid the special tax under a penalty of up to five years imprisonment and a fine of no more than $2,000. Rules promulgated by the Treasury Department permitted only medical professionals to register, and they had to maintain records of the drugs they dispensed. It was concern with federalism—the police powers of the central government being constitutionally limited—that led Congress to use the taxing authority of the federal government to respond to the problem of controlling drugs. At the turn of the century, federal authority to regulate narcotics and the prescription practices of physicians was generally thought to be unconstitutional (Musto 1973). In 1919 the use of taxing authority to regulate drugs was upheld by the Supreme Court.

In 1923, legislation was introduced to ban the importation of opium for the manufacture of heroin, a virtual ban on heroin in the United States. (By 1956, Congress declared all heroin to be contraband.) However, there was still no federal legislation dealing with marijuana. The Federal Bureau of Narcotics, operating under a Depression-era budget, was reluctant to take on the additional responsibilities that would accompany outlawing marijuana at the federal level. Himmelstein (1983) states that it was the hope of Harry J. Anslinger, FBN commissioner from 1930 until his retirement in 1962, that the states would act against marijuana, leaving the Bureau free to concentrate on heroin and cocaine. In order to get the states to act, argues Himmelstein, the Bureau dramatized the dangers of marijuana—but the plan backfired. The states were reluctant to take action in such trying economic times, and the Bureau was forced by its own propaganda campaign to act. At the urging of Anslinger, Congress passed the Marijuana Tax Act of 1937.

In 1972 the (presidentially appointed) National Commission on Marijuana and Drug Abuse recommended that possession of marijuana for personal use or noncommercial distribution be decriminalized. The following year Oregon became the first state to abolish criminal penalties for the possession of one ounce or less of marijuana, replacing incarceration with relatively small fines. In 1975 California made possession of one ounce or less of marijuana a citable misdemeanor with a maximum penalty of $100, and there were no increased penalties for recidivists. By 1978 eleven states had decriminalized marijuana, a position supported by President Jimmy Carter (Himmelstein 1983) but opposed by the President's Commission on Organized Crime (1986a), which was appointed by President Ronald Reagan.

In the years immediately preceding the Second World War, it was perceived that the Federal Bureau of Narcotics had the drug problem well under control. Commissioner Anslinger released statistics indicating a significant drop in the addict population. Then came the war: opiate smuggling dwindled, and those Americans of an age most susceptible to drug use were in Europe and Asia. Drug use was viewed as unpatriotic as well as illegal. Alcohol, barbiturates, and amphetamines were the substances most widely abused during the war years as the price of opiates increased dramatically. The heroin addict population appeared to reach an all-time low.

At the end of the war an epidemic of drug use was feared as American soldiers began to return from the Far East, where opiates were endemic. Morgan (1981) notes that the epidemic failed to materialize. The FBN became a victim of its own propaganda and apparent success, and Congress would not increase the drug-fighting budget. Then, in 1950 and 1951, a spate of news stories on drug abuse reported that the use of heroin was spilling out of the ghetto and into the middle-class environs, where it was poisoning the minds and bodies of America's youth.

On the basis of statistics showing that between 1946 and 1950 there was a 100 percent increase in the number of narcotics-related arrests, and that over a five-year period the average age of persons committed to a public health service hospital for drug abuse had declined from 37.5 to 26.7 years, Congress concluded that drug addiction was increasing and that penalties for drug trafficking were inadequate. In 1951, Congress passed the Boggs Act, increasing penalties for violations of drug laws. Once again, using rather dubious statistical data, Congress concluded that the increased penalties of the Boggs Act had successfully reduced drug trafficking. As a result, in 1956 Congress passed the Narcotic Control Act, which further increased the penalties for drug violations— for example, the sale of heroin to individuals under eighteen years of age was made a capital offense—and increased the authority of the Federal Bureau of Narcotics and agents of the Customs Bureau (PCOC 1986c). State legislatures, responding to the federal initiative, significantly increased their penalties for drug violations.

During the 1960s, concern over the diversion of dangerous drugs from licit sources increased. Congress enacted the Drug Abuse Control Amendments of 1965, which mandated recordkeeping and inspection requirements for depressant and stimulant drugs throughout the chain of distribution, from the basic manufacturer to (but not including) the ultimate consumer. The enforcement aspects of the 1965 legislation were given to a newly created agency, the Bureau of Drug Abuse Control within the Department of Health, Education and Welfare's (HEW) Food and Drug Administration.

Comprehensive Drug Abuse Prevention and Control Act of 1970

As the end of the decade approached, alarming statistics (of dubious validity) were publicized. The drug problem had become a major political issue, and in 1968 President Lyndon Johnson decried the fragmented approach to drug law enforcement. With congressional approval, the president abolished the Federal Bureau of Narcotics and the Bureau of Drug Abuse Control, and transferred their responsibilities to a newly created agency, the Bureau of Narcotics and Dangerous Drugs (BNDD) in the Department of Justice. Revenue and importation aspects of drug trafficking remained within the Treasury Department's Internal Revenue Service and Bureau of Customs. In 1970, President Richard Nixon further clarified the responsibilities of the federal agencies involved in drug control, announcing that BNDD "controls all investigations involving violations of the laws of the United States relating to narcotics, marijuana and dangerous drugs, both within the United States and beyond its borders." Several months later guidelines were promulgated that provided increased authority for the Customs officials at ports and borders.

The two-pronged approach to dealing with drug abuse—investigating and prosecuting traffickers, and reducing demand by preventing addiction and treating addicts—became firm policy. Legislation in 1970 authorized HEW to increase its efforts at prevention and rehabilitation through a program of grants to special projects. The National Institute of Mental Health (NIMH) became the agency with primary responsibility for drug education and prevention activities. The legislation also established five schedules into which all controlled substances could be placed according to their potential for abuse. It imposed additional reporting requirements for manufacturers, distributors, and dispensers, created new regulations for the importation of controlled substances, and established a Commission on Marijuana and Drug Abuse. The BNDD was authorized to increase its strength by three hundred agents.

The 1970 legislation represented a new legal approach to federal drug policy—it was predicated not on the constitutional power to tax but upon federal authority over interstate commerce. The PCOC (1986c: 228) notes that

---

Figure 9.1. Schedules of Controlled Substances

Schedule I

A. The drug or other substance has a high potential for abuse.
B. The drug or other substance has no currently accepted medical use in treatment in the United States.
C. There is a lack of accepted safety for use of the drug or other substance under medical supervision.

Schedule II

A. The drug or other substance has a high potential for abuse.
B. The drug or other substance has a currently accepted medical use in treatment in the United States or a currently accepted medical use with severe restrictions.
C. Abuse of the drug or other substances may lead to severe psychological or physical dependence.

Schedule III

A. The drug or other substance has a potential for abuse less than the drugs or other substances in Schedules I and II.
B. The drug or other substance has a currently accepted medical use in treatment in the United States.
C. Abuse of the drug or other substance may lead to moderate or low physical dependence or high psychological dependence.

Schedule IV

A. The drug or other substance has a low potential for abuse relative to the drugs or other substances in Schedule III.
B. The drug or other substance has a currently accepted medical use in treatment in the United States.
C. Abuse of the drug or other substance may lead to limited physical dependence or psychological dependence relative to the drugs or other substances in Schedule III.

Schedule V

A. The drug or other substance has a low potential for abuse relative to the drugs or other substances in Schedule IV.
B. The drug or other substance has a currently accepted medical use in treatment in the United States.
C. Abuse of the drug or other substances may lead to limited physical dependence or psychological dependence relative to the drugs or other substance in Schedule IV.

Source: Drug Enforcement Administration.

---

this shift had enormous implications for the way in which the federal government would approach drug enforcement in the future. The Act "set the stage for an innovation in Federal drug law enforcement techniques. That innovation was the assigning of large numbers of Federal narcotic agents to work in local communities. No longer was it necessary to demonstrate interstate traffic to justify Federal participation in combatting illegal drug use." The new approach was sustained by decisions of the Supreme Court, and the National Conference of Commissioners on Uniform State Laws drafted a model act based on the 1970 statutes, which has been adopted by most states.

A reorganization plan in 1973 led to the creation of the Drug Enforcement Administration (DEA) within the Department of Justice. All drug control investigative and enforcement responsibilities, except those related to ports of entry and borders, were given over to the new agency. In 1982 the Federal Bureau of Investigation (FBI) was given concurrent jurisdiction with the DEA for drug investigation and law enforcement. In addition, the DEA director was required to report to the director of the FBI, who was given responsibility for supervising drug law enforcement efforts and policies. That same year the Department of Defense Authorization Act included a provision outlining military cooperation with civilian authorities. This provision was designed to improve the level of cooperation by delineating precisely that assistance military commanders could provide, and also permitted military personnel to operate military equipment that had been lent to civilian drug enforcement agencies (PCOC 1986c).

The Comprehensive Crime Control Act of 1984 supplemented the Comprehensive Drug Abuse Prevention and Control Act of 1970 by authorizing the

ANTI-DIVERSION LEGISLATION

The principal statute to control the diversion of precursor and essential chemicals for the manufacture of drugs is the Chemical Diversion and Trafficking Act, Subtitle A of the Anti-Drug Abuse Amendments of 1988. The act established record-keeping requirements and enforcement standards for more than two dozen precursor and essential chemicals. State and federal statutes make the unauthorized trade in any of the listed substances equivalent to trafficking in the actual illegal drugs. There are three basic requirements for all manufacturers and distributors:

1. They must keep retrievable records of the distribution, receipt, sale, importation, or exportation of any of the chemicals or machines on a special list prepared pursuant to the act.

2. They must report certain unusual or suspicious orders for these substances to the DEA.
3. They must obtain proof of identity for customers, whether individuals or companies.

The DEA is authorized to stop the import or export of precursor and essential chemicals if their use cannot be shown to have legitimate medical, scientific, or commercial purposes.

Source: Charles B. DeWitt, *Controlling Chemicals Used to Make Illegal Drugs: The Chemical Action Task Force and the Domestic Chemical Action Group*. Washington, DC: National Institute of Justice, 1993.

doubling of a sentence for drug offenders with prior domestic or foreign felony drug convictions. The Anti-Drug Abuse Act of 1986 imposes mandatory prison sentences for certain drug offenses, and a mandatory doubling of the minimum penalties for offenders with prior felony drug convictions. In 1988 the military's role in drug law enforcement was substantially increased, and Congress enacted another drug abuse act that mandates greater control over precursor chemicals and devices used to manufacture drugs, such as encapsulating machinery.

The Anti-Drug Abuse Amendments of 1988 created a complex and extensive body of civil penalties that were aimed at casual users. These included withdrawal of federal benefits, such as mortgage guarantees. The penalties could result in the loss of a pilot's license or stockbroker's license at the discretion of a federal judge. Fines of up to $10,000 could be imposed for illegal possession of even small amounts of controlled substances. There are special penalties for the sale of drugs to minors. The statute permits the imposition of capital punishment for murders committed as part of a continuing criminal enterprise or for the murder of a law enforcement officer during an arrest for a drug-related felony. The statute also established an Office of National Drug Policy headed by a director appointed by the president. The director was charged with coordinating federal drug supply reduction efforts, including international control, intelligence, interdiction, domestic law enforcement, treatment, education, and research.

The Hobbs Act

The earliest statutes designed to deal with "racketeering" are collectively known as the Hobbs Act (18 U.S.C. Sections 1951–55). Since 1946 they have been amended several times. The Hobbs Act makes it a federal crime to engage in criminal behavior that interferes with interstate commerce:

> Whosoever in any way or degree obstructs, delays, or affects commerce or the movement of any articles or commodity in commerce, by robbery or extortion or attempts or conspires to do so, or commits or threatens physical violence to any person or property in furtherance of a plan or purpose to do anything in violation of this section shall be fined not more than $10,000 or imprisonment for not more than twenty years or both.

The statute has been broadly interpreted so as to permit the successful prosecution of more than sixty Chicago police officers for extorting payoffs from the owners of saloons. The six-year investigation (1970–76) by the U.S. Department of Justice was based on the part of the Hobbs Act that makes extortion that in *any* way affects interstate commerce a federal crime: Federal attorneys "reasoned that because taverns sold beer and liquor, much of which was either delivered from or manufactured in states other than Illinois, extortion of a tavern owner would be a violation of the Hobbs Act" (Biegel and Biegel 1977: 7).

The Hobbs Act also prohibits foreign or interstate travel or the use of interstate facilities, for example, the mails or telephones, to advance illegal activities such as gambling, drug trafficking, extortion, and bribery. This interpretation permitted the federal government to prosecute corrupt officials and lawyers in Cook County, Illinois, "Operation Greylord," in the late 1980s and early 1990s. Section 1954 defines as criminal a union official who misuses an employee benefit plan. An official who

> receives or agrees or solicits any fee, kickback, commission, gift, loan, money, or thing of value because of or with intent to be influenced with respect to, any of the actions, decisions, or other duties relating to any question or matter concerning such plan or any persons who directly or indirectly gives or offers, or promises to give or offer, any fee, kickback, commission, gift, loan, money, or thing of value prohibited by this section, shall be fined not more than $10,000 or imprisoned for not more than three years, or both.

Conspiracy

Conspiracy is an agreement between two or more persons to commit a criminal act; it is the *agreement* that becomes the *corpus* (body) of the crime. Conspiracy requires proof (beyond a reasonable doubt) that two or more persons planned to violate the law and that at least one overt act in furtherance of the conspiracy was made by a conspirator; for example, the purchase of materials to aid in the transportation or dilution of the drugs. Conspiracy statutes provide valuable tools for prosecuting persons in organized crime since:

1. Intervention can occur prior to the commission of a substantive offense.
2. A conspirator cannot shield him- or herself from prosecution because of a lack of knowledge of the details of the conspiracy or the identity of co-conspirators and their contributions.
3. An act or declaration by one conspirator committed in furtherance of the conspiracy is admissible against each co-conspirator (an exception to the hearsay rule).
4. Each conspirator is responsible for the substantive crimes of his or her co-conspirators; even late joiners can be held liable for prior acts of co-conspirators if the agreement by the latecomer is made with full knowledge of the conspiracy's objective.

The charge of conspiracy, which federal prosecutors generally include whenever a case involves multiple defendants (Campane 1981a), is particularly effective against upper-echelon OC figures: "The fundamental essence of a conspiracy," notes Earl Johnson (1963: 2), "obviates the necessity of establishing that the organization leader committed a physical act amounting to a crime or that he even committed an overt act in furtherance of the object of the conspiracy. It is sufficient if he can be shown to have been a party to the conspiratorial agreement." Its usefulness can be seen in the following incident:
Two young men entered an Italian restaurant and approached the table of an elderly gentleman who was sipping anisette with a large burly individual.

After he acknowledged them, the two sat down at the table. They were members of a powerful crime Family; he was the boss. The young men explained that they had just discovered a large-scale gambling operation that was not tied to OC—an "outlaw" game. They wanted to "license" the operation and asked for his approval. The boss gestured with his hands and face, saying nothing, but conveying approval. The two young men excused themselves and left. With several other members of the Family, they proceeded to assault and threaten to kill the owner of the gambling operation, extorting several thousand dollars from him. They returned and shared the money with their boss, who knew nothing of the details of what had occurred.

There are three basic types of conspiracy:

1. *Wheel Conspiracies.* One person at the "hub" conspires individually with two or more persons who make up the "spokes" of the wheel. For the conspiracy to be (legally) complete, the wheel needs a "rim": each of the spokes must be aware of and agree with each other in pursuit of at least one objective.
2. *Chain Conspiracies.* Like the lights on a Christmas tree, each conspirator is dependent on the successful participation of every other member. Each member is a "link" who understands that the success of the scheme depends upon everyone in the chain.
3. *Enterprise Conspiracies.* The RICO enterprise conspiracy avoids the practical limitations inherent in proving wheel and chain conspiracies. The statute makes it a separate crime to conspire to violate state or federal law as the result of an agreement to participate in an enterprise by engaging in a *pattern of racketeering activity.* Members of the conspiracy need not know each other, or even be aware of each other's criminal activities. All that needs to be shown is each member's agreement to participate in the organization—the "enterprise"—by committing two or more acts of racketeering such as gambling or drug violations within a ten-year period (a pattern of racketeering). The enterprise conspiracy facilitates mass trials with each member of the enterprise subjected to the significant penalties—twenty years imprisonment on each count—that can result from a conviction.

Prosecuting criminal conspiracy cases can be problematic. In a 1974 case (*United States v. Sperling* 506 F.2d 1323, 1341, 2d Cir.) the court noted that

> it has become too common for the government to bring indictments against a dozen or more defendants and endeavor to force as many of them as possible to trial in the same proceeding on the claim of a single conspiracy when the criminal acts could more reasonably be regarded as two or more conspiracies, perhaps with a link at the top.

This creates the risk of "guilt by association" wherein a jury, confronted by a large number of defendants and a great volume of evidence, is unable to give each defendant the individual consideration that due process requires. In such situations, a finding of guilty brings with it the risk of being reversed on appeal. Jerome Campane (1981b: 30) notes that constitutional guarantees of a fair trial "make it imperative to determine whether the evidence establishes one large conspiracy as opposed to multiple smaller ones."

Another considerable problem is that conspiracy cases usually require direct testimony of eyewitnesses; these are often participants in the conspiracy who agree to testify ("flip") against their co-conspirators in exchange for leniency or immunity from prosecution. Thus, Campane (1981b: 29) advises: "An investigator should therefore be prepared to locate witnesses (often immunized co-conspirators) who are willing to testify and are able to explain the complicated or intricate nature of the unlawful activity, and as a consequence, the stake in the venture or mutual dependence each participant has with each other."

RICO

The Racketeer Influenced and Corrupt Organizations statute (18 U.S.C. Sections 1961–68), usually referred to as RICO, has clearly become the most important single piece of legislation ever enacted against organized crime. Part of the Organized Crime Control Act of 1970, RICO defines "racketeering" in an extremely broad manner, and it includes many offenses that do not ordinarily violate any federal statute: "any act or threat involving murder, kidnapping, gambling, arson, robbery, bribery, extortion, or dealing in narcotic or other dangerous drugs, which is chargeable under State law and punishable by imprisonment for more than one year." In addition, there is a "laundry list" of federal offenses that are defined as "racketeering":

- Hobbs Act violations
- Bribery
- Sports bribery
- Counterfeiting
- Embezzlement from union funds
- Loansharking
- Mail fraud
- Wire fraud
- Obstruction of (state or federal) justice
- Contraband cigarettes
- White slavery (Mann Act violations)
- Bankruptcy fraud (scam)
- Drug violations

Obscenity was added in 1984.

RICO has provided the federal government with jurisdiction that heretofore had been exclusively that of state and local law enforcement, which is often ineffective in dealing with organized crime. As a result, the FBI has become the lead agency in organized crime law enforcement.

The thrust of RICO is to prove a pattern of crimes conducted through an organization. Under RICO it is a separate crime to *belong* to an enterprise, for example, an OC unit, that is involved in a "pattern of racketeering," even if the "racketeering" was committed by other members.

> It shall be unlawful for any person employed by or associated with any enterprise engaged in, or the activities of which affect, interstate or foreign commerce, to conduct or participate, directly or indirectly, in the conduct of such enterprise's affairs through a pattern of racketeering activity or collection of an unlawful debt.

In order for "racketeering" to be a RICO violation there must be a "pattern":

> A pattern of racketeering requires at least two acts of racketeering activity, one of which occurred after the effective date of this chapter and the last of which occurred within ten years (excluding any period of imprisonment) after the commission of a prior act of racketeering activity.

The criminal penalties for violating RICO are substantial: "Whoever violates any provision of section 1962 of this chapter shall be fined not more than $25,000 or imprisoned not more than twenty years, or both." In addition to the criminal penalties, there are civil forfeiture provisions, requiring the violator to forfeit to the government any business or property he or she has acquired in violation of RICO. The government can also freeze a defendant's assets before trial.

Under the provisions of RICO, the government can file a petition in federal district court seeking to have a branch (local) of a labor union, or even the leadership of the union itself, removed and the entity placed in receivership. As noted in chapter 8, this was done with Local 560 of the International Brotherhood of Teamsters (the "Tony Pro local") and Local 54 of the Hotel Employees and Restaurant Employees Union. Similar action was taken with respect to two construction union locals in New York City.

RICO also has provisions by which private citizens can sue for damages: "Any person injured in his business or property by reason of a violation of section 1962 of this chapter may sue therefore in any appropriate United States district court and shall recover threefold damages he sustains and the cost of the suit, including a reasonable attorney's fee."

While it took some time for federal prosecutors to fully understand and incorporate RICO into their array of prosecutorial tools, it has become clear that the use of the statute has been quite effective. By 1990, more than 1,000 major and minor organized crime figures had been convicted and given lengthy prison sentences. "The hierarchies of the five New York LCN Families have been prosecuted, and similar prosecutions have dented the LCN hierarchies in Boston, Cleveland, Denver, Kansas City, Milwaukee, New Jersey, Philadelphia, Pittsburgh and St. Louis" (Pennsylvania Crime Commission 1990: 18). In fact, the threat of lengthy imprisonment under RICO provides a "stick" that has been used to gain the cooperation of defendants. Rudolph W. Giuliani (1987: 106), former U.S. attorney for the Southern District of New York, who has successfully used RICO in prosecuting OC cases, states:

> The federal prosecutor derives a variety of benefits from the RICO statute's definitions of enterprise and racketeering activity. For example, it is the only

RICO AND THE COLOMBO CRIME FAMILY

Fourteen defendants were indicted as either leaders, members, or associates of the Colombo Family of La Cosa Nostra. In setting forth the "enterprise," the indictment identified the three "Bosses" of the Family and five "Capos," who were all charged with supervising and protecting the criminal activities of the subordinates of the Family. The leadership as well as the lower-ranking members were included within the Family "enterprise" as a group of individuals associated in fact. The ongoing nature of the enterprise was demonstrated by the fact that the Family selected an Acting Boss to direct its criminal activities while the Boss was in jail. Reliance entirely upon traditional conspiracy law without RICO would not have enabled the Government to include all of these individuals within a single prosecution or to identify each of their specific roles within the enterprise.

In addition, RICO's requirement of proving a "pattern of racketeering activity" and its broad definition of "racketeering activity" allowed the prosecution to join in a single indictment the widely diverse state and federal crimes the Colombo Family has engaged in over the past fifteen years. Thus, the indictment included charges that the Family had engaged in extortion, labor racketeering, drug trafficking, gambling, loansharking, and both state and federal bribery violations. The prosecution was also able to include as predicate acts of racketeering the prior federal bribery convictions of three of the defendants.

Moreover, venue in RICO cases permits the prosecution of a continuing offense in any district in which such offense was begun, continued, or completed. Thus, the prosecution was able to include crimes committed in the southern and eastern districts of New York, as well as Florida and New Jersey.

Finally, because of RICO's broad definition of a pattern of racketeering activity, it was possible for the prosecutors to include predicate offenses in which the criminal conduct occurred at a time beyond the reach of the general federal five-year statute of limitations. In this regard, all that RICO requires is that one act of racketeering have occurred after the effective date of the statute (October 15, 1970), and that the last or most recent predicate act have occurred within ten years of a prior act of racketeering. Given these provisions, the prosecution was permitted to charge a 1970 heroin transaction as well as extortions that took place in 1975.

Source: Rudolph W. Giuliani, "Legal Remedies for Attacking Organized Crime." In *Major Issues in Organized Crime Control*, edited by Herbert Edelhertz. Washington, DC: U.S. Government Printing Office, 1987: 106–107; edited.

criminal statute that enables the Government to present a jury with the whole picture of how an enterprise, such as an organized crime family, operates. Rather than pursuing the leader of a small group of subordinates for a single crime or scheme, the Government is able to indict the entire hierarchy of an organized crime family for the diverse criminal activities in which that "enterprise" engages. Instead of merely proving one criminal act in a defendant's life, it permits proof of a defendant's whole life in crime.

Giuliani provides an example: the successful prosecution of the Colombo Family.

Criticism of RICO

Four basic criticisms of RICO have been raised:

1. It is overreaching, leading to the prosecution of persons who, although they may have been involved in criminal behavior, are not by any stretch of the imagination connected to organized crime.
2. Invoking RICO can result in assets being frozen even before a trial begins, an action that can effectively put a company out of business. The threat of freezing assets can induce corporate defendants to plead guilty even when they believe themselves to be innocent.
3. A RICO action brings with it the stigma of being labeled a "racketeer," which may be inappropriate given the circumstances at issue.
4. RICO permits lawsuits for treble damages when ordinary business transactions, not organized crime or racketeering, are at issue.

The Organized Crime Act (of which RICO is a part) fails to define *organized crime*, and RICO fails to define *racketeer*. The lack of precision coupled with the substantial penalties has made RICO a tempting tool for federal prosecutors to use against persons who are not connected to organized crime, no matter how widely that term is defined. In Chicago, for example, a deputy sheriff and clerk in traffic court have been convicted under RICO for helping to fix parking tickets. In New York, the U.S. attorney used RICO against a small commodities firm for what Edward J. Epstein (1988a: 46) calls so commonplace a transaction "that on some days they account for a third of the volume on the New York Stock Exchange." In 1988, the government brought a RICO indictment against Princeton/Newport Partners, a securities firm, seeking $500,000 in illegal profits. Prosecutors insisted, however, on a bond of $24 million, forcing the company to liquidate before a trial even began (Nocera 1988).

Supporters argue that RICO has been very effective in combatting corporate crime that has traditionally proven difficult to prosecute successfully (Waldman and Gilbert 1989). Illegal business practices—*crime*—can certainly be defined as *organized* if they are sufficiently large-scale and are continuously performed by specialists, even in the absence of violence and/or corruption. For example, securities violations involving prestigious brokerage firms have been successfully prosecuted using RICO.

Since 1986, about one thousand civil racketeering suits have been filed each year by private plaintiffs seeking to recover triple their damages from a variety of defendants—business competitors, swindlers, securities brokers, and unions. (The government averages about one hundred a year.) There are so many cases, notes Epstein (1988a), that the practice has spawned its own publication: *RICO Law Reporter*. In 1989, a federal appeals court ruled that under RICO twenty-six anti-abortion demonstrators who used coercive tactics against a clinic in Philadelphia were liable for $43,000 in damages and $65,000 in lawyer's fees, despite the fact that no criminal charges had been brought in the case (Lewin 1989).

While private cases have generally proven hard to win, critics argue that the threat of triple damages—and of being referred to as a "racketeer"—causes many defendants to settle. Furthermore, the triple-damage provision encourages contingency lawyers to sue when under ordinary circumstances the potential reward would not be worth the commitment of time. The courts, however, have fined lawyers for bringing frivolous racketeering claims (Diamond 1988). Edward O'Brien (1986) argues that in contract disputes attorneys routinely add RICO violations, thereby removing their cases from state court and overloading federal courts. Robert Blakey (1986), the author of RICO, argues that the civil sections provide a powerful tool for persons victimized by swindlers to recover their losses while serving as a deterrent. To avoid the problem of inappropriate labeling, Michael Waldman and Pamela Gilbert (1989) recommend that the term *racketeer* be removed from the civil aspects of the statute.

In the first case to limit the scope of a state RICO law, the Supreme Court ruled that the inventory of a Fort Wayne, Indiana, adult bookstore could not be subjected to seizure in advance of an obscenity conviction. In a unanimous decision, the Court referred to prohibitions against "prior restraint" of publications that have not been judged to be obscene. In a 6–3 vote, however, the Court rejected a claim that the First Amendment prohibits the use of RICO to prosecute obscenity cases, and left open the possibility that the materials could be confiscated after obscenity is proven at trial (*Fort Wayne Books, Inc. v. Indiana, et al.*, 488 U.S. 445, 1989). That same year, the Supreme Court unanimously refused to limit the scope of RICO with respect to private suits (*H.J., Inc. v. Northwestern Bell Telephone Co.*, 492 U.S. 229).

Consumer Credit Protection Act (CCPA)

The 1968 Consumer Credit Act (18 U.S.C. Sections 891–94) was designed to combat loansharking. It provides a definition of a loanshark debt as

> any extension of credit with respect to which is the understanding of the creditor and the debtor at the time it is made that delay in making repayment or failure to make repayment could result in the use of violence or other criminal means to cause the harm to the person, reputation, or property of any person.

The statute chose the term *understanding*, note Ronald Goldstock and Dan Coenen (1978: 65), "in an obvious effort to catch the many loansharks who operate purely on the basis of implication and veiled suggestion." The critical element of the offense is the *understanding* that violence "could result" if repayment is not timely. The statute even provides for an alternative to direct evidence. An implied threat can be assumed:

> The state must show the debtor's reasonable belief that the creditor had used, or had a reputation for using, "extortionate means" to collect or punish nonpayment. Second, if direct evidence of this sort is unavailable (as when the victim is dead or too frightened to testify) and certain other prerequisites are met, the court may allow evidence tending to show the creditor's reputation as to collection practices to show the "understanding" element. (Goldstock and Coenen 1978: 110–11)

The CCPA also contains a provision intended to make it possible to prosecute upper levels of the OC hierarchy who, although they may not make the loans themselves, are often the original source of funding for extortionate credit transactions made directly by underlings (18 U.S.C. Section 893):

> Whoever willfully advances money or property, whether as a gift, as a loan, as an investment, pursuant to a partnership or profit-sharing agreement, or otherwise, to any person, with the reasonable grounds to believe that it is the intention of that person making extortionate extensions of credit, shall be fined not more than $10,000 or an amount not to exceed twice the value of the money or property so advanced, whichever is greater, or shall be imprisoned not more than 20 years, or both.

The same penalties hold for the loanshark actually making the loan or those who assist in attempting to collect an extortionate extension of credit.

Forfeiture

For obvious reasons—funds without taxation—governments have found forfeiture very attractive. In 1972, Hawaii enacted civil RICO legislation with the seizure and forfeiture provision and by 1989, twenty-five other states had enacted similar legislation. Interest in forfeiture has generated several periodicals; for example, the National Association of Attorneys General publishes the monthly *State Civil RICO Enforcement Newsletter*, while the Police Executive Research Forum publishes the *Asset Forfeiture Bulletin*. In 1985, the Department of Justice established the National Assets Seizure and Forfeiture Fund. The total amount of seized assets so far is about $3 billion, with between 30,000 and 40,000 seizures a year. The law requires that the proceeds from resold property be spent on the fight against drugs, so much of the money resulting from forfeiture goes back into state and local law enforcement efforts. Automobiles seized are usually transferred to law enforcement agencies for undercover use.

Section 881 of the Comprehensive Drug Abuse Prevention and Control Act of 1970 provides for the seizure of assets under certain conditions. The reach of Section 881 was extended through amendments in 1978 and 1984. The statute now permits forfeiture of all profits from drug trafficking and all assets purchased with such proceeds or traded in exchange for controlled substances. It authorizes the forfeiture of all real property used in any manner to facilitate violations of drug statutes, including entire tracts of land and all improvements regardless of what portion of the property facilitated the illegal activities. Currency, buildings, land, motor vehicles, and airplanes have all been confiscated (Stahl 1992).

A seizure can be made incident to an arrest or customs inspection or upon receipt of a seizure order. To obtain a seizure order—actually a warrant—the government must provide sworn testimony in an affidavit spelling out the property to be seized and why there is reason to believe that it is being used to commit crimes or was acquired with money from criminal activity—the same process used in securing a search warrant. The filing of criminal charges against the owner is not required. Except for personal residence, the owner of the property is not informed of the action until his or her property is seized by U.S. marshals pursuant to the court order. The owner of the property has a right to contest the seizure only after it has occurred; he or she must prove that the money or property was earned through legal enterprise. In 1993, the Supreme Court (*United States v. Good*, No. 92-1180) ruled that the government may not seize real estate without providing the owner a hearing. "Current case law requires a firm nexus [tie or link] between asset(s) subject to forfeiture and narcotics activity, but it allows that nexus to be built on circumstantial evidence. The courts are construing the proceeds provisions in a manner that permits tracing in general, as opposed to specific acts of narcotics trafficking" (Bryant 1988: 8).

Civil forfeiture is an *in rem* proceeding in contrast to the *in personam* proceedings used in criminal forfeiture. As such, the action is against the property, not the person, so that even an acquittal on the criminal charges does not preclude civil forfeiture. Under federal statutes, an order to seize property can be issued on a showing of probable cause, a relatively low level of evidence. If the forfeiture is contested, once probable cause has been established by the government the burden of proof shifts to the defendant, who must prove that his or her property is not subject to seizure by a higher standard of proof, the preponderance of the evidence. This shift in the burden of evidence also diminishes the Fifth Amendment privilege against self-incrimination. The Supreme Court has refused to apply the Fifth Amendment's Double Jeopardy Clause or the Sixth Amendment's right to confront witnesses to *in rem* forfeiture (Stahl 1992). Since the process is quasi-criminal, however, the exclusionary rule is applicable, and evidence seized in violation of the Constitution cannot be considered in establishing probable cause (*One 1958 Plymouth Sedan v. Pennsylvania* 380 U.S. 691, 701 [1965]).

Section 881 provides for an innocent owner defense: the violation occurred without the owner's knowledge. The burden is on the owner to prove inno-

Figure 9.2. Verified Complaint for Forfeiture

```
          IN THE UNITED STATES DISTRICT COURT
             NORTHERN DISTRICT OF ILLINOIS
                  EASTERN DIVISION
```

UNITED STATES OF AMERICA
    Plaintiff,

        v.

A 1987 ROLLS-ROYCE CORNICHE
VIN SCAZDO2A4HCX20937,

$152,645.00 in UNITED
STATES CURRENCY seized
from SAFE DEPOSIT BOX
6265 at CLYDE FEDERAL,

$30,040 in UNITED STATES
CURRENCY seized from
SAFE DEPOSIT BOX 5660
at WESTERN NATIONAL BANK,

$22,400 in UNITED STATES
CURRENCY seized from
SAFE DEPOSIT BOX 8805-N
AT OAK PARK TRUST AND
SAVINGS BANK, and

UNITED STATES CURRENCY in
THE AMOUNT OF $120,023.00
      Defendants

NO.

89C1250

FEB 15 1989

JUDGE
JUDGE NORGLE

MAGISTRATE LEFKOW

VERIFIED COMPLAINT FOR FORFEITURE

    The United States of America, by its attorney, Anton R. Valukas, United States Attorney for the Northern District of Illinois for its complaint states:

    1.) This is a forfeiture action under Title 21, United States Code Section 881 (a) (6) and this Court has jurisdiction under Title 28, United States Code, Sections 1345 and 1355.

2.) The defendants named in the caption were seized on land within the Northern District of Illinois and will remain within this Court's jurisdiction throughout the pendency of this action.

3.) On February 7, 1989, a search warrant arising from a narcotics investigation of an individual known as Rufus Sims was executed at a residence at 2606 South Boeger in Westchester, Illinois. The search resulted in the seizure of a large quantity of weapons and twenty-three (23) bags containing cocaine repackaged for sale commingled with United States Currency in the amount of $4,301.00.

4.) During the execution of the warrant at the residence, the police discovered title to the defendant 1987 Rolls Royce Convertible, VIN SCAZDO2A4HCX20937. Review of records at Steve Foley Cadillac revealed that the purchase price of the cadillac was $176,681, of which $129,461 was paid in currency and the remainder of the purchase price came from Sims' trade-in of another Rolls-Royce owned by him.

5.) During the execution of the search warrant at Sims' residence, the police discovered a number of keys to safe deposit boxes at banks in the Chicago area. One of the keys seized was for safe deposit box 2655 at the Forest Park National Bank. On February 10, 1989, police officers stopped Andrea Thomas, Sims' common-law wife, and Estelle Greenfield, Sims' mother, outside the Forest Park National Bank with $120,023.00 in United States Currency which they had just taken from box 2655. Both women disavowed knowledge of the money (even though it filled a large satchel which Estelle Greenfield was carrying) and each claimed that it did not belong to them.

6.) On February 11, 1989, Magistrate Bucklo issued seizure warrants ordering the Federal Bureau of Investigation to seize the contents of the other safe deposit boxes for which keys had been found at the Sims' residence. The warrants resulted in the seizure of $152,645.00 from box 6265 at Clyde Federal, $30,040 from box 5660 at Western National Bank, and $22,400 from Box 8805–N at Oak Park Trust and Savings Bank.

7.) Rufus Sims is unemployed and has no known legitimate source of income. Although he is unemployed, he purchased a 1987 Rolls-Royce worth $176,681, owns real estate and numerous other vehicles, and had safe deposit boxes containing over $320,000.00 in cash.

8.) The affidavit of Chicago Police Sergeant Robert M. Lombardo verifying this complaint is appended hereto and incorporated herein.

9.) By reasons of the foregoing, and as detailed more specifically in the attached affidavid, the defendants constitute proceeds of narcotics trafficking and are therefore subject to forfeiture pursuant to Title 21, United States Code, Section 881 (a) (6).

WHEREFORE, for the reasons described above, the United States prays:

1.) That the defendants be proceeded against for forfeiture and condemnation;

2.) that a warrant of seizure and monition issue;

3.) that due notice be given to all interested parties to appear and show cause as to why the forfeiture should not be decreed; and,

4.) that this Court adjudge and decree that the defendants be forfeited to the United States of America, and that they be properly disposed of according to law.

cence by a preponderance of the evidence. The government can overcome claims of innocence by showing that it would be reasonable to believe that the owner was aware. In addition, notes Marc Stahl (1992: 288), some courts have required the owner to prove that he or she took all reasonable steps to prevent the violation. There is also a remission procedure—the claimant can file a petition with the attorney general, who can order the return of property if there are mitigating circumstances. However, remission is a discretionary act.

A great deal of criticism has been leveled at forfeiture. The normally conservative *Chicago Tribune*, for example, in an editorial (April 1, 1993) stated that while forfeiture can be an effective punishment for crime, when used appropriately, "a growing number of innocent parties and two-bit players are being swept up in the net. And those who are unfairly trapped find that forfeiture laws turn due process on its head." In 1993, the Supreme Court ruled unanimously that the Eighth Amendment's protection against "excessive fines" requires that there must be a relationship between the gravity of the offense and the value of the property seized (*Austin v. United States*, 113 S. Ct. 2801).

Until 1988, the act permitted the Department of Justice to prosecute attorneys and seize fees from tainted sources. Defense attorneys argued that this created a situation "in which a defendant cannot retain an attorney because of the government's threat of criminal and civil sanctions against any attorney who takes the case" (Weinstein 1988: 381). The defendant was left without a free choice of attorneys and was dependent on a public defender, who was not always able to defend against the often complex nature of RICO prosecutions. Supporters of this legislation argue that criminals who have grown wealthy from crime are not entitled to any greater consideration with respect to legal representation than their less successful criminal colleagues, who are often represented by a public defender. On November 18, 1988, President Ronald Reagan signed an anti-drug abuse bill that contained an amendment to 18 U.S.C. Section 1957. The amendment excluded defense attorney's fees from the criminal money laundering provisions. Thus, while criminal defense fees could still be subject to forfeiture, the attorneys who accept tainted fees are exempt from criminal prosecution. In 1988, the Supreme Court, in a 5–4 decision, ruled that under the Comprehensive Forfeiture Act, the government can freeze the assets of criminal defendants before trial (*Caplin and Drysdale v. United States*, 491 U.S. 617; *United States v. Monsanto*, 491 U.S. 600).

Money Laundering

Prior to the passage of the Money Laundering Control Act of 1986 (Title 18 U.S.C. sections 1956 and 1957), money laundering was not a federal crime, although the Department of Justice had used a variety of federal statutes to successfully prosecute money-laundering cases. The act, notes Adam Weinstein (1988), consolidated these statutes with the goal of increasing prosecutions for this offense. Money laundering was made a separate federal offense punishable by a fine of $500,000 or twice the value of the property involved, whichever is greater, and twenty years imprisonment. Title 18 U.S.C. Section 981 provides for the civil confiscation of any property related to a money-laundering scheme. Legislation enacted in 1988 allows the government to file a suit claiming ownership of all cash funneled through operations intended to disguise their illegal source. The courts can issue an order freezing all contested funds until the case is adjudicated. An amendment to the Drug Abuse Act of 1988 requires offshore banks to record any U.S. cash transactions in excess of $10,000 and to permit U.S. officials to have access to the records. Off-shore banks that fail to comply can be banned from holding accounts in U.S. banks and denied access to U.S.-dollar clearing and money-transfer systems (Egan 1991).

Under the Currency and Foreign Transactions Reporting Act (31 U.S.C. Sec. 5311, as amended), the United States can compel other countries to maintain certain financial records similar to those required under the Bank Secrecy Act. The Bank Secrecy Act requires recordkeeping by financial institutions (including gambling casinos) and currency transaction reports for certain deposits, withdrawals, or exchanges of currency or monetary instruments in excess of $10,000. If a country fails to negotiate an acceptable records system, its financial institutions can be denied access to the U.S. banking system. There are problems implementing this legislation:

> Very few countries, apart from developed countries with exchange control laws, have legislation requiring their banks and other financial institutions to collect and report such information to a government agency. . . . [I]n those countries that collect such information, there is no specific attention given to United States dollar transactions and generally there are tight limits on the dissemination of cash reports to third parties. (Chaiken 1991: 505)

A person is guilty of money laundering if he or she knows that the property involved represents the proceeds of some illegal activity, attempts to conceal or disguise the nature, the location, the source, the ownership, or the control of the proceeds, or attempts to avoid a transaction-reporting requirement. Furthermore, a person is guilty of money laundering if he or she transports or attempts to transport a monetary instrument or funds out of the United States with the intent to carry out an unlawful activity. If a person has the knowledge that the monetary instrument or funds involved represent the proceeds of some form of unlawful activity, or attempts to conceal or disguise the nature, location, source, ownership, or control of the proceeds, or to avoid a transaction-reporting requirement, he or she is guilty of money laundering. For a conviction under section 1957, notes Weinstein (1988), the prosecutor must prove the following:

1. The defendant engaged in a monetary transaction in excess of $10,000.
2. The defendant knew the money was the fruit of criminal activity.
3. The money was in fact the fruit of a specified unlawful activity.

LAW ENFORCEMENT

General police responsibility is a function of a "full-service" municipal department—there is no national police force in the United States. The primary responsibility of state police forces is highway traffic enforcement. Most of the resources of a municipal police department go into uniformed services such as patrol; only a small portion goes into plainclothes or detective units. In larger cities, such units include specialties such as "vice" (gambling and prostitution) and drug enforcement. In this function, local police do apprehend some of the participants in organized criminal activity. Organized crime, however, is rarely a priority item for a municipal department. Resources devoted to OC detract from the department's ability to respond to citizen demands for police services. Justin Dintino and Frederick Martens (1980: 67) point out:

> Few local departments have the luxury of developing a sophisticated organized crime control program. Obviously, the daily realities of police work at the grass-roots level mitigates against a well-developed execution of an organized crime control strategy. Since organized crime is often synonymous with vice enforcement—gambling, prostitution, narcotics, and loansharking—there are few incentives for a police administrator to allocate limited and valuable resources toward this particular form of criminality. Often the investment of personnel to enforce laws which govern "consensual relationships" between customer and supplier are met with judicial indifference and public apathy; and as demonstrated through numerous studies and investigations, it is highly questionable from a purely cost-benefit analysis whether the benefits outweigh the costs incurred.

Accordingly, most investigative and law-enforcement efforts against OC are found at the federal level.

An important exception is in New York, where under the direction of Ronald Goldstock the Organized Crime Task Force has been responsible for developing important cases against persons involved in organized crime. The Task Force is an independent investigative agency with a mandate to investigate and prosecute multi-county organized criminal activity and to assist local law enforcement agencies in their efforts against organized crime. The Task Force has statewide jurisdiction and is divided into three regional offices. Each office is comprised of teams that are assigned to investigate a specific type of OC activity such as labor racketeering or narcotics. Each team is comprised of an attorney, an accountant, an investigative analyst, and a senior investigator who supervises investigations using personnel from the state police. Other states, for example, New Jersey, Pennsylvania, and New Mexico, have established investigating or crime commissions in response to organized criminal activity.

Because the police are the most visible agents of governmental power, and because Americans have historically distrusted government in general and the federal government in particular, there has never been serious consideration of a federal police force. Over the decades, however, necessity led to the creation

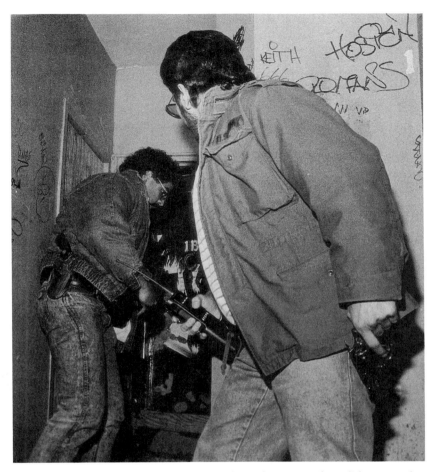

Plainclothes police officers break down the door of a suspected crack house in the Bronx. Only in larger cities do plainclothes and detective units include specialties such as vice and drug enforcement.

of a number of specialized federal enforcement agencies in an unplanned and uncoordinated manner. Thus, while they all have the same nominal boss, the president, federal law enforcement is fragmented. The result is a confusing number of agencies in several departments—Justice, Treasury, Transportation, Labor, and Defense—whose responsibility for OC law enforcement lacks systematic coordination.

Department of Justice (DOJ)

Clearly, the most important federal department dealing with organized crime is the Department of Justice, which is headed by the attorney general, a member of the president's cabinet. Each of the ninety-four judicial districts has a U.S. attorney appointed by the president for a period of four years. The U.S. attorneys and about 2,000 assistant U.S. attorneys prosecute cases for all federal enforcement agencies. Within the DOJ is the Organized Crime and Racketeering Section (OCRS), which is responsible for coordinating and developing nation-wide programs for responding to organized crime.

Federal Bureau of Investigation (FBI)

The FBI is the closest thing to a federal police force in the United States. Its origins date back to the establishment of the Department of Justice in 1870. Until 1908, the department used private detectives or borrowed men from the Secret Service. In that year, President Theodore Roosevelt directed the attorney general to develop an investigative unit within the Justice Department: it was named the Bureau of Investigation. In 1935, Congress renamed it the Federal Bureau of Investigation.

After the First World War, the bureau was involved in a great deal of "anti-radical" activity at the direction of Attorney General A. Mitchell Palmer. The FBI conducted raids and arrested thousands of people in what became known as the "Red Scare of 1919." The "Palmer Raids" were the subject of a congressional investigation and were strongly defended by the bureau's assistant director, John Edgar Hoover, who was appointed director of the FBI in 1924 and remained at its head until his death in 1972.

Over the years, the bureau was given the responsibility of investigating interstate shipment of stolen vehicles, kidnapping, bank robbery, interstate fugitives, espionage, and sabotage. After the Second World War, FBI resources were directed towards the perceived threat posed by domestic Communism. The problem of organized crime was left unattended. Sanford Unger (1975: 391) argues that "the Director was simply clever enough to steer clear of the toughest problems—the ones less likely to produce prompt and stunning results, that might test conflicts of loyalty among agents, or that would require them to be exposed to the seamier side of life (and, as with many policemen, tempt them into corruption)." (Anthony Summers 1993 presents a more sinister set of explanations for Hoover's lack of activity against organized crime.) This changed when President Kennedy appointed his brother Robert attorney general. The FBI has since become the major law enforcement agency combatting traditional organized crime. In 1982 its broad investigative mandate was expanded when the FBI was given concurrent jurisdiction with the Drug Enforcement Administration for drug law enforcement and investigation.

Drug Enforcement Administration (DEA)

In 1914, the commissioner of the Internal Revenue was placed in charge of upholding the Harrison Act, and in 1915, 162 collectors and agents of the Miscellaneous Division of the Internal Revenue Service were given the responsibility for enforcing drug laws. In 1919, a Narcotics Division was created within the Bureau of Prohibition with a staff of 170 agents and an appropriation of $270,000. There was "public dissatisfaction with the activities of the Narcotics Division, which was tainted by its association with the country's anti-liquor laws. The public dissatisfaction intensified because of a scandal involving falsification of arrest records and charges relating to payoffs by, and collusion with, drug dealers" (PCOC 1986c: 204). Responding in 1930, Congress removed drug enforcement from the Bureau of Prohibition and established the Federal Bureau of Narcotics (FBN) as a separate agency within the Department of the Treasury. "Although the FBN was primarily responsible for the enforcement of the Harrison Act and related drug laws, the task of preventing and interdicting the illegal importation and smuggling of drugs remained with the Bureau of Customs" (PCOC 1986c: 205). As noted above, in 1973 responsibility for enforcing federal drug statutes was given to the DEA, which was placed in the Department of Justice.

The DEA is a single-mission agency responsible for enforcing federal statutes dealing with controlled substances by investigating alleged or suspected major drug traffickers. The DEA is also responsible for regulating the legal trade in controlled substances such as morphine, methadone, and barbiturates. Diversion agents conduct accountability investigations of drug wholesalers, suppliers, and manufacturers. They inspect the records and facilities of major drug manufacturers and distributors, and special agents investigate instances where drugs have been illegally diverted from legitimate sources. DEA special agents are also stationed in other countries, where their mission is to gain cooperation in international efforts against drug trafficking and to help train foreign enforcement officials.

The basic approach to DEA drug law enforcement is the *buy and bust* or the *controlled buy*. Typically, a drug agent is introduced to a seller by an informant. The agent arranges to buy a relatively small amount and then attempts to move further up the organizational ladder by increasing the amount of drugs purchased. "The agent prefers to defer an arrest until he can seize a large amount of drugs or can implicate higher-ups in the distribution system or both" (Wilson 1978: 43). When arrests are made, DEA agents attempt the "flip"—convince a defendant to become an informant, particularly if the person has knowledge about the entire operation so that a conspiracy case can be effected. As discussed earlier, the use of informants is problematic. The DEA, usually with the aid of state and local enforcement agencies, monitors airports in an effort to interdict drugs being smuggled by "mules."

Immigration and Naturalization Service (INS)

The primary role of the INS is to prevent the illegal entry of persons into the United States, and to apprehend those who have entered illegally. This is particularly important in the fight against OC when illegal aliens are used to strengthen the ranks and operations of criminal organizations. Border patrol officers check suspicious persons within one hundred miles of border areas most

"MULE SKINNING"

DEA special agents, working with state and local police agencies, monitor airports at key junctions for drugs entering the United States. In addition to primary ports of entry such as South Florida, Los Angeles, and New York, they also cover secondary routes such as Atlanta and Chicago, where travellers frequently change planes. Using a *drug courier profile*, which has been developed over the past fifteen years, the agents look for specific clues (primary and secondary characteristics) that have been shown to distinguish persons ("mules") most likely to be carrying wholesale quantities of illegal substances.

There are seven primary characteristics:

1. Arrival from or departure to an identified foreign source country, for example, Colombia, or domestic source city, such as Miami.
2. Carrying empty suitcases, or little or no luggage.
3. Unusual travel patterns, for example, short turnaround times for lengthy airplane trips.
4. Use of an alias.
5. Possession of large amounts of currency.
6. Purchase of airline tickets with cash using small bills.
7. Unusual display of nervousness.

And there are four secondary characteristics:

1. Exclusive use of public transportation, particularly cabs, to and from the airport.
2. A phone call made immediately after deplaning.
3. Provision of a phony telephone number when purchasing airline tickets.
4. Excessive travel to source country or distribution city or cities.

While these primary and secondary traits can be consistent with lawful behavior, they characterize a person toward whom inquiries should be directed. Passengers meeting enough profile characteristics may be approached and questioned—asked for identification and travel documentation. Agents are particularly interested in signs of excessive nervousness. If such signs are observed, agents will ask the passenger to consent to a search for drugs. A refusal, which is rare, can result in detention and the securing of a drug-sniffing dog and/or search warrant. At times the agents discover large amounts of cash that cannot be accounted for; it is seized until its "lawful" owner appears to claim it, a highly unlikely event. If a courier is arrested, efforts are made to "flip" the mule in order to implicate the person picking up the drugs (Hedgepeth 1989).

Although its use is rather controversial, the "profile" permits drug agents to act in the absence of specific information. The use of the profile and any evidence discovered as a result has been upheld by the courts as a legitimate law enforcement tool, the Fourth Amendment notwithstanding. On April 3, 1989, the Supreme Court, in a 7–2 decision, ruled that the profile provides a "reasonable basis" to suspect that a person is transporting drugs. The case involved Andrew Sokolow; in July of 1984, he flew from Honolulu to Miami and then returned to Hawaii after forty-eight hours. Dressed in a black jumpsuit with gold jewelry, Sokolow purchased two airline tickets in Miami for $2,100 in cash, taken from a roll of $20 bills containing about twice that amount. He was traveling under a name that did not match his telephone listing. Sokolow did not check any luggage and appeared quite nervous. After stopping him in Honolulu, drug agents, with the help of a drug-sniffing dog, discovered 1,063 grams of cocaine in Sokolow's carry-on luggage.

Writing for the Court, Chief Justice William H. Rehnquist stated, "While a trip from Honolulu to Miami, standing alone, is not a cause for any sort of suspicion, here there was more: surely few residents of Honolulu travel from that city for twenty hours to spend forty-eight hours in Miami during the month of July." The Court, however, did not base its decision on the existence or use of the DEA drug profile. According to the decision agents must justify their decision to stop a suspect on the basis of their own observations and experiences (Elsasser 1989; Greenhouse 1989b).

Sources: William Hedgepeth, "Mule Skinner." *Atlanta*, March 1989: 61–62, 93–101; Glen Elsasser, "Suspicion is Ruled Ample Basis for Drug Search." *Chicago Tribune*, April 4, 1989: 3; Linda Greenhouse, "High Court Backs Airport Detention Based on 'Profile.'" *New York Times*, April 4, 1989: 1, 10.

likely to be used as illegal crossing points, and they often arrest persons transporting drugs.

Marshals Service

The Marshals Service is the oldest federal law enforcement agency, dating back to 1789. During the period of westward expansion, the U.S. marshal played a significant role in the "Wild West," where he was often the only symbol of law and order. In the past marshals have also been used as an alternative to military intervention in civil disturbances. Today, they provide security for federal court facilities, transport federal prisoners, serve civil writs issued by federal courts, which can include the seizure of property under the provisions of RICO, and they investigate and apprehend certain federal fugitives. Their most important task relative to organized crime, however, is responsibility for administering the Witness Protection Program, discussed later in this chapter.

Department of the Treasury

The primary responsibility of the Department of the Treasury is the collection of revenues due the federal government. In carrying out these responsibilities, the Treasury Department employs law enforcement personnel in several agencies. Three of these have an important role in dealing with OC.

Internal Revenue Service (IRS)

The mission of the IRS is to encourage and achieve the highest possible degree of voluntary compliance with tax laws and regulations. When such compliance is not forthcoming or not feasible, as in the case of persons involved in organized criminal activity, the Criminal Investigation Division receives the case. Agents examine bank records, cancelled checks, brokerage accounts, property transactions, and purchases, compiling a financial biography of the subject's lifestyle in order to prove that proper taxes have not been paid (according to the net worth theory discussed earlier). As a result of the excesses

469

revealed in the wake of the Watergate scandal, Congress enacted the Tax Reform Act of 1976, which reduced the law enforcement role of the IRS and made it quite difficult for law enforcement agencies other than the IRS to gain access to income-tax returns. Amendments in 1982 reduced the requirements and permit the IRS to better cooperate with the efforts of other federal agencies investigating organized crime, particularly drug traffickers.

Bureau of Alcohol, Tobacco and Firearms (ATF)

ATF traces its origins to 1791, when a tax was placed on alcoholic spirits. Eventually, the Prohibition Bureau evolved. With the repeal of Prohibition, it became known as the Alcohol Tax Unit. In 1942, the bureau was given jurisdiction over federal firearms statutes, and in 1970, over arson and explosives. ATF agents are empowered to seize and destroy contraband and illegal liquor production facilities, and they are responsible for combatting contraband cigarette smuggling from a low-tax state to a high-tax state—North Carolina to New York, for example—an activity often engaged in by persons in OC and the bootlegging of untaxed tobacco products.

Through enforcement of federal firearms and explosives statutes and regulations, ATF has been involved in the investigation of outlaw motorcycle clubs. The Anti-Arson Act of 1982 increased the bureau's jurisdiction over arson. (The FBI has jurisdiction in arson or bombings that occur at federal buildings or other institutions that receive federal funds, and in incidents that fit the Department of Justice's definition of terrorism.) ATF's National Response Teams investigate cases of arson and bombings in conjunction with state and local agencies. Each is composed of special agents, a forensic chemist, and an explosives specialist. The teams are equipped with sophisticated, state-of-the-art equipment.

Customs Service

The Customs Service was established in 1789 to collect duties on various imports. Customs inspectors examine cargoes and baggage, articles worn or carried by individuals, and vessels, vehicles, and aircraft entering or leaving the United States. Special teams of inspectors and canine enforcement officers concentrate on cargo and conveyances determined to be high risk. In 1981 the Customs Service established an Office of Intelligence to better manage information and target suspects. The service participates in several multi-agency programs designed to combat organized drug trafficking. The service works with commercial carriers, often signing cooperative agreements, to enhance the carriers' ability to prevent their equipment from being used to smuggle drugs. Special agents of the Customs Service are responsible for carrying out investigations involving drug smuggling and currency violations as part of laundering schemes.

The Customs Service is not hampered by the Fourth Amendment protections that typically restrain domestic law enforcement. Customs agents do not need probable cause or warrants to engage in search and seizure at ports of entry; a variety of degrees of suspicion will suffice. The typical Customs case is a "cold border bust," the result of an entry checkpoint search. Since it is impractical, if not impossible, to subject most vehicles and persons entering the United States to a thorough search, Customs agents have developed certain techniques for minimizing inconvenience to legitimate travelers and shippers, while targeting those most likely to be involved in smuggling activity. They are vigilant for any signs of nervousness and incongruities. In addition to various cues that act as tipoffs, officials at border crossing points have computers containing information about known or suspected smugglers such as license plate numbers and names. Persons arrested by the Customs Service become targets for plea bargaining deals in an effort to gain their cooperation for follow-up enforcement efforts by the Drug Enforcement Administration—they are pressured to become informants in return for some form of leniency.

Donald Goddard (1988: 158) states:

> Customs cases almost always began with a seizure. If the smugglers were amateur, bringing in the stuff for their own use, or to finance their vacation or mortgage arrears, then the buck usually stopped there. But if they were professional couriers, the specialized skill and the standard procedure of the Customs agent was to flip them . . . and carry out a controlled delivery with a view toward arresting their employers, and perhaps moving on from there, widening the net, to pull in the whole operation, from source to final customer.

Department of Transportation/Coast Guard

The Coast Guard in the Department of Transportation is responsible for drug interdiction on the sea. Its vessels conduct continuous surface patrols and frequent surveillance flights over waters of interest, and its personnel board and inspect suspect vessels at sea. Coast Guard personnel are law enforcement officers who do not have to establish probable cause prior to boarding a vessel.

> Responsible in large part for U.S. drug interdiction efforts, the Coast Guard's strategy has been mainly directed toward intercepting motherships as they transit the major passes of the Caribbean. To effect this "choke point" strategy, the Coast Guard conducts both continuous surface patrols and frequent surveillance flights over waters of interest, and boards and inspects vessels at sea. In the past major Coast Guard resources have been concentrated in the "choke points" traditionally transversed [sic] by traffickers. Cutters now more frequently patrol the Bahamas, the eastern passes of the Caribbean, and the Gulf, Atlantic and Pacific coastal areas. (PCOC 1986c: 313)

A typical seizure begins with the sighting of a suspect plane by a Coast Guard plane 250 miles away. The radar plane informs an intelligence center, where the suspect plane's flight track is compared with flight plans submitted to the Federal Aviation Administration. If a flight plan has not been filed, a two-engine Coast Guard tracking plane is dispatched. The tracking plane picks up the suspect plane on radar, and then turns it off to avoid being detected by a "fuzz-buster." The tracker follows behind and above the suspect aircraft, maintaining surveillance with an infrared device that senses heat but does not send out an electronic beam. When the suspect plane prepares to land, the tracker notifies officers aboard a waiting helicopter, and they move in to make arrests. If the plane makes a drop at sea for pick-up by boat, a Coast Guard helicopter or patrol boat makes the seizure. Coast Guard personnel are sometimes assigned to Navy ships, because military personnel are prohibited to make arrests of civilians by the Posse Comitatus Act.

The Coast Guard and Customs service are hampered by the need to patrol more than 12,000 miles of international boundary, over which more than 420 billion tons of goods and 270 million persons cross each year. In 1987 the Coast Guard succeeded in seizing almost 15,000 pounds of cocaine, although it estimates that the seizures represent only 5 to 7 percent of the cocaine smuggled into the United States (Halloran 1988).

Department of Defense (DOD)

The primary role of the Department of Defense is obviously to protect the security of the United States from hostile military activities of foreign powers. In more recent years, however, it has been drawn into the fight against drug trafficking, and this role is controversial.

In the wake of the Reconstruction era, when the Union Army occupied the states of the Confederacy, Congress enacted the 1878 Posse Comitatus Act prohibiting the U.S. Army from performing civilian law enforcement. In 1956, Congress added the Air Force to the Posse Comitatus Act, while the Navy and Marines promulgated administrative restrictions. Until 1981, the DOD limited its involvement in law enforcement to lending equipment and training civilian enforcement personnel in its use. In that year, as part of a new "War on Drugs," Congress amended the Posse Comitatus Act, authorizing a greater level of military involvement in civilian drug enforcement, particularly the tracking of suspect ships and airplanes and the use of military pilots and naval ships to transport civilian enforcement personnel. As a result of this legislation, the DOD provides surveillance and support services, using aircraft to search for smugglers and Navy ships to tow or escort vessels seized by the Coast Guard to the nearest U.S. port. The 1981 legislation authorized the military services to share information that is collected during routine military operations with law enforcement officials, and to make facilities and equipment available to law enforcement officials.

Further amendments to the 1981 legislation led to the use of military equipment and personnel in interdiction efforts against cocaine laboratories in Bolivia. These amendments permit the use of such personnel and equipment if the secretary of state or the secretary of defense and attorney general jointly determine that emergency circumstances exist—if the scope of specific criminal activity poses a serious threat to the interests of the United States. Combined operations involving U.S. Army Special Forces, DEA agents, U.S. border patrol officers, and Bolivian police and military officers have been successful in destroying hundreds of coca-paste laboratories in the coca-growing Champare region. The U.S. Department of State uses former military pilots to fly helicopter gunships, transport planes, and cropdusters used by U.S. and foreign drug agents in countries where U.S. military operations are barred.

Almost every day in 1987, the Air Force used sophisticated AWACS surveillance aircraft to look for smugglers, who crossed the Mexican border or the coastlines in low-flying planes. Two smugglers were apprehended. Other Air Force operations in 1987 led to the arrest of an additional eight persons. The Navy expended 2,500 "man-days" on ships and sent out 2,100 aerial sorties in the 1987 antidrug effort. They discovered twenty-seven smuggling ships, leading to the arrest of fifty-seven persons and the seizure of 168,000 pounds of marijuana and 1,900 pounds of cocaine. The total cost of the military's antidrug activities in 1987 was $389 million (Halloran 1988). By 1992, DOD antidrug expenditures had reached more than $1 billion annually.

Until 1988 federal efforts against airborne drug smuggling were coordinated by the Customs Service and the Coast Guard, with the DOD using radar to help detect smugglers. The following year, Congress designated the DOD as the lead agency in these efforts, but a report by the General Accounting Office stated that the equipment used was costly, operated poorly in bad weather, and required frequent maintenance. Furthermore, airborne smugglers responded to the DOD activities by switching airports and finding other ways of entering the country (Berke 1989).

Early in 1990, hundreds of members of the National Guard were deployed to search for drugs along the border with Mexico and at ports of entry. U.S. military officials have traditionally opposed the involvement of the armed forces in law enforcement: it was viewed as inappropriate because the goal of military operations is to kill and destroy, and law enforcement could potentially undermine its primary mission. Other fears include a threat to civil liberties, and the potentially corrupting influence of drug traffickers on the military. In 1993, for example, Army personnel were accused of smuggling hundreds of pounds of cocaine from Panama into the United States using military transport. The traditional anti-law enforcement position of military officials has been tempered by the reality of military budget cutbacks, the result of the breakup of the Soviet Union. The use of the military in the war on drugs justifies a level of funding that might otherwise be difficult to defend before Congress and the public. For example, in 1989 Congress refused to fund a $243 million radar system for the military. In 1990 the system resurfaced in the Pentagon's proposed antidrug budget. Later that year, the Middle East exploded with the Iraqi invasion of Kuwait—and the war on drugs was placed on the back burner. But not for long: In 1992, $1.2 billion was budgeted for military efforts against drug trafficking.

Other Federal Enforcement Agencies

In addition to the agencies already discussed, a number of other federal agencies have an investigative or law enforcement role that at times may

Art theft is a highly organized international crime. Each month INTERPOL distributes a poster depicting stolen art treasures to the international law enforcement community. Many of these works have been recovered.

involve its personnel with organized crime. The *Secret Service* in the Treasury Department, in addition to its primary role of providing executive protection, is responsible for investigating counterfeiting; the *Department of Labor*, Office of the Inspector General, employs special agents in its Organized Crime and Racketeering Section who investigate compliance with federal labor laws and labor racketeering activities; and the *Postal Inspection Service* has the responsibility of ensuring the integrity of the mails, and in this role investigates the use of the mails to further racketeering or the unlawful shipment of controlled substances.

INTERPOL

The International Police Organization, known by its radio designation INTERPOL, assists law enforcement agencies with investigative activities that transcend national boundaries. It was founded in 1923 through the efforts of the police chief of Vienna. The organization became dormant during the Second World War, but was reorganized at a conference in Brussels in 1946. A stormy relationship existed between the director of the FBI and leaders of INTERPOL, and in 1950 the FBI withdrew from participation. The Treasury Department, anxious to maintain international contacts to help with its drug enforcement responsibilities, continued an informal liaison with INTERPOL.

Until 1968, "INTERPOL meant very little to the United States law enforcement community and was virtually unknown" (Fooner 1985: 19). In that year, Iran announced that it was going to end its ban on opium production. At the same time, there appeared to be an epidemic of drug use in the United States. A U.S. National Central Bureau (NCB) with a connection to INTERPOL was quickly activated in Washington, and by 1970 the NCB was handling about three hundred cases a year. In the mid-1970s, a turf battle ensued between the Treasury Department and Justice Department: the attorney general, after decades of neglect, decided that he wanted to deal with INTERPOL, but the Treasury Department resisted. An agreement—a memorandum of understanding—was effected between the two departments in 1977; they would share the responsibility of representing the United States to INTERPOL and of operating the NCB.

There are currently 167 INTERPOL members. A government announces its intention to join in order to become a member. In each country there is an NCB that acts as a point of contact and coordination with the General Secretariat in Lyons, France. INTERPOL has a headquarters staff of about 250 persons, about sixty of whom are law enforcement officers from about forty different countries. A large communications facility links seventy-two of the member countries into a radio network; other nations use telex or cable facilities. INTERPOL is under the day-to-day direction of a secretary general; it is a coordinating body and has no investigators or law enforcement agents of its own.

The U.S. receives about 12,000 requests for assistance from federal, state, and local law enforcement agencies each year. The requests are checked and coded by technical staff and entered into the INTERPOL Case Tracking System (ICTS), a computer-controlled index of persons, organizations, and other crime information items. The ICTS conducts automatic searches of new entries, retrieving those that correlate with international crime. The requests are forwarded to senior staff members who serve as INTERPOL case investigators, usually veteran agents from a federal agency whose experience includes work with foreign police forces. Each investigator is on loan from his or her principal agency.

Requests for investigative assistance, notes Michael Fooner (1985: 6), range "from murder, robbery, narcotics violations, illicit firearms traffic, and large frauds, to counterfeiting, stolen works of art, bank swindles, and locating fugitives for arrest and extradition. The bureau also receives investigative requests for criminal histories, license checks, and other ID verifications. Sometimes locations of persons lost or missing in a foreign country are also requested." The Financial and Economic Crime Unit at INTERPOL headquarters facilitates the exchange of information stemming from credit card fraud, airline ticket counterfeiting, computer crime, off-shore banking, commodity futures, and money-laundering schemes. The monitoring of this type of activity can sometimes lead to the identification of suspects involved in drug trafficking or other types of organized crime who had previously escaped detection.

INVESTIGATIVE TOOLS IN ORGANIZED CRIME LAW ENFORCEMENT

Enforcing the law against organized criminal activity requires highly trained agents and prosecutors using sophisticated investigative and enforcement tools. In this section we will examine these tools, their advantages, disadvantages, and their limitations.

Intelligence

The collection of information about organized crime, its evaluation, collation, analysis, reporting, and dissemination, is referred to as *intelligence* (Dintino and Martens 1983). It is laborious and usually unexciting work that requires a great deal of expertise. The *American Heritage Dictionary* (1992) defines intelligence as the work of gathering secret information about an enemy, and Justin Dintino and Frederick Martens (1983: 9) conceive of intelligence as "(1) a process through which information is managed which (2) will hopefully increase our knowledge of a particular problem (3) resulting in preventive and/or informed public policy."

Intelligence data are collected for two main purposes—tactical and strategic. At times, these two categories overlap (Godfrey and Harris 1971). *Tactical intelligence* is information that contributes directly to the achievement of an immediate law-enforcement objective, such as arrest and prosecution. *Strategic intelligence* is information that contributes to producing sound judgment with respect to long-range law-enforcement objectives and goals. The information is collected over time and put together by an intelligence analyst to reveal new (or newly discovered) patterns of organized crime activity. The information may be unsubstantiated ("raw") data and require further investigation for confirmation (thus becoming "hard" data).

Robert Stewart (1980: 54) notes the common sources of intelligence data:

- court records
- other public agency documents such as real estate, tax, and incorporation records
- business records
- old case records in the intelligence unit's files
- investigative and intelligence files of other law-enforcement agencies
- newspapers, periodicals, books
- utility company records
- documents and items recovered during searches or subpoenaed by the grand jury, administrative agencies, and legislative committees
- electronic surveillance evidence
- information and material produced voluntarily by citizens
- statements and/or testimony obtained from accomplices, informants, victims, and law enforcement personnel

This material can be collected overtly or covertly. Covert collection involves the accumulation of information from subjects who are unaware that they are being observed or overheard. Since this type of collection is usually quite expensive in terms of the personnel required, it is usually tied directly to the goal of securing evidence that can be used in prosecution; that is, it is more tactical than strategic.

Drexel Godfrey and Don Harris (1971) refer to *analysis* as the "heart" of the intelligence system. An analyst uses the methods of social science research, and central to this approach is the hypothesis. The analyst develops a hypothesis, an "educated guess," about the relevance of the information that has already been collected, collated, and stored. The investigators are then told to seek data that will permit "hypothesis testing." If the hypothesis does not withstand an adequate test, alternative hypotheses must be developed and tested. A hypothesis that has been supported by the data after rigorous testing becomes the basis for an *intelligence report*. The report guides tactical and/or strategic law enforcement efforts.

Intelligence gathering lacks many of the exciting aspects of law enforcement—there are no television series based on the adventures of intelligence analysts. The results produced by strategic intelligence are never immediate and seldom dramatic. They fail to impress those who allocate funds for law enforcement agencies, and intelligence personnel often have little status in agencies such as the DEA. There have been abuses as well:

> A basic principle in collecting information for a criminal intelligence file is that such information should be restricted to what an agency needs to know in order to fulfill its responsibility to detect and combat organized crime in its jurisdiction. The ethnic origin or the political or religious beliefs of any individual, group, or organization should never be the reason for collecting information on them. Criminal activities or associations must be the key factors. If associations are found not to be criminal in nature, the data collected on them should be dropped from the files. (Task Force on Organized Crime 1976: 122)

For several decades this was not the practice. In many urban police departments and the FBI, extensive intelligence efforts were directed against political groups and personalities. In Los Angeles, this type of activity was accomplished under the cover of the Organized Crime Intelligence Division, which "maintained secret Stalinesque dossiers, some of them kept in privately rented units; there were files on virtually every mover and shaker in Southern California" (Rothmiller and Goldman 1992: 9). "Red squads" and similar units would sometimes "leak" raw data whose source was untrustworthy. However, when such data move through a respected law enforcement agency, there is a "cleansing" effect, and the now "laundered" information takes on new importance, particularly when reported by the news media. Law enforcement intelligence files frequently contain news clips whose source is the agency itself—known as *circular sourcing*. Restrictions on what information may be kept in intelligence files and "Freedom of Information" statutes have resulted to correct such abuses.

Electronic Surveillance

"The great majority of law enforcement officials believe that the evidence necessary to bring criminals to bear consistently on the higher echelons of organized crime will not be obtained without the aid of electronic surveillance techniques" (President's Commission on Law Enforcement and Administration of Justice 1968: 468). The Task Force on Organized Crime (1976: 148) points out, "Because of their organization and methods of organization, organized crime activities require sophisticated means of evidence gathering. Often witnesses will not come forward, and members are bound by either an oath of silence or threats of violence. Often the use of informants is of limited value, and many organizations are difficult, if not impossible, for undercover agents to penetrate to the point where they can obtain useful evidence." One way to break through these conspiratorial safeguards, notes the Task Force, is through the use of electronic surveillance.

The technology to accomplish electronic surveillance has become increasingly sophisticated, and the temptation to use technology to gain information that is none of the state's business has proven quite strong. In recent years wiretapping has been complicated by technological advances in communications. Conversations via high-capacity digital lines (human voices are translated

ELECTRONIC SURVEILLANCE

Telephone Tap: An extension is hooked into a line at a telephone switching station.

Simple Transmitter: A microphone about the size of a small wooden match box. The batteries need to be changed every forty-eight hours. More sophisticated devices can be turned on and off from a remote location using a microwave signal.

Telephone Transmitter: A microphone wired inside a telephone from which it draws its power. Some devices are activated by an outside telephone call and can transmit voices as well as telephone conversations.

Laser Interceptors: These devices can be pointed at a window to record vibrations on the glass caused by indoor conversations. A computer interprets the vibrations into conversations.

Satellite Relays: Some microphones can transmit by way of a space satellite to a ground receiver.

Fiber Optics: Micro-sized fiber optic filaments are embedded into walls. They draw power from a building's electrical system, and are used to intercept conversations.

into numbers) and fiber-optic lines (which use pulses of light), for example, cannot be intercepted using conventional wiretap equipment. In response, the Justice Department has requested a weakening of the systems so they can be subjected to law enforcement surveillance. This has engendered strong opposition from Congress and telephone companies. They argue that making the devices more susceptible to FBI surveillance would also make them more vulnerable to illegal penetrations while retarding advances in communications technology (Ramirez 1993).

Legal definitions of just what may be part of law enforcement's business have been evolving since the first wiretap case confronted the United States Supreme Court in 1928. In *Olmstead v. United States* (277 U.S. 438), telephone wiretaps were used to prosecute persons involved in large-scale Prohibition violations. The interception of Olmstead's telephone line was accomplished without trespass. Chief Justice William Howard Taft, writing for the majority, determined that since telephone conversations are not tangible items, they cannot be the subject of an illegal seizure, and thus wiretapping is not prohibited by the Fourth Amendment. Shortly after the *Olmstead* decision, Congress prohibited interception of telephonic communication without judicial authorization.

The first case to reach the Supreme Court under the Congressional restrictions was *Goldman v. United States* (316 U.S. 129), in 1942. The Court, consistent with *Olmstead*, ruled that a dictaphone placed against an office wall did not violate the Fourth Amendment since there was no trespass. In

Typical surveillance equipment includes portable radios, video cameras, night vision scopes, 35-mm cameras, binoculars, and tape recorders.

Silverman v. United States (365 U.S. 505, 1961), a foot-long spike with a microphone attached was inserted under a faceboard and into the wall until it made contact with a heating duct that ran through Silverman's house. The Court found this activity unconstitutional, not because of trespass, but based on actual intrusion into "a constitutionally protected area." In 1967 the Supreme Court ruled (*Berger v. New York* 388 U.S. 41) that a New York State law authorizing "eavesdropping" was unconstitutional. The case involved the conviction of Ralph Berger, a Chicago public relations man, who was convicted of conspiracy to bribe the chairman of the New York State Liquor Authority. The evidence consisted of conversations intercepted by bugs and wiretaps pursuant to a court order. According to the Court, the statute failed to require warrants to state the specific crime being committed and the place or the persons to be surveilled. Also, no time limits were placed on the order once incriminating conversation was secured.

Later in 1967, the case of *Katz v. United States* (389 U.S. 347) came before the Supreme Court. In violation of the Hobbs Act, Katz transmitted wagering information on the telephone (McGuinness 1981: 27):

> In *Katz*, the Government, acting without a warrant or other judicial authorization, intercepted defendant's end of telephone conversations by means of two microphones attached by tape to the top of two adjoining public telephone booths from which Katz regularly made calls. Katz was subsequently prosecuted for the interstate transportation of wagering information by telephone in violation of a Federal statute, and tape recordings of the intercepted telephone calls were introduced in evidence over his objection. The Government argued

that since no physical intrusion was made into the booth and since it was not a "constitutionally protected area" (the defendant having no possessory interest as such in the booth), a search for Fourth Amendment purposes did not occur. In holding that there was a search, the Court stated that it was erroneous to resolve questions of Fourth Amendment law on the basis of whether a constitutionally protected area is involved. For the Fourth Amendment protects people, not places." This being the case, the reach of the "Amendment [also] cannot turn upon the presence or absence of a physical intrusion into any given enclosure." The Court thus concluded that the Government's activities "violated the privacy upon which [the defendant] *justifiably relied* while using the telephone" (emphasis added), and hence a search within the meaning of the Fourth Amendment had taken place.

The key to understanding *Katz* and subsequent decisions concerning surveillance and the Fourth Amendment, notes Robert McGuinness (1981), are the terms: "reasonable expectation of privacy," "legitimate expectation of privacy," and "justifiable expectation of privacy." As Kimberly Kingston (1988: 22–23) notes, the Supreme Court "redefined the term 'search' to include any governmental action which intrudes into an area where there is a reasonable expectation of privacy." However, she points out (1988: 24), it is not the subjective expectation of privacy that is protected but rather "only those that society as a whole is willing to recognize and protect." Thus, while a drug-trafficking defendant may have had a subjective expectation that his trash was private, it was not an expectation of privacy that society was willing to recognize and protect—the defendant had exposed his garbage to the public and that included the police (*California v. Greenwood* 107 S.Ct. 3260, 1987).

During the 1960s, the FBI used electronic surveillance extensively, often without the benefit of judicial authorization. Kevin Krajick (1983: 30) points out:

> Numerous Congressional committees and criminal court judges in the 1960s found that the FBI and local police had for decades used illegal electronic surveillance to supplement their investigations. And, worse, they had used taps and bugs to spy on and disrupt the activities of law-abiding citizens and organizations. Civil rights leader Martin Luther King, Jr., for one, was the subject of extensive electronic surveillance in the 1960s.

Furthermore, private wiretapping received greater coverage in the press: "The publicity continued to grow, and by the mid-1960s there were regular exposures of industrial espionage and of electronic surveillance operations by private detectives" (National Commission for the Review of Federal and State Laws Relating to Wiretapping and Electronic Surveillance 1976: 39; hereafter Wiretap Commission).

As a result of this activity, and in order to bring some uniformity into the use of electronic surveillance, Congress enacted Title III of the Omnibus Crime Control and Safe Streets Act in 1968 (18 U.S.C. Sections 2510-20). It was the first time in history that Congress had sanctioned electronic surveillance (Lapidus 1974).

> Pressures had been mounting on Congress to enact legislation regulating electronic surveillance, but the scope of the controls could not be agreed to. *Berger* and *Katz* not only forced some legislative action by ruling out law enforcement use of electronic microphones without judicial warrant, but also outlined the scope of the privacy which was protected by the Fourth Amendment and sketched the guidelines for adequate warrant protection. (Wiretap Commission 1976: 38)

Title III bans all private eavesdropping and authorizes federal officials, and prosecutors in states whose laws conform to the federal statute, to petition for court authorization to intercept wire or oral communications provided that:

1. There is probable cause for belief that an individual is committing, has committed, or is about to commit, a particular offense that is enumerated in Title III.
2. There is probable cause for belief that particular communications concerning that offense will be obtained through such interception.
3. Normal investigative procedures have been tried and have failed, or reasonably appear unlikely to succeed if tried, or are too dangerous.
4. There is probable cause for belief that the facilities in which, or the place where, the oral communications are to be intercepted is being used, or is about to be used, in conjunction with the commission of such offense, or is leased to, listed in the name of, or commonly used by persons believed to commit such offenses.

The Title III judicial order terminates in thirty days or less, unless extended by the issuing judge:

> No order entered under this section may authorize or approve the interception of any wire or oral communication for any period longer than necessary to achieve the objective of the authorization, nor in any event longer than thirty days. Extensions of an ʿorder may be granted, but only upon the application for an extension made in accordance with subsection (1) of this section [essentially the four points listed above]. . . . The period of extension shall be no longer than the authorizing judge deems necessary to achieve the purposes for which it was granted and in no event for longer than thirty days. Every order and extension thereof shall contain a provision that the authorization to intercept shall be executed as soon as practicable, shall be conducted in such a way as to minimize the interception of communications not otherwise subject to interception under this chapter, and must terminate upon attainment of the authorization objective, or in any event in thirty days.

The *minimization* noted above requires that great care be taken in order to avoid intercepting conversations that are not relevant to the judicial order. In order to ensure that an unauthorized interception does not occur, the eavesdropping equipment must be monitored at all times. If the monitoring agent should hear a privileged conversation between doctor and patient or attorney and client, or a personal conversation between husband and wife unrelated to the judicial order, he or she must discontinue the interception. Agents usually wear earphones, and these are taken off and placed where the conversation cannot be overheard—usually in a box provided for that purpose. Each time a conversation is intercepted, the agent is permitted to listen only briefly, long enough to establish if the nature of the conversation is within the scope of the judicial order. A monitoring agent who is distracted or falls asleep and causes the recording of a privileged conversation jeopardizes the results of the investigation. Title III requires that the target(s) of the judicial order be notified that their conversations have been intercepted within ninety days after termination of the order. Judges and prosecutors are required to file reports on their use of Title IIIs with the Administrative Office of the United States Courts (AOUSC) in Washington, D.C., and the AOUSC must submit an annual report on Title III with Congress.

Although Title III regulates the interception of wire and oral communications, Congress did not explicitly provide any authority for the surreptitious placement of a listening device ("bug") to intercept oral communication—a "black bag job." Federal courts remained in conflict over the issue until *Dalia v. United States* (441 U.S. 238, 1979). FBI agents pried open a window in the New Jersey office of Lawrence Dalia in order to install a bug in his ceiling. As a result of the intercepted conversations, Dalia was convicted of violating the Hobbs Act by receiving property stolen from an interstate shipment. The Supreme Court concluded that a Title III warrant for eavesdropping implicitly grants authority for covert entry.

DOUBLE JEOPARDY

In 1982, the FBI bugged the home of Angelo Ruggiero, a Gambino soldier in the crew headed by then-*caporegime* John Gotti. They subsequently placed a bug in the home of Family boss Paul Castellano. The tapes implicated Ruggiero in drug trafficking and he was recorded being critical of Castellano's leadership, even impugning his manhood. Castellano was heard referring to the Gotti faction as a bunch of brainless gorillas. Legal procedure requires that the results of electronic surveillance be made available to defendants prior to trial. Before they could be revealed, however, the Gotti faction, fearing retribution from the boss, executed Castellano.

Source: Joseph F. O'Brien and Andris Kurins, *Boss of Bosses: The FBI and Paul Castellano*. New York: Dell, 1991.

Title III is sometimes criticized by law enforcement officials because of the extensive investigation and documentation required to secure a warrant, although there are emergency exceptions built into the statute:

> Any investigative or law enforcement officer, specially designated by the Attorney General, or by the principal prosecuting attorney of any State or subdivision thereof acting pursuant to a statute of that State, who reasonably determines that (a) an emergency situation exists with respect to conspiratorial activities threatening the national security interests or to conspiratorial activities characteristic of organized crime that requires a wire or oral communication to be intercepted before an order authorizing such interception can with due diligence be obtained, and (b) there are grounds which an order could be entered under this chapter to authorize such interception may intercept such wire or oral communication if an application for an order approving the interception is made in accordance with this section within forty-eight hours after the interception has occurred, or begins to occur.

Any wire or oral communication may be intercepted legally (although some states, for example, Illinois, have restrictions) without a court order if one of the parties to the communication gives prior consent. Thus, law enforcement officers and informants may be "wired" to secure incriminating conversation without a court order. In 1979, the Supreme Court (by a 5–3 vote) ruled that the police do not need a search warrant to record the numbers dialed from a particular telephone—there is an absence of a "reasonable expectation of privacy" since the telephone company routinely maintains such information for billing purposes. In *Smith v. Maryland* (442 U.S. 735), the Court affirmed the robbery conviction of a man linked to the crime by a pen register which, when installed at a telephone company switching station, can record the numbers dialed from a particular phone.

Since Title III was enacted in 1968, a majority of states have passed statutes permitting electronic surveillance. However, some rarely make use of the law, and cost is a major reason. In addition to the investigative costs of securing the order, the monitoring ties up at least two law enforcement officers, over three shifts for thirty days or more on a continuous basis, at an average cost in excess of $40,000. There have been cases in which the cost exceeded $2 million, and less than 20 percent actually produce incriminating evidence. Persons in organized crime frequently limit conversations that could be subjected to interception to code phrases. John Gotti, boss of the Gambino Family, was recorded as advising a young associate about telephone conversations: "Don't ever say anything you don't want played back to you some day" (Mustain and Capeci 1988: 115). Conversations may be in a foreign language, so monitors have to be fluent in that language, or the conversation may be in a dialect or contain colloquial expressions that are difficult for outsiders to translate.

Material from electronic bugs often must be enhanced by specialists to reduce background noise from radios or televisions. The conversations must then be transcribed, and usually only the monitoring agents are familiar enough with the subjects' manner of speech to be able to accomplish this tedious task, which can take months of effort.

Grand Jury

In the federal system, a grand jury is a body of twenty-three citizens empowered to operate with a quorum of sixteen, and requiring twelve votes for an indictment. In the state system, however, the number of jurors varies considerably. Nowhere does the maximum of grand jurors exceed twenty-three. While some states adhere to the federal rule of twelve for an indictment, in others the range is anywhere from four to nine. Like those serving on a petit or trial jury, grand jurors are selected from the voting rolls; however, they meet in *secret* to consider evidence presented by the prosecutor.

Since the members of a grand jury are not agents of the government—they act as direct representatives of the citizenry—the extensive due process rights typically enjoyed by a criminal defendant are not necessarily relevant to grand jury proceedings. Their activities are secret, and only sixteen states permit the subject of a grand jury inquiry to have an attorney present, and then only to give advice. In the remaining states and the federal system, an attorney is not even permitted to accompany his or her client at a grand jury hearing. There is no right to present evidence or cross-examine adverse witnesses. While the subject can refuse to answer any questions whose answers may be incriminating, he or she can be granted immunity and required to testify under the threat of being jailed for contempt.

The grand jury can receive virtually any type of information, even that which would not be admissible at a trial, such as certain types of hearsay and evidence that was secured in violation of the Fourth Amendment—the exclusionary rule does not apply to the grand jury (*United States v. Calandra* 414 U.S. 338, 1974). In every state and the federal system, the grand jury may be utilized for investigative purposes, and when so used has broad investigative authority, including the power to subpoena persons and documents. In those states where statutes permit and in the federal system, the grand jury is used to investigate the operations of law enforcement and other government agencies, particularly when corruption is suspected, and to investigate the activities of organized crime.

The Organized Crime Control Act of 1970 requires that a *special grand jury* be convened at least every eighteen months in federal judicial districts of more than 1 million persons. It can also be convened at the request of a federal prosecutor, and its typical life, eighteen months, may be extended to thirty-six months. The *special grand jury* and grand juries of several states have the power to publish reports at the completion of their terms on certain types of noncriminal misconduct by public officials. While such reports cannot command any particular action, the widespread publicity they typically enjoy usually encourages action by government officials.

According to Robert Stewart (1980: 124), the investigative grand jury is the single most useful tool by which to attack the traditional forms of organized crime. For example, convicted drug pushers, bookmakers, numbers writers and runners, prostitutes, weapons offenders and petty thieves can be summoned before the grand jury, immunized, and questioned about the higher-ups in a particular enterprise or activity. If the witness is not already under charges, there is little likelihood that the grant of immunity will jeopardize any prosecution. If the witness testifies truthfully, that witness will be ostracized from the criminal community and thereby neutralized as an organized crime operative. Moreover, the defection of one member of an organization may serve as a catalyst which forces others within the organization to defect and cooperate with the state. Whenever any appreciable number of lower-level offenders are summoned before an investigative grand jury, the higher-ups in the organized crime structure can never be sure what, if anything, is being said. This alone is sufficient to generate severe tensions within the organized crime structure.

Immunity

The Fifth Amendment to the United States Constitution provides that no person "shall be compelled in any criminal case to be a witness against himself." This is an important protection for the individual against the coercive powers of the state, and it can be partially neutralized by a grant of immunity. There are two types of immunity:

1. *Transactional immunity* provides blanket protection against prosecution for crimes about which a person is compelled to testify; and
2. *Use immunity* prohibits the information provided by a person from being used against him or her, but the person can still be prosecuted using evidence obtained independently of his or her compelled testimony.

In many states and the federal system, the court or the prosecutor may grant immunity to reluctant witnesses. Legislative or administrative bodies investigating criminal activity can also request a grant of immunity. A witness who, after being granted immunity, refuses to testify can be subjected to civil or criminal contempt.

The civil contempt proceeding is summary in nature and relatively simple. First the witness is immunized. Upon refusing to answer in the grand jury [or other authorized body] the witness appears before the court. The prosecutor makes an oral application and the court instructs the witness to testify. The witness returns to the grand jury room; and, if recalcitrant, is directed to reappear before the court. The prosecutor then makes an oral application for the court to enforce its previous order, which the witness has disobeyed. The prosecutor explains what has occurred before the grand jury, and the foreperson or reporter testifies about these facts. The witness is given an opportunity to be heard; and thereafter the court decides whether the witness is in contempt and should be remanded. (Stewart 1980: 239)

"The remand order normally specifies that the witness shall remain confined until he offers to purge himself of the contempt by agreeing to testify or for the life of the grand jury, whichever is shorter" (1980: 240). The term of a grand jury is usually eighteen months. Legislative committees and administrative bodies, of course, have indefinite terms. In 1970, as a result of his refusal to testify before a New Jersey investigating committee after being immunized, Jerry Catena (then acting boss of the Genovese Family) was imprisoned for contempt—and he remained imprisoned for five years, never testifying.

The *criminal contempt* proceeding is quite different, since it requires a formal trial, and the witness is entitled to the full array of due process rights enjoyed by any criminal defendant. Being found guilty of criminal contempt, however, can result in a substantial sentence of imprisonment: "The purpose of the remand is coercive [to compel testimony], while the purpose of the criminal contempt sentence is punitive and deterrent" (Stewart 1980: 246). Of course, a witness, whether immunized or not, is subject to the laws against perjury.

In 1972 the Supreme Court decided the case of *Kastigar v. United States* (406 U.S. 441), which involved several persons who had been subpoenaed to appear before a federal grand jury in California in 1971. The assistant U.S. attorney, believing that the petitioners in *Kastigar* were likely to assert their Fifth Amendment privilege, secured from the federal district court an order directing them to answer all questions and produce evidence before the grand jury under a grant of immunity. Nevertheless, the persons involved refused to answer questions, arguing that the "scope of the immunity provided by the statute was not coextensive with the scope of the privilege against self-incrimination, and therefore was not sufficient to supplant the privilege and compel their testimony." The Supreme Court, in upholding the immunity order, quoted from the federal immunity statute:

> The witness may not refuse to comply with the order on the basis of his privilege against self-incrimination; but no testimony or other information compelled under the order (or any information directly or indirectly derived from such testimony or other information) may be used against the witness in *any criminal case*, except a prosecution for perjury, giving a false statement, or otherwise failing to comply with the order. [Emphasis added]

The Supreme Court concluded that since the statute prohibited the prosecutorial authorities from using the compelled testimony in *any* respect, it therefore ensured that the testimony could not lead to the infliction of criminal penalties on the witness. In a dissenting opinion, Justice Thurgood Marshall pointed to the possibility of using the testimonial information for investigative leads designed to secure evidence against the witness. The Court majority agreed that the statute barred such use of the testimony.

Civil action against a criminally immunized witness, however, is possible, and has been upheld by the appellate courts (Rhodes 1984). In addition, a grant of immunity does not protect the witness from a loss of social status, employment, and most important, revenge from those against whom he or she is forced to testify. Rufus King (1963: 651) raises additional issues:

> The immunity bargain is a somewhat unsavory device per se, inaccurate and potentially very unfair; it should be used only sparingly and where it is absolutely required. Immunity grants are always exchanges, a pardon for crimes that would otherwise be punishable, given in return for testimony that could otherwise be withheld. In every case the interrogating authority must enter into a special "deal" with a wrongdoer to buy his testimony at the price of exoneration for something [for which] he would otherwise deserve punishment. . . .
>
> Such bargains are always somewhat blind. Ordinarily the witness will be hostile, so that his examiners cannot be sure in advance exactly what value the withheld testimony will have. And at the same time, especially in broad legislative or administrative inquiries, it is impossible to tell beforehand just what crimes are likely to be exonerated. Conceivably, the witness may have a surprise ready for his questioners at every turn of the proceedings.

Because of the potentially undesirable repercussions, some prosecutors have developed guidelines for consideration when making an immunity decision. The following guidelines are from the New Jersey Division of Criminal Justice (quoted in Committee on the Office of Attorney General 1978: 27):

1. Can the information be obtained from any source other than a witness who wants to negotiate immunity?
2. How useful is the information for the purposes of criminal prosecution?
3. What is the likelihood that the witness can successfully be prosecuted?
4. What is the relative significance of the witness as a potential defendant?
5. What is the relative significance of the potential defendant against whom the witness offers to testify? In other words, is the witness requesting immunity more culpable than those against whom she or he is agreeing to testify? Are they in a position to provide evidence against the witness, or superior evidence against others?
6. What is the value of the testimony of the witness to the case (is it the core evidence upon which the prosecution is based)?
7. What impact will immunity have on the credibility of the witness at trial? Are the terms of the immunity agreement so favorable to the witness that the jury will not accept the testimony? Rhodes notes, however, "that a grant of immunity has a favorable impact on a jury. It makes a defendant's testimony more credible. A prosecutor can point to the witness with a sordid record and say to the jury, 'What reason does Mr. X have to lie? His immunity is assured and if he lies he will be prosecuted for perjury!' " (Rhodes 1984: 193).
8. What impact will immunity have on the prosecutor's personal credibility and that of his or her office?

Witness Protection/Security Program

Because of the potentially undesirable consequences for a witness who testifies in an organized crime case—either voluntarily or compelled by immunity—

efforts have been made to protect such witnesses from OC retribution. The Witness Protection Program was authorized by the Organized Crime Control Act of 1970:

> The Attorney General of the United States is authorized to rent, purchase, modify or remodel protected housing facilities and to otherwise offer to provide for the health, safety, and welfare of witnesses and persons intended to be called as Government witnesses, and the families of witnesses and persons intended to be called as Government witnesses in legal proceedings instituted against any person alleged to have participated in an organized criminal activity whenever, in his judgment testimony from, or a willingness to testify by, such a witness would place his life or person, or the life or person of a member of his family or household in jeopardy. Any person availing himself of such an offer by the Attorney General to use such facilities may continue to use such facilities for as long as the Attorney General determines the jeopardy to his life or person continues.

The program was given over to the U.S. Marshals Service to administer, a logical arrangement (Permanent Subcommittee on Investigations 1981c: 54; hereafter PSI):

> Law enforcement officers wanted the protecting and relocating agency to be in the criminal justice system but to be as far removed as possible from both investigating agents and prosecution. That way the Government could more readily counter the charge that cooperating witnesses were being paid or otherwise unjustifiably compensated in return for their testimony.

However, the Marshals Service was not prepared for these new responsibilities since its typical duties were related to support of the judicial system (court security, transporting prisoners, and serving subpoenas). Moreover, the educational requirements and training of deputy U.S. marshals were not rigorous. This has changed. Marshals Service personnel are better trained, and a new position, that of inspector, was created specifically for the Witness Security Program. However, officials had not anticipated the number of persons who would enter the program; they had expected about two dozen annually, not the more than three hundred brought into the program each year.

Some critics of the program have charged that the Marshals Service shields criminals, not only from would-be assassins, but also from debts and lawsuits. In an attempt to remedy this, an amendment to the 1984 Comprehensive Crime Control Act directs the Justice Department to stop hiding witnesses who are sued for civil damages, and participants linked to new crimes are to be dropped from the program. But the program still provides career criminals with "clean" backgrounds that they can use to prey on or endanger an unsuspecting public.

The problem is obvious: "the marshals are often dealing with men and women who have never done an honest day's work in their lives. Many of them were skilled criminals—burglars, embezzlers, arsonists, physical enforcers—accustomed to lucrative financial rewards and a high standard of living," a standard that is not going to be duplicated by the program (PSI 1981c: 53–54). Once the immediate physical danger has passed, some of these protected witnesses begin to yearn for the excitement and financial rewards that crime

WAYWARD WITNESSES

During the 1970s, Michael Hellerman helped to convict more than thirty organized crime figures, stockbrokers, and politicians on a variety of charges. He went into the Witness Protection Program and emerged as Michael Rapp, a restaurant operator in Massachusetts. The high-living gambler and his associates went on a rampage, swindling financially ailing banks throughout the country out of millions of dollars by using worthless securities as collateral. The biggest "killing" involved a Flushing, New York, saving bank; Hellerman took out $8 million in loans in the names of twenty-two separate individual and corporate borrowers during a seven-month period in 1984 (Willoughby 1986).

Charles J. McDonald, in order to "work off a beef," spent two years as an FBI undercover operative, taping conversations with his associates in the Colombo Family. He and his family were provided with new Social Security cards, phony job records, a military service record, references from nonexistent employers, and school records for his children. The three hundred pound career criminal emerged as Charlie Bertinelli, and with his associates posed as Teamster Union pension officials, bilking legitimate businessmen in the United States and Canada out of an estimated $1.5 million (Coates 1986).

Arthur Katz, in order to avoid imprisonment for insurance fraud, provided information in a Phila-

delphia OC case. He subsequently entered the Witness Protection Program and emerged as Arthur Kane. When he lost $6 million in the October 1987 stock market crash, Kane shot and killed the local Merrill Lynch brokerage manager and badly wounded another broker before turning the gun on himself ("Insurer Won't Pay on Federal Witness" 1987).

Vito Arena was a vicious three hundred pound hitman for the Gambino crime Family who delighted in dismembering victims. He was placed in the program for his testimony against Paul Castellano. In 1991, Arena was killed trying to hold up a supermarket in Houston (Coffey and Schmetterer 1991).

On March 4, 1993, James Allen Red Dog, a thirty-nine-year-old Sioux, was executed by lethal injection in Delaware. While in the Witness Protection Program, Red Dog murdered an acquaintance, then kidnapped a woman and raped her.

Sources: Jack Willoughby, "A License to Steal," *Forbes*, September 22, 1986: 146, 148; James Coates, "Another Bad Apple Spoils Witness Protection Image." *Chicago Tribune*, March 2, 1986: 4; "Insurer Won't Pay on Federal Witness." *Chicago Tribune*, December 9, 1987: 10; Joseph Coffey and Jerry Schmetterer, *The Coffey Files: One Cop's War Against the Mob.* New York: St. Martin's, 1991.

brought to their lives. Having few if any noncriminal skills, it is not surprising that some of them return to criminal activity even if it places both their freedom and their lives, and that of their families, at risk.

In some cases estranged spouses have been unable to visit their own children. This was dramatically portrayed in the 1980 movie *Hide in Plain Sight*, starring James Caan. In the case of Anthony Prisco, the government relocated his ex-wife and young daughter to a secret location in 1983. His ex-wife married a drug trafficker who became a government witness, but Prisco hired a private investigator, who found out she and his daughter were in the Witness Security Program. In 1984, Congress amended the law to provide greater rights to parents in such cases. They now permit Prisco monthly visits monitored by marshals, but he has no input into his daughter's upbringing (Tulsky 1987).

REVIEW QUESTIONS

1. How is organized crime law enforcement limited by constitutional restraints and jurisdictional limitations?
2. Why is corruption a problem associated with organized crime law enforcement?
3. What is the problem inherent in using informants in organized crime law enforcement?
4. What are the most important federal statutes used in organized crime control?
5. What were the historically significant changes instituted by the drug control legislation of 1970?
6. What are the major provisions of the Hobbs Act?
7. What is a conspiracy, and what are the three forms that a conspiracy can take?
8. How can "guilt by association" become a problem in a conspiracy prosecution?
9. Why does a conspiracy prosecution usually require an informant to testify?
10. What are the required elements for a RICO prosecution?
11. Why has RICO been criticized?
12. According to forfeiture statutes, under what conditions can the government seize property?
13. What are the levels of evidence applicable in a forfeiture proceeding?
14. What are the provisions of anti-money laundering statutes?
15. Why is most organized crime law enforcement at the federal level?
16. What are the two primary responsibilities of the Drug Enforcement Administration?
17. What agencies of the Department of Justice are responsible for organized crime law enforcement?
18. What are the agencies of the Department of the Treasury that have responsibilities for organized crime law enforcement?
19. What are the unusual powers enjoyed by Customs Service agents?

20. What are the responsibilities and special powers of the Coast Guard?
21. Why is the use of military personnel to fight drug trafficking controversial?
22. What is meant by intelligence in law enforcement and what are the two types of intelligence?
23. What does federal law ("Title III") require with respect to electronic surveillance?
24. Why are there exceptional costs attached to using electronic surveillance?
25. How is the grand jury used against organized criminal activities?
26. How are immunity statutes used in organized crime law enforcement?
27. Why was the Witness Protection Program given over to the U.S. Marshals Service to administer?
28. Why is the Witness Protection Program controversial?

10

Organized Crime: Committees, Commissions, and Policy Issues

Public policy on organized crime is the result of the interaction of the news media, public opinion, and government. Government can influence the media by providing "anonymous sources," by "leaking" information, or by holding press conferences and public hearings. Investigations by fact-finding bodies, congressional committees, and presidential commissions have often provided the grist for news media mills, which in turn forms public opinion about organized crime. This has led to increased allocations for investigative agencies and new laws for dealing with OC. A symbiotic relationship exists between media representations, including fictional accounts such as *The Godfather*, public reaction, and governmental activity; one (or more) can trigger activity by others.

LIFE IMITATING ART

The media influences persons in organized crime. In his study of fence Vincent Swaggi (a pseudonym), Carl Klockars (1974) notes that Swaggi believed that film characters strongly influence the style if not the techniques of criminals. The notorious Joseph ("Crazy Joe") Gallo copied actor George Raft, who copied Bugsy Siegel; Gallo later copied Richard Widmark. Robert Delaney, an undercover detective for the New Jersey State Police testified before the Permanent Subcommittee on Investigations 1981b: 372:

> *Mr. Delaney*: The movies *Godfather I* and *Godfather II* have had an impact on these crime families. Some of the members and associates would inquire of me, had I seen the movie? I said yes. They would reply that they'd seen it three and four times. One young man said he'd seen it ten times.
>
> At dinner one night at a restaurant, Patrick Kelly and I were with Joseph Doto, who is the son of Joseph Adonis,[1] and known as

---

1. Joseph ("Joe Adonis") Doto was an important racketeer who sided with Joe ("The Boss") Masseria during the Castellammarese War. He is reputed to have been one of the

Movie actor George Raft (right) stands with an arm around Benjamin (Bugsy) Siegel at the latter's preliminary hearing in 1944 on charges of bookmaking. Raft, who testified under court subpoena, became so emphatic in his answers that the district attorney warned him: "Don't get yourself in contempt."

> *Mr. Delaney* Joey Adonis, Jr. Joey Adonis, Jr. gave the waiter a pocketful of
> *cont.:* quarters and told him to play the juke box continuously and to play
> the same song, the theme music from the "Godfather." All
> through dinner, we listened to the same song, over and over.

men who murdered Masseria in 1931 (Messick 1973). During Prohibition, Adonis was a partner in the liquor business with Meyer Lansky, Bugsy Siegel, and Lucky Luciano (Cressey 1969). The owner of a Brooklyn restaurant, "Joe's Italian Kitchen," which was frequented by politicians, he served as an intermediary between the syndicate in Brooklyn and police and political officials (Nelli 1976). A ranking member of the Anastasia (later Gambino) Family, his power as a racketeer extended into New Jersey, where he headed a large-scale gambling operation in Bergen County. In 1932, Harry Bennett of the Ford Motor Company signed a contract to haul new cars with Adonis' Automotive Conveying Company of New Jersey (Fox 1989). In 1951 Adonis was convicted of gambling violations, and in 1953, after his release from New Jersey State Prison, was deported to Italy.

495

THE GODFATHER

Crime boss Joseph Colombo agreed to aid the filming of the *The Godfather* if the production company hired some of his men as extras and if the film avoided the use of the terms Mafia and *Cosa Nostra*. "The actor James Caan, who played Sonny Corleone, spent so much time hanging out with [Colombo Family captain] Carmine ("The Snake") Persico that undercover government agents briefly mistook him for an aspiring mobster."

Source: Alessandra Stanley, "When the Gangster Becomes the Gangster Movie." *New York Times,* February 21, 1992: B1, 9.

> *Senator Nunn:* In other words, you are saying sometimes they go to the movie to see how they themselves are supposed to behave, is that right?
> *Mr. Delaney:* That is true. They had a lot of things taught to them through the movie. They try to live up to it. The movie was telling them how.

One organized crime figure, while being interviewed, pointed to Gay Talese's book *Honor Thy Father* (1971) and began discussing its central character, Joseph Bonanno. He had also read Peter Maas' biography of Joseph Valachi. He said that he had never heard the term *Cosa Nostra* (although he is Italian and understood the meaning) until it was popularized by Valachi—after which, he stated, low-level OC figures began using the term. Renee Buse (1965: 206) reports that when ("Big") John Ormento, a *caporegime* in the Genovese Family, was arrested for drug trafficking, federal agents found a copy of Frederic Sondern's book *Brotherhood of Evil* (1959) in his home in Lido Beach, New York. "It had obviously been read carefully, as dog-eared pages and underlined passages marked the text which dealt with Ormento." On March 15, 1981, Philadelphia crime boss Philip Testa was killed by a bomb blast at his south Philadelphia home. Peter Lupsha, an expert on organized crime from the University of New Mexico, states that when law enforcement officers entered Testa's house after the bombing, they found two videos, *Godfather I* and *Godfather II*, next to the VCR. On the side of Testa's favorite chair was a copy of Demaris' book on Jimmy Fratianno, *The Last Mafioso* (1981), in which Testa had been making marginal notes and comments (personal correspondence).

THE KEFAUVER CRIME COMMITTEE

The importance of organized crime as a national political issue was recognized by Tennessee Senator Estes Kefauver in 1950. The five-term congressmember

Crime crusader Senator
Estes Kefauver riding
high in public opinion.

had been elected to the Senate in 1948 despite the vigorous opposition of the
political machine headed by notorious "Boss" Ed Crump of Memphis. In an
advertisement placed in newspapers throughout Tennessee, Crump referred to
Kefauver as a "pet coon," a veiled message to readers that "Kefauver was
pretending to be a loyal American when he was in truth a Red agent"
(Steinberg 1972: 129). The ad brought the Kefauver campaign to life, and the
otherwise reserved candidate began sporting a coonskin cap: "I may be a coon,"
he would tell audiences, "but I'm not Mister Crump's pet coon."

On January 5, 1950, Kefauver introduced Senate Resolution 202 "to
investigate gambling and racketeering activities" by a special subcommittee.
The impetus for this legislation was the highly publicized findings of several
private municipal crime commissions, particularly the Chicago Crime Commission (Moore 1974). Kefauver (1951b) writes that he was influenced by an
American Municipal Association (AMA) resolution calling on the federal
government for action against interstate crime operations that affect local
governments. In response to the AMA, Attorney General J. Howard McGrath
convened a conference of mayors and law enforcement officials, which met in
Washington on February 15, 1950. The attorney general, however, stressed the
need for local remedies, and soon afterward conference mayors began to

complain about federal inaction on what they saw as a serious *national* problem—interstate organized crime (Moore 1974). The crime committee was established by Senate resolution but not without a fight, notes William Moore (1974).

Senator Joseph McCarthy of Wisconsin attempted to "hijack" the resolution; he wanted the investigative responsibility turned over to the Special Investigations Committee on which he served. The attempt failed, and McCarthy quickly moved on to the issue of domestic communism and his own widely publicized hearings. Bosses of big-city machines were concerned that an investigation might look into their activities. The chair of the Judiciary Committee, Pat McCarren of Nevada, was apparently worried about the impact of an investigation on his native state; he held Kefauver's bill captive for several months. On April 6, 1950, Charles Binaggio, the gambling boss of Kansas City, Missouri, and one of his men were murdered in a Democratic party clubhouse. This helped spur passage of the legislation, and on May 10, 1950, Estes Kefauver became chair of the Special Committee to Investigate Organized Crime in Interstate Commerce, launching the first major congressional investigation into the phenomenon.

The committee was charged with making a full and complete study and investigation

> to determine whether organized crime utilizes the facilities of interstate commerce or whether it operates otherwise through the avenues of interstate commerce to promote any transactions which violate federal law or the law of the state in which such transactions might occur.
> The committee was also charged with an investigation of the manner and extent of such criminal operations if it found them actually to be taking place and with the identification of the persons, firms, or corporations involved.
> A third responsibility which was assigned to the committee was the determination as to whether such interstate criminal operations were developing corrupting influences in violation of federal law or the laws of any state. (Kefauver 1951b: 24)

This charge was made all the more dramatic by a new element in public hearings, extensive television coverage that the final report praised "for the public spirit of this relatively new medium" (Kefauver 1951b: 25).

More startling than the committee's conclusions, notes Theodore Wilson (1975: 353), was the extent of public interest in the televised hearings:

> One factor, television, was largely responsible for fixing the public consciousness upon this one investigation. . . . For the first time millions of Americans (some 20 million by one estimate) observed the periodic outbursts of drama and boredom which comprised a congressional hearing as it unfolded. Americans gaped as the denizens of other worlds—bookies, pimps, and gangland enforcers, crime bosses and their slippery lawyers—marched across their television screens. They watched and were impressed by the schoolmasterish

Estes Kefauver, the dignified Tennessean who was the committee's first chairman, as he condemned criminals and the system of ineffective law enforcement, graft, and popular apathy which permitted them to thrive.

The first hearing was conducted on May 26, 1950. Before Kefauver's term as chair would end on May 1, 1951, the committee heard more than six hundred witnesses in Miami, Tampa, New Orleans, Kansas City, Cleveland, St. Louis, Detroit, Los Angeles, San Francisco, Las Vegas, Philadelphia, Washington, Chicago, and New York (Kefauver 1951a). This whirlwind of activity led the committee to conclude:

> Crime is on a syndicated basis to a substantial extent in many cities. The two major crime syndicates in this country are the Accardo-Guzik-Fischetti syndicate, whose headquarters are in Chicago; and the Costello-Adonis-Lansky syndicate based in New York. . . .
>
> There is a sinister criminal organization known as the Mafia operating throughout the country with ties in other nations in the opinion of the committee. The Mafia is the direct descendant of a criminal organization of the same name originating in the island of Sicily. In this country, the Mafia has also been known as the Black Hand and the Unione Siciliano [sic]. The membership of the Mafia today is not confined to persons of Sicilian origin. The Mafia is a loose-knit organization specializing in the sale and distribution of narcotics, the conduct of various gambling enterprises, prostitution, and other rackets based on extortion and violence. The Mafia is the binder which ties together the two major criminal syndicates as well as numerous other criminal groups throughout the country. (Kefauver 1951a: 1–2)

The committee reported that widespread corruption allowed the syndicates to flourish.

While the committee demonstrated extensive interstate contact and investments between gambling figures, notes Moore (1974: 101), "it failed to show extensive interstate control of gambling operations." He argues, however, that the committee's conclusions about gambling had intellectual sincerity based on substantial if not always convincing evidence. Such was not the case with its conclusions about the Mafia: "Inadequate evidence and the necessity to reach some conclusion rushed the committee into fuzzy and ill-founded statements that brought the senators sensational headlines but left an ugly popular misunderstanding in the country" (1974: 114). The Mafia, according to Kefauver (1951b: 19), is "the shadowy international organization that lurks behind much of America's organized criminal activity," a conclusion for which he credits the Federal Bureau of Narcotics. In fact, the committee's final report contained a great deal of nonsense, for example (Kefauver 1951a):

- The Mafia was originally one of many secret societies organized in Sicily to free the island from foreign domination.
- As early as the 1880s, New Orleans was the focal point of Mafia activity.

- The lynching of eleven Italians in New Orleans in 1891 temporarily broke the power of the Mafia in that city. (The committee failed to condemn this murderous outrage.)

According to Dwight Smith (1975: 85), there is an American preoccupation with conspiracy, from the "Bavarian Illuminati" of 1798 to the "Red Scare" of 1919. One of the conditions required for an "alien conspiracy" theory is a set of "facts" or assumptions that can be constructed into evidence supporting a conspiratorial explanation. Such "facts" often make fascinating reading: they sell newspapers, books, and magazines. Smith argues that the conspiracy theory provided the Federal Bureau of Narcotics with an explanation for failure: "The notion of total suppression of illegal narcotics use through importation control was a self-proclaimed mission, and it had not been attained. How better to explain failure (and, incidentally, to prepare the ground for increased future budgets) than to argue that, dedicated though it might be, the bureau was hard-pressed to overcome an alien, organized, conspiratorial force which, with evil intent and conspiratorial methods, had forced its way on an innocent public?" In this era of McCarthyism, the search for alien conspiracies proved to be good politics.

Moore (1974: 211) concludes that the committee's "most constructive work had been the documenting of widespread corruption at the local and state level and the exposing of attempts by law enforcement officials to conceal their malfeasance or ineptitude behind a maze of conflicting, overlapping jurisdictional boundaries." Unfortunately, notes Moore, committee preoccupation with ethnic conspiracies detracted from these findings and some of its constructive policy recommendations. The committee tied organized crime and the Mafia inextricably, thereby equating Italians with organized crime—a theory that was put forth by Harry Anslinger, Director of the Federal Bureau of Narcotics.

Kefauver stepped down as committee chair on May 1, 1951, four months before the committee's mandate ended. The hearings made the Tennessee senator a national political figure—he appeared on the cover of *Time* magazine on March 12, 1951—and contender for the Democratic presidential nomination in 1952. However, the hearings proved to be a source of embarrassment for President Harry S. Truman, a product of the corrupt Kansas City Pendergast machine (although the committee hearings in Kansas City were generally seen as a "whitewash"). Democratic party officials from many urban areas denied Kefauver the nomination, which went instead to Adlai Stevenson of Illinois. In 1956, Kefauver became the Democratic candidate for vice president on the second unsuccessful ticket of Adlai Stevenson. On August 10, 1963, at age sixty, while serving his third term, Senator Kefauver died of a heart attack in Bethesda, Maryland.

THE MCCLELLAN COMMITTEE

In 1956 the Senate Permanent Subcommittee on Investigations began an inquiry into the Teamsters Union, an effort that met with union recalcitrance (see chapter 8). The Senate responded by establishing the Select Committee on Improper Activities in the Labor or Management Field. The findings of the Select Committee led to the passage of the 1959 Labor-Management Reporting and Disclosure Act, usually called the Landrum-Griffin Act after its two sponsors. The Select Committee expired in 1960, but Senator McClellan remained chair of the Permanent Subcommittee on Investigations (PSI). In 1963, the PSI held televised hearings on organized crime and introduced the public to its star witness, Joseph Valachi. Peter Maas (1968: 40) states that Senator McClellan visited Valachi privately at the District of Columbia jail just before the hearings began: "According to Valachi, the senator requested he skip any mention of Hot Springs, in McClellan's home state," which was notorious for its wide-open gambling operations.

Joseph Valachi

In 1962, Joseph Valachi, a convicted drug trafficker and member of the Genovese Family, was serving a sentence for drug trafficking at the U.S. Penitentiary in Atlanta, Georgia. A fellow inmate accused Valachi of being an informer for the Federal Bureau of Narcotics. His accuser was also a "made-guy," and this made the accusation very serious—life threatening. On June 22, 1962, Valachi was approached by an inmate he thought was Joseph DiPalermo ("Joe Beck"), an enforcer for the Genovese Family. Valachi attacked the inmate with a lead pipe—the wrong man, as it turned out—and beat him to death. A little more than one year later, during September and October 1963, Valachi was in Washington, D.C. appearing before the McClellan (PSI) Committee.

Valachi was inducted—"made"—into the Maranzano faction during the Castellammarese War, and had been a soldier for more than thirty years. The career criminal told of a secret society which insiders referred to as *Cosa Nostra*, "Our Thing," replete with blood oaths and murders. He discussed the Castellammarese War, Luciano's murder of Joe Masseria, Salvatore Maranzano, and some forty [sic] "mustache Petes" (see chapter 3). Valachi outlined the structure of each crime Family and explained how they were linked together through a national commission—the "Supreme Court of Organized Crime." Once the television lights were turned on, notes Peter Maas (1968: 41), senators bombarded Valachi with questions designed to score points with the voters back home. Nebraska Senator Carl Curtis, for example, asked about organized crime in Omaha:

> After a moment's reflection, Valachi carefully cupped his hand over his mouth, turned to a Justice Department official sitting next to him, and whispered something. Those viewing the scene could be forgiven for supposing that Senator Curtis had hit on a matter of some import which Valachi wanted to check before answering. He was in fact asking, "Where the hell is Omaha?"

Virgil Peterson, a former FBI agent and almost legendary executive director of the Chicago Crime Commission for twenty-seven years, points out

501

that Valachi made a remarkable impact on organized crime literature (1983a: 425):

> In fact, it was Valachi who quite likely coined the name *Cosa Nostra*, using it to denote an Italian criminal organization. During the years following his revelations, the great majority of published books, articles, and news items that have attempted to describe the structure of organized crime in America clearly reveal a heavy reliance on Valachi. Likewise, his disclosures have been accepted without much questioning by many official agencies as well. On some occasions, writers either misinterpreted portions of Valachi's testimony or attributed to him statements he never made at all.

Valachi was a barely literate, low-echelon soldier whose first-hand knowledge of organized crime was limited to street-level experiences. Much of the information attributed to him is obviously well beyond his personal experience. Peterson notes that some of Valachi's testimony was extremely vague, confusing, and inconsistent. "Not infrequently, it would appear, he either withheld facts that should have been known to him or deliberately lied" (1983a: 425). Nevertheless, this did not prevent his disclosures from becoming the core of a chapter on organized crime in the final report of the President's Commission on Law Enforcement and Administration of Justice.

PRESIDENT'S COMMISSION ON LAW ENFORCEMENT AND ADMINISTRATION OF JUSTICE

In 1964, Lyndon B. Johnson was serving the remainder of John F. Kennedy's term and seeking election as president. The Republicans had nominated Senator Barry M. Goldwater of Arizona, who launched what has come to be known as a "law-and-order" campaign: the Republicans attacked the Democratic administration for being "soft on crime." Johnson won a landslide victory, but the issue of "crime in the streets" lingered on. In order to blunt criticism (and, Richard Quinney (1974) argues, to divert attention away from the Vietnam conflict), Johnson launched his own "war on crime." On March 8, 1965, in a message to the Eighty-ninth Congress—"Crime, Its Prevalence and Measures of Prevention"—President Johnson announced: "I am establishing the President's Commission on Law Enforcement and Administration of Justice. The commission will be composed of men and women of distinction who share my belief that we need to know far more about the prevention and control of crime." The president appointed Attorney General Nicholas deB. Katzenbach to head the commission. Nine different task forces were established, including the Task Force on Organized Crime headed by Charles H. Rogovin, with Donald R. Cressey and Ralph Salerno serving as consultants. Cressey (1969) and Salerno (1969) extended the influence of the president's commission (and Joseph Valachi) by writing books on organized crime.

In its report to the commission, the Task Force on Organized Crime (1967: 6) stated:

Today the core of organized crime in the United States consists of twenty-four groups operating as criminal cartels in large cities across the nation. Their membership is exclusively men of Italian descent, they are in frequent communications with each other, and their smooth functioning is insured by a national body of overseers. To date, only the Federal Bureau of Investigation has been able to document fully the national scope of these groups, and the FBI intelligence indicates that *the organization as a whole has changed its name from the Mafia to Cosa Nostra.* (emphasis added)

The last statement was obviously based on the revelations of Joseph Valachi.

The task force continued what the Kefauver Committee had begun, equating organized crime with Italians. The only new wrinkle was a name change (Messick 1973: 8): "La Cosa Nostra was created [by the FBI via Valachi] as a public image. This simple device of giving the Mafia a new name worked wonders. Hoover was taken off the limb where he had perched for so long, and citizens had a new menace to talk about with tales of blood oaths, contracts for murder, secret societies." Hank Messick argues that this picture was thirty years out of date. More important, however, were the policy implications.

The task force recommended a witness protection program, special federal grand juries, and legislation permitting electronic surveillance—recommendations that were enacted into law. The task force noted the inadequacy of budgetary allocations devoted to dealing with organized crime and the lack of coordination among agencies charged with combatting OC activity. Accordingly, budgetary allocations were increased to deal with the "new" menace, and in 1967 federal organized crime strike forces were established in each city with an "LCN Family." In 1968 the Omnibus Crime Control and Safe Streets Act was enacted providing law enforcement agencies with legal guidelines for electronic surveillance. In 1970, Congress passed the Organized Crime Control Act which contains the RICO provisions discussed in chapter 9.

The task force concluded that the major income for OC is derived from gambling, with loansharking second. Little attention was given to other sources of income, in particular, drug trafficking and labor racketeering. After the task force disbanded, the Permanent Subcommittee on Investigations, chaired first by Senator McClellan, and later by William Roth (R-Delaware) and Sam Nunn (D-Georgia), remained the congressional committee most interested in organized crime, although it was eclipsed for several years by the President's Commission on Organized Crime. (In government, a committee is a legislative unit, while a commission is part of the executive branch.)

PRESIDENT'S COMMISSION ON ORGANIZED CRIME (PCOC)

The Reagan administration era was extraordinary with respect to organized crime. The man who welcomed the support of the International Brotherhood of Teamsters and who appointed Jackie Presser to his interim planning staff also issued *Executive Order Number 12435* of July 28, 1983, creating the President's Commission on Organized Crime.

> The commission shall make a full and complete national and region-by-region analysis of organized crime; define the nature of traditional organized crime as well as emerging organized crime groups, the sources and amounts of organized crime's income, and the uses to which organized crime puts its income; develop in-depth information on the participants in organized crime networks; and evaluate federal laws pertinent to the effort to combat organized crime.

The commission was charged with advising the president on "actions which can be taken to improve law enforcement efforts directed against organized crime, and make recommendations concerning appropriate administrative and legislative improvements in the administration of justice." The commission was given thirty-three months and $5 million to accomplish these tasks.

During the nearly three years of its life, the commission produced five reports:

1. *The Cash Connection: Organized Crime, Financial Institutions, and Money Laundering* (1984)
2. *The Edge: Organized Crime, Business and Labor Unions, Appendix* (1985)
3. *The Edge: Organized Crime, Business and Labor Unions* (1986)
4. *America's Habit: Drug Abuse, Drug Trafficking, and Organized Crime* (1986)
5. *The Impact: Organized Crime Today* (1986)

The results of seven hearings were also published.

PCOC began and ended in controversy. First Irving R. Kaufman of the U.S. Court of Appeals for the Second Circuit (NY) was appointed as chair. Judge Kaufman's sole connection to efforts against organized crime consisted of his role as presiding judge at the 1959 conspiracy and obstruction of justice trial of some of the men who were arrested at the infamous "Apalachin Crime Convention" in 1957 (discussed in chapter 3). In a *New York Times Magazine* article, President Reagan (1986: 84) recalled the judge's role, particularly his statements at the sentencing hearing: "The judge called them 'hardened, sophisticated criminals who thought of themselves as a group above the law, men who placed loyalty to each other above loyalty to their country and its law-abiding citizens.'" The convictions of the men, however, were reversed in 1960, and Judge Kaufman was criticized by the Court of Appeals for having allowed "a prosecution framed on such a doubtful basis" to proceed to trial (*United States v. Buffalino et al.* 285 F.2d. 408). On May 30, 1985, the U.S. Court of Appeals for the Eleventh Circuit in Atlanta ruled that Kaufman's service as chair of the President's Commission violated constitutional separation of powers. The decision, however, was successfully appealed, and Judge Kaufman remained chair until the commission expired in 1986.

Philip Shenon (1986: 9) notes that "discord was a dominant characteristic of the commission." Peter Vaira, a former U.S. attorney and the first executive director, resigned before the commission began its work, reportedly the result of a disagreement with Judge Kaufman. After a second candidate for executive director was rejected by the Justice Department, James D. Harmon, Jr., was selected and served until the commission completed its work. During the first year there was a conflict with the Justice Department over the commission's independence and personnel. As a result, the commission was unable to fulfill its mandate to evaluate federal prosecutorial efforts. Finally, on July 17, 1984, the commission was given subpoena power.

Many important OC figures were subpoenaed. As expected, they invoked the Fifth Amendment or presented some novel arguments for their refusal to respond to commission questions. When he appeared on April 23, 1985, Jackie Presser invoked the Fifth Amendment in response to commission questions. Robert Cantazaro, the head of a dental insurance plan formerly used by the International Union of Allied Novelty and Production Workers, which represents about 20,000 workers in the Chicago area, was incarcerated for refusing to answer commission questions after having been granted immunity from prosecution. (The vice president of the union, John Serpico, is a leader of the Chicago Outfit.) The commission was interested in the extraordinary contract Cantazaro had with the union, a contract that allowed his company to keep about 67 percent of the premiums paid in (the norm for the insurance industry is 20 to 25 percent). One subpoenaed witness, Lorenzo Scaduto, refused to testify after being granted immunity, and he was sentenced to one year of imprisonment by a federal judge in Miami. Scaduto, however, was already serving a sixty-two year prison sentence for drug trafficking.

The seven public hearings held by the PCOC generated a great deal of media coverage. They were denounced by some as mere publicity stunts, particularly when witnesses were produced wearing black hoods to hide their identities. Lawyers for Roy L. Williams, the convicted former president of the Teamsters Union, urged a federal judge to allow him to remain free because he had been subpoenaed to testify before the President's Commission, and this, they argued, would jeopardize his life. Federal District Judge Prentice Marshall of Chicago "ridiculed the notion that anyone would be worried that Mr. Williams might testify before the Kaufman commission, which he said was 'powerless to do anything other than to examine a bunch of characters dressed up like witches'" (Shipp 1985b: 12). Some of these anonymous witnesses provided dubious information and identified persons without any criminal records as being involved in organized crime, information that was duly reported in the newspapers without any corroboration. Alleged dropouts from Asian gangs told of Vietnamese gangs in several major cities, including Chicago. "But when the Chicago police tried to track down the gang here, they couldn't find a trace of it" (Koziol and O'Brien 1985: 4). In one case an anonymous witness identified the vice chairman of a New York Chinatown bank as an "organized crime figure," causing a run on the bank and the resignation of the vice chairman ("Chinatown Bank Official, Cited at Hearing, Quits" 1984).

PCOC highlighted the problem of money laundering, the continuing problem of labor-union racketeering, and drew attention to the problem of "mob lawyers." A staff study (PCOC 1985b: 3)

> confirmed the existence of a small group of attorneys who have become integral parts of criminal conspiracies, using their status as sworn officers of the court to advance the criminal purposes of these criminal organizations. It is clear that traditional organized crime and narcotics traffickers depend upon and could not effectively operate without these attorneys.

While the commission revealed little that was new, it avoided an overemphasis on Italian-American organized crime, presented information on Colombian cocaine cartels, and examined to a lesser degree other criminal organizations including outlaw motorcycle clubs. In fact, there was so little attention paid to traditional OC that the commission failed to determine how many crime units/Families were actually operating in the United States—it used the figure twenty-four, which dates back to 1967 and the Task Force on Organized Crime.[2] The commission concluded that drug trafficking was the greatest money-maker for OC. As opposed to its predecessor, the Task Force on Organized Crime, the President's Commission found existing laws generally adequate for dealing with OC, although it found significant deficiencies in carrying out the statutes.

The President's Commission's (1986c: 463) most highly-publicized recommendation was related to drug policy. Since "drug trafficking and abuse are the most serious organized crime problems in America today," the commission stated,

> Government contracts should not be awarded to companies that fail to implement drug programs, including suitable drug testing. . . . Government and private sector employers who do not already require drug testing of job applicants and current employees should consider the appropriateness of such a testing program. (1986c: 483, 485)

The recommendation generated an angry response from some commissioners who had not seen the drug report or its recommendations prior to its release to the media.

The final report was submitted to President Reagan in draft form in April 1986, but was not published until early 1987. In the report, ten of the panel's

---

2. So little information was gathered about traditional OC that just before the commission was to disband, I was asked to provide extensive information on the state of Italian-American organized crime and was given thirty days to research and respond.

nineteen commissioners were critical of the work of the commission. "Poor management of time, money and staff," they concluded, "has resulted in the commission's leaving important issues unexamined, most notably the questions of the effectiveness of federal and state anti-organized crime efforts" (PCOC 1986a: 173). Lupsha (1987: 283) notes that commission reports appear thrown together, a collection of written statements, depositions, and consultant's papers with little or no organization. There is an absence of summary volumes "bringing together all of the salient points." Lupsha points out that key names were misspelled and factual errors abound, the result of a failure to check primary sources.

Unlike the political impact of the Task Force on Organized Crime, the President's Commission created hardly a ripple—new legislation was not forthcoming, nor did new initiatives result. The policy that was in place before the commission was established remained in place.

ORGANIZED CRIME POLICY

Four basic (but not mutually exclusive) policy changes could be made in response to organized crime:

1. Increase the risks of involvement in OC by increasing OC law enforcement resources.
2. Increase the risks of involvement in OC by expanding the authority of OC law enforcement.
3. Reduce the economic lure of involvement in OC by making legitimate opportunity more readily available.
4. Decrease organized criminal opportunity (decriminalization).

Increasing OC law enforcement resources requires that tax revenue be shifted away from other areas and into OC law enforcement—a difficult task to accomplish under present economic and political conditions. Shortly after his inauguration, President George Bush, in response to a reporter's question, stated that the thrust of his antidrug initiative would be in the area of prevention, since additional resources were not available for increasing drug law enforcement. However, an increase in the budget of the Internal Revenue Service would return tax revenue many times the increase. Richard Neely (1982: 28) points out, however:

> Cheating on federal and state income taxes is pervasive in all classes of society; except among the compulsively honest, cheating occurs in direct proportion to opportunity. Why, then, do we not expand the Internal Revenue Service and its state counterparts? Every new revenue agent pays his salary and overhead at least eight times. The answer is that we do not really want Rhadamanthine enforcement of the tax laws.

We could take advantage of *control theory* (discussed in chapter 2) and shift the focus of law enforcement efforts away from "headhunting," concentrating instead on those most likely to be deterred—the young associates of organized criminal groups who aspire to insider/membership status. Such persons are most vulnerable to enforcement efforts, and since they have not yet been granted full entry into the OC subculture, are the most likely targets of control theory law enforcement. Since the continuity of an OC group is dependent on its ability to successfully recruit able members, this approach has strategic value beyond that accomplished by efforts aimed at incapacitating current OC leadership.

Expanding the authority of OC law enforcement is an inexpensive response—at least with respect to tax dollars. It requires the enactment of legislation that would make it easier to investigate, prosecute, and punish persons involved in organized criminal activity. For example, we could provide a "good faith" exception to the exclusionary rule in prosecutions involving RICO violations. Legislation to accomplish this was passed by the House of Representatives in 1988 (in the guise of a bill to deal with drug trafficking) during the heat of a presidential campaign, although it was deleted from the final bill enacted into law. Title III could be amended so that electronic surveillance could be more easily accomplished, and we could give the FBI and DEA complete access to federal income-tax returns. While these changes would enhance the efficiency of law enforcement efforts against organized crime, it would be at the expense of our concern for privacy and liberty

Reducing the economic lure of involvement in OC requires providing improved legitimate economic opportunity for persons in deprived circumstances who are most likely to become part of OC. We are referring to a reduction of the *strain* (see chapter 2) experienced by ambitious young persons whose opportunity structure is such that they perceive organized criminal activity as a viable career choice. While obviously a more positive approach to dealing with OC, increasing opportunity is expensive and, many would argue, should be based on social and political goals much broader than combatting organized crime.

Decreasing organized criminal opportunity was one argument for the legalization of certain types of gambling, in particular the state lottery, beginning in New Hampshire in 1964, followed by New York in 1967. The first financially successful lottery, however, was the fifty-cent weekly established by New Jersey in 1971 (Gambling Commission 1976). Most lottery states now have a variety of games: instant winners, daily drawings, and weekly drawings with payoffs in the millions of dollars. This form of gambling was originally offered as a way of reducing the income of the illegal lottery—numbers—and capturing those monies for public use. Without a doubt, the lottery has aided states. Thirty-four states and the District of Columbia by 1992 used lotteries to increase their revenues: more than $20 billion in sales annually (Smothers 1992).

There is no evidence, however, that the legal lotteries have diminished the revenues of their illegal counterparts. In fact, publicity may have actually increased illegal revenues along with those of state lotteries. The introduction

LOTTERY DREAMS

In a poverty-wracked neighborhood on Chicago's South Side, a fifty-five-year-old mother of seven and grandmother of fifty-nine emptied a small cellophane bag of quarters onto the counter of a small clothing store. The pile amounted to $5, enough to purchase five tickets in the state's lottery, which because of several rollovers reached over $60 million. The woman had promised herself that if she won she would repay the state some of what she has gotten during the twenty-nine years she has been on public aid. The next customer paid $15 in Social Security money for fifteen lottery tickets. He was followed by the father of seven who had recently won $500—after spending about $25 per week over the past few years. Outside, another man—unemployed since triple-bypass surgery in 1980—checked a handful of instant winner tickets he had just purchased.

Source: Ann Marie Lipinski, "Poor Dream Impossible Lotto Dream." *Chicago Tribune*, April 13, 1989: Section 2: 1, 6.

of a legal lottery serves to educate persons who heretofore did not know the intricacies of numbers gambling (Blount and Kaplan 1989). Illegal operators typically provide better odds, do not report the winnings to tax officials, and accept bets on credit, over the telephone, and in amounts of less than $1. Furthermore, the daily lottery provides illegal operators with a winning number in which bettors have confidence and offers a free layoff service so that numbers banks can always balance their bets (see chapter 6). The illegal lottery, however, does not encourage people to gamble by an unseemly spate of advertising.[3]

In 1976, a federal commission warned that "the availability of legal gambling creates new gamblers." Therefore, "a government that wishes merely to legitimize illegal wagering must recognize the clear danger that legalization may lead to unexpected and ungovernable increases in the size of the gambling clientele" (Gambling Commission 1976: 2). In the constant quest for new revenues without having to raise taxes, states such as New York have introduced new forms of lottery such as Keno, an electronic game in which bettors pick one or more numbers and win if the computer comes up with their numbers. Instead of a weekly or daily drawing, Keno picks a new number every five minutes—the compulsive gambler's nightmare.

Off-track betting (OTB) in New York has been less than a resounding success and is struggling to cover its expenses, although it has created plenty of patronage jobs. OTB did succeed in reducing illegal betting on horses, as few

---

3. I have a strong bias against government-inspired gambling.

bookmakers in New York accept bets on horse-racing. Like a number of other states, OTB in New York is considering the introduction of sports betting. Some fear that the introduction of sports betting will serve to educate more persons on the intricacies of gambling. Since illegal operators typically provide better odds (their overhead is significantly lower), do not report the winnings to tax officials, and accept bets on credit and over the telephone, legalized sports betting may succeed in recruiting new bettors for the bookmakers. There is also legalized casino gambling. As far as New Jersey's efforts to keep OC out "While it may be true that mobsters haven't yet found their way into the casino counting rooms—as they once did in Las Vegas—almost anywhere you look in the city you'll find a wiseguy or one of his associates. The mob is on the floor of every casino in the city. It's in the restaurants and the casino lounges. It controls the labor unions whose workers make the big casino-hotels go" (Anastasia 1991: 163).

There is also the question of decriminalizing drug use, since drug trafficking appears to provide the greatest profits for organized crime. Decriminalizing cocaine and heroin would dramatically impact on emerging organized crime groups. This issue is quite complex, and will be considered in our examination of drug policy in the United States.

DRUG POLICY

Before examining the possibility of changing our current drug policy, we need to note some incongruities. Of the most widely used psychoactive drugs, heroin and cocaine (except for limited topical use) are banned; barbiturates, tranquilizers, and amphetamines are highly restricted; and alcohol, caffeine, and nicotine products are freely available. These inconsistencies make convincing young people that they should not use drugs for recreational purposes difficult. Nicotine and alcohol are clearly dangerous psychoactive chemicals—*drugs*. Statutory vocabulary and social folklore have established the fiction that alcohol and nicotine are not drugs at all, notes the National Commission on Marijuana and Drug Abuse (1973). Furthermore, the commission points out that to do otherwise would be inconsistent with our stated policy goal of eliminating drug abuse—an admission that we can never eliminate the problem.

The scientific truth is that not all drug use is misuse, notes Norman Zinberg (1984: 200), but since this contravenes formal social policy, those who present this message run the risk that "their work will be interpreted as condoning use." Society's response to easily abused substances is not based on the degree of danger inherent in their use. For example, measured on any scale, alcohol is a more serious drug of abuse than marijuana, although this fact is not reflected by our legal system. Many dangerous substances, such as amphetamines, barbiturates, and a variety of sedatives, were actively promoted by "pushers" in the drug industry and their medical accomplices for use in dealing with anxiety, stress, obesity, or insomnia.

Why some drugs have been outlawed while others are legally and widely available should be examined beyond scientific or medical reasons. The tobacco industry, the alcoholic beverage industry, the drug manufacturing industry, and the media have influenced drug policy. The public's knowledge of and response to the "drug problem" is mediated through newspapers and television. As Joseph Gusfield (1975: 5) notes: "The attention of public media to a problem gives it status as an issue. The attention of government and other public agents to a problem accentuates, in turn, its position on the public agenda."

What are the policy alternatives available to the United States?

Drug Maintenance and Legalization

John Kaplan (1983: 101) poses the following policy question: "Could we not lower the total social costs of heroin [and cocaine] use and the government response to it by allowing the drug to be freely and cheaply available in liquor stores or as an over-the-counter drug?" Such a policy would be consistent with the American approach to other unhealthy habits such as cigarette smoking, drinking alcohol, and overeating, or to sports such as mountain climbing, skydiving, automobile and motorcycle racing, football, and boxing—an acknowledgment of the freedom of an individual to enjoy himself or herself, or to earn money, even when it may be injurious to that person's health. The deliberate engagement in dangerous pursuits can be explained by the release of potentially reinforcing (pleasure producing) neurotransmitters such as endorphin, which acts like heroin, and dopamine, which acts like cocaine (Abadinsky 1993). Furthermore, as Edward Brecher (1972: 528) notes, most of the harmful aspects of heroin use are the result of its being illegal:

> Many American morphine and heroin addicts prior to 1914 led long, healthy, respectable, productive lives despite addiction—and so do a few addicts today. The sorry plight of most heroin addicts in the United States results primarily from the high price of heroin, the contamination and adulteration of the heroin available on the black market, the mainlining of the drug instead of safer modes of use, the laws against heroin and the ways in which they are enforced, the imprisonment of addicts, society's attitudes toward addicts, and other nonpharmacological factors.

"Our attempt to protect drug users from themselves," notes James Ostrowski (Committee on Law Reform 1987: 6), "has backfired, as it did during the prohibition of alcohol. We have only succeeded in making drug use much more dangerous and driving it underground, out of the reach of moderating social influences."

Advantages of Decriminalization

The practical advantages of a decriminalization policy are impressive:

1. There would be a reduction in the resources necessary for drug law enforcement. According to Ethan Nadelmann, federal, state, and local governments spend an

estimated $8 billion a year on direct drug law enforcement costs. This does not include indirect but expensive costs such as imprisonment, probation, and parole (*Time* 30 May 1988: 14). These resources could be shifted to other areas of crime control, or could be used for drug treatment and education.

2. The low cost of psychoactive substances would curtail secondary criminality, performed to support an expensive drug habit.

3. Criminal organizations supported by drug trafficking would no longer remain viable (unless they moved into other criminal activities). In Colombia, the government drive against major drug cartels left many henchmen and assassins scampering for other sources of income, leading to a dramatic increase in kidnappings; there were 1,274 kidnappings in 1990 as opposed to 789 in 1989 (Brooke 1991a).

4. Those dependent on heroin, cocaine, or other currently illegal psychoactive substances could lead more normal lives. The time and energy needed to maintain the habit could be channeled into more constructive pursuits, and abusers would have an opportunity to become contributing members of society. With respect to heroin, it is not the drug but the law that makes heroin hazardous to the addict. Opiates, like widely prescribed sedatives, provide relief from anxiety, distress, and insomnia to persons who would have difficulty functioning normally in the absence of such substances (Chein et al. 1964). Similar arguments can be made for cocaine and amphetamines.

5. The intravenous use of heroin would not necessarily involve the danger of hepatitis or AIDS since each user would have his or her own hypodermic kit. In the United States, while the incidence of AIDS among the homosexual population has stabilized, the disease is spreading quickly among drug addicts. Decriminalization would also make many drugs available in liquid form for oral ingestion. Under government oversight, drugs would be distributed in precisely measured doses free of any dangerous contaminants; the chance of a drug overdose would be reduced.

6. Decriminalization would enable the use of social controls that inhibit antisocial, albeit lawful, behavior. Because drugs are illegal, users avoid detection and are shielded from social pressure. "Therefore, illicit drug users generally escape the potent forms of social control that are applied to smokers and drunk drivers" (Alexander 1990: 8).

Disadvantages of Decriminalization

There are, of course, important negative consequences:

1. Cocaine, heroin, and other potentially dangerous substances that are freely available to adults could be abused by youngsters as easily as cigarettes and alcohol are. Restrictions on these items have not proven effective in keeping the substances away from young people. Of course, it is unlikely that those adolescents motivated toward drug use are currently being thwarted by legislative acts and law enforcement efforts—drug use typically begins during adolescence.

2. More persons would be tempted to try legalized controlled substances, and abuse-related problems might increase accordingly. There is a higher rate of drug abuse among medical practitioners than among the general population because of easier access. James Q. Wilson (1975: 142) argues that "all evidence suggests that the easy availability of heroin would lead to a sharp increase in its use." The PCOC (1986c: 331) states that "legalization would almost certainly increase demand, and therefore spread this destruction." Isidor Chein and his colleagues (1964: 348)

argue, however, that "opiates are not inherently attractive, euphoric, or stimulant substances." That is, they are not seductive substances that "hook" the unsuspecting and the innocent. A study of 11,882 hospital patients treated with painkilling drugs revealed that only four became addicted. A study of more than 10,000 burn victims who received injections of narcotics for weeks or months did not find a single case of addiction attributed to this treatment (Melzack 1990). Russell Portnoy, M.D., director of analgesic studies in the Pain Service at Sloan-Kettering Memorial Hospital, points out, "Just as the vast majority of people who drink do not become alcoholics, those who are treated with opioid for pain do not become addicts" (Goleman 1987: 10). While two out of every three Americans consume alcohol, 10 percent of the drinkers account for half of all the alcohol consumed in the United States.

3. Legalizing all psychoactive substances would signal an acceptance of their use similar to the acceptance of alcohol and tobacco. Most users of alcohol do not become addicted, but Kaplan (1983) argues that we do not know whether this will hold true for drugs such as heroin. Studies indicate that rats and monkeys perform considerable amounts of work to earn injections of heroin or cocaine, but not alcohol. However, many persons have used opiates without becoming addicted: hospital patients experiencing pain, "chippers" and "weekenders" who use heroin much as a social drinker uses alcohol. Soldiers returning to the United States who used high-quality heroin while in Vietnam usually discontinued use when they no longer felt the anxiety and depression that apparently was endemic to the Vietnam experience, and when the cheap, high-quality heroin to which they had grown accustomed was no longer available (Robins 1973, 1974; Robins et al. 1980). The availability of cheap heroin in the United States, argues Wilson (1990), might have kept these veterans addicted.

Kaplan (1984) points out that several conventions have developed around alcohol use that limit its abuse potential: using it only at ceremonial occasions or when at dinner with the family, never drinking alone, and avoiding intoxication— being "a drunk." He warns that while conventions may develop around the use of heroin, the cultural model might turn out to be that of the "junkie." Kaplan fails to deal with the disease theory of addiction. What if some persons take heroin or cocaine to compensate for a physiological deficiency? Is this not analogous to the diabetic's use of insulin? Erich Goode (1972: 212) recommends abandoning efforts to eliminate or even drastically reduce drug abuse: *Live with it and make sure that drug users do not seriously harm themselves and others*" (original emphasis). This is a reasonable suggestion if one accepts physiological theories—the disease model of drug abuse or the concept of an "addictive personality" (see Abadinsky 1993).

Some researchers have found a strong correlation between poor mental health and drug abuse. Drugs are frequently self-prescribed by persons to deal with their mental problems "primarily to improve their level of affect and/or functioning." Psychoactive drugs do alleviate, at least temporarily, psychological discomfort, enabling the person to relax and/or function more effectively: "[To the] extent that drug use is, or at least perceived as being, an effective strategy for improving one's mental health, there will be strong motivation for the user to persist in drug use" (Gove, Geerken, and Hughes 1979: 587).

4. The easy and legal availability of heroin, cocaine, and other currently illegal psychoactive substances would reduce the incentive for those already addicted or habituated to enter drug treatment or otherwise to seek a drug-free existence. Of

course, there is no reason to believe that a drug-free existence would facilitate a constructive, crime-free life-style in most persons currently using psychoactive substances. Most heroin addicts, for example, go right on using heroin despite the threat or actuality of imprisonment, and despite efforts to cure the affliction.

The legal availability of heroin, however, could prolong heroin addiction beyond the age at which spontaneous remission typically occurs (thirty-five to forty). Furthermore, as Zinberg (1984: 13) notes, the availability of cheap, high-grade heroin in Vietnam helps explain its widespread use by American servicemen: "Heroin was so potent and inexpensive that smoking was an effective and economical method to use, and this no doubt made it more attractive than if injection had been the primary mode of administration.... The decreased availability of heroin in the United States (reflected in its high price) and its decreased potency (which made smoking wholly impractical) made it difficult for the returning veterans to continue use."

In order to develop a policy that responds to these serious concerns, we need to understand the causes of drug use. Are some persons more vulnerable than others? We do not know why some persons abuse drugs while others with similar access do not. We do not know why some persons who experiment with certain drugs become dependent while others do not. Any discussion of drug policy is conditioned on views of drug abuse and on the particular theory that one adopts:

1. Drug abuse is a disease with a physiological basis.
2. Drug abuse is a psychological condition or personality disorder.
3. Drug abuse is a response to oppressive social conditions.
4. Drug abuse is simply the pleasure-seeking activity of hedonistic persons.

We do know that there is a very high correlation between urban poverty and heroin and cocaine use. A great deal of drug use, it seems, feeds upon human misery. A serious effort to deal logically with drugs would require greater efforts to reduce the ills of urban America. Chein and his colleagues (Chein et al. 1964: 381) extend this argument further: "Is a society which cannot or will not do anything to alleviate the miseries which are, at least subjectively, alleviated by drugs better off if it simply prevents the victims of these miseries from finding any relief?" Furthermore, Zinberg (1984) reminds us that much of the damage inflicted today under the aegis of drugs is the result of their illicit status and not from their pharmacology. Post-Harrison Act efforts against certain psychoactive chemicals were based on their potential for harm. These efforts come full circle when the user is the target of vigorous enforcement efforts, as in the case of current drug policy: "We must focus responsibility and sanctions on illegal drug users" (White House Conference for a Drug Free America 1988: 9).

Kaplan (1983) argues that our inability to predict the consequences of making heroin freely available mitigates against a policy of drug legalization. Ethan Nadelmann (1988: 91) disagrees: "The case for legalization [of heroin, cocaine, and marijuana] is particularly convincing when the risks inherent in alcohol and tobacco use are compared with those associated with illicit drug use." Chein et al. (1964) and Trebach (1982) recommend a more modest policy: placing greater trust in the medical profession. Physicians should be allowed to treat addicts with a variety of drugs, including heroin. They recommend the establishment of clinics to implement this policy. (Such clinics have never been popular with community residents, and it would be difficult to open them in most neighborhoods.) Any person shown to be addicted to heroin could receive prescriptions for this drug. Determining whether or not a person is addicted and how much heroin he or she should be given would be left to the medical profession. Trebach notes that some drugs would be diverted into the black market, but there is already a considerable market in illegal heroin. Legalization would reduce the price of heroin, thereby reducing the incentive for dealing in the substance. This policy, Trebach argues, would attract heroin addicts in large numbers and cause significant decreases in crime. Such clinics would also offer a wide variety of social services, including help in becoming drug-free (which would be encouraged—but not imposed—by clinic staff). Trebach has not suggested a similar program with respect to cocaine, currently the major illicit drug of abuse.

One source of strong opposition to drug decriminalization is the leadership of the African-American community. Many have expressed the view that such programs are designed to tranquilize members of the minority community who would use the drug to alleviate their social and psychological frustrations. Some would abandon protest and political activity for the "easy fix," and such programs would saddle the minority community with life-long addicts robbed of the incentive to give up drug use.

THREE MODELS OF LEGALIZATION/DECRIMINALIZATION

1. Dangerous drugs can be dispensed only through government-controlled clinics or specially licensed medical personnel and only for short-term treatment purposes. Unauthorized sale or possession entails criminal penalties. Long-term maintenance is limited to the use of methadone. This is basically the approach currently used in England.
2. Dangerous drugs can be prescribed by an authorized medical practitioner for treatment or maintenance. Criminal penalties are imposed for sale or possession outside of medical auspices. This is the old British system.
3. Dangerous drugs can be sold and used in a similar fashion to tobacco and alcohol products; that is, nonprescription use by adults is permitted. This was the case in the United States prior to the Harrison Act.

Changes in our drug policy would help destroy heroin and cocaine cartels that are a threat to the integrity and stability of a number of nations faced with Marxist insurgencies, while reducing the everyday dangers to which we expose our drug law enforcement agents. Indeed, government officials in cocaine-producing countries such as Colombia and Peru endorse legalization or decriminalization, since they bear the brunt of the insurgencies and U.S. condemnation: "Either we legalize drugs and regulate and tax them, or we completely internationalize the fight against the drug traffickers," states a Colombian assistant attorney general (de Lama 1988d). *Internationalization*, notes George de Lama (1988d), "is the new South American code in the producer nations of Peru, Bolivia and Columbia. . . . It means merging various national law enforcement and customs agencies into a multinational antidrug police force." This, of course, would require the renunciation of certain aspects of sovereignty—and foreign police officers operating in the United States would probably not be acceptable to Congress, the president, and the public.

Another suggested response involves military action—"Let's call out the troops!"

Using the Military

In 1878, congressional Democrats enacted the Posse Comitatus Act to prevent Republican presidents from using the Army to further Reconstruction in the former Confederate states. The act provides that:

> whoever, except in cases and under circumstances expressly authorized by the Constitution or Act of Congress willfully uses any part of the Army or Air Force as a posse comitatus or otherwise to execute the laws shall be fined not more than $10,000 or imprisoned not more than two years or both. (18 USCA sec. 1385, 1984)

The Navy and Marines promulgated administrative restrictions that parallel the act.

As noted in chapter 9, until 1981 the DOD limited its involvement in drug law enforcement to lending equipment and training civilian enforcement personnel in the use of military equipment. In that year, as part of a new "War on Drugs," Congress amended the Posse Comitatus Act, authorizing a greater level of military involvement in civilian drug enforcement, particularly the tracking of suspect ships and planes and the use of military pilots and naval ships to transport civilian enforcement personnel. Further amendments to the 1981 legislation liberalized the use of military equipment and personnel in interdiction efforts.

The 1981 statute maintained the prohibition against U.S. military personnel involvement in arrest and seizure activities. This prohibition is based on fear that further DOD involvement in drug law enforcement could:

1. compromise American security by exposing military personnel to the potentially corrupting environment of drug trafficking;
2. impair the strategic role of the military; and
3. present a threat to civil liberties: "The very nature of military training precludes any considerations of due process or civil rights" (Marsh 1991: 63).

"Furthermore," Harry Marsh notes, "civilian casualties ["collateral damage"], although unwanted, are often an inevitable result of military operations." Despite this fear, in 1988 legislation was overwhelmingly approved to dramatically expand the role of the military and allow the arrest of civilians under certain circumstances.

Controlling Drugs at Their Source

Our current policy of attempting to control drugs at their source has had unintended consequences. The successful effort to force Turkey to curtail its production of opium in the 1970s resulted in a concomitant rise in production in Mexico and Southeast Asia. The United States has provided weaponry to the government of Burma to deal with drug trafficking in its part of the Golden Triangle. These armaments enabled the brutal Burmese military to be more effective against indigenous populations fighting for independence from Rangoon. In response, the opium growers and drug traffickers under control of the independence movements in this area increased their drug trafficking activities in order to secure better weaponry (for example, ground-to-air missiles to use against American-supplied helicopters) and the cycle continues (Nietschmann 1987).

Most of the money given to Colombia to fight the cocaine cartels has been used instead by the military to fight Marxist insurgencies (de Lama 1989; Lane et al. 1992). A similar situation exists in Peru, where U.S. military assistance is used to fight leftist insurgents. At the end of 1991, the United States began withholding drug-fighting aid to Peru because of charges that the Peruvian military was aiding cocaine traffickers. Army units have reportedly fired on police helicopters engaged in antidrug missions (Krauss 1991b). U.S. advisors in Bolivia believe that many of the military conscripts they are training for antidrug enforcement will eventually be employed by the traffickers—their training makes them a valuable resource (Lane et al. 1992).

There is concern that the fight against drugs is simply a way for the United States to finance a sub-rosa war against leftist insurgents without incurring strong congressional opposition (Shenon 1990; Krauss 1991). Such opposition would focus attention on the excesses of foreign government forces. The Peruvian military, which has a primary role in fighting the cocaine business, has earned widespread condemnation for rampant corruption and the violation of basic human rights. The government response to terrorists, particularly Shining Path guerillas, has grown indiscriminate and sadistic, as dramatized by a 1991 incident: a medical student on his way to a study session and two unfortunate teenagers were arrested and shoved into the trunks of police cars. The incident was videotaped by a news reporter. Their bodies were later found with multiple bullet wounds (Nash 1991). It is reported that "Peru leads the world in documented cases of disappearances of people taken prisoner by security forces" (Brooke 1991c: 6).

Our criticism of the government of Mexico for not doing enough about drug trafficking has caused a great deal of ill-will. Mexican officials respond that their efforts have been extraordinary. They argue that the United States has failed to deal with the consumption end of the problem (Rohter 1988). Peter Smith (1987: 130) states that the "Mexican government has made a good faith effort to eradicate narcotic production and trade. Thousands of police and about 25,000 military troops have been assigned to this campaign; hundreds have been wounded or have lost their lives." He points out that the Mexican establishment has no reason to permit the consolidation of narcotic kingdoms, an empire within an empire, because "Drug-trade patronage lies outside the control of the regime... and, in times of declining resources, it therefore threatens the regime."

The danger of using the military in efforts against drug trafficking is highlighted by the following incident: On April 11, 1988, commandos from the Mexican military attacked a welding shop in a sedate residential neighborhood in Caborca, Mexico, a prosperous farming town sixty miles south of Arizona. The soldiers were apparently targeting the organization of Miguel Caro Quintero, brother of the imprisoned drug kingpin Rafael Caro Quintero, but they only managed to kill four young apprentices with machine-gun fire. The Caro Quinteros do not own the welding shop, although they do own many legitimate businesses in the area. Under rising pressure from Washington to do something about drugs flowing into the United States from Mexico, "but burdened by limited budgets, training and intelligence-gathering capabilities," Larry Rohter (1988b: 7) notes, the Mexican military "often end up antagonizing the very citizens they are charged with defending, and whose rights they are supposed to respect." In 1991, Mexican soldiers killed seven Mexican drug agents who were preparing to raid a Colombian plane that had landed on a rural air strip (Golden 1991a, 1991b). In 1990, the Mexican government launched a media campaign in the United States to present its version of the fight against drugs. In fact, Mexican antidrug efforts have led to a rise in poppy production in neighboring Guatemala, whose government is ill-equipped to respond to the problem (Sheppard 1990a).

The United States has imposed customs restrictions on passengers and shipments that originate, or even stop, in Colombia. Avianca Airlines has suffered millions of dollars in U.S.-imposed fines. But policymakers in Washington do not have to deal with the reality that is Colombia: "First, drug traffickers murdered the security chief of Avianca, Colombia's largest privately owned airline, two days after he had seized $5 million worth of cocaine that had been smuggled aboard a Miami-bound cargo jet.... Then several days later, two of the victim's colleagues received death threats, one in the form of a miniature casket delivered to his doorstep and the other a funeral mass card bearing his name" (Wiedrich 1988: 1). Both resigned.

The cocaine business has been detrimental to the Colombian economy, in contrast to its effect on poorer countries. In Cartagena, for example, drug-inspired terrorism led to travelers' advisory warnings by the U.S. and Canadian governments, causing a severe economic downturn in this tourist port city of about 500,000. Apparently, government leniency for traffickers has brought an end to this violence and tourism has returned ("Colombian City Basks in Terror's End" 1991). In addition to the cost of government efforts to fight the traffickers, the stigma on Colombian products and the associated security mechanisms add enormous costs to exporting Colombian products ("Colombian Growth Hurt By Cocaine" 1991). Crackdowns, insofar as they have succeeded in Colombia, have had an unintended result—displacement. As noted in chapter 7, Ecuador and Brazil now have cocaine-processing laboratories; Argentina, Uruguay, and Chile have emerged as major money-laundering centers; drug-related corruption scandals have hit Argentina and Venezuela, which along with Chile serve as major cocaine transshipment centers. Traffickers in Peru and Bolivia have begun to bypass the Colombians, refining coca and shipping directly to the United States and Europe.

Colombian officials, like the Mexican government, criticize the United States for doing little to stem consumption. During the Colombian presidential election of 1990, campaign speeches frequently made angry references to Marion Barry, the mayor of Washington who was videotaped by federal agents smoking crack (Brooke 1990c). His misdemeanor conviction on only one of fourteen charges relating to drug use further inflamed Colombian public opinion (Brooke 1990d). To place the issue in perspective, Peter Bourne points out that "more Colombians die from the effects of U.S. tobacco products than the number of Americans who die from Colombian cocaine. Yet we are

HYPOCRISY?

"What is the difference between exporting a pound of coke from a producer country and exporting an AR-15 and its ammunition from the U.S. to murder innocent people in developing countries? Why are countries such as Germany free to export materials used to refine cocaine? Why do countries like Switzerland, Panama, and even the U.S. protect money whose origin is dubious?"—Cali cocaine cartel leader Gilberto Rodriguez Orejuela.

Source: John Moody, "A Day with the Chess Player," *Time*, July 1, 1991: 34–36.

519

unwilling to lift even a twig to curb the trafficking of this drug whose cultivation is subsidized by U.S. taxpayers" (1990: 11). Colombians can also justifiably complain about the smuggling of firearms from the United States into their country, a trade encouraged by weak U.S. gun control laws. In 1989, firearms purchased in Miami gun shops were used to assassinate three Colombian presidential candidates. The United States is a primary source of weapons for Latin American drug traffickers: ships and planes with drug cargoes easily load up on firearms for the return trip (Rohter 1991b).

Politics, Patronage, and Terrorism

The economics of coca in poor countries raises important policy issues. The Bolivian economy is dominated by coca, with an estimated 300,000 jobs generating annual economic activity worth about $1.5 billion (Medina 1990). The business of cocaine serves to support not only those directly involved in the trafficking but also their dependents and the legitimate businesses that depend on their patronage. U.S. drug dollars brought into poor Latin America countries keep the *narcomafia* in luxury but also provide benefits for poorer people. In the coca-growing regions of Peru and Bolivia, the *coqueros* or *firmas* provide a level of income that would otherwise be unavailable to the peasants who cultivate and process the leaves for the illegal market. Government attempts to curtail coca cultivation encounter often violent opposition. Inhabitants are strongly opposed to American-inspired efforts to eradicate their most important cash crop. Both countries face serious Marxist insurgencies that are particularly strong in these remote regions. In 1987, thousands of coca growers blocked roads and staged demonstrations to express their opposition to the presence of fourteen military instructors from the United States who had been sent to help Bolivian authorities train members of their antidrug force. The growers were from a region where the soil is not considered good enough to grow anything *but* coca bush (Christian 1987). Despite these threats, that year U.S. military personnel and aircraft assisted the Bolivian authorities in a series of raids against traffickers in north-central Bolivia, where much of the world's cocaine is produced.

In 1987, the United States cut aid to Bolivia in retaliation for that country's failure to curtail coca cultivation. Such action may do more harm than good, notes Lupsha (1990). It may increase the influence of the rich drug-trafficking cartels over these governments. Unfortunately, in addition to providing a livelihood for Bolivian farmers, cocaine brings an estimated $600 million in U.S. currency into Bolivia, more than all legal exports combined ("U.S. to Cut Bolivian Aid Over Drug-War Failures" 1987). In Peru's Upper Huallaga Valley, which extends for two hundred miles along the Huallaga River, an estimated 60,000 families depend on coca as a cash crop for their survival. Large-scale eradication, notes Alan Riding (1988b: 6), could "provoke a social convulsion, forcing thousands of families to leave the area and creating deep resentment that Shining Path [guerillas] will be ready to exploit." And

American helicopter gunships on loan to Peru carried anti-drug police in the Upper Huallaga Valley in 1990. The helicopters, equipped with door-mounted M-60 machine guns, were used during a firefight with Shining Path guerillas, who said they were defending coca leaf growers.

"coca is Peru's largest export, earning more than one billion dollars a year. As many as one million of the country's twenty-one million citizens are involved in the trade" (Massing 1990: 26). Despite millions of dollars in American aid to eradicate coca in Peru, the effort has not been successful. By the end of 1990 there had been a 25 percent increase in coca cultivation (Brooke 1991d). RAND analyst Peter Reuter points out an ironic twist: "Increasing the risks of growing coca [and thereby reducing quantities] might raise the price needed to induce farmers to grow it" (Passell 1991: C2).

Steven Wisotsky (1987: 57) states:

> In both Peru and Bolivia, the failure of coca control is not a temporary aberration but a function of culture, tradition, and the weakness and poverty of underdevelopment. These basic social conditions render effective enforcement against coca impossible. Widespread corruption in the enforcement agencies, the judiciary, and elsewhere in government is endemic. Indeed, the central governments do not necessarily control major portions of coca-growing countryside, where the traffickers rule like feudal lords.

Effective law enforcement against cocaine laboratories in Bolivia led to a steep decline in prices for raw coca leaves—about $20 for 100 pounds in early 1988,

COCALAND

ROBERTO FERNANDEZ, BOLIVIAN FATHER AND COCA GROWER

Roberto Fernandez is a Bolivian who earns the equivalent of $1 a day as a mine-entrance watchman. "Some days, if I don't have enough work, I can't buy each of my children a whole bread roll. I have to cut the breads in half. Or, if I eat one bread roll myself, my daughter Erica [age six] has no breakfast. I have to work 16 hours a day so that Erica can have her breakfast."

"When Roberto Fernandez considers whether to cultivate the coca plant," notes James North, "he does not visualize despairing crack addicts in far-off American cities that he will never be able to visit. . . . No, he sees his daughter Erica" (North 1988: 21).

In the Upper Huallaga Valley

"An old barefoot Indian man walked into one of the showrooms recently, carrying a large sack on his back. He looked around a moment, spotted a little blue pickup, and asked the price. The dealer named a sum, the equivalent in (1980) Peruvian soles of about U.S. $10,000. Fine, the old man said. He would take it. He opened his sack, took out a heap of crumpled bills and counted out the money. The dealer handed him the keys and the sale was over" (Morales 1989: xvi).

Sources: James North, "Meet Roberto Fernandez, A Bolivian Father and Coca User." *Chicago Tribune*, September 7, 1988: 21; Edmundo Morales, *Cocaine: White Gold Rush in Peru*. Tucson: University of Arizona Press, 1989.

down from $100 in 1986 and $350 in 1984—but the planting of coca did not decrease. Shirley Christian (1988b: 6) notes that despite financial assistance from the United States, a "severe shortage of money for the government to carry out crop substitution and relocation programs leave the peasants with almost no option but to continue planting coca, even with the price uncertainty." Growers have become much more vulnerable and receptive to the blandishments of insurgent Marxist guerilla movements. Participation in the illicit cocaine economy, writes Edmundo Morales (1986: 157), "is inevitable. Not only is the natives' traditional way of life intertwined with coca, but their best cash crop is the underground economy for which no substitute has yet been provided."

Crop Substitution

As part of the effort to control drugs at their source, crop substitution programs have met with only limited success. As long as demand remains high, the price offered for poppy or coca will be many times that received for conventional crops. In 1991, the leader of a Peruvian coca growers association who had agreed to a crop substitution program was murdered, reputedly by corrupt government officials earning money from the cocaine business (Strong 1992). Attempts to eradicate the crop by cutting or burning results in healthier and more bountiful growth, while uprooting coca plants causes the soil to become unproductive for as long as eight to ten years (Morales 1989). An eradication program in the Upper Huallaga Valley was established with U.S. funding in 1982, but since that time about forty of its workers have been murdered, and the U.S. subsequently suspended the program (Massing 1990). An alternative is the use of aerial herbicides that are either sprayed or dropped as pellets that melt into the soil when it rains. A major difficulty is finding environmentally safe herbicides, and the United States has been conducting research on a variety of such substances. In 1988 it was revealed that the U.S. Department of Agriculture had secretly been growing coca as part of an intensive effort to find an effective means of eradicating the crop abroad (May 1988b). The most successful herbicides, however, kill many species of plants, including crop plants, and they remain in the soil, affecting future plantings. Environmentalists have raised objections to the use of herbicides, and the companies that produce them are concerned about potential liability and fear that their employees in South America may become targets of retribution by trafficking organizations (Riding 1988b).

Furthermore, Lee McIntosh (1988: 26) has found that a "single genetic mutation can give rise to complete resistance in a similar herbicide. This implies it may be necessary continually to spray different classes of herbicides in the future." The human and political dangers inherent in this approach to drug control should serve as a restraining influence. Nevertheless, in 1988 the director of the Drug Enforcement Administration announced that his agency would begin to spray paraquat—a highly toxic chemical that can cause serious harm when inhaled or absorbed by human beings or animals—on private land in the United States used for growing marijuana. The chemical has already been banned for the same purpose in national forests ("U.S. Plans to Resume Using Paraquat to Eradicate Marijuana" 1988: 26).

While Mexico "was once considered as having one of the most successful crop eradication programs in the world," the comptroller general (1988: 8) notes that "it has been unable to significantly reduce illegal cultivation despite more than $118 million in U.S. and Mexican funding between 1984 and 1987 to support a bilateral aerial eradication program." Use of herbicides in Mexico has led growers to develop techniques to make aerial eradication more difficult:

> In 1977, when eradication of almost 10,000 hectares [1 hectare = 2.47 acres] of opium poppies was reported, fields were large and in open flat areas. Cultivators reacted to the aerial eradication program by decreasing the size of their fields and planting in more remote areas, often at higher altitudes and often on the sides of steep ravines, under trees, or otherwise camouflaged.

CROP SUBSTITUTION

When George Bush met with the leaders of cocaine-exporting countries in Cartagena, Colombia, on February 15, 1990 the leader of 200,000 Peruvian peasant coca farmers unsuccessfully attempted to meet with the president. He wanted to tell President Bush that the United States should be spending less on law enforcement in Latin America and more on economic development. The peasants, he argued, want to grow, process, and export fruits and vegetables, not coca. But to do this they need support from the United States.

Source: Joseph B. Treaster, "A Peruvian Peasant Fails to See Bush." *New York Times*, February 16, 1990: 9.

Spraying the higher, more remote fields required greater aircraft capacity for fuel and herbicides. . . . [And] farmers were often able to wash off the herbicides sprayed on their plants. (Comptroller General 1988: 19)

Latent Effects of Drug Policy

Lupsha (1990) notes that if all of the coca that the producing countries of Latin America have publicly committed themselves to eradicate over the next few years were actually eradicated, the effect in the United States would be minimal. It is likely that African, Middle Eastern, and Southwest Asian areas would be able to cultivate enough to meet consumer demand in coca indefinitely, as they have with opium. Edward J. Epstein (1988b: 25) points out that "the entire cocaine market in the United States can be supplied for a year by a single cargo plane." Attempting to drive up the price of cocaine and thereby reduce consumption by attacking it at its source is a doomed strategy. As the figures in chapter 7 reveal, the share of the final retail price of cocaine accounted for "at the farm" is negligible—much less than 1 percent (Reuter 1992). If we curtail importation but fail to affect demand, an incentive for greater domestic efforts is created, leading to the production of synthetic analogs for cocaine and heroin and stronger strains of marijuana. The highly inventive marijuana horticulturists of California are using a new, faster-growing, highly potent strain that matures in three months (older strains require four months). This new strain has been discovered in the national forests of northern California. (Growing marijuana on federal lands was made a felony in 1987, punishable by a prison term of up to ten years.)

In response to law enforcement efforts against marijuana, some innovative growers have established elaborate underground farms equipped with diesel powered lights and ventilation systems. Their use of hydroponic technology—growing plants in water—has helped make marijuana the number one cash crop in the United States. In response, the DEA has been subpoenaing the records of businesses selling hydroponic equipment in order to discover indoor marijuana growers. These records contain the names of mostly legitimate growers paying by check or credit card who may be subjected to DEA inquiries—marijuana traffickers usually pay in cash (Bishop 1991).

Richard Cowan (1986: 27) argues that federal efforts against cocaine led to the development of crack: *"The iron law of drug prohibition is that the more intense the law enforcement, the more potent the drug will become. The latest stage of this cycle has brought us the crack epidemic."* Free market conditions provide an incentive for traffickers to improve the attractiveness of their product. Jeffrey Fagan and Ko-lin Chin (1990) point out that crack was the subject of an ingenious production and marketing strategy (see also Witkin 1991). A glut of cocaine forced prices down in 1983, but even lower prices could not keep up with production:

> At this point, a new product was introduced which offered the chance to expand the market in ways never before possible: crack, packaged in small quantities and selling for $5 and sometimes even less—a fraction of the usual minimum for powder—allowed dealers to attract an entirely new class of consumers. Once it took hold this change was very swift and very sweeping. (Williams 1989: 7)

By 1990 there was evidence that the crack epidemic had peaked, but that heroin use was on the increase. Because heroin had lost its dominant market position to cocaine, purity levels had increased substantially, allowing new users to snort or smoke the substance instead of injecting it intravenously in the more traditional manner. These changes, however, may eventually lead to an increase in price and a decrease in purity, causing many addicts to shift to the more economic (and more dangerous) intravenous ingestion (Treaster 1990c).

There is evidence that U.S. efforts against drug trafficking are often secondary to foreign policy considerations. The Anti-Drug Abuse Act of 1986, for example, requires the president to "certify" to Congress that producer and transshipment nations have made adequate progress in attacking drug production and trafficking. Without certification, a country can lose aid, loans, and trade preferences. Elaine Sciolino (1988) reports that the law has numerous loopholes allowing several nations to be certified despite their failure to cooperate in the war against drugs. In 1990, of the twenty-four major drug-producing and drug-transiting countries, only four—Afghanistan, Burma, Iran, and Syria—were denied certification. At the other extreme, the United States has turned to the Guatemalan military to take the lead in efforts against trafficking. The Guatemalan military, however, has been responsible for human rights abuses that have plagued the country (Gruson 1990). For many years, we tolerated the drug-trafficking activities of our Central American ally, General Manuel Noriega. When his politics took on a decidedly anti-U.S. tone, the general was indicted and apprehended following the "Operation Just Cause" invasion of Panama. (For a discussion of Noriega, his relationship with the United States, and drug dealing, see John Dinges 1990; Kempe 1990.)

Peter Andreas and his colleagues note, "After more than a decade of U.S. efforts to reduce the cocaine supply, more cocaine is produced in more places than ever before. Curiously, the U.S. response to failure has been to escalate rather than reevaluate.... The logic of escalation in the drug war is in fact strikingly similar to the arguments advanced when U.S. counterinsurgency strategies, undercut by ineffective and uncommitted governments and security forces, were failing in Vietnam: 'We've just begun to fight.' 'We're turning the corner.'" Andreas and his colleagues argue that "since failure can so easily be used to justify further escalation, how do we know whether we are really turning the corner or simply running around [in] a vicious circle?" (Andreas et al. 1991–92: 107).

The Problem of Synthetic Drugs

The issues discussed so far in this chapter concern substances that (except for marijuana) originate outside of the United States. However, there are a number of controlled substances that are manufactured—legally and illegally—in the United States, for example, synthetic opioids such as pethidine, methadone, and propoxyphene (Darvon). The synthetic drug fentanyl citrate, which is often used intravenously in major surgery, works exactly like morphine: it kills pain, produces euphoria, and if abused leads to addiction. The substance is easy to produce for persons skilled in chemistry. As noted in chapter 7, fentanyl compounds are often sold as "China White," the street name for the finest Southeast Asian heroin, to addicts who cannot tell the difference. Synthetic substances chemically similar to cocaine produce the same euphoric response when taken intranasally as does cocaine in experienced cocaine users. In recent years, methamphetamine ("speed") has enjoyed a growing popularity among those who might otherwise abuse cocaine. Its effects are similar, longer-lasting, and the substance is cheaper. Chemicals costing less than $200 can be converted into one pound of speed, which can be diluted to two pounds and sold for more than $30,000. The popularity of the drug has been enhanced by a crystallized form of speed that can be smoked (Gross 1988).

Greater control of poppy and coca plants at their source, or enhanced interdiction efforts, will not impact on synthetic drugs except that greater control and interdiction of the former will increase the demand for—and thus production of—the latter.

CONCLUSION

Responding in a rational manner to organized crime requires a sense of proportion and an appreciation of American history. Organized crime in America can be conceived of as one stage along a continuum. Our colonial forebears exhibited many of the activities currently associated with organized crime: bribery, usury, and monopoly, not to mention seizure of land by force, indentured servitude, and slavery. Early American adventurers cheated and killed native Americans, and chartered pirates—privateers—plundered the high seas. During the War of 1812, and later during the Civil War, profiteers accumulated fortunes while the less fortunate suffered and died. The range wars in the West and the frauds, bribery, violence, and monopolistic practices of the "robber barons" are all part of the context in which we must understand modern forms of organized crime. The cost of organized crime must be measured against the cost of corporate crime, which has the potential to harm far more persons, both financially and physically (see, for example, Clinard et al. 1979; Mokhiber 1988).

Organized crime has provided economic opportunity for certain groups, allowing them to move into legitimate society on a level that would otherwise not be readily available. There are, of course, ethical and moral objections to "blasting" or "thieving" into the middle or upper strata, even though this has been a feature of U.S. history from the earliest days. Very few management-level members of OC have been able to escape either assassination or significant prison terms. Indeed, law enforcement efforts against OC are impressive, constrained as they are by the requirements of a democratic system that provides a great deal of legal protection to even its criminal citizens. With this in mind, we should proceed with a great deal of caution when contemplating changes in policy with respect to organized crime.

Organized crime evolved out of moralistic laws that created opportunity for certain innovative actors. As circumstances changed, so did available opportunity, and organized crime exhibited great flexibility. Beginning as essentially a provider of "goods and services," it entered racketeering and legitimate business, adapting to changing laws and social and economic conditions. Policy for responding to organized crime must be based on an appreciation of history, an understanding of the "side effects" of proposed policy changes, and the realization that organized crime has proven to be quite a dynamic phenomenon.

REVIEW QUESTIONS

1. How can the government influence the public, via the media, with respect to organized crime?
2. What were the conclusions of the Kefauver Committee?
3. What important conclusion of the Task Force on Organized Crime agreed with the findings of the Kefauver Committee?

4. What recommendations of the Task Force on Organized Crime were enacted into law?
5. How did the findings of the President's Commission on Organized Crime differ from those of the Task Force on Organized Crime?
6. What would be the advantages of decriminalizing heroin and cocaine?
7. What would be the disadvantages of decriminalizing heroin and cocaine?
8. What are the political difficulties encountered in trying to eradicate drugs at their source countries?
9. Why haven't herbicides proven successful in eradicating coca and poppy crops at their source?
10. How does the problem of synthetic drugs impact on our policy with respect to drug trafficking?

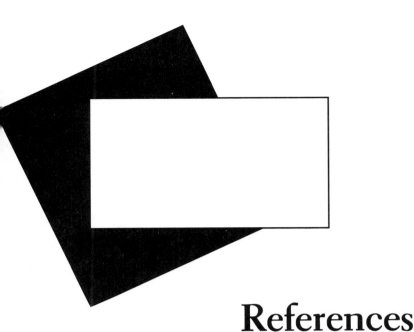

References

Abadinsky, Howard
1993   *Drug Abuse: An Introduction*, 2nd ed. Chicago: Nelson-Hall.
1991   *Law and Justice: An Introduction to the American Legal System*. Chicago: Nelson-Hall.
1987   "The McDonald's-ization of the Mafia." Pp. 43–54 in *Organized Crime in America: Concepts and Controversies*, edited by Timothy Bynum. Monsey, NY: Criminal Justice Press.
1983   *The Criminal Elite: Professional and Organized Crime*. Westport, CT: Greenwood.
1981a   *The Mafia in America: An Oral History*. New York: Praeger.
1981b   *Organized Crime*. Boston: Allyn and Bacon.

Abel, Ernest L., ed.
1978   *The Scientific Study of Marijuana*. Chicago: Nelson-Hall.

Ackerman, Kenneth D.
1988   *The Gold Ring: Jim Fisk, Jay Gould, and Black Friday, 1869*. New York: Harper and Row.

Adams, James Ring and Douglas Frantz
1992   *A Full Service Bank: How BCCI Stole Billions Around the World*. New York: Pocket Books.

Albanese, Jay S.
1989   *Organized Crime in America*, 2nd ed. Cincinnati, OH: Anderson.
1988   "Government Perceptions of Organized Crime: The Presidential Commissions, 1967 and 1987." *Federal Probation* 52 (March): 58–63.

Albini, Joseph L.
1971   *The American Mafia: Genesis of a Legend*. New York: Appleton-Century-Crofts.

Alexander, Bruce K.
1990   "Alternatives to the War on Drugs." *Journal of Drug Issues* 20 (1): 1–27.

Alexander, Herbert E. and Gerald E. Caiden
1985   *The Politics and Economics of Organized Crime*. Lexington, MA: D.C. Heath.

Alexander, Shana
1988   *The Pizza Connection: Lawyers, Money, Drugs, Mafia*. New York: Weidenfeld and Nicolson.

Allsop, Kenneth
1968   *The Bootleggers: The Story of Prohibition*. New Rochelle, NY: Arlington House.

Allum, P. A.
1973   *Politics and Society in Post-War Naples*. Cambridge: Cambridge University Press.

REFERENCES

Altman, Lawrence K.
1988   "Cocaine's Many Dangers: The Evidence Mounts." *New York Times* (January 26): 18.

Anastasia, George
1991   *Blood and Honor: Inside the Scarfo Mob—The Mafia's Most Violent Family.* New York: William Morrow.

Anastasia, George and Laurie Hollman
1992   "Mob Hit Raises Leadership Questions." *Philadelphia Inquirer* (February 2): B1, B2.

Anbinder, Tyler
1992   *Nativism and Slavery: The Northern Know-Nothings and the Politics of the 1850s.* New York: Oxford University Press.

Anderson, Annelise Graebner
1979   *The Business of Organized Crime: A Cosa Nostra Family.* Stanford, CA: Hoover Institution Press.

Anderson, Robert T.
1965   "From Mafia to Cosa Nostra." *American Journal of Sociology* 71 (November): 302–10.

Andreas, Peter R., Eva C. Bertram, Morris J. Blackman, and Kenneth E. Sharpe
1991–92 "Dead End Drug Wars." *Foreign Policy* (Winter): 106–28.

Andrews, Wayne
1941   *The Vanderbilt Legend.* New York: Harcourt, Brace.

Arlacchi, Pino
1986   *Mafia Business: The Mafia Ethic and the Spirit of Capitalism.* London: Verso.

Aronson, Harvey
1978   *Deal.* New York: Ballantine Books.
1973   *The Killing of Joey Gallo.* New York: Putnam's.

Asbury, Herbert
1950   *The Great Illusion: An Informal History of Prohibition.* Garden City, NY: Doubleday.
1942   *Gem of the Prairie: An Informal History of the Chicago Underworld.* Garden City, NY: Knopf.
1928   *Gangs of New York.* New York: Knopf.

Aschmann, Homer
1975   "The Persistent Guajiro." *Natural History* 84 (March): 28–37.

Atlas, Terry
1988   "U.S. Losing Its War on Drugs Along the Afghan-Pakistani Border." *Chicago Tribune* (May 9): 6.

Attorney General's Commission on Pornography
1986   *Final Report.* Washington, DC: U.S. Government Printing Office.

Audett, James Henry
1954   *Rap Sheet: My Life Story.* New York: William Sloane.

Ausubel, David P.
1980   "An Interactional Approach to Narcotic Addiction." Pp. 4–7 in *Theories on Drug Abuse: Selected Contemporary Perspectives,* edited by Dan J. Lettieri, Mollie Sayers, and Helen Wallenstein Pearson. Rockville, MD: National Institute on Drug Abuse.
1978   *What Every Well-Informed Person Should Know About Drug Addiction.* Chicago: Nelson-Hall.

Bailey, Pearce
1974   "The Heroin Habit." Pp. 171–76 in *Yesterday's Addicts; American Society and Drug Abuse, 1865–1920,* edited by Howard Wayne Morgan. Norman, OK: University of Oklahoma Press.

Baquet, Dean
1992   "Tips on B.C.C.I. Flowed Freely for Years." *New York Times* (August 27): C1, C2.

Baquet, Dean and Jeff Gerth
1992   "Lawmaker's Defense of B.C.C.I. Went Beyond Speech in Senate." *New York Times* (August 26): 1, C2.

Barboza, Joe and Hank Messick
1975   *Barboza.* New York: Dell.

Barzini, Luigi
1977   "Italians in New York: The Way We Were in 1929." *New York* (April 4): 34–38.
1972   *The Italians.* (paperback ed.) New York: Bantam.
1965   *The Italians.* New York: Atheneum.

Basler, Barbara
1988   "Hong Kong Gangs Wield Vast Power." *New York Times* (December 12): 4.

Beaty, Jonathan and Sam Gwynne
1993   *The Outlaw Bank: A Wild Ride Into the Heart of BCCI.* New York: Random House.

Beeching, Jack
1975   *The Chinese Opium Wars.* New York: Harcourt Brace Jovanovich.

Bell, Daniel
1964   *The End of Ideology.* Glencoe, IL: Free Press.
1963   "The Myth of the Cosa Nostra." *The New Leader* 46 (December): 12–15.

Bell, Ernest A., ed.
1909   *War on the White Slave Trade.* Chicago: Thompson.

Bennett, David H.
1988   *The Party of Fear: From Nativist Movements to the New Right in American History.* Chapel Hill, NC: University of North Carolina Press.

Bennett, Harry
1951   *We Never Called Him Henry.* New York: Gold Medal.

Bequai, August
1979   *Organized Crime: The Fifth Estate.* Lexington, MA: D. C. Heath.

Berger, Meyer
1957   "Anastasia Slain in a Hotel Here: Led Murder, Inc." *New York Times* (October 26): 1, 12.

1944   "Lepke's Reign of Crime Lasted Over 12 Murder-Strewn Years." *New York Times* (September 21): 1, 20.

1940   "Gang Patterns: 1940." *New York Times Magazine* (August 4): 5, 15.

1935   "Schultz Reigned on Discreet Lines." *New York Times* (October 25): 17.

Berke, Richard L.
1989   "U.S. Attack on Airborne Drug Smuggling Called Ineffective." *New York Times* (June 9): 10.

Biegel, Herbert and Allan Biegel
1977   *Beneath the Badge: A Story of Police Corruption.* New York: Harper and Row.

Bishop, Jim
1971   *The Days of Martin Luther King, Jr.* New York: Putnam's.

Bishop, Katherine
1991   "Business Data Is Sought in Marijuana Crackdown." *New York Times* (May 24): B9.

1990   "Military Takes Part in Drug Sweep and Reaps Criticism and a Lawsuit." *New York Times* (August 10): 11.

Blakey, G. Robert
1986   "RICO's Triple Damage Threat: The Public's Secret Weapon vs. Boesky." *New York Times* (December 7): F3.

Blakey, G. Robert, Ronald Goldstock, and Charles H. Rogovin
1978   *Rackets Bureau: Investigation and Prosecution of Organized Crime.* Washington, DC: U.S. Government Printing Office.

Blau, Peter M.
1964   *Exchange and Power in Social Life.* New York: Wiley.

1956   *Bureaucracy in Modern Society.* New York: Random House.

Blau, Robert and John O'Brien
1991   "Rise and Fall of the El Rukns—Jeff Fort's Evil Empire." *Chicago Tribune* (September 8): Sec. 2: 1, 2.

Bloch, Max and Ron Kenner
1982   *Max the Butcher.* Secaucus, NJ: Lyle Stuart.

Block, Alan A.
1991   *The Business of Crime: A Documentary Study of Organized Crime in the American Economy.* Boulder, CO: Westview.

1979   *East Side-West Side: Organizing Crime in New York, 1930–1950.* Swansea, U.K.: Christopher Davis.

1978   "History and the Study of Organized Crime." *Urban Life* 6 (January): 455–74.

1975   "Lepke, Kid Twist and the Combination: Organized Crime in New York City, 1930–1944." Ph.D. dissertation, University of California at Los Angeles.

Block, Alan A. and Frank R. Scarpitti
1985   *Poisoning for Profit: The Mafia and Toxic Waste.* New York: William Morrow.

Blok, Anton
1974   *The Mafia of a Sicilian Village, 1860–1960: A Study of Violent Peasant Entrepreneurs.* New York: Harper and Row.

Blount, William E. and H. Roy Kaplan
1989   "The Impact of the Daily Lottery on the Numbers Game: Does Legalization Make a Difference." Paper presented at the Annual Meeting of the Academy of Criminal Justice Sciences, March 29, Washington, DC.

Blum, Howard
1992   "The Cop They Call the Mob's Mole." *New York Times* (May 3): 30–34, 84.

1977   "New York Gang Reported to Sell Death and Drugs." *New York Times* (December 16): 1, D12.

Blum, Howard and Leonard Buder
1978   "The War on 130th Street." *New York Times* (six articles appearing on page 1 from December 18 through December 23).

Blum, Richard H.
1984   *Offshore Haven Banks, Trusts, and Companies: The Business of Crime in the Euromarket.* New York: Praeger.

Blumenthal, Ralph
1992   "When the Mob Delivered the Goods." *New York Times Magazine* (July 26): 22–23, 31–34.

1988a   *Last Days of the Sicilians: At War With the Mafia: The FBI Assault on the Pizza Connection.* New York: Times Books.

1988b   "Dozens Seized in New U.S.-Italian Anti-drug Sweep." *New York Times* (December 2): 1, 8.

Blumenthal, Ralph and Celestine Bohlen

1989   "Soviet Emigre Outlaws Fusing Into a New Mob." *New York Times* (June 4): 1, 16.

Bohlen, Celestine

1993   "Russia [sic] Mobsters Grow More Violent and Pervasive." *New York Times* (August 16): 1, 4.

Boissevain, Jeremy

1974   *Friends of Friends: Networks, Manipulators and Coalitions.* Oxford: Basil Blackwell.

Bonanno, Joseph and Segio Lalli

1983   *A Man of Honor: The Autobiography of Joseph Bonanno.* New York: Simon and Schuster.

Bonnie, Richard J. and Charles H. Whitebread II

1970   "The Forbidden Fruit and the Tree of Knowledge: An Inquiry Into the Legal History of American Marijuana Prohibition." *Virginia Law Review* 56 (October): 971–1203.

Booth, Martin

1990   *The Triads: The Growing Global Threat From the Chinese Criminal Societies.* New York: St. Martin's.

Bopp, William J.

1977   *O.W. Wilson and the Search for a Police Profession.* Port Washington, NY: Kennikat Press.

Bourne, Peter

1990   "Our Dubious Crusade in Colombia." *Chicago Tribune* (July 2): 11.

Bowden, Charles

1991   "La Virgen and the Drug Lord." *Phoenix* (March): 96–103.

Bowden, Mark

1987   *Doctor Dealer.* New York: Warner Books.

Bowman, Jim

1984   "The Long Hot Summer When Chicago Erupted in Violence." *Chicago Tribune Magazine* (August 29): 7.

1983a   "Beer, Bribery, and Bullets: 'Spike' O'Don-nell's Chicago." *Chicago Tribune Magazine* (October 2): 8.

1983b   " 'Greasy Thumb' Guzik: From Brothel to Bookkeeper for Al Capone's Gang." *Chicago Tribune Magazine* (March 8): 10.

Boyd, Kier T.

1977   *Gambling Technology.* Washington, DC: U.S. Government Printing Office.

Brashler, William

1981   "Two Brothers From Taylor Street." *Chicago* (September): 150–56, 194.

1977   *The Don: The Life and Death of Sam Giancana.* New York: Harper and Row.

Brecher, Edward M. and the Editor of *Consumer Reports*

1972   *Licit and Illicit Drugs.* Boston: Little, Brown.

Brenner, Marie

1990   "Prime Time Godfather." *Vanity Fair* (May): 109–15, 176–81.

Bresler, Fenton

1980   *The Chinese Mafia.* New York: Stein and Day.

Brill, Steven

1978   *The Teamsters.* New York: Simon and Schuster.

Broder, Jonathan

1984   "As a Tradeoff, Soviets Let Afghan Heroin Flow." *Chicago Tribune* (September 2): 12.

Brooke, James

1993   "In a 'Dirty War,' Former Drug Allies Are Terrorizing Escobar." *New York Times* (March 4): 4.

1992   "Drug Seizures Up in Latin Countries." *New York Times* (January 15): 5.

1992b   "With Graft Rife, Nation Reins in Cocaine King." *New York Times* (July 22): 2.

1992c   "Trafficker is Still Feared in Colombia." *New York Times* (January 21): 5.

1992d   "How Escobar, a Rare Jailbird, Lined His Nest." *New York Times* (August 5): 1, 2.

1992e   "Colombians Kill Drug Lord's Aide." *New York Times* (October 29): 5.

1992f   "Venezuela Joins the Drug Route." *New York Times* (November 10): 4.

1991a   "Colombia's Rising Export: Fake U.S. Money." *New York Times* (April 21): 4.

1991b   "Cali, the 'Quiet Cocaine Cartel,' Profits Through Accommodation." *New York Times* (July 14): 1, 6.

1991c   "Marxist Revolt Grows Strong in the Shantytowns of Peru." *New York Times* (November 11): 1, 6.

1991d   "Peru, Its U.S. Aid Imperiled, Plots a New Drug Strategy." *New York Times* (January 14): 2.

1990a   "In the Capital of Cocaine, Savagery Is the Habit." *New York Times* (June 7): 4.

1990b   "Was the Beautiful Agent a Cartel Spy?" *New York Times* (December 24): 7.

1990c   "Bogotá Chief Tells of Drug War's Toll." *New York Times* (May 27): 4.

1990d   "Near-Acquittal of Barry is Outraging Colombians." *New York Times* (August 27): 4.

1990e   "Peru Suggests U.S. Rethink Eradication in Land Where Coca is Still King." *New York Times* (November 18): 3.

1990f   "U.S. Anti-Drug Pilots in Peru Battle Guerillas." *New York Times* (April 12): 1, 8.

Brooks, Thomas R.
1971   *Toil and Trouble: A History of American Labor.* New York: Dell.

Bryant, Wanda G.
1988   "Use Net Worth to Build the Nexus Between Assets and Illegal Drug Activity." *Asset Forfeiture Bulletin* (October): 6–8.

Buenker, John D.
1973   *Urban Liberalism and Progressive Reform.* New York: Scribner's.

"Bugs Moran Dies in Federal Prison"
1957   *New York Times* (February 26): 59.

Bullough, Vern L.
1965   *The History of Prohibition.* New Hyde Park, NY: University Books.

Burkholz, Robert
1987   "Pain: Solving the Mystery." *New York Times Magazine* (September 27): 16–19; 32–35.

Burns, John F.
1990   "Afghans: Now They Blame America." *New York Times Magazine* (February 4): 23–29, 37.

Buse, Renee
1965   *The Deadly Silence.* Garden City, NY: Doubleday.

Butterfield, Fox
1990   "2 Indicted in New England As Core of Organized Crime." *New York Times* (March 27): 8.

"By Order of the Mafia"
1888   *New York Times* (October 22): 8.

Byck, Robert, ed.
1974   *Cocaine Papers: Sigmund Freud.* New York: Stonehill.

Byron, Christopher
1992a   "Conning the Media." *New York* (August 31): 28–37.

1992b   "Sky Writing." *New York* (October 12): 16–17.

California Board of Corrections
1978   *Prison Gangs in the Community.* Sacramento.

Campane, Jerome O.
1981a   "Chains, Wheels, and the Single Conspiracy: Part 1." *FBI Law Enforcement Bulletin* (August): 24–31.

1981b   "Chains, Wheels, and the Single Conspiracy: Conclusion." *FBI Law Enforcement Bulletin* (September): 24–31.

Campbell, Rodney
1977   *The Luciano Project.* New York: McGraw-Hill.

Cantalupo, Joseph and Thomas C. Renner
1990   *Body Mike.* New York: St. Martin's Paperbacks.

Capeci, Jerry
1978   "Tieri: The Most Powerful Mob Chieftain." *New York* (August): 22–26.

"Capone Dead at 48; Dry Era Gang Chief."
1947   *New York Times* (January 26): 7.

Caputo, David A.
1974   *Organized Crime and American Politics.* Morristown, NJ: General Learning Press.

Carroll, Brian
1991   "Combatting Racketeering in the Fulton Fish Market." Pp. 183–98 in *Organized Crime and Its Containment: A Transatlantic Initiative*, edited by Cyrelle Fijnaut and James Jacobs. Deventer, Netherlands: Kluwer.

Carter, Hodding, IV
1991a   "King of the Jungle." *M Inc.* (March): 84–91.

1991b   "Day of the Triads." *M Inc.* (June): 68–73.

Cartey, Desmond
1970   "How Black Enterprisers Do Their Thing: An Odyssey Through Ghetto Capitalism." Pp. 19–47 in *The Participant Observer*, edited by Glenn Jacobs. New York: George Braziller.

Cashman, Sean Dennis
1981   *Prohibition.* New York: The Free Press.

Catanzaro, Raimondo
1992   *Men of Respect: A Social History of the Sicilian Mafia.* New York: Free Press. Translated by Raymond Rosenthal.

Chafetz, Henry
1960   *Play the Devil: A History of Gambling in the United States from 1492 to 1955.* New York: Clarkson Potter.

Chaiken, David A.
1991   "Money Laundering: An Investigatory Perspective." *Criminal Law Forum* 2 (Spring): 467–510.

Chaiken, Marcia R. and Bruce D. Johnson
1988   *Characteristics of Different Types of Drug-Involved Offenders.* Washington, DC: National Institute of Justice.

Chambliss, William
1975   "On the Paucity of Original Research on Organized Crime: A Footnote to Galliher and Cain." *American Sociologist* 10 (August): 36–39.
1973   *Functional and Conflict Theories of Crime.* New York: MSS Modular Publications.
Chandler, David Leon
1975   *Brothers in Blood: The Rise of the Criminal Brotherhoods.* New York: Dutton.
Chapman, Stephen
1991   "Prohibition—From Alcohol to Drugs—Is a Costly Failure." *Chicago Tribune* (September 1): Sec. 4: 3.
Chein, Isidor, Donald L. Gerard, Robert S. Lee, and Eva Rosenfeld
1964   *The Road to H: Narcotics, Delinquency, and Social Policy.* New York: Basic Books.
Chernow, Ron
1990   *House of Morgan.* New York: Atlantic Monthly Press.
Chicago Crime Commission (CCC)
1990   *Organized Crime in Chicago: 1990.* CCC.
Chin, Ko-lin
1990   *Chinese Subculture and Criminality: Non-Traditional Crime Groups in America.* Westport, CT: Greenwood.
Chin, Ko-lin and Jeffrey Fagan
1990   "The Impact of Crack on Drug and Crime Involvement." Paper presented at the annual meeting of the American Society of Criminology, Baltimore, November.
"Chinatown Bank Official, Cited at Hearing Quits."
1984   *New York Times* (November 10): 11.
"Choice of Poisons, A."
1988   *Newsweek* (December 9): 62.
Christian, Shirley
1992   "Why Indulge Drug Lord? Colombia Pressed to Tell." *New York Times* (July 29): 3.
1991   "Central America a New Drug Focus." *New York Times* (December 16): 6.
1988a   "Drug Trafficking and Output Rising Sharply in Argentina." *New York Times* (April 28): 4.
1988b   "Bolivian Drug Lord Reportedly in Financial Straits." *New York Times* (May 9): 5.
1987   "Bolivians Fight Efforts to Eradicate Coca." *New York Times* (July 27): 3.
Chubb, Judith
1982   *Patronage, Power, and Poverty in Southern Italy.* Cambridge, England: Cambridge University Press.

Clarke, Donald Henderson
1929   *In the Reign of Rothstein.* New York: Grosset and Dunlap.
Clinard, Marshall B., Peter C. Yeager, Jeanne Brissette, David Petrashek, and Elizabeth Harries
1979   *Illegal Corporate Behavior.* Washington, DC: Government Printing Office.
Cloward, Richard A. and Lloyd E. Ohlin
1960   *Delinquency and Opportunity.* New York: Free Press.
Cloyd, Jerald W.
1982   *Drugs and Information Control: The Role of Men and Manipulation in the Control of Drug Trafficking.* Westport, CT: Greenwood.
Coates, James
1986   "Another Bad Apple Spoils Witness Protection Image." *Chicago Tribune* (March 2): 4.
Cockburn, Leslie
1987   *Out of Control: The Story of the Reagan Administration's Secret War in Nicaragua, the Illegal Arms Pipeline, and the Contra Drug Connection.* New York: Morgan Entrekin/Atlantic Monthly Press.
Coffey, Joseph and Jerry Schmetterer
1991   *The Coffey Files: One Cop's War Against the Mob.* New York: St. Martin's.
Coffey, Thomas A.
1975   *The Long Thirst: Prohibition in America: 1920–1933.* New York: Norton.
Cohen, Mickey
1975   *Mickey Cohen: In My Own Words.* Englewood Cliffs. NJ: Prentice-Hall.
Cohen, Stanley
1977   *The Game They Played.* New York: Farrar, Straus and Giroux.
Collins, Randall
1975   *Conflict Sociology.* New York: Academic Press.
"Colombian City Basks in Terror's End"
1991   *New York Times* (December 12): 9.
"Colombian Growth Hurt By Cocaine"
1991   *New York Times* (February 19): C1.
"Colombian Heroin May Be Increasing"
1991   *New York Times* (October 27): 10.
Colombo, Furio
1983   "Meaning of Italy's Vote." *New York Times* (July 13): 21.
Commission on the Review of the National Policy Toward Gambling
1976   *Gambling in America.* Washington, DC: U.S. Government Printing Office.

Committee on Law Reform of the New York County
Lawyers Association
  1987   "Advisory Reports. Part I: Why Cocaine
             and Heroin Should be Decriminalized. Part
             II: Why Cocaine and Heroin Should Not
             Be Decriminalized." New York: Photocopied.

Committee on the Office of Attorney General
  1978   *Witness Immunity.* Raleigh, NC: National
             Association of Attorneys General (NAAG).
  1977   *State Grand Juries.* Raleigh, NC: NAAG.
  1974   *Prosecuting Organized Crime.* Raleigh, NC:
             NAAG.

Comptroller General
  1988   *Drug Control: U.S.-Mexico Opium Poppy
             and Marijuana Aerial Eradication Program.*
             Washington, DC: General Accounting Of-
             fice.
  1983   *Federal Drug Interdiction Efforts Need a
             Strong Central Oversight.* Washington, DC:
             General Accounting Office.

Conklin, John E., ed.
  1977   *The Crime Establishment.* Englewood Cliffs,
             NJ: Prentice-Hall.

Connable, Alfred and Edward Silberfarb
  1967   *Tigers of Tammany: Nine Men Who Ruled
             New York.* New York: Holt, Rinehart and
             Winston.

Contreras, Joseph
  1989   "With the Shining Path: A Rare and Risky
             Encounter with Peru's Fanatic Guerilla
             Movement." *Newsweek* (April 24): 44–49.

Cook, Fred J.
  1979   "Shaking the Bricks at the FBI." *New York
             Times Magazine* (March 25): 31–40.
  1973   *Mafia!* New York: Fawcett.
  1972   "Purge of the Greasers." Pp. 89–109 in
             Mafia, U.S.A., edited by Nicholas Gage.
             New York: Dell.

Coppola, Vincent
  1989   "Georgia's High Sheriffs." *Atlanta* (March):
             15.

Coram, Robert
  1981   "Colombia's Pot Peninsula—a Hot, Deadly,
             Lawless Land." *Chicago Tribune* (May 3):
             8.
  1978   "The Colombian Gold Rush of 1978."
             Esquire (September): 33– 37.

Courtwright, David T.
  1982   *Dark Paradise: Opiate Addiction in America
             Before 1940.* Cambridge, MA: Harvard Uni-
             versity Press.

Covington, Dennis
  1992   "Kidnapping Rips Open a Town's Secrets
             and Fears." *New York Times* (January 13):
             10.

Cowan, Richard C.
  1986   "A War Against Ourselves: How the Narcs
             Created Crack." *National Review* (Decem-
             ber 5): 26– 31.

Cowell, Alan
  1993a   "Heroin Pouring Through Porous Euro-
             pean Borders." *New York Times* (February
             9): 3.
  1993b   "Italy Intensifies Crackdown on Organized
             Crime." *New York Times* (May 14): 5.
  1993c   "Busting the Mafia: Italy Advances in War
             on Crime." *New York Times* (June 27): 3.
  1992a   "Inquiry Into Sicilian Slaying Looks For
             Mafia Link to Colombia Drug Cartel."
             New York Times (June 21): 3.
  1992b   "A Top Sicilian Politician Is Slain; Pre-
             Election Mafia Warning Seen." *New York
             Times* (March 12): 2.
  1992c   "Defying Fear of Reprisal, 40,000 in Palermo
             Protest Mafia's Grip." *New York Times* (June
             22): 6.
  1992d   "Mafia Throws the Gauntlet in Italy's Face."
             New York Times (July 21): 5.
  1992e   "Sicilian Symbolizes Mob's Survival." *New
             York Times* (August 2): 8.
  1992f   "Italians Defying Shakedowns Pay With
             Lives." *New York Times* (November 12): 5.
  1992g   "Italy Arrests 75 in Mafia Roundup." *New
             York Times* (November 18): 3.
  1992h   "Some Surprising Allies Fighting Sicily's
             Mafia." *New York Times* (November 29): 4.

Cressey, Donald R.
  1972   *Criminal Organization: Its Elementary
             Forms.* New York: Harper and Row.
  1969   *Theft of the Nation.* New York: Harper and
             Row.
  1967a   "The Functions and Structure of Criminal
             Syndicates." Pp. 25–60 in *Task Force on
             Organized Crime.* Washington, DC: U.S.
             Government Printing Office.
  1967b   "Methodological Problems in the Study of
             Organized Crime as a Social Problem."
             Annals 374 (November): 101–12.

Crossette, Barbara
  1990   "U.S.-Pakistani Bone of Contention: Nar-
             cotics." *New York Times* (December 8): 7.

1987 "An Opium Warlord's News Conference Spurs Burma and Thailand to Battle Him." *New York Times* (February 22): 11.

Crouse, Russel
1947 "The Murder of Arnold Rothstein: 1928." Pages 184–200 in *Sins of New York*, edited by Milton Crane. New York: Grosset and Dunlap.

Daley, Robert A.
1978 *Prince of the City.* Boston: Houghton Mifflin.

Dannen, Federic
1992a "The Untouchable? How the FBI Sabotaged Competing Prosecution Teams in the Race to Nail Alleged Mob King John Gotti." *Vanity Fair* (January): 27–44.
1992b "Revenge of the Green Dragons." *The New Yorker* (November): 76–99.

David, John J.
1988 "Outlaw Motorcycle Gangs: A Transnational Problem." Paper presented at the Conference on International Terrorism and Transnational Crime, Chicago, August 1988.

Davis, John H.
1993 *Mafia Dynasty: The Rise and Fall of the Gambino Crime Family.* New York: Harper Collins.

Davis, Roger
1981 "Social Network Analysis: An Aid in Conspiracy Investigation." *FBI Law Enforcement Bulletin* (December): 11–19.

De Franco, Edward J.
1973 *Anatomy of a Scam: A Case Study of a Planned Bankruptcy by Organized Crime.* Washington, DC: U.S. Government Printing Office.

Defus, R. L.
1928 "The Gunman Has an Intercity Murder Trade." *New York Times* (July): XX 3.

De La Rosa, Mario, Elizabeth Y. Lambert, and Bernard Gropper, eds.
1990 *Drugs and Violence: Causes, Correlates, and Consequences.* Rockville, MD: National Institute on Drug Abuse.

de Lama, George
1989 "Most Antidrug Aid for Colombia Used Against Rebels." *Chicago Tribune* (October 31): 1, 8.
1988a "For Colombian Officials, Nowhere is Safe." *Chicago Tribune* (November 21): 1, 12.
1988b "Besieged Colombia Becoming the Lebanon of Latin America." *Chicago Tribune* (November 20): 5.

1988c "U.S. Pilots Risk Lives in Peru's Drug War." *Chicago Tribune* (November 6): 18.
1988d "South Americans' Idea for Drug War May Upset U.S." *Chicago Tribune* (November 25): 23, 26.

Delaney, Paul
1988 "Drug Trafficking for Northern Europeans is Overwhelming Spanish Ports." *New York Times* (November 9): 6.

Delaney, William P.
1977 "On Capturing an Opium King: The Politics of Law Sik Han's Arrest." Pp. 67–88 in *Drugs and Politics*, edited by Paul E. Rock. New Brunswick, NJ: Transaction Books.

Demaris, Ovid
1981 *The Last Mafioso: The Treacherous World of Jimmy Fratianno.* New York: Bantam.
1969 *Captive City: Chicago in Chains.* New York: Lyle Stuart.

Department of Justice
1975 *Report on the National Conference on Organized Crime.* Washington, DC: U.S. Government Printing Office.

Department of Justice and Department of Transportation
1972 *Cargo Theft and Organized Crime.* Washington, DC: U.S. Government Printing Office.

De Quincey, Thomas
1952 *The Confessions of an English Opium Eater.* London: J.M. Dent. First published in 1821.

DeWitt, Charles B.
1993 *Controlling Chemicals Used to Make Illegal Drugs: The Chemical Action Task Force and the Domestic Chemical Action Group.* Washington, DC: National Institute of Justice.

Diamond, Stuart
1988 "Steep Rise Seen in Private Use of Federal Racketeering Law." *New York Times* (August 1): 1, 15.

Diapoulos, Peter and Steven Linakis
1976 *The Sixth Family.* New York: Dutton.

Dickson, Clarence
1988 "Drug Sting in Miami." *FBI Law Enforcement Bulletin* 57 (January): 1–6.

Dickson, Donald T.
1977 "Bureaucracy and Morality: An Organizational Perspective on a Moral Crusade." Pp. 31–52 in *Drugs and Politics*, edited by Paul E. Rock. New Brunswick, NJ: Transaction Books.

Dictionary of Criminal Justice Data Terminology
1981   Washington, DC: U.S. Government Printing Office.

Dinges, John
1990   *Our Man in Panama: How General Noriega Used the United States—and Made Millions in Drugs and Arms.* New York: Random House.

Dintino, Justin J. and Frederick T. Martens
1983   *Police Intelligence Systems and Crime Control.* Springfield, IL: Charles C. Thomas.
1980   "Organized Crime Control in the Eighties." *Police Chief* (August): 66–70.

Dobyns, Fletcher
1932   *The Underworld of American Politics.* New York: Fletcher Dobyns.

Dorsett, Lyle W.
1968   *The Pendergast Machine.* New York: Oxford University Press.

Douglas, Paul H.
1974   "Introduction," *Bosses in Lusty Chicago*, by Lloyd Wendt and Herman Kogan. Bloomington, IN: Indiana University Press.

Drew, Christopher
1993   "Privacy Leaves Cops a Key." *Chicago Tribune* (April 17): Sec. 2: 1, 2.

Drug Abuse and Drug Abuse Research
1987   Rockville, MD: National Institute on Drug Abuse.

Drug Enforcement Administration
1991a   *Worldwide Heroin Situation.* Washington, DC: DEA.
1991b   *Worldwide Cocaine Situation.* Washington, DC: DEA.
1988   *Crack Cocaine Availability and Trafficking in the United States.* Washington, DC: DEA.

"Drug Gangs, The"
1988   *Newsweek* (March 28): feature story.

"Drug Smugglers Used Cuban Base For U.S. Shipment, Jury Charges"
1988   *New York Times* (February 27): 6.

"Drugs of Abuse"
1979   *Drug Enforcement* (July; entire issue).

Drugs of Abuse
1977   Washington, DC: Drug Enforcement Administration.

Duggan, Christopher
1989   *Fascism and the Mafia.* New Haven, CT: Yale University.

Durk, David and Ira Silverman
1976   *The Pleasant Avenue Connection.* New York: Harper and Row.

Durkheim, Emile
1951   *Suicide.* New York: Free Press.

Duster, Troy
1970   *The Legislation of Morality: Law, Drugs, and Moral Judgment.* New York: Free Press.

Eadington, William R.
1993   "Casinos Are No Economic Cure-All." *New York Times* (June 13): F13.

Eddy, Paul, Hugo Sabogal and Sara Walden
1988   *The Cocaine Wars.* New York: Norton.

Egan, Jack
1991   "How BCCI Banked on Global Secrecy." *U.S. News and World Report* (August 19): 58–59.

Egan, Timothy
1988   "U.S. Agents Aid Drug Fight in Seattle." *New York Times* (July 15): 6.

Ehrenfeld, Rachel
1990   *Narco-Terrorism.* New York: Basic Books.

Elliott, Delbert S., David Huizinga, and Suzanne S. Ageton
1985   *Explaining Delinquency and Drug Use.* Beverly Hills, CA: Sage.

Elliott, Dorinda
1992   "Russia's Goodfellas: The Mafia on the Neva." *Newsweek* (October 12): 50, 52.

Elsasser, Glen
1989   "Suspicion is Ruled Ample Basis for Drug Search." *Chicago Tribune* (April 4): 3.

Engelberg, Stephen
1988   "Nicaragua Rebels Tell of Drug Deal." *New York Times* (April 8) L6.

Engelmann, Larry
1979   *Intemperance: The Lost War Against Liquor.* New York: Free Press.

English, T. J.
1990   *The Westies: Inside the Hell's Kitchen Irish Mob.* New York: G.P. Putnam's.

Epstein, Edward Jay
1988a   "Marrying the Mob to Wall Street." *Manhattan, Inc.* (October): 43–47.
1988b   "The Dope Business." *Manhattan* (July): 25–27.
1977   *Agency of Fear: Opiates and Political Power in America.* New York: Putnam's.

Epstein, Leon D.
1986   *Political Parties in the American Mold.* Madison, WI: University of Wisconsin Press.

Erie, Steven P.
1988   *Rainbow's End: Irish-Americans and the Dilemmas of Urban Machine Politics, 1840–1985.* Berkeley, CA: University of California Press.

REFERENCES

Erlanger, Steven
  1988   "Burma's Political Unrest and Weather are Helping Opium Flourish." *New York Times* (December 11): 8.

Fagan, Jeffrey and Ko-lin Chin
  1991   "Social Processes of Initiation Into Crack." *Journal of Drug Issues* 21: 313–43.

Faison, Seth
  1993   "How Betrayal Snagged a Chinatown Gang Leader." *New York Times* (August 31): 12.

Fay, Peter Ward
  1975   *The Opium War: 1840–1842.* Chapel Hill: University of North Carolina Press.

"FBI Says Los Angeles Gang Has Drug Cartel Ties"
  1992   *New York Times* (January 10): 8.

Feinberg, Alexander
  1959   "Genovese Is Given 15 Years in Prison in Narcotics Case." *New York Times* (April 18): 1, 15.
  1950   "A Who's Who in New York's Gambling Inquiry." *New York Times* (October 29): IV 6.
  1944   "Lepke Is Put to Death, Denies Guilt to Last; Makes No Revelation." *New York Times* (March 5): 1, 30.

Fijnaut, Cyrelle and James Jacobs, eds.
  1991   *Organized Crime and Its Containment: A Transatlantic Initiative.* Deventer, Netherlands: Kluwer.

Finley, M.I., Denis Mack Smith, and Christopher Duggan
  1987   *A History of Sicily.* New York: Viking.

Fisher, Ian
  1993   "In New York City's Underworld: A Window on Immigrant Crime." *New York Times* (June 17): 13.

Fisher, Sethard
  1975   "Review of the 'Black Mafia.'" *Contemporary Sociology* 4 (May): 83–84.

Fitzgerald, F. Scott
  1925   *The Great Gatsby.* New York: Scribner's.

Flinn, John J.
  1973   *History of the Chicago Police.* New York: AMS Press. Originally published in 1887.

Foderaro, Lisa W.
  1988   "A Drug Called 'Ecstasy' Emerges in Nightclubs." *New York Times* (December 11): 26.

Fogelson, Robert M.
  1977   *Big City Police.* Cambridge, MA: Harvard University Press.

Fong, Mak Lau
  1981   *The Sociology of Secret Societies: A Study of Chinese Secret Societies in Singapore and Peninsular Malaysia.* Oxford, England: Oxford University Press.

Fong, Robert S.
  1990   "The Organizational Structure of Prison Gangs: A Texas Case Study." *Federal Probation* 54 (March): 36–43.

Fooner, Michael
  1985   *A Guide to Interpol.* Washington, DC: U.S. Government Printing Office.

"$4,000,000 Narcotics Seized Here Tied to Rothstein Ring."
  1928   *New York Times* (December 19): 1.

Fox, Stephen
  1989   *Blood and Power: Organized Crime in the Twentieth Century.* New York: William Morrow.

Frank, Blanche, Gregory Rainone, Michael Maranda, William Hopkins, Edmundo Morales, and Alan Kott
  1987   "A Psyco-Social View of 'Crack' in New York City." Paper presented at the American Psychological Association Convention, New York City, August 28.

"Frank Costello Dies of Coronary at 82; Underworld Leader."
  1972   *New York Times* (February 19): 1, 21.

Franklin, Stephen
  1993   "Teamsters Move on Local." *Chicago Tribune* (June 17): Sec. 2: 1, 2.

Franks, Lucinda
  1977   "An Obscure Gangster Is Emerging as the New Mafia Chief in New York." *New York Times* (March 17): 1, 34.

Frantz, Douglas and Chuck Neubauer
  1983   "Teamster Pension Fund Just Fine After Surgery." *Chicago Tribune* (May 29): 1, 10.

Franzese, Michael and Dary Matera
  1992   *Quitting the Mob.* New York: Harper Paperbacks.

Freeman, Ira Henry
  1957   "Anastasia Rose in Stormy Ranks." *New York Times* (October 26): 12.

French, Howard W.
  1992   "Violence Makes Jamaican Fear for Tourism." *New York Times* (February 25): 4.
  1991   "Filthy Rich With a Drug Connection." *New York Times* (August 6): 6.

Freud, Sigmund
1933   *New Introductory Lectures on Psycho-Analysis.* New York: W.W. Norton.

Fried, Albert
1980   *The Rise and Fall of the Jewish Gangster in America.* New York: Holt, Rinehart and Winston.

Fried, Joseph P.
1993   "Government Sues to Seize Gotti's Remaining Assets." *New York Times* (January 15): 16.
1993b   "Indictment Links the Mafia to Trash-Hauling Industry." *New York Times* (April 20): B16.
1992   "Inside Man for U.S. Oversees Union at Kennedy in War on Airport Rackets." *New York Times* (May 17): 21.

Friedman, Allen and Ted Schwarz
1989   *Power and Greed: Inside the Teamsters Empire of Corruption.* New York: Watts.

Friel, Frank and John Gunther
1990   *Breaking the Mob.* New York: Warner.

Fuller, Robert H.
1928   *Jubilee Jim: The Life of Colonel James Fisk, Jr.* New York: Macmillan.

Gage, Nicholas
1976   "Five Mafia Families Open Rosters to New Members." *New York Times* (March 21): 1, 40.
1975   "Carlo Gambino Dies in His Long Island Home at 75." *New York Times* (October 16): 26.
1974   "Questions Are Raised on Lucky Luciano Book." *New York Times* (December 17): 28.
1971a   *The Mafia Is Not an Equal Opportunity Employer.* New York: McGraw-Hill.
1971b   "Gallo-Colombo Feud Said To Have Been Renewed." *New York Times* (June 29): 21.

Gage, Nicholas, ed.
1972   *Mafia, U.S.A.* New York: Dell.

Gallagher, James P.
1992a   "As Law Enforcement Crumbles, Russian Crime, Gangs Proliferate." *Chicago Tribune* (September 2): 6.
1992b   "Chechens Stir Bloody Cauldron in Caucasus." *Chicago Tribune* (January 10): 20.

Galliher, John F. and James A. Cain
1974   "Citation Support for the Mafia Myth in Criminology Textbooks." *American Sociologist* 9 (May): 68–74.

Gallo, Patrick J.
1981   *Old Bread, New Wine: A Portrait of the Italian-American.* Chicago: Nelson-Hall.

Galvan, Manuel
1982   "Capone's Yacht Sails Calmer Seas Today." *Chicago Tribune* (February 16): Section 2: 1.

Gambino, Richard
1977   *Vendetta.* Garden City, N.Y.: Doubleday.
1974   *Blood of My Blood: The Dilemma of the Italian-American.* Garden City: Doubleday.

"Gamblers Hunted in Rothstein Attack."
1928   *New York Times* (November 6): 1.

Gambling Commission, see Commission on the Review of the National Policy Toward Gambling.

"Gang Kills Suspect in Alien Smuggling."
1931   *New York Times* (September 11): 1.

"Gang Linked to Union Charged at Trial."
1934   *New York Times* (January 31): 8.

"Gangster Shot in Daylight Attack."
1928   *New York Times* (July 2): 1.

Gardiner, John A.
1970   *The Politics of Corruption: Organized Crime in an American City.* New York: Russell Sage Foundation.

Geary, Nori
1987   "Cocaine: Animal Research Studies." Pp. 19–47 in *Cocaine Abuse: New Directions in Treatment and Research,* edited by Henry I. Spitz and Jeffrey S. Rosecan. New York: Brunner/Mazel.

Genzman, Robert W.
1988   "Press Release." October 11.

Giancana, Antoinette and Thomas C. Renner
1985   *Mafia Princess: Growing Up in Sam Giancana's Family.* New York: Avon.

Giancana, Sam and Chuck Giancana
1992   *Double Cross: Inside Story of the Mobster Who Controlled America.* New York: Warner Books.

Gibson, Sonny
1981   *Mafia Kingpin.* New York: Grossett and Dunlop.

Gies, Joseph
1979   *The Colonel of Chicago: A Biography of the Chicago Tribune's Legendary Publisher Colonel Robert McCormick.* New York: E.P. Dutton.

REFERENCES

Giuliani, Rudolph W.
1987   "Legal Remedies for Attacking Organized Crime." Pp. 103–30 in *Major Issues in Organized Crime Control*, edited by Herbert Edelhertz. Washington, DC: U.S. Government Printing Office.

Glaberson, William
1989   "U.S. Loses Round in Bid to Curb Mob at Fish Market." *New York Times* (January 25): 12.

Goddard, Donald
1988   *Undercover: The Secret Lives of a Federal Agent.* New York: Times Books.
1980   *All Fall Down.* New York: Times Books.
1978   *Easy Money.* New York: Farrar, Straus and Giroux.
1974   *Joey.* New York: Harper and Row.

Godfrey, E. Drexel, Jr. and Don R. Harris
1971   *Basic Elements of Intelligence.* Washington, DC: U.S. Government Printing Office.

Gold, Allan R.
1989   "Dead Officer, Dropped Charges: A Scandal in Boston." *New York Times* (March 20): 9.

Gold, Mark S.
1984   *800-Cocaine.* New York: Bantam.

Gold, Mark S., Charles A. Dackis, A.L.C. Pottash, Irl Extein and Arnold Washton
1986   "Cocaine Update: From Bench to Bedside." *Advances in Alcohol and Substance Abuse* 5 (Fall/ Winter): 35–60.

Gold, Mark S., Arnold M. Washton, and Charles A. Dackis
1985   "Cocaine Abuse: Neurochemistry, Phenomenology, and Treatment." Pp. 130–50 in *Cocaine Use in America: Epidemiologic and Clinical Perspectives*, edited by Nicholas J. Kozel and Edgar H. Adams. Rockville, MD: National Institute on Drug Abuse.

Golden, Tim
1993   "Violently, Drug Trafficking in Mexico Rebounds." *New York Times* (March 8): 3.
1991a   "Killing of 7 Mexican Drug Agents Raises Fear." *New York Times* (November 30): 5.
1991b   "Mexican Panel Faults Army in Death of Drug Agents." *New York Times* (December 7): 3.

Goldstein, Joseph
1982   "Police Discretion Not to Invoke the Criminal Process." Pp. 33–42 in *The Invisible Justice System: Discretion and the Law*, 2nd ed., edited by Burton Atkins and Mark Pogrebin. Cincinnati, OH: Anderson.

Goldstein, Paul J.
1985   "The Drugs/Violence Nexus: A Tripartic Conceptual Framework." *Journal of Drug Issues* 15 (Fall): 493–506.

Goldstock, Ronald and Dan T. Coenen
1978   *Extortionate and Usurious Credit Transactions: Background Materials.* Ithaca, NY: Cornell Institute on Organized Crime.

Goleman, Daniel
1987   "Brain Defect Tied to Utter Amorality of the Psychopath." *New York Times* (July 7): 13, 16.

Gomez, Linda
1984   "America's 100 Years of Euphoria and Despair." *Life* (May): 57–68.

Goode, Eric
1972   *Drugs in American Society.* New York: Knopf.

Goozner, Merrill
1992   "Thugs Avenge a Movie's Insults." *Chicago Tribune* (June 4): 4.

"Gordon Made by Dry Era."
1933   *New York Times* (December 2): 6.

Gordon, Michael R.
1992   "U.S. Military Long a Part of the Narcotics Battle." *New York Times* (August 2): 10.

"Gordon Says He Got up to $300 a Week."
1933   *New York Times* (December 1): 14.

Gosch, Martin and Richard Hammer
1974   *The Last Testament of Lucky Luciano.* Boston: Little, Brown.

Gosnell, Harold
1977   *Machine Politics: The Chicago Model.* Chicago: University of Chicago. Originally published in 1937.

Gottfried, Alex
1962   *Boss Cermak of Chicago.* Seattle: University of Washington Press.

Gove, Walter R., Michael Geerken, and Michael Hughes
1979   "Drug Use and Mental Health Among a Representative Sample of Young Adults." *Social Forces* 58 (December): 572–90.

Graham, Fred
1977   *The Atlas Program.* Boston: Little, Brown.

Graham, Hugh Davis and Ted Robert Gurr, eds.
1969   *The History of Violence in America: A Report to the National Commission on the Causes and Prevention of Violence.* New York: Bantam.

Grant, Madison and Charles S. Davison, eds.
1930   *The Alien in Our Midst: Or Selling Our Birthright for a Mess of Pottage.* New York: Galton Publishing Co.

Greenberg, Norman
1981   *The Man With a Steel Guitar: Portrait of Desperation, and Crime*. Hoover, NH: University Press of New England.

Greenhouse, Linda
1989a   "In Spotless Switzerland, Dirty Money is Washed." *New York Times* (April 4): 6.
1989b   "High Court Backs Airport Detention Based on 'Profile.'" *New York Times* (April 4): 1, 10.
1989c   "Racketeering Law Limited in Pornography Cases." *New York Times* (February 22): 12.

Grinspoon, Lester
1979   *Psychedelic Drugs Reconsidered*. New York: Basic Books.

Grinspoon, Lester and James B. Bakalar
1985   *Cocaine: A Drug and Its Social Evolution: Revised Edition*. New York: Basic Books.
1976   *Cocaine: A Drug and Its Social Evolution*. New York: Basic Books.

Grinspoon, Lester and Peter Hedblom
1975   *The Speed Culture: Amphetamine Use and Abuse in America*. Cambridge, MA: Harvard University Press.

Gross, Jane
1988   "Speed's Gain in Use Could Rival Crack, Drug Experts Warn." *New York Times* (November 27): 1, 14.

Gruson, Lindsey
1990   "U.S. Pinning Hopes on Guatemalan Army for Stability and War Against Drugs." *New York Times* (July 5): 4.

Grutzner, Charles
1969   "Genovese Dies in Prison at 71; 'Boss of Bosses' of Mafia Here." *New York Times* (February 15): 1, 29.

Gugliotta, Guy and Jeff Leen
1989   *Kings of Cocaine: Inside the Medellín Cartel—An Astonishing True Story of Murder, Money, and International Corruption*. New York: Simon and Schuster.

Gusfield, Joseph R.
1975   "The (F)Utility of Knowledge? The Relation of Social Science to Public Policy Toward Drugs." *Annals* 417 (January): 1–15.
1963   *Symbolic Crusade: Status Politics and the American Temperance Movement*. Urbana, IL: University of Illinois Press.

Haberman, Clyde
1985   "TV Funeral for Japan's Slain Godfather." *New York Times* (February 1): 6.

Haden-Guest, Anthony
1990   "Medellin East." *Vanity Fair* (May): 82–92.

Hagerty, James A.
1933   "Assassin Fires into Roosevelt Party at Miami; President-Elect Uninjured; Mayor Cermak and 4 Others Wounded." *New York Times* (February 16): 1.

Haley, Bruce
1990   "Burma's Hidden Wars." *U.S. News and World Report* (December 10): 44–47.

Haller, Mark H.
1991   *Life Under Bruno: The Economics of an Organized Crime Family*. Conshohocken, PA: Pennsylvania Crime Commission.
1990a   "Illegal Enterprise: A Theoretical and Historical Interpretation." *Criminology* 28 (May): 207–35.
1990b   "Policy Gambling, Entertainment, and the Emergence of Black Politics: Chicago from 1900 to 1940." *Journal of Social History* 24: 791–38.
1985a   "Bootleggers as Businessmen: From City Slums to City Builders." Pp. 139–57 in *Law, Alcohol, and Order: Perspectives on National Prohibition*, edited by David E. Kyvig. Westport, CT: Greenwood.
1985b   "Philadelphia Bootlegging and the Report of the Special Grand Jury." *Pennsylvania Magazine of History and Biography* 109 (April): 215–33.
1974   "Bootlegging in Chicago: The Structure of an Illegal Enterprise." Paper presented at the annual meeting of the American Historical Association, December 28, Chicago.
1971–72 "Organized Crime in Urban Society: Chicago in the Twentieth Century." *Journal of Social History* 5: 210–34.

Halloran, Richard
1988   "U.S. Odds Reported to Favor Cocaine Smugglers." *New York Times* (December 8): 14.

Hammer, Richard
1982   *The Vatican Connection*. New York: Holt, Rinehart and Winston.
1975   *Playboy's Illustrated History of Organized Crime*. Chicago: Playboy Press.

Hampson, Rick
1993   "Mob-linked Eatery Warms to Watchdog." *Chicago Tribune* (May 13): 14.

Handelman, Stephen
1993   "Inside Russia's Gangster Economy." *New York Times Magazine* (January 24): 12–15, 30–31, 34, 40, 50.

Hanley, Charles J.
1993   "Drug Bust May Signal Colombia-Russia Link." *Chicago Tribune* (May 14): 31.

REFERENCES

Hapgood, Norman and Henry Moskowitz
  1927   *Up From the Streets: Alfred E. Smith.* New York: Harcourt, Brace.

Harker, R. Phillip
  1978   "Sports Bookmaking Operations." *FBI Law Enforcement Bulletin* (September); FBI reprint.
  1977   "Sports Wagering and the 'Line.'" *FBI Law Enforcement Bulletin* (November); FBI reprint.

Harmon, Dave
  1993   "Ex-Agent: Drug Sales Aided Contras." *Chicago Tribune* (January 26): 3.

Hayes, Monte
  1987   "Peru's Maoists Join Drug Lords." *Chicago Tribune* (December 21): 13.

Hayner, Don
  1990   "Chinatown Gambling: Inside Story." *Chicago Sun-Times* (September 2): 1, 20–21.

Hays, Constance L.
  1991   "Drug Lord? This Man? Impossible." *New York Times* (August 25): 15.

Hazarika, Sanjoy
  1993   "Indian Heroin Smugglers Turn to New Cargo." *New York Times* (February 21): 8.

Hedgepeth, William
  1989   "Mule Skinner." *Atlanta* (March): 61–62, 93–101.

Helmer, John
  1975   *Drugs and Minority Oppression.* New York: Seabury Press.

Henkel, Ray
  1986   "The Bolivian Cocaine Industry." Pp. 53–80 in *Drugs in Latin America*, edited by Vinson H. Sutlive, Nathan Altshuler, Mario D. Zamora, and Virginia Kerns. Williamsburg, VA: College of William and Mary.

Henriques, Diana B. and Dean Baquet
  1993   "Investigators Say Bid-Rigging Is Common in Milk Industry." *New York Times* (May 23): 1, 12.

Herndon, Booton
  1969   *Ford: An Unconventional Biography of the Men and Their Times.* New York: Weybright and Talley.

Hershkowitz, Leo
  1978   *Tweed's New York: Another Look.* New York: Anchor.

Hess, Henner
  1973   *Mafia and Mafiosi: The Structure of Power.* Lexington, MA: D.C. Heath.

Hibbert, Christopher
  1966   *Garibaldi and His Enemies.* Boston: Little, Brown.

Hijazi, Ihsan A.
  1991   "Army in Lebanon Seizes Militia's Smuggling Ports." *New York Times* (March 12): 4.

Hill, Henry, with Douglas S. Looney
  1981   "How I Put the Fix In." *Sports Illustrated* (February 16): 14–21.

Hills, Stuart, L., ed.
  1987   *Corporate Violence: Injury and Death for Profit.* New York: Barnes and Noble.
  1969   "Combatting Organized Crime in America." *Federal Probation* 33 (March): 23–28.

Himmelstein, Jerome L.
  1983   *The Strange Career of Marijuana: Politics and Ideology of Drug Control in America.* Westport, CT: Greenwood.

Hirschi, Travis
  1969   *Causes of Delinquency.* Berkeley: University of California Press.

Hobsbawm, Eric J.
  1976   "Mafia." Pp. 90–98 in *The Crime Society*, edited by Francis A.J. Ianni and Elizabeth Reuss-Ianni. New York: New American Library.
  1971   *Bandits.* New York: Dell.
  1969   "The American Mafia." *The Listener* 82 (November): 685–88.
  1959   *Social Bandits and Primitive Rebels.* Glencoe, IL: Free Press.

Hoffman, Paul
  1983   "Italy Gets Tough with the Mafia." *New York Times Magazine* (November 13): 164–67, 170, 180.
  1976   *To Drop a Dime.* New York: Putnam's.

Hofstadter, Richard
  1956   *The Age of Reform: From Bryan to F.D.R.* New York: Knopf.

Hofstadter, Richard and Michael Wallace, eds.
  1971   *American Violence: A Documentary History.* New York: Vintage.

Hogan, William T.
  1976   "Sentencing and Supervision of Organized Crime Figures." *Federal Probation* 40 (March): 21–24.

Hohimer, Frank
  1975   *The Home Invaders.* Chicago: Chicago Review Press.

Holbrook, Stewart H.
  1953   *The Age of Moguls.* Garden City, NY: Doubleday.

Homans, George C.
  1961   *Social Behavior: Its Elementary Forms.* New York: Harcourt, Brace and World.

Homer, Frederic D.
1974   *Guns and Garlic*. West Lafayette, IN: Purdue University Press.

Horne, Louther
1932   "Capone's Trip to Jail Ends a Long Battle." *New York Times* (May 8): IX 1.

Horrock, Nicholas
1975   "Roselli Describes His Role in CIA Plot on Castro." *New York Times* (June 25): 1.

Humphries, Drew and David F. Greenberg
1981   "The Dialectics of Crime Control." Pp. 209–54 in *Crime and Capitalism*, edited by David F. Greenberg. Palo Alto, CA: Mayfield.

Ianni, Francis A.J.
1974   *The Black Mafia: Ethnic Succession in Organized Crime*. New York: Simon and Schuster.
1972   *A Family Business: Kinship and Social Control in Organized Crime*. New York: Russell Sage Foundation.

Iannuzzi, Joseph
1993   *Joe Dogs: The Life and Crimes of a Mobster*. New York: Simon and Schuster.

Ihde, Aaron J.
1982   "Food Controls Under the 1906 Act." Pages 40–50 in *The Early Years of Federal Food and Drug Control*, edited by James Harvey Young. Madison, WI: American Institute of Pharmacy.

Inciardi, James A.
1986   *The War on Drugs: Heroin, Cocaine, Crime, and Public Policy*. Palo Alto, CA: Mayfield.
1975   *Careers in Crime*. Chicago: Rand McNally.

Inciardi, James A. and Anne E. Pottieger
1991   "Kids, Crack, and Crime." *Journal of Drug Issues* 21: 257–70.

"Insurer Won't Pay on Federal Witness"
1987   *Chicago Tribune* (December 9): 10.

Inverarity, James M., Pat Lauderdale, and Barry Field
1983   *Law and Society: Sociological Perspectives on Criminal Law*. Boston: Little, Brown.

Irey, Elmer L. and William T. Slocum
1948   *The Tax Dodgers*. Garden City, NY: Doubleday.

Iwai, Hiroaki
1986   "Organized Crime in Japan." Pp. 208–33 in *Organized Crime: A Global Perspective*, edited by Robert J. Kelly. Totowa, NJ: Rowman and Littlefield.

Jackson, David
1990   "Bad Company." *Chicago* (February): 91–95, 109–10.

"Jail Informer's Admissions Spur Inquiry."
1989   *New York Times* (January 3): 10.

James, George
1993   "Man Tied to Crime Family is Shot to Death in Queens." *New York Times* (October 22): 12.

Jenkins, Philip and Gary W. Potter
1985   *The City and the Syndicate: Organizing Crime in Philadelphia*. Lexington, MA: Ginn Custom Publishing.

Jennings, Dean
1967   *We Only Kill Each Other*. Englewood Cliffs, NJ: Prentice-Hall.

Joe, Karen
1992   "Chinese Gangs and Tongs: An Exploratory Look at the Connection on the West Coast." Paper presented at the Annual Meeting of the American Society of Criminology, November 4–7, New Orleans.

"Johnny Torrio, Ex-Public Enemy 1, Dies; Made Al Capone Boss of the Underworld."
1957   *New York Times* (May 8): 32.

Johnson, Earl, Jr.
1963   "Organized Crime: Challenge to the American Legal System." *Criminal Law, Criminology, and Police Science* 54 (March): 1–29.

Johnson, Kirk
1986   "Manhattan Gang is Tied to 30 Unsolved Killings." *New York Times* (December 17): 19.

Johnson, Malcolm
1972   "In Hollywood." Pp. 325–38 in *Mafia, U.S.A.*, edited by Nicholas Gage. New York: Dell.

Johnston, David
1993   *Temples of Chance: How America Inc. Bought Out Murder Inc. to Win Control of the Casino Business*. Garden City, NY: Doubleday.
1986   "Credibility of Drug Book Challenged." *Los Angeles Times* (October 2): 2, 30–33.

Johnston, Michael
1982   *Political Corruption and Public Policy in America*. Monterey, CA: Brooks/Cole.

Jolidon, Laurence
1992   "Panama's Free, But Drug Trade, Crime Thrive." *USA Today* (April 3): 7.

Jones, Alex S.
1990   "Lotto Winner is a Hoax! Reporters Duped Again." *New York Times* (January 9): 13.

Jones, Malcolm and Ray Sawhill
1992   "Just Too Good to be True." *Newsweek* (May 4): 68.

REFERENCES

Jones, Reese T.
   1980   "Marijuana, Human Effects: An Overview."
           Pp. 54–80 in *Marijuana: Research Find-*
           ings, 1980. Rockville, MD: National Insti-
           tute on Drug Abuse.

Joselit, Jenna Weissman
   1983   *Our Gang: Jewish Crime and the New York*
           Jewish Community, 1900–1940. Blooming-
           ton, IN: Indiana University Press.

Josephson, Matthew
   1962   *The Robber Barons.* New York: Harcourt,
           Brace and World. Originally published in
           1934.

Kamin, Blair
   1987   "Cheers! Brewery Born Again." *Chicago*
           Tribune (September 18): Sec. 2: 3.

Kamm, Henry
   1988   "In Wild West Not Far From the Khyber
           Pass, Shots Ring Out." *New York Times*
           (March 18): 7.
   1982a   "A Modern Mafia Stirs Rage and Fear."
           New York Times (September 12): E3.
   1982b   "Pope Begins Visit to Mafia Stronghold."
           New York Times (November 21): 3.
   1982c   "Gang War in Naples Laid to Jailed Chief."
           New York Times (April 4): 11.

Kaplan, David E. and Alec Dubro
   1986   *Yakuza: The Explosive Account of Japan's*
           Criminal Underworld. Reading, MA: Ad-
           dison-Wesley.

Kaplan, John
   1983   *The Hardest Drug: Heroin and Public Policy.*
           Chicago: University of Chicago Press.

Katcher, Leo
   1959   *The Big Bankroll: The Life and Times of*
           Arnold Rothstein. New York: Harper and
           Brothers.

Katz, Leonard
   1973   *Uncle Frank: The Biography of Frank*
           Costello. New York: Drake Publishers.

Kefauver, Estes (Special Committee to Investigate Organized Crime in Interstate Commerce)
   1951a   *Third Interim Report.* Washington, DC:
           U.S. Government Printing Office.
   1951b   *Crime in America.* Garden City, NY:
           Doubleday.

Kelly, David
   1990   "U.S.: Syrians Aid Supply of Heroin."
           Chicago Tribune (December 7): 13.

Kelly, Robert J., ed.
   1986   *Organized Crime: An International Perspec-*
           tive. Totowa, NJ: Rowman and Littlefield.

Kelly, Robert J., Ko-lin Chin, and Jeffrey A. Fagan
   1993   "The Dragon Breathes Fire: Chinese Or-
           ganized Crime in New York City." *Crime,*
           Law and Social Change 19: 245–69.

Kempe, Frederick
   1990   *Divorcing the Dictator: America's Bungled*
           Affair with Noriega. New York: Putnam.

Kennedy, Robert F.
   1960   *The Enemy Within.* New York: Popular
           Library.

Kerr, Peter
   1988a   "Cocaine Glut Puts New York in Drug
           Rings' Tug-of-War." *New York Times* (Au-
           gust 24): 14.
   1988b   "Chinese Criminals Move to Broaden Role
           in U.S." *New York Times* (January 4): 1,
           12.
   1988c   "Cocaine Ring Holding Fast in Colombia."
           New York Times (May 21): 1, 5.
   1987   "New Breed of Ethnic Gangs Smuggling
           Heroin." *New York Times* (March 21): 1,
           11.
   1987b   "Chinese Now Dominate New York Her-
           oin Trade." *New York Times* (August 9): 1,
           16.

Kidner, John
   1976   *Crimaldi: Contract Killer.* Washington, DC:
           Acropolis Books.

Kihss, Peter
   1979   "John Dioguardi (Johnny Dio), 64, a Leader
           in Organized Crime, Dies." *New York Times*
           (January 16): B6.

Kilian, Michael, Connie Fletcher, and Richard P. Ciccone
   1979   *Who Runs Chicago?* New York: St. Mar-
           tin's Press.

Kimeldorf, Howard
   1988   *Reds or Rackets? The Making of Radical*
           and Conservative Unions on the Waterfront.
           Berkeley, CA: University of California Press.

Kinder, Douglas Clark
   1992   "Shutting Out the Evil: Nativism and Nar-
           cotics Control in the United States." Pp.
           117–42 in *Drug Control Policy: Essays in*
           Historical and Comparative Perspective,
           edited by William O. Walker. University
           Park, PA: Pennsylvania State University.

King, Rufus
   1969   *Gambling and Organized Crime.* Wash-
           ington, DC: Public Affairs Press.
   1963   "The Fifth Amendment Privilege and Im-
           munity Legislation." *Notre Dame Lawyer*
           38 (September): 641–54.

Kingston, Kimberly A.
    1988   "Reasonable Expectation of Privacy Cases Revive Traditional Investigative Techniques." *FBI Law Enforcement Bulletin* (November): 22–29.
Kinzer, Stephan
    1988   "Trust in Honduran Leaders Plummets with Drug Arrest." *New York Times* (May 25): 9.
Kirk, Donald
    1981   "Death of Japan Crime Boss Breeds Fear." *Miami Herald* (July 27): 17.
    1976   "Crime, Politics and Finger Chopping." *New York Times Magazine* (December 12): 60–61, 91–97.
Klatt, Wayne
    1983   "The Unlucky Love of King Mike McDonald." *Chicago Reader* (September 23): 8–9, 30–34.
Klein, Malcolm, Cheryl L. Maxson, Lea C. Cunningham
    1991   "'Crack,' Street Gangs, and Violence." *Criminology* 29 (November): 623–50.
Klein, Maury
    1986   *Life and Times of Jay Gould.* Baltimore, MD: Johns Hopkins University Press.
Klockars, Carl B.
    1974   *The Professional Fence.* New York: The Free Press.
Knapp, Whitman et al.
    1972   *Report of the Commission to Investigate Alleged Police Corruption.* New York: Braziller.
Kobler, John
    1971   *Capone: The Life and World of Al Capone.* Greenwich, CT: Fawcett.
Kobrin, Solomon
    1966   "The Conflict of Values in Delinquency Areas." Pp. 151–60 in *Juvenile Delinquency: A Book of Readings*, edited by Rose Giallombardo. New York: Wiley.
Kogan, Rick and Toni Ginnetti
    1982a   "Skin Flicks Are Reeling in Millions." *Chicago Sun-Times* (August 17): 1, 8.
    1982b   "Adult Bookstores: Source of Money for the Mob." *Chicago Sun-Times* (August 16): 1, 14.
Kornhauser, Ruth Rosner
    1978   *Social Sources of Delinquency: An Appraisal of Analytic Models.* Chicago: University of Chicago Press.
Koziol, Ronald
    1988   "U.S. May Expel Chief 'Crime Boss.'" *Chicago Tribune* (October 6): Section 3: 2.

Koziol, Ronald and Edward Baumann
    1987   "How Frank Nitti Met His Fate." *Chicago Tribune* (June 29): Sec. 5: 1, 7.
Koziol, Ronald and George Estep
    1983   "Fresh Insight Into February 14 Killings." *Chicago Tribune* (February 14): 13.
Koziol, Ronald and John O'Brien
    1992   "Reputed Mob Boss Accardo Dies." *Chicago Tribune* (May 28): Sec. 2: 1, 8.
    1988   "Tapes Detail Life Inside the Mob's Porn World." *Chicago Tribune* (September 19): 1, 6.
    1985   "Mob Inquiry's Road Show Set for Chicago Debut." *Chicago Tribune* (April 21): Sec. 2: 1, 4.
Kraar, Louis
    1988   "The Drug Trade." *Fortune* (June 20): 26–29, 32–33, 36–38.
Krajick, Kevin
    1983   "Should Police Wiretap?" *Police Magazine* (May): 29–32, 36–41.
Kramer, Jane
    1992   "Letter From Europe." *New Yorker* (September 21): 108–24.
Krauss, Clifford
    1992   "U.S. Plans to Aid Army in Peru to Fight Cocaine." *New York Times* (January 25): 4.
    1991a   "U.S. Military Team to Advise Peru in War Against Drugs and Rebels." *New York Times* (August 7): 1, 6.
    1991b   "U.S. Withholding Aid to Peru." *New York Times* (November 11): 6.
Kristof, Nicholas D.
    1993   "China Police Are Linked to Gangs in Hong Kong." *New York Times* (April 9): 7.
Kurtis, Bill
    1980   "The Caviar Connection." *New York Times Magazine* (October 26): 132–33, 136–37, 141.
Kwitny, Jonathan
    1979   *Vicious Circles: The Mafia in the Marketplace.* New York: Norton.
Labaton, Stephen
    1993   "Justices Restrict Ability to Seize Suspects' Goods." *New York Times* (June 29): 1, 8.
    1989a   "Bank to Plead Guilty to Laundering Drug Money." *New York Times* (August 11): 1, 10.
    1989b   "Banking's Technology Helps Drug Dealers Export Cash." *New York Times* (August 14): 1, 10.

Lacey, Robert
1991   *Little Man: Meyer Lansky and the Gang-ster Life.* Boston: Little, Brown.

Lamour, Catherine and Michael R. Lamberti
1974   *The International Connection: Opium From Growers to Pushers.* New York: Pantheon.

Landesco, John
1968   *Organized Crime in Chicago.* Chicago: University of Chicago Press. Originally published in 1929.

Lane, Charles, Douglas Waller, Brook Larmer, and Peter Katel
1992   "The Newest War." *Newsweek* (January 6): 18–23.

Langlais, Rudy
1978   "Inside the Heroin Trade: How a Star Double Agent Ended Up Dead." *Village Voice* (March 13): 13–15.

Lapidus, Edith J.
1974   *Eavesdropping on Trial.* Rochelle Park, NJ: Hayden Book Co.

Lasswell, Harold D. and Jerimiah B. McKenna
1972   *The Impact of Organized Crime on an Inner-City Community.* New York: Policy Sciences Center.

Latimer, Dean and Jeff Goldberg
1981   *Flowers in the Blood: The Story of Opium.* New York: Franklin Watts.

Lavigne, Yves
1987   *Hell's Angels: Taking Care of Business.* Toronto, Canada; Deneua and Wayne.

Le Vine, Steve
1990   "Alleged Drug Kingpin's Election Sends a Signal to Pakistan," *Chicago Tribune* (January 2): 6.

Lee, Felicia R.
1991   "Best Seller is a Fake, Professor Asserts." *New York Times* (October 4): 14.

Lee, Henry
1963   *How Dry We Were: Prohibition Revisited.* Englewood Cliffs, NJ: Prentice-Hall.

Lee, Rensselaer W., III
1992   "Colombia's Cocaine Syndicates." Pp. 93–124 in *War on Drugs,* edited by Alfred W. McCoy and Alan A. Block. Boulder, CO: Westview Press.

Lens, Sidney
1974   *The Labor Wars.* Garden City, NY: Doubleday.

Lerner, Steven E.
1980   "Phencyclidine Abuse in Perspective." Pp. 13–23 in *Phencyclidine Abuse Manual,* edited by Mary Tuma McAdams, Ronald L. Linder, Steven E. Lerner, and Richard Stanley Burns. Los Angeles, CA: University of California Extension.

Levine, Edward M.
1966   *The Irish and Irish Politicians.* Notre Dame, IN: University of Notre Dame Press.

Levine, Michael
1990   *Deep Cover.* New York: Delacorte.

LeVine, Steve, Betsy McKay, and Natasha Lebedeva
1993   "A Long Bloody Summer." *Newsweek* (August 30): 38–39.

Levins, Hoag
1980   "The Kabul Connection." *Philadelphia* (August): 114–20.

Lewin, Tamar
1989   "Abortion Foes Lose Appeal on Racketeer Law." *New York Times* (March 4): 1, 9.

Lewis, Norman
1964   *The Honoured Society.* New York: Putnam's.

Light, Ivan
1977   "The Ethnic Vice Industry, 1880–1944." *American Journal of Sociology* 42 (June): 464–79.

Lindberg, Richard C.
1991   *To Serve and Collect: Chicago Politics and Police Corruption From the Lager Beer Riot to the Summerdale Scandal.* New York: Praeger.

Linder, Ronald L., Steven E. Lerner, and R. Stanley Burns
1981   *PCP: The Devil's Dust.* Belmont, CA: Wadsworth.

Lindersmith, Alfred C.
1968   *Addiction and Opiates.* Chicago: Aldine.

Lipinski, Ann Marie
1989   "Poor Dream Impossible Lotto Dream," *Chicago Tribune* (April 13): Section 2: 1, 6.

Lippman, Walter
1962   "The Underworld as Servant." In *Organized Crime in America,* edited by Gus Tyler. Ann Arbor: University of Michigan Press. (Article originally published in 1931.)

Lloyd, Henry Demerest
1963   *Wealth Against Commonwealth.* Edited by Thomas C. Cochran. Englewood Cliffs, NJ: Prentice-Hall.

Logan, Andy
1970   *Against the Evidence: The Becker-Rosenthal Affair.* New York: McGraw-Hill.

Lohr, Steve
1992   "Where the Money Washes Up: Offshore Banking in the Cayman Islands." *New York Times Magazine* (March 29): 26–29, 32, 46, 52.
1985   "Taiwan Trial: Verdict, But No Motive." *New York Times* (April 10: 6.

Lombardo, Robert M.
1979   "Organized Crime and the Concept of Community." Department of Sociology, University of Illinois at Chicago. Photocopied.

Lorch, Donatella
1990   "Mourners Shot Back at Funeral." *New York Times* (July 30): 9.

Loth, David
1938   *Public Plunder: A History of Graft in America.* New York: Carrick and Evans.

Lubasch, Arnold H.
1993   "Gambino Trial Opens With Focus on Witnesses Defense Calls Liars." *New York Times* (February 2): C19.
1992a   "Death Penalty Sought At a Trial in Brooklyn." *New York Times* (April 14): 16.
1992b   "U.S. Moves to Break Up Trash Cartel." *New York Times* (August 18): B12.
1992c   "U.S. Prosecutors Say That Gotti Is Still a Functioning Crime Boss." *New York Times* (September 16): 18.
1992d   "Mobster Testifies of Bribing Juror." *New York Times* (November 5): 13.
1991a   "Ex-Mob Leader Tells Court of Killings." *New York Times* (April 26): 16.
1991b   "Jury in Windows Trial Convicts 3 of Lesser Charges and Acquits 5." *New York Times* (October 19): 12.
1986   "11 Reputed Members of Bamboo Gang Going on Trial." *New York Times* (July 30): 6.

Lundberg, Ferdinand
1968   *The Rich and the Super-Rich: A Study in the Power of Money Today.* New York: Lyle Stuart.

Lupsha, Peter A.
1991   "Drug Lords and Narco-Corruption: The Players Change But the Game Continues." *Crime, Law and Social Change* 16: 41–58.
1990   "The Geopolitics of Organized Crime: Some Comparative Models From Latin American Drug Trafficking Organizations." Paper presented at the annual meeting of the American Society of Criminology, Baltimore, November.
1987   "The President's Commission on Organized Crime." *Corruption and Reform* 2: 279–91.
1983   "Networks Versus Networking: Analysis of an Organized Crime Group." Pp. 59–87 in *Career Criminals,* edited by Gordon P. Waldo. Beverly Hills, CA: Sage.
1981   "Individual Choice, Material Culture, and Organized Crime." *Criminology* 19: 3–24.

Lupsha, Peter A. and Kip Schlegel
1980   "The Political Economy of Drug Trafficking: The Herrera Organization (Mexico and the United States)": Department of Political Science, University of New Mexico at Albuquerque. Photocopied.

Maas, Peter
1968   *The Valachi Papers.* New York: Putnam's.

MacDougall, Ernest D., ed.
1933   *Crime for Profit: A Symposium on Mercenary Crime.* Boston: Stratford.

"Mafia Poised for East Europe"
1992   *Chicago Tribune* (July 19): Sec. 7: 7.

Malcolm, Walter D. and John J. Curtin, Jr.
1968   "The New Federal Attack on the Loan Shark Problem." *Law and Contemporary Problems* 133: 765–85.

Mallowe, Mike
1993   "Disorganized Crime." *Philadelphia Magazine* (January): 72–75.

Maltz, Michael D.
1990   *Measuring the Effectiveness of Organized Crime Control Efforts.* Chicago: Office of International Criminal Justice, University of Illinois.
1976   "On Defining 'Organized Crime.'" *Crime and Delinquency* 22 (July): 338–46.

Manca, John and Vincent Cosgrove
1991   *Tin for Sale: My Career in Organized Crime and the NYPD.* New York: William Morrow.

Mangione, Jerre
1985   *A Passion for Sicilians: The World Around Danilo Dolci.* New Brunswick, NJ: Transaction Books.

Mangione, Jerre and Ben Morreale
1992   *La Storia: Five Centuries of the Italian American Experience*. New York: Harper Collins.

Mann, Arthur
1965   *La Guardia Comes to Power: 1933*. Philadelphia: Lippincott.

Markoff, John
1993   "U.S. As Big Brother of Computer Age." *New York Times* (May 6): C1, 2.

Marriott, Michel
1992   "A Mob Witness Describes Murder as a Business Tool." *New York Times* (May 28): 13.

Marsh, Harry L.
1991   "Law Enforcement, the Military, and the War on Drugs: Is the Military Involvement in the War on Drugs Ethical." *American Journal of Police* 10 (No. 2): 61–75.

Marshall, Eliot
1978   "State Lottery." *The New Republic* (June 24): 20–21.

Martin, Raymond V.
1963   *Revolt in the Mafia*. New York: Duell, Sloan, and Pearce.

Marx, Gary
1992   "Bolivia's 'Coca Diplomacy' Aims to Lift Ban." *Chicago Tribune* (December 6): 28.
1991a   "Cautious Optimism in Colombia." *Chicago Tribune* (August 4): 1, 13.
1991b   "Drug Lord, or Ghost, Stalks Colombian Town." *Chicago Tribune* (July 28): 4.
1991c   "Drug Money, Poverty Fuel Medellín's Cycle of Death." *Chicago Tribune* (February 18): 1, 6.
1991d   "Drug Trade Spreads in S. America." *Chicago Tribune* (August 18): 1, 15.
1990   "Drug War Puts Bolivian Farmers on Front Line." *Chicago Tribune* (July 16): 1, 6.

Mass, Robert
1991   "Law Enforcement Approaches to Organized Crime Infiltration of Legitimate Industry." Pp. 37–47 in *Organized Crime and Its Containment: A Transatlantic Initiative*, edited by Cyrelle Fijnaut and James Jacobs. Deventer, Netherlands: Kluwer.

Massing, Michael
1990   "In the Cocaine War, the Jungle Is Winning." *New York Times Magazine* (March 4): 26, 88, 90, 92.

May, Clifford D.
1988   "Coca-Cola Discloses an Old Secret." *New York Times* (July 1): 25, 29.

1988b   "U.S. Secretly Grows Coca to Find Way to Destroy Cocaine's Source." *New York Times* (June 12): 1, 17.

McCaffrey, Lawrence J.
1976   *The Irish Diaspora in America*. Bloomington, IN: Indiana University Press.

McClellan, John L.
1962   *Crime Without Punishment*. New York: Duell, Sloan, and Pearce.

McConaughy, John
1931   *From Cain to Capone: Racketeering Down the Ages*. New York: Brentano's.

McCoy, Alfred W.
1991   *The Politics of Heroin: CIA Complicity in the Global Drug Trade*. Brooklyn, NY: Lawrence Hill Books.
1972   *The Politics of Heroin in Southeast Asia*. New York: Harper and Row.

McFadden, Robert D.
1988   "Anthony Provenzano, 71, Ex-Teamster Chief, Dies." *New York Times* (December 13): 22.
1983   "Meyer Lansky Is Dead at 81; Financial Wizard of Organized Crime." *New York Times* (January 16): 21.

McGuinness, Robert L.
1981   "In the Katz Eye: Use of Binoculars and Telescopes." *FBI Law Enforcement Bulletin* (June): 26–31.

McGuire, Michael
1993   "Airborne Police Wage Losing Battle in Colombia Poppy Fields." *Chicago Tribune* (April 4): 6.

McGuire, Phillip C.
1988   "Jamaican Posses: A Call for Cooperation Among Law Enforcement Agencies." *Police Chief* (January): 20–27.

McIntosh, Lee
1988   "Letter to the Editor." *New York Times* (June 39): 26.

McKinley, James C., Jr.
1990   "17 Charged in Raids of Brooklyn 'Posse' Linked to 10 Deaths." *New York Times* (December 8): 1, 7.

McMahon, Colin
1992   "Illegal Wagers Now Are Safer Than Ever." *Chicago Tribune* (November 15): 1, 17.

McPhaul, Jack
1970   *Johnny Torrio: First of the Gang Lords*. New Rochelle, NY: Arlington House.

Medina, Samuel Doria
1990   "Bolivia is Trying to Dismantle Its Coca Economy." Letter to the *New York Times* (May 17): 18.

Melzack, Ronald
1990   "The Tragedy of Needless Pain." *Scientific American* 262 (February): 27–33.
Mendelson, Wallace B.
1980   *The Use and Misuse of Sleeping Pills: A Clinical Guide.* New York: Plenum.
Merlin, Mark David
1984   *On the Trail of the Ancient Opium Poppy.* Rutherford, NJ: Fairleigh Dickinson University Press.
Mermelstein, Max
1990   *The Man Who Made It Snow.* New York: Simon and Schuster.
Merriam, Charles Edward
1929   *Chicago: A More Intimate View of Urban Politics.* New York: Macmillan.
Merton, Robert
1967   *On Theoretical Sociology.* New York: The Free Press.
1964   "Anomie, Anomia, and Social Interaction." Pp. 213–42 in *Anomie and Deviant Behavior,* edited by Marshall B. Clinard. New York: Free Press.
1938   "Social Structure and Anomie." *American Sociological Review* 3: 672–82.
Meskil, Paul
1977   "Meet the New Godfather." *New York* (February 28): 28–32.
1973   *Don Carlo: Boss of Bosses.* New York: Popular Library.
Messick, Hank
1979   *Of Grass and Snow: The Secret Criminal Elite.* Englewood Cliffs, NJ: Prentice-Hall.
1973   *Lansky.* New York: Berkley.
1967   *The Silent Syndicate.* New York: Macmillan.
"Mexico: A Profile."
1985   *Drug Enforcement* (Summer): 11–18.
Mieczkowski, Thomas
1986   "Geeking Up and Throwing Down: Heroin Street Life in Detroit." *Criminology* 24 (November): 645–66.
Miller, Walter B.
1958   "Lower Class Culture as a Generating Milieu of Gang Delinquency." *Journal of Social Issues* 14: 5–21.
Mills, James
1986   *The Underground Empire: Where Crime and Governments Meet.* New York: Dell.
Mirante, Edith T.
1989   "How Opium Became Burma's Cash Crop." Letter to the *New York Times* (January 13): 24.

Mitchell, Alison
1992   "Russian Émigrés Importing Thugs to Commit Contract Crimes in U.S." *New York Times* (April 11): 1, 18.
Mokhiber, Russell
1988   *Corporate Crime and Violence: Big Business Power and the Abuse of the Public Trust.* San Francisco: Sierra Club Books.
Moldea, Dan E.
1978   *The Hoffa Wars.* New York: Charter Books.
Moody, John
1991   "A Day with the Chess Player." *Time* (July 1): 34–36.
Moore, Mark H.
1987   "Organized Crime as a Business Enterprise." Pp. 51–64 in *Major Issues in Organized Crime Control,* edited by Herbert Edelhertz. Washington, DC: U.S. Government Printing Office.
Moore, Robin and Barbara Fuca
1977   *Mafia Wife.* New York: Macmillan.
Moore, William Howard
1974   *The Kefauver Committee and the Politics of Crime.* Columbia, MO: University of Missouri Press.
Morales, Edmundo
1989   *Cocaine: White Gold Rush in Peru.* Tucson: University of Arizona Press.
1986   "Coca and Cocaine Economy and Social Change in the Andes of Peru." *Economic Development and Social Change* 35: 144–61.
Morgan, Howard Wayne
1981   *Drugs in America: A Social History, 1800–1980.* Syracuse, NY: Syracuse University Press.
Morgan, Howard Wayne, ed.
1974   *Yesterday's Addicts: American Society and Drug Abuse, 1865–1920.* Norman: University of Oklahoma Press.
Morgan, John
1985   *Prince of Crime.* New York: Stein and Day.
Morgan, John P.
1979   "The Clinical Pharmacology of Amphetamine." Pp. 3–10 in *Amphetamine Use, Misuse, and Abuse,* edited by David E. Smith. Boston, MA: G. K. Hall and Co.
Morgan, Thomas
1989   "16 Charged in Scheme to Launder Drug Millions." *New York Times* (May 14): 24.
Mori, Cesare
1933   *The Last Struggle with the Mafia.* London: Putnam.

Moseley, Ray
    1992   "Cold War's End Opens Door for Mafia in Europe." *Chicago Tribune* (December 29): 1, 6.

Mowatt, Twig
    1991   "For Killers Who Seek a New Job." *New York Times* (August 14): 4.

Mustain, Gene and Jerry Capeci
    1992   *Murder Machine: A True Story of Murder, Madness, and the Mafia.* New York: Dutton.
    1988   *Mob Star: The Story of John Gotti, The Most Powerful Criminal in America.* New York: Franklin Watts.

Musto, David
    1973   *The American Disease: Origins of Narcotic Control.* New Haven, CT: Yale University Press.

Myers, Gustavus
    1936   *History of Great American Fortunes.* New York: Modern Library

Nadelmann, Ethan A.
    1988   "U.S. Drug Policy: A Bad Export." *Foreign Policy* 70 (Spring): 83–108.

Nash, Nathaniel C.
    1992   "Cocaine Invades Chile, Scorning the Land Mines." *New York Times* (January 23): 6.
    1991a   "10 Die a Day, Or Disappear, and Peru Goes Numb." *New York Times* (July 14): 2E.
    1991b   "Peru Takes Bigger Role in Production of Cocaine," *New York Times* (July 29): 2.

Nash, Robert J.
    1981   *People to See.* New Brunswick, NJ: New Century.
    1975   *Bloodletters and Badmen: Book 3.* New York: Warner Books.

National Advisory Commission on Causes and Prevention of Violence
    1969   *Staff Report: Crimes of Violence.* Washington, DC: U.S. Government Printing Office.

National Advisory Commission on Civil Disorders
    1968   *Report.* New York: Bantam.

National Advisory Commission on Criminal Justice Standards and Goals
    1975   *A National Strategy to Reduce Crime.* New York: Avon.

National Association of Attorneys General
    1977   *Organized Crime Control Units.* Raleigh, NC: Committee on the Office of Attorneys General.

National Commission on Law Observance and Enforcement
    1931   *Report on Police.* Washington, DC: U.S. Government Printing Office.

National Commission on Marijuana and Drug Abuse
    1973   *Drug Abuse in America: Problem in Perspective.* Washington, DC: U.S. Government Printing Office.

National Commission for the Review of Federal and State Laws Relating to Wiretapping and Electronic Surveillance
    1976   *Electronic Surveillance.* Washington, DC: U.S. Government Printing Office.

Navasky, Victor S.
    1977   *Kennedy Justice.* New York: Atheneum.

Neely, Richard
    1982   "The Politics of Crime." *Atlantic Monthly* (August): 27–31.

Neff, James
    1989   *Mobbed Up: Jackie Presser's High Wire Life in the Teamsters, the Mafia, and the F.B.I.* New York: Atlantic Monthly Press.

Nelli, Humbert S.
    1976   *The Business of Crime.* New York: Oxford University Press.
    1969   "Italians and Crime in Chicago: The Formative Years; 1890–1920." *American Journal of Sociology* 74 (January): 373–91.

Nelson, Jack E., Helen Wallenstein Pearson, Mollie Sawyers and Thomas J. Glynn
    1982   *Guide to Drug Abuse Research Terminology.* Rockville, MD: National Institute on Drug Abuse.

"New Gang Methods Replace Those of Eastman's Days."
    1923   *New York Times* (September 9): Sec. 9: 3.

New Jersey State Commission of Investigation (NJSCI)
    1987   *Report and Recommendations on Organized Crime-Affiliated Subcontractors at Casino and Public Construction Sites.* Trenton, NJ: NJSCI.

New York State Commission of Investigation (NYSCI)
    1978   *A Report on Fencing: The Sale and Distribution of Stolen Property.* New York: NYSCI
    1970   *Racketeer Infiltration Into Legitimate Business.* New York: NYSCI.

New York State Organized Crime Task Force (NYSOCTF)
    1988   *Corruption and Racketeering in the New York City Construction Industry.* Ithaca, NY: Cornell University School of Labor and Industrial Relations.

Newell, Barbara Warne
    1961   *Chicago and the Labor Movement: Metropolitan Unionism in the 1930s.* Urbana, IL: University of Illinois Press.

Newfield, Jack
    1979   "The Myth of Godfather Journalism." *Village Voice* (July 23): 1, 11–13.

Nicodemus, Charles and Art Petacque
1981   "Mob Jewel Fencing Investigated." *Chicago Sun-Times* (November 29): 5, 76.

Nietschmann, Bernard
1987   "Drugs-for-Guns Cycle Produces Bitter Ironies," Letter to the *New York Times* (August 28): 22.

"Nigerian Connection, The"
1991   *Newsweek* (October 7): 43.

Nocera, Joseph
1988   "Drexel: Hanged Without a Trial." *New York Times* (December 30): 19.

Nolan, Frederick
1992   *The Lincoln County War: A Documentary History*. Norman: University of Oklahoma Press.

Nordheimer, Jon
1986   "Police Arrests Plague South Florida." *New York Times* (August 3): 15.

North, James
1988   "Meet Roberto Fernandez, a Bolivian Father and Coca User." *Chicago Tribune* (September 7): 21.

O'Brien, Edward I.
1986   "RICO's Assault on Legitimate Business." *New York Times* (January 5): Sec. F2.

O'Brien, John
1992   "74-Year-Old South Suburban Crime Boss Gets 32 Years." *Chicago Tribune* (March 27): Sec. 2: 4.

1988   "Car-Theft Figure Slain at His Home." *Chicago Tribune* (August 16): Sec. 2: 3.

1983   "Gambling Boss Ken Eto Tells of Mob Murder and Intrigue." *Chicago Tribune* (May 16): Sec. 2: 1.

O'Brien Joseph F. and Andris Kurins
1991   *Boss of Bosses: The FBI and Paul Castellano*. New York: Dell.

O'Brien, Robert and Sidney Cohen
1984   *Encyclopedia of Drug Abuse*. New York: Facts on File.

O'Connor, Len
1984   "Give Me That Old-Time Politics." *Chicago Magazine* (February): 114–19.

O'Connor, Matt
1993a "2 Ex-Chicago Heights Officers Get 30 Years." *Chicago Tribune* (February 26): Sec. 2: 3.

1993b "2nd Officer Admits Case Was Bogus." *Chicago Tribune* (March 10): Sec. 2: 2.

O'Connor, Philip J. and Maurice Possley
1982   "Thai Envoy Seeking Immunity in Drug Case." *Chicago Sun-Times* (May 30): 34.

O'Connor, Richard
1962   *Gould's Millions*. Garden City, NY: Doubleday.

1958   *Hell's Kitchen*. Philadelphia: Lippincott.

Okada, Daniel W.
1992   "Asian Gangs: What Are We Talking About?" Paper presented at the Annual Meeting of the American Society of Criminology, November, New Orleans.

O'Neill, Gerard and Dick Lehr
1989   *The Underboss: The Rise and Fall of a Mafia Family*. New York: St. Martin's.

Overly, Don H. and Theodore H. Schell
1973   *New Effectiveness Measures for Organized Crime Control Efforts*. Washington, DC: U.S. Government Printing Office.

Packer, Herbert L.
1968   *The Limits of the Criminal Sanction*. Stanford, CA: Stanford University Press.

Palsey, Fred D.
1971   *Al Capone: The Biography of a Self-Made Man*. Freeport, NY: Books for Libraries Press. Originally published in 1931.

Pantaleone, Michele
1966   *The Mafia and Politics*. New York: Coward and McCann.

Passell, Peter
1991   "Coca Dreams, Cocaine Reality." *New York Times* (August 14): C2.

PCOC, see President's Commission on Organized Crime.

Pear, Robert
1992   "2 Nations Seize 165 Linked to Drug-Cash Laundering." *New York Times* (September 29): 1, 7.

1989a "Cubans Disclose A Drug Network." *New York Times* (June 24): 1, 4.

1989b "Cuban General and Three Others Executed for Sending Drugs to U.S." *New York Times* (July 14): 2.

Pearce, Frank
1981   "Organized Crime and Class Politics." Pp. 157–81 in *Crime and Capitalism*, edited by David F. Greenberg. Palo Alto, CA: Mayfield.

Pennsylvania Crime Commission (PCC)
1992   *Racketeering and Organized Crime in the Bingo Industry*. Conshohocken, PA: PCC.

1991   *1991 Report*. Conshohocken, PA: PCC.

1990   *Organized Crime in Pennsylvania: A Decade of Change, 1990 Report*. Conshohocken, PA: PCC.

1989   *1989 Report*. Conshohocken, PA: PCC.

1988   *1988 Report*. Conshohocken, PA: PCC.

1980   *A Decade of Organized Crime: 1980 Report*. Saint Davids, PA: PCC.

Permanent Subcommittee on Investigations (PSI)

1984   *Profile of Organized Crime: Great Lakes Region*. Washington, DC: U.S. Government Printing Office.

1983a   *Crime and Secrecy: The Use of Offshore Banks and Companies*. Washington, DC: U.S. Government Printing Office.

1983b   *Organized Crime in Chicago* (March 4). Washington, DC: U.S. Government Printing Office.

1983c   *Profile of Organized Crime: Mid-Atlantic Region* (February 15, 23, 24). Washington, DC: U.S. Government Printing Office.

1983d   *Staff Study of Crime and Secrecy: The Use of Offshore Banks and Companies*. Washington, DC: U.S. Government Printing Office.

1982   *Hotel Employees and Restaurant Employees International Union: Part I* (June 22, 23). Washington, DC: U.S. Government Printing Office.

1981a   *International Narcotics Trafficking*. Washington, DC: U.S. Government Printing Office.

1981b   *Waterfront Corruption*. Washington, DC: U.S. Government Printing Office.

1981c   *Witness Security Program*. Washington, DC: U.S. Government Printing Office.

1980a   *Organized Crime and the Use of Violence: Part I*. Washington, DC: U.S. Government Printing Office.

1980b   *Organized Crime and the Use of Violence: Part II*. Washington, DC: U.S. Government Printing Office.

1978   *Organized Crime Activities: South Florida and United States Penitentiary, Atlanta, Georgia (August 1, 2, 3, 9, 10): Part I*. Washington, DC: U.S. Government Printing Office.

1971   *Organized Crime and Stolen Securities: Part I*. Washington, DC: U.S. Government Printing Office.

Petacco, Arrigo

1974   *Joe Petrosino*. New York: Macmillan.

Petacque, Art and Hugh Hough

1983   "'Banker' Holds Lansky Secrets." *Chicago Sun-Times* (January 23): 9.

Peterson, Virgil

1983a   *The Mob: 200 Years of Organized Crime in New York*. Ottawa, IL: Green Hill Publishers.

1983b   "The Career of a Syndicate Boss." Pp. 506–26 in *Hotel Employees and Restaurant Employees International Union: Organized Crime in Chicago*. Hearings of the Permanent Subcommittee on Investigations. Washington, DC: U.S. Government Printing Office.

1969   *A Report on Chicago Crime for 1968*. Chicago Crime Commission.

1963   "Chicago: Shades of Capone." *Annals* 347 (May): 30–39.

1962   "Career of a Syndicate Boss." *Crime and Delinquency* 8 (October): 339–49.

Physicians' Desk Reference

1988   Oradell, NJ: Medical Economics Co.

1987   Oradell, NJ: Medical Economics Co.

Pileggi, Nicholas

1985   *Wise Guy: Life in a Mafia Family*. New York: Pocket Books.

1982   "There's No Business Like Drug Business." *New York* (December 13): 38–43.

Pistone, Joseph D.

1992   *The Ceremony: The Mafia Initiation Tapes*. New York: Dell.

1987   *Donnie Brasco: My Undercover Life in the Mafia*. New York: New American Library.

Pitkin, Thomas Monroe and Francesco Cordasco

1977   *The Black Hand: A Chapter in Ethnic Crime*. Totowa, NJ: Littlefield, Adams.

Plate, Thomas and the Editors of *New York*, eds.

1972   *The Mafia at War*. New York: New York Magazine Press.

Poethig, Margaret

1988   "Q & A: Seizing the Assets of Drug Traffickers." *Compiler* 8 (Winter): 11–12.

"Police Blotter"

1979   *New York Times* (May 17): B4.

Pooley, Eric

1992   "Cop Stars." *New York* (March 16): 43–49.

Posner, Gerald L.

1988   *Warlords of Crime: Chinese Secret Societies—the New Mafia*. New York: McGraw-Hill.

Post, Henry

1981   "The Whorehouse Sting." *New York* (February 2): 31–34.

Potter, Gary, Larry Gaines, and Beth Holbrook

1990   "Blowing Smoke: An Evaluation of Marijuana Eradication in Kentucky." *American Journal of Police* 9: 97–116.

1989   "The Retail Pornography Industry and the Organizing of Crime." Paper presented at the annual meeting of Academy of Criminal Justice Sciences, Washington, DC, March 28–April 1.

Potts, Mark, Nicholas Kochan, and Robert Whittington
1992   *Dirty Money. BCCI: The Inside Story of the World's Sleaziest Bank.* Washington, DC: National Press Books.

Powis, Robert E.
1992   *The Money Launderers.* Chicago: Probus.

Prall, Robert H. and Norton Mockridge
1951   *This is Costello.* New York: Gold Medal Books.

President's Commission on Law Enforcement and Administration of Justice
1968   *The Challenge of Crime in a Free Society.* New York: Avon.

President's Commission on Organized Crime (PCOC)
1986a   *The Impact: Organized Crime Today.* Washington, DC: U.S. Government Printing Office.

1986b   *The Edge: Organized Crime, Business, and Labor Unions.* Washington, DC: U.S. Government Printing Office.

1986c   *America's Habit: Drug Abuse, Drug Trafficking, and Organized Crime.* Washington, DC: U.S. Government Printing Office.

1985a   *Organized Crime and Labor-Management Racketeering in the United States.* Washington, DC: U.S. Government Printing Office.

1985b   *Materials on Ethical Issues for Lawyers Involved With Organized Crime Figures.* Photocopied.

1984a   *Organized Crime and Cocaine Trafficking.* Washington, DC: U.S. Government Printing Office.

1984b   *Organized Crime of Asian Origin.* Washington, DC: U.S. Government Printing Office.

1984c   *The Cash Connection: Organized Crime, Financial Institutions, and Money Laundering.* Washington, DC: U.S. Government Printing Office.

"Profaci Dies of Cancer, Led Feuding Brooklyn Mob."
1962   *New York Times* (June 8): 32.

PSI (See Permanent Subcommittee on Investigations)

Quinney, Richard
1974   *Critique of the Legal Order.* Boston: Little, Brown.

Raab, Selwyn
1993   "FBI Arrests a Mafia Boss in New Jersey." *New York Times* (January 20): B1, B6.

1992a   "Mafia Family in New York Linked to Newspaper Fraud." *New York Times* (July 8): C3.

1992b   "'Most Dangerous Mafia Left' at Helm of Lucchese Crime Family." *New York Times* (November 28): 14.

1992c   "Top Member of Colombo Crime Family Is Ambushed in Brooklyn." *New York Times* (December 30): 13.

1990   "Racketeering Held to Persist at New York's Fish Market." *New York Times* (August 9): B12.

1989   "Mafia-Aided Scheme Evades Millions in Gas Taxes." *New York Times* (February 20): 1, 7.

1987   "Floating Museum is Called Target of Racketeers." *New York Times* (April 4): 9.

1984a   "The Drug Pipeline From Europe to New York." *New York Times* (May 21): 1, 13.

1984b   "U.S. Inquiry Finds Gangsters Hold Grip on Kennedy Cargo." *New York Times* (September 30): 1, 18.

"Racket Chief Slain by Gangster Gunfire." *New York Times*
1931   (April 16): 1.

Rakove, Milton L.
1975   *Don't Make No Waves, Don't Back No Losers.* Bloomington: Indiana University Press.

Ramirez, Anthony
1993   "F.B.I.'s Proposal on Wiretaps Draws Criticism From G.S.A." *New York Times* (January 15): 8.

Rangel, Jesus
1988   "10 Are Convicted for Corruption." *New York Times* (November 20): 25.

Ray, Oakley
1978   *Drugs, Society, and Human Behavior.* St. Louis: C.V. Mosby.

Reagan, Ronald
1986   "Declaring War on Organized Crime." *New York Times Magazine* (January 12): 26, 28, 47, 55–57, 62, 65, 84.

Reckless, Walter
1969   *Vice in Chicago.* Montclair, NJ: Patterson Smith.

Reece, Jack
1973   "Fascism, the Mafia, and the Emergence of Sicilian Separatism." *Journal of Modern History* 45 (June): 261–76.

Reedy, George E.
1991   *From the Ward to the White House: The Irish in American Politics.* New York: Scribner's.

Rehfeld, Barry
1984   "The Crass Menagerie." *New York* (October 15): 50–53.

Reid, Ed
1970   *The Grim Reapers.* New York: Bantam.

Reid, Ed and Ovid Demaris
1964   *The Green Felt Jungle.* New York: Cardinal Paperbacks.
1953   *The Shame of New York.* New York: Random House.

Reif, Rita
1984   "Gould Jewels to be Sold at Auction." *New York Times* (January 3): 21.

Reinhold, Robert
1989   "California Shaken Over an Informer." *New York Times* (February 17): 9.

Reisman, W. Michael
1979   *Folded Lies: Bribery, Crusades, and Reforms.* New York: Free Press.

Repetto, Thomas A.
1978   *The Blue Parade.* New York: Free Press.

Reuter, Peter
1992   "The Limits and Consequences of U.S. Foreign Drug Control Efforts." *Annals* 521 (May): 151–62.
1987   *Racketeering in Legitimate Industries: A Study in the Economics of Intimidation.* Santa Monica, CA: RAND Corporation.
1983   *Disorganized Crime.* Cambridge, MA: MIT Press.

Reuter, Peter, Robert MacCoun, and Patrick Murphy
1990   *Money From Crime: A Study of the Economics of Drug Dealing in Washington, D.C.* Santa Monica, CA: RAND.

Reuter, Peter, Jonathan Rubinstein, and Simon Wynn
1983   *Racketeering in Legitimate Industries: Two Case Studies. Executive Summary.* Washington, DC: U.S. Government Printing Office.

Rhodes, Robert P.
1984   *Organized Crime: Crime Control vs. Civil Liberties.* New York: Random House.

Rice, Berkeley
1988   "The Cocaine Express." *The Business World (New York Times Special Magazine,* March 27): 74–76.

Richardson, James F.
1975   "The Early Years of the New York Police Department." Pp. 15–23 in *Police in America*, edited by Jerome Skolnick and Thomas C. Gray. Boston: Little, Brown.

Ridenhour, Ron
1992   "Capitalism in the Underworld." *New Orleans Magazine* (October): 47–49, 90–96.

Riding, Alan
1989   "Rebels Disrupting Coca Eradication Efforts." *New York Times* (January 26): 6.
1988a   "Brazil Now a Vital Crossroad for Latin Cocaine Traffickers." *New York Times* (August 28): 1, 8.
1988b   "Drug Lords Acquire Colombian Ranches and Win New Allies." *New York Times* (December 21): 1, 6.
1987a   "Colombian Envoy Shot in Budapest." *New York Times* (January 14): 5.
1987b   "Colombia Effort Against Drugs Hits Dead End." *New York Times* (August 20): 4.
1984   "Shaken Colombia Acts at Last on Drugs." *New York Times* (September 11): 1, 6.

Ring, Wilson
1991   "Robinson and 6 Rukns Guilty of Murder." *Chicago Tribune* (September 2): 1, 6.
1989   "Poppy Fields Sprout Crisis in Guatemala." *Chicago Tribune* (July 23): 19.
1988   "Local Hero Can't Run From His Reputation as Drug-Dealer King." *Chicago Tribune* (March 2): 16.

Riordon, William L.
1963   *Plunkett of Tammany Hall.* New York: Dutton.

Robbins, Lee N.
1974   *The Vietnam Drug User Returns.* Washington, DC: U.S. Government Printing Office.
1973   *A Followup of Vietnam Drug Users.* Washington, DC: U.S. Government Printing Office.

Robbins, Lee N., John E. Helzer, Michi Hesselbrock, and Eric Wish
1980   "Vietnam Veterans Three Years After Vietnam: How Our Study Changed Our View of Heroin." Pp. 213–30 in *The Yearbook of Substance Use and Abuse*, vol. 2, edited by Leon Brill and Charles Winick. New York: Human Sciences Press.

Robbins, William
  1988   "Armed, Sophisticated and Violent, Two Drug Gangs Blanket Nation." *New York Times* (November 25): 1, 9.
  1984   "Trial Offers a Glimpse Inside the Mafia." *New York Times* (October 29): 15.

Roberton, Robert J.
  1986   "Designer Drugs: The Analog Game." Pp. 91–96 in *Bridging Services: Drug Abuse, Human Services and the Therapeutic Community,"* edited by Alfonso Acampora and Ethan Nebelkopf. New York: World Federation of Therapeutic Communities.

Roberts, Sam
  1992   "In This Corner of New York, Tammany Still Reigns." *New York Times* (September 28): A13.
  1984   "A Profile of the New American Mafia: Old Bosses and New Competition." *New York Times* (October 4): 1, 18.

Robinson, Linda
  1991   "Still a Cocaine Crossroads." *U.S. News and World Report* (April 15): 47–48.

Robinson, Louis N.
  1933   "Social Values and Mercenary Crime." Pp. 13–31 in *Crime for Profit: A Symposium on Mercenary Crime*, edited by Ernest D. MacDougall. Boston: Stratford Company.

Roebuck, Julian and Wolfgang Frese
  1976   *The Rendezvous: A Case Study of an After Hours Club.* New York: Free Press.

Rohter, Larry
  1991a   "A Cocaine Baron's Tales of Intrigue and Greed Liven Up Noriega's Trial." *New York Times* (November 24): E3.
  1991b   "From Brazil to Peru to Jamaica, Gun Smugglers Flock to Florida." *New York Times* (August 11): 1, 13.
  1990   "Drug Fight Targets U.S. Chemicals." *New York Times* (May 13): 4.
  1989a   "Bandit Wears a Halo in an Unsaintly City." *New York Times* (May 11): 7.
  1989b   "Mexico Captures Top Drug Figure and 80 Policemen." *New York Times* (April 11): 1, 6.
  1988   "Who Is the Enemy in Mexico Drug War?" *New York Times* (July 24): 7.

Rome, Florence
  1975   *The Tattooed Men.* New York: Delacorte.

Romoli, Kathleen
  1941   *Colombia.* Garden City, NY: Doubleday, Doran.

Rosecan, Jeffrey S., Henry I. Spitz, and Barbara Gross
  1987   "Contemporary Issues in the Treatment of Cocaine Abuse." Pp. 299–323 in *Cocaine Abuse: New Directions in Treatment and Research*, edited by Henry I. Spitz and Jeffrey S. Rosecan. New York: Brunner/Mazel.

Rosen, Charles
  1978   *Scandals of '51: How the Gamblers Almost Killed College Basketball.* New York: Holt, Rinehart and Winston.

Rosenthal, Andrew
  1988   "Inquiry Raises Questions on Anonymous Sources." *New York Times* (June 27): 9.

Ross, Irwin
  1992   *Shady Business: Confronting Corporate Corruption.* New York: Twentieth Century Fund Press.
  1980   "How Lawless Are the Big Companies?" *Fortune* (December 1): 57–58, 62–64.

Rothmiller, Mike and Ivan G. Goldman
  1992   *L.A. Secret Police: Inside the LAPD Elite Spy Network.* New York: Pocket Books.

Rottenberg, Dan
  1983   "Book Review of 'Wall Street Journal: The Story of Dow Jones and the Nation's Business Newspaper.'" *Chicago* (January): 90–91.

Rowell, Earle Albert and Robert Rowell
  1939   *On the Trail of Marijuana: The Weed of Madness.* Mountain View, CA: Pacific Press.

Royko, Mike
  1971   *Boss: Richard J. Daley of Chicago.* New York: Dutton.

Rubinstein, Jonathan
  1973   *City Police.* New York: Farrar, Straus and Giroux.

Rubinstein, Jonathan and Peter Reuter
  1978a   "Fact, Fancy, and Organized Crime." *Public Interest* 53 (Fall): 45–67.
  1978b   "Bookmaking in New York." New York: Policy Sciences Center (Preliminary, unpublished draft).
  1977   "Numbers: The Routine Racket." New York: Policy Sciences Center (Preliminary, unpublished draft).

Rudolph, Robert
  1992   *The Boys from New Jersey.* New York: Morrow.

Ruggerio, Vincenzo
1993   "The Camorra: 'Clean' Capital and Orga-
        nised Crime." Pp. 141–61 in *Global Crime
        Connections: Dynamics and Control*, edited
        by Frank Pearce and Michael Woodiwiss.
        Toronto, Canada: University of Toronto Press.

Rugoff, Milton
1989   *America's Gilded Age: Intimate Portraits
        from an Era of Extravagance and Change,
        1850–1890*. New York: Henry Holt.

Russell, Francis
1975   *A City in Terror—1919—The Boston Police
        Strike*. New York: Viking.

Salerno, Joseph and Stephen J. Rivele
1990   *The Plumber*. New York: Knightsbridge Pub-
        lishing Co.

Salerno, Ralph and John S. Tompkins
1969   *The Crime Confederation*. Garden City,
        NY: Doubleday.

Saney, Parviz
1986   *Crime and Culture in America: A Compar-
        ative Perspective*. New York: Greenwood.

Sanger, David E.
1992   "Top Japanese Party Leaders Accused of
        Links to Mobsters." *New York Times* (Sep-
        tember 23): 1, 4.

Sann, Paul
1971   *Kill the Dutchman: The Story of Dutch
        Schultz*. New York: Popular Library.

Sante, Luc
1991   *Low Life*. New York: Vintage.

Sawyers, June
1988a   "A 'King' Who Had Us In His Pocket."
        Chicago Tribune Magazine (October 2): 10.
1988b   "Who, Everyone Wanted to Know, Killed
        McSwiggin?" *Chicago Tribune Magazine*
        (November 27): 9.
1987   "Hinky Dink and Bathhouse John's 'Carni-
        val of Evil.'" *Chicago Tribune Magazine*
        (January 25): 7.

Saxon, Wolfgang
1990   "Harry Bridges, Docks Leader, Dies at 88."
        New York Times (March 31): 11.

Schatzberg, Rufus
1993   *Black Organized Crime in Harlem: 1920–
        1930*. New York: Garland.

Schelling, Thomas C.
1971   "What Is the Business of Organized Crime?"
        American Scholar 40 (Autumn): 643–52.

Schmetzer, Uli
1993   "China Official Decries Ills Ignited by Re-
        form." *Chicago Tribune* (April 9): 6.

1991a   "'Nigerian Connection' Ties Chicago to
        Asian Drugs." *Chicago Tribune* (December
        21): 1, 11.
1991b   "Slave Trade Survives, Prospers Across Asia."
        Chicago Tribune (November 15): 1, 18.
1990   "'Prince of Death' Is a Wanted Man."
        Chicago Tribune (March 21): 21.
1988a   "Sicily: Artist Packs 'em in Despite His
        Many Brushes With the Law." *Chicago
        Tribune* (January 13): 16.
1988b   "Defiant Mayor Vows to Hit Sicily's Ma-
        fia." *Chicago Tribune* (October 9): 18.
1987   "Godfather's Shadow Still Darkens Town
        Notorious for Death." *Chicago Tribune* (De-
        cember 28): 14.
1985   "A City Whose Kids are Hired to Kill."
        Chicago Tribune (October 13): 4.
1982   "Naples Mafia—Slaughter With a Venge-
        ance." *Chicago Tribune* (March 7): Sec. 3:
        1.

Schmidt, William E.
1984   "New Era, New Problems for South's Sher-
        iffs." *New York Times* (September 10): 1,
        15.

Schneider, Keith
1988   "Marijuana Once Reigned as King." *New
        York Times* (January 26): 8.

Schnepper, Jeff A.
1978   *Inside the IRS*. New York: Stein and Day.

Schodolski, Vincent J.
1988   "In Soviet Union, Mob Czars Are Sticking
        to the Script." *Chicago Tribune* (December
        26): 5.

Schoenberg, Robert J.
1992   *Mr. Capone*. New York: William Morrow.

Schorr, Mark
1979   "The .22 Caliber Killings." *New York* (May
        7): 43–46.
1978   "Gunfight in the Cocaine Corral." *New
        York Times Magazine* (September 25): 48–57.

"Schultz Aide Slain; 7th in Five Months."
1931   *New York Times* (June 22): 2.

"Schultz Product of Dry Law Era."
1933   *New York Times* (January 22): 23.

"Schultz Succumbs to Bullet Wounds Without Naming
Slayers."
1935   *New York Times* (October 25): 1.

Schur, Edwin H.
1962   *Narcotic Addiction in Britain and America*.
        Bloomington, IN: Indiana University.

Schwartz, Herman
1968   "Wiretapping Problem Today." Pp. 156–68 in *Criminological Controversies*, edited by Richard Knudten. New York: Appleton-Century-Crofts.

Sciascia, Leonard
1963   *Mafia Vendetta*. New York: Knopf.

Sciolino, Elaine
1989   "U.S. Urging Afghan Rebels to Limit Growing of Opium." *New York Times* (March 26): 6.
1988   "Diplomats Do Not Hurry to Enlist in the War on Drugs." *New York Times* (February 21): E3.

Sciolino, Elaine and Stephen Engelberg
1988   "Narcotics Effort Foiled by U.S. Security Goals." *New York Times* (April 10): 1, 10.

Sciolino, Elaine and Jeff Gerth
1992   "Bank Charges Embarrass the Saudis." *New York Times* (August 2): 11.

Scott, W. Richard
1981   *Organizations: Rational, Natural, and Open Systems*. Englewood Cliffs, NJ: Prentice-Hall.

Scott, Peter Dale and Jonathan Marshall
1991   *Cocaine Politics: Drugs, Armies, and the CIA in Central America*. Berkeley: University of California Press.

Seedman, Albert A.
1974   *Chief!* New York: Arthur Fields.

Seidman, Harold
1938   *Labor Czars: A History of Labor Racketeering*. New York: Liveright.

Seigel, Max H.
1977   "14, Including Alleged Charter Member of Purple Gang, Charged in Heroin Conspiracy." *New York Times* (December 20): 27.

Serao, Ernesto
1911a   "The Truth About the Camorra." *Outlook* 98 (July 28): 717–26.
1911b   "The Truth About the Camorra: Part II." *Outlook* (August 50): 778–87.

Serio, Joseph
1992a   "Organized Crime in the Soviet Union and Beyond." *Low Intensity Conflict and Law Enforcement* 1 (Autumn): 127–51.
1992b   "Shunning Tradition: Ethnic Organized Crime in the Former Soviet Union." *CJ International* 8 (November-December): 5–6.

Serrin, William
1989   "Jackie Presser's Secret Lives Detailed in Government Files." *New York Times* (March 27): 1, 11.

Servadio, Gaia
1976   *Mafioso: A History of the Mafia from its Origins to the Present Day*. Briarcliff Manor, NY: Stein and Day.
1974   *Angelo LaBarbera: The Profile of a Mafia Boss*. London: Quartet Books.

Shannon, Elaine
1991   "New Kings of Coke." *Time* (July 1): 29–33.
1988   *Desperados: Latin Drug Lords, U.S. Lawmen, and the War America Can't Win*. New York: Viking.

Shannon, William V.
1989   *The American Irish: A Political and Social Portrait*. Amherst, MA: University of Massachusetts.

Shapiro, Margaret
1993   "Perils of Kiosk Capitalism." *Washington Post* (August 28): 15, 18.

Shaw, Clifford and Henry D. McKay
1972   *Juvenile Delinquency and Urban Areas*. Chicago: University of Chicago Press. Originally published in 1942.

Shaw, David
1984   *Press Watch*. New York: Macmillan.

Shawcross, Tim and Martin Young
1987   *Men of Honour: The Confessions of Tommaso Buscetta*. London: Collins.

Shenon, Philip
1990   "Peru Drug Fund Used in War, Aide Says." *New York Times* (June 21): 3.
1988   "Enemy Within: Drug Money is Corrupting the Enforcers." *New York Times* (April 11): 1, 8.
1986   "U.S. Crime Panel: Discord to the End." *New York Times* (April 6): 9.

Sheppard, Nathaniel Jr.
1993   "Drug Money Clouds Skyline of Panama City." *Chicago Tribune* (January 31): 21.
1992   "Panama Still Conduit for Drugs and Money." *Chicago Tribune* (April 11): 1, 6.
1991a   "In Panama, Drug War is Corrupted." *Chicago Tribune* (May 26): 19.
1991b   "In Panama's Drug Capital, Small Police Unit Faces Uphill Fight." *Chicago Tribune* (January 31): 23.
1990a   "Guatemalan Climate: Good for Poppy Fields, Drug Traffickers." *Chicago Tribune* (September 23): 12.
1990b   "Drug Lords Easily Flee Panama Jails." *Chicago Tribune* (October 7): 22.

Sheridan, Walter
1972   *The Fall and Rise of Jimmy Hoffa*. New York: Saturday Review Press.

Sherman, Lawrence W.
1978   *Scandal and Reform: Controlling Police Corruption*. Berkeley: University of California Press.
1974   *Police Corruption: A Sociological Perspective*. Garden City, NY: Doubleday.

Shipp, E. R.
1985a   "Chicago Gang Sues to be Recognized as Religion." *New York Times* (December 27): 8.
1985b   "Former Chief of Teamsters Ordered to Jail Next Month." *New York Times* (April 25): 12.

Short, James F., Jr., ed.
1968   *Gang Delinquency and Delinquent Subcultures*. New York: Harper and Row.

Siciliano, Vincent
1970   *Unless They Kill Me First*. New York: Hawthorn Books.

"Siegel, Gangster, Is Slain on Coast."
1947   *New York Times* (June 22): 1.

Simmons, Marlise
1984a   "Peruvian Rebels Halt U.S. Drive Against Cocaine." *New York Times* (August 13): 1, 6.
1984b   "Revolt in Bolivia Embarrasses U.S." *New York Times* (July 17): 1, 5.

Sinclair, Andrew
1989   "J.P. Morgan, Where Are You Now That We Need You?" *Manhattan, Inc.* (March): 88–93.
1962   *The Era of Excess: A Social History of Prohibition Movement*. Boston: Little, Brown.

Skolnick, Jerome H.
1978   *House of Cards: Legalization and Control of Casino Gambling*. Boston: Little, Brown.

Skolnick, Jerome H., Theodore Correl, Elizabeth Navarro, and Roger Rabb
1990   "The Social Structure of Street Drug Dealing." *American Journal of Police* 9: 1–41.

Sloane, Arthur A.
1992   *Hoffa*. Cambridge, MA: MIT Press.

Smith, Alson J.
1962   "The Early Chicago Story." Pp. 138–46 in *Organized Crime in America*, edited by Gus Tyler. Ann Arbor: University of Michigan Press.

Smith, David E., ed.
1979   *Amphetamine Use, Misuse, and Abuse*. Boston, MA: G.K. Hall and Co.

Smith, Dwight C., Jr.
1982   "Paragons, Pariahs, and Pirates: A Spectrum-Based Theory of Enterprise." *Crime and Delinquency* 26 (July): 358–86.
1978   "Organized Crime and Entrepreneurship." *International Journal of Criminology and Penology* 6: 161–77.
1975   *The Mafia Mystique*. New York: Basic Books.

Smith, Dwight C., Jr., and Ralph Salerno
1970   "The Use of Strategies in Organized Crime Control." *Journal of Law, Criminology and Police Science* 61: 101–11.

Smith, Peter H.
1987   "Uneasy Neighbors: Mexico and the United States." *Current History* 86 (March): 97–100, 130–32.

Smith, Richard Austin
1961a   "The Incredible Electrical Conspiracy." *Fortune* (May): 161–64, 210, 212, 217–18, 221–24.
1961b   "The Incredible Electrical Conspiracy." *Fortune* (April): 132–37, 170, 175–76, 179–80.

Smith, Richard Norton
1982   *Thomas E. Dewey and His Times*. New York: Simon and Schuster.

Smith, Sherwin D.
1963   "35 Years Ago Arnold Rothstein Was Mysteriously Murdered and Left a Racket Empire Up for Grabs." *New York Times Magazine* (October 27): 96.

Smothers, Ronald
1992   "Many State Lotteries Feel the Pinch of Recession, and Perhaps Monotony." *New York Times* (February 2): 10.

Snyder, Solomon H.
1989   *Brainstorming: The Science of Politics and Opiate Research*. Cambridge, MA: Harvard University Press.
1977   "Opiate Receptors and Internal Opiates." *Scientific American* (March): 44–56.

"Son Gains Control of Mob, FBI Says: Bureau Asserts Patriarca is New England Mafia Chief."
1984   *New York Times* (October 28): 31.

Sondern, Frederic, Jr.
1959   *Brotherhood of Evil: The Mafia*. New York: Farrar, Straus and Cudahy.

Special Committee to Investigate Organized Crime in Interstate Commerce
1951   *Kefauver Crime Report*. New York: Arco.

Spence, Richard T.
   1989   *Current Substance Abuse Trends in Texas.* Austin: Texas Commission on Alcohol and Drug Abuse.
Spergel, Irving
   1964   *Racketville, Slumtown, Haulberg.* Chicago: University of Chicago Press.
Spiering, Frank
   1976   *The Man Who Got Capone.* Indianapolis: Bobbs-Merrill.
"Spotlight"
   1981   *Chicago Crime Commission Searchlight* (October): 8.
Stahl, Marc B.
   1992   "Asset Forfeiture, Burdens of Proof and the War on Drugs." *Journal of Criminal Law and Criminology* 83: 274–337.
Stanley, Alessandra
   1992   "When the Gangster Becomes the Gangster Movie." *New York Times* (February 21): B1, 9.
State Commission of Investigation
   1989   *Solid Waste Regulation.* Trenton, NJ: New Jersey State Commission of Investigation.
Steffens, Lincoln
   1957   *The Shame of the Cities.* New York: Hill and Wang. Originally published in 1904.
   1931   *The Autobiography of Lincoln Steffens.* New York: Chautauqua Press. Republished by Harcourt, Brace & World in 1958.
Steinberg, Alfred
   1972   *The Bosses.* New York: New American Library.
Sterling, Claire
   1990   *Octopus: The Long Reach of the Sicilian Mafia.* New York: Simon and Schuster.
Sterngold, James
   1992a   "Japan Takes on Mob, and the Mob Fights Back." *New York Times* (June 15): 1, 6.
   1992b   "Mob and Politics Intersect, Fueling Cynicism in Japan." *New York Times* (October 21): 1, 4.
   1992c   "Corporate Japan's Unholy Allies." *New York Times* (December 6): Sec. 3: 1, 6.
Stewart, Robert C.
   1980   *Identification and Investigation of Organized Criminal Activity.* Houston: National College of District Attorneys.

Stevens, Jay
   1987   *Storming Heaven: LSD and the American Dream.* New York: Atlantic Monthly Press.
Stille, Alexander
   1993   "Letter From Palermo: The Mafia's Biggest Mistake." *New Yorker* (March 1): 60–73.
Stone, Michael
   1992   "After Gotti." *New York* (February 3): 23–30.
Strong, Josiah
   1976   "Perils—the Boss, the Machine, the Immigrant: A Nineteenth-Century View." Pp. 14–17 in *The City Boss in America: An Interpretive Reader,* edited by Alexander B. Callow, Jr. New York: Oxford University Press.
Strong, Simon
   1992   "Peru is Losing More Than the Drug War." *New York Times* (February 17): 11.
"Strong Synthetic Heroin Sold in Pittsburgh Area."
   1988   *New York Times* (December 26): 11.
Stutman, Robert M. and Richard Esposito
   1992   *Dead on Delivery: Inside the Drug Wars, Straight From the Street.* New York: Warner.
Sullivan, Joseph F.
   1991   "Casino Union Yields Power As Its Leaders Accept Curbs." *New York Times* (April 13): 7.
   1988   "New Jersey Teamster Local Elects Slate Tied to the Mob." *New York Times* (December 8): 16.
Summers, Anthony
   1993   *Official and Confidential: The Secret Life of J. Edgar Hoover.* New York: Putnam's.
Supreme Court of the State of New York
   1942   *A Presentment Concerning the Enforcement by the Police Department of the City of New York of the Laws Against Gambling.* New York: Arno Press Reprint, 1974.
Suro, Roberto
   1988   "Sicilian Mafia, After Crackdown, Revives with a Wave of Killings." *New York Times* (October 9): 1, 4.
   1987   "338 Guilty in Sicily in a Mafia Trial; 19 Get Life." *New York Times* (December 17): 1, 2.
   1986   "Sicily and the Mafia." *New York Times Magazine* (May 18): 47, 62–65.
Sutherland, Edwin H.
   1973   *Edwin H. Sutherland: On Analyzing Crime.* Edited by Karl Schuessler. Chicago: University of Chicago Press.

1972   *The Professional Thief.* Chicago: University of Chicago Press. Originally published in 1937.

Suttles, Gerald D.
1968   *The Social Order of the Slum.* Chicago: University of Chicago Press.

Swanberg, W. A.
1959   *Jim Fisk: The Career of an Improbable Rascal.* New York: Scribner's.

Taft, Philip and Philip Ross
1969   "American Labor Violence: Its Causes, Character, and Outcome." Pp. 281–395 in *The History of Violence in America*, edited by Hugh Davis Graham and Ted Robert Gurr. New York: Bantam.

Takahashi, Sadahiko and Carl B. Becker
1985   "Organized Crime in Japan." Osaka, Japan: Kin'ki University, photocopied.

Talese, Gay
1971   *Honor Thy Father.* New York: World Publishing.
1965   *The Overreachers.* New York: Harper and Row.

Talmadge, Eric
1988   "All Is Not Well Within Japan's Underworld." *Southtown Economist* (December 15): Sec. 2: 4.

Task Force on Organized Crime
1976   *Organized Crime.* Washington, DC: U.S. Government Printing Office.
1967   *Task Force Report: Organized Crime.* Washington, DC: U.S. Government Printing Office.

Taylor, Ian, Paul Walton, and Jock Young
1973   *The New Criminology.* New York: Harper and Row.

Teresa, Vincent, and Thomas C. Renner
1973   *My Life in the Mafia.* Greenwich, CT: Fawcett.

Terry, Charles E. and Mildred Pellens
1928   *The Opium Problem.* New York: The Committee on Drug Addictions, in collaboration with the Bureau of Social Hygiene, Inc.

Texas Commission on Alcohol and Drug Abuse (TCADA)
1987   *Drug Abuse Trends in Texas.* Austin: TCADA.

Thomas, Jo
1984   "Islands' Bank Secrecy is Lifted for U.S." *New York Times* (July 27): 3.

Thomas, Ralph C.
1977   "Organized Crime in the Construction Industry." *Crime and Delinquency* 23: 304–11.

Thompson, Craig and Allan Raymond
1940   *Gang Rule in New York.* New York: Dial.

Thompson, Hunter S.
1966   *Hell's Angels: A Strange and Terrible Saga.* New York: Random House.

Thornburgh, Dick
1989   "Statement Before the U.S. Senate Committee on the Judiciary Concerning Organized Crime Strike Forces." September 8.

Thrasher, Frederic Milton
1968   *The Gang: A Study of 1,313 Gangs in Chicago.* Chicago: University of Chicago Press. (Abridged version.) Originally published in 1927.

Tindall, George Brown
1988   *America: A Narrative History: Volume Two.* New York: Norton.

Toby, Jackson
1958   "Hoodlum or Businessman: An American Dilemma." Pp. 542–50 in *The Jews: Social Patterns of an American Group*, edited by Marshall Sklare. Glencoe, IL: Free Press.

Touhy, Roger
1959   *The Stolen Years.* Cleveland: Pennington.

"Town That's Addicted to Drug Money, A" *New York*
1991   *Times* (May 16): 7.

Toy, Calvin
1992   "A Short History of Asian Gangs in San Francisco." *Justice Quarterly* 9 (December): 647–65.

Train, Arthur
1922   *Courts and Criminals.* New York: Scribner's.
1912   "Imported Crime: The Story of the Camorra in America." *McClure's Magazine* (May): 83–94.

Traub, James
1987   "The Lords of Hell's Kitchen." *New York Times Magazine* (April 5): 38, 40, 42, 44, 85.

Treaster, Joseph B.
1993a   "A Dozen Killings Tied to Colombia." *New York Times* (May 16): 1, 10.
1993b   "U.S. Says Top Trafficker is Seized in Puerto Rican Connection." *New York Times* (June 5): 7.
1992a   "Nigerian Connection a New Threat in Heroin War." *New York Times* (February 15): 1, 10.
1992b   "Jailbreak Dramatizes Drug-Policy Failures." *New York Times* (July 26): E3.
1991a   "New York City's Top Cocaine Smugglers Are Arrested in Raids, Police Say." *New York Times* (December 7): 10.
1991b   "Cocaine is Again Surging Out of Panama." *New York Times* (August 13): 1, 4.

1991c   "U.S. Seizes Suspect in New York in 40 Colombian Drug Slayings," *New York Times,* September 27: 1, 7.

1990a   "Eager for Good Press, Drug Bosses Sacrifice Laboratory in Colombia." *New York Times* (February 15): 1, 6.

1990b   "A Peruvian Peasant Fails to See Bush," *New York Times* (February 16): 9.

1990c   "Cocaine Users Adding Heroin to Their Menus." *New York Times* (July 21): 1, 10.

1989a   "A Nice Place (Just Ask Drug Barons)." *New York Times* (May 23): 6.

1989b   "In Bolivia, U.S. Pumps Money Into the Cocaine War, But Victory is Elusive." *New York Times* (June 11): 10.

1984   "Jamaica, Close U.S. Ally, Does Little to Halt Drugs." *New York Times* (September 10): 1, 8.

Treaster, Joseph B. and Steven Lee Myers
1993   "A Dozen Killings Tied to Colombia." *New York Times* (May 16): 1, 10.

Trebach, Arnold S.
1987   *The Great Drug War: Radical Proposals that Could Make America Safe Again.* New York: Macmillan.

1982   *The Heroin Solution.* New Haven, CT: Yale University Press.

Trujillo, Stephen G.
1992a   "Peru's Maoist Drug Dealers." *New York Times* (April 8): 17.

1992b   "Corruption and Cocaine in Peru." *New York Times* (April 7): 19.

Tucker, Richard K.
1991   *The Dragon and the Cross: The Rise and Fall of the Ku Klux Klan in Middle America.* Hamden, CT: Archon Books.

Tuite, James
1978   "Would Benefits of Legalized Betting on Sports Outweigh the Drawbacks?" *New York Times* (December 19): B21.

Tully, Andrew
1958   *Treasury Agent: The Inside Story.* New York: Simon and Schuster.

Tulsky, Frederic N.
1987   "U.S. Witness Protection Program Hides a Daughter From Her Father." *Chicago Tribune* (March 5): Sec. 5: 3.

Turkus, Burton and Sid Feder
1951   *Murder, Inc.: The Story of the Syndicate.* New York: Farrar, Straus and Young.

Turner, Wallace
1984   "U.S. and Nevada Agents Crack Down on Casinos." *New York Times* (January 28): 1, 7.

"21 Killings Ridicule Talk of Surrender by Escobar" *New York*
1992   *York Times* (October 11): 4.

"$2,000,000 Lottery Unmolested Here." *New York Times*
1935   (March 4): 1.

"2 Women Wounded as Gang Opens Fire in Upper Broadway."
1933   *New York Times* (May 25): 1.

Tyler, Gus
1975   "Book Review of 'The Black Mafia.'" *Crime and Delinquency* 21 (April): 175–80.

Tyler, Gus, ed.
1962   *Organized Crime in America.* Ann Arbor: University of Michigan Press.

Uelmen, Gerald F. and Victor G. Haddox, eds.
1983   *Drug Abuse and the Law.* New York: Clark Boardman.

Uhlig, Mark A.
1990   "Panama Drug Smugglers Prosper As Dictator's Exit Opens the Door." *New York Times* (August 21): 1, 4.

1989a   "As Colombian Terror Grows, The Press Becomes the Prey." *New York Times* (May 22): 1, 4.

1989b   "In 'Machine-Gun City,' Life's Not Worth a Song." *New York Times* (June 7): 4.

1989c   "Drug Wars: U.S. Weighs a Military Escalation." *New York Times* (July 9): E3.

"U.N. Accord on Drug Trafficking is Signed, A" *New York*
1988   *Times* (December 21): 6.

Ungar, Sanford
1975   *The FBI.* Boston: Little, Brown.

"Unger Indicted in Drug Conspiracy."
1928   *New York Times* (December 11): 1.

United States General Accounting Office
1981   *Stronger Federal Effort Needed in Fight Against Organized Crime.* Washington, DC: U.S. Government Printing Office.

United States Senate Subcommittee on Administrative Practice and Procedure
1978   *Hearings on Oversight of the Witness Protection Program.* Washington, DC: U.S. Government Printing Office.

"U.S. Looking Into Undercover Drug Manipulation."
1988   *New York Times* (November 30): 9.

"U.S. Plans to Resume Using Paraquat to Eradicate Marijuana"
1988   *New York Times* (July 14): 26.

"U.S. Seizes Florida Properties Seen as Profits of Drug Trade"
1987   *New York Times* (December 2): 18.

"U.S. to Cut Bolivian Aid Over Drug-War Failures"
1987   *Chicago Tribune* (September 22): 12.

"Usury Racket Stirred Gang War."
1935   *New York Times* (October 25): 17.

Van Devander, Charles W.
1944   *The Big Bosses.* New York: Howell, Soskin, Publishers.

Van Dyke, Craig and Robert Byck
1982   "Cocaine." *Scientific American* 246 (March): 139–41.

Villano, Anthony
1978   *Brick Agent.* New York: Ballantine.

Volsky, George
1979   "Indictment in Miami Depicts Rise and Fall of Narcotics-Smuggling Gang." *New York Times* (May 6): 26.

Vulliamy, Ed
1992   "Mafia, Inc.: Italy's Underworld Extends Its Reach." *World Press Review* (December): 11–14.

Waldman, Michael and Pamela Gilbert
1989   "RICO Goes to Congress: Keep the Teeth in the White-Collar Law." *New York Times* (March 12): F2.

Walker, Samuel
1980   *Popular Justice: A History of American Criminal Justice.* New York: Oxford University Press.

Wall, Joseph Frazier
1970   *Andrew Carnegie.* New York: Oxford University Press.

Wallace, Anise
1983   "Morgan's Bold Plan for the Teamsters." *New York Times* (December 4): C3.

Wallace, Irving and David Wallechinsky
1983   "The Palisades Massacres." *Parade* (January 23): 18.

Wallance, Gregory
1982   *Papa's Game.* New York: Ballantine.

Walsh, Marilyn E.
1977   *The Fence.* Westport, CT: Greenwood.

Walston, James
1986   "See Naples and Die: Organized Crime in Campania." Pp. 134–58 in *Organized Crime: A Global Perspective*, edited by Robert J. Kelly. Totowa, NJ: Rowman and Littlefield.

Walter, Ingo
1990   *Secret Money: The World of International Financial Secrecy.* New York: Harper Business.

Washburn, Charles
1934   *Come Into My Parlor: Biography of the Aristocratic Everleigh Sisters of Chicago.* New York: Knickerbocker Publishing Co.

"Washington Talk"
1986   *New York Times* (January 18): 8.

"Waxey Gordon Dies in Alcatraz at 63."
1952   *New York Times* (June 25): 1.

"Waxey Gordon Guilty; Gets 10 Years. Is Fined $80,000 for Tax Evasion."
1933   *New York Times* (December 2): 1.

Weber, Max
1958   *Protestant Ethic and the Spirit of Capitalism.* New York: Scribner's.

Webster, Barbara and Michael S. McCampbell
1992   *International Money Laundering: Research and Investigation Join Forces.* Washington, DC: National Institute of Justice.

Weingarten, Paul
1989   "Drug War Battle Lines Shift to Rio Grande." *Chicago Tribune* (April 16): 1, 6.
1989b   "Drug Cash Flows Over U.S. Border." *Chicago Tribune* (December 10): 25.

Weinstein, Adam K.
1988   "Prosecuting Attorneys for Money Laundering: A New and Questionable Weapon In the War on Crime." *Law and Contemporary Problems* 51 (Winter): 369–86.

Weisman, Alan
1989   "Dangerous Days in the Macarena." *New York Times Magazine* (April 23): 40–48.

Weisman, Steven R.
1991   "Is Business Too Cozy With the Mob?" *New York Times* (August 29): 11.

Weiss, Murray and Jim Nolan
1993   "Scrub Out! Top Mobster Nabbed in the Shower." *New York Post* (January 20): 7.

Wendt, Lloyd and Herman Kogan
1974   *Bosses in Lusty Chicago: The Story of Bathhouse John and Hinky Dink.* Bloomington, IN: Indiana University Press. Originally published in 1943.

Werner, M. R.
1928   *Tammany Hall.* Garden City, NY: Doubleday, Doran.

Wessel, Milton R.
1963   "The Conspiracy Charge as a Weapon Against Organized Crime." *Notre Dame Lawyer* 38 (September): 689–99.

Wesson, Donald R. and David E. Smith
1985   "Cocaine: Treatment Perspectives." Pp. 193–203 in *Cocaine Use in America: Epidemiologic and Clinical Perspectives*, edited by Nicholas J. Kozel and Edgar H. Adams. Rockville, MD: National Institute on Drug Abuse.
1977   *Barbiturates: Their Use, Misuse, and Abuse.* New York: Human Sciences Press.

562

Westrate, David L.
1985   "Drug Trafficking and Terrorism." *Drug Enforcement* (Summer): 19–24.

Wethern, George and Vincent Colnett
1978   *A Wayward Angel*. New York: Marek Publishers.

Whitaker, Mark, Elaine Shannon, and Ron Moreau
1985   "Colombia's King of Coke." *Newsweek* (February 25): 19–22.

White, Frank Marshall
1908   "The Bands of Criminals of New York's East Side." *New York Times* (November 8): V9.

White, Peter T.
1989   "An Ancient Indian Herb Turns Deadly: Coca." *National Geographic* 175 (January): 3–47.

White House Conference on a Drug Free America
1988   *Final Report*. Washington, DC: U.S. Government Printing Office.

"Who Took the Stone of Alphonse Capone?"
1981   *Chicago Tribune Magazine* (September 6): 6.

Whyte, William Foote
1961   *Street Corner Society*. Chicago: University of Chicago Press.

"Widening the Drug War"
1991   *Newsweek* (July 1): 32–43.

Wiebe, Robert H.
1967   *The Search for Order: 1877–1920*. New York: Hill and Wang.

Wiedrich, Bob
1988   "Airlines Taking the Rap for Drug Smugglers." *Chicago Tribune* (July): Sec. 4: 1, 6.

Williams, Jay R., Lawrence J. Redlinger, and Peter K. Manning
1979   *Police Narcotics Control: Patterns and Strategies*. Washington, DC: U.S. Government Printing Office.

Williams, T. Harry
1969   *Huey Long*. New York: Bantam.

Williams, Terry
1989   *The Cocaine Kids: The Inside Story of a Teenage Drug Ring*. Reading, MA: Addison-Wesley.

Willoughby, Jack
1986   "A License to Steal." *Forbes* (September 22): 146, 148.

Wilson, James Q.
1978   *The Investigators*. New York: Basic Books.
1975   *Thinking About Crime*. New York: Basic Books.

Wilson, Theodore
1975   "The Kefauver Committee, 1950." Pp. 353–82 in *Congress Investigates: 1792–1974*, edited by Arthur M. Schlessinger, Jr. and Robert Burns. New York: Chelsea House.

Winick, Charles and Paul M. Kinsie
1971   *The Lively Commerce*. Chicago: Quadrangle.

Wiretap Commission, see National Commission for the Review of Federal and State Laws Relating to Wiretapping and Electronic Surveillance.

Wishart, David
1974   "The Opium Poppy: The Forbidden Crop." *Journal of Geography* 73 (January): 14–25.

Wisotsky, Steven
1987   *Breaking the Impasse in the War on Drugs*. Westport, CT: Greenwood.

Withers, Kay
1982   "Cardinal Leads Drive to Crush Sicily's Mafia." *Chicago Tribune* (September 29): 5.

Witkin, Gordon
1991   "The Men Who Created Crack." *U.S. News and World Report* (August 19): 44–53.

Woetzel, Robert K.
1963   "An Overview of Organized Crime: Mores versus Morality." *Annals* 347 (May): 1–11.

Wolf, Daniel R.
1991   *The Rebels: A Brotherhood of Outlaw Bikers*. Toronto: University of Toronto Press.

Wolf, Eric R.
1966   "Kinship, Friendship, and Patron-Client Relations in Complex Societies." Pp. 1–22 in *The Social Anthropology of Complex Societies*, edited by Michael Banton, London: Tavistock Publications.

Wolfgang, Marvin E. and Franco Ferracuti
1967   *The Subculture of Violence: Toward an Integrated Theory in Criminology*. London: Tavistock.

"Woman, 2 Men, Slain as Gang Raids Home in Coll Feud."
1932   *New York Times* (February 2): 1.

Woodiwiss, Michael
1988   *Crime, Crusades and Corruption: Prohibitions in the United States, 1900–1987*. Totowa, NJ: Barnes and Noble.
1987   "Capone to Kefauver: Organised Crime in America." *History Today* 37 (June): 8–15.

Worthington, Rogers
1990   "Town Revved Up As 250,000 Bikers Roar In." *Chicago Tribune* (August 10): 6.

REFERENCES

Wright, Michael
    1979   "Phenix City, Ala., Leaves Ashes of Sin in the Past." *New York Times* (June 18): 14.

Wyman, Mark
    1984   *Immigrants in the Valley: Irish, Germans, and Americans in the Upper Mississippi Country, 1830–1860.* Chicago: Nelson Hall.

Yates, Ronald E.
    1987   "Afghanistan Invasion Propels Pakistan to Top in Opium Trade." *Chicago Tribune* (February 12): 32.

    1985   "Lawmen's Dispute on Gangs Rages Over Pacific." *Chicago Tribune* (December 8): 5.

Young, James Harvey
    1961   *The Toadstool Millionaires: A Social History of Patent Medicines In America Before Federal Regulation.* Princeton, NJ: Princeton University Press.

Zilg, Gerard Colby
    1974   *Du Pont: Behind the Nylon Curtain.* Englewood Cliffs, NJ: Prentice-Hall.

Zinberg, Norman E.
    1984   *Drug, Set, and Setting: The Basis for Controlled Intoxicant Use.* New Haven, CT: Yale University Press.

Zinberg, Norman E. and John A. Robertson
    1972   *Drugs and the Public.* New York: Simon and Schuster.

Author Index

Subject Index

PHOTO CREDITS

p. 5. Historical Pictures/Stock Montage

p. 7. Gene Mustain

p. 14. Cappelli Editore

p. 38. Joseph O'Brien

p. 53. David Strick/Onyx

p. 68. Bettmann Archive

p. 76. Brown Brothers

p. 82. AP/Wide World

p. 91. Brown Brothers

p. 113. UPI/Bettmann

p. 120. AP/Wide World

p. 122. UPI/Bettmann

p. 124. UPI/Bettmann

p. 134. (*left to right*) *Top:* AP/Wide World; AP/Wide World; UPI/Bettmann. *Bottom:* AP/Wide World; AP/Wide World; AP/Wide World

p. 135. (*left to right*) *Top:* AP/ Wide World; UPI/Bettmann; UPI/Bettmann. *Middle:* AP/Wide World; UPI/Bettmann. *Bottom:* AP/Wide World; AP/Wide World.

p. 140. AP/Wide World

p. 147. New Jersey Newsphotos

p. 160. Chicago Historical Society

p. 166. Chicago Historical Society

p. 167. (*left to right*) *Top:* Chicago Historical Society; *Middle:* Chicago Historical Society; *Bottom:* AP/Wide World; William J. Helmer.

p. 174. Chicago Historical Society

p. 179. Chicago Historical Society

p. 187. AP/Wide World

p. 189. UPI/Bettmann

p. 202. UPI/Bettmann

p. 224-27. Federal Bureau of Investigation

p. 238. AP/Wide World

p. 243. AP/Wide World

p. 250. Howard W. French/NYT Pictures

p. 252. Bernard Krisher

p. 257. Royal Hong Kong Police

p. 266. Mel Evans/NYT Pictures

p. 290. NYT Pictures

p. 302. AP/Wide World

p. 312. Las Vegas News Bureau

p. 317. AP/Wide World

p. 322. Chicago Historical Society

p. 323. Charles Batewood/ Magnum

p. 332. Historical Pictures/Stock Montage

p. 345. AP/Wide World

p. 363. Ray Stubblebine/NYT Pictures

p. 367. Vera Lentz/Black Star

p. 380. Ed Buryn/Jeroboam

p. 382. Terrence McCarthy/NYT Pictures

p. 386. Joyce Dopkeen/NYT Pictures

p. 398. AP/Wide World

p. 409. UPI/Bettmann

p. 411. UPI/Bettmann

p. 427. NYT Pictures

p. 438. Reuters/Bettmann

p. 465. Angel Franco/NYT Pictures

p. 474. Courtesy: INTERPOL

p. 480. Courtesy: City of Beachwood, Ohio

p. 495. AP/Wide World

p. 497. Time

p. 521. James Brooke/NYT Pictures

About the Author

Howard Abadinsky is professor/associate director of criminal justice at Saint Xavier University, Chicago. He was a parole officer and senior parole officer for the State of New York for almost fifteen years, and an inspector for the Cook County Sheriff's Office for eight years. The author is a graduate of Queens College of the City University of New York, holds an M.S.W. from Fordham University, and a Ph.D. in sociology from New York University. He is the author of numerous books on crime and justice and served as a consultant to the President's Commission on Organized Crime. Dr. Abadinsky welcomes comments on his work, and can be reached at Saint Xavier University, 3700 W. 103rd Street, Chicago, IL 60655.